# STUDENTS! HOW TO VIEW THE VIDEO CASES THAT GO ALONG WITH THIS TEXT

## Explore Teaching in Action

Are you interested in what *really* happens in the classroom? Do you want to know how teachers handle challenging situations? Watch the **Houghton Mifflin Video Cases** and see how new and experienced teachers apply concepts and strategies in real K–12 classrooms. These four- to six-minute video clips cover a variety of different topics that today's teachers face, and allow you to experience real teaching in action.

***To access the Houghton Mifflin Video Cases:***

- Using your browser, go to: **college.hmco.com/pic/ryanTSL**
- Select the **Online Study Center**
- Go to the General Resources and click on **HM Video Cases**
- You will be prompted to enter the passkey below and to choose a username and password
- Select a video case from the list of options

**Passkey:** E5VY72FT1BOKM

Free access is available with the purchase of a **new** textbook, and will expire six months after first use. Access can also be purchased via the website. If you have a problem accessing the website with this passkey, please contact Houghton Mifflin Technical Support through: **http://college.hmco.com/how/how_techsupp.html**.

## Enhance Your Learning Experience

Houghton Mifflin video cases are integrated into your new copy of Ryan/Cooper/Tauer, ***Teaching for Student Learning*** through boxed features in the text. The cases include video clips and a host of related materials to provide a comprehensive learning experience.

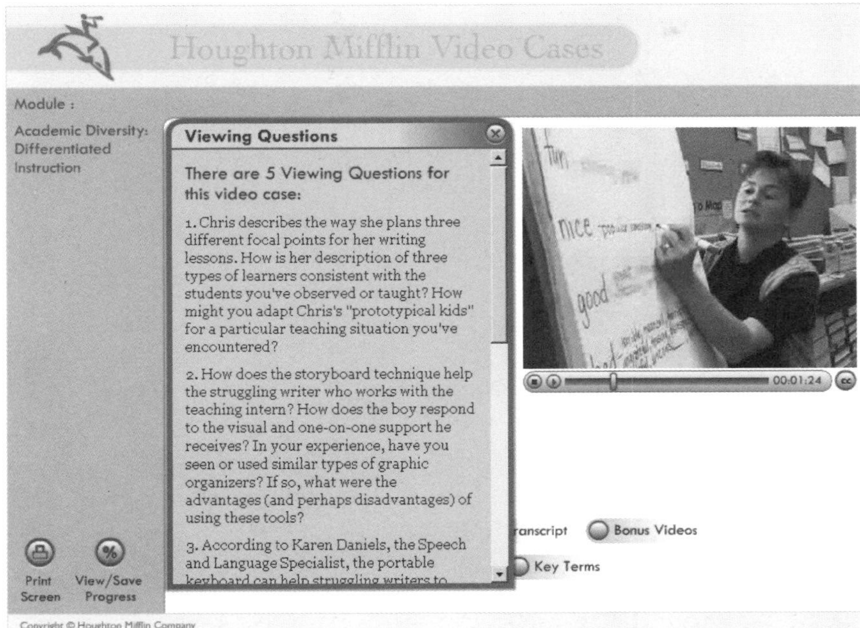


Reflect on the teacher's approach and assess how you might handle the situation by considering the **Viewing Questions.**

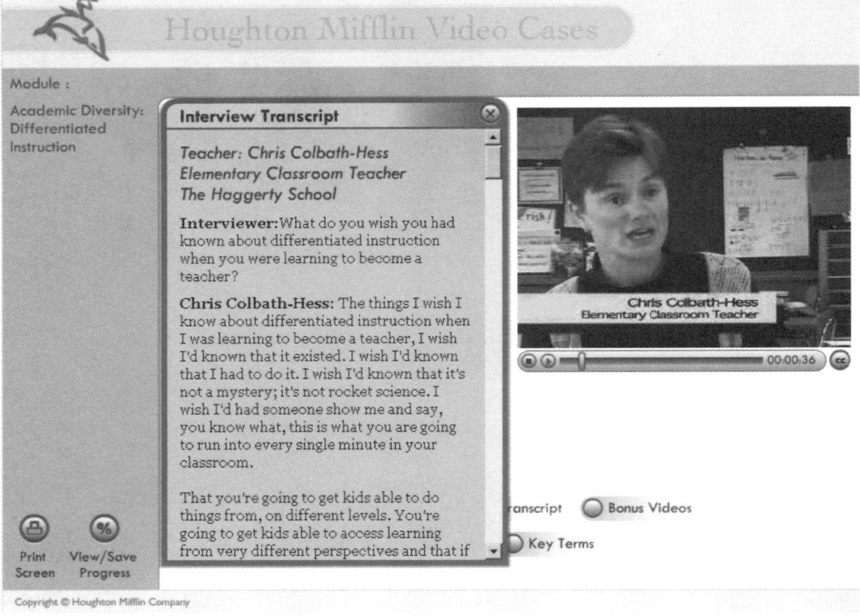


Read detailed **interviews with the teachers** as they explain their approach, how they engage students, and how they resolve issues.

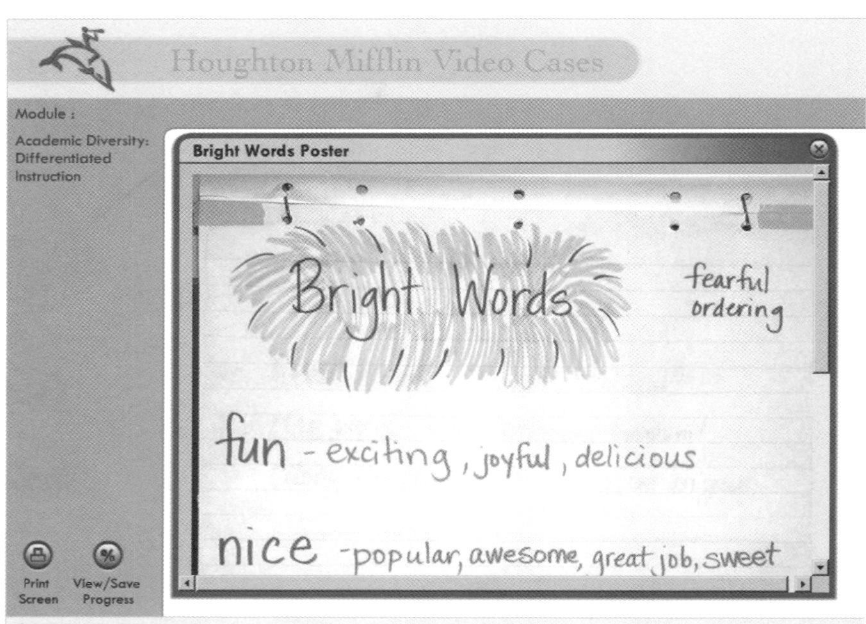


View **handouts and materials used in the class,** and gain ideas for your own portfolio.

# TEACHING *for* STUDENT LEARNING

## *Becoming a Master Teacher*

**KEVIN RYAN**
Boston University

**JAMES M. COOPER**
University of Virginia

**SUSAN TAUER**
Framingham State College

**Houghton Mifflin Company** Boston New York

Executive Publisher: Patricia Coryell
Executive Editor: Mary Finch
Marketing Manager: Amy Whitaker
Senior Development Editor: Lisa Mafrici
Senior Project Editor: Jane Lee
Senior Art and Design Coordinator: Jill Haber
Cover Design Manager: Anne S. Katzeff
Senior Photo Editor: Jennifer Meyer-Dare
Composition Buyer: Chuck Dutton
New Title Project Manager: James Lonergan
Editorial Assistant: Dayna Pell
Editorial Assistant: Carrie Parker

Cover Image: Copyright © Don Bishop/Getty Images

Photo Credits: p. 5: © Elizabeth Crews; p. 14: © Gideon Mendel/Corbis; p. 16: © Laura Dwight; p. 23: © Susie Fitzhugh; p. 26: © Royalty-Free/Corbis; p. 31: © Michael J. Doolittle/The Image Works; p. 43: © Susie Fitzhugh; p. 45: © Elizabeth Crews; p. 58: © Susie Fitzhugh; p. 61: © Ellen Senisi/The Image Works; p. 68: © Elizabeth Crews/The Image Works; p. 74: © Susie Fitzhugh; p. 80 (left): © Bettmann/Corbis; p. 80 (right): © Michael Newman/PhotoEdit; p. 82: © Charles Gupton/Corbis; p. 95: © Ellen Senisi/The Image Works; p. 104: © Laura Dwight; p. 112: © Monika Graff/The Image Works; p. 114: © Michael Newman/PhotoEdit; p. 126: © Elizabeth Crews; p. 128: © Bob Daemmrich; p. 149: © Susie Fitzhugh; p. 156: © Peter Hvizdak/The Image Works; p. 165: © Laura Dwight; p. 172: © David Grossman/The Image Works; p. 179: © Elizabeth Crews; p. 186: © David Young-Wolff/PhotoEdit; p. 193: © Laura Dwight; p. 202: © Susie Fitzhugh; p. 206: © Laura Dwight; p. 213: © Bob Daemmrich/PhotoEdit; p. 216: © Ellen Senisi/The Image Works; p. 232: © Ellen Senisi/The Image Works; p. 235: © Susie Fitzhugh; p. 246: © Laura Dwight; p. 252: © Michael Zide; p. 258: © Bob Daemmrich/PhotoEdit; p. 264: © Rachel Epstein/The Image Works; p. 270: © Michael Newman/PhotoEdit; p. 278: © Ellen Senisi/The Image Works; p. 286: © Laura Dwight; p. 287: © Michael Newman/PhotoEdit; p. 297: © Elizabeth Crews; p. 306: © Bob Daemmrich; p. 316: © Susie Fitzhugh; p. 317: © David Young-Wolff/PhotoEdit; p. 329: © Susie Fitzhugh; p. 331: © Susie Fitzhugh; p. 346: © Michael Zide; p. 354: AP/Wide World Photos.



Printed in the U.S.A.

Library of Congress Control Number: 2006940971

Instructor's exam copy:
ISBN 13: 978-0-618-83338-2
ISBN 10: 0-618-83338-2

For orders, use student text ISBNs:
ISBN 13: 978-0-618-43400-8
ISBN 10: 0-618-43400-3

123456789-CRK-11 10 09 08 07

# Brief Contents

# Contents

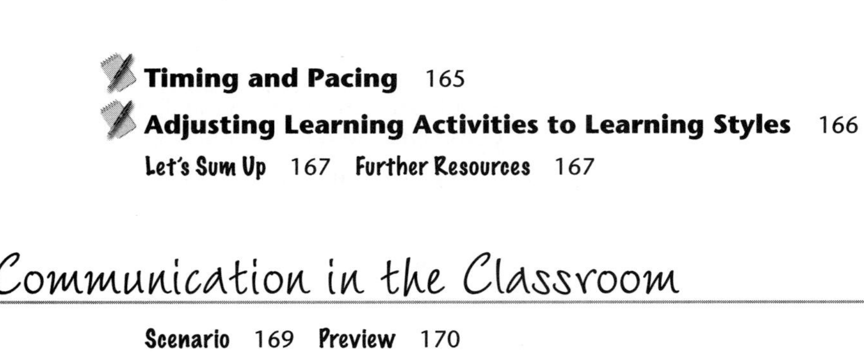

# Preface

*Teaching For Student Learning: Becoming A Master Teacher* is a new text for a recent development in education: the growth of accelerated teacher education programs and alternative licensure programs, such as Teach for America, Troops to Teachers, and the New Teacher Project.

America needs teachers and it needs them now. Demand for teachers (especially at middle and high school levels) is greatest in inner cities and outlying rural areas of the country and in the fields of mathematics, the sciences, and special education. In some areas of the country, this critical teacher shortage is resulting in a wide variety of crash courses, emergency licensure programs, and alternative licensure programs.

According to the National Center for Education Information, every state in the nation is now facing the challenge of creating alternatives to the traditional college route for licensing teachers. States, cities, and private groups are scrambling to develop intensive, reality-based workshops and short courses to prepare new teacher recruits for their classroom responsibilities. Also, traditional college and university teacher education programs are now streamlining their programs to get candidates out into the classrooms as efficiently as possible.

*Teaching For Student Learning: Becoming A Master Teacher* grew out of a conversation between Houghton Mifflin editors and two of the text's authors, who were discussing the revision of another book, *Those Who Can, Teach,* which is geared toward students who are beginning their traditional teacher education programs. We realized that the new alternative teacher licensure population needed options to the traditional textbook. Current publications, including *Those Who Can, Teach* and most introductory education and general teaching methods texts, do not address the problems facing this group of students. We set out to fill those needs.

## Purpose and Audience

This innovative text is for those who are already teaching or about to teach, not those who are just thinking about perhaps teaching someday! It is for student teachers at the end of their traditional program or new in-service teachers who are part of an alternative licensure program. These students may be more experienced than traditional "introduction to education" students (for whom we believe *Those Who Can, Teach* is the ideal choice). They require materials that will help them be competent in the classroom—immediately.

We created *Teaching for Student Learning* to help our users meet their goals via the following features:

- **Focus on the essential tasks of teaching.** Topics such as instruction, assessment, and classroom control are coupled with get-the-job-done problem-solving skills a new teacher needs. We aim to immerse soon-to-be or early-career teachers in the sometimes tough realities of teaching. We give them focused advice that will help them avoid common pitfalls and directly lead to classroom competence. It is our hope that this "real world" issue and problem focus will help make the theory-to-practice connection much tighter for both students and instructors.
- **Flexibility in content coverage and content presentation.** We have distilled the fundamental information and professional insights

that all teachers need for the demanding requirements of today's schools, and we present them in a series of twenty-five brief, easy-to-read and easy-to-reference modules rather than the more traditional fifteen or sixteen longer chapters often found in educational survey texts. This series of modules allows instructors to put together a combination that fits their course and the needs of their students. By offering these modules in a perforated, three-hole-punched format, instructors can select and sequence the materials in a ready-to-reference binder to suit their different needs. The flexible format also allows instructors to add school- or state-specific materials to their personal reference collection.

- **An "interactive" text.** We have carefully woven together the printed material in this book with links to in-depth information or supporting teaching and learning materials available through the Online Study Center and Online Teaching Center developed for this book. A key feature of the online component of *Teaching for Student Learning* is the integration of extraordinarily rich Houghton Mifflin Video Cases, which help new teachers see key concepts put into action by real teachers in real classrooms.
- **Clear connection to standards.** The No Child Left Behind Act and the Standards for Beginning Teacher Licensing and Development, issued by the Interstate New Teacher Assessment and Support Consortium (INTASC), have gone a long way toward delineating what a new teacher should know and be able to do. They also continue to have a guiding impact on the new teacher licensing process in many states. As we wrote the various modules for this text, we had these new standards and requirements firmly in mind. The Online Study Center helps users correlate content from *Teaching for Student Learning* to the proficiencies and standards that have been identified by key states.

## Content

*Teaching for Student Learning* was selected as this book's title to emphasize that teaching should have a "results orientation."

Effective teachers bring about intended learning outcomes. They manage students' behavior in the classroom, organize instruction, assess student learning, and adjust learning activities in response to students' needs and abilities. The goal of these activities is to ensure that all students learn what is expected of them.

The core goal of an effective teacher, helping students learn, is enmeshed in several layers of relationships such as those with students and students' families, the teacher's colleagues and administrators, and even with the laws of our country. A successful teacher must manage all of these relationships effectively.

The modules of this book are designed to help new teachers thrive in their first years of teaching and to assist them on their way to becoming master teachers who can handle all of these tasks:

- Module 1, Reflective Teaching for Student Learning, introduces the book, the current climate for teachers, and the essential skills of effective teachers.
- Modules 2 through 5 help users to develop an understanding of their students that is a key foundation for all other characteristics of effective teaching. Module 2, Understanding Student Differences, lays a foundation for teachers to grasp the extent and importance of diversity among

their students. Specific sources of diversity are the focus of Module 3, Teaching Culturally Diverse Learners, Module 4, Teaching Students with Disabilities, and Module 5, Teaching Academically Diverse Learners.

- Module 7, School Culture, Module 8, Establishing the Classroom Environment, Module 9, Maintaining the Classroom Environment, and Module 13, Communication in the Classroom, are designed to help readers master the essentials of managing the classroom behavior of their students.
- Module 6, Key Principles of Learning, Module 10, Planning What to Teach, Module 11, Planning Lessons, Module 12, How to Teach, and Module 14, Teaching and Technology, are intended to offer essential theoretical footing and solid, practical advice to prepare the users of this book for the core work of their profession: teaching for student learning.
- Module 15, Assessment for Learning, and Module 16, Tools for Assessment, provide background on the essential task of determining how well students are learning.
- Module 17, Working with Your Students' Families, Module 18, Working with Colleagues, Module 19, School Governance and Funding, and Module 20, Professional Performance Assessment, will get users up to speed quickly with information about the key relationships teachers need to maintain.
- Module 21, The Ethics of Teaching, Module 22, Educational Law, Module 23, Hiring, Firing, and Educational Law, and Module 25, Professionalism in Teaching, help readers understand the larger context of teaching as a profession; the role teachers play in society; and the way society—particularly the laws our of society—affects teachers.
- Module 24, The First Year, offers both a realistic preview and sensible advice for not just making it through, but making the most of the first few years of teaching.

## Design Features

We have made this book interactive to provide many opportunities for readers to test their knowledge, respond to questions, and engage with the book. To accomplish this engagement, the modules have a number of different features.

- **Opening scenarios** illustrate some of the issues discussed in the module and are referred to often throughout the module.
- **Preview** provides an overview of the major points addressed in the module, culminating in a bulleted format of key topics for the module.
- **Key Terms** appear in boldface, and the definitions for these terms are provided in the margins beside the text reference. Flashcards, available at the Online Study Center, provide additional reinforcement of the key terms.
- **Now You Do It** features are designed to prompt and allow opportunities for readers to consolidate the knowledge and to reflect more on key topics. Each feature asks the reader to respond to questions or suggestions.
- **In Your Classroom** boxes provide practical ideas and application tips for use in classrooms.

- **Video Case** boxes refer readers to selected **HM Video Cases** (described in the next section) and provide readers with questions to help them relate key module topics to video content, and to their own practice as teachers.
- **Let's Sum Up** gives a summation of the major points of the module, along with reassuring parting words of advice.
- **Further Resources** provide a set of additional readings and websites to investigate further the major ideas of the module.

## Accompanying Teaching and Learning Resources

*Teaching for Student Learning: Becoming a Master Teacher* is accompanied by an extensive package of instructor and student resources, all well integrated with the textbook.

- **Instructor's Resource Manual,** prepared by Amy Alvarado of the University of Virginia, is offered at the Online Teaching Center website and includes sample syllabi, student objectives, chapter overviews, supplementary lecture and discussion topics, class activities, student study guides, assessment questions, and selected references and web resources.
- **Online Teaching Center.** We have developed an Online Teaching Center to help instructors make the best use of *Teaching for Student Learning* for them and their students. At the Online Teaching Center, instructors may access the Instructor's Resource Manual, PowerPoint slides to use in class, information that correlates the text content to the INTASC Standards, and all student materials.
- **Online Study Center.** In addition to the text, *Teaching for Student Learning,* an Online Study Center has been created specifically for this book. At the website students can find additional resources, web links, and materials to give more in-depth and enhanced coverage of the book's topics. Look for the Online Study Center symbol throughout the book. When you see it, you will know that there is more information available to you at **college.hmco.com/pic/ryanTSL.**

- **Houghton Mifflin Video Cases.** Of particular interest at the Online Study Center is the array of **HM Video Cases.** Specific video cases, illustrating important ideas and issues, are identified throughout the book and can be accessed at the Online Study Center. These video cases show real-life classroom examples of problems, methodology, and teaching styles that add another layer of richness to the book. They are intended to help prospective or new teachers understand better the realities of schools, classrooms, and students. Each video clip or "case" lasts four to six minutes and is accompanied by questions to help the viewer get the most out of the case. The video cases also contain bonus videos, classroom artifacts, teacher interviews, and key terms to enhance the viewing experience. They allow students to experience and reflect on the complex problems and opportunities that teachers face every day.

## Acknowledgments

Creating a new book is a cooperative process. We would like to acknowledge the team at Houghton Mifflin for their help throughout the process: Lisa Mafrici, Senior Development Editor; Mary Finch and Sue Pulvermacher-Alt,

Senior Sponsoring Editors; and Jane Lee, Senior Project Editor. We'd also like to offer a special thanks to developmental editor, Sheralee Connors, whose insightful suggestions and contributions made her a true part of the author team.

We greatly appreciate the advice and insights offered by members of our advisory review board:

Stanley P. Burcham, McKendree College
Jennifer M. Coronado, Texas A&M International University
Maryann Dickar, New York University
Barbara J. Divins, Franklin College
Dion J. Dubois, Dallas Independent School District
Holly C. Gould, Sweet Briar College
Victoria Huffman, Bradley University
Arthur McLin Jr., Arkansas State University
Susan M. Seely-Miley, The Pennsylvania State University
Amy S. Rushneck, Mesa State College
Ronald Stanfield, Utah State Office of Education
Eva Weisz, DePauw University
Amy E. White, Central Piedmont Community College

The suggestions of the following reviewers were also invaluable to us as we shaped this book:

Deborah Butler, Wabash University
Larnell Flanagan, Clayton State University
Jacqueline Frierson, University of Maryland
Charlene Haar, Education Policy Institute, Washington DC
Robert Lane, Wichita State University
Bill Larmer, Tarleton State University
Robert MacDonald, University of Montana, Bozeman
Ronda Neilson, Utah State Office of Education
Patti Pettigrew, California State University, San Marcos
Charles Robinson, Bridgewater State University
Miriam Sherin, Northwestern University
Bill Suttles, Inner City Teaching Corps, Chicago

Creating a new book is also a time-consuming process that requires a large investment of energy and emotion in addition to the intellectual endeavors of research, writing, and revisions. We would all like to thank friends and family members who invested their support in us while were making those investments of time and energy. Sue would particularly like to thank Ken, Alice, Yvon, Karen, and especially Dick, whose "belief in me, much greater than my own, inspired me to accomplishments I never would have reached on my own."

Finally, we acknowledge the students for whom this book is written. Your new learning as you become teachers is central to our work as authors. We value your feedback on how we are doing and invite you to respond by sending us your comments through the Houghton Mifflin Online Study Center.

Kevin Ryan
James M. Cooper
Susan M. Tauer

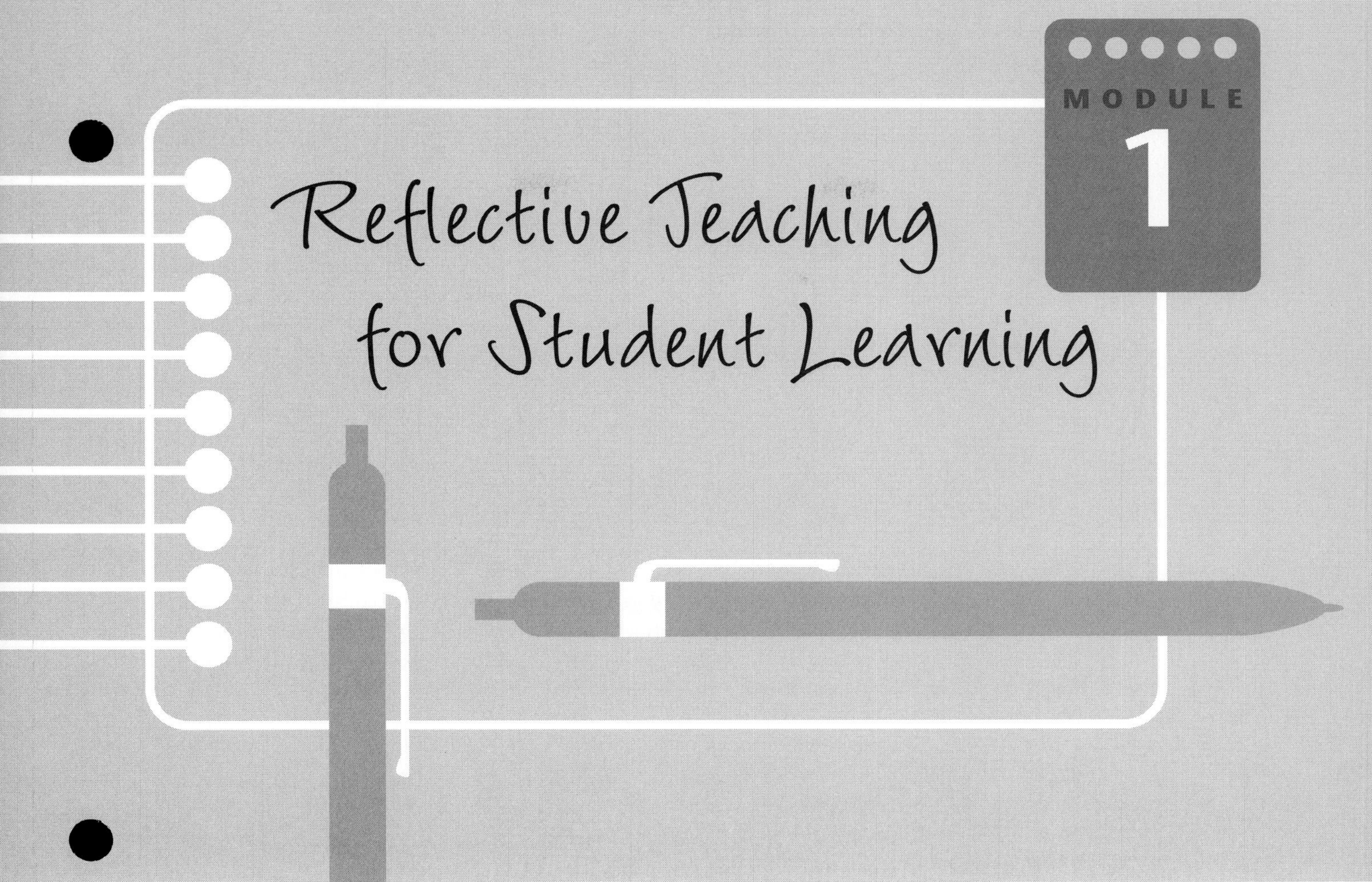


Scenario

It was late at night, and Richard Yee hadn't been this nervous since his wedding day. Tomorrow was the start of school and his first day as a teacher. After being a computer engineer for ten years, Richard had gradually come to realize that his heart wasn't in it. After a lengthy period of soul-searching, he had finally decided that what he really wanted to do was teach high school mathematics. Following that decision, Richard had spent the past year working through an alternative licensure program for people, like himself, who were entering teaching after some time in another career. Now, he was about to become a teacher in an urban high school.

Richard had always been good at mathematics, so he wasn't worried about understanding the subject he was going to teach. What made him nervous was whether he would be able to organize and run a classroom full of sixteen- and seventeen-year-olds, many of whom came from backgrounds that were very different from his own. Would they like him? Would they even listen to him? What about his colleagues—how would he get along with them? What if he needed help—whom could he approach for assistance? Would his teacher salary be enough for him and his family to live on? But most of all, Richard worried that he would not be able to teach the students what they needed to know to pass the state standards of learning. Would he be a good teacher? New questions and new worries kept popping into his head as he tossed and turned. Looking at the clock, Richard realized he would soon have the answers to many of his questions; it was already almost tomorrow.

Preview

Like Richard Yee, most teachers choose to enter teaching because they want to work with young people and believe they can make a difference in their students' lives. They also recognize teaching as important work that contributes significantly to society. The potential for these intrinsic rewards, as well as others, such as simply enjoying the process of teaching, attract people to the profession more strongly than the extrinsic rewards, such as salary and summers off.

Upon entering the profession, many teachers do, in fact, find the intrinsic satisfactions they sought. Nearly all new teachers agree, for instance, that teaching is work they love to do, and nearly two-thirds report that they get a lot of satisfaction from teaching.[1] But even so, approximately 30–50 percent of America's new teachers leave the classroom within the first five years. Why?

The reasons for leaving teaching are often related to the reasons for entering the field. Although salaries are important in retaining teachers, most of those who leave teaching report doing so because of factors more intrinsic to the work. The most common complaints include lack of administrative and parental support, problems with student motivation and discipline, and limited teacher input into and influence over school policies.[2] Some teachers, it seems, find that they do not enjoy working with young people as much as they thought they would, or they discover that the work of teaching is not what they thought it would be.

This book will, we hope, give you a start in developing the understanding and skills to overcome the problems that plague so many beginning teachers. There is no doubt that teachers who possess the knowledge and skills to be effective enjoy teaching more than those who struggle to develop these competencies. And, as their competencies develop and become more sophisticated, the satisfaction they derive from teaching increases.

**This module emphasizes that:**

- **Although teaching is a wonderful profession, teachers face many challenges, including pressure to ensure that all students learn.**
- **Teachers need many skills to be effective in ensuring that their students learn.**
- **To be effective, teachers must continuously grow, develop new knowledge and skills, and adopt a reflective stance that enables them to improve more and more over time.**
- **The federal government, through the No Child Left Behind Act, is holding states accountable for ensuring student learning as measured by success on a state-mandated test. This accountability reaches down to the school and its teachers.**

# Knowledge, Skills, and Attitudes You Need to Be an Effective Teacher

Richard's concerns are shared by many teachers as they prepare for the start of the school year. Whether in their first year or much later in their careers, teachers often wonder at the start of a new school year whether they will be able to teach effectively.

Let's look more closely at what we mean by an "effective teacher." An effective teacher brings about intended learning outcomes. He or she manages students' behavior in the classroom, organizes instruction, assesses student learning, and adjusts learning activities in response to students' needs and abilities. The goal of these activities is to ensure that all students learn what is expected of them. The core work of an effective teacher, helping students learn, is enmeshed in several layers of relationships—with your students, with their families, with your colleagues and administrators, and even with the laws of our country—and you must function successfully in all of these relationships if you are to be an effective teacher. Excelling in them also enables you to avoid some of the disillusionment common among new teachers, so that you are more likely to experience the satisfactions at the center of the job. Because if teaching isn't personally satisfying, why not just stay a software engineer?

The modules of this book are designed to help you thrive in your first years of teaching and to assist you on your way to becoming a master teacher who can handle all of these tasks:

- Modules 2–5 will help you to understand your students, a key foundation for all other characteristics of effective teaching.
- Module 6 presents an overview of the key principles of learning to help to frame your instructional and assessment strategies, and Module 7 assists you in understanding the purposes of schools and what cultures in schools are like.
- Modules 8 (Establishing the Classroom Environment), 9 (Implementing the Classroom Environment), and 13 (Communication in the Classroom) are designed to help you master the essentials of managing classroom behavior.
- Modules 10 (Planning What to Teach), 11 (Planning Lessons), 12 (How to Teach), and 14 (Teaching and Technology) are intended to prepare you for the core work of your profession, teaching for student learning.
- Modules 15 (Assessment for Learning) and 16 (Tools for Assessment) provide background on the essential task of determining how well your students are learning.
- Modules 17–24 will get you up to speed quickly with information about the key relationships you will need to maintain.

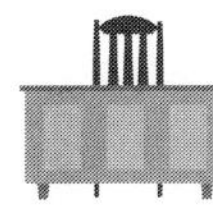

## Now You Do It

Take a few moments to page through the book while considering your current level of preparation and competency. Target the modules of most interest to you, those that you expect to fill some of the key gaps in your current knowledge and skills. Plan to pay special attention when you are assigned to study these modules, and if they are not assigned to you, plan to study them on your own.

## Reflective Teaching

**Reflective teaching** a teacher's habit of examining and evaluating his or her teaching on a regular basis.

**Teaching portfolios** collections of items (such as research papers, pupil evaluations, teaching units, and videos of lessons) that reflect the quality of a teacher's teaching. Portfolios can be used to illustrate to employers the teacher's proficiency or to obtain national board certification.

One characteristic of professional career teachers is the ability to grow and develop on the job. A key element in continued growth is reflection on the problems and issues of practice. New teachers are like learning sponges, soaking up information, skills, and experience. Everything is new, and you will be eager to learn so you can be an effective teacher. After a few years, however, there is a danger that you may fall into a "comfort zone." You may stop being open to learning new methods and instead rely on patterns of teaching that seem to have worked in the past. Before you know it, you may find yourself resembling one of the drab, dull teachers that Hollywood likes to characterize in movies.

How can you avoid this complacency and stagnation? An important element is to develop the habits of inquiry and reflection. You need to become a lifelong student of teaching by continually examining your assumptions, attitudes, practices, effectiveness, and accomplishments. This process of examination and evaluation is often called **reflective teaching,** and it is the key to becoming a master teacher.

### In Your Classroom

#### Tools for Reflective Teachers

Reflection on the practice of teaching can take many forms.

- *Teaching journal.* Some teachers keep a journal to record their thoughts and reactions to the events of the day. Writing about events that occur in your classroom gives you the opportunity to reexamine these events in a calmer and less distracting setting (after school hours, for example) and to propose solutions to problems that may have arisen. A journal can also provide you, as a new teacher, with a potentially rewarding record of growth in your thinking and problem-solving ability.
- *Video recordings.* Videos provide a visual and aural reminder of what happened in the classroom and act as triggers for recalling feelings, events, and intentions. They also seem to "objectify" the teaching, allowing teachers to feel less defensive and more willing to consider alternatives. Viewing a video of your own teaching nearly always reveals patterns of behavior that you didn't know existed. Some patterns you'll like and others you'll want to change.
- *Teaching portfolios.* **Teaching portfolios** consist of artifacts (videos, tests, lesson plans, student work, and other teacher-created materials) that provide a record of a teacher's professional growth and development. You can choose what items you want to include in your portfolio, justifying to yourself why you want to include particular items and what they say about you and your teaching. Reviewing their portfolios enables teachers to reflect on their teaching practices, see where they need to make changes, and recognize areas in which they are performing well. Teaching portfolios can be digitized or in hard copy.
- *Colleagues.* Reflection is easier when you work with a colleague to obtain another's perspective and to get new ideas. By revealing your teaching to another teacher, you make your ideas explicit and open for examination. Observe your colleagues, too, if you can. Watching others can spur reflection about your own practices, as well as providing you with new ideas.

Teachers, like many other professional practitioners, make assumptions that undergird their actions. By reflecting on their actions, teachers can bring to the surface some of these assumptions, which might otherwise go unrecognized. The accompanying "In Your Classroom" feature suggests several techniques you might use to kick-start your own reflection process. Once aware of their assumptions, reflective teachers can critique and examine these tacit understandings and can make adjustments to them as they become more knowledgeable about the subjects and the students they teach as well as the school setting. Such continuing reflection and improvement establishes a self-reinforcing habit of being thoughtful about your teaching.

## The No Child Left Behind Act

*Teaching for Student Learning* was selected as this book's title to emphasize that teaching should have a "results orientation." A few decades ago, the relationship between teaching and student learning was less often examined. Teachers taught, and some students learned while others did not. Although reflective teachers have always been concerned about their effectiveness, there was less official recognition of the teacher's central role in student learning. The teacher's effectiveness was not really considered, because learning was seen as primarily the responsibility of the student, not the teacher.

Today, this expectation has changed. In 1983, a highly influential report titled *A Nation at Risk* highlighted the "mediocrity" of American schooling and called for raising both expectations and learning standards in U.S. schools. Since then, the nation has been engaged in numerous attempts to reform the schools. States increased graduation requirements for high school students, required more time in school, and expected more of their teachers. A federal educational reform act called *Goals 2000: Educate America Act* was signed into law in 1994; it provided states with funding to develop comprehensive plans to improve the educational outcomes of their students.

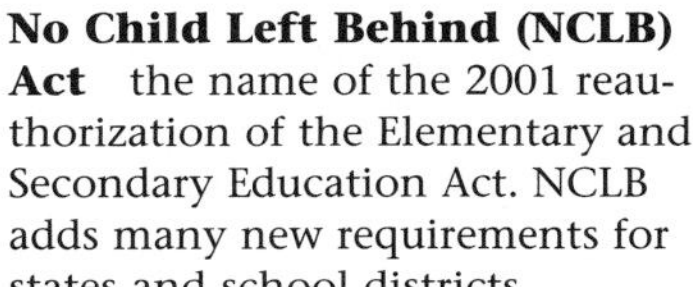

**No Child Left Behind (NCLB) Act** the name of the 2001 reauthorization of the Elementary and Secondary Education Act. NCLB adds many new requirements for states and school districts.

The most recent, and one of the most visible, major reform effort is the federal **No Child Left Behind (NCLB) Act.** Passed by Congress in 2001 and signed into law in 2002, NCLB is a reauthorization of the Elementary and Secondary Education Act (ESEA), which is the federal government's largest investment in K–12 education. The No Child Left Behind Act greatly increased the federal government's presence in education by putting into

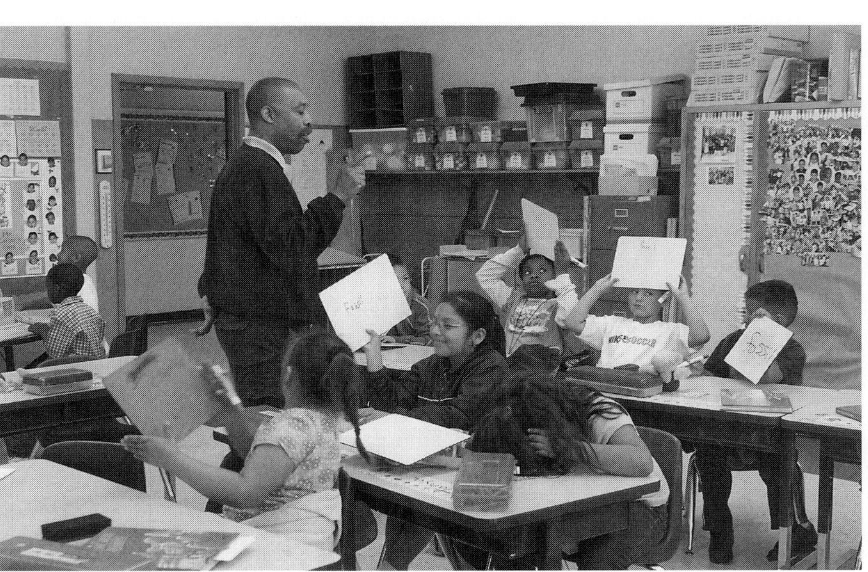

Our nation needs teachers with energy, commitment, and professional knowledge.

**Highly qualified teacher** a teacher who has been licensed (via traditional or alternative routes) and has demonstrated a high level of competence in the subjects that he or she teaches.

**Adequate yearly progress** annually demonstrable improvement toward meeting state standards. The federal No Child Left Behind Act specifies that schools with students who do not make adequate yearly progress are subject to a variety of corrective measures.

place requirements that reach into just about every public school in the country. In order for states to receive federal dollars for their schools, they must meet all of the following requirements of NCLB:

- Annual testing in reading and mathematics for all students in grades three to eight
- A high school exit exam that students must pass in order to earn their diplomas
- A **highly qualified teacher** in every classroom

The law applies pressure to school districts to turn around low-performing schools by specifying a series of consequences for schools that persistently fail to demonstrate **adequate yearly progress** toward having all students meet state content standards. These and other important NCLB concerns for teachers are summarized in Table 1.1.

## TABLE 1.1 Key Provisions of the No Child Left Behind Act

| NCLB Term | What This Means to You as a Teacher |
|---|---|
| State testing | States must design and administer tests, aligned with their state standards in core subjects, on NCLB's required schedule:<br>Language Arts/Reading<br>• Annually: All students in grades three through eight<br>• At least once during grades ten through twelve<br>Mathematics<br>• Annually: All students in grades three through eight<br>• At least once during grades ten through twelve<br>Science<br>• At least once in each of elementary, middle, and high school |
| Disaggregated data | Schools must separate and report the test results of students in as many as thirty different income, racial, special education, and English proficiency groups, in order to track gaps in performance among groups. |
| Adequate yearly progress | States must set minimum performance thresholds and ensure, within twelve years, that all students meet them. Test scores must show progress toward thresholds each year. Schools that fail to demonstrate adequate yearly progress are labeled as failing schools. |
| Failing schools | Schools that fail to meet adequate yearly progress goals face the following consequences:<br>• Two years of inadequate progress: technical assistance from school district, and school must offer students the option of transferring to another public school<br>• More than two years: possible reconstitution of school |
| Highly qualified teachers | All public school teachers of core subjects must:<br>• Be licensed by their state in the subject they teach<br>• Demonstrate high competence in their subjects |

Sources: U.S. Department of Education, "Introduction: No Child Left Behind." Available at: **http://www.ed.gov/nclb/overview/intro/index.html;** "An ESEA Primer," *Education Week,* January 9, 2002, pp. 28–29.

Copyright © John Trever

**Video Case**

In the video case, *Teacher Accountability: A Student Teacher's Perspective,* you'll see how student teacher Caitlin Hollister gains insights about teacher accountability from her principal and other teachers. As you watch the clips and study the artifacts in the case, reflect on the following questions.

**QUESTIONS**

1. The chart displaying students' math scores can seem overwhelming to a new teacher. Has viewing this video case changed your mind about using large data sets to track student progress? Why or why not?
2. Principal Mary Russo remarked that "every piece of data has a name and a face." What strikes you about her statement?
3. In your opinion, what's the best piece of advice that was given to Ms. Hollister?

***Online Study Center***

## Issues Related to NCLB

NCLB has proved quite controversial, for several reasons.

- *Funding.* Many states have complained that the requirements of the act have resulted in an *unfunded mandate* from the federal government (a law that requires organizations or states to implement policies or procedures but provides them with no or little money to carry out the policies); the states must spend larger amounts of money to comply with the law than they receive from the federal government for doing so. Although NCLB promised monies to the states, much of that funding has never been included in the federal budget. Some states have sued the federal government in hopes of recovering additional monies.
- *Labeling of schools.* If any of almost thirty subgroups of the students in a school fails to achieve passing scores on the state's tests for two consecutive years, then the whole school is labeled as failing to make adequate yearly progress. In some schools, the subgroup of students who fail to make adequate yearly progress may represent only a small percentage of the students in the school and hence may give a skewed perception of the progress made by the large majority of students in the school. Many educators also believe this provision is unduly punishing, holding them and the school accountable for social, cultural, and economic factors that may affect the performance of certain groups of students on statewide tests.
- *Unintended consequences.* Under the provisions of NCLB, students who attend such a failing school can opt to leave the school to attend any other public school, taking with them federal and state education monies. Ironically, in the first few years, larger percentages of high-achieving students than struggling ones took advantage of the transfer privilege, and this was certainly not the intent of the law.
- *Pressure toward lowering state standards.* Although NCLB is a federal law, it is important to note that each state sets its own content standards, designs its own assessments, and establishes its own passing scores.

Thus, states that have set high standards and require high scores to pass their assessments are more likely to have a higher failure rate among their students than states that have lower standards and lower pass scores. This fact encourages states to set lower standards and lower pass scores. Also, because each state's tests differ from those of the other states, it is impossible to make student achievement comparisons across states.

Whatever shifts these ongoing concerns may bring about in the future, it is a fact that NCLB in many ways now defines your job as a teacher. Teachers are now expected to bring about learning in students, and that learning is primarily measured by high-stakes state tests. If a sufficiently large number of students do not pass key tests, then educators and schools are held accountable for improving their scores. Your effectiveness as a teacher, therefore, is measured explicitly in terms of your students' results. Our hope is that studying this book and its accompanying materials will help prepare you to undertake all of the key tasks that will help you deliver these results.

More and more policymakers have become convinced that the single most important element in educational reform is the individual teacher. They have come to believe that all policy innovations will fall short of their goals if the classroom teacher isn't doing a good job of teaching for student learning. As a result of this insight, policymakers have promoted higher and higher expectations for teachers. To help you meet these high expectations, we have prepared this book, which contains essential knowledge for the beginning teacher. We hope you will find the information it contains useful in your first year as a teacher. But your continued success as a career professional teacher depends on the quality of your reflection, growth, and willingness to work at being the best teacher you can imagine. The work is difficult, but the reward is great.

## Further Resources

- Charlotte Danielson, *Enhancing Professional Practice: A Framework for Teaching* (Alexandria, VA: Association for Supervision and Curriculum Development, 1996). A useful book, organized around a framework of professional practice and based on the PRAXIS III criteria, including planning and preparation, classroom environment, instruction, and professional responsibilities.

- Thomas L. Good and Jere E. Brophy, *Looking in Classrooms*, 9th ed. (Boston: Allyn & Bacon, 2003). This excellent book provides teachers with skills that will enable them to observe and interpret the classroom behavior of both teachers and students.

- Clare R. Kilbane and Natalie B. Milman, *The Digital Teaching Portfolio Handbook: A How-To Guide for Educators* (Boston: Allyn & Bacon, 2003). An excellent guide to creating a digital teaching portfolio.

- *Teaching for Student Learning* Online Study Center. Be sure to include visits to your Online Study Center as part of your study of each module. You can link to the Video Cases from there, find links to Further Resources not listed in the book, and access many other resources that will help prepare you to be a master teacher.

- Kenneth M. Zeichner and Daniel P. Liston, *Reflective Teaching: An Introduction* (Mahwah, NJ: Lawrence Erlbaum Associates, 1996). An excellent introduction to the concept and practice of teacher reflection.

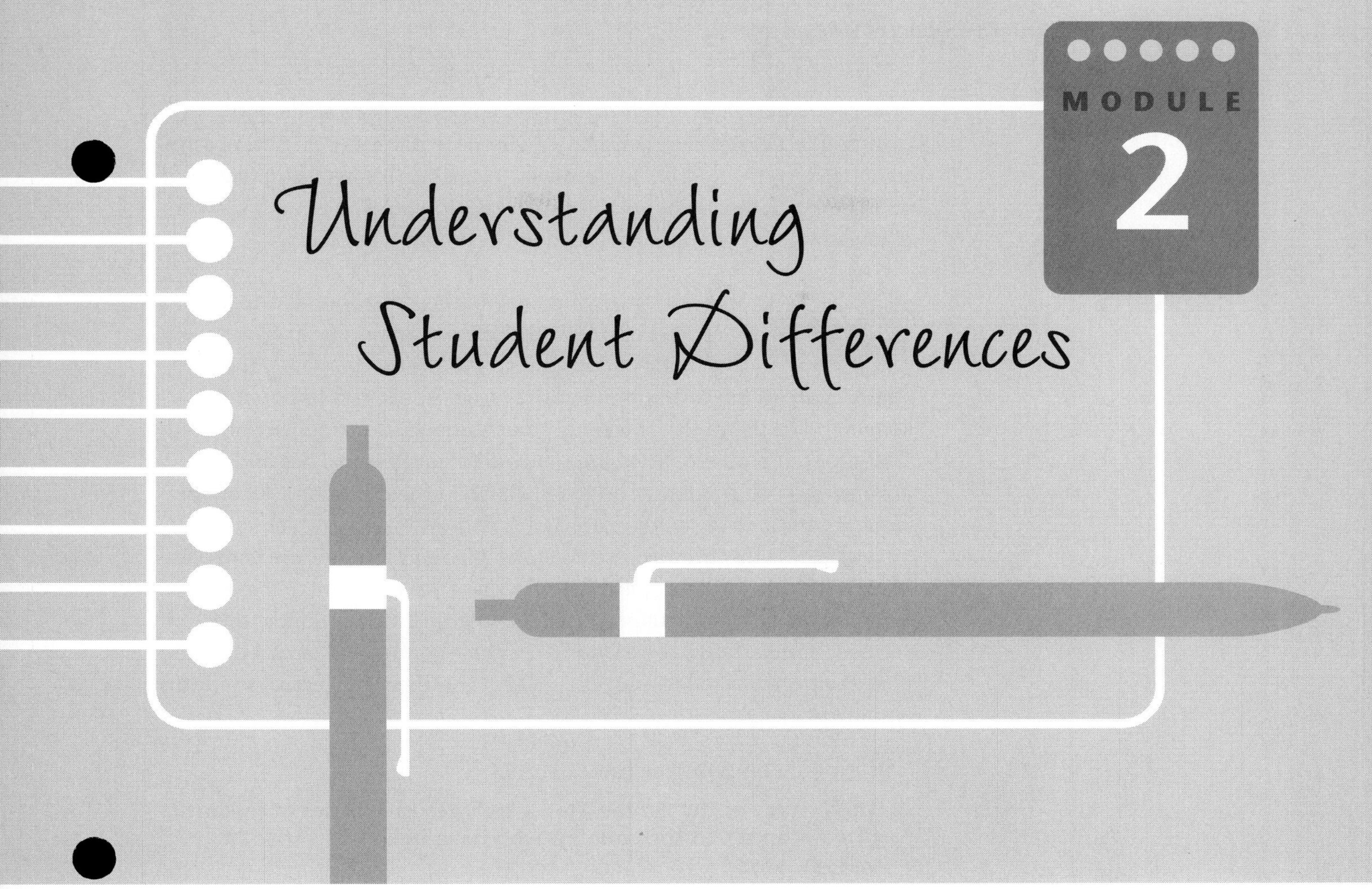

MODULE 2

# Understanding Student Differences

Scenario

The day has come! It's the first day of school. Sporting your new school clothes and clean, crisp, and nearly empty school pack, you disembark from the school bus and march off confidently toward your new classroom. You know where it is because you visited the building at the end of the last school year. From behind, you hear your name being called by your best friend, who wants to spend some time hanging out before the bell rings. You smile, adjust your pack, and head off with your friend to the start of a great new year.

This scenario may be a lot like one that you experienced. Or, you may have experienced a first day more like this one.

Scenario

As you get off the school bus, the hordes of people overwhelm you. You stop and stare, uncertain where to go or whom to ask. You remain frozen in anxiety until you feel a push from behind. As you turn, a group of young people go rushing past you, shouting something. You think they are yelling at you, but you don't know what they said. You shuffle along in the general direction of the crowd of people, but you still have no idea where you are supposed to go. You hear a lot of voices, laughter, and shouts of excitement—all of which makes you feel even more alone and isolated. You look around and, after a while, realize that an adult seems to be talking to you. The adult moves toward you, still talking, although you understand none of what is being said to you. The adult takes your elbow and leads you into the building. Your fear intensifies.

Preview

Just as *your* first day in the classroom as a teacher may fill you with feelings ranging from nervous anticipation to fear and dread, many of your students are going through much the same ordeal. It is important to keep in mind the range of feelings your students are experiencing. That range is emblematic of the many different personalities and abilities you will encounter on a daily basis in the classroom. All of your students are unique, quirky, capricious, and (at times) problematic individuals. In this module, we will take a look at some of the variables that contribute to the uniqueness of each of your students. These variables include their cultural, racial, and ethnic backgrounds, their socioeconomic status, their languages, their gender and sexual orientation, their physical abilities or disabilities, and their intellectual strengths and learning styles.

**This module emphasizes that:**

- **The history of the United States includes the stories of millions of newcomers to the country, who have been welcomed in various ways.**
- **Many groups of students were underserved until social and legal changes starting in the 1960s began to address their needs.**
- **The United States and its school classrooms continue to grow more and more racially and ethnically diverse. Teachers must understand the racial and cultural backgrounds of their students if they are to teach them effectively.**
- **Schools have taken many approaches to teaching students whose first language is not English. The current trend is toward immersing these students in regular classrooms, so teachers must be ready to help English language learners.**
- **Students' economic backgrounds can affect their school performance, and teachers must understand the role of family income.**
- **Teachers need to treat both male and female students fairly in the classroom. Teachers must also create a safe climate for students (and their family members) of all sexual orientations.**
- **An ongoing effort to include students with disabilities in regular classrooms means that teachers must be ready to work with students who have disabilities and to collaborate with families and special educators to the help meet the needs of these students.**
- **Your students will have a range of academic strengths and weaknesses, challenging you to help each one achieve to the best of her or his potential.**

# How We Got Here: A Brief History of U.S. Cultural Diversity

Throughout the history of the United States, people from many different countries have come to the United States for a host of reasons. Some came willingly, including many European immigrants who were seeking adventure, economic prosperity, or escape from famine. Others came here by force, as was the case for many African Americans. Still others came to escape an oppressive government or threats of genocide. Whatever the reason, tens of millions of people from scores of countries have immigrated to the United States.

Over the course of the past 200 years, America has welcomed immigrants with changing degrees of openness. Two periods of heavy immigration, in particular, demonstrate changes in the ways newcomers have been received. During one of the first major waves of immigration, between 1880 and 1930, over 27 million immigrants came to the United States, most of them from Western Europe. More recently, from 1960 to 2000, the number of immigrants exceeded 23 million people, most coming from Southeast Asia, Asia, Mexico, and Central and South America.[1] Not only did the cultural and racial makeup of the immigrant population change between these two immigration periods, but the responses of American school systems changed radically as well.

## The Melting Pot Idea

**Melting pot** an approach to receiving and educating immigrants based on the belief that immigrants would be most successful if they were able to assimilate into the dominant American culture.

During the earlier wave, the approach to receiving and educating immigrants was grounded in the belief that immigrants would be most successful if they were able to assimilate into the dominant American culture, which at that time was principally the white, Anglo-Saxon, Protestant (WASP) culture. The metaphor most often used to describe this approach to assimilating immigrants was the **melting pot,** which was taken from the play *Melting Pot,* written by Israel Zangwill in 1909. In a melting pot, different ingredients, unique and distinguishable—for example, different metals—are melted together to create a new compound. In the same way, people from many different cultures and backgrounds were expected to merge together to become part of their new culture, the American culture. Following this mindset, immigrants were encouraged to adopt the customs and traditions of their new host country, and many immigrants, either consciously or gradually, abandoned many of the traditions of their homelands in favor of American ways.

In a similar way, immigrants, especially the younger ones, were expected to adopt the language of their new country. Many youngsters were strongly encouraged to become fluent in English by their parents, who believed, often correctly, that the path to financial success in the United States was easier for English speakers. American schools responded in kind and taught immigrant students in English only. Stories abound of young immigrants who spoke no English being placed in an English-only classroom, where they were expected to learn, without assistance, not only English but all the other subjects as well! They may have experienced a first day of school like the one described in Scenario Two at the beginning of this chapter.

***McGuffey Readers*** a six-volume series of readers developed by William Holmes McGuffey that sold more than 100 million copies between 1836 and 1906. These books served to create a common curriculum for many students.

Lessons that promoted American beliefs and values were also an integral part of the curriculum. The ***McGuffey Readers,*** a series of readers first developed in 1836 and used in thirty-seven states in the late 19th century, were filled with stories that taught specific social behaviors and desirable character traits. These early textbooks taught American lore and promoted American customs and holidays. These beliefs and values were instilled in all students, American-born and immigrant, with no acknowledgement of any other culture.

**Assimilation** the absorption of an individual or a group into the cultural tradition of a population or another group.

Despite the predominance of the melting pot, or **assimilationist,** approach, most major cities had ethnic neighborhoods in which the language, customs, and traditions of the immigrant residents prevailed. Many of these neighborhoods also hosted bilingual schools, run most often by a religious group or church, which provided an easier transition for immigrant children who spoke no English.

## Moving Away from the Melting Pot

The most recent wave of immigration began in the tumultuous period of the 1960s and 1970s, when every aspect of American culture was called into question, and American social priorities became oriented toward the self-fulfillment of the individual. Many schools reflected this change by loosening their graduation requirements and broadening curriculum offerings. The combination of fewer graduation requirements and a new range of courses, in fields such as arts and literary genres, allowed high school students to craft a course of studies that appealed to their unique interests.

This period also saw demands for greater inclusiveness of all Americans, especially those whose cultural traditions were not grounded in the dominant WASP tradition or whose socioeconomic status placed them far from middle-class America. Schools have been a key arena for extending this inclusiveness to several key groups, including low-income students, members of racial and ethnic minority groups, English language learners, and students with disabilities.

***Low-Income Students*** In 1964, President Lyndon Johnson launched a far-reaching program called the War on Poverty. One of its cornerstones was the **Elementary and Secondary Education Act (ESEA)** of 1965, a law that has since become the major vehicle for federal funding of schools and is now known ast the No Child Left Behind Act (see Module 1, Reflective Teaching for Student Learning, for a full description of No Child Left Behind). The ESEA provided funding for extra, **compensatory education** services for "educationally deprived" children, predominantly children from low-income families. Another compensatory education program, Head Start, offered its first summer program in 1965 to increase the school readiness of children from low-income families. It has since expanded into a full-year program for preschool children.

**Elementary and Secondary Education Act (ESEA)** the federal government's single largest investment in elementary and secondary education, including Title I. Originally passed in 1965 and periodically reauthorized by Congress, most recently in 2001 as the No Child Left Behind Act.

**Compensatory education** educational support to provide a more nearly equal educational opportunity for disadvantaged students through such activities as remedial instruction and early learning.

***Brown* v. *Board of Education of Topeka*** U.S. Supreme Court ruling in 1954 holding that segregated schools are inherently unequal.

***Racial and Ethnic Minorities*** The ESEA, along with the landmark ***Brown* v. *Board of Education of Topeka*** Supreme Court decision, also aimed to address racial inequities and to protect and promote the constitutional rights of all Americans, especially African Americans. The most visible of these programs were the forced integration of all-white schools and the forced busing of African Americans to these schools. After an intensive effort to integrate schools during the 1970s and 1980s, the effort lost steam during the 1990s and early 21st century. Today, the average white student attends a school that is 80 percent white, while the average African American student attends a school that is 67 percent African American.[2]

***English Language Learners*** In 1968, a reauthorization of the ESEA included Title VII, the Bilingual Education Act, a law that provided federal money to

**Limited English proficiency (LEP)** a term used to describe students whose native language is not English and who have difficulty understanding and using English.

**English language learners (ELL)** students whose first language is other than English and who must learn English at school.

**P.L. 94-142, the Education for All Handicapped Children Act** a federal law that guaranteed a "free and appropriate public education" for all students with disabilities. In 1990, the name of the act was changed to the Individuals with Disabilities Education Act.

**Individuals with Disabilities Education Act (IDEA)** the 1990 enactment and subsequent reauthorizations of the Education for All Handicapped Children Act.

**Inclusion** the commitment to educate each child, to the maximum extent appropriate, in the regular school and classroom, rather than moving children with disabilities to separate classes or institutions.

school districts for teaching students with **limited English proficiency (LEP)** in their native languages. A 1974 Supreme Court ruling, in the case *Lau* v. *Nichols,* went even further. The Court declared it unconstitutional to deprive any student of equal access to education as a consequence of language barriers. The ruling required schools to provide equal opportunities for **English language learners (ELL)** either by helping students develop proficiency in the language of instruction (English) or by providing instruction in the students' dominant language. As we'll see later in this module, schools have responded in a range of ways to this directive.

***Students with Disabilities*** A 1975 federal law known as **P.L. 94-142, the Education for All Handicapped Children Act** began a revolution in the treatment of students with disabilities. Before that time, students with disabilities were segregated from the rest of the school population. This law and several subsequent ones have led to full **inclusion** of students with disabilities in many schools. The change has been costly and disruptive, but it has also been one of the truly noble moments in the history of American education. And, as we will see later in this module, as well as in Module 4, Teaching Students with Disabilities, this revolution is still going on, as administrators, teachers, and students struggle to work out the most effective and just procedures to meet the educational needs of students with disabilities.

The demands and requirements placed on schools to provide equal educational opportunities to all students have changed and expanded over the years, but the expectation that the schools will provide equal educational opportunities has not. The actual delivery of "equal educational opportunities" is your job as a teacher. It is therefore a teacher's special professional responsibility to be, first, sensitive to, and then responsive to, the conditions and special situations of your students. The rest of the module summarizes some of those situations.

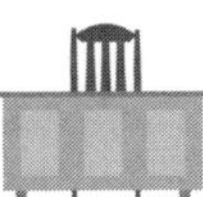

### Now You Do It

Have you personally benefited from any of these efforts to expand educational opportunities? Do you have any friends or family members who have benefited? If so, in what ways? What problems or difficulties still remain?

## Diversity in Today's Classrooms

You can see the direct results of the increasing cultural diversity of the population in your classroom today, where you will find a wide range of differences among the students in your class. Every student is an individual, with his or her own personality and characteristics, and we urge you to get to know all of the students in your class.

Cultural differences (sometimes related to racial or ethnic backgrounds), socioeconomic differences, gender differences, and differences in physical and mental abilities all can influence student learning, and you must be prepared to respond to these differences in learning.

## Racial and Ethnic Diversity

As the most recent wave of immigration continues, the population of the United States continues to become more and more diverse. About 32 percent of the entire U.S. population are members of racial or ethnic minority groups, and the number of school-age children who are members of minority groups is even greater, estimated to be about 40 percent.[3] As a result, your classroom is very likely to have students of various races and ethnic origins.

**Race** a physiological descriptor for people with a common ancestry and physical characteristics.

**Ethnicity** shared history, traits, and customs.

**Culture** shared characteristics among a group of people, such as language, customs, political and economic interests, and often religion, that affect how they perceive and interact with the world.

**Race** is a physiological descriptor for people with a common ancestry and physical characteristics. **Ethnicity,** in contrast, refers to a group of people who share such characteristics as language, customs, political and economic interests, and (often) religion—in other words, people who share a common **culture.** Tied into one's ethnicity are ways of perceiving and interacting with the world. Such perceptions are manifested in language expression and thinking processes and have a significant impact on how an individual learns.

***Teacher–Student Disparity*** Women constitute about 75 percent of all public school teachers. Furthermore, almost 91 percent of public school teachers are white, and most are from middle-class backgrounds.[4] About 40 percent of students in public schools are from racial and ethnic minorities, and many of them live in poverty. Thus the typical teacher, a white female, comes from a very different background than many of the students she teaches. There is an achievement gap between white students and students of African American and Hispanic background in the United States, and at least some of that gap can be attributed to disparities between school and home cultures.

It is easier for most teachers to work with students who share a similar background. The more alike students and teachers are in social and cultural characteristics, the more they share tacit, unspoken expectations about behavior and academic performance, which greatly streamlines and enhances teacher–student communications. When social and cultural characteristics of the teacher and students differ, however, teacher and student expectations at school may not match as well. The teacher in this situation needs training to be able to understand her students—and to help them understand her expectations—in order to help the students achieve and succeed.

**Culturally responsive teaching** a method of embracing students' cultural backgrounds by modifying classroom conditions or activities to include elements related to the students' culture.

One way that teachers can acknowledge and accommodate cultural diversity in the classroom is through **culturally responsive teaching.** The school's middle-class culture often places students from other cultures at a

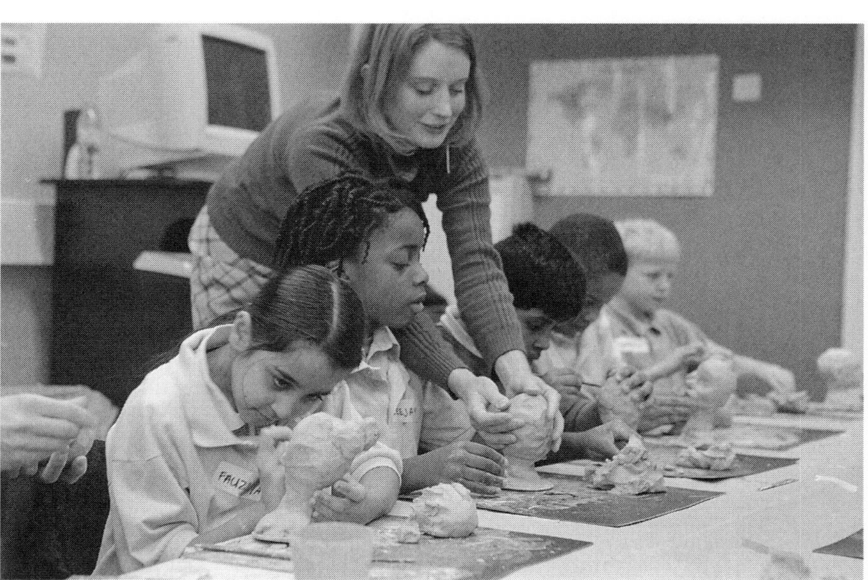

Students from many different ethnicities and cultures can be found in our nation's classrooms.

## In Your Classroom

### Coping with Cultural Disparities

*Prospective Teachers*

Seeking to broaden your own cultural background will help you understand more of your students.

- Seek experiences to broaden your understanding of societal and cultural commonalities and differences (for example, travel to foreign countries).
- Volunteer in organizations and clubs located in communities that differ from those in which you grew up.
- Volunteer in schools that differ from those you attended.

*Practicing Teachers*

Here are some guidelines to help you address diversity once you have your own classroom:

- Learn about and appreciate the values and backgrounds of your students.
- Try to use culturally responsive teaching by incorporating elements of the students' culture into your learning activities.
- Focus on students' strengths, rather than weaknesses, and teach to those strengths rather than making the students feel incapable or deficient. Find ways for all students to receive recognition from you and their peers for being good at something.
- Differentiate your instruction so that students with different approaches to learning can find suitable ways to learn. (See Module 5, Teaching Academically Diverse Learners, for more on differentiated instruction.)
- Coordinate expertise and support with the students' homes so that students get a consistent message.
- Recognize that school's middle-class values, such as individual learning and competition, may clash with the values of some students' cultures. Teachers need to help students learn to bridge the gaps between the two worlds.

disadvantage in understanding the school's codes and communication styles. By using instructional materials and practices that incorporate important aspects of students' family and community, teachers can respond to and reflect their students' cultures in their classrooms. For example, if a class consists of many Latino immigrant children, teachers can place maps of students' home countries and of the United States around the room, provide magazines and games in both Spanish and English, or play salsa music as background for certain activities. The "In Your Classroom" feature provides further suggestions for bridging cultural gaps between you and your students. Knowing and understanding your students' cultural backgrounds can help you make your classroom more inviting and increase student achievement.

## Linguistic Diversity

Whereas cultural differences may be enigmatic and deceiving, linguistic differences are generally quite prominent. Approximately 5 million of the 49.6 million students enrolled in K–12 schools in the United States are English language learners.[5] That means that about one in ten students in the K–12 student population faces the scary first day of school described in Scenario Two at the beginning of this module. About three-fourths of English language learners speak Spanish as their primary language. Other languages represented in American schools include Vietnamese, Hmong, Korean, Arabic, Haitian Creole, Cantonese, Tagalog, Russian, Navajo, and Khmer (Cambodian).

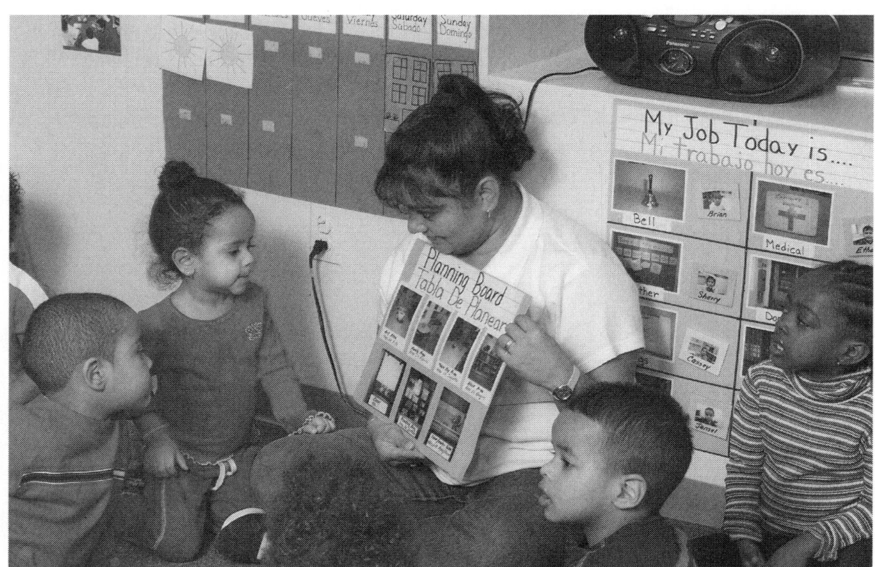


Both English and Spanish are used to help preschool children become ready for kindergarten.

Not all of these students are recent immigrants. Many students who have lived their whole lives in the United States come from homes or neighborhoods where they have had little opportunity to hear or practice English. Students who are new to the United States need help in understanding the culture as well as in learning English. But *all* English language learners have the double task of learning not just a new language but also at least some new ways of thinking, acting, and behaving that correspond to the social and linguistic norms of the dominant American culture.

Schools have responded to these needs in a variety of ways. Approaches to teaching English language learners fall into three broad categories: bilingual education programs, English-as-a-second-language programs, and immersion-type programs.

**Bilingual education** educational programs in which students of limited English proficiency attend classes taught in English as well as in their native language.

1. *Bilingual education programs.* **Bilingual education** programs provide academic instruction in students' dominant language, while also providing English language instruction to help the students develop their fluency in English. Many bilingual education programs are meant to be *transitional*, providing students with decreasing amounts of instruction in their dominant language and increasing amounts of instruction in English. This approach was devised on the basis of the underlying belief that as students became more fluent in English, they could begin to be taught other subjects in English, too.

   In recent years, however, bilingual education programs have become controversial. Many parents, students, and lawmakers were dissatisfied with programs in which transitions to English occurred very slowly, or sometimes not at all. As a result, voters in several states (including California, Arizona, and Massachusetts) have approved the elimination of bilingual education programs in favor of English-as-a-second-language programs or limited-time sheltered English programs, such as those described below.

**English as a second language (ESL)** a program in which English language learners are assigned to a mainstream classroom and then given specialized instruction in English, usually in a resource room with a specially trained teacher.

**Mainstream classroom/mainstreaming** the practice of placing special education students and English language learners in general education classes for at least part of the school day, while also providing additional services, programs, or classes as needed.

2. *English-as-a-second-language (ESL) programs.* Especially in schools with fewer than twenty students of the same linguistic background, educators often respond to the needs of ELL students by teaching **English as a second language (ESL).** ELL students are assigned to a **mainstream classroom** and then given specialized instruction in English, usually in a resource room with a specially trained teacher. Students receive ESL support for varying amounts of time during the school day, depending on their level of fluency in English.

**Immersion** programs for English language learners in which the students are placed in language-rich, mainstream classrooms with their fluent-English-speaking classmates. Through this maximum exposure to the English language, they are expected to learn it.

**Sheltered immersion** immersion programs in which the English used is simplified and the classrooms consist entirely of English language learners.

3. *Immersion programs and sheltered immersion programs.* For some years, immersion programs were more aptly called *submersion* or *sink-or-swim* programs. Many educators and school administrators believe that young learners learn a second language with relative ease, so they do not require special instruction or a specialized environment to help these students learn the target language. Thus, in **immersion** programs, English language learners are placed in language-rich, mainstream classrooms with their fluent-English-speaking classmates. From maximum exposure to the English language, they are expected to learn it. These programs are more likely to be found in elementary schools, because younger learners seem to acquire new languages with more ease than older ones.

   In response to immersion programs, **sheltered immersion** programs were developed. Sheltered English classrooms are also English-only, language-rich environments, but the English used is simplified to make it more accessible and understandable to English language learners. In addition, the student population is made up entirely of English language learners, a format that allows these students only limited contact with their native English-speaking classmates.

Your school may have some type of bilingual education program to help ELL students become more fluent in English—or it may not. In either case, you are almost certain to have students whose first language is not English in your classroom for at least part of the day. The "In Your Classroom" feature offers some guidelines that may help you work more effectively with these students.

## In Your Classroom

### Working with Students Whose First Language Is Not English

1. *Students may understand more than they can say.* Students' *receptive* skills, listening and reading, are often more advanced than their *productive* skills, speaking and writing. ELL students may be in the preproduction phase of their language development; they understand what they hear but are not yet ready to respond. Therefore, if a student does not answer aloud, you should refrain from assuming that the student does not understand what you have told him or her to do. Instead, look for another indicator that will tell you whether students understand, such as a sample of their work.

2. *As with other students, talking in class is not the same as doing the work.* Understanding academic language and instructional materials is generally harder than understanding an everyday conversation. Second language learners often develop basic interpersonal communicative skills (BICS) before they develop cognitive/academic language proficiency (CALP).[6] Remember that even students who are very competent communicators may still need support to help them develop appropriate academic language.

3. *Show, don't just tell.* Just as much as, if not more than, most other students, ELL students need visual or nonverbal cues to help them understand words and concepts. Provide information using visuals as often as possible.

4. *Focus on reading comprehension, not just pronunciation.* Reading a text aloud is not necessarily an indication that the student understands what he or she is reading. Decoding—associating a sound with a particular symbol (letter)—is a mechanical skill in which ELL students may develop fluency quite readily. Comprehension is a separate reading skill that needs to be fostered and developed among ELL students.

## Socioeconomic Diversity

**Socioeconomic status (SES)** a term used by the U.S. Bureau of the Census to describe a person's occupational status, income, and (often) educational attainment.

**Video Case**

The video case, *Bilingual Education: An Elementary Two-Way Immersion Program*, introduces two teachers and their students who are involved in a two-way bilingual program. That is, all students learn to read, write, and communicate in *both* English and Spanish in all subject areas. As you watch the clips and study the artifacts in the case, reflect on the following questions.

**QUESTIONS**

1. Which of the models described here does this classroom most resemble? Why?
2. How are these teachers demonstrating the teaching tips listed here?
3. Do you agree with the teacher's assessment of the pros and cons of her program? Why or why not? What would you add?

*Online Study Center*

**Socioeconomic status (SES)** is a term that the U.S. Bureau of the Census uses to describe a person's occupational status, income, and (often) educational attainment. It is probably not a surprise to you that people of high socioeconomic status usually have well-paying jobs and high levels of education. People of low socioeconomic status often have low-paying jobs and may not have very much education.

Many sociologists insist that socioeconomic class is as much a cultural group as is ethnicity. They suggest that, like other cultural groups, different SES groups have distinct customs, beliefs, and values. For example, people of high socioeconomic status often consider high educational attainment a worthwhile goal, whereas people of low socioeconomic status may not place as much value on educational attainment. Other differences may include variations in work ethic, family structure, or norms of interacting between the young and adults.

One researcher, Shirley Brice Heath, has documented differences among families from different SES groups in the ways that adults speak to children and in the importance the families place on helping preschool children develop literacy skills.[7] In lower-SES families, Heath found that there was less verbal interaction, overall, between adults and children than in middle-SES families. The nature of the interactions differed, too. In a low-SES family, the purpose of conversation between parents and children is more often knowledge gathering. A parent might ask a child, "Where's your brother?" or "Who broke the window?" In middle-SES families, the verbal interaction between parents and children was often knowledge building, a type of communication that more closely resembles school discourse. A parent in a middle-SES family might ask a child to identify an object, a letter, or a word, in order to help the child build knowledge. Students who have had this type of "practice" at home often begin school better prepared for the style of conversation they will encounter there, as well as armed with more of the basic skills for learning school subjects, such as how to read. These are the kinds of students who seem to fit in effortlessly on the first day of school, as described at the beginning of this module.

Ruby Payne has written about mismatches that often occur between children from impoverished backgrounds and our schools. Payne asserts that whereas schools value academic learning, delayed gratification, and other middle-class values, children from poverty tend to value survival, entertainment, and relationships. Unless educators understand these "hidden rules" that tend to govern the behavior of children of poverty, they will not be effective in educating them.[8]

Teachers who find themselves teaching in a school district with students from a range of SES groups need to keep in mind that students from different socioeconomic groups may not share the same practices or values. Heath's research, for example, suggests that young students from lower-SES groups may need more explicit explanation of how the school environment works than will those from middle-SES backgrounds.

## Gender and Sexual Orientation

Another important difference in students is related to their gender. Although debate still rages about whether differences between males and females are biological or socially created, it is agreed that there are different expectations for males and females in our society, despite the evolving gender roles of recent decades. For our purposes here, we will acknowledge that differences in learning, motivation, and attitude can often be related to gender. In addition,

## Video Case

In the video case, *Gender Equity in the Classroom: Girls and Science*, you'll see how middle school teacher Robert Cho promotes science learning for all his students, boys *and* girls. As you watch the clips and study the artifacts in the case, reflect on the following questions.

**QUESTIONS**

1. Toward the end of the main video in the case, Mr. Cho, the middle school teacher, talks about girls shying away from science because of stereotypes that it is not a "girl job." This module also discusses the effects of gender stereotypes on academic performance. Besides the one mentioned, about science, what are some other gender stereotypes related to academic subjects?
2. Do you agree that it is important for students to have gender or ethnic-minority role models in different academic and career areas, as the teachers in the video case suggest? Why or why not?

***Online Study Center***

a number of sociolinguists claim that there are distinct differences in discourse patterns between genders. This kind of diversity is less likely to lead to misunderstanding than cultural diversity, but its potential to disrupt the educational process is significant, especially if there are students who are insensitive to individual differences.

Research indicates that teachers do tend to treat boys and girls differently.[9] Whereas there was great concern during the 1980s and early 1990s that schools were favoring boys over girls, in recent years more concern is being expressed that boys are falling behind. Although boys continue to outperform girls in science and higher mathematics, girls outperform boys in reading and writing, take more credits in academic subjects, and are more likely to attend college. Boys also constitute two-thirds of the students receiving special education services.

Teachers need to ensure that they treat boys and girls equitably by not stereotyping gender roles, by providing equal opportunity to participate in classroom discussions, by eliminating the assignment of sex-stereotyped tasks, and by modeling sex-equitable behavior.

If you are teaching in middle school or high school, you are likely to encounter students who are still struggling to figure out their sexual identity. As many of your middle school youth begin to explore attractions to classmates of the opposite sex, some will begin to wonder about their lack of attraction to these classmates or their stronger attraction to classmates of the same sex. By the time these students reach high school, many have begun to realize that they do not think, feel, or act like their same-sex classmates.

The issue of homosexuality is extremely controversial in our society. There is considerable evidence that gay and lesbian students often face a hostile environment in school, as well as in the larger society. As educators, however, we have the responsibility to avoid promoting any particular social agenda in favor of promoting the emotional well-being of all of our students. This means that all your students, regardless of sexual orientation, have the right to a safe and supportive learning environment.

## Diverse Abilities

As you get to know your students, you will certainly notice differences in their performance and participation in the classroom. These differences can be linked to a number of variables: their innate ability, the match of their innate ability with the performance demands placed on them in the classroom, and their interest in performing well at school. Some of your students may have physical or learning disabilities that affect their classroom participation. As we noted earlier in this module, the education of students with disabilities has been mandated and regulated by federal legislation since the 1970s, and the trend in recent years has been to include these students in regular classrooms. Thus you will find yourself teaching students with a range of disabilities. Module 4, Teaching Students with Disabilities, discusses your role in meeting the needs of these students. You can be certain that even in a homogenous classroom, you will have students who represent a range of abilities, learning styles, and motivations to learn. Trying to keep *all* students engaged and challenged requires extensive planning and preparation, which we describe in detail in Module 5, Teaching Academically Diverse Learners.

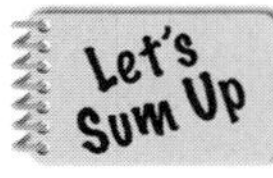


Most beginning teachers express concern about their ability to address the various kinds of diversity that we have touched on in this module. "How can I, as a beginning teacher, meet the needs of my students who possess these various characteristics, when I'm just learning how to teach?" This is a legitimate concern, but it should not be discouraging to you. Learning to teach is a gradual process, and it will take you both time and reflection to become effective with most of your students. In the beginning, be aware that these differences do exist and affect how children will learn. Try to incorporate student differences into your lesson plans, in the activities you provide, and in how you assess student learning. Give students choices that enable them to learn in ways that play to their strengths, rather than demonstrate their shortcomings. There are many resources available that can help you incorporate student differences into your teaching; some of these resources are listed in the next section. Also keep in mind that just as surely as there are many differences among children, there are also many common elements. We all have basic psychological and physical needs that span racial, cultural, and gender boundaries. Understanding these stages of development and areas of common needs will help you to understand student behavior and to develop appropriate classroom experiences.

## Further Resources

- Lisa Delpit, *Other People's Children: Cultural Conflict in the Classroom* (New York: The New Press, 1995). The author asserts that most classrooms are dominated by a white perspective and that too few teachers acknowledge that children of color have perspectives of their own.

- Geneva Gay, *Culturally Responsive Teaching: Theory, Research, and Practice* (New York: Teachers College Press, 2000). This book describes how teachers can use culturally responsive teaching to improve the school performance of underachieving students of color.

- The Hall of Multiculturalism. Available at: **http://www.tenet.edu/halls/multiculturalism.html.** This site provides a list of multicultural resources for K–12 teachers and students.

- *National Clearinghouse for English Language Acquisition*. Available at: **http://www.ncela.gwu.edu.** Funded by the U.S. Department of Education, this site contains hundreds of articles, links, databases, and online assistance in the area of English language acquisition.

- Carol Ann Tomlinson and Jay McTighe, *Integrating Differentiated Instruction & Understanding by Design: Connecting Content and Kids* (Alexandria, VA: Association for Supervision and Curriculum Development, 2006). This book addresses two major concerns of teachers: how to craft a powerful curriculum in an age of standards-based reform and ensuring academic success for the wide variety of learners.

- University of Virginia, *Office of Special Education: A Web Resource for Special Education.* Available at: **http://curry.edschool.virginia.edu/go/specialed.** This website at the Curry School of Education at the University of Virginia contains much information about special education, including the history of the field and a review of the types of disabilities. It also offers discussion groups, electronic addresses of special educators, and much more.

- Guadalupe Valdes, *Learning and Not Learning English* (New York: Teachers College Press, 2001). The author addresses the difficulties of learning and teaching English for second language learners by focusing on the lives and experiences of four Mexican children in an American middle school.

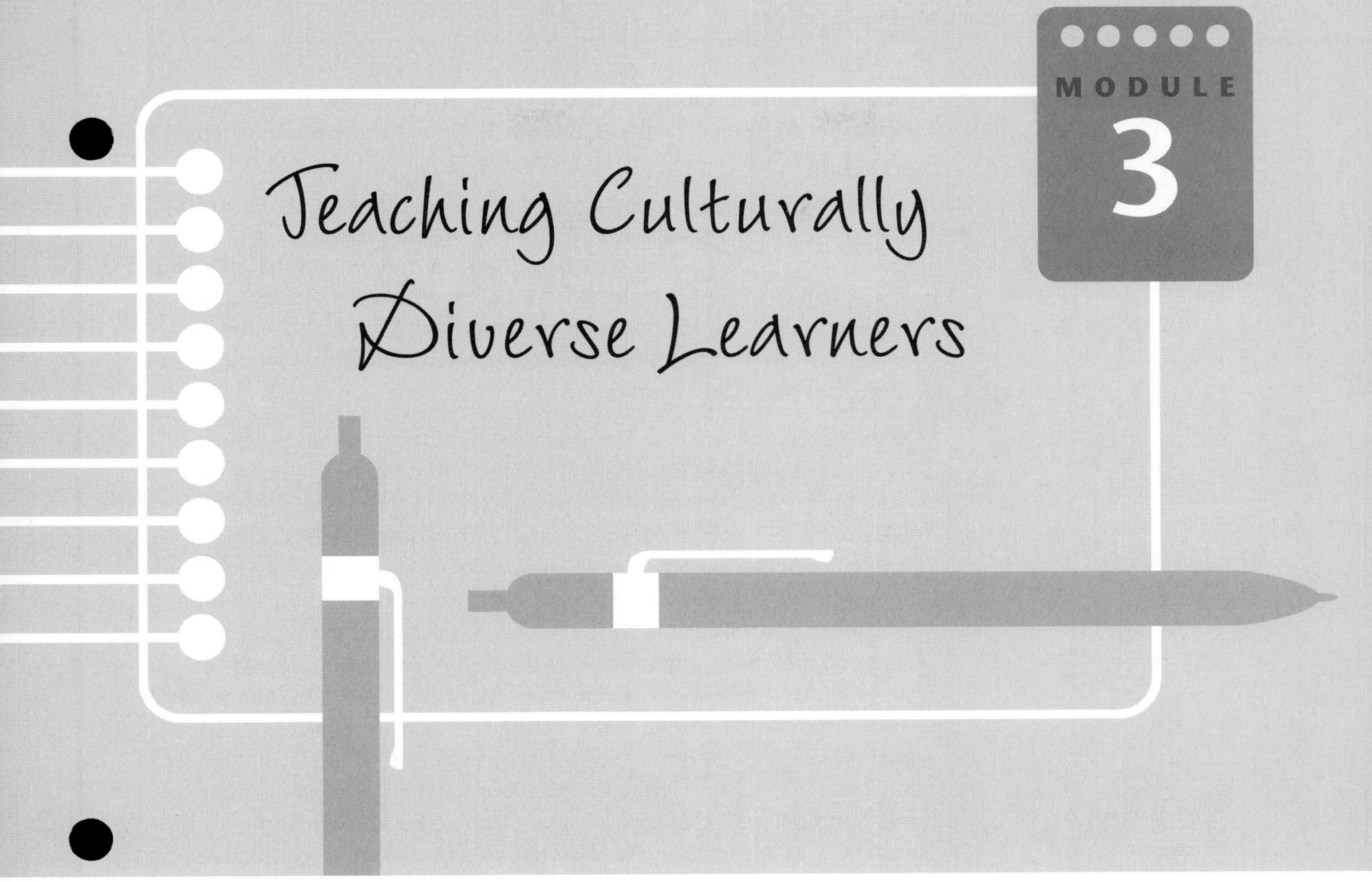


# Teaching Culturally Diverse Learners

Scenario

Mary Jane Gibson, a first-year, third-grade teacher at Frontier Elementary School in Chula Vista, California, scheduled an appointment to talk to Mr. Edwards, the school principal, about the cheating she had discovered in her classroom.

"Mr. Edwards," she said, "I think that several of my children have been turning in homework that is not their own. In fact, I think that some of the children have done the homework of others in the class and have received help from older siblings. Before I take any action, I wanted to talk over the matter with you."

"Ms. Gibson, I'm glad you've come to see me. What are the names of these children?"

"The four students are Yao Thao, Pa Hang, Mai Lor, and Choua Vang. I think they are all Hmong students."

"I see," said Mr. Edwards. "Are you aware, Ms. Gibson, that within Hmong society, there is a strong expectation that students will help one another and younger siblings? They don't see helping one another as inappropriate, and they certainly don't see it as cheating."

"Really?" said Ms. Gibson, "I had no idea. Maybe I need to make it clearer to the students when it is OK to help one another and when I expect them to do their own work."

Preview

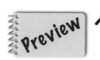

This fictional scenario demonstrates that different cultures have different expectations for appropriate behavior and that you, as a teacher, need to be aware of some of these cultural differences that might affect student behavior and learning.

As we noted in Module 2, Understanding Student Differences, the American population, especially the school population, is among the most racially and ethnically diverse populations in the world. You are likely to have in your classroom students from other nations, some of whom are fluent in English and others who are not. These students will need your help to learn the culture of your school and your classroom. Of course, you will also have students who have lived in the United States all their lives. These students will also need varying degrees of your help to learn the culture of your school and classroom. Some may speak English only as their second language, because their family speaks another language at home. Even students who show fluency in English, however, may have different expectations for the classroom environment and different understandings of both verbal and nonverbal exchanges, because they are likely to come from a variety of socioeconomic and ethnic backgrounds. You must master the art of communicating with *all* of your students, whether their cultural background matches yours or not.

In this module, we describe how to avoid several of the potential pitfalls of intercultural communication, and we introduce you to multicultural education and culturally responsive teaching.

**This module emphasizes that:**

- **Mastering intercultural communication requires teachers to be aware of—and to avoid—potential misunderstandings that stem from culturally based differences in verbal communication, nonverbal communication, time orientation, social values, and instructional formats and learning processes.**
- **The term *multicultural education* encompasses a host of programs, practices, and philosophies.**
- **Researchers and educators disagree about the effectiveness and the appropriateness of multicultural education in general, as well as about specific multicultural education programs.**
- **Culturally responsive teaching requires teachers to know the cultures of their students, to understand their own attitudes toward different cultural groups, and to incorporate elements of students' cultures into the classroom.**

# Intercultural Communication

As we have noted, cultural differences among your students are likely to include linguistic diversity. Although linguistic diversity is obvious when students speak a language other than English, or when they use an accent other than the one most common in the region, people fluent in English can also have trouble talking to each other because of differences in culture. You can teach all of your students more effectively if you are sensitive to key principles of intercultural communication, the process by which people from different cultures attempt to exchange messages.

According to researcher Christine Bennett, there are five aspects of culture that present the potential for misunderstanding: verbal communication, nonverbal communication, time orientation, social values, and instructional formats and learning processes.[1] To maximize the educational experiences of all students in your classroom, you should clarify the meaning of routine gestures and expression, common words and commands, and expectations for behaviors and social interactions. Taking time to develop shared understanding of these elements will make communication and learning that much more effective for all.

## Verbal Communication

Even among your students who speak English, there may be varying expectations in verbal communication, especially among students from different ethnic backgrounds. One level of verbal misunderstanding is tied to the *connotations* we attribute to words, the meanings we attach to them beyond their simple dictionary definitions. Words that may have a neutral meaning to one person may have a negative connotation to another. A comment as simple as "Good work" from the teacher may be interpreted by one student to be an indication of praise and by another to be a sign of disappointment. A derogatory comment from one African American student to another may

Working together in an after-school mentoring program, students develop an understanding and appreciation for their cultural differences.

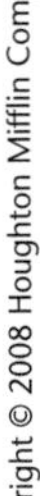

be taken in fun, whereas the same comment from a white student may be interpreted as an insult.

A second level of verbal misunderstandings is related to discourse patterns, or styles of talking. Misunderstandings based on discourse patterns occur quite regularly among people of different ethnic or cultural groups whose first language is English. Think about the different ways a request can be made. Let's say you want someone to empty the wastebasket. You could explicitly tell the person, "[Please] empty the wastebasket." You could make it a request, asking, "Would you mind emptying the wastebasket?" Or you could be more indirect and say, "The wastebasket is full," with the assumption that the person will act on that observation.

In some cultures, the typical discourse pattern is direct, or even abrupt, whereas other cultures prefer a more indirect discourse pattern. In an indirect discourse, a conversation may meander for fifteen or twenty minutes before the purpose of the interaction is made known. And even after the purpose or topic is made known, its unveiling may take another substantial period of time. Often, one of the speakers will drop hints to suggest the purpose or topic of the meeting, and the other speaker will, through seeking the answers to suggestive questions, become aware of the message. However, in most classrooms, teacher communication tends to be direct rather than circuitous. Be aware that a direct communication style may be jarring to some children who are unaccustomed to such directness.

A third level of verbal misunderstanding combines the characteristics of differing connotations and discourse patterns. Certain topics of conversation that may be acceptable in one culture may be considered the height of disrespect or inappropriateness in another. One good example comes from the experience of one of the authors in West Africa. At one point, a tribal king had died, but the announcement of his death stated that the king had a broken leg. Not only would it have violated cultural norms to say explicitly that the king had died, but revealing this information early in the conversation would have been a second violation.

## Nonverbal Communication

We communicate as much information with our gestures, facial expressions, postures, silences, and pauses as with our words. In fact, many sociolinguists maintain that we communicate more nonverbally than we do verbally. If you ask someone for directions, for example, and the person tells you to take a right but points to the left, are you more inclined to go right or left when you get to the intersection in question? More people will follow the nonverbal direction, which is seen as a more reliable source of information.

Like verbal communication, nonverbal communication is culturally defined. Europeans, especially the Italians and French, are well known for their expansive use of gestures in communication. Four aspects of nonverbal communication are vulnerable to the greatest misunderstanding or discomfort in intercultural communication. These include personal and physical space, physical contact, eye contact, and use of gestures.

- *Personal and physical space.* Americans love their space! Some cultural anthropologists attribute this to the wide-open country and abundance of land that our forebears found when they first came to the continent and continued to explore it. This love of open vistas seems to translate into an expectation for a large personal space, the distance individuals like to keep between themselves and other people. When Americans engage in conversation, they generally remain two to three feet away from their conversation partners. Europeans, Asians, and Africans do not have the same preference or need for personal space. Therefore, when engaging in conversation, many non-Americans stand much closer to their conversation partners than Americans do. This physical proximity often makes many Americans feel uncomfortable or nervous. Do not be surprised if your non-American or minority students place themselves much closer to you than you find comfortable.

There are also cultural differences in attitudes toward one's physical space. In the classroom, this translates into one's desk area, one's locker or cubby space, and even one's backpack and lunch box. Some people are very protective of their physical space and don't want others to intrude, whereas children from some cultures that are used to crowded environments don't feel that sense of spatial ownership and are more willing to share space.

- *Physical contact.* Along with physical proximity goes physical contact. Mainstream Americans tend to shun physical contact just as they shun physical proximity. Europeans and South Americans are often much more open about physical contact, and it is not uncommon to see heterosexual men holding hands in many South American and Middle Eastern cities. Non-American students may find physical contact with the teacher appropriate. If you find it unnerving, be sure to explain that to your students. Do not expect them to know dominant cultural norms.

- *Eye contact.* "Look at me when I talk to you!" How many times have we heard or said this? In the dominant American culture, eye contact is an important part of honest and open communication. The common perception is that eye contact allows people to assess the validity of the verbal message being conveyed. Thus, Americans are often suspicious of a conversation partner who does not make eye contact. "He must have been lying. He wouldn't even look me in the eyes."

  In many non-Western cultures, however, making eye contact is a sign of *disrespect,* especially in a hierarchical relationship. In other words, a child who makes eye contact with an adult is showing a disregard for the position of the adult. Telling students from these cultures to "look at" the teacher directly would be forcing them to show disrespect for you.

- *Gestures.* We make no attempt to present an exhaustive guide to culturally defined behaviors and gestures, but we want to present a few examples to show the range of meanings that gestures or behaviors can have from one culture to another.

  - *Come here.* Although it is common in the dominant American culture to beckon a person to "come here" by motioning with the index finger with the palm up, such a gesture can be insulting to many Asians and Middle Easterners and may be without meaning to Africans. In these cultures, the beckoning gesture involves the whole hand, palm down, with all fingers motioning.

  - *Good-bye.* Americans often wave good-bye by waving their hands palms outward in the direction of the recipient. For some Europeans and Asians, this gesture means, "No," or "Stop it."

  - *OK.* Another frequently used gesture among Americans is the OK sign, formed with the thumb and index finger. Teachers sometimes use this gesture to indicate that a student has done

Gestures can be easily misunderstood. Is this person pointing upward, or saying "one," or saying "Wait just a moment"?

acceptable or even good work. In some cultures, however, the teacher's compliment is understood as an obscenity, and in others, it indicates worthlessness (the thumb and index finger make a zero).

- *Counting.* Even something as simple as counting on one's hand is culturally bound. Americans usually have a closed fist facing outward and lift one finger at a time, starting with the index finger and ending with the thumb; Europeans have a closed fist facing inward and lift the thumb first and end with the little finger. Asians have an open hand, palm up, and fold in fingers, starting with the thumb and ending with the little finger. (The numbers six through ten are counted by lifting the fingers starting with the little finger and ending with the thumb.)

And these are just the international differences! Remember that different ethnic or student groups may have developed their own meaningful gestures, too. Because of the ambiguity of nonverbal communication, you should never assume that students understand the meaning of familiar gestures and common nonverbal communication patterns. At the beginning of the year, spend some time introducing students to the gestures you will use in the classroom. At first, model the gesture and look for students' reactions. If any student seems troubled or surprised by the gesture, you may want to consider using a different gesture. In any case, be sure to spend some time modeling the gesture and explaining its meaning. "When I do this (raise hand in the air), it means I want you all to stop talking and listen to me. When you do the same (raise hand in air), I'll know that you have something you want to tell the class."

### Now You Do It

Working with a fellow prospective teacher from a different culture, take an inventory of some of the gestures, expressions, and phrases you often use in your communication. Ask your colleague whether any of them are likely to be offensive to some students. Are any of them ambiguous in meaning? That is, could they be interpreted to mean something other than what you intended?

## Time Orientation

Non-Americans are often amused by the American obsession with time. "For you Americans, 'Time is money,' right?" is a comment frequently made by our European, African, and Latino neighbors. This obsession with time is instilled in Americans at a very early age. It is particularly evident in the school setting, where students are often punished for coming late to class and are encouraged to work quickly (and quietly, but that's another issue).

In the classroom, expect that some of your students whose culture differs from the dominant American culture will not understand your negative reactions to their tardiness or slowness in getting started with work in the classroom. To help them be more successful, explain your expectations regarding punctuality and time management, so that students can realize the importance of these traits in your classroom. Ensuring that they understand the importance of these traits in the dominant American culture may also help them be more successful in their future school career.

## Social Values

In addition to the "time is money" attitude, two other traits are often cited as being of special value in the dominant American culture: individualism and competition. The self-made person is a hallmark of American history and culture, and the "rags to riches" story is one of the most popular in American folklore. The rugged pioneers who helped to settle what are now the midwestern and western regions of the United States are equally legendary for their independent spirit and drive. This "every man for himself" sentiment is often found not only in American business but in schools as well, where students are often pitted against one another and graded on individual, rather than collective, performance.

American culture also thrives on competition, the mainstay of the powerful American economic system. This love of competition is encouraged in most American schools, where students regularly compete for the best grades, the highest awards, the winningest team.

Students from different cultural backgrounds may not, however, be driven by the same values. Students from some Native American, Asian, and African cultures are taught that loyalty to others is more important than individual gain. These students may feel a strong responsibility for helping classmates of the same ethnic origin succeed in schoolwork. In addition, some cultures discourage competition among students, encouraging instead cooperation and collaboration. For example, in many Asian cultures, students are regularly expected to work in teams to solve problems, like the Hmong students described in the opening scenario of this module. Much emphasis is placed on developing in students a sense of loyalty to their work group and a sense of responsibility for the success of all members in the group. In an American classroom, these same students may find themselves being punished for adhering to the cultural expectations of their homes or native schools. This can create confusion and even disengagement among these students, leading to poor academic performance.

## Instructional Formats and Learning Processes

Despite pockets of change, the instructional approach typically used in most American classrooms is teacher-directed, large-group lessons. The teacher presents material and then later checks the level of understanding of individual students by asking questions or through a test or written assignment (such as a worksheet) or by oral questioning. This approach, however, can conflict with the teaching and learning approaches preferred by other cultural groups. For example:

- The aural presentation of information that tends to dominate American classrooms is, for some students from nondominant American cultures, a readily accessible mode of delivery. But students from oral-tradition cultures in Africa or South America may have problems with the linear and direct presentation of information favored by American teachers and curriculum publishers. They may be accustomed to a more indirect discourse pattern, as we noted earlier.
- As we have discussed, students from cultures in which collaboration is highly valued may have difficulty with the independent work encouraged in many American schools. In the classroom, these differing social

values may translate into such practices as one student helping another, or asking for help from a neighbor, on a test, which many teachers interpret as cheating, as Ms. Gibson did in the opening scenario. These are reasonable and acceptable practices from the students' cultural perspective, which obligates them to help their classmates or encourage collaboration. As a teacher, you can help students by making a clear distinction, in advance, between the activities where you allow cooperation and those where it is forbidden.

- Students who are new to American schooling may not be familiar with such staples as cooperative learning groups, manipulatives in mathematics instruction, and instructional videos. (They may be shocked to learn that they are encouraged to watch TV in school!) Students who are unfamiliar with a group-learning approach to instruction may assume it is similar to a group study session in which they would normally assist their classmates in ways that American teachers may find troubling.

As a teacher of students from different cultures, you must perform a balancing act. One the one hand, you should explain, clearly and in detail, your expectations for behaviors and performance, to help these students understand how your classroom works. At the same time, you will need to realize that many of your students have different understandings of and expectations for appropriate behaviors. You can, and should, make allowance for these differences if they do not compromise students' academic performance or the classroom stability. For example, if a student keeps his head down rather than looking you in the eye when you talk to him, you can realize that the student is still showing respect and that there is no need to make the student change this particular behavior.

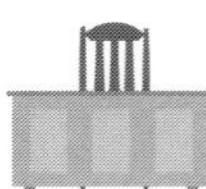

### Now You Do It

Choose a particular topic that you would teach in your subject area. Plan a learning activity that would include both competitive and cooperative aspects. Did you find it easier to plan competitive or cooperative activities? What does that tell you?

## Cultural Pluralism

At one time the United States was considered a "melting pot" of different people and cultures. Immigrants were expected to give up the language and customs of their homelands and adopt the language and customs of their new country. Schools were expected to socialize and acculturate immigrant children to American ways. The goal was to create one dominant culture—the white, Anglo-Saxon, Protestant (WASP) culture. This process of incorporating an immigrant group into the mainstream culture is called **assimilation.** Many European immigrant groups were easily assimilated, but people of color were often prevented from doing so.

**Assimilation** the absorption of an individual or group into the cultural tradition of a population or another group.

**Cultural pluralism** an approach to the diversity of individuals that calls for understanding and appreciating cultural differences.

The concept of the melting pot has generally been replaced by the notions of **cultural pluralism.** Cultural pluralism calls for an understanding and appreciation of the cultural differences and languages among the nation's citizens. The goal is to create a sense of society's wholeness based on the unique strengths of each of its parts. The cultural pluralist understands

**Separatism** the philosophical position that each cultural group should maintain its own identity without trying to fit into an overall American culture.

that America has provided a home for many different groups and honors the contributions that each group has made to our common American culture. Cultural pluralism rejects both assimilation and **separatism,** the idea that each group should maintain its own identity without trying to fit into an overall American culture. The pluralists look for a richer, common culture, whereas the separatists believe that no common culture is possible or desirable.

Although many people advocate cultural pluralism as a desirable goal, it remains an elusive target. Although racial, ethnic, and cultural diversity exists, equality among the various groups does not. In general, racial and ethnic minorities do not share equal political, economic, or educational opportunities with those of the dominant culture. Schools are the primary institution charged with promoting and supporting cultural pluralism, but too often minority groups have failed to receive the full range of benefits.

Schools committed to cultural pluralism try to promote diversity and to avoid the dominance of a single culture. These schools infuse their curricula with the contributions and histories of diverse groups. They use instructional activities that incorporate the cultural patterns of the students. They may use the multicultural education approaches described below. Students in these schools are expected to be comfortable within their own cultures and in others as well. Students from all groups are expected to participate in the school's various academic, social, governmental, and athletic activities. Disparities in academic achievement between the various racial, ethnic, and cultural groups are addressed, and attempts are made to eradicate them. In short, the goal for schools aspiring to cultural pluralism is that no group dominate the school's activities and that no group be excluded from them.

## Multicultural Education

**Multicultural education** a philosophy of teaching and learning that aims to ensure that all students, regardless of their race, gender, or ethnic origin, are provided equal educational opportunities to achieve their full potential.

**Multicultural education** has become an umbrella term for a host of programs, practices, and philosophies. Spurred by the civil rights movement of the 1960s, multicultural education is a response to economic inequality, racism, and sexism in American culture. Originally used in conjunction with improving conditions for people of color, particularly African Americans, the term has expanded to include gender, disability, and other forms of diversity. Its goals include reducing prejudice and fostering tolerance, improving the academic achievement of minority students, building commitment to the American ideals of pluralism and democracy, and incorporating minority groups' perspectives into the curricula of the schools. It charges the schools and the people working in them to be active participants in creating a more just, unbiased, and equitable American society. Multiculturalists insist that schools are the most appropriate and effective venue for bringing about large-scale social change to right the social injustices of our society, because schools themselves are a creation of the society the multiculturalists wish to reform.

Many proponents of multicultural education believe that the dominant model of schools in the United States is biased to favor students from white, middle-class upbringings. They cite such evidence as the following to support their argument that changes need to be made in our schools.

- The gap in academic achievement between white students and students of color remains wide in spite of recent gains by African American and Hispanic students.

- Only about 50 percent of African American, Native American, and Hispanic students graduate from high school, compared to 75–80 percent of whites and Asian Americans.
- African American, Hispanic, low-income, and disabled students are very underrepresented in gifted and talented programs, relative to their proportions in the total school population.
- African American students are almost three times as likely as white students to be suspended or expelled from schools.
- African American students are overrepresented in special education classes.

Proponents of multicultural education call for redesigning historically and currently biased curriculum materials, instructional activities, and school policies to eliminate any content or practices that favor one racial or social group of students over another and perpetuate social inequities. Thus, multicultural education has also become an approach to educational reform.

## Approaches to Multicultural Education

Some multiculturalists insist that all students need greater knowledge and understanding of cultures other than their own. Others argue that minority students can achieve greater academic success if instructional activities are designed to address their particular learning preferences. From these two perspectives have emerged a range of approaches to multicultural education.

One of the leading figures in multicultural education, James A. Banks, describes four common approaches to multicultural education, ranging from those that "add on" multicultural content to approaches that integrate multicultural education more thoroughly into the curriculum and activities in the classroom:

- *Contributions.* In this "add-on" approach, students celebrate the contributions of culturally different groups and individuals at opportune moments during the academic year (for example, during Black History Month), while most activities and curriculum materials remain unchanged.
- *Additive.* The teacher adds units of study on nondominant groups to the basic curriculum (for example, the role of African American soldiers during the various world wars). Although it adds content beyond the dominant culture, this approach remains a supplemental one.
- *Transformational.* This approach requires a change in the curriculum and instructional activities to weave in new content and perspectives that reflect the cultural background of the students being taught. For example, in studying the Mexican–American War of 1846–48, the teacher might try to incorporate the Mexican perspective and the resentments that existed as a result of Mexico's losing so much territory to the United States.
- *Social action and awareness.* Educators who take a social-action approach seek to bring about significant long-term change not just to the school environment, but eventually to the greater society as well. Social issues such as racism, sexism, and classism are directly addressed through the curriculum.[2]

"Add-on" approaches to multicultural education, such as festivals, do not change the basic assumptions of the curriculum.

In the first two approaches, teachers promote the inclusion in the curriculum of content about different cultural groups in order to increase all students' knowledge and understanding of these different groups. Some schools or districts add to the standard curriculum the study of cultural heroes or holidays with events during Black History Month and Women's History Month or with annual multicultural festivals featuring different foods, games, or songs from a range of countries. In the additive approach, teachers may integrate a series of multicultural materials and themes into the curriculum, offering, for example, a unit on Latino literature as part of a world literature course or one on African history in a world history course. The contributions and additive approaches, however, have little power to change or reform education. The transformation and social action approaches possess much greater potential to change thinking, attitudes, and actions.

The transformation approach changes the basic assumptions of the curriculum by enabling students to see issues, themes, and problems from several ethnic/cultural perspectives and points of view. The social-action approach includes all the elements of the transformation approach but also gives students an opportunity to make decisions and take actions related to the issue or problem they have been studying. For example, if students were studying prejudice and discrimination in American history, they might undertake a study of these constructs in their own school by gathering data, analyzing the data collected, and discussing what the data suggest. They might then follow up with some actions designed to explain the discovery of any prejudices or inequities that emerged from the data and ultimately to reduce them.

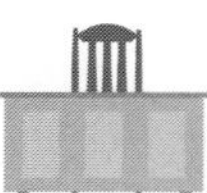

## Now You Do It

What have been your experiences with multicultural education? What non-Western curricular offerings were available in your high school? Did your undergraduate education require that you take a non-Western history, literature, art, or music course? What arguments would you advance to support the inclusion of non-Western cultures and civilizations in the K–12 curriculum? What arguments would you advance to oppose the inclusion of these courses?

## Evaluating Multicultural Education

Although not much research has yet been done to assess the results of multicultural education, preliminary findings suggest that students reap real benefits from some multicultural programs. Some researchers have reported improved self-images, positive racial attitudes, and increased academic achievement among students exposed to multicultural education.[3] One program in particular, the Kamehameha Early Education Program (KEEP), was found to have very positive effects on the reading abilities of native Hawaiian children. Teachers in this program adapted their communication and teaching styles to the learning styles of young native Hawaiians. As a result, the students showed significant improvements in social and academic skills, and their average reading scores jumped from the 13th to the 67th percentile in four years.[4]

Like nearly all educational practices and policies, multicultural education has critics as well as supporters. Among the criticisms of multicultural education are the following:

- It may undermine any sense of common traditions, values, purposes, and obligations in our country.
- It may divert schools from focusing on their basic purposes of educating for civic, economic, and personal effectiveness.
- It addresses minority student underachievement by focusing on increasing minority students' self-esteem rather than on encouraging hard work.
- It substitutes the "relevance" of subjects studied for instruction in solid academics.
- Separatist multicultural programs that focus on a single cultural group, such as Afrocentric schools, create reverse discrimination and can lead to greater misunderstandings among different social groups.

Some critics of multicultural education accept the need to preserve and value the achievements of different groups in our country but reject the idea that everything is of equal value. These critics argue that there are limits to pluralism and that school leaders need to articulate what the core curriculum is and what is not in the curriculum. Other critics of multiculturalism completely reject the concept of cultural pluralism, preferring an assimilationist perspective whereby schools are charged with creating one dominant American culture in which English is the only acceptable language.

The battles between proponents and critics of multicultural education can be read in newspapers or heard on radio talk shows almost every day as issues related to immigration, bilingual education, and "English only" are discussed and debated. In all these debates, however, it is clear that schools need to accommodate larger minority populations in a way that removes barriers while preserving the basic purposes of schooling.

### Video Case

The video case, *Diversity: Teaching in a Multiethnic Classroom,* shows a second-grade teacher and a Japanese language teacher working with a second-grade class that has a large percentage of Japanese students. As you watch the clips and study the artifacts in the case, reflect on the following questions.

**QUESTIONS**

1. The teacher mentions that he wishes he had learned more about how to communicate with the students who spoke little English. Based on the discussion earlier in this module, what advice would you give him?
2. This teacher also suggests that multicultural education adds to, rather than takes away from, what we often think of as core curriculum topics, such as reading instruction. Do you agree with this teacher's assessment of the value of multicultural education? Why or why not? Would your opinion be different if he were discussing a different grade level? If so, how?

**Online Study Center**

## Culturally Responsive Teaching

**Culturally responsive teaching** a method of embracing students' cultural backgrounds by modifying classroom conditions or activities to include elements related to the students' culture.

One form of the transformational approach to multicultural education is **culturally responsive teaching.** This approach to instruction is grounded in the belief that culture affects not just values and beliefs but also ways of thinking and processing information. Supporters suggest that students can learn better if their ways of thinking and seeing the world are taken into consideration in the teaching/learning process.[5]

They also suggest that culturally responsive teachers integrate information about their students' cultural perspectives into the curriculum and into classroom activities. For instance, in a unit on voting rights, students can trace the history of voting privileges in the United States for their own gender or racial/ethnic group. They can study what the barriers were to "universal suffrage" at various points in our nation's history and can determine what forces finally enabled their particular group to acquire voting privileges. Supporters of this approach say that, by grounding instruction in students' cultural backgrounds, teachers create more productive learning environments for their students. In addition to letting students know that their own cultures are valued, this approach helps students understand the dominant culture and see comparisons to their own cultures. You can view another example of culturally responsive teaching in the accompanying video case.

To help them recognize students' culturally based ways of learning, and to successfully integrate the cultures of their students into the curriculum, culturally responsive teachers must learn about their students' cultures. Take the time to ask your students or their families about their background, or use the Internet or library to learn more about the cultural heritages of your students.

If your goal is to become a culturally responsive teacher, you must also consider your own attitudes about different cultures and about your students. Teachers who are successful in this approach have an appreciation and respect for cultural diversity. They have clarified their attitudes and beliefs about culture and learning, and they can look objectively at the heritages of different cultures. They see students from different cultures not as possessing deficiencies to be overcome but, rather, as exhibiting different styles of learning and knowledge that can contribute to the whole class. Culturally responsive teachers also communicate high expectations for all students. These teachers are able to create caring, respectful, and inclusive classrooms. They seek, listen to, and use student voices and life experiences in the classroom, rather than just expecting students to parrot answers the teacher would like to hear.

They also reach beyond the classroom, striving to develop positive relationships with the parents and families of their students and to actively involve them in the schooling process. Furthermore, many of these teachers believe that by promoting a socially conscious environment in the classroom, they can help bring about positive social changes in society at large.

### Video Case

The video case, *Culturally Responsive Teaching: A Multicultural Lesson for Elementary Students,* shows a literacy specialist working on a writing project in which students describe their cultural origins. As you watch the clips and study the artifacts in the case, reflect on the following questions.

**QUESTIONS**

1. How does this project reflect the principles of culturally responsive teaching described here?
2. Dr. Hurley, the literacy specialist, advises new teachers to learn more about the world than they already know. How can you go about acquiring more knowledge of the world and its people?

***Online Study Center***

Your school may or may not have a specific multicultural education program, but it probably has a student body that is culturally diverse. You may or may not have had a course in multicultural education as part of your teacher preparation program, but we hope this module has equipped you to recognize the diversity of behaviors, mannerisms, values, and beliefs that students from different cultural groups represent. Although you may not know for certain that a gesture you often use to call for your students' attention is insulting to students from a particular country, you now can and should know that the gesture you use *may* have another meaning for students from other cultural groups. You should also recognize that Jung Yee's annoying habit of always saying "yes" every time you ask a yes-or-no question does not mean that Jung Yee cannot tell truth from fiction, that he is a pathological liar, or that he does not understand these two words. It might simply mean he is determined to be polite to you.

Teachers should also recognize the diversity within a cultural group. Latinos generally speak some variation of Spanish and can usually understand one another as well as Americans can understand Brits or Australians. Keep in mind, however, that Dominicans and Venezuelans are separate cultural groups, as are Vietnamese and Laotians and Chinese, even though the latter may all be ethnic Chinese. Grouping them into one cultural entity may be as insulting as putting Red Sox and Yankees fans in the same group because they all enjoy baseball.

Pragmatically, then, how does a teacher respond to the different cultures in a classroom? How does a teacher teach effectively, knowing that there may be up to ten different ethnic, linguistic, and/or cultural heritages represented in the classroom? We offer the following suggestions as guiding principles for your classroom.

1. Find out as much as you can about all of your students. Students' behaviors and responses to situations and questions will be affected by many variables, one of which is their culture. The better you know each person in your room, the more you will understand his or her behavior and how you can best help your students to learn.
2. Create in your students the mindset that your classroom has its own way of doing things. When you correct behavior, for example, use the classroom as a context: "In this classroom, we . . ." or "In this classroom, we do not . . . ." This strategy can help students from other cultures understand the behavior they must adopt in your classroom, and appreciate the cultural differences underlying it, without thinking that the behaviors and beliefs they brought with them from their dominant cultures are in any way inferior.
3. Focus on the similarities among cultural groups rather than on the differences. Avoid highlighting what is different about a child from a particular heritage. Instead, make note of how students are all similar to one another.

## Further Resources

- James A. Banks, *Cultural Diversity and Education: Foundations, Curriculum, and Teaching,* 5th ed. (Boston: Pearson Education, 2006). One of the major scholars in multicultural education provides an excellent overview of the various forms of multicultural education.
- Leonard Davidman and Patricia T. Davidman, *Teaching with a Multicultural Perspective: A Practical Guide,* 3d ed. (Boston: Addison-Wesley, 2000). A practical, useful book on how to incorporate multicultural teaching in the classroom.
- Geneva Gay, *Culturally Responsive Teaching: Theory, Research, and Practice* (New York: Teachers College Press, 2000). An excellent source for using culturally responsive teaching to improve the school performance of underachieving students of color.

- The Hall of Multiculturalism. Available at: **http://www.tenet.edu/halls/multiculturalism.html.** This site provides a list of multicultural resources for K–12 teachers and students.

- Multicultural Pavilion. Available at: **http://www.edchange.org/multicultural/index.html.** This site also provides excellent resources for teachers, research, and articles on multicultural education.
- Christine E. Sleeter and Carl A. Grant, *Turning on Learning: Five Approaches for Multicultural Teaching Plans for Race, Class, Gender, and Disability,* 4th ed. (John Wiley & Sons, 2007). This practical, lesson-based companion to *Making Choices for Multicultural Education,* by the same authors, contains many ready-to-use lesson plans covering a variety of subject areas for grades K–12.

# Teaching Students with Disabilities

Scenario

"And to think I was looking forward to this school year," Chelsea said to herself with a sigh. "I don't know why I thought this year would be so much easier. I kept hearing about the challenges that Marilyn had with this group last year."

Chelsea was in her fifth year of teaching at the Brown School, a K–8 school in an upper-middle-class community. She had always had a few students with individualized education programs, or IEPs, the documents required for a student to receive special education services, but this year it was nearly half her class! Nine of the 19 students in her fifth-grade class had IEPs, for a whole host of reasons. Four students had specific learning disabilities. Two had such severe attention deficit disorders that they had IEPs and received services, as well as psychological counseling. Then there was Ashley who had Asperger's syndrome, Shannon who suffered from severe anxiety, and Jonah who had been diagnosed with something called oppositional defiant disorder.

"At least Ashley has a full-time aide who is willing to help out when she can," Chelsea thought to herself, "but I still need more support to deal with all of the needs of all these students, not to mention those students who are *not* on IEPs. Someone will have to work with the four who have learning disabilities.

Then, I'll have to talk to the school counselor about Shannon and Jonah. I'd better start sending 'gentle reminders' to the Learning Resource Room and the principal to make sure I get the assistance I am sure I will need. And I'd better check that I have the most recent IEPs for all of these students."

Preview

Chelsea's situation may seem a bit extreme, but more and more, it is becoming the norm as classroom teachers are being asked to rise to new challenges and to share the tasks of educating students with a host of disabilities.

Only a few decades ago, millions of American students who did not fit the standard profile of normal learners were treated in our schools as second-class citizens. Often students with very different disabilities, from mental retardation to poor hearing, were placed together in "the special class," given only cursory instruction, and kept in isolation from the rest of the students in the school. To avoid this treatment, other students with learning difficulties presented themselves as "normal." With no special assistance or support in regular classes, however, these students struggled.

Things have changed, and they continue to change. The revolution in special education began with the federal **P.L. 94-142, The Education for All Handicapped Children Act**, passed in 1975. Since that time, the act has been reauthorized many times, most recently in 2004. It has also been renamed the **Individuals with Disabilities Education Improvement Act**, which is abbreviated as **IDEA.**

**Individuals with Disabilities Education Improvement Act (IDEA)** the successor to the Education for All Handicapped Children Act.

**Least restrictive environment (LRE)** a requirement of the Education for All Handicapped Children Act that students with disabilities should participate in regular education programs to the greatest extent appropriate.

The original law stated that public schools must provide all students with disabilities a "free and appropriate public education" (FAPE) in the "**least restrictive environment (LRE).**" Over the years since this law was written, schools have refined their definitions of these terms. A free and appropriate public education for students with disabilities has been understood to mean one in which students are provided special educational services that help them compensate for their identified disabilities. The least restrictive environment is most often understood to be the regular classroom.

This means that regular classroom teachers such as Chelsea—and you—can expect to have students with a variety of disabilities in their rooms for a large part of each day. As you will see, regular classroom teachers receive aid and support from disability specialists, but you undoubtedly will need to understand and be able to respond to a range of physical, mental, and emotional challenges that students will bring to your classroom.

**This module emphasizes that:**

- **Virtually every classroom teacher will have students with disabilities of one kind or another.**

- Federal and state laws require schools to identify students with disabilities and to prepare an individualized education program (IEP) to provide them with support they need.
- Students with a variety of disabilities are included in regular classrooms today, where they are supported by a combination of accommodations made by their regular teachers and the services of specialists who come into the room to help. The practice of inclusion has both strong supporters and critics.
- Schools are having a hard time paying for all the services they must, by law, provide to students with disabilities. The costs of providing special education have risen dramatically, but the federal government has yet to pay its promised share of the expenses.
- As a classroom teacher, you have the ultimate responsibility to provide all your students with the services and support they need.

## Learners with Disabilities

Currently almost 5.9 million students in the United States, or 12 percent of the school-age population, receive some kind of special education support.[1] The federal law known as IDEA specifies a number of disabilities that qualify a student for special education services. Table 4.1 summarizes the approximate numbers of students receiving services for different *qualifying*

**TABLE 4.1 Specific Disabilities Among Children Ages 6–21: Total and Percentage for Each Category***

| Disability | Number | Percentage† |
|---|---|---|
| Specific learning disabilities | 2,887,115 | 49.2% |
| Speech or language impairments | 1,093,581 | 18.6% |
| Mental retardation | 605,267 | 10.3% |
| Emotional disturbance | 477,627 | 8.1% |
| Other health impairments | 338,658 | 5.8% |
| Multiple disabilities | 128,552 | 2.2% |
| Autism | 97,904 | 1.7% |
| Orthopedic impairments | 73,821 | 1.3% |
| Hearing impairments | 71,222 | 1.2% |
| Developmental delay | 45,128 | 0.8% |
| Visual impairments | 25,845 | 0.4% |
| Traumatic brain injury | 20,748 | 0.4% |
| Deaf-blindness | 1,615 | 0% |
| ALL DISABILITIES | 5,867,078 | 100% |

*Based on data from *Twenty-Fifth Annual Report to Congress on the Implementation of the Individuals with Disabilities Education Act* (Washington, DC: U.S. Department of Education, 2005).
†Percentages may not add up to 100 percent due to rounding.

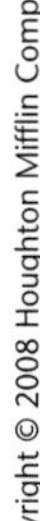

*disabilities*, and we describe several of the most common disabilities here. For more complete descriptions of these disabilities, visit the website of the Council for Exceptional Children, **http://www.cec.sped.org,** particularly the Teaching and Learning Center section.

## Specific Learning Disabilities

**Specific learning disability** a neurologically based disorder that affects a student's ability to access and produce language, either oral or written or both.

**Dyslexia** a language-based disability causing the student difficulties decoding and understanding words and sentences.

**Dyscalculia** a mathematical disability that impairs a person's ability to solve arithmetic problems.

**Dysgraphia** a writing disability in which an individual finds it hard to form letters or write within a defined space.

As in Chelsea's class, nearly half of the students who receive special education services have a **specific learning disability (SLD),** which is defined as a neurologically based disorder that affects the student's ability to access and produce language, either oral or written or both. These disabilities generally are not curable and persist throughout a person's lifetime. Among the most common learning disabilities are

- **Dyslexia,** a language-based disability that causes the student difficulties decoding and understanding words and sentences. Between 2 percent and 8 percent of elementary students are diagnosed with some form of dyslexia.
- **Dyscalculia,** a mathematical disability that impairs an individual's ability to solve arithmetic problems.
- **Dysgraphia,** a writing disability in which a person finds it hard to form letters or write within a defined space.

Specific learning disabilities are often linked to perceptual processing disorders, such as auditory or visual processing disorders, which are described next. As a teacher, it is important for you to remember, however, that a learning disability does not affect a student's overall intellectual or thinking abilities, nor is it an indicator of an individual's cognitive or intellectual ability.

## Visual or Auditory Processing Disorders

**Perceptual processing disorders** impairments in the brain's ability to receive or transmit information that is seen, information that is heard, or both.

**Visual processing disorders** difficulties processing information received through the eyes.

Learners with **perceptual processing disorders** have difficulty properly receiving or transmitting information through the key senses of vision and/or hearing. These disorders are not physical disabilities; they do not indicate how well a person can see or hear. They are psychological disabilities that affect how the brain processes the information received and how well the brain can produce language, either orally or in writing or both.

**Visual processing disorders** involve difficulty with information received through the eyes. They can manifest themselves in a host of ways. You may notice students who have the following problems:

- *Difficulty "seeing" symbols correctly or reproducing them accurately.* These students may reverse letters and see *b* as *d,* for example, or write the number 3 as a capital *E*.
- *Problems with direction.* Students may reverse entire words or may instinctively begin reading from right to left rather than from left to right.
- *Difficulty differentiating between similar letters,* such as *n* and *m,* or between similar objects, such as squares and rectangles.
- *Poor visual recognition or visual memory.* For these students, letters or numbers learned one day may be unrecognizable the next day or the next week.
- *Motor coordination problems.* Some individuals will have an impaired sense of distance or depth, causing them to misjudge distances between themselves and objects, or they may have difficulty with fine motor skills.

**Auditory processing disorders** disabilities that interfere with a person's ability to make sense of information received through the ears.

**Auditory processing disorders** interfere with a person's ability to make sense of information received through the ears. Auditory processing difficulties can directly affect an individual's speech and language, as well as her or his ability to read, write, and spell. Some learners with an auditory processing disability may have difficulty recognizing differences in *phonemes*, the sounds that are put together to make words. They may, for example, be unable to isolate sounds within a word, such as the short *a* vowel sound in the word *hat*. Other learners may have problems with auditory memory, not being able to recall things they hear (such as directions or a story read aloud), just minutes after hearing it.

Because most of school learning relies on information that is seen and heard, visual and auditory processing disorders can seriously compromise a learner's progress. Special education services generally help learners develop compensatory strategies so that they can function effectively in spite of the disorder.

## Speech or Language Impairments

**Speech impairments** disabilities that affect spoken language.

**Language impairment** a disability that can affect any phase of the communication process, from receiving messages to the production of language.

Speech or language impairments impede students' ability to communicate effectively. The cause of the impairment can be neurological, cognitive, or physical. **Speech impairments** are disabilities that affect spoken language. Common speech disorders include stuttering and chronic mispronunciation of certain sounds or syllables. Voice disorders, which may be caused by irregularities in the vocal cords, are also considered speech impairments. A **language impairment** can affect any phase of the communication process, from receiving messages to the production of language. In some young children, both receptive and expressive abilities are affected, causing delays in the child's development of language.

Learners in your class who have speech and language impairments may receive specialized services from speech and language pathologists. They will probably leave class regularly for private, one-on-one sessions devoted to helping them overcome their specific speech or language impairments.

## Developmental Disabilities

**Developmental disability** a condition involving severe mental or physical impairments that limit an individual's ability to participate fully in normal activities of daily life.

About 2 percent of all children under 18 years old have a **developmental disability.** These children suffer mental or physical impairments, sometimes severe, that limit their ability to participate fully in major life activities, such as communication, mobility, learning, and independent living as an adult. A developmental disability can be present at birth, caused perhaps by genetic irregularities, or it can begin at any time during an individual's life as a consequence of an accident or illness. Developmental disabilities include mental retardation, autism spectrum disorders, orthopedic disorders, and hearing loss or vision impairment.

**Mental retardation** the most common developmental disability, characterized by low IQ, slow learning pace, and a limited ability to develop cognitively.

***Mental Retardation*** **Mental retardation** is the most common developmental disability. One common cause of mental retardation is Down syndrome, a disorder resulting from a genetic problem that originates at conception. An individual with mental retardation has an IQ, or general intelligence score, that is significantly below average. The low IQ contributes to a slow learning pace and a limited ability to develop cognitively. As a result, a mentally retarded person's ability to perform key life functions is often significantly compromised. The individual may have limited ability to communicate, to reason and remember, or to live independently or even within a community.

The services provided for students with mental retardation depend in large part on the degree of mental retardation and the age of the student. A student with mental retardation may require full-time educational support in a mainstream classroom. Services provided to high school students with mental retardation often focus on preparing students for the transition to independent living, including vocational training that would enable the student eventually to be self-supporting.

**Autism spectrum disorders (ASD)** disabilities caused by unusual brain development that most often affect an individual's social and communication skills, including both verbal and nonverbal communication. Include autism, Asperger's syndrome, Rett syndrome, and pervasive developmental disorder (PDD).

***Autism Spectrum Disorders*** **Autism spectrum disorders (ASD)** are caused by unusual brain development and most often affect an individual's social and communication skills, including both verbal and nonverbal communication. Under the umbrella of ASD are autism, Asperger's syndrome, Rett syndrome, and pervasive developmental disorder (PDD).

Symptoms of ASD can vary significantly, and rarely do two individuals with ASD exhibit the same symptoms. Most will, however, have some problems in the following general areas:

- *Speech and language.* About 40 percent of individuals with ASD do not talk at all. Others may have *echolalia,* in which they habitually repeat something said to them. Some speak with no intonation in their voices, or they may speak more loudly than needed.
- *Social skills.* Individuals with ASD often have underdeveloped or impaired social skills and may not interact with others well. People with Asperger's syndrome, a kind of autism, are unable to read social cues or nonverbal communications.
- *Need for routines or repeated behaviors.* Some children with severe difficulties may repeat behaviors that actually hurt themselves, such as banging their head against things. In addition, any change to a routine is often deeply unsettling and may be met with anxiety attacks or even violence.

Treatments of students with ASD vary as much as the symptoms of the disorders. Your students may be receiving various dietary or biomedical treatments. Oftentimes, treatment is focused on modifying problematic behaviors and improving communication skills. Depending on the severity of the student's autism, he or she may require a full-time educational assistant who can constantly enforce and reinforce the behavior therapy established. Ashley, the student with Asperger's syndrome described at the beginning of this module, had such an aide. Some autistic students have responded positively to complementary therapies involving the arts or interaction with animals, such as dogs or horses.

***Orthopedic Impairments*** Orthopedic impairments include physical malformations or malfunctions of limbs or other body parts. These problems may have been present since birth or may have arisen as a result of accidents or diseases.

**Cerebral palsy** an orthopedic impairment that affects body and muscle coordination.

Perhaps the most common orthopedic impairment is **cerebral palsy (CP),** a disorder that affects body and muscle coordination and afflicts approximately half a million people in the United States. Symptoms of CP generally include difficulty with motor skills. The condition can affect gross motor skills, such as keeping one's balance, walking, or running, or fine motor skills, such as writing or using small tools. Other complications may include specific learning disabilities, speech and language impairments, or even mental retardation, depending on the degree and location of damage to the brain.

Learners with orthopedic impairments need varying degrees of help, depending on their impairment and its severity. Some may require only certain accommodations to address their limited mobility; others may need a full-time educational assistant. Treatment of cerebral palsy often includes physical therapy to address the weakened muscles and improve motor coordination, occupational therapy to help the student learn to do specific daily functions, and speech and language pathology if speech is affected.



## Emotional Disturbances

**Emotional disturbances (ED)** mental health conditions that often cause difficulties at home, at school or work, and with peer relations.

**Emotional disturbances (ED)** are mental health conditions that often cause difficulties at home, at school or work, and with peer relations. These conditions include mood disorders, anxiety disorders, and oppositional defiant disorder (ODD), which is an ongoing pattern of uncooperative, defiant, and hostile behavior toward authority figures that seriously interferes with the youngster's day-to-day functioning. Like students with specific learning disabilities, students with emotional disturbances may be highly intelligent and have well-developed cognitive skills. Their emotional disorders, however, can impede their learning and limit their academic success. Students with ED may be prone to episodes of extreme anger, anxiety, or depression. These emotional episodes may hamper their ability to focus on academic studies or to interact productively with peers or adults. In addition, these students often exhibit low tolerance for frustration. Some may simply "shut down" in the classroom if their frustration levels are too high. Others may share their frustration overtly, leading to an unproductive classroom environment during these periods.

Treatment often includes medication to stabilize mood swings or lessen feelings of anxiety. In addition, your students with emotional disturbances may be receiving psychological or counseling services, or special education services, such as behavior modification training to help them develop coping strategies to deal with anxieties or frustrations. The nature of this category of disorders often calls for comprehensive programs that involve cooperation and consistency between school and home, so you should be sure to learn how a student's parents, support staff, and family recommend that you work with the student.

## Other Health Impairments

Nearly 6 percent of students receiving special education services have what federal laws refer to as "other health impairments." These are defined as problems that cause an individual to have "limited strength, vitality or alertness, including a heightened alertness to environmental stimuli, that result in limited alertness with respect to the educational environment, that . . . adversely affects a child's educational performance."‡ Among the most common conditions in this category are **attention deficit disorder (ADD)** and **attention deficit/hyperactivity disorder (ADHD),** neurological disorders caused by deficiencies of a certain neurotransmitter in the brain. This deficiency affects an individual's ability to control impulses, both verbal and behavioral, or to remain focused for normal periods of time. Students with these attention disorders may have a hard time sitting still during school or keeping themselves from calling out or misbehaving in class.

**Attention deficit disorders** imbalances in brain chemistry that affect an individual's ability to control impulses or remain focused for normal periods of time. Include attention deficit disorder (ADD) and attention deficit/hyperactivity disorder (ADHD).

The most common treatment for attention deficit disorders is medication to adjust neurotransmitter levels. In addition, many students with these disorders are involved in behavior modification programs to help them recognize and adjust problem behaviors. As is the case with emotional disturbances, you may need to tailor your classroom treatment of students with attention disorders to fit into a comprehensive program that involves both school and home.

‡34 Code of Federal Regulations § 300.7(c)(9) (hereinafter C.F.R.).

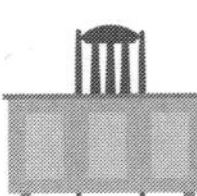

## Now You Do It

Think of a person (fellow student, relative, or acquaintance) who has one of the disabilities described here. Does that person manifest the characteristics/symptoms described or some other characteristics? If you had that person as a student in your class, how would you go about trying to accommodate his or her disability? What challenges would you face?

# Educating Students with Disabilities: Responsibilities of Schools

The education of students with disabilities has been mandated and regulated by federal legislation since the mid-1970s. In addition, many states have guidelines for the education of these students.[§] Currently, public schools are responsible for identifying students with disabilities and providing them with special education services that meet their individual needs, while including them in regular classes to the greatest extent possible. As you'll see, schools also have to find ways to pay for these services.

## Identifying Learners with Disabilities

Back in 1975, the Education for All Handicapped Children Act made school districts responsible for identifying students from as young as 3 years of age who may have disabilities and may need special educational services. Classroom or specialist teachers, social workers, school counselors, or even parents who notice that a student is struggling in school can request that the student be evaluated to see whether he or she has a disability that may require special education services. Teachers must refer for testing students whose educational progress lags behind that of their classmates.

School districts must carry out relevant and appropriate testing of these students. An evaluation team, including a specialist in the area of the suspected disability, will test the student and examine his or her records before making a recommendation about special services. Schools are also required to evaluate annually the academic, physical, or social progress being made by the students who are already receiving special services, and to adjust these services as needed.

## Providing Special Education Services

**Individualized education program (IEP)** a legally binding document that identifies the specific qualifying disability or disabilities the student has and outlines the services that the school or school district will provide for the student.

If testing shows that the student has one (or more) of the qualifying disabilities listed in IDEA, a team of people involved with the student's education draft an **individualized education program (IEP)** that specifies the services the school and its agents will provide, sets measurable benchmarks the student will be expected to achieve, and explains how the student's progress will be assessed. The IEP is a legally binding document. Once it is signed by

[§]We are not able to discuss all the state laws here, but you should find out, through your state department of education or local school district, which laws will affect you as a teacher in your state.

Learners with different disabilities require assistance specific to their needs. Technology may help you meet the needs of some learners, whereas others need different kinds of modifications.

the student's parents or guardian, as well as by an agent of the school, the school is legally responsible for meeting its obligation to provide the services that the IEP describes.

Because regular education teachers may be responsible for implementing some of the services specified in the IEP, their participation in the development of the IEP is essential. The team that develops the IEP must also include several other people:

- The parents or guardian of the student
- The student, if appropriate
- At least one of the student's special education teachers
- Other services providers, as appropriate
- One representative of the school or school district
- Any other person who may have knowledge of the student's disability or who may be an expert on the student's disability

A sample IEP template developed by the New York State Education Department can be found at **http://www.vesid.nysed.gov/specialed/publications/policy/iep/2005-sampleschoolage.doc.** The content of IEPs is mandated by IDEA, so your school or school district will probably use a similar template when you are involved in preparing IEPs. You can receive help in preparing IEPs from special educators or school psychologists. An IEP must contain the following information:

- *Current performance.* The IEP must describe how the student is doing academically at the time that the IEP is being developed or revised. It should also address how the student's disability affects his or her participation in the general curriculum.
- *Annual goals.* The IEP must specify goals that the student can reasonably be expected to achieve within a year. These goals, which may be academic, social, or behavioral, are further broken down into short-term measurable objectives.
- *Services.* The IEP must list all the services that the student will receive. The description of services must specify where the services will be provided, how often these services will be provided, and how long each interaction will last.
- *Exceptions to participation with students without disabilities.* The IEP must explain any school-related or school-sponsored activities that the student will not participate in with his or her classmates without disabilities.
- *Statewide testing.* Federal law requires states to administer standardized tests to students annually to ensure that they are making adequate yearly progress. The IEP must indicate what modifications, if any, to the state-mandated tests will be made for the student. If the state-mandated test is not an appropriate tool to assess the student, the IEP must justify that position and explain what alternative testing will be used to assess the student's learning.

- *Transition services.* If the student is in high school, the IEP must include a plan to help the student transition from high school to the next phase of education or the world of work.
- *Progress.* The IEP will state how the student's progress will be monitored and measured, as well as how parents will be notified of the progress being made.

One other law, in addition to IDEA, that plays a role in the education of students with disabilities is Section 504 of the Rehabilitation Act of 1973. Whereas IDEA mandates that the school provide remedial services to students with specific disabilities, the focus of Section 504 is ensuring that students with disabilities must have the same educational opportunities as their classmates without disabilities.

Schools must eliminate any barrier that may prevent students from benefiting to the same extent as their classmates without disabilities from the educational programs offered. As a teacher, you must help provide equal education opportunities by implementing **accommodations,** or adaptations of regular school activities, for students in your class who have disabilities. Examples of such accommodations include

**Accommodations** adaptations of regular school activities that make the benefits of these activities as accessible to students with disabilities as to students without disabilities.

- Providing adaptive equipment in the physical education facilities to enable students with limited mobility to participate in athletic activities.
- Arranging special seating in the classroom for students whose vision limitations require that they sit close to objects, such as chalkboard, video screens, computer monitors, and so on, or acquiring specialized computers or other **adaptive technologies** for visually impaired students.
- Hiring or working with signers for deaf students.
- Creating a distraction-free work area or providing special reminders at the end of the day, to eliminate barriers to academic growth for students with attention deficit disorders.

**Adaptive technologies** (also known as **assistive technologies**) the array of devices and services that help people with disabilities perform better in their daily lives. Such devices include motorized chairs, remote control units, computers, and speech synthesizers.

The "In Your Classroom" feature offers a few more general guidelines that may help you devise appropriate accommodations as part of your regular lesson planning.

## Now You Do It

Go to the website **http://trainland.tripod.com/sample.htm** for a sample IEP for a child with autism. On the basis of this sample, complete an IEP for a hypothetical student, using the form found at **http://www.vesid.nysed.gov/specialed/publications/policy/iep/2005-sampleschoolage.doc.** Choose the grade level and type of disability. As you work on this activity, think about who else would be working with you on a real-life IEP, and be sure to note what knowledge you might be lacking. Where would you go to get this information for a real student?

## Including Students with Disabilities

**Mainstream classroom** (also known as **mainstreaming**) placing special education students in general education classes for at least part of the school day, while also providing additional services, programs, or classes as needed.

Prior to 1997, it was not uncommon for students with moderate to severe disabilities to be placed in a special education classroom where they would receive most of their educational services. Depending on the severity of their disabilities, these students would be **mainstreamed** in the regular education classroom for certain periods of the school day. These students might join

## In Your Classroom

### Adapting to Students with Disabilities

There are very likely to be students with disabilities in your classroom. How will you deal with their different needs?

- *Do not stereotype these students.* For example, consider two students identified as having learning disabilities. One may have below-average intelligence and have difficulty in mathematics; the other may have high intelligence and have trouble reading. Although each has learning disabilities, you would need to provide different instruction for each.
- *Get to know them.* Learn all you can about each student's limitations and potential and about what instructional approaches and technologies might be particularly effective.
- *Consult the special education teachers in your school.* The more you and the special education teacher can coordinate instruction and services for your students with disabilities, the better the students' educational experiences will be.
- *Try to co-teach with a special education teacher* whenever feasible.
- *Insist that any needed services be provided.* After all, it is the law.
- *Pair students who have disabilities with students without disabilities who can help them.*
- *Use a variety of teaching strategies,* including hands-on activities, peer tutoring, and cooperative learning strategies.



their classmates without disabilities for electives, lunch and recess, or instruction in some disciplines. Decisions for mainstreaming were generally based on the academic and social abilities and needs of the students with disabilities. Many parents and educators argued, however, that students with disabilities were often stigmatized by the segregated placements, leading to even lower academic progress and underdeveloped social skills.

Their concerns were addressed by the U.S. Congress when it reauthorized IDEA in 1997. The law was changed to state that "Schools may place children with disabilities in separate classrooms or schools only when supports and

Inclusion practices even extend to physical education games.

services are not enough to help the child learn in a regular classroom."** It discouraged the "pulling out" of students with disabilities to send them to another room or school for specialized services. The new practice of inclusion became the standard for educating students with disabilities.

**Inclusion** the practice of placing all students with disabilities in the regular education classroom.

**Full inclusion** the practice of providing all educational services for students with disabilities in the regular classroom, with the help of specialists who come into the room as needed, rather than pulling out students for special services.

**Co-teaching** the assignment of two teachers, often a regular education teacher and a special education teacher, to teach in the same classroom.

**Inclusion** places all students with disabilities in the regular education classroom. Some inclusion classrooms are still combined with pull-out services, when students leave the classroom for specialized services. Other schools practice **full inclusion,** in which students receive all of their educational services in the classroom, with the help of specialists who come into the room as needed. Some schools assign two teachers, a regular education teacher and a special education teacher, to teach in the same full-inclusion classroom. These **co-teaching** situations combine the subject-matter expertise of the regular education teacher with the special education teacher's strengths in adapting content and pedagogy to meet the educational needs of the students with disabilities.

As a practice, inclusion has been steeped in controversy. Advocates of inclusion point to benefits for both students with disabilities and their classmates without disabilities. According to this view, students with disabilities who are placed in the regular classroom no longer feel marginalized or stigmatized as being less of a participant in the educational process or less of a member of the school community. They also develop social skills through interactions with all their classmates. And classmates without disabilities gain a greater understanding of students with disabilities and become more accepting of these students.

**Section 614(d)(1)(A)(iii).

Opponents argue that the academic and educational needs of students with disabilities risk being compromised in an inclusion classroom and that there is little gain in social development to compensate for this risk. These critics maintain that the distractions in the regular classroom make the special education services delivered there less effective than they would be in a separate special education classroom. Furthermore, they point out that the stigma of requiring specialized services can persist when the specialist comes into a regular classroom.

In spite of the controversy, including students with disabilities in the regular classroom, except under special circumstances, is the law of the land. Administrators, teachers, students, and parents must embrace this requirement and ensure that effective learning occurs for *all* students. It's our duty as educators.

**Video Case**

What does an inclusion classroom look like? How does a skillful teacher work with specialists, such as an occupational and physical therapist, to optimize learning for each student? In the video case, *Inclusion: Classroom Implications for the General and Special Educator,* you will see how veteran third-grade teacher Chris Colbath-Hess collaborates with her colleagues to help every child succeed as a reader and writer. As you watch the clips and study the artifacts in the case, reflect on the following questions.

QUESTIONS

1. How do the modifications described by the specialists and the regular teacher compare to those listed above? Are there any other adaptations you have seen used in the classroom?
2. Ms. Colbath-Hess stresses the importance of regular classroom teachers working closely with specialists to help include students with disabilities. How can you prepare now to work well with the specialists you will meet?

*Online Study Center*

## Paying for Special Education Services

Schools have been worried about how to pay for the education of students with disabilities since the passage of PL 94-142 over three decades ago. The law promised federal funding for 40 percent of the costs of special services that schools were required to provide to students with disabilities. However, IDEA has been chronically underfunded from the beginning. The federal government has never contributed enough money for more than 18 percent of the costs, leaving individual school districts and states to pay for over 80 percent of specialized services. The 1973 Rehabilitation Act, which also affects special education services, is completely unfunded. Schools receive no money at all for what are, in some cases, extremely high expenses, such as the purchase of adaptive technologies.

At the same time, the financial burden of providing special services has risen steadily. The number of students requiring specialized services has increased rapidly in recent years, and the services provided to these students have become more and more specialized—and expensive. If, for example, a student with an emotional disturbance requires placement in a specialized school, the school district is responsible for paying the school fees of the student, which can be up to $100,000 per year. Likewise, school districts are often responsible for the cost of special transportation to and from school. Federal laws also require school districts to pay for services for students who live in the district but attend private schools.

Still, school districts are often faced with difficult decisions on how to meet the needs of the students with disabilities *and* still provide a quality educational experience for all of the students enrolled in the schools. The challenge is great, and in some instances, the decisions and responses are not pleasing to all. Some schools and districts may be reluctant to comply with federal laws when compliance would mean additional expense, and they may look for ways to limit the level of services they are obligated to provide. Some districts have, for example, challenged in court the need for certain accommodations.

Other districts cannot afford as many special education teachers as they need, so schools may be understaffed with (overworked) specialists. In this situation, regular classroom teachers may feel they have to compete with one another for support from the special education department, and specialist teachers feel themselves pulled in many different directions. Some financially unstable school districts may compromise on the services provided by hiring assistants rather than licensed special education teachers to work with students. They may also rely on the regular classroom teacher to provide some of the services, perhaps under the supervision of a special education teacher.

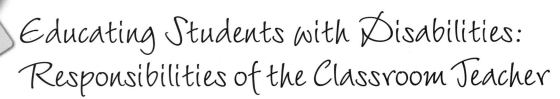

# Educating Students with Disabilities: Responsibilities of the Classroom Teacher

Ultimately, the classroom teacher is responsible for making sure that all accommodations specified in a student's IEP are provided. Making such accommodations often requires classroom teachers to adapt learning activities to make them accessible to students with disabilities. In Chelsea's class (described in the scenario at the beginning of this module), for example, a student whose specific learning disability causes problems recognizing words may need help in reading directions for an assignment, whereas one with dysgraphia may require a scribe to write responses for the same activity. Shannon and Jonah, the students with emotional disturbances, may need to have the assignment broken down into smaller tasks, to help them avoid becoming overwhelmed and frustrated by it.

Failure to provide the services specified in a student's IEP can be grounds for a lawsuit. Parents can sue only the school district, not individual teachers, but provoking a lawsuit by a parent is not something you want to have in your personnel file.

In addition to avoiding lawsuits, we assume that your professional goals include doing your best to meet the needs of all your students. To help you do that, we strongly urge classroom teachers to be proactive. Become as well informed as possible about the students in your classroom at the start of the school year, and keep learning about them as the year goes on. The accompanying "In Your Classroom" feature offers specific recommendations.

## In Your Classroom

### Complying with Special Education Law

- *Attend all IEP meetings that concern students in your classroom.* At the IEP meeting, you can find out what services the student will receive, who will provide these services, and what accommodations need to be made for the student. You can also voice any concerns you have about the feasibility of providing proposed services. This meeting may help you get to know the specialists who will be working with you as they provide services for the student, especially if you teach a content area that has a mandated state assessment at the end of the school year.
- *Get copies of current IEPs of the students in your classroom.* Make sure you know what services these students are to receive, not just in your classroom, but from specialists as well. Like Chelsea, you may have to send "gentle reminders" to the special education department to make sure the services from specialists are, in fact, delivered.
- *Maintain frequent and open contact with parents or legal guardians of students with IEPs.* Keep them abreast of their children's progress, and alert them to any changes. You want to work in collaboration with these parents and to keep them as allies in educating students with disabilities.
- *Keep written records of meetings with parents.* Your records do not need to be "official" in any sense; they should serve primarily as reminders for you of these meetings. Jotting down the substance of conversations with parents and family members of your students can help you recall important information later, as you plan activities and accommodations.

## In Your Classroom

### Strategies for Working with Students with Disabilities

You'll find that many of the strategies you learn for working with students with disabilities, including the following, are effective strategies for educating *all* your students.

1. *Show* and *tell.* As much as possible, use multiple modalities to present information. Try to make all your instructions and lessons accessible through at least two different senses. For example, tell students what they are to do, and then put written instructions on the board. When introducing a new concept, explain the concept verbally, use manipulatives or objects to show the concept, and then write key understandings on the overhead or board. Making use of these different modalities helps all students, but especially students with such disabilities as processing disorders, who have trouble using one of their senses for learning. Presenting information more than once can also be beneficial to students with ADHD whose abilities to concentrate wax and wane throughout the day.
2. *Tell it again (and again).* Not only do you want to provide instruction and directions in more than one modality, but you should also provide the information more than one time. Repeat the information verbally, show the concept, and have students read the instructions more than one time. For some students, the repetition helps them to internalize the information better.
3. *Stick to the routine.* Develop and maintain routines for activities that you do regularly, such as handing in papers or forming small groups. All students benefit from routines, but they are especially helpful for some students with disabilities. Predictability gives students the security and comfort of knowing what materials to access, what activities and expectations they will encounter, and, most important, what mindset to prepare. In addition, routines can help some students learn essential organizational skills.
4. *Control the climate.* Create and maintain an even-tempered, safe, and productive classroom environment. Students with disabilities, in particular those with severe emotional disturbances, need a calm, predictable classroom environment. And all students are more willing to take risks and stretch their abilities when they are confident that the response to their attempts will be encouraging rather than critical, supportive rather than blaming. We are by no means advocating a classroom with no rules or no consequences for breaking the rules. We are suggesting that the rules and consequences be predictable and be administered to students in an even-tempered, clear manner.
5. *Stay flexible.* You may need to adjust classroom practices and policies to meet the needs of your students with disabilities. You may have to make an exception to a no-calculator policy in mathematics for a student with severe dyscalculia, for example, or to a no-computer policy for certain writing tasks for students with dyslexia or dysgraphia. Adapting learning activities to accommodate students with disabilities will also require you to be flexible. Activities that you design as individualized tasks may have to be changed to "pair work" for some students, or a student who has problems working in groups might need an individual version of a group task. When you are planning accommodations, consider the purpose of the learning activity, determine whether a change in classroom practice will affect the primary purpose of the activity, and ponder how you can adapt the activity and still achieve the original purpose.
6. *What's fair?* You may need to rethink the concept of "fairness." Some students without disabilities may question or even protest when you allow exceptions to policies or change activities to accommodate those who have disabilities. Be ready to explain or even defend the accommodations that you allow.

We also urge you to ask for help when you need it! Sometimes, schools may unknowingly expect regular education teachers to provide more services to students with disabilities than they are able to do effectively with twenty-five or more other students in the classroom. Regular education teachers may also be expected to provide services for which they have not been appropriately trained. If you find yourself in one of these situations, find diplomatic ways of sharing your concerns with the school administration and the special education department. If promises of support from the special education team are made, be sure to follow up with the special education teachers to get the classroom support that was promised.

Let's Sum Up

Few teachers would disagree that the recent move toward greater inclusion of students with disabilities in the regular education classroom has led to significant challenges for teachers. As a classroom teacher, you will need to plan learning activities thoughtfully, taking into consideration the strengths and limitations of the students with disabilities in your classroom. You must coordinate the delivery of special services for these students with the specialists and must support the development of compensatory and coping strategies that can help these students perform at their highest levels. You may even need to seek out additional training or information to better understand the challenges that students with disabilities face and better support the efforts of these students to be successful.

Although including students with special needs demands more planning, coordination, and training from you, many teachers are convinced of the benefits that the inclusive classroom confers, not just for students with disabilities, but also for their classmates without disabilities.

**Video Case**

In the video case, *Inclusion: Grouping Strategies for Inclusive Classrooms,* you'll see how teacher Sheryl Cebula works with an inclusion specialist and additional support staff to make sure that each child in her fourth- and fifth-grade inclusion classroom succeeds in a unit on the Caribbean. As you watch the clips and study the artifacts in the case, reflect on the following questions.

QUESTIONS

1. How does Ms. Cebula's lesson planning reflect the guidelines presented in this chapter?
2. What are some ways in which you can apply these guidelines in the subject areas and with students of the age you'll be teaching?

## Further Resources

- Council for Exceptional Children. Available at: **http://www.cec.sped.org.** This website of the national professional organization for special education contains many helpful resources.
- Daniel P. Hallahan and James M. Kauffman, *Exceptional Learners: Introduction to Special Education* (Boston: Allyn & Bacon, 2006). A comprehensive overview of the field of special education, including descriptions of various disabilities.
- Samuel A. Kirk, James J. Gallagher, Nicholas J. Anastasiow, and Mary Ruth Coleman, *Educating Exceptional Children,* 11th ed. (Boston: Houghton Mifflin Co., 2006). This leading textbook provides practical applications on how to adapt teaching methods, curriculum, and settings to meet the needs of students with disabilities.
- Judy W. Kugelmass, *The Inclusive School* (New York: Teachers College Press, 2005). The author examines a public elementary school that provides a creative, inclusive educational environment and still meets the demands of state content standards.
- Janet Lerner and Frank Kline, *Learning Disabilities and Related Disorders, Characteristics and Teaching Strategies,* 10th ed. (Boston: Houghton Mifflin, 2006). The authors provide theory, case studies, and practical advice on issues related to learning disabilities.
- University of Virginia, *Office of Special Education: A Web Resource for Special Education.* Available at: **http://curry.edschool.virginia.edu/go/specialed.** This website at the Curry School of Education, University of Virginia, contains much information about special education, including discussion groups.

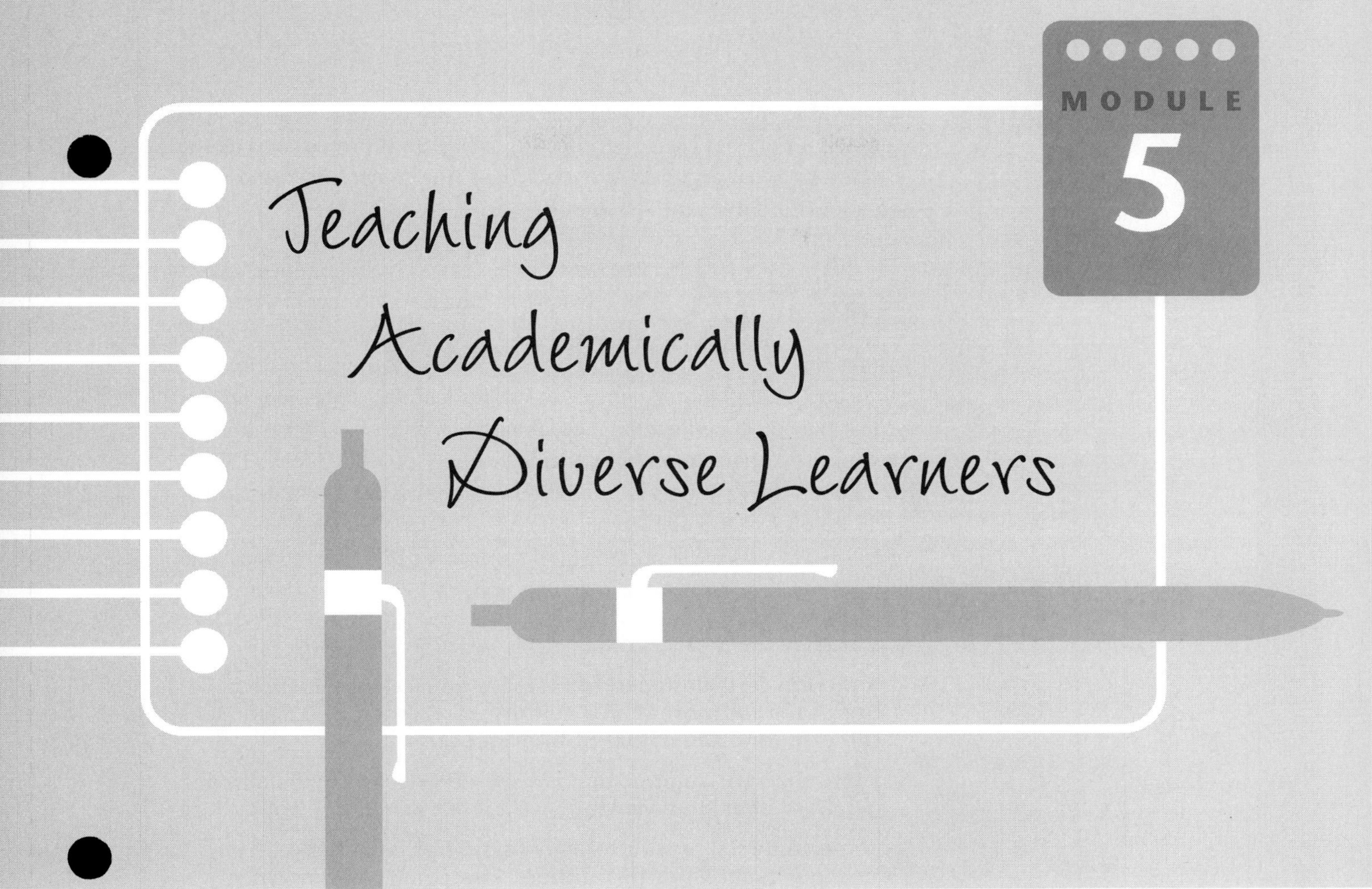


# Module 5: Teaching Academically Diverse Learners

**Scenario**

It is the second day of teacher meetings, prior to the school year beginning tomorrow. For first-year teacher Maria Muñoz, her sixth-grade class list is still just a sea of names. But not to her new friends, who, between them, have taught most of the students on the list. As they peer at her list, Maria's abstract notion of "her class" takes on very specific dimensions! "Oh, you've got Ramon. He's quiet, but he can draw anything . . . scenes from stories, faces of other students. He's amazing!"

"Look out for Annemarie. She's a real social butterfly. She could make a friend of a stone. You'll have to work to keep her on task."

"You've got Heather Cook, too. I had her last year. Nice kid. She is really gifted athletically. She can do anything with her body, but she really struggles with math."

"And, look out! You've got Elroy Nichols, the school brain! He'll be great, but he'll keep you busy keeping him busy!"

"Maria, you've got quite a class! Some of our highs and some of our lows. Some of our 'ins' and some of our 'outs.' You're in for a very interesting year."

As they all went back to the final session of the teacher meeting, Maria's mental map of "her class" had been radically transformed, and as she reflected on what and how she would teach this year, she realized she had a lot more thinking ahead of her.

Preview

What Maria experienced has happened to most new teachers. However, in recent years the discussion of students' varying and various abilities has become much more precise. Conversations about intelligence and multiple intelligences, as well as learning styles, are now a regular part of the educational psychology landscape. Among these theories are Robert Sternberg's triarchic theory of intelligence (1977), Howard Gardner's theory of multiple intelligences (MI) (1983), and David Kolb's experiential learning theory (ELT) and learning styles inventory (LSI). We will present brief summaries of these theories and look at their implications for teaching and learning in the classroom.

**This module emphasizes that:**

- **Although tests designed to measure general intelligence have been used for more than a century, researchers and theorists are still exploring the nature of intelligence.**
- **Some theorists suggest that we should refer to several intelligences, rather than viewing intelligence as a single ability.**
- **Some students, by almost any measure of intelligence, have stronger capabilities than others. These *gifted* and *talented* students require special teaching attention.**
- **Individual students approach learning in different ways. Several theorists have tried to categorize these learning styles and to recommend teaching techniques that work well with students' varying learning styles.**
- **Teachers can hold all students accountable for the same content but provide them with a range of options for mastering that content by differentiating instruction.**

# What Is Intelligence?

**Intelligence** mental capabilities, such as reasoning, problem solving, and abstract thinking, and the ability to use them.

What exactly do we mean when we talk about a child being "really smart" or "an average student"? How do we define intelligence?

Various definitions of **intelligence** usually include mental capabilities, such as reasoning, problem solving, and abstract thinking. Some definitions focus more on the ability to *acquire* knowledge and store it in memory, and others look at the ability to *apply* new knowledge in practical or unfamiliar situations. More recently, some cognitive psychologists have talked about intelligences in the plural rather than the singular.

## General Intelligence: IQ

Many views of intelligence see it as a single quality that people possess in varying amounts, independent of the context. That is, some people are more intelligent, and others are less intelligent, all the time, at school and everywhere else. These views generally also see intelligence as biologically based, something one is born with.

If intelligence is a single thing that can occur in varying levels, that suggests we can measure it. Alfred Binet was one of the first researchers to attempt to measure intelligence. In the early twentieth century, he and Theodore Simon developed a series of thirty tasks of increasing complexity that they thought children at different ages should be able to accomplish. The easier tasks could be accomplished by all children of a certain age, whereas the most complex tasks could be accomplished only by the "most intelligent" of children at that age. On the basis of how well the child performed on these tasks, Simon and Binet calculated a numerical score for the child, which became his or her **intelligence quotient (IQ).**

**Intelligence quotient (IQ)** a numerical score used to describe intelligence levels on the basis of test performance.

IQ tests based on Binet's test are still in use today. They include the Stanford-Binet IQ test, designed to measure the intelligence of children, and the Wechsler Adult Intelligence Scale, to measure the intelligence of adults. In schools, IQ tests are used to give teachers information about the intellectual capacities of their students, whether they are gifted or intellectually limited. Teachers use this information to plan instruction at the appropriate levels for their students. There are, however, different theories of intelligence, and these have different implications for instruction.

## Triarchic Theory of Intelligence

Psychologist Robert Sternberg believes that intelligence consists of practical and creative abilities, as well as the academic skills that many people think of as intelligence. Sternberg's **triarchic theory of intelligence**[1] considers three aspects of intelligence:

**Triarchic theory of intelligence** a theory of intelligence, promulgated by Robert Sternberg, that divides general intelligence into three parts: analytical, creative, and practical.

- *Analytical.* The internal mental processes that are the more familiar aspects of intelligence (verbal and mathematical skills, and logical reasoning and problem-solving skills).
- *Creative.* How well an individual responds to unfamiliar problems in novel situations.
- *Practical.* The ability of an individual to adapt to or shape his or her environment. People who have high practical intelligence can "read" their environment well, which helps them determine the most appropriate course of action to be successful: adjust to the environment, shape it to their liking, or find an alternative environment in which they can be successful.

Sternberg believes that all three types of intelligence can be developed through education and training, but he suggests that intelligence is best measured by assessing how well students perform on realistic tasks, rather than noting how high they score on a test.

Sternberg also calls attention to cultural influences on the definition of intelligence. Because different societies or cultures may have different views on what constitutes success, and may value successful performance on different tasks as indicators of intelligence, they also have differing views on intelligence. For example, in highly developed Western societies, advanced computer skills might be considered a sign of intelligence, whereas in developing, agricultural societies, people might demonstrate their intelligence through their ability to understand the behavior of farm animals or the effects of weather on crops.

## In Your Classroom

### Using Sternberg's Triarchic Theory of Intelligence

Sternberg criticizes the typical classroom in which students' analytical abilities are the primary, and often sole, focus. He urges teachers to design and implement learning activities that draw on students' creative and practical abilities, as well as on their analytical abilities. A creative lesson could encourage students to design a new tool to measure mass; a practical lesson might have students use trigonometry to decide where to anchor a buoy in a sea cove. Encouraging students to work in groups can also help develop their practical abilities. The negotiation and compromise that are a part of group work can develop students' abilities to adapt to or shape their environment.

## Multiple Intelligences Theory

**Multiple intelligences (MI)** a theory of intelligence, advanced by Howard Gardner, that identifies at least eight dimensions of intellectual capacities that people use to approach problems and create products.

Howard Gardner, a leading psychologist, has developed a theory of **multiple intelligences (MI).**[2] According to this view, intelligence is not one single characteristic. Instead, Gardner suggests that we all have strengths, weaknesses, and unique combinations of cognitive abilities.

Gardner has identified eight separate intelligences. He points out that all humans have all of these intelligences to varying degrees, but some individuals have exceptional strength in a particular intelligence. These intelligences are as follows:

1. *Verbal/linguistic intelligence* draws on the individual's language skills, oral and written, to express what is on the person's mind and to understand other people.
2. *Logical-mathematical intelligence* is a person's ability to understand principles of some kind of causal system, as a scientist does, or to manipulate numbers, quantities, and operations, as a mathematician does.
3. *Spatial intelligence* is the ability to represent the spatial world internally in the mind, as a chess player or sculptor does.
4. *Bodily-kinesthetic intelligence* is the capacity to use one's whole body or parts of one's body to solve a problem, make something, or put on some kind of production, such as that of an athlete or a performing artist.
5. *Musical intelligence* is the capacity to "think" in music, to hear patterns, and to recognize, remember, and manipulate them.
6. *Interpersonal intelligence* is the ability to understand other people, an ability that we all need but that is particularly important for teachers, salespeople, and politicians.
7. *Intrapersonal intelligence* consists of understanding oneself and knowing one's preferences, capabilities, and deficiencies.
8. *Naturalist intelligence* consists of the ability to discriminate among living things (plants and animals) and to be sensitive to features of the natural world, such as rock formations and clouds.[3]

Some psychologists and educators criticize Gardner's theory as lacking in rigor and scientific precision. The individuality and variability of assessments make it difficult to compare students' knowledge and skills against a national standard, for example. Others suggest that the qualities Gardner

## In Your Classroom

### Using Multiple Intelligences Theory

Gardner and his associates believe that many American schools focus too much on linguistic and logical-mathematical intelligences, to the exclusion of the others. They recommend that teachers instead use a variety of activities and projects that require a range of intelligences to teach course content. Gardner's MI classroom has students engaging in activities that target the visual-spatial, bodily-kinesthetic, or musical-rhythmic intelligences, in addition to the more familiar linguistic and mathematical intelligences. These activities should require students to work in groups at times and, at other times, to work alone to address both the interpersonal and intrapersonal intelligences. All students should be expected to complete all activities, not just those students who are strong in the intelligence that the activity targets.

Gardner and his colleagues suggest, however, that teachers identify learners' strengths and use these strengths to help them understand concepts or perform tasks that require an intelligence in which they are weaker. For example, a math teacher might teach fractional parts through musical notes to help learners with strong musical-rhythmic but weak mathematical intelligence.

Likewise, Gardner urges teachers to develop a range of assessment tools that speak to the different intelligences so that no student or group of students is favored over another in the assessment process. Some students may be able to convey their understanding of concepts more fully through a medium other than written expression, for example.



labels "intelligences" may more appropriately be defined simply as abilities or skills. Another criticism is that Gardner's definitions of intelligences are culture-specific, which limits the universal applicability of the theory.

Other educators are concerned about the use of MI theory in the classroom (see the "In Your Classroom" feature). These critics believe that teachers are spending too much valuable time and resources on MI learning activities, detracting from instruction in key concepts and skills that students need to know for state-mandated standardized tests. They suggest that MI activities are compromising, rather than enhancing, student learning.

Whatever criticism the theory may engender, many classroom teachers have found the theory useful for explaining and addressing the varying student abilities they encounter in their classrooms. Many teachers, such as the one shown in the accompanying video case, ground their pedagogical decisions in the theory of multiple intelligences and offer a range of options when assigning a task or a project.

## One Definition of Intelligence—the Gifted and Talented

Nearly 3 million students, or just over 6 percent of the students in public elementary and secondary schools, have been identified as gifted or talented.[4] These two terms are defined in a host of different ways. Generally, however, a **gifted student** is one who has exceptional intellectual ability, whereas a **talented student** may excel in another ability, such as musical or artistic ability. Some students, however, are both gifted and talented.

**Gifted student** a student who possesses cognitive (intellectual) superiority, creativity, and motivation of sufficient magnitude to set the child apart from most age-mates.

**Talented student** a student who exhibits a special ability, aptitude, or accomplishment.

Joseph Renzulli, director of the National Research Center on the Gifted and Talented, speaks of two types of giftedness: "schoolhouse" giftedness and creative productive giftedness. Schoolhouse giftedness is based on standardized tests and is what is most commonly associated with the concept of

## Video Case

In the video case, *Multiple Intelligences: Elementary School Instruction,* you'll see how teacher Frederick Won Park draws on the theory of multiple intelligences to help his students improve their writing abilities. As you watch the clips and study the artifacts in the case, reflect on the following questions.

**QUESTIONS**

1. How does this teacher's emphasis on the ability to solve problems compare to general-ability theories of intelligence and to Sternberg's triarchic theory?
2. How does the writing activity link multiple intelligences with one another?
3. In your opinion, does this teacher use multiple intelligences activities in a way that supports standard learning goals or in a way that detracts from achieving standards? Why do you think so?
4. Do you feel comfortable with the idea of using multiple intelligences activities in the ways this case describes? Could you, for instance, act out a math problem? How could you become more comfortable with this approach to teaching?

**Acceleration** an instructional program that allows gifted students to learn at a pace that fits their aptitudes and abilities. These students cover more material, and more advanced material, than their classmates.

**Enrichment** offering students the opportunity to explore curricular topics in greater depth and breadth or to engage in independent inquiry on topics of particular interest to them.

"giftedness"—superior cognitive and reasoning ability. Creative productive giftedness involves the "development of original ideas, products, artistic expressions, and areas of knowledge that are purposefully designed to have an impact on one or more target audiences."[5]

The many ways of defining the terms *gifted* and *talented* lead to a great deal of variability among states and school districts in identifying students. As a consequence of different criteria, for example, less than 2 percent of the student population in Vermont is labeled as gifted or talented, compared to nearly 14 percent of the students in Oklahoma. Identification of gifted and talented students usually relies on a number of different assessments, including cognitive ability tests, achievement tests, observational data, and anecdotal evidence from parents, teachers, and other adults who interact with the student on a regular basis. When intelligence tests are used as a measure, an IQ score of 130 or higher is typically required for a student to be identified as gifted. Approximately 2–3 percent of the student population in the United States score at this level.[6]

Many educators express concern that the common methods of identification are unsuccessful for bilingual and minority students. A longitudinal survey found that, although African Americans and Hispanics made up about 25 percent of the student population in U.S. public schools, they represented only about 10 percent of the student population identified as gifted and talented. White students, by contrast, represented 71 percent of the student population but 82 percent of those identified as gifted and talented.[7] Minority educators and advocates are calling for a more inclusive definition of giftedness, as well as for more sensitive and culturally appropriate assessment measures for determining giftedness.[8]

Specific programs for the education of gifted and talented students are as varied as the criteria by which students are selected for these programs. Schools take all of the following approaches:

- Some school districts establish separate classrooms (or, if numbers warrant, a separate school) and a separate course of study for these students.
- Some programs group gifted students for part of the school day or school week.
- Other schools have a tailor-made approach, designing special services, such as one-on-one tutoring for students in their areas of greatest strength. For example, a middle school student who excels in mathematics might have individualized instruction in advanced mathematics while his or her classmates have math class.
- Some schools do not offer any special services to gifted and talented students. Because schools are not required to address the needs of gifted students, parents of gifted students may opt out of the public school system and seek a charter or private school where the academic programs more fully address the needs of gifted students.

The two main instructional approaches to teaching gifted and talented students are **acceleration** and **enrichment.** An accelerated curriculum allows gifted students to learn at a pace that fits their aptitudes and abilities. These students cover more material, and more advanced material, than their classmates. An enrichment program offers students the opportunity to explore curricular topics in greater depth and breadth or to engage in independent inquiry on topics of particular interest to the students.

In an era of sparse educational resources, both material and human, gifted and talented programs are often underfunded at best and, at worst, are not funded at all. Unlike students with disabilities, gifted students are not protected by any federal legislation, nor are specialized educational services mandated for them. As a result, funding for gifted and talented programs may be reallocated to other needs, to the detriment of the educational experiences of these gifted students. In addition, a philosophical opposition is often raised to gifted and talented programs, which may be seen as classist or elitist, catering to a small group of students who, by some standards, already have real advantages over other students. Some educators also believe that mixed-ability grouping is a more productive and beneficial approach to educating *all* students, including gifted students.

No matter what type of program your school uses, like Maria Muñoz in the opening scenario, you are likely to be the one primarily responsible for

## In Your Classroom

### Working with Gifted and Talented Students

Most gifted and talented students *are* exceptional students who require special educational services. Knowing more about the learning abilities and styles of gifted and talented students will help you to understand their unique needs and to design effective learning experiences for them.

1. *Gifted students usually learn very quickly and easily.* They are easily bored with lower-level thinking tasks but thrive on higher-level thinking, such as analysis and synthesis.
2. *Some gifted students are "big-picture" learners.* These students may not be very detail-oriented. Some will not have a good grasp of basic facts, nor will they see the necessity of learning these basic facts. For example, many gifted students would rather think about strategies for solving mathematics problems than put in the drudgework of learning the multiplication tables. Be flexible in your expectations for students, and clarify for yourself what learning goals and objectives you are setting for these students and what measures you will use to assess students' progress toward these goals.
3. *Gifted students are ever curious,* always asking for in-depth explanations of phenomena or events. Because the constant questions can be wearying for you, anticipate these students' needs and have available independent resources, such as reference books or Internet portals, that these students can access to seek answers to their queries. Tap into your own creativity to propose creative and unique projects for your gifted students to undertake.
4. *Some gifted students may need guidance in developing the strategies and skills that are needed for self-directed learning.* Do not assume that, just because a student learns quickly and easily, the student knows how to learn efficiently and effectively.
5. *Gifted students may be perfectionists.* Some gifted students become obsessed with achieving an unattainable level of perfection. They may be easily frustrated or may refuse to engage in a learning activity for fear of not achieving their desired level of perfection. These students need to know that mistakes are a natural part of life and that these mistakes can form the basis of new knowledge. Show these students that everyone—including you, the teacher—makes mistakes.
6. *Each one is different.* There is no universal profile of gifted students; individuals are typically gifted in vastly different ways. The strengths and interests of one student are more than likely very different from those of another gifted student. If your school does not have a listing, develop your own listing of specialized resources within the school and community that you can call on to work with and mentor your gifted students.

educating the gifted and talented students in your classes. Some teachers may naively assume that gifted students, who do not struggle with learning, are self-motivated to learn and need less of their attention than some of the other students in the class. Unfortunately, the danger is that gifted students who are left unchallenged can, and often do, become unmotivated underachievers who turn into problem students and are prone to dropping out. In fact, gifted students drop out at rates that exceed those of their classmates who are not gifted. The "In Your Classroom" feature offers advice to help you keep this from happening.

Having focused here on students with high IQs and special gifts and talents, we need to remember that most students are average students for whom schoolwork is demanding. In addition, there are those of limited academic intelligence and skills for whom classroom life is a constant struggle and often the source of immense frustration. They cry out for teachers of great compassion and creativity.

# Learning Styles

**Learning styles** learners' preferred ways of acquiring, processing, and then making use of new knowledge.

Theories of intelligence tend to focus on *how much* learners can learn. Psychologists and educators have also studied *how* we learn. These researchers have identified several models of **learning styles,** learners' preferred ways of acquiring, processing, and then making use of new knowledge. These models suggest that teachers should present information in all of the ways that are most meaningful to students with a variety of learning styles. Different models, however, focus on different learning-style priorities.

We present two popular views of learning styles in this module, but there are many more. One popular model, used heavily in business, is the Myers-Briggs Type Indicator (MBTI). The MBTI is based on a theory of sixteen distinctive personality types, each of which has direct implications for

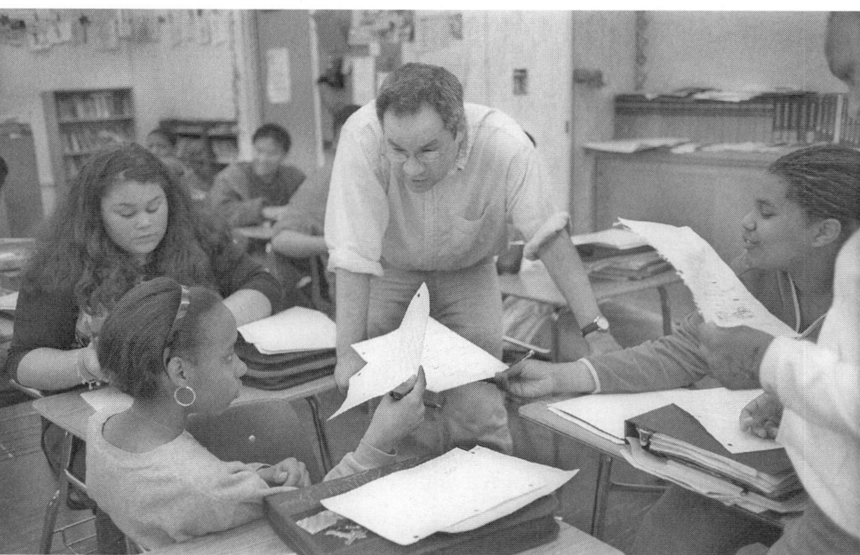

Cooperative learning activities encourage students with different learning styles to contribute to group goals.

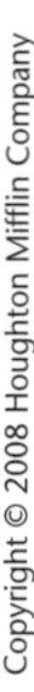

teachers and their students. Visit the Online Study Center to read about the MBTI.

## VAK

**VAK** a learning styles model that suggests learners receive new information through one of three senses: visual, auditory, or kinesthetic.

The **VAK** model, developed by Neil Fleming,[9] claims that learners receive new information through one of three senses: visual, auditory, or kinesthetic. (VAK is an acronym made up of the first letters of these senses.) Fleming suggested that most learners have a general preference for one sense but that some learners are *multimodal*, their preference for a particular mode depending on the demands of the situation or the task.[10]

***Visual*** Some visual learners may have a preference for verbal or linguistic input, whereas others are spatial-visual learners.

- *Verbal-visual learners* learn best through written language and remember information better when they see it written down. In the school setting, verbal-visual learners may take copious notes during a lecture or when reading a textbook. They are often list-writers, although they may or may not need to see the list once it has been written. In the classroom, verbal-visual learners benefit from outlines or other graphic organizers, and from teachers who make use of the blackboard or overhead to list key elements of a lecture or discussion. These learners often find flashcards useful for remembering words or facts.
- *Spatial-visual learners* prefer visuals, such as graphs, charts, or videos. They easily visualize faces and places by using their imagination and seldom get lost in new surroundings. In the classroom, spatial-visual learners benefit from visual aids such as film, video, maps, and charts to help them access new information. In a textbook, the spatial-visual learner is more likely to study a chart or a map than to read the text. Spatial-visual learners can also benefit from flashcards that use symbols, diagrams, or pictures rather than words.

***Auditory*** Auditory learners learn best by hearing things. They prefer listening and talking to reading and writing. When trying to recall previously acquired knowledge, auditory learners can often "hear" the way the information was originally presented. Auditory learners often need to interact verbally with others in order to internalize the new information presented. In the classroom, auditory learners may listen to lectures without taking notes and still be able to recall key information. They may have to "talk through" concepts with a partner or group in order to clarify their understanding of them. They may also read their notes aloud when they are studying for a test or exam.

***Kinesthetic*** Kinesthetic learners prefer to move or touch objects as they access new information. Some kinesthetic learners are tactile learners and need to touch or handle objects as they learn about them. They benefit most from "hands-on" lessons or field explorations and observations. These learners may have difficulty remaining physically passive while learning. They may need to get up and walk around or stand as they complete assigned tasks in the classroom. They may lose focus or concentration without some kind of external stimulation or movement. When studying for a test, kinesthetic learners can benefit from information on index cards that they can put in order or manipulate in some other way.

## In Your Classroom

### Teaching for Different Learning Styles

As a mentor teacher once told one of our student teachers, "Always present information in three ways: say it, write it, and show it." We might add to that advice: "Plan hands-on activities as much as possible for the kinesthetic learners." For example, in a lecture or discussion on the underground railroad during the U.S. Civil War, as you discuss key concepts, you can write them on the board. You might also distribute a graphic organizer, on which students can write these concepts. You can present maps of routes that escaped slaves would have followed or a chart showing the numbers of runaway slaves helped to freedom by the underground railroad. In addition, you might have students enact some of the cramped living quarters or other experiences of runaway slaves on the underground railroad.

## Now You Do It

Some students, even high school students, may need assistance in understanding their preferred sensory learning modality. They may have an intuitive sense that they are more visual or more auditory, but they may not have very effective learning strategies to support these modalities. In some cases, they may have been discouraged from drawing on their preferred learning style by previous teachers or their primary caretakers, who may not have recognized these subtle differences in learning. How would you respond to parents who make comments like the following?

- "I've told Jason a thousand times to take notes on the lectures and to take notes on his reading. But he just won't listen to me. He keeps saying he remembers what is said in class without writing it down."
- "I keep telling Melinda she should write down important concepts on index cards. Then she can go through the cards and sort the information when it's time for an exam. She says her notes are fine, but how can they be fine? Look how messy they are!"
- "Before a test, I tell Eric to recite aloud all the words he has to know in Spanish, but he won't. How else are you going to remember the words if you don't keep saying them over and over?"

## Kolb's Learning Styles Model and Experiential Learning Theory (ELT)

**Kolb's learning styles model** a four-phase learning cycle that consists of a *concrete experience,* which provides a basis for *reflective observation,* which is followed by *abstract conceptualization,* which, in turn, is followed by *active experimentation.*

David **Kolb's learning styles model** includes four learning styles, which are based on a four-phase cycle of experiential learning.[11] Kolb suggested that the cycle begins with a *concrete experience*, which provides a basis for *reflective observation*. From this observation emerges *abstract conceptualization*, followed by *active experimentation*. When learning to ride a bicycle, for example, the learner is first presented with a concrete experience, an actual bicycle to examine, although he or she may or may not attempt to ride the bike. Then the learner spends time observing others riding a bicycle and thinking about various aspects of the bike-riding experience. From these observations, the learner formulates abstract ideas about how to ride a bicycle. When ready, the learner actively engages in the experience, experimentally implementing the ideas formulated in advance.

Kolb noted, however, that learners tended to show a preference for one phase of the learning cycle over the others. Some learners are more inclined to jump right in and experiment in a new situation, for example, whereas others prefer to observe before attempting any action. Kolb revised his theory on the basis of these observations. He suggested four different learning styles based on people's preferences for doing (active experimentation) versus watching (reflective observation) and for thinking (abstract conceptualization) versus feeling (concrete experience). He labeled these four styles diverging, assimilating, converging, and accommodating.

- *Diverging* learners combine concrete experience and reflective observation. Learners with a diverging style learn best when they are able to observe others at work rather than participating in an activity. Learning activities that will appeal to them include brainstorming sessions, journal writing, and analyses. They do not do well with tight deadlines. Instead, they need time to review what has happened, to reflect on what they have learned, and to think about implications and possible applications. Individuals with this learning style are able to look at situations from different perspectives. They tend to be emotional and sensitive, with an artistic side. They prefer to work in groups rather than alone, although they generally do not like to have leadership responsibilities.
- *Accommodating* learners favor a combination of concrete experience and active experimentation. Individuals with this learning style take a practical, experiential approach to solving problems. Activities that appeal to these learners include simulations, case studies, and exploration of new concepts. They relish experimenting without researching beforehand, and they do not do well with following directions or procedures. Although these learners would rather make use of others' analyses than carry out their own, they do not have much time for reading texts or listening to long lectures. Learners with the accommodating style learn best when they work with others to solve problems or complete tasks, and they prefer to be in charge of the experimenting.
- *Assimilating* learners tend to combine abstract conceptualization and reflective observation. These learners are analytical, logical, and concise. Learning activities that will appeal to them include lectures,

Kinesthetic and converging learners prefer "hands-on" learning.

**Video Case**

In the video case, *Academic Diversity: Differentiated Instruction,* you'll see how third-grade teacher Chris Colbath-Hess strives to meet one of the greatest challenges for teachers in teaching students in heterogeneous classrooms: designing instruction that meets the needs of different types of learners. As you watch the clips and study the artifacts in the case, reflect on the following questions.

**QUESTIONS**

1. Do the techniques demonstrated in this case address content, process, or product?
2. How are all students held accountable for mastering the same writing-skills content, even though they approach the task differently?
3. What are some ways in which you might differentiate lessons in the subject area and grade level you teach?

***Online Study Center***

classroom discussion, and analogies. Assimilating learners tend to focus on theories and abstract concepts rather than on practical approaches, and they sometimes come up with interesting ideas that may or may not have immediate relevance to the task at hand. They learn best, however, when they have a very specific task, with a clear goal, to accomplish. They do not do well with experimentation unless they have first developed a knowledge base to frame the experiment. Learners with the assimilating style are more focused on ideas than on people, and they prefer to work on their own.

- *Converging* learners mix abstract conceptualization and active experimentation. Individuals with this learning style are pragmatic and practical. They are good at finding practical and applicable solutions to problems. Learners with the converging style learn best when they are given enough information and a challenging task. Tasks that are not purposeful and meaningful, however, can make these learners impatient. Learning activities that appeal to them include fieldwork, observations, and laboratory experiments. Converging learners do not do well with abstract or theoretical discussions, preferring to test out ideas and theories. They have a preference for technical tasks and would rather solve problems on their own than work in a team or group situation.

## Teaching Students with Diverse Learning Styles

As a teacher, it is important for you to recognize the diversity in learning styles that your students will bring to your classroom. You also need to realize that many of your students will have learning styles that differ from your own preferred learning style. According to learning style researchers, imposing on students a standard way of performing a task, or expecting them all to use and excel with a particular strategy, could compromise their learning. Teachers should recognize this diversity and propose activities that can maximize the learning of all students.

We do *not*, however, advocate designing separate learning activities for students on the basis of their individual learning styles. Instead, teachers should organize and implement a variety of activities that can be approached through a range of learning styles. Such variety gives learners the opportunity to explore learning modalities outside their usual preferences, as well as some activities that "fit" their preferred modality.

# Addressing Intelligences and Learning Styles Through Differentiated Instruction

**Differentiated instruction** a teaching philosophy based on the premise that teachers should adapt instruction to student differences in reading readiness, learning preferences, and interests.

The academic diversity of students in today's classrooms is growing, and one instructional approach is very unlikely to work for all students. **Differentiated instruction** is a teaching philosophy based on the premise that teachers should adapt instruction to student differences in reading readiness, learning preferences, and interests. In its simplest form, differentiated instruction advocates responding to individual students, rather than imposing a standardized approach to teaching that assumes all learners in a class are essentially alike. In a classroom that adopts differentiated instruction, students have choices among learning activities, although they are all still expected to master the same concepts.

According to Carol Tomlinson, a national expert on differentiated instruction, teachers can differentiate three aspects of the curriculum: content, process, and product.[12]

- *Content* is made up of the concepts, principles, and skills that teachers want students to learn. All students should be given access to the same core content, Tomlinson believes. However, teachers can provide different means (for example, texts, lectures, and demonstrations) to give students access to skills and knowledge.
- *Process* consists of the activities that help students make sense of and "own" the knowledge being taught. Teachers can vary the activities to provide some students with access to more complexity and to offer others more support, depending on their readiness levels, interests, and learning preferences.
- *Products* are the culminating projects that students develop to demonstrate and extend what they have learned. These products can vary

## In Your Classroom

### Differentiating Instruction

Many teachers acknowledge the desirability of differentiated instruction but don't know how to go about doing it. Here are some of the many strategies that teachers can use.

| | |
|---|---|
| *Stations* | Setting up different spots in the classroom where students can work on different tasks at the same time, which encourages flexible grouping because not all students have to go to all stations all the time. |
| *Compacting* | Assessing students before beginning a unit of study to see what they already know so they won't have to waste time learning something they have already learned. |
| *Complex Instruction* | Uses challenging materials, open-ended tasks, and small instructional groups. Teachers circulate as students work, asking questions and stimulating student thinking. |
| *Choice Boards* | Teachers write work assignments on cards that are placed in hanging pockets. Students are asked to select a card from a particular row of pockets, which gives the students some circumscribed choices. The different rows represent work at different levels of complexity. |
| *Problem-based Learning* | Teachers place students in an active role solving problems. |
| *Entry Points* | Using Howard Gardner's MI theory, students explore a given topic through as many as five avenues: narrational (presenting a story), logical-quantitative (using numbers or deduction), foundational (examining philosophy and vocabulary), aesthetic (focusing on sensory properties), and experiential (hands-on). |
| *Orbital Studies* | Consists of independent investigations, usually lasting several weeks, related to some aspect of the curriculum. Students select topics, and the teacher guides them during the investigation. |

Source: Adapted with permission from *The Differentiated Classroom: Responding to the Needs of All Learners* by Carol Tomlinson, Chapters 7 and 8: ASCD, 1999. Copyright © 1999 by the Association for Supervision and Curriculum Development. The Association for Supervision and Curriculum Development is a worldwide community of educators advocating sound policies and sharing best practices to achieve the success of each learner. To learn more, visit ASCD at **www.ascd.org.**

depending on students' interests or learning preferences. For example, some students might prefer to work as a member of a group producing a play about the topic being studied, whereas others might prefer to work alone and write a term paper.

Differentiating content, process, and product for students requires teachers to know their students, their subject, and their materials. There is no formula for differentiation—no single way to address student differences. Rather, differentiating instruction is a commitment to start with students and to make a match between the learner and the material to be learned. Although its primary goal is to maximize the learning of each student, an important secondary goal is to give students training in ways of learning that don't come naturally to them. Differentiating instruction "stretches" students and increases their capacities to grow and learn.

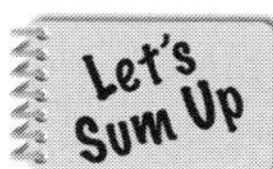


Although there may be nearly endless combinations of variables that affect learning, there are a predictable number of combinations of academic skills that are found most often in learners. Likewise, there are a predictable number of learning activities and strategies to present to your students. The key, we would argue, is to establish certain learning routines so that students develop and practice important skills and habits of mind. Not every lesson should be routine, however. We also suggest that you aim to vary some percentage of students' learning experiences, planning a range of activities. Teaching is something of a balancing act. Sometimes we need to design instruction to play to students' learning strengths, and sometimes we need to stretch them into what are, for them, new and important ways of learning. This is one of the important features of teaching that is ever fascinating, ever challenging.

## Further Resources

- Association for Supervision and Curriculum Development (ASCD). Available at: **http://www.ascd.org.** ASCD has many resources on multiple intelligences and learning styles. Click on Education Topics, Multiple Intelligences, for more resources on this topic.

- Experimental Learning Cycle. Available at: **http://www.learningandteaching.info/learning/experience.htm.** This website provides a rich explanation of David Kolb's theory of learning and knowing. Its visuals show the cycles and the interrelationships among the phases.
- Howard Gardner, *Frames of Intelligence* (New York: Basic Books, 1985) and Howard Gardner, *Multiple Intelligences: The Theory in Practice* (New York, Basic Books, 1993). These two books are the most complete statements of the multiple intelligences theory.
- Carol Ann Tomlinson and Jay McTighe, *Integrating Differentiated Instruction & Understanding by Design* (Alexandria, VA: Association of Supervision and Curriculum Development, 2006). This book combines a curriculum design model that focuses on what we teach with an instructional approach that focuses on whom and how we teach.

- VARK, A Guide to Learning Styles. Available at: **http://www.vark-learn.com/english/index.asp.** This website allows visitors to analyze their preferred learning style via an online or downloaded questionnaire. It also suggests strategies for learning that are aligned with particular learning styles.

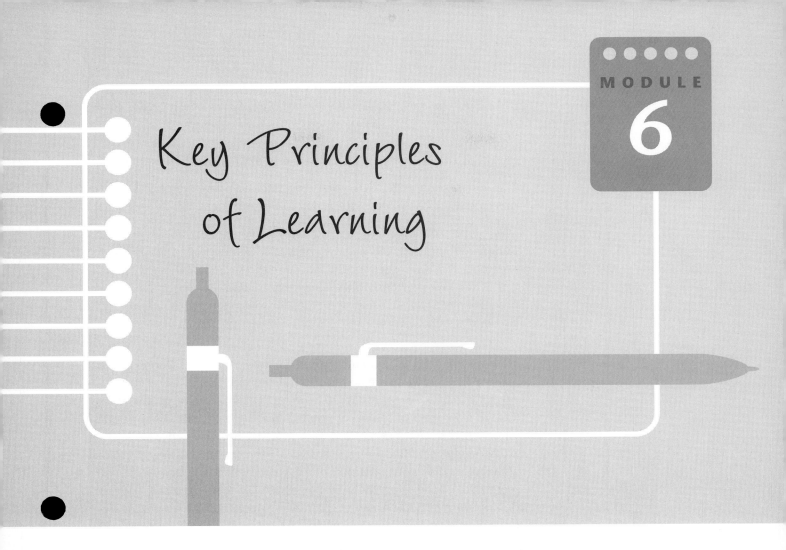

Scenario

Franklin Jones, a middle school science teacher, is in the middle of an astronomy unit with his seventh graders. The current focus of study is the sun-earth-moon dynamics, in particular the phases of the moon. Today, Franklin has asked his students to investigate the interaction among these three celestial bodies and to come up with some hypotheses to explain the moon's phases. Franklin has gathered a variety of resources for students to use in their investigations: yearly charts showing the phases of the moon, a scaled physical model of the sun-earth-moon, flashlights, different-sized plastic balls, globes, resource books, and a bank of computers. He explains the task to the students, lists the resources available, and sets a time limit for the investigation. He tells students that they can work either individually or in groups and that during the last part of the class session, they will share their findings and hypotheses.

After a few minutes, most of the students seem to be busily engaged in their investigations. Some are using the plastic balls and flashlights to test their ideas about shadows on the moon. Others are on the computer searching different websites, while still others are studying the moon charts. One group, however, seems too talkative to be discussing phases of the moon. Franklin approaches their table to redirect them. "Do you all really want to get a point today?" he asks the group. The school recently adopted a point system to address student behavior. When a student "earned" ten points, he or she had to go to a Saturday session, a three-hour work session on Saturday morning. "Sorry, Mr. Jones," mumble group members as they get up to consult some of the reference books Franklin had gathered.

"Mr. Jones, can you help us? We think shadows cause the phases of the moon, but we can't figure out a way to test our ideas."

"Well, look around," Franklin suggests. "Do you see anyone in here doing anything that might cause shadows?" Suddenly the group's members seem to notice for the first time the students who are using the plastic balls and flashlights. They excitedly get up to observe the process a little more closely, and Franklin smiles as he continues to circulate about the room.

Preview

Students in Franklin Jones's class are *learning*; they are acquiring new knowledge about the moon. This act of learning is at the core of your work as a teacher, so it is important for you to have some idea what happens when we learn. Although you have been learning your entire life and are certainly very effective at it, answering the question of how individuals acquire new knowledge presents a greater challenge than it may seem. Philosophers, psychologists, and, yes, teachers have been pondering this question of how we gain new knowledge, or how we learn, since at least the time of the ancient Greeks, well over 2,000 years ago.

Over the centuries, various thinkers have advanced a number of theories to try to unravel the mysteries of the learning process. All of the current major learning theories have their strengths and weaknesses for explaining how people learn, and we will see that none of them can fully explain how all people learn all subjects, all of the time.

We'll explore in this module several theories from two main schools of thought that have been influential in American schools and describe some instructional activities that are grounded in each school of thought. In one school of thought is *behaviorism,* which focuses on observable behaviors. In the other are *cognitive theories*, which focus on mental activities. We'll also describe social learning theory, which combines elements of both views. You'll be presented with the basics of each theory, its application in the classroom, and information about its strengths and weaknesses.

**This module emphasizes that:**

- **Learning is an idiosyncratic process, so no one approach to learning is best for all learners.**
- **Behaviorist theories suggest that we learn as the result of our past experiences.**

- Some cognitive theories describe sequences of changes in learners' thinking as they age and develop. Others stress the social and cultural context surrounding the student.
- Constructivism, which applies ideas from cognitive learning theories, is popular among many educators.
- Social learning theory suggests that we learn by observing the experiences of others.

## Now You Do It

Because learning theories can be very abstract, we suggest that you make a special effort to think about possible real-life uses of these theories. As you read about each learning theory presented in this module, mentally plan an instructional activity based on that theory. Try to think of an activity that takes advantage of the strengths of the theory and avoids its weaknesses, something that would actually work in your classroom.

# Behaviorist Theories

**Conditioning** developing a link between some stimulus in our environment and a behavior or other response.

**Classical conditioning** the process of creating automatic associations between certain stimuli in the environment and our responses.

**Operant conditioning** the process of making behaviors more or less likely to recur, based on the consequences, reinforcing or punishing, that follow the behavior.

Behaviorists believe that learning is a result of past experiences. Behaviorists often refer to learning as **conditioning,** developing a link between some stimulus in our environment and a response, or a particular behavior. **Classical conditioning** consists of automatic associations between certain stimuli in the environment and our responses, whereas **operant conditioning** accounts for behaviors we acquire as the result of past successes and failures. As we'll see, both types of conditioning can operate in your classroom.

## Classical Conditioning

The Russian psychologist Ivan Pavlov (1846–1936) was the first to formally study the link between stimulus and response. Pavlov noticed that some dogs in his laboratory began to salivate when they heard a sound signaling the appearance of their food. After studying this phenomenon, Pavlov found that the dogs could be trained to begin salivating when they heard the sound, whether food appeared or not. They were *conditioned* to salivate in response to the stimulus of the sound alone. Pavlov's conditioning became known as *classical conditioning*. Classical conditioning can be seen in students' automatic response to school bells or buzzers. As soon as the bell rings, the students have hoisted their belongings and are on their way out the door, even though the teacher may not have finished talking.

## Operant Conditioning

Influenced by Pavlov's ideas, American psychologist B. F. Skinner (1904–1999) expanded them to develop his own, highly influential behaviorist theory of operant conditioning. Skinner's theory suggests that people "learn" behaviors

Praise and attention can serve as reinforcers for desired student behaviors. Be careful, however, that you do not accidentally reinforce undesired behavior.

based on the response they receive to a particular action. A positive response is likely to encourage the behavior, while a negative response is thought to discourage the behavior. Operant conditioning rests on two key principles:

- *Reinforcement.* If a person's behavior is followed by a positive response, which Skinner termed **positive reinforcement,** or if the behavior eliminates an undesirable condition, a situation Skinner labeled **negative reinforcement,** then that person is more likely to repeat the behavior.
- *Punishment.* If a behavior is followed by **punishment,** an undesirable or adverse response, the person is less likely to repeat the behavior.

**Positive reinforcement** in operant conditioning, occurs when a person's behavior is followed by a rewarding consequence, making the behavior more likely in the future.

**Negative reinforcement** in operant conditioning, occurs when a person's behavior causes an undesirable situation to end, making the behavior more likely in the future.

**Punishment** in operant conditioning, occurs when a person's behavior is followed by an undesirable or adverse response, making the behavior less likely to occur in the future.

**Behavior modification** a behaviorist technique in which teachers carefully control responses in order to create desired behaviors in their students.

From the theory of operant conditioning evolved the practice of **behavior modification.** In behavior modification, teachers carefully control responses in order to shape behaviors of their students. If Billy, a third-grade student, consistently fails to hand in his homework, his teacher might implement a behavior modification plan to get him to start doing the homework. Each day that Billy hands in his homework, he gets a sticker. If Billy forgets any of his homework, he must give back one sticker. At the end of the week, he can "cash in" his stickers in the school store. Results in such programs are often gradual. During the first few weeks of the program, Billy might have to give back some stickers, but after several weeks, he may be earning five stickers each week by handing in his homework every day. Other plans may include a point system, in which desirable or appropriate behaviors are rewarded by the awarding of points; undesirable, inappropriate behaviors are discouraged by the removal of points. Students can "buy" goods or privileges (such as a homework-free day or extra time at the computer) with their points.

## Behaviorist Influences in the Classroom

The key to learning for a behaviorist is the environment, and it is the teacher's responsibility to set up and maintain an environment that is conducive to learning. Indeed, many teachers rely heavily on behaviorist techniques for classroom management, implementing behavior modification programs designed to reinforce appropriate behaviors and eliminate inappropriate ones. Depriving students of their recess time if they fail to complete work during class is a common approach to helping students develop the appropriate classroom habits and behaviors.

Behaviorism can also be applied to instruction. Learning activities based on behaviorist theories have several key features, including the following:

- *Repetition.* Behaviorists believe that learners learn best through repetition. A common behaviorist teaching technique, therefore, is "drill and practice," used more often perhaps at the younger grades, but still found throughout the K–12 curriculum. On any given day in almost any school, students may be heard reciting their "times tables," reading a passage in union, reciting foreign-language words, or repeating definitions of certain concepts. Other versions of drill and practice include completing worksheets and using computer-based drill software.

- *Prompt feedback.* Skinner himself proposed a behaviorist instructional approach that he called *programmed instruction.*[1] This approach, one of the first attempts to automate instruction, used teaching machines in the instructional process. Precursors to today's computers, these teaching machines would present students with a question related to a particular unit of study. Students would receive immediate feedback from the machine for their answers. The immediacy of the feedback was the crucial element, according to Skinner, because it provided the necessary reinforcement to help solidify accurate information in the students' minds.

  From Skinner's teaching machines has evolved computer-assisted instruction (CAI), an approach that makes use of computer programs to teach concepts or skills. Many of these programs function in a similar manner, providing students with immediate feedback on the accuracy of their answers to questions. Continuing advances in computer graphics and animation allow for lively, attractive feedback, as well as for engaging and motivating games and scenarios.

- *Specific, measurable (and measured) learning objectives.* Behaviorists recommend dividing the curriculum into discrete units of study, organized sequentially. Each unit of study is further divided into topics with specific and measurable learning objectives. Learning is measured primarily through objective, multiple-choice tests that allow for clear and quick feedback. The learner is rewarded in the form of high grades for remembering information that has been presented and is punished with low grades for not remembering.

  In the early 1960s, Benjamin Bloom, a well-known educational psychologist, applied these behaviorist principles to an approach called **mastery learning.**[2] Mastery learning is based on the belief that all students can master concepts if they are taught appropriately and given sufficient time to master the content. Appropriate teaching, according to Bloom, consists of systematic instruction on discrete units of study, a sequenced curriculum, adequate time and support for student learning, clear criteria for mastery, and prompt and specific feedback. In mastery learning, students are regularly tested to determine their levels of mastery. Bloom believed that with enough time, some 90–95 percent of students using this method could master the content they need to know.

  **Mastery learning** a behaviorist learning approach consisting of systematic instruction in discrete units of study, a sequenced curriculum, adequate time and support for student learning, clear criteria for mastery, frequent evaluation of progress, and prompt and specific feedback.

  Many of today's computer tutorials, programs designed to teach or re-teach students concepts or skills, follow the model of mastery learning by presenting concepts or skills in short, sequenced units on which students are immediately assessed. A typical tutorial begins with a teaching component, followed by a guided practice phase during which students work through items and receive not just feedback, but also explanations of the correct and incorrect responses. This phase is followed by an assessment with immediate feedback and, frequently, with opportunities to revisit material if the test results reveal that the student did not completely master a concept.

### Evaluation of Behaviorism

Like all other educational theories, behaviorism has its proponents and opponents. Proponents insist that behaviorism is the most efficient approach to developing important and foundational skills and concepts. Because students practice a skill until they achieve a level of mastery, they have truly "learned" the skills.

Opponents argue that the system of rewards and punishments in the behaviorist approach can backfire. Instead of its leading to mastery learning of skills and concepts, students quickly lose interest in learning and focus only on the rewards. On tests, students figure out how to *select* the right answer without necessarily *knowing* the right answer. In many computer learning games, students often look for ways to "game the game," bypassing the instructional or assessment component to get the rewards screens.

An even more basic criticism of behaviorism questions the very premise of the theory. These critics insist that human behavior cannot be explained only in terms of responses to external stimuli and that learning cannot be reduced to drills practice. They argue that consideration must be given to mental activity—remembering and thinking—as well. We discuss this cognitive viewpoint next.

## Cognitive Theories

Behaviorists focus principally on external and visible responses to stimuli. In contrast, *cognitivists* focus on understanding the role of the brain—that is, one's cognitive functions—in the learning process. They are interested in how learners process the stimuli they receive and in what thought processes learners use to decide on and execute their responses. Two of the more influential early cognitive theorists were the Swiss psychologist Jean Piaget (1896–1980) and the Russian psychologist Lev Vygotsky (1896–1934). We'll summarize each of these major theories and discuss the cognitivist education movement known as constructivism.

### Piaget's Theory of Cognitive Development

Jean Piaget's theory[3] suggests that humans have two inherent intellectual tendencies:

**Schemes** cognitive structures for organizing knowledge.

1. *Organization.* People tend to organize their knowledge using cognitive structures that Piaget called **schemes.** This organizational system enables a person to recall information and events.
2. *Acquisition of new information.* People add new information to their existing schemes throughout their lives, and as they do so, these schemes expand and become more complex.

**Equilibration** Piaget's term for a state of mental balance and harmony.

Piaget also suggested that, just as the body adjusts to any change in body temperature to return it to normal, the brain also looks to reestablish **equilibration,** or balance and harmony, when new information is introduced.

**Adaptation** Piaget's term for incorporating new information into our mental organizational schemes.

**Assimilation** Piaget's term for adding new information to existing mental schemes.

**Accommodation** Piaget's term for changes in mental schemes made when new information conflicts with existing knowledge.

Piaget labeled this process of finding equilibration **adaptation.** His theory proposes two methods of adaptation:

- ***Assimilation.*** In some instances, the new information presented creates only minimal, if any, disruption to a learner's schemes, and the learner is able to easily add, or assimilate, that information to the existing schemes.
- ***Accommodation.*** In other instances, when the new information conflicts with existing knowledge, it creates considerable disruption. In this situation, the learner has to find some way to change his or her schemes to accommodate the new information. Suppose a young child growing up in French-speaking Africa has in her scheme the knowledge that Africans speak French. On a trip to the United States, she hears African Americans speaking English. This new information creates a disruption in her knowledge base. She now has to adjust her schemes to accommodate this new information and to allow for English-speaking African Americans.

According to Piaget, the learning process consists of the continual adaptation of new information into one's schemes by either assimilating the new information or making accommodations to the new information, to one's schemes, or both.

All learners have these tendencies of organization and adaptation, but Piaget noted differences in the learning process depending on the age of the learner. Piaget proposed that all learners pass through four distinct stages of cognitive development.[4]

1. *Sensorimotor stage.* Piaget suggested that for the first two years of life, we receive most new information through our senses—what we can see, hear, touch, or pick up and taste—or by trying out different physical, or motor, activities.
2. *Preoperational* stage.* In Piaget's second stage, preoperational learners (from age 3 to 7) have more developed schemes and are able to store in their minds images and symbols (such as letters and words). Sources of new information can also be more symbolic than they are for babies. It is in this period, for example, that children usually begin to read. Although learners start to develop organizational patterns in their schemes, the organization tends to be largely illogical, at least from an adult's perspective.
3. *Concrete operational stage.* Piaget suggested that the concrete operational stage lasts from age 7 to 11, a period when most learners are in elementary school. During this third stage, learners' schemes continue to become more complex and their organization starts to take on an adult-like logic. The most readily accessible source of new information, however, is still actual experiences or concrete objects. In addition, Piaget believed that concrete operational learners are not quite ready to engage in abstract reasoning, such as drawing conclusions or making inferences from specific events or information.
4. *Formal operational stage.* The fourth stage is that of formal operations, which is characteristic of teens and young adults aged 11 to 18. During this stage, schemes grow progressively more complex and take on a more logical

*Piaget used the word *operational* to mean "logical." The preoperational stage can be understood as being prelogical, the stage before logical thinking has developed in the learner.

## In Your Classroom

### Applying Piaget's Stages to Lesson Planning

Piaget's theory suggests that tasks assigned to learners should match their developmental stage, an idea known as *developmentally appropriate learning.*

- Most elementary learners function in the concrete operational stage, so learning tasks should involve working with concrete objects and concepts as much as possible. For example, teachers who encourage elementary students to use manipulatives in mathematics or who plan hands-on science lessons are looking to address the developmental needs of learners in the concrete operational stage.
- Secondary learners have begun to move into the formal operational stage, so instructional activities should be designed to help learners hone their developing logical and abstract thinking skills. For example, a compare-and-contrast essay in English requires that students generalize behaviors, characteristics, or events in two or more pieces of literature in such a way as to examine the *form* rather than the specific *content.*

## Video Case

In the video case, *Vygotsky's Zone of Proximal Development: Increasing Cognition in an Elementary Literacy Lesson,* you will see how developmental psychologist Dr. Francis Hurley draws on this theory to support students' abstract thinking in a lesson on poetry. As you watch the clips and study the artifacts in the case, reflect on the following questions.

**QUESTIONS**

1. Which of the Vygotskian instructional techniques is Dr. Hurley describing when she talks about building the children's knowledge in stepwise fashion from day to day? How would this step-by-step approach apply to the students and subject you will be teaching?
2. How does this teacher determine the original knowledge level of her students? How can you determine the zone of proximal development for each of your students?

*Online Study Center*

organization of information that allows for efficient recall of knowledge. Piaget described the learner's thinking at this stage as "formal" because the learner can look at the *form* of the problem, not just the *content* of the problem. This focus on form means that learners can begin to abstract from a specific problem to make generalizations, inferences, and conclusions, skills that are frequently encouraged in high school courses.

Piaget noted that the age spans he suggested are, at best, approximations and that individual development varies greatly. Some learners at the middle school age range may still need to work with concrete models, while others will be ready to engage in more abstract thinking and reasoning. Further, he cautioned that people's schemes become progressively more complex at a relatively slow pace. It may be more appropriate to say that learner's schemes generally show the characteristics described for a particular stage by the end of the stage, rather than at the beginning.

## Vygotsky's Sociocultural Perspective

The Russian psychologist Lev Vygotsky, a contemporary of Piaget, describes the process of cognitive development as dependent on and defined by two principal variables.[5]

- *Cultural context.* The ways in which people organize their knowledge and how they think are defined and determined by their culture. Americans categorize knowledge in a particular way because that organizational structure is valued in the American culture and modeled to young learners. Other cultures value different ways of organizing knowledge and will teach these ways to their youth.

  Consider, for example, how people tell stories. American stories are most often linear; the story has a clear beginning, middle, and end. In societies with stronger oral traditions, including many Native American and African cultures, stories more often exhibit a cyclical organization, in which events may recur and the story does not necessarily have a beginning or an end. Students are taught this story structure throughout their elementary school career.

- *Social interaction.* We learn and develop our thinking through social interaction: engaging in conversation with others. Interacting with a more knowledgeable person, such as an adult or even a more knowledgeable peer, helps learners make sense of the events and actions around them. This interaction also helps learners know what information or knowledge is valued by the culture and begin to organize their cognitive structures in culturally appropriate ways.

  Language is key to this learning process. Vygotsky suggests that language, which serves an obvious social function of communication, also reflects a culture's patterns of thinking and ways of organizing knowledge, which then influence how we learn. Vygotsky maintains that language actually becomes thinking, as we engage in what he called "inner speech," or talking to ourselves. In young learners, inner speech is often verbalized; they may talk aloud to themselves as a way of making the transition from the purely social use of language to using it for thinking.

**Zone of proximal development** the gap between what learners can do on their own and what they can do with the guidance or collaboration of another.

***Vygotsky's Influence in the Classroom*** Vygotsky believed that learning occurs when the learner is given tasks that fall within the **zone of proximal development**, the gap between what learners can do on their own and what they can do with the guidance or collaboration of another. If a learner can already do a task on her own, no new learning takes places. If the task given the learner is too complex or beyond the intellectual capacity of the learner, no learning takes place unless the learner engages in the task with the assistance of someone who can complete the task successfully. To plan assignments within their students' zone of proximal development, teachers must know the current status of the students' skills and have a good idea about their capacities.

In keeping with the theory's emphasis on social interaction, teachers who use a Vygotskian instructional approach provide frequent opportunities for students to interact with others using such strategies as

**Scaffolding** an instructional technique in which the teacher at first provides the learner with structured support for a task and then gradually reduces the support as the learner becomes more proficient.

**Reciprocal learning** (also known as **reciprocal teaching**) An instructional technique in which the teacher and students take turns leading small-group discussions. First the teacher models questioning strategies, and then the students gradually assume the teaching role, following the model of the teacher.

**Peer collaboration/cooperative learning** an instructional approach in which students work together, or collaborate, to complete tasks or assignments.

**Constructivism** a cognitive-based educational theory suggesting that learners must "construct" their own interpretations of new knowledge from information they encounter in order to add it to their existing knowledge base.

- ***Scaffolding.*** At first, the teacher provides the learner with structured support for a task. The support is gradually reduced as the learner becomes more proficient with a skill or concept and able to do the work with less help.
- ***Reciprocal learning.*** In reciprocal learning, which is also called reciprocal teaching, the teacher and students take turns leading small-group discussions. First the teacher models questioning strategies, and then the students gradually assume the teaching role, following the model of the teacher.
- ***Peer collaboration/cooperative learning.*** As students interact with one another to complete a task, they develop their communication and thinking skills.

## Constructivism: Applying Cognitive Theories

These cognitive theories on how we learn have merged into a kind of umbrella theory called **constructivism.** As the name implies, this theory states that when learners encounter new information, they use it to make, or "construct," new knowledge, which they add to their existing knowledge base. According to constructivists, knowledge is not simply passed from teacher to learner. Instead, learners have to take this new information, make sense of it, and then attach it in some way to what they already know.

**Discovery learning** an instructional approach in which teachers set up investigative activities, and students engage in methodical inquiry to find answers or solutions to the problems presented.

**Project-based learning** a pedagogical approach in which students work on an open-ended project that allows for the integration of information from various disciplines.

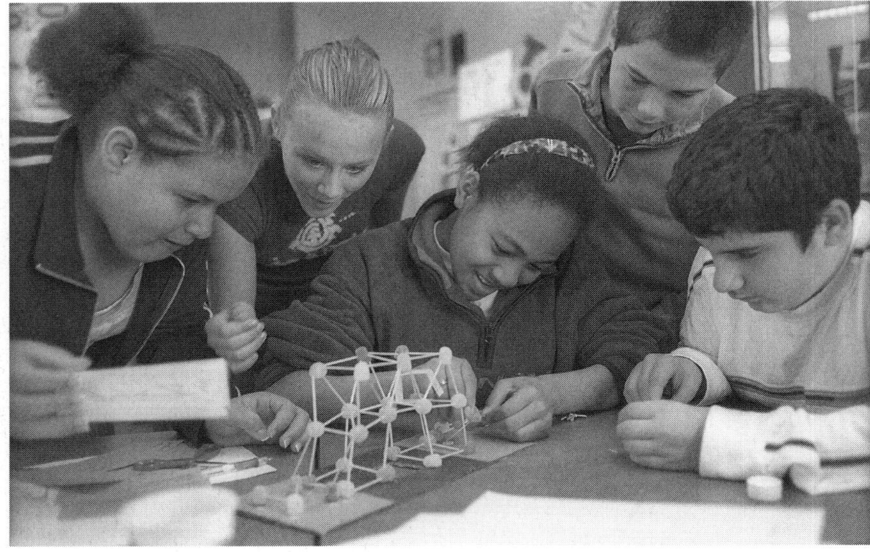

Students work collaboratively to explore concepts and gain understanding.

***Constructivist Influence in the Classroom*** Constructivist ideas have been very influential in recent decades in American education. Because the theory combines elements of several cognitive learning theories, constructivists also use several of the methods that stem from those theories. The "In Your Classroom" feature describes two approaches, discovery learning and project-based learning.

## In Your Classroom

### Constructivist Instructional Approaches

Two teaching and learning approaches popular among educators who take a constructivist approach are discovery learning and project-based learning.

- ***Discovery Learning.*** Developed by American psychologist Jerome Bruner, discovery learning is based on the idea that learners learn best when they have the opportunity to discover new information, classify that information, and store it appropriately.[6] In this approach, teachers set up investigative activities and students engage in methodical inquiry to find answers or solutions to the problem presented.

  The moon investigation presented at the beginning of this module is an example of discovery learning. Students were given a question to investigate: "Why does the moon seem to have these different shapes?" They used information they already had learned about the different phases of the moon to formulate hypotheses to explain the phases. Then they could use the different materials and resources that Franklin Jones had supplied them to test their hypotheses.

- ***Project-Based Learning.*** Originally the brainchild of William Heard Kilpatrick, the goal of project-based learning (PBL) is to make the process of education "worthy living itself."[7] Instead of being presented with discrete topics of study, students undertake a purposeful project. Students may or may not decide on the project itself, but in all cases, it should be something meaningful to them. Project-based learning integrates elements of Piaget's theory and Vygotsky's approach. In the course of carrying out their projects, students encounter new information, interact with it, and adapt it to their current schemata. In addition, students work on their projects in groups and later share their new knowledge with their peers.

## In Your Classroom

In all their planning, constructivist teachers tend to focus on the following key ideas:

- *Learner focus.* For constructivists, the focus of schooling cannot be on coverage of the curriculum, because that does not necessarily lead to meaningful learning for students. The focus instead has to be on the learners.
- *Active learning.* Constructivists believe that learners have to be able to interact, to get "down and dirty" with new information being presented. They need to be actively engaged in making sense of this information, not passively receiving it. This means that learners need opportunities to touch, see, handle, or mold objects in order to "understand" them, as Franklin Jones's students are doing when they study the phases of the moon. They need to be able to see how objects are similar or different, how they fit together or come apart, how they work or do not work.
- *Context.* New information also needs to be presented in a context or situation to which learners can relate. Learners do not find information, such as scientific facts or formulas, as meaningful if it is presented without a context, such as an opportunity to use the formula, or perhaps a background story about how the fact was discovered.
- *Activating prior learning.* By creating a situation or setting in which the learning is to take place, the teacher can help students think about what they already know about a given topic, so that they can make sense of the new information presented.



### Evaluation of Cognitive Theories

In recent years, cognitive theories have gained a more pronounced following among teachers and educators. Proponents of these theories notice that students show greater interest in learning when they are more interactively involved in it. They also find that with constructivist tasks, students often take more ownership in and responsibility for learning the content. Because students are more interested and more engaged, constructivist educators argue that they are also learning more.

Some educators disagree with the core idea of constructivism, that all learners construct their own meaning from information presented. Others are concerned that if students are encouraged to make their own meaning, they may misunderstand or misinterpret the information, and the meaning they make could be inaccurate. Many critics argue instead for a more "transmittal" form of instruction so that the key concepts are presented clearly and specifically to students, reducing the possibility of students' misinterpretations.

From a practical standpoint, constructing new knowledge often takes time. Students need time to explore, hypothesize, and test ideas. Teachers may feel unable to make such a time commitment when they are under pressure to cover a great deal of material so that students will meet state standards or benchmarks.



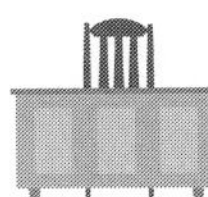

## Now You Do It

How might one of the constructivist instructional approaches or practices be implemented in your classroom? Explain how this activity would embody the principles of constructivism. What would be the pros and cons of the activity, in terms of time and materials needed, compared with the quality of student learning?

# Social Learning Theory: Combining Behaviorism with Cognition

Social learning theory is attributed in large part to psychologist Albert Bandura (1925– ).[8] Social learning theorists suggest that people learn from vicarious experiences—that is, by watching others—as well as from actual or direct experiences. The students in Franklin Jones's class, at the beginning of this module, who went to watch another group use balls and flashlights were engaging in social learning.

Bandura's theory combines elements of behaviorism and cognitivism. Like the behaviorists, Bandura believed that a person's behaviors are largely

## In Your Classroom

### Using Social Learning Theory

Unlike behaviorism, social learning theory has not been translated into many formal instructional programs commonly found in schools. Still, you can apply much from social learning theory in your classroom.

- *Be a behavior model.* As a teacher, you hold a position of influence in many of your students' lives. Although high-school-aged students might vehemently deny it, many of them look to you to help them sift through the range of possible responses to situations in order to understand what constitutes appropriate and inappropriate responses. If you shout at or belittle a student for a wrongdoing, or if you are discourteous to a student or colleague, this behavior becomes validated and acceptable to mimic. Instead, be sure to exhibit the kind of behavior that you would like to see the students emulate.
- *Think aloud.* Teachers can model problem solving in many different areas by thinking aloud as they demonstrate a skill or concept. For example, a second-grade teacher might help students develop strategies for figuring out an unfamiliar word by modeling the thinking process. Let's say the word is *frigid:* "What's this word? I can sound it out. But what does it mean? The sentence it is in says, 'The frigid wind made Ana shiver even under her big winter coat.' Hmm, I shiver when I'm cold. I'll bet *frigid* must mean 'really cold.'"
- *Encourage social learning when it is appropriate.* Students may not realize that it's OK for them to "copy" others in the class unless you tell them. Be sure to specify when you expect students to work alone and when imitation is acceptable. Be sure to be as explicit as you can about this to avoid confusion.
- *Talk them through it.* Provide verbal instructions and support for all four steps of social learning. Start by drawing students' attention to exactly what behavior you want them to notice and repeat. Help them to remember the behavior by reminding them to "rehearse" it, or repeat it their minds. Be sure to offer encouragement or verbal persuasion that the learner can faithfully reproduce the desired behaviors. For example, you want to offer intellectual "pep talks" before tests, convincing the less confident students of their ability to perform as well as they have seen others do. Finally, provide feedback that motivates the students to keep trying to reproduce the desired behavior or lets them know they have succeeded at it.

dependent on his or her environment and are shaped largely in response to it. But he also believed that psychological processes, including attention, memory, and thinking, explain how the learner can store experiences and use them later to decide on an appropriate behavior in a given situation.

According to Bandura, the following four elements are required for social learning to take place.

- *Attention.* The learner must notice and pay attention to the behavior. In order for the learner to be attentive to experiences, she or he must be rested, relaxed, and focused.
- *Retention.* The learner needs to remember the behavior. Learners use their memories to predict the consequences of a particular response to a stimulus. Then they can use their predictions to decide on a behavior. If last week Juan observed you praising Dean for raising his hand to answer a question, Juan can use his memory of that occasion to predict that you will reward hand-raising. On the basis of this prediction, Juan may decide to raise his hand when he wants to speak.
- *Reproduction.* The learner recalls stored images of the behavior and translates them to reproduce the behavior. Social learning theory supposes that the learner has the ability to produce the behavior in the first place. If Juan has a physical disability that prevents him from raising his hand, he will not be able to repeat Dean's behavior.
- *Motivation.* The learner wants to reproduce the behavior. If the experiences are vicarious, the model plays a big role in motivation. We are more likely to want to imitate the behavior of someone who is attractive, prestigious, and/or similar to us. If Dean is unpopular among his classmates, Juan may avoid imitating Dean's hand-raising behavior.

  Self-image also affects motivation. The learner must be confident that he or she is capable of reproducing the desirable behaviors. The more confident one is, the more likely one is to persevere in one's attempt to model behavior, and the more likely it is that one will learn. Juan should have a reasonable expectation that you will call on him if he raises his hand. If you call only on students in the front of the room and Juan sits in back, he may give up raising his hand and just shout out his answers.

**Video Case**

In the video case, *Modeling: Social Cognitive Theory in a High School Chemistry Lesson,* you'll see how high school chemistry teacher Jerusha Vogal models a lesson for students and how they respond. You'll also hear Jerusha's reflections on why and how she uses the modeling technique. As you watch the clips and study the artifacts in the case, reflect on the following questions.

**QUESTIONS**

1. How does this teacher incorporate the four elements necessary for successful modeling into her science classes?
2. When and how do you anticipate using modeling in the classes you will teach?

## Evaluation of Social Learning Theory

Observational learning is a very powerful form of learning. After all, we spend the first two years or so of our lives observing and listening before we begin to talk, walk, and do other things. Many of the behaviors we do are learned from watching those around us. As a teacher, you must make sure you model appropriate behaviors for your students. You may also want to point out which behaviors you want your students to imitate and find ways to discourage them from mimicking undesirable acts. The challenge for teachers is making sure that the behavior being observed, retained, and reproduced is desirable or appropriate and not one that is to be discouraged.

Remember, also, that no two learners learn the same thing from the same experience in the same way. What may capture the attention of one learner leaves another indifferent. What motivates one learner is of little interest to another. Again, it is up to you to determine individually, for each of your students, what and who will work best as a model for various behaviors you'd like them to acquire.

Let's Sum Up

The reason why we have summarized so many theories in this module is that there is no "one right way," no single "one-size-fits-all" learning theory that fits all students in all subjects. People come in a variety of shapes and forms, and they learn things in a variety of ways. As teachers, we need to be able to draw on our knowledge of many learning theories in order to plan the right activities at the right time to help each student learn what he or she needs to know. As abstract as the various theories may seem, they have fundamental importance and usefulness in our classrooms. We need to develop the habit of mentally moving back and forth between "what" we are trying to teach and "how" our students learn. Perhaps our greatest gift to our students is not the subject matter we teach them, but the help we give them in becoming more skillful learners.

Let us offer a note of caution to remember when planning and implementing learning activities. By the time people reach adulthood, most have individually established certain learning styles and habits, such as those described in Module 5, Teaching Academically Diverse Learners. Most of us have found our preferred approach to learning and have been successful in making that approach work for us. Keep in mind, however, that just because your way works best for you, it may not work best for others. Don't be fooled into thinking that "your way is *the* way."

## Further Resources

- *Online Study Center* — Association for Direct Instruction. Available at: **http://www.adihome.org/phpshop/members.php.** Insights from a group interested in this behaviorist technique.
- *Online Study Center* — The B. F. Skinner Foundation. Available at: **http://www.bfskinner.org.** The Foundation provides information about the behavioral sciences.
- C. Brainerd, *Piaget's Theory of Intelligence* (Englewood Cliffs, NJ: Prentice-Hall, 1978).
- Jerome Bruner, *Toward a Theory of Instruction,* New Ed edition (Cambridge, MA: The Belknap Press of Harvard University Press, 2004). Bruner presents his views on learning and teaching.
- Siegfried Engelmann and Geoff Colvin, *Rubric for Identifying Authentic Direct Instruction Programs,* 2006. Retrieved at: **http://www.zigsite.com/PDFs/rubric.pdf.** Engelmann and Colvin offer a list of criteria for evaluating programs that claim to be direct instruction programs.
- Howard Gruber and Jacques Vonèche, *The Essential Piaget: An Interpretive Reference and Guide* (Dunmore, PA: Jason Aronson, 1997). The editors have compiled key essays by Piaget, framed by background information about Piaget and the work that led to the essays.
- Thomas R. Guskey and Terra Schulz, *Implementing Mastery Learning,* 2d ed. (Belmont, CA: Wadsworth Publishing, 1996). Guskey and Schulz offer many examples and illustrations of effective mastery learning programs.
- *Online Study Center* — The Jean Piaget Society. Available at: **http://www.piaget.org/index.html.** Established in 1970, this group of scholars and researchers studies the developmental nature of human knowledge.
- *Online Study Center* — Theory Into Practice. Available at: **http://tip.psychology.org/index.html.** This website contains summaries of major theories of teaching and learning.

Scenario

Take a look at the two public school classrooms shown on the following page. One is from the late 1800s, and one shows a high school of today. What similarities and differences do you notice? What messages do these classrooms send to students? What do the goals of each school seem to be? What does life seem to be like for the students in each school?

Preview

Schools are institutions created by societies to serve the needs of each society. In the United States, public schools are charged with educating young Americans to be productive workers, knowledgeable and contributing citizens, and good neighbors to help maintain American culture and way of life. The diversity of American culture, however, ensures that there will be disagreements about the best way to achieve these goals. In fact, the way that schools interpret and carry out this mission has been a source of debate and controversy for most of the nearly 400 years that schools have been in existence in the United States. Despite continuing debate and minor variations, however, you can see from the photos that open this module that there is a strong national school culture in the United States. In some ways, that culture continues to reflect the schools from over a century ago.

This module will explore how schools reflect the values of the larger culture in which they operate, as well as helping to establish those values through the school culture they establish.

**This module emphasizes that:**

- **Schools have reflected and passed along the American culture since the founding of the country.**
- **In the United States today, schools serve intellectual, democratic, economic, and social purposes.**
- **Schools, as a group and individually, have a culture of their own that both reflects and shapes the larger culture in which they operate.**

## Historical Purposes of U.S. Schools

The purpose for establishing schools in America was initially a religious one: to help the young learn to read the Christian Bible. The first public schools in America were established in the Massachusetts Bay Colony in 1647, when the General Court of the Colony decreed that every township of at least fifty families was to set up and fund an elementary school and that every town of one hundred families should have a secondary school. The purpose of this decree, referred to as the **Old Deluder Satan Act,** was to ensure that the children living in the colony learned to read—especially to read the Bible—so that they could avoid being tempted and deceived by that "Old Deluder," Satan. The act called for public oversight and public funding of these schools, requiring "the parents or masters of such children, or . . . the inhabitants in general," to pay the wages of the teachers hired. The act even included a hefty fine for failure to comply with it.

**Old Deluder Satan Act** a Massachusetts law passed in 1647 that required every town of fifty or more families to pay a teacher to teach the children reading and writing so they could read the Bible and thwart Satan, who would try to keep people from understanding the scriptures.

During the forming of the new nation in America after the war for independence from England, schools took on another purpose—a political or civic purpose. The founders of the United States of America also created a form of government best described as a representative republic, inspired by the ideals of democracy in the Greek tradition of Athens. Some early leaders, including Thomas Jefferson and Noah Webster, argued that the success of this new form of governance, in which all citizens were able to participate, resided in the citizens' ability to make informed decisions. In order to make informed

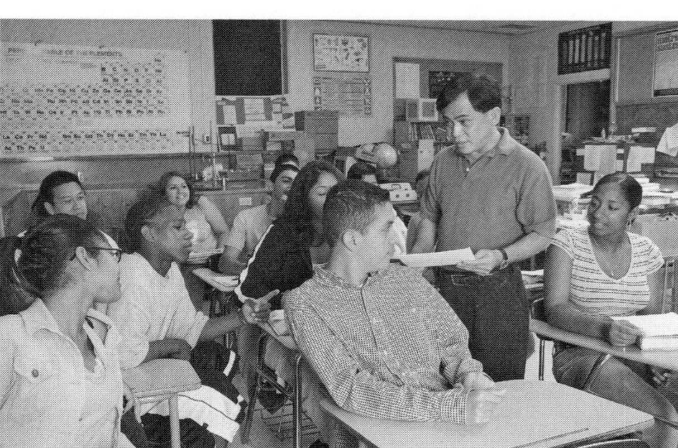

In the American schools, much has changed and much has not changed.

decisions, the citizens would need to be literate, as well as to understand the governing process and the beliefs and values that the process embodies.

Over the years, U.S. public schools have been assigned other purposes depending on the political and social climate and the needs of the country. The religious purpose also has been de-emphasized as a goal of public education over the years, particularly in the wake of court decisions, starting in the late 1950s and early 1960s, that discouraged prayer and other religious practices in public schools.

# Purposes of Today's American Schools

Today, we can identify four basic purposes served by public schools in America:

- intellectual
- political and civic
- economic
- social

Most public schools fulfill more than one, and often all four, of these purposes, but they usually see one of the purposes as primary and the others as secondary.

**Intellectual purpose of schools** one of the primary reasons for having schools, which is to develop the intellectual capacities and knowledge base of students. Many people believe this is the primary purpose of schooling.

## Intellectual Purposes

When most people think of schools, they think of learning (or being taught) about different topics: history, algebra, chemistry, a foreign language; or learning how to read, write, solve mathematical problems, and reason critically. Thus, one of the most recognizable purposes of schools is the intellectual purpose, to develop the intellectual capacities of students through academic achievement. In fact, for many parents, the intellectual purpose is the *sole* purpose of public schools. These parents want the schools to prepare their children for academic advancement, and they place primary responsibility for their children's success (as often measured by acceptance for admission to prestigious institutions of higher learning) on the schools.

Most schools identify an intellectual purpose in their mission statements, which often include such goals as helping students develop critical thinking skills or life-long learning habits, or providing an academically rich or challenging curriculum. Some schools require that students take a full course load of core academic courses with few, if any, offerings in the other areas. These schools see their paramount purpose as intellectual.

**No Child Left Behind Act** the 2001 reauthorization of the Elementary and Secondary Education Act, which is the federal government's greatest contribution to public education.

The federal **No Child Left Behind Act,** which relies on curriculum standards and state-mandated testing for both students and teachers, also stresses the intellectual purpose of schools. It "demands that schools close the achievement gap"[1] between white and minority students by making schools more accountable for the academic performance of *all* of the students they educate.



**Political and civic purpose of schools** to prepare students to be functioning citizens in a democratic society.

## Political and Civic Purposes

As we mentioned earlier, the founders of the United States believed that public education was essential to the well-being of their newly created, democratic form of governance. If citizens were to be granted the power to participate in the decision-making process, they had to accept the responsibility of

School elections and participation in student government familiarize students with the democratic process, fulfilling the political and civic purposes of the school.

becoming informed on the issues about which they were to make decisions. Being well informed requires not just a certain level of literacy, but also the reasoning skills to think through the different views on the issues under debate.

Most public schools in the United States have upheld this legacy of educating future citizens. Not only are students taught about the founding of the United States and the structure, organization, and operation of the three branches of government in the United States, but they are also given opportunities to participate in governance through student government organizations. Through campaigns, elections, and limited decision-making authority on school issues, students become familiar with the democratic process.

In addition to developing the intellectual skills needed to participate in a democracy, the founders believed that future citizens should develop at school the personal virtues needed to support a democracy, such as honesty, self-discipline, and a commitment to justice. Public schools were expected to instill in students a civic responsibility to help others.

This legacy continues today. Through everything from clothing drives to organized trips to nursing homes or homeless shelters, many educators aim to foster in students an appreciation for addressing the needs of the less fortunate in society. A number of secondary schools throughout the country have imposed a community service requirement for graduation, formalizing the expectation that all students will contribute to the well-being or even betterment of their communities.

**Economic purpose of schools** to prepare students to earn a living and to provide a work force for American businesses and industry.

## Economic Purposes

Another responsibility that society has placed on schools is to make good workers. Much of the structure and organization of the school day is designed to help fulfill this goal. Students learn to obey rules and respect authority, as they will be expected to do in the workplace. They are given tasks with set deadlines, or due dates, and failure to meet a deadline is usually penalized by points deducted from the grade for the course. Students are expected to produce quality work and are rewarded with good grades for doing so, not unlike workers who receive bonuses for meeting their objectives. Finally, students are expected to adhere to a daily schedule and to be punctual and well prepared for their "work."

Nearly all schools work to instill in students these basic workplace habits, and some sociologists suggest that the economic purpose of schools reaches even further. In their view, schools differentiate and select students to prepare them for the different socioeconomic levels in the work force. This sorting is most evident from the secondary level on, when students are grouped according to identified criteria that are usually linked to their academic performance. Students placed in the honors or college courses are expected to become professionals or middle/upper managers, whereas those placed in general or vocational education courses are directed toward the skilled or unskilled labor force.

This differentiation leads to students acquiring different workplace skills. In some schools, for example, bells ring to mark the end of one class period and the start of another. It is not uncommon to see students rushing into the classroom just as the bell rings, much like factory workers begin and end their shifts when the whistle blows. Other schools have no bells to mark the start or end of periods, and students move from class period to class period on their own or when their teachers dismiss them, a setting that more resembles a professional work environment where the professionals themselves decide on the work flow of the day.

In this view, work expectations that differ from one academic level to another also serve to prepare students for the different work demands they will encounter at their respective socioeconomic levels. Students in honors or college-level courses are often given more long-term assignments, requiring them to plan and schedule on their own the work tasks needed to complete the assignment. Students in general or vocational education courses are given day-to-day homework assignments and more frequent quizzes and tests.

Schools not only influence the work futures of groups of students but also sort students individually. Through their twelve-year "apprenticeship" periods, students are groomed for their potential economic roles. Teachers and schools determine which students will be "good" workers and which will not. They also determine who will hold positions of responsibility and authority and who will make up the corps of workers. The classroom "leaders" are identified early in their school careers and encouraged to take on leadership roles both in school and, later, in the work force.

**Social purposes of schools** to prepare students to become functioning members of society by learning and adapting to social conventions.

## Social Purposes

The fourth purpose of schooling is to promote the healthy social development of students. At an early age, students are taught to interact with their classmates and with adults other than their parents in ways that their culture considers appropriate. In the United States, for example, students learn how to share, take turns, and wait patiently. They learn acceptable and appropriate behaviors and norms of interactions with friends, familiar adults, and less familiar adults, such as other teachers, school administrators, and community members. They learn the importance of making eye contact when interacting with an adult, of personal space, of punctuality, and of appropriate language and nonverbal communication.

At the secondary level, schools often try to promote students' social development by offering co-curricular and extracurricular activities that help develop understanding of and empathy for the challenges that others may face. Schools may sponsor clubs, for example, that focus on race relations, diversity, and equity issues, while sports teams emphasize good sportsmanship. All of these activities and clubs share the goal of instilling in students desirable qualities and attitudes so that they will be compassionate and caring adult members of their communities.

***Promoting Moral Development*** Historically, American schools were also charged with the moral development of their students, clearly an echo of the religious purpose that colonial America attributed to public schools. Until the 1920s the curriculum in many public schools was overtly Christian, with religious and moral lessons integrated into students' daily lessons. The widely used *McGuffey Readers,* for example, included excerpts from the Bible, as well as lessons on morality and ethics. Students would often begin the school day with a prayer, and references to biblical teachings were common. Starting in the 1920s, various social movements gradually led to the elimination of such overt religious references and practices in schools, although, as described in Module 22, Educational Law, religious questions continue to raise legal issues.

**Values clarification** a movement of the 1960s and 1970s that presented students with game-like activities involving choices and asked them to solve the dilemmas as a means to clarify what values they held. No particular values were deemed to be more or less important, but each individual would come to understand his or her values better.

In the 1970s, the spread of a movement called **values clarification** led to the removal, from many school curricula, of overt involvement in the moral development of students. Grounded in existentialist ideas of the late 1950s and 1960s, values clarification takes a philosophical view known as moral relativism, which suggests that one's moral beliefs should be individually formed, rather than imposed by society. Thus the values clarification movement promotes the self-discovery of beliefs and values among students. The program is essentially a set of game-like techniques. Students are presented with a hypothetical situation involving a choice, such as "If you were given a thousand dollars with no strings attached, what would you do with it?" or provocative questions, such as "Do you think convicted serial killers deserve to be put to death?" Then they are asked to make a decision. All answers are accepted without criticism or judgment. Critics of values clarification believe that the adult community, and especially teachers, have a responsibility to pass on the nation's core moral values and principles, not just to leave young Americans totally on their own and ignorant of our moral heritage.

**Moral education** See *Character education.*

**Character education** efforts by the home, the school, the religious community, and the individual student to help the student know the good, love the good, and do the good, and, in the process, to foster qualities such as courage, respect, and responsibility.

Over the last couple of decades, a countermovement, originally called **moral education** and more recently termed **character education,** has arisen. Proponents of character education aim to reestablish in the schools a responsibility for the moral or character development of students. They argue that the schools have historically had this responsibility and that the need for such teaching is now even greater, because the families of students are, in many instances, unable or unwilling to attend to the ethical and moral development of their young people.

***Socialization and Social Class*** Another aspect of the social purpose of school is socialization into the adult society. Schools teach students about the society in which they will soon become adult members and about the expectations that society will have of them. In American schools, as we have noted, students learn appropriate workplace attitudes and behaviors, as well as the importance of participating in the democratic process and being a contributing member of a community.

Some sociologists, however, see this social purpose of schooling as more akin to social engineering than to socialization. They suggest that schools, as socialization agents, serve to maintain the status quo. In other words, students who attend school in working-class districts are prepared for continuing to live and work in working-class environments, while those in upper-middle-class school districts are socialized into upper-middle-class environments. Some educators, such as the Brazilian Paolo Freire, accuse the schools of intentionally socializing students into their current socioeconomic class as a way of maintaining political power and control. Although we would not ascribe such a sinister intention to most schools, many policies and curriculum materials in use may unintentionally reinforce current inequities. As a teacher, you should be constantly alert to avoid perpetuating class distinctions or making unfounded assumptions about the capabilities or destinies of students on the basis of their assigned track or the location of the school.

## Now You Do It

One way to learn more about how schools and districts view their primary purpose is to read their mission statements. Look at the following mission statements from six different public school districts throughout the country. What does each statement seem to say is the district's main purpose? What other purposes does each district embrace?

- The mission of the Framingham Public Schools, a system that understands and values our diversity, is to educate each student to learn and live productively as a critically thinking, responsible citizen in a multicultural, democratic society by providing academically challenging instructional programs taught by a highly qualified and diverse staff and supported by comprehensive services in partnership with our entire community. (Framingham, Massachusetts)
- The mission of the Omaha Public Schools is to provide educational opportunities which enable all students to achieve their highest potential. (Omaha, Nebraska)
- The mission of the West Orange Public Schools is to engage in an energetic partnership with all components of this culturally diverse community, to marshal resources that promote highest-quality intellectual and human relations development to our pupils, and to instill in all students the knowledge and decision-making skills essential to make appropriate choices and successfully meet the challenges they will encounter as productive members of society. (West Orange, New Jersey)
- The Ann Arbor Public Schools, working with families and the community, will educate and empower every student to succeed in a changing environment as a responsible participant in a democratic society. (Ann Arbor, Michigan)
- This vision is supported by a mission to educate all students to meet high academic standards and to prepare all students to be responsible citizens in the twenty-first century. (Fairfax County Public Schools, Fairfax County, Virginia)
- Walla Walla Public Schools will provide academically challenging programs to meet the diverse needs of all students in a safe, supportive environment and, in partnership with families and the community, prepare students to become competent, creative, and contributing citizens of a rapidly changing world. (Walla Walla, Washington)

# School Culture



**Culture** the integrated pattern of human behavior that includes thought, speech, action, and artifacts and depends on the human capacity for learning and transmitting knowledge to succeeding generations. The customary beliefs, social forms, and material traits of a racial, religious, or social group.

**School culture** the prevailing mores, values, and rituals that permeate a school.

Although it might seem strange to talk about schools as "cultures," a strong argument can be made that they do indeed function like a distinct culture. **Culture** is a "system of shared beliefs, values, customs, behaviors, and artifacts that the members of society use to cope with their world and with one another, and that are transmitted from generation to generation through learning."[2] Another rather folksy, but accurate, definition of culture is "the way we do things 'round here."

Certainly the artifacts of the **school culture** are readily identifiable: structures for students to sit on and to work at, such as desks and chairs; and structures on which information and ideas can be displayed, such as blackboards, white boards, and even SMART Boards™, overhead projectors, computers, or other new technologies. We can also see that the school culture is transmitted from generation to generation. In fact, as the photos at the beginning of this module demonstrate, allowing for updating of equipment and technologies, a classroom of the twenty-first century does not look all that different from a nineteenth-century classroom. The culture evolves, but it stays relatively stable.

We do not want to suggest that all schools are carbon copies of one another in which the teachers teach the same lessons in the same way at the same time. There was a story told about one minister of education in France who claimed that at any given time on any given day, he knew exactly what lesson was being taught in any grade in any school in France. On the contrary, just as the American culture is a rather loosely defined set of beliefs, values, and behaviors, so too is the school culture. Under the umbrella of school culture, we can find variations due to geography, socioeconomic status of the district, grade level, and philosophy of the school or district leaders.

Nevertheless, there are particular behaviors that are unique to schools. Lining up, moving from one place to another *en masse*, and asking permission to move, talk, or go to the bathroom are behaviors found rarely outside of a school building or school-sponsored event. Each of these behaviors is grounded in a belief and value system that seems to be commonly found in schools.

## Values of Schools

Educational researchers have also identified several other key values and behaviors that, for better or worse, make up the school culture in the majority of American schools.

- *Compliance.* Students quickly learn that compliance is a valued quality in the school culture. Starting in kindergarten, students are taught that their personal desires and wants are subordinate to the instructions and directives of the teacher or other adults in the school. They are rewarded for being obedient and punished for being noncompliant. Some leeway is granted to younger students, but by the middle elementary years, students are expected to have internalized fully this value and the corresponding behaviors, such as raising hands to talk, lining up to move from one place to another, and walking quietly in the hallways. Failure to demonstrate these compliant behaviors often results in prompt discipline.

- *Competitiveness.* This value may be less noticeable at the elementary level in some schools or districts, but it is generally a strong presence at the middle school and high school levels. Students learn to compete for the teacher's attention, for placement in a higher learning group or an honors course, and for better grades within the school. They also learn to compete with students from other schools through sports or academic competitions. Although students are often encouraged to "work together," to "work as a team," or to carry out a cooperative learning project that requires sharing of resources, information, and abilities, the stronger value communicated to them tends to be that of competition.

- *Order.* With a ratio of, on average, twenty-two students to one adult, the potential for chaos in schools is significant; hence order is a highly prized value. Students learn to be orderly as they work in the classroom, pass from one classroom to the next in the hallways, and enter or leave different classrooms. Many of the behaviors that instill student compliance are designed to bring about order.

Culture is also very localized, as we noted earlier. Regional and local cultures abound in the United States. Distinct differences in customs and celebrations, norms of interaction, and even speech patterns can be noted from one region of the United States to another. In a similar way, school cultures vary from one school district to the next and, to a lesser degree, from one school to another. The particular beliefs and values that define a school culture are shaped not just by the beliefs and values of the community in which the school is located, but equally as powerfully by the educators—the teachers and administrators—in the school.

## Clues to a School's Culture

It is important to your effectiveness as a teacher to be able to "read" the culture of the school and interpret the messages it sends to those who work in or attend the school about what is important and valued. These messages, some of which are overt and some hidden, help explain why some schools are joyful, exciting places, whereas others breed alienation and boredom.

The physical plant of the school is a good place to start when trying to get a sense of the school culture. The overall appearance of the school building can give you some idea of how much the community values education. A well-maintained, even if old, school building tells you that despite limited resources, the community is concerned about the schooling of its young people. Look also at the inside of the school building. The cleanliness of the hallways at the end of a school day can provide important insights into how students treat the physical plant, and into the attitudes that are communicated—in sometimes subtle and sometimes explicit ways—by the school personnel.

Student expectations within the school community are another source of information about the school culture. In some schools, students are responsible for keeping their classrooms and other areas neat and clean. We know of one upper-middle-class middle school in which students are required to wipe their tables and sweep the floor around their tables in the lunchroom before they leave the cafeteria. In Japanese schools, students wash their classrooms—the desks, floors, and walls—every week! In other schools, student responsibilities are limited to academic tasks. Each of these approaches communicates which priorities the school and community consider most important for students.

Teacher expectations also contribute to the school culture. When teachers are assigned duties beyond the classroom, such as monitoring the lunchroom, the hallways between classes, or study halls, they may be viewed as workers and monitors, rather than as professional educators. On the other hand, some may interpret the assigning of such duties as a way of creating a community in which the school takes responsibility for the academic and social development of the students. Schools that limit teacher responsibility to academic tasks may suggest a culture that believes strongly in students' intellectual development.

School policies are another good source of information on the school culture. For example, in some suburban communities, high schools may have an "open campus" policy that allows juniors and seniors to come to school later or leave earlier than other students if they do not have a class scheduled. This practice is viewed as a way of preparing students for the independence of college studies and reflects the assumption that all (or nearly all) of the students in the school are destined for college. It also suggests a belief that students will act wisely and make good and safe decisions.

At the same time, some urban schools have a locked-door policy, in which the doors of the school are locked from shortly after the start of the school day until shortly before its end. This practice is viewed as essential to protect students from potential dangers that the community presents and reflects the belief that schools need to provide a safe haven for students. It also suggests that the school has less confidence in students' ability to make good decisions and protect themselves from the potential threats in the community.

## Now You Do It

In the two scenarios that follow, cite the artifacts or behaviors that can help you identify the beliefs and values of the school. Then reflect on your answers to the questions at the end of the box.

### Scenario One

Suburban Middle School has five one-story buildings, each housing one academic department, and an expansive two-story building that houses the administrative offices, the library, and the performance areas. The academic buildings are labeled for the discipline they house, so the math department is in the M-building and the foreign language department is located in the L-building.

Although the school itself was built in the late 1950s, the buildings have been renovated regularly so that they maintain an appearance of cleanliness and order. The last renovation was five years ago, and during it the classrooms were refurnished with new student and teacher desks and carpeting. Wiring for new technologies was installed, and the school made a significant financial investment in desktop and laptop computers, as well as in other new technologies, such as SMART Boards™, LCD displays, and projectors. Each academic building benefited from a fixed number of computers, set up either in a computer lab or as rolling class sets of computers. All classrooms are equipped with internal communication systems, which enable teachers to communicate with the main office or any other classroom in the school.

The classrooms themselves are spacious and brightly lit. Each classroom has one wall of windows providing natural light, in addition to full banks of overhead fluorescent lights. The doors to the classrooms all have a large, clear window in the upper half of the door. Most classrooms have desks for twenty-five students, but the average class size is eighteen. No matter which academic building you find yourself in, you are likely to notice a striking similarity in the arrangement of desks. The desks tend to be clustered in groups of four or five or arranged in semicircles, two or three rows deep, around the blackboard.

The hallways are also wide and well lit. Full-size lockers line the bottom half of the hallway, and the upper half is filled with posters of various sorts. Some remind students of appropriate behavior within the school. Others announce upcoming events, and still others are reminders of expectations and responsibilities of all students within the school. The wall space around classroom doors often displays student projects or student-made posters. The hallways and classrooms appear well kept, with no visible signs of graffiti, trash, or vandalism.

The silence of the hallway is suddenly broken as students emerge from classrooms on their way to their next class. No bell or siren announces the end of a given period, but students appear with a precision reminiscent of a drill team. They move at a steady pace, occasionally stalled by a student visiting his or her locker or a group of students talking. No teachers are seen in the hallways, but the classroom doors are open and students peer quickly into certain classrooms as they pass by.

Then, just as quickly, silence is restored as the students file into their next class. One or two stragglers rush through the hall to their classroom, even though, once again, no bell or siren marks the start of the class period.

### Scenario Two

The Oxford Middle School, the largest of the three middle schools in the city, is located on the edge of a commercial zone in the predominantly Portuguese-speaking, low-income area of the city. The school is an imposing multistory brick building constructed around the turn of the twentieth century. The numerous additions to the side and back have given the school a patchwork look, with no clear architectural style. A large double-door entrance serves as the sole access to the building, making the start of the school day a particularly chaotic time, when more than a thousand fifth- through eighth-graders attempt to gain entry into the building all at once.

Just inside the imposing front door is the atrium, a large open area that serves as the hub for school traffic. Three hallways, one to the right, one to the left, and one straight ahead, lead to different grade or academic wings of the school, and two stairways, one on either side, provide access to the upper levels of the building. The main office is off to the left, its location indicated by a sign, easily lost among the morass of old and current announcements, on the bulletin board facing the main entrance.

The walls of the atrium, once an off-white color, have acquired a dingy hue from daily wear and tear and infrequent painting. Wooden panels covering the bottom halves of the walls have, over the years, lost their luster. The limited light comes from a set of fluorescent fixtures. A large EXIT sign over the front doors casts a reddish hue on the space.

The three hallways emanating from the atrium show little differentiation. Lockers stacked three high line the right side of each corridor, and the left side is covered with wood paneling similar to that found in the atrium. Above the lockers and the wood paneling, the walls are painted a familiar beige color that shows the same aging as the walls in the atrium. Many of the lockers are adorned with stickers, graffiti, or other marks of current or previous ownership. Some have no doors, others no lock, and others dented doors. The chipped and cracked linoleum flooring also shows its age. Bits of papers, especially gum wrappers, fill the dingy edges and corners of the floors.

The classrooms that line the hallways are unmarked, except for a number placed above the solid wood doors. The doors, made of the same dark wood as the paneling, burst open as the bell rings to signal the end of a class period, filling the otherwise somber hallways with shafts of light from the classrooms. Along with the light comes the onslaught of noisy students piling out of the classroom as the bell shatters the silence. Teachers line the hallways, mechanically reminding students to "keep it down," although these exhortations go virtually unnoticed by the students, who freely call up or down the hallways to classmates. Students rush to catch up with their friends, bouncing like pinballs off other students who have stopped at their lockers or in conversation.

The classrooms themselves are uniformly rectangular, encouraging a matrix-like arrangement of desks. In some rooms, the desks are pushed together in uninterrupted rows or groups of two or three; in others, each desk stands alone. In each room, a large blackboard, framed in the school's signature dark wood, fills the front wall, and a bulletin board of similar size fills the back wall. The windows that line the upper half of the outer wall date from the mid-1950s and still sport the large, opaque emergency response shades from the Cold War era. Both the inside and the outside of the windows are covered with a sooty film, muting the natural lighting in the room. The walls in most rooms are filled with various commercially made, worn posters explaining grammar rules, scientific processes, or mathematical formulas.

The doors to the school are locked shortly after the morning bell rings, requiring any visitor to ring a doorbell to be let in. School staff accompany all visitors to the front office, where they must sign the register and get a visitor pass before venturing into the rest of the building. The front office has seen little renovation or upgrading since the last expansion of the school nearly twenty years before. Although computers have become fixtures in the office, the requisite electrical upgrading has yet to take place, and tangled wires and cables litter the desks and floor.

How would you describe the school cultures of these two schools? Specifically, think about these questions:

1. In which of these two schools would you rather teach? Why?
2. What are some of the hidden messages that each school communicates to students and teachers via the physical plant, the policies, practices, and routines, and the way the classrooms are set up?
3. Make a list of adjectives to describe each school.
4. Which of these schools more closely resembles schools you attended? In what ways?
5. How do you suppose teaching differs in these two schools?

Classrooms provide even more information on the school culture. A classroom in which desks are arranged in rows suggests a different classroom and school culture than one in which the desks are grouped together. A class in which students are able to move freely within the classroom and around the school during class time presents a different learning environment and a different school culture than one in which student movement is strictly monitored and controlled.

School leaders are particularly influential in defining the school culture. The way the principal interacts with faculty and students sets the tone for the interactions between faculty and students or faculty and community members. A principal who knows the names of all of the faculty members and students in the school and who makes himself or herself seen throughout the school communicates an open and responsive environment.

In a high school, even the student parking lot can provide important insights into the school culture. Is there a separate student parking area or do students and teachers park in the same lot? If there is a separate student lot, where is it located? What kinds of cars are in the student parking lot? Is it fenced in or open?

Schools are places that "educate" young people, but as we have tried to show in this module, that education may look and, in fact, *be* very different at different schools, depending on the purposes that the community and the school personnel ascribe to the school. These purposes also help to define the school culture. As a teacher, you must learn to decipher clues that tell you about the values and culture of a school. Unless you are willing to put up with a school culture you disagree with, while subtly and carefully working to change that culture, it is vitally important that your values as a teacher reasonably match the values and messages of the school. Otherwise, you will find yourself disaffected and working at cross-purposes to the school's messages. During job interviews, you should ask questions that will give you a sense of whether there will be a good match between yourself and the school. Talk with other teachers, as well as with the principal, to understand what the school is all about. And if the fit is not a good one, don't be afraid to turn down a job offer to find a better fit.

## Further Resources

- Ernest Boyer, *Basic School: A Community for Learning* (Princeton, NJ: The Carnegie Foundation for the Advancement of Teaching, 1995). Practical wisdom is woven into a clear description of the kind of schools we can and should have.
- Terrence Deal and Kent Peterson, *Shaping School Culture* (San Francisco: Jossey-Bass, 1999). The authors explore how schools reflect the culture and are themselves culture shapers.

- Education World. Available at: **http://www.educationworld.com/a_admin/admin/admin275.shtml.** The article "Is Your School's Culture Toxic or Positive?" offers guidelines and examples to help you assess whether a school culture is healthy or sick.
- Richard Rothstein, *Class and Schools* (Washington, DC: Economic Policy Institute, 2004). An excellent examination of how social class characteristics influence learning in our schools and how we can close the achievement gap among different social classes.
- Allison Zmuda, Robert Kuklis, and Everett Kline, *Transforming Schools: Creating a Culture of Continuous Improvement* (Alexandria, VA: ASCD, 2004). This book is a highly readable, fictional account of how a group of educators changed the culture in a school to improve student achievement and lead to higher student and teacher satisfaction.

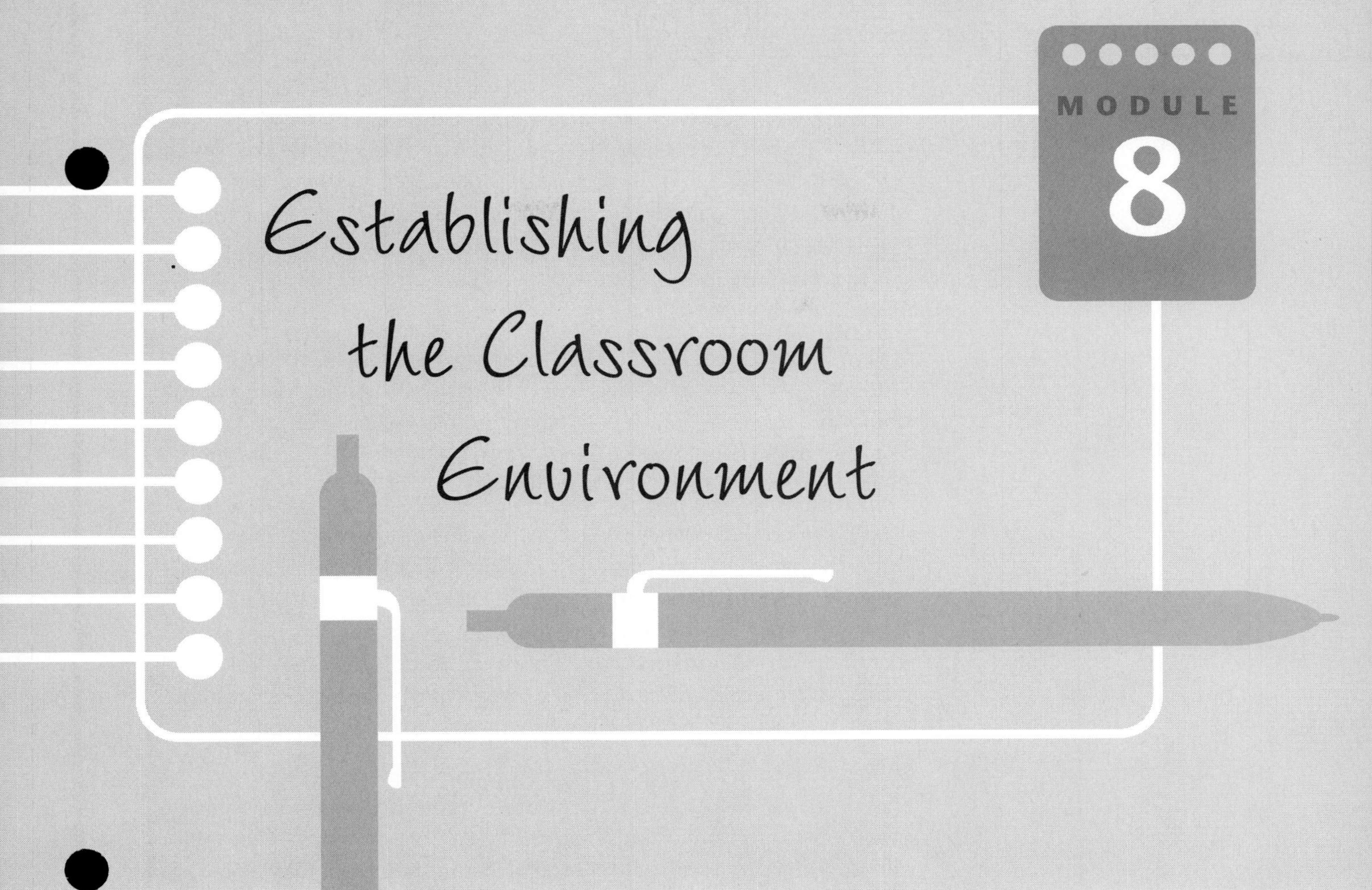


Scenario

Students file into the classroom, muttering greetings to Ms. Edwards, who is seated at her desk in the front of the classroom. They take their seats quietly, in desks arranged in single rows. Ms. Edwards peers up over her glasses, nodding in response to the students' mutterings, and glaring at those students who violate the unwritten code of silence that prevails in the classroom. Students sheepishly slink to their seats as they catch "the look" from Ms. Edwards. As soon as the bell rings, Ms. Edwards stands up and moves to the front of her desk. "Good day, ladies and gentlemen. Are you ready to begin?" On cue, students take out their notebooks and pens, poised to begin writing as Ms. Edwards starts her lecture. Throughout the fifty-two minutes of the class, the students silently and obligingly write as, Ms. Edwards talks. Five minutes before the end of the class, Ms. Edwards concludes her lecture, assigns homework for the evening, and reminds students of long-term assignments. She asks a few students about their progress on the long-term assignment. As the bell rings, Ms. Edwards reminds the students of the upcoming test. "Don't forget the test next Friday. Come with questions tomorrow and we'll review. Have a good day!" As students file out, they mumble incoherently to Ms. Edwards, presumably in response to her good-bye.

Scenario

Students are seated in clusters of four or five, chatting to one another in the cluster or to others across the room, while waiting for Mr. Josiah to come in. Just as the bell rings, Mr. Josiah strolls in and greets the students with a cheery, "All right, then, everyone ready to get to work?" He in turn is greeted with calls of, "Hey Mr. J!" and "How's it going, Mr. J?"

"Okay, kids, let's get settled," Mr. Josiah says as he starts the lesson. With little additional prodding, students get out their books and notebooks to begin the class. "Let's see, where did we leave off yesterday?" asks Mr. Josiah. A number of hands shoot up as students flip through their notebooks to refresh their memories.

After a ten-minute review, Mr. Josiah presents a new project in which students will work in groups doing research. As Mr. Josiah distributes the research topics to each group, he reviews expectations for group work, lists information sources students could use, and finally specifies the time frame for the project. "You'll have the rest of this week and through Wednesday of next week to work on this project. Presentations will begin on Thursday. Any questions? Okay. Let's get to work."

Students assemble in their study groups quickly and begin to get organized. Mr. Josiah goes from group to group to talk through each group's plans for organizing their work. With two minutes left in the period, Mr. Josiah instructs the groups to put their work folders in the "Projects" basket.

Scenario

The classroom has a cluttered look about it even when no students are present. Grouped in clusters in the middle of the classroom, the desks are covered with alphabet strips, number lines, and students' names. In the middle of each cluster of desks sit various containers that hold pencils, crayons, and markers. On the right side of the room, by the bank of windows, is a carpeted area with a straight-back wooden chair at one end. An assortment of pillows is strewn about the area in a marginally organized manner. Around the walls of the classroom are different areas marked for study of the various topics: a science center, a math center, a listening center, a reading center, and an arts center. Other designated areas around the perimeter of the classroom include a classroom correspondence center, along with spaces for "Finished Papers" and "Work in Progress." A series of two-shelf bookcases houses various classroom supplies in large plastic bins.

As the bell rings to begin the day, students stroll in, in most cases with a folder in hand. As they enter, they stop at a tin full of sticks, find the one with their name, and place the stick in the tin right next to it. Then they stop at the Milk Board to indicate their milk preference for the day (white, chocolate, or strawberry). Next, they drop off their folders in a basket marked "Homework Folders" and pick up new papers from the

"Morning Work" basket. Finally, the students head to their desks and begin to do their morning work while waiting for everyone in the class to arrive. The teacher, Mr. Anderson, greets the students as they come in, reminding the occasional student who forgets to do one of the morning routines.

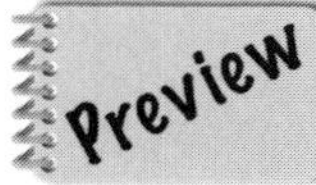

These three scenarios give you some idea of the variability of classroom climates. Although one of these classrooms may be more appealing to you than the others, each represents an environment in which students can learn. In this module, we explore what makes all three classrooms, despite their obvious differences, productive learning environments.

The tone and feel of the classroom is largely determined by the teacher. Productive classrooms rarely happen by accident. Effective teachers carefully and consciously craft the environment in their classrooms. They invest thoughtful planning and consistent effort in creating and then maintaining the classroom culture they believe will help students reach key learning goals.

As a teacher, you can work proactively to create a particular classroom culture that will fit with the kinds of learning activities in which you want your students to engage. Or you can allow the classroom to take on a character of its own—which may or may not support student learning.

Your decisions not only help you craft your classroom environment but also send particular messages to your students about what is—and what is not—important, acceptable, and permissible in your classroom. In this module, we examine the messages sent to students by various elements of the classroom environment and the decisions teachers need to make about the classroom environment.

**This module emphasizes that:**

- **Teachers make decisions that establish the tone and feel of their classrooms.**
- **A good starting point for establishing the classroom environment is to consider the learning activities that will happen in the classroom.**
- **The physical arrangement of the classroom provides students with clues to the behavior that is expected and hence can support or impede learning activities.**
- **Classroom rules help to establish an orderly environment where learning can happen. Teachers need to consider who makes the rules, how many rules they should have, and what the rules should cover.**
- **Like rules, classroom procedures and routines support order so that learning activities go more smoothly.**
- **Rules, procedures, classroom set-up, and activities should send consistent messages to students and should work in harmony with school policies.**

# Learning Activities

A clear view of your instructional goals will help you decide what kind of classroom you want. Begin by considering your learning goals for the students and thinking about the kinds of activities that will happen in your classroom to help students meet those goals. Lectures, demonstrations, group meetings, individual seat work, and computer research are just some of the activities that might take place in your classroom. In Module 10, Planning What to Teach, and Module 11, Planning Lessons, we discuss the importance of considering state standards in planning your goals and identifying the kinds of lessons that will help students meet those goals. Then you can determine how to arrange the room physically and establish rules and procedures that support the activities you plan.

Here are some specific questions to consider as you think about activities that will help students meet set learning goals.

- Will students be expected to listen attentively and take notes from lectures delivered by you or other speakers?
- Will they watch demonstrations or carry out activities on their own?
- Will they be expected to talk to one another and to work together, or will they usually work independently?
- Will all of these learning activities take place at once or at different times?
- What expectations will you set for your students?

Before you start making any decisions, it is important to look at the implicit messages conveyed to students by different learning activities. A lecture, such as the one given by Ms. Edwards in Scenario One at the beginning of the module, suggests that the teacher is the main source of knowledge. It may also suggest an inherent hierarchy within the classroom, with the teacher in a superior position. Ms. Edwards's room certainly seems to operate under this hierarchical pattern. At the same time, it may also convey the message of expediency and efficiency, because the lecture format is the fastest way to convey large amounts of information.

A demonstration lesson may also send a message of efficiency and order. Having the teacher do a demonstration in front of the class is certainly more expedient than having a group of twenty or twenty-five students perform the same activity. The results are more predictable as well, suggesting a certain predetermined outcome of learning. At the same time, however, a demonstration lesson might convey a distrust of students' ability to carry out the activity or experiment on their own. Students may suspect that the teacher believes they will get the wrong results and, as a consequence, not learn the concept correctly, or that they will be too distractible to focus on the activity. Many teachers are particularly wary about allowing students to carry out activities that involve materials that present even the slightest possibility of causing injury (such as certain chemicals) or creating a mess in the classroom (anything that has quantities of water).

Sometimes, of course, the decision to do a demonstration lesson has very little to do with conscious choice on the part of the teacher and everything to do with the availability of adequate materials or equipment. If a school has limited resources or space, a demonstration lesson may be the only way to teach certain concepts.

## Now You Do It

What other learning activities are you considering besides lectures and demonstrations? What implicit messages may be communicated by implementing the kinds of lessons you are considering?

# Physical Arrangement of the Classroom

Once you know what you might be doing in the classroom, consider how the physical arrangement of the classroom can support the activities you envision. Some teachers will have more options for arranging the room than others. Most elementary grade teachers, for example, will have their own rooms. Middle school and high school teachers may not have their own rooms or may be limited by furniture or equipment that is fixed in place. They may need to adapt their plans rather than adapting the classroom set up.

Assuming you have some control over the physical classroom, how do you envision your classroom set-up? How will you arrange the students' desks? Where will you put your desk? What other furniture would you like to have? Will you partition the classroom for different activities (such as a writing center or a class library)? What about the walls—what will you have on the walls or on the bulletin boards? As with lessons, the arrangement of the classroom can convey implicit messages to students about what you expect from them while they are in the room.

Student desks arranged in single rows, like those in Ms. Edwards's room, tell students that they are expected to work independently and in silence. They are not encouraged to interact with their classmates during class time.

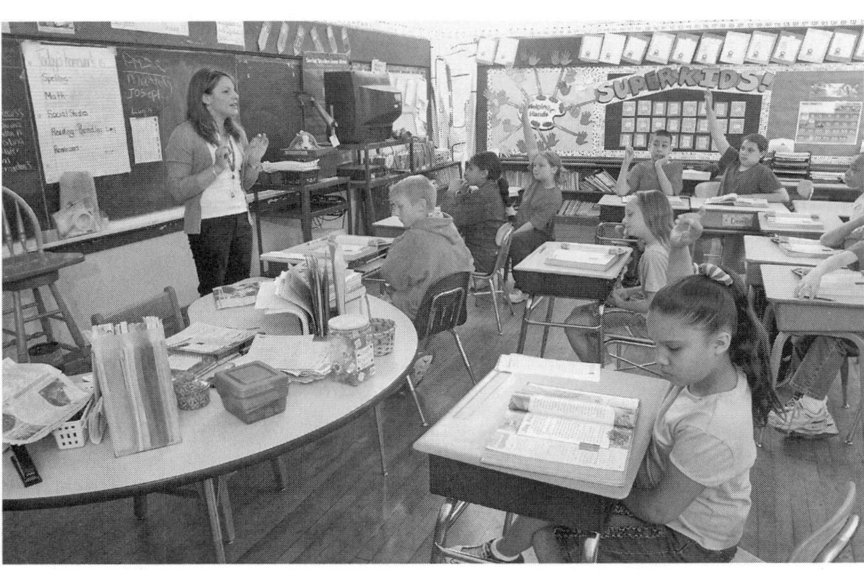


The physical arrangement of the classroom conveys expectations for classroom behavior.

**Figure 8.1**
**Classroom Arrangements**

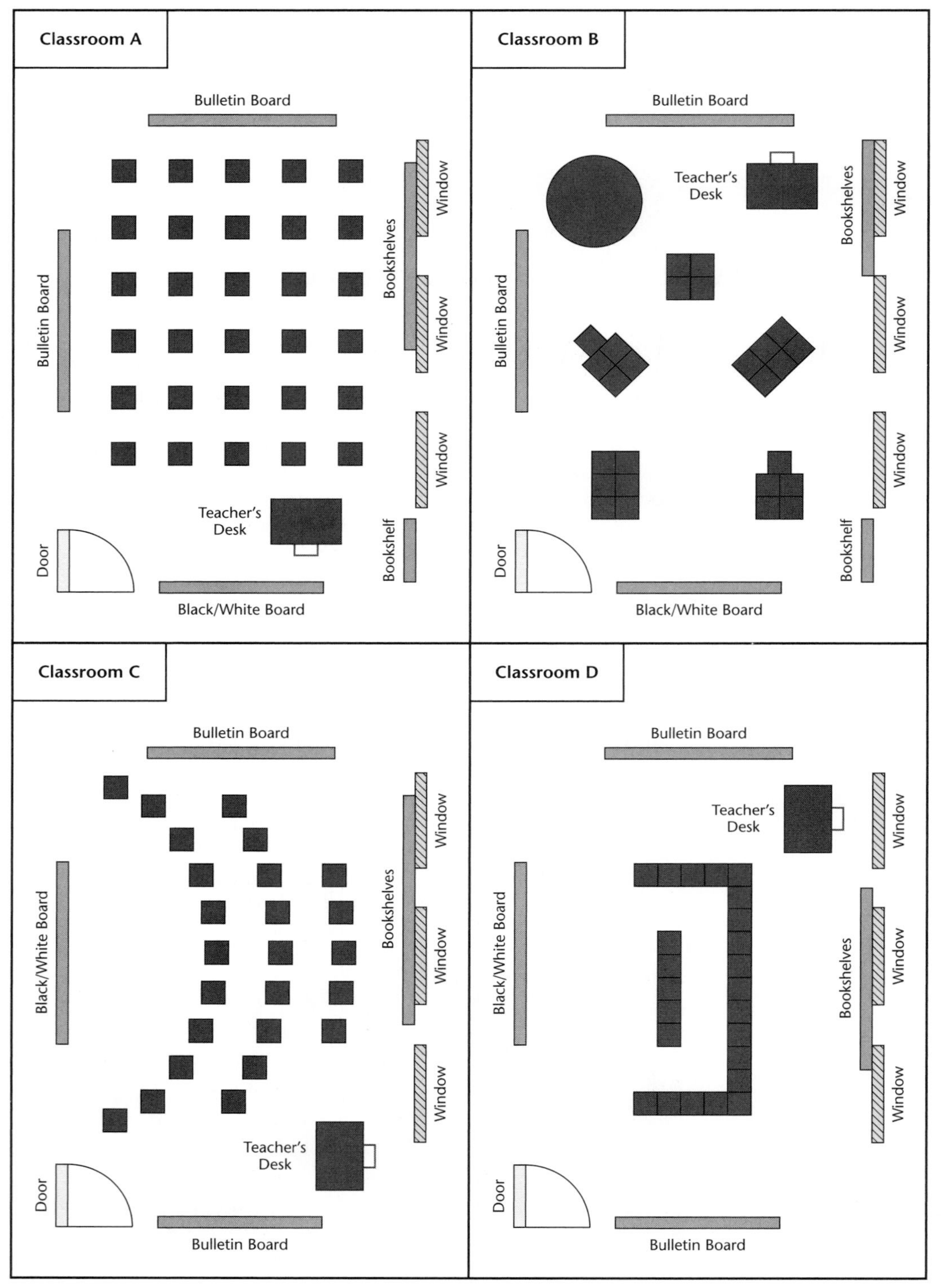


Look at the diagrams of different classroom physical arrangements. What kind of instruction do these physical arrangements encourage? What message does each of these physical arrangements convey to students? Which of these physical arrangements most closely reflects the way you would like to have your classroom? What changes, if any, would you make?

In fact, the expectation is that the dominant discourse pattern is between student and teacher. The teacher asks questions; the students answer. Occasionally the student queries the teacher, who provides clarification or further explanation. Other students are not necessarily expected to respond to what their classmates are saying. They are, however, expected to be attentive to the interactions going on.

When desks are arranged in clusters, as in Mr. Josiah's room, the implicit message is that students can and should work together to complete tasks, such as the group projects Mr. Josiah assigns. Collaboration is encouraged and, depending on the cluster arrangement, enhanced, especially if students are facing one another. Clusters may also suggest to students that social interaction is acceptable in the classroom. The more desks in a cluster, the more social interaction is implicitly accepted. If you do not want students to talk to one another or to work collaboratively, then perhaps you do not want to arrange desks in groups!

Another arrangement of desks is in a horseshoe shape or open U around the blackboard. This set-up tells students that discourse will take place not just between individual students and the teacher but among all students and the teacher. It suggests that students are to listen and respond to the comments of their classmates. This arrangement also conveys that the teacher is not the sole source of information; knowledge resides in other students as well. This set-up requires students to engage actively in the classroom conversation at all times. It is not uncommon for students to passively resist these built-in requirements for face-to-face contact and active participation. They may, for example, "naturally" converge to a second row.

What about the teacher's desk? Consider three of the possible options:

- *Teacher in front.* The teacher's desk placed at the front of the classroom, like Ms. Edwards's desk, tells students that the teacher is in charge. It also suggests a certain hierarchical structure, with the teacher having greater authority and decision-making responsibility than the students. More than likely, the flow of information will be from the teacher to the student.

- *Teacher in back or to the side.* Placing the teacher's desk off to the side or in the back of the classroom suggests that there is less of a hierarchy in this classroom. There may be some decision-making responsibility accorded to the students. The information flows not just from teacher to student, but also from student to student, and the sources of information may be varied.

- *Multiple teacher stations.* Some teachers like to have a table or a student desk in the front of the class, with the teacher's desk off to the side or in the back of the classroom. Particularly if the teacher uses a student desk, this set-up can suggest that even though the teacher is still clearly directing the learning activities, there is an attempt to de-emphasize the hierarchical character of the relationship between teacher and students.

## Now You Do It

Think about some of the other physical aspects of your current or future classroom. Consider, for example, the walls and bulletin boards, reading/listening centers, and computers. How will you use them and what messages will they send to the students? How will you use or arrange these parts of the room? What will these arrangements tell students about the classroom culture you want to create?

# Classroom Rules and Policies

As a teacher, you are charged with supervising from 20 to upward of 200 students a day. Keeping all of your charges moving in the same direction is not unlike a cowhand moving a herd of cattle. Any lack of clarity in your guidance can lead to unexpected, and most often undesirable, results. (Nothing is more unpleasant than experiencing, or even witnessing, a stampede of your metaphorical herd!)

**Classroom rules** explicit statements to students about what behavior is acceptable and desirable in the classroom.

**Classroom rules** are one important way of providing clear guidance to your students. Rules and policies are explicit statements to students about what behavior is acceptable and desirable in the classroom. Effective rules are essential to maintaining a safe, orderly, and fair environment. Developing a set of effective rules requires you to make a number of careful decisions.

Some of these decisions may already have been made for you by school policies and practices. Others were made when you designed your classroom set-up. Remember that you need to achieve consistency among the school policies, the physical set-up of the classroom, and the norms and expectations you set for own classroom. Consistency is one of the keys to a productive, enjoyable classroom environment, and you can avoid a fair number of classroom management difficulties if you are careful not to send conflicting messages to students. As we have noted, for example, a teacher who does not want students to talk to one another or to ask classmates for help should not put student desks in clusters.

It is also important to realize that rules are key elements of the classroom climate. In addition to their face value as statements of expectations, rules send implicit messages about what is valued in your class. The questions you'll need to answer when developing rules include

- Who makes the rules?
- How many rules do we need?
- What should the rules cover?

## Who Makes the Rules?

Will you as the teacher decide on the rules and share them with (or impose them on) your students? Or will the rules be formulated and agreed on by the class as a whole? When the teacher makes the rules, it is easier for the teacher to be sure that the classroom rules match the school rules. That consistency is critical. When students participate in the rule-making process, the teacher may need to guide them to rules that are acceptable to the school community as a whole. A benefit of student participation is that students may feel a greater sense of "ownership" of the rules and may be more inclined to follow rules that they themselves created. Another workable option might be for the teacher to decide on some rules and the students to formulate additional ones.



## How Many Rules?

A number of veteran teachers insist that the most important principle for classroom rules is KISS—keep it so simple! These teachers believe that the fewer the rules, the easier it is for students to remember them and the easier it is for the teacher to implement them. Perhaps more important than the number of rules, however, is their clarity. Rules must be explicit and clear; and

## In Your Classroom

### Guidelines for Developing Class Rules

Here are a few guidelines that can be useful in helping you decide on classroom rules.

1. *Make rules whose purpose and necessity are easy to explain and obvious.* A good question to ask yourself is "Why do we need this rule in the classroom?" Can you easily explain how the rule will help to make the classroom environment a productive one? If not, maybe you should rethink the rule.
2. *Make rules that can be consistently implemented.* Rules are useless if they are not implemented or, even worse, cannot be implemented. When deciding on rules, be sure to ask yourself, "How will I ensure that this rule is effectively and fairly implemented?"
3. *If possible, phrase rules in the positive rather than the negative.* Tell students what they should or must do, not what they shouldn't or mustn't do.
4. *Establish clear consequences for violating the rules.* Rules are most readily enforceable when the consequences for violating them are clear and explicit. Consequences should also be reasonable and capable of being implemented. Do not, for example, threaten after-school detention if the school has a policy prohibiting any after-school presence.
5. *Post the rules in the classroom so that they can be seen as a reminder of classroom expectations.* If your class includes students whose first language is not English, you may want to help them follow rules by posting a copy written in their own language.



the consequences of violating them reasonable, understandable, and consistently enforced. The "In Your Classroom" feature offers some guidelines for developing rules.

You can link to several examples of rules and policies from teachers' classrooms from your Online Study Center. Studying existing examples such as these can be useful when you put together your own classroom rules and policies.

## What Should Rules Cover?

Most classroom rules reflect expectations for student behavior in the classroom or during class time, with the goal of helping to ensure a productive and pleasant environment for teacher and students. The behaviors often addressed in rules include asking or answering questions, movement inside and outside the classroom, punctuality, and work flow.

***Responding to or Asking Questions*** The dominant practice in classrooms around the country is to require students to raise their hands when they want to talk, whether to ask a question or to answer one posed by the teacher. There are several reasons why hand-raising is so common.

- *Order.* Many teachers believe that requiring students to raise their hands imposes a certain order in what would otherwise be a very chaotic environment. If students were free to speak whenever they wanted, it could be hard for the teacher to hear anyone clearly. Students also might not be able to hear what the teacher says or what their classmates ask, leading to redundancy in questions asked or comments made. (Even with hand-raising, redundancy tends to be a chronic problem.) This is a compelling reason for hand-raising in the classroom.

- *Skill-building.* Some teachers feel that hand-raising helps to instill in students acceptable discourse behavior. Children learn to be respectful of others who are talking, to wait their turn, and to control impulses.
- *Fairness.* Hand-raising can help ensure a more equitable distribution of time, making it easier for all students to participate in the class discussion. Because the teacher determines who will speak next, overly talkative students can be controlled to some extent. Teachers can also keep better track of which students have been called on, to ensure equitable participation.

There are also several potential drawbacks to requiring students to raise their hands to speak.

- *Spontaneity.* Requiring students to raise their hands before they talk may reduce the spontaneity of their thoughts. Students may forget what they wanted to say if they have to wait until they can speak. And their comment may be related to a point made earlier, which interrupts the continuity of the discussion.
- *Exclusion.* Some students may be less inclined to participate if their perception is that they "never get called on" when they raise their hands. Also, students from some cultural backgrounds may be reluctant to volunteer answers for fear that they will be perceived as being too assertive. Module 12, How to Teach, offers suggestions for ensuring fairness when you call on students to answer questions.
- *Skill-building.* In normal conversation, we do not raise our hands when we want to make a comment, and somehow people are able to convey their ideas and points of view in a timely manner—generally without interrupting others. Allowing students to contribute to the discussion without raising their hands more closely mimics normal conversation and, some argue, is more effective at teaching students how to take turns.

Thus, if you establish as a practice that students raise their hands if they want to talk, your implicit message is one of order, efficiency, and respectfulness. If you do not require that students raise their hands, your message may be that the classroom is a natural environment characterized by a free-flowing exchange of ideas and points of view, unencumbered by the formality of asking permission to speak. Again, your personal style, the learning goals you envision for your students, and the activities you plan, as well as the norms at your school and the personalities and expectations of the students themselves, are all likely to contribute to your procedures for managing conversation in the classroom.

***Student Movement*** Another category of rules that you should establish early on are those that govern student movement within and beyond the classroom. Within the classroom, students will need to get up to sharpen pencils, retrieve articles from various locations, dispose of waste paper, select reference books, and make use of different work areas that you may have set up in the classroom. Beyond the classroom, students will need to go to the bathroom, their lockers, the main office, or the nurse's office. Movement is inevitable and even necessary, especially for elementary-level students who are often in the same classroom, and even the same seat, for extended periods of time. The key for you as the teacher is to decide how to manage this movement and how much freedom you will give to students. The "In Your Classroom" feature summarizes some possible options for managing student movement.

Will you require that students ask permission for any and all movement, either within or beyond the classroom? Once again, the reason for requiring

## In Your Classroom

Here are some options for managing student movement. Keep in mind that some of these decisions might be moot if school policies cover student movement within and beyond the classroom. You want to be sure that your practices are consistent with school policy. If you aren't sure, ask an experienced colleague.

- *Movement requires permission.* You may want to insist that students ask permission for any movement within and beyond the classroom. If so, you'll need to think about *how* you want students to request permission. Having students raise their hands is one possibility. The problem with this approach is that you won't know whether the student raising his or her hand wants to answer the question posed or ask permission to go to the bathroom. Some teachers propose that students indicate a request for movement via silent signals—a particular way of raising one's hand or some other sign.
- *Movement is allowed only at specific times.* This practice may be dictated by school policies and procedures. In some schools, more often middle schools and high schools, students are allowed to use bathrooms only at designated times, such as between classes. Elementary schools may have similar procedures. One school familiar to us has bathroom and drink breaks, when all students in the class are escorted to the bathroom and water fountain.
- *Students are free to move without requesting permission.* You may want to grant students total freedom, or you can set a limit on how many students can be out of the classroom at a time. We know of numerous classrooms where one boy and one girl may be out at the bathroom at any one time. Students are free to go if no one else is out. Otherwise, they must wait for the boy or girl to come back from the bathroom before they can go.
- *Different procedures govern movement within and beyond the classroom.* You could allow students to move freely about the classroom so that they can make optimal use of the different learning areas you may have set up, and, at the same time, have strict procedures for any movement beyond the classroom. This option is especially useful in schools where policies and procedures for movement beyond the classroom are explicit and/or rigid, requiring, for example, that students request permission, sign in and out, or have a hall pass to leave the classroom.

permission for movement is often linked to order and efficiency. If students are free to get up and move around whenever they want, your classroom may sometimes become a very chaotic environment.

At the same time, some movement *is* inevitable, and if you require students to ask permission to move about the classroom, your lesson could be constantly disrupted by requests to sharpen pencils; get a pen, a piece of paper, or a calculator; go to the bathroom; get last night's homework; and so on.

In managing student movement, remember to plan for the different work areas you have designated within the classroom: computer stations, listening centers, reading/library area, and so on. You will want to establish procedures to allow equal access to these work areas for all students. Some management strategies to consider include posting a sign-up sheet that allots each student so much time each week or assigning weekly times to all students.

Remember, too, that along with the management of student movement comes the monitoring of this movement. With twenty or more students in a given classroom, teachers often have a hard time keeping track of when a particular student left the classroom. Still, teachers are responsible for all students during that time they are in that teacher's class. Unsupervised students could sustain injury while outside the room or, perhaps more likely, engage in behaviors that violate school rules. In any case, you don't want the principal or vice-principal to see one of your students roaming the hallways, seemingly without purpose.

Some teachers monitor student movement beyond the classroom by having students sign out each time they leave the classroom and sign back in when they return. The teacher can later look at these sign-out/sign-in times to note any student's chronic absence from the classroom for extended periods of time.

Other teachers note, themselves, the time that a student leaves the classroom. If a student is not back within five minutes, the teacher can send another student to find him or her. Still others do not actively monitor student movement; rather, they assume the students will not abuse the movement policy and will return to class promptly. Students who abuse this trust and privilege are dealt with individually.

Before you make a decision on managing and monitoring student movement, consider the messages conveyed through these different options. Requiring that students ask permission, allowing movement only at specified times, and timing students who leave the classroom suggest a structured, disciplined environment with clear accountability. Many teachers believe that teaching students to be organized and disciplined in procedures and practices may help them to incorporate similar efficiency and discipline in their thinking.

At the same time, however, such an approach to student movement may send a message of distrust to some students, because it grants them little to no autonomy or decision-making ability within the classroom. Many teachers suggest that such messages have negative effects on student learning and development. In classrooms where students have more freedom of movement, teachers place the responsibility for their actions on the students themselves. The implicit message to students can be one of trust and responsibility. Teachers are trusting students to act responsibly, to get up when they need to, not to disturb the lesson being taught, and not to abuse the freedom they are granted.

Some educators also argue that allowing freedom of movement helps students to better focus on learning. The argument is that when students are free to decide when and for how long they can move, they may be better able to realize their learning needs and structure their learning in more productive ways. If students know that they can get up and move around as they need to, they don't have to divert productive psychic energy into thinking up reasons why they should be allowed to get up from their seats. In some instances, students who have been sitting for extended periods may just need some physical movement to help them refocus on the tasks at hand.

**Choice theory** the theory, articulated by psychiatrist William Glasser, that humans have fundamental needs, such as survival, love, power, freedom, and fun, and that throughout our lives our actions are attempts to satisfy these needs.

This approach to classroom movement stems from a psychological theory called **choice theory.** Developed by psychiatrist William Glasser, choice theory is based on the concept of helping people to identify their needs for survival, love and belonging, power, freedom, and fun and to make conscious decisions for meeting these needs.[1] Glasser suggests, for example, that many students try to meet their needs for love and belonging by interacting with their friends at school. If they are not allowed freedom of movement in the classroom, their need for belonging may be unmet, which may provoke disruptive behaviors. Glasser argues that when students have the freedom to make choices, they can learn to control their own reactions to events and take greater responsibility for their behaviors.

***Punctuality*** Concerns about students arriving at class on time are more of an issue at the middle school and high school levels where students change

## Now You Do It

Which of the classroom rules and policies described above appeal to you most? Why? What additional rules and policies do you expect to have? What messages are implicit in the other rules and policies that you propose?

classrooms each period, but upper elementary school teachers may want to establish such rules, as well. These rules may be dictated by school policy, so you may not have much flexibility here. If you do have the option to develop your own policies regarding punctuality, what rules will you establish? Will you allow middle school or high school students to come to class after the bell has rung and you have started your class?

Many teachers believe that imposing a strict rule regarding punctuality teaches students to be accountable. The message might be that the students have a responsibility to arrive on time. Requiring promptness prepares students for the working world, where they will be expected to arrive at work on time. If, however, the consequence for breaking this rule is that the student is marked absent for that day of class, the message communicated may be that being punctual is more important than learning the content of the day's lesson.

A more relaxed implementation of punctuality rules may be understood by students to mean that the content of the lesson is more important than being on time: a "better-late-than-never" message. Some students see this attitude as a more humane approach to the hectic school life at the middle school and high school levels, where students usually have no more than four minutes to move from one class to the next. The risk, however, is that the students may also conclude that the information being presented or the learning expected to take place is not that important, so they can show up whenever they want.

### Video Case

The video case, *Classroom Management: Best Practices,* shows several teachers discussing their rules and how they establish the classroom culture. As you watch the clips and study the artifacts in the case, reflect on the following questions.

**QUESTIONS**

1. The first teacher emphasizes the length of time it takes for students to understand classroom rules and procedures. Were you surprised by her time estimate? How long do you believe it will take your students to internalize rules and procedures?
2. How will you establish a feeling of "community" in your classes?

**Online Study Center**

***Work Flow*** Work flow includes tasks such as submission of papers, homework, or other student assignments. Some teachers have very strict policies regarding submission of assignments. A common policy, for example, is to lower the grade on a paper by half a grade for each day the paper is late. Those who impose rigid timelines reinforce the value of responsibility, accountability, and discipline. Those who are more lenient may be sending the message that the quality of work is more important than timeliness.

One potential danger with rigid timelines is the need to allow for exceptions. There really are legitimate reasons why a student's homework or paper may not be handed in on time. If you have a rigid policy, you'll need to enforce it equitably. You should plan ahead and develop a policy for the legitimate exceptions, such as catastrophic family events. How much evidence will you require to substantiate a legitimate excuse, for example, and how much extra time will you allow in such cases?

## Organizational Tasks

We cannot overemphasize the importance of organization in the classroom. Teachers face an almost overwhelming number of tasks every day that, though not part of instruction, are necessary to keep the classroom and school running, so that instruction may take place. Developing effective

**Classroom routines and procedures** policies or regulations the teacher establishes for getting things done, such as how to hand in papers, how to request a bathroom visit, or where and how to line up to go to lunch.

**class routines and procedures** for handling these tasks will save you countless hours and headaches. The specific tasks for which you will need to develop routines tend to vary by grade level.

## Organization at the Elementary Level

At the elementary level, the myriad tasks that need to be done on a daily basis can be daunting. These include taking and reporting attendance and, in many schools, taking lunch counts; making morning announcements; setting up activities; distributing and collecting materials for specific activities (math manipulatives, calculators, art supplies, and the like); and moving the students to different locations for various activities, such as art, music, and physical education. (You never thought moving a group of 10-year-olds from one classroom to another could be so challenging, did you?) Then there is the task of managing the never-ending work flow: papers to be graded, recorded, and returned; papers or projects in progress; homework coming in and being returned; class/seatwork; and school-to-home correspondence, just to name a few. In addition, a series of housekeeping tasks need to be addressed, such as cleaning the board and erasers, picking up papers from the floor, straightening up the classroom library, and keeping desks and chairs arranged.

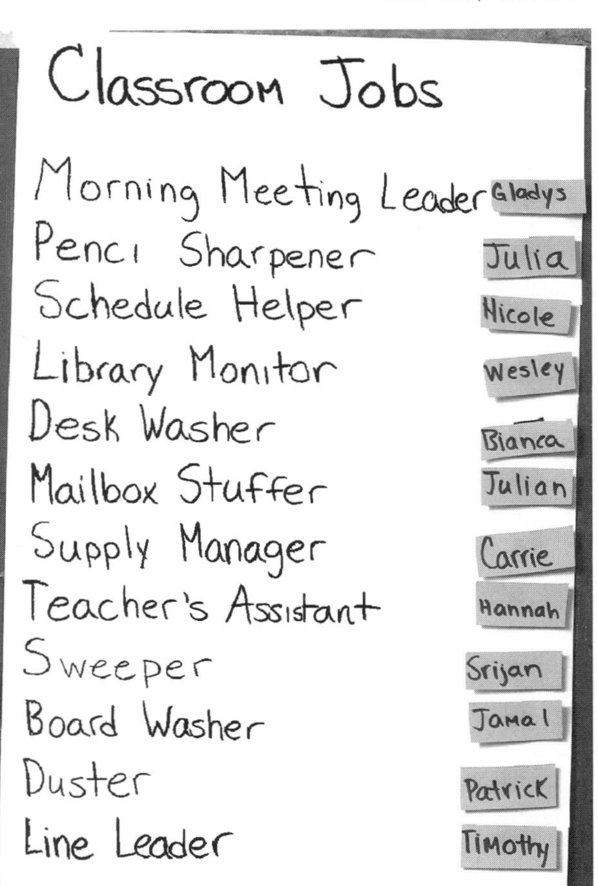


Chore charts such as this one are a popular method for rotating classroom job assignments in many elementary schools.

Some teachers find it most efficient and effective to carry out all these diverse tasks themselves. This decision may lead to long hours spent in the classroom, however, especially after school.

Other teachers may charge the students with responsibility for many aspects of classroom management. Mr. Anderson, whose morning routines were described at the beginning, has students indicate their daily presence by moving their name sticks from one can to another. In such a classroom, students might be responsible for retrieving whatever classroom supplies they may need, for keeping their desks and the area around them neat and paper-free, and for returning books appropriately to the classroom library.

Another option is to set up rotating classroom jobs. Students are assigned various tasks, such as line leader, door holder, paper distributor, blackboard cleaner, or attendance reporter. They are responsible for these tasks for a period of time, such as a day, a week, or a month, and then the jobs are reassigned. Elementary school students generally enjoy the recognition and responsibility that comes with being given a task.

## Organization in Middle School and High School

At the middle school and high school levels, the classroom organization is equally important but presents other challenges. Because students generally move from one classroom to the next, they often feel no "ownership" for any particular classroom environment. As a result, it may be more common for teachers at these levels to take responsibility for all of the logistical tasks. On the other hand, some teachers like to place responsibility on individual students to maintain order in the classroom in the same way that elementary teachers do. For example, students in some middle school and high school classrooms are expected to keep the area around their desks neat during the class and to make sure the area is picked up before leaving class.

**Class prefect** a student leader charged with special responsibilities to assist the teacher, including monitoring other students' behavior.

Some interesting practices employed in other countries are worth noting here. In many European middle schools and high schools, each class has a **class prefect**—a class leader or liaison who is responsible for monitoring the behavior of his or her classmates. This individual is in charge of much of the discipline of the class. In many Asian schools, students are responsible for the housekeeping of the classroom. At the end of the school day, the students sweep the floor and clean the desks. At the end of the week, students are expected to wash the classroom, often including the walls!



### Messages to Students

Like many other decisions you make as a teacher, the organization of the "daily chores" also sends messages to your students and their families, as well as to your colleagues and supervisors. If you decide that you will handle most of the logistics yourself, the message to students and their families might be that the primary task of students is acquiring knowledge, so they should not be distracted by mundane activities. If you decide to involve the students in the daily logistics of the classroom by setting individual expectations or assigning tasks, the message received might be one of responsibility and accountability, either individual or shared. Students learn that belonging to a community requires a commitment from all to participate in the life of that community.

## Clashing Cultures: When Classroom Culture and School Culture Collide

We've made frequent reference throughout this chapter to consistency in messages sent to students. The classroom set-up, policies and practices, and learning activities all need to send a consistent message to your students. Inconsistency can lead to significant challenges in establishing and maintaining a productive learning environment.

This same need for consistency applies throughout the school. Your classroom rules must be consistent with the school policies and rules. This is no problem if you agree with school policies. But let's say that you disagree with certain school policies. What is the danger of having classroom policies or rules that are inconsistent with school policy? Let's look at one example.

Suppose your school has a rule that no student can be in the hallway without a pass. As you read through the school policies and rules in the course of establishing rules for your classroom, you decide that this policy is too heavy-handed and controlling. After all, you reason, students at this age (whatever age they may be) need to develop responsibility and trust. You decide that your classroom policy will be that students can go to their lockers during the first five minutes of class without a pass. You also think that students should be able to go to the bathroom whenever they need to. Besides, you do not want the constant interruption of students asking for hall passes.

What messages are you sending your students with your policy? One message might be that of trust and responsibility. You trust that they will go out of the classroom for a specific purpose and return immediately. You believe that they are responsible enough to be able to monitor their own behavior outside of the classroom.

You might, however, be unintentionally sending an even more powerful message: that rules do not have to be followed. If students are aware of the school rule about hall passes, your policy tells them it's okay to break that rule. If you send the message that the school's rules and policies do not have to be followed, though, wouldn't that same message apply for *your* classroom rules? It will be hard for you to expect students to follow your rules if you do not follow school rules.

That is why it is important to know the school environment before taking a teaching position in the school. You have to be willing to support fully the learning environment of the school and to create a classroom environment that is consistent with (although not necessarily identical to) the school environment. If you cannot fully support the school policies, you might want to consider working at a different school.

As you finish this chapter, we recommend that you revisit the "Now You Do It" boxes throughout the chapter. If you haven't already reflected on your answers, do so now. If you have been answering as you went along, now is a good time to tie together all of your separate responses.

We've already mentioned the importance of consistency and uniformity of message. Take some time now to evaluate the consistency of the decisions you've made about your classroom environment. Consider the following questions:

- *Learning Activities.* What learning activities are you considering? What messages do they send to the learners?
- *Classroom Layout.* What messages are you sending students via your classroom layout? How do the physical arrangements support the learning activities that you envision?
- *Classroom Rules, Routines, and Policies.* What messages are you sending students with the classroom routines, rules, and policies that you have chosen? How do your routines and procedures support the learning activities you plan? How do your routines, rules, and policies mesh with the school rules and policies?

## Further Resources

- Paul Burden, *Classroom Management: Creating a Successful Learning Community,* 2d ed. (New York: John Wiley & Sons, 2003). The author emphasizes how to use classroom management to foster successful learning.

- Education World. Available at: **http://educationworld.com/a_curr/archives/classmanagement.shtml.** This website includes a database of teacher resources related to classroom management.
- Wilford A. Weber, "Classroom Management," in James M. Cooper (ed.), *Classroom Teaching Skills,* 8th ed. (Boston: Houghton Mifflin, 2006), pp. 235–285. This chapter examines different approaches to classroom management and includes practice exercises to improve classroom management skills.
- Carol Simon Weinstein and Andrew J. Mignano, Jr., *Elementary Classroom Management: Lessons from Research and Practice,* 3d ed. (New York: McGraw-Hill, 2003). A practical book that addresses the major issues in establishing and maintaining effective learning environments. Ms. Weinstein has a secondary version entitled *Secondary Classroom Management* (2003), also published by McGraw-Hill.

MODULE 9

# Maintaining the Classroom Environment

Scenario

The twenty-eight students in Betty Caldwell's eighth-grade social studies class are working in cooperative learning groups to complete an assignment about China. The students are discussing the questions, but the overall noise level is quite tolerable. Two students get up quietly from one of the groups, one student going to the dictionary and the other one going to the atlas. Ms. Caldwell is circulating around the room, eavesdropping on the conversations of each expert group.

At one of the tables, Sam starts dropping a pen repeatedly on the tabletop. Ms. Caldwell hears the noise and unobtrusively goes to Sam's table, where she gently holds the pen down on the tabletop, sending Sam a message to leave the pen still.

The groups continue working until Ms. Caldwell indicates that the period is about over and that students need to hand in their homework from the previous night. One student at each table collects the homework from the students at that table, and then one student collects the papers from each of the seven tables and puts them in a basket on Ms. Caldwell's desk. At that point, the bell rings and class ends.

Preview

Ms. Caldwell's students are learning in a well-managed classroom environment. Managing a classroom is really managing the individuals in that classroom—idiosyncratic, unpredictable individuals. Some of the students in any class may have little interest in school at all, let alone your class, and they may be less than cooperative in the classroom. In fact, there are probably a fair number of students, especially at the secondary levels, who resent, either overtly or covertly, the school environment and by extension the teacher (it's not personal, really). Among these students are those who seem to have made it a life study to passively resist any attempt to socialize them into the learning environment. Still others consider themselves champions at outsmarting and outmaneuvering the teacher.

At the same time, you will have many students who are exemplars of scholarly behavior in school: always attentive, dutiful, obliging, and even proactive in their schoolwork. You'll also have students whose commitment to the learning process is stellar, although their ability to achieve remains problematic.

With such a range of individuals, the strategies and techniques you use successfully with one student or group of students may or may not work with another. What works one day may not work another day. To manage in the ever-changing conditions in your classroom, you will need to use a lot of different practices and approaches. Indeed, the key to a successful management program is having as large a storehouse of tools as possible. We recommend that you work continuously throughout your career as a teacher to amass a varied set of strategies and techniques that are consistent with your philosophy of teaching and learning. The more tips and techniques you have, the more likely you are to find something that works with a particular group of students in a particular situation.

Does that mean that you have to come up with an individualized management program for each student? We'd argue that the situation is not quite that complex. There are some generalizations that hold for all students and can help you frame your managing of the classroom environment. In this module, we offer you those generalizations, as the foundation upon which to build your personal storehouse of specific tips and techniques.

**This module emphasizes that:**

- **Psychologists have proposed that all people have basic needs and motivations. If you are aware of these needs, you can help motivate students to find acceptable ways of meeting them.**
- **Getting students focused on learning activities and keeping them focused minimizes the potential for misbehavior in the classroom.**
- **To prevent misbehavior, teachers should model desirable behavior, treat students consistently, and be proactive in preventing undesirable behavior.**

- When students do occasionally misbehave, teachers should be clear, firm, and calm in correcting the behavior. The focus of their corrections should be on the behavior, rather than the student, and teachers may need to repeat and clarify rules.
- Teachers must think strategically to deal with students who repeatedly violate classroom rules.

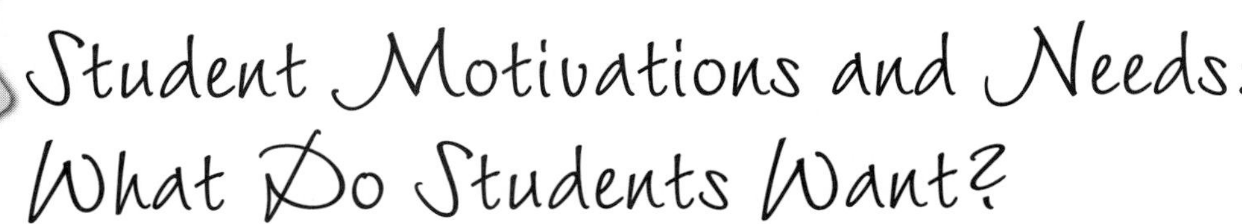

# Student Motivations and Needs: What Do Students Want?

Your learning objectives for the class may not always match the students' desires. In fact, students may want or need something completely different from the classroom experience you intend them to have. When students' desires are unmet by the activities you have planned, they find it harder to focus on those activities. Their attention may wander, opening up avenues for behaviors you would rather they avoid. If you know what motivates your students, however, you can engage them in learning activities that help fulfill their needs, rather than causing them frustration. Allowing students to meet their needs through the learning activities that you present will thus make your job as a classroom manager much easier.

**Maslow's hierarchy of needs** the theory, formulated by Abraham Maslow, that as humans meet "basic needs," they seek to satisfy successively "higher needs" that occupy a set hierarchy.

The noted psychologist Abraham Maslow (1908–1970) formulated the **hierarchy of needs** shown in Figure 9.1. Maslow suggested that needs at the lower levels of the hierarchy must be met before those at higher levels can be satisfied. At the most basic level in Maslow's hierarchy are physiological needs, such as the need for water, air, and food. Once these needs are met, individuals look to satisfy their needs for safety and security, followed by their needs for love and belonging, and their self-esteem needs. At the top of the hierarchy is self-actualization, the full realization of one's potential.[1]

Maslow's hierarchy suggests that students need to have their basic needs—physiological, safety, belonging—met before they are able to focus on

**Figure 9.1**
**Maslow's Hierarchy of Needs**

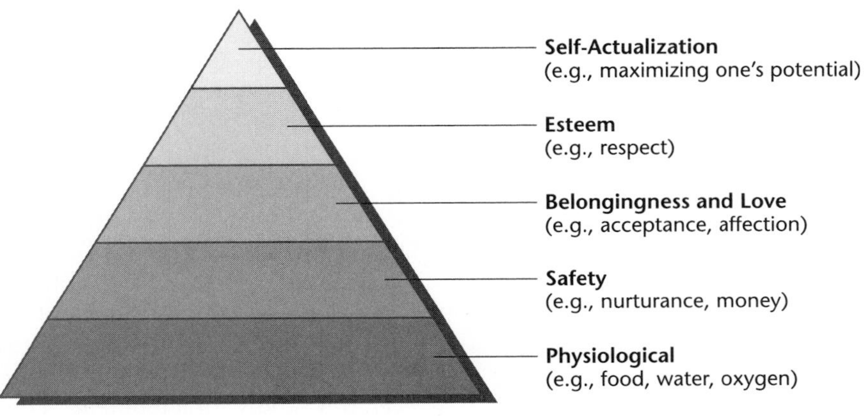


Source: Reprinted from A. H. Maslow, "Some Theoretical Consequences of Basic Need-Gratification," *Journal of Personality* 16 (1948): 402–416, by permission of Blackwell Publishing.

learning. Unfortunately, teachers do not have much control over students' lives outside their classrooms. This means that some students may come to school not ready or able to learn because their basic needs are still unmet (for example, if they are chronically hungry). To help satisfy some of these basic needs, many schools offer free lunch and breakfast programs. Most schools and teachers also take steps to ensure that students feel physically safe at school. These steps include locking the school doors once all students have entered for the day and carefully monitoring visitors who enter the school during the school day.

In order to create an environment that optimizes students' learning in your classroom, you should also help address basic needs to the greatest extent possible. You should strive to make students feel emotionally "safe" and to find ways to address your students' needs for love and belonging. Keep in mind the needs of all the students in your class, and recognize that students from different cultures may need you to marshal different strategies or actions to make them feel a sense of safety and belonging. As noted in Module 2, Understanding Student Differences, for example, students from different cultures or socioeconomic backgrounds may have had different school experiences and may not share the same outlook on school as you do. It is up to you to to find out what will make these students feel at home in your class.

Carl Rogers (1902–1987), another well-known psychologist, identified three attitudes or qualities that teachers should possess to help students learn.[2]

- *Realness.* Teachers who are real allow students to see them as actual people; they do not deny their individuality and don't play roles.
- *Acceptance.* Accepting means the teacher accepts the learners as they present themselves—their feelings, their opinions, and their persons—and does not demand that they change basic aspects of their personalities in order to gain the teacher's approval.
- *Empathy.* Empathy is the ability to understand the learner without judging or evaluating. Statements such as "You must be feeling frustrated" or "I heard you say . . ." are examples of nonjudgmental or reflecting statements.

In addition to being real, accepting, and empathic, you should also convey to your students that you notice, respect, and appreciate them as individuals.

- *Notice your students.* How can you *not* notice this room full of students? But there's a difference between noticing a room full of students and noticing individual students. Of course, there are always those students whom you cannot help but notice. But there are many others who do not call attention to themselves. Look around the classroom. You might notice that Manuela always sits in the back of the room, her head down, avoiding eye contact with anyone. Or you might notice that Greg seems to have grown five inches in two weeks.

  In her book *Caring* (1984), educational philosopher and researcher Nel Noddings points out that noticing one's students does not require an extensive time commitment, but it does require that the teacher be "totally and nonselectively present to the student"[3] during the exchange. The student must know that he or she has your undivided attention, even if it is only for a moment. A quick comment or a greeting is often enough. For Manuela, it might simply be a brief comment: "How are you today?" or "How did you like the story you read last night?" For Greg, commenting on how much he's grown may do the trick.

Noticing takes very little time or effort, but it can pay incredible dividends. You as a teacher are highly influential in many of your students' lives, even some of those hard-to-crack teens. A comment about an area known to be of interest to the student—"How did the team do this weekend?" "How'd the play go?" "What did you think about the [name the sport] game last night?"—will often light up students' faces by letting them know that you've noticed them. (*You* don't have to love soccer; you just have to have noticed that the *student* does.)

Some teachers make a practice of standing at the door to greet students individually as they enter or leave the room, working hard to have a good word for each. "Hey, Paul, you got a haircut. Looking good!" "Nice work today, Patrice. You really participated well." These personal encounters can aid immensely in establishing rapport with students who are often overlooked at school.

- *Respect your students.* This may seem like backward piece of advice. After all, aren't the students the ones who are supposed to show respect for the teacher? Most assuredly, but respect is mutual. Students often need to be shown respectful behavior so that they can act respectfully. One teacher we know has just three classroom rules: "Respect yourself," "Respect others," and "Respect your and others' property." He constantly models his high regard for students as individuals, framing his directions in a respectful manner, and even asking a student's permission before taking a book off the student's desk to show to the class. His students soon learn to be equally respectful toward him and their classmates. As a result, he rarely has any discipline issues.

  You can model respect in the classroom by treating students the way you want them to treat you and others. If they are to listen attentively to you without interrupting, shouldn't you be doing the same? If your desk is off limits to students, shouldn't you try to treat their desks with a similar courtesy? Naturally, there will be differences, but many of these basic interactions can be mutually respectful. A quick request ("Mind if I read a passage from your paper?") sends a very powerful message to students about respect for others. Allowing students to explain their actions when they have broken a rule conveys your willingness to hear them out, which is then viewed as being respectful. (It doesn't, however, mean that they evade punishment if it is warranted.)

- *Appreciate your students.* Your students are fascinating individuals who have wit, insight, and intellect. Take the time to get to know them and to appreciate what they can offer as individuals. Listen to their stories (in moderation) and respond to them. You can even at times laugh with them.

## Video Case

The video case, *Classroom Management: Handling a Student with Behavior Problems,* shows two teachers working with a student support coach to design strategies and interventions to cope with a particular student's disruptive behavior. As you watch the clips and study the artifacts in the case, reflect on the following questions.

**QUESTIONS**

1. The support coach mentions the importance of helping students feel a sense of belonging. What are some ways you hope to help your students feel they belong?
2. The support coach also mentions the importance of noticing and appreciating students. Besides those mentioned above, what are some specific ways in which you might be able to notice your students?

***Online Study Center***

Appreciating your students, however, does not mean that you become their equal. Teachers may be friendly and appreciate their students, but they must always maintain an appropriate social distance and keep in mind their position as the person in charge of the classroom. This is often especially difficult for young teachers, who may be close in age to their students if they teach high school, or who may not have much experience being in charge. Appreciating your students also does not mean that you can become their confidante. If a student tells you about anything inappropriate, you must act on that information.

## Getting, and Keeping, Students Focused

Your classroom environment needs to be one in which your students will be motivated and encouraged to learn, as well as able to focus with minimal distractions on the learning process. A useful model to keep in mind is that of an actor on stage. Just as the actors have to engage the passive audience in the story being told on stage, you need to engage your students in the learning being presented in class.

The complicating variable in the equation is your students' ability to maintain sustained focus on the tasks at hand. It is not unusual for students to lose focus or become bored after short periods of time. The younger the students, the more fidgety they are likely to become, and the sooner, but no matter what their age, all students find it challenging to sit for long periods of time. Seven to ten minutes is about the longest time many students can stay fully focused.

Here are some suggestions for preventing boredom and helping students maintain their focus.

1. *Move around the classroom.* If students cannot move freely around the classroom, you, the teacher, need to move. Your movement not only helps break up the monotony of the lesson (although we certainly do not mean to suggest that your lessons are boring!), but more important, it provides some vicarious relief from the inactivity that students must endure during the school day. As you move around the classroom, the students will follow you, and this will require that they shift their gaze and their positions in their seats.

A productive classroom environment helps students stay motivated and on task.

2. *Make eye contact.* Making eye contact with your students helps to engage them in the class activity. It also tells them that you "see" them as individuals. Be sensitive, though, to cultural differences regarding eye contact. (See Module 2, Understanding Student Differences, for more details.)

3. *Use signals.* Make ample use of nonverbal cues and other signals that clue students in to appropriate behaviors. Some teachers turn off the lights when it's time to transition between activities; some will raise two fingers in a "V" to indicate a need for silence. Still other teachers have some kind of auditory signal, a bell or a buzzer, to get students' attention. You can also make use of nonverbal cues, such as facial expressions or hand signals, to address students' misbehavior. A quick glare or stern look can often improve behavior quickly and efficiently without disrupting the ongoing learning activity.

4. *Manipulate your voice.* In addition to nonverbal cues, you can provide students with verbal cues to help them negotiate expectations and demands. Learn to vary your intonation, tone, speed, and volume in consistent ways so that students can associate a particular verbal pattern with a task. Whenever you ask a question that you want students to answer, present it in such a way that student know they are expected to answer the question. (And then be sure to insist that students answer the question. Don't answer it yourself!) When giving directions, use another consistent voice pattern so that students realize you are giving directions. When you are modeling thinking, or strategizing problem-solving processes, use yet a different verbal pattern.

5. *Wait.* In managing the classroom, patience is essential. After asking a question, wait at least ten seconds and, when few to no hands are raised, wait up to sixty seconds before calling on students to respond. This wait time helps students in two ways. First, some students need the time to think about the question asked and to formulate their answer. Without that wait time, the necessary thought processes may fail to be fully engaged, and student learning is compromised. Second, some students are quite adept at waiting the teacher out, putting their thought processes on hold in the hopes of not having to engage them at all. If the teacher habitually allows little wait time, these students quickly calculate that they face a very small likelihood of being called on and/or being expected to answer a question; the quick responders will probably satisfy the teacher's need for an answer. Allowing for wait time requires more, if not all, students to engage in the thinking process. Therefore, cultivate that most important of teacher virtues, the courage to tolerate silence.

6. *Make use of physical proximity.* In addition to moving about the classroom, you occasionally want to move close to students. Depending on the student and the culture of your classroom, you may even at times gently place your hand on a student's shoulder or arm. For potentially misbehaving students, your close proximity can keep their behavior in check. For other students, your close physical presence may help them to feel a greater sense of belonging. Think back to the scenario of Ms. Caldwell when she walked over to Sam's table and gently stopped him from dropping his pen on the tabletop.

7. *Keep your distance.* Well, which is it? Stay close or keep your distance? Both are helpful at different times and for different reasons. When a student is talking, we recommend that you stay fairly far from that student. This may seem counterintuitive. In normal conversation, we usually move closer to our partner to make it easier to hear one another. But school discussion is not normal conversation. A teacher's goal is often to

Pay attention to your proximity to students. Moving nearer can help encourage good behavior, but stay at some distance if you want a student's comments to be heard by all.

create a group discussion. The farther away you are from a particular student who is speaking, the louder that student must speak, allowing more of the other students in the room to hear. The effect is that the listening students become silent participants in the discussion, creating a larger learning environment in which more students are engaged. At the same time, being close to those students who are *not* active participants in the discussion helps to keep them more alert and involved in the discussion.

8. *Plan seating carefully.* Because most students have at least occasional problems with impulse control and discipline, they need as much help as you can give them. This means placing temptations and distractions as far from students as possible. One of the greatest distracters for students is other students. Thus, the seating arrangement is an important tool to help you keep students focused and engaged. If you decide to assign seats (and we would strongly encourage you to do so), think strategically about which student can sit next to which other students. Students sometimes whine and complain about not being able to sit next to their friends, but many are relieved of the pressure to attend to their friends rather than their work. Sometimes it is helpful to change the seating arrangements on a regular basis to keep students from forming relationships with their neighbors that could distract them from the learning process.

9. *Give appropriate and specific verbal feedback.* Providing meaningful feedback is an important aspect of your responsibilities as a teacher. It helps students assess themselves and gauge how well they are meeting the learning goals you have set. It also provides a critical source of motivation for students. What you want to think about is what kind of feedback will best serve these two purposes. You also want to think about how often you will give feedback and on what kinds of learning activities you will give feedback. Some teachers are reluctant to indicate that a student's answer is incorrect for fear that this information will be interpreted as criticism. Don't be afraid to say when an answer is incorrect (you don't want other students to think that an incorrect response is correct), but do so with tact and respectfulness. Perhaps give the student a helpful hint so that she or he can answer correctly.

   Various points of view have been offered regarding feedback. Haim Ginott, a well-known psychologist and educator, cautions teachers to make judicious use of praise.[4] He urges teachers to praise the act, but not the student. For example, the teacher might mention the improvement in a student's writing ("Good job choosing action verbs in this story"), rather than offering global praise to the student, such as, "You're becoming an excellent writer." Praising the act maintains a focus on the learning activity, rather than on any particular personality or intellectual quality the student may possess. Praising the student, many argue, not only misplaces the focus on inherent qualities, but also can quickly create a classroom environment of inequality in which some students feel discouraged because they see themselves as unable to compete with their "more talented" classmates.

Rudoph Dreikurs (1897–1972), a German psychologist, urged teachers to refrain from praising either students' work or their global characteristics. Instead, he urged teachers to encourage and praise students' effort.[5] Dreikurs argued that praise for effort was more egalitarian, because effort is a controllable response; all students can work hard. Intelligence and other personal characteristics are not so controllable, and not all students can achieve high scores on tests.

Other educators recommend that teacher feedback be framed from an "I" perspective, as in "I like the way you _____." This format for feedback provides specific information regarding the work done, so that students can self-assess. Proponents claim that it also maintains an egalitarian environment in the classroom, because the teacher can usually find something of value in all students' work, even if it's as simple as "I like the way you worked quietly at your desk during the activity."

### Now You Do It

Think back to your own schooling. What techniques or approaches did your teachers use to keep you focused on your work? Which techniques seemed most effective? Were there any that turned you off?

# Preventing Misbehavior

As we noted earlier, many students lack the ability to stay focused for long periods of time. It may even be possible that something happening in the class could be boring. (Well, it's *possible*!) Whatever the reason, the attention of all students wanders from time to time, and they may become tempted to behave in ways that you would rather they didn't. The following practical guidelines should help you help students avoid the inevitable temptations of misbehavior.

## Model Desirable Behaviors

Haim Ginott, whose ideas on praise we mentioned earlier, believes that the teacher's own behavior is the most important element in implementing effective classroom management. Teachers must not only make clear to students their expectations for appropriate behavior; they must also embody these behaviors.

Your impact as a model cannot be underestimated. As we pointed out in Module 8, Establishing the Classroom Environment, the message you send regarding appropriate behaviors is only as effective as it is visible in your own interactions with your students, colleagues, and superiors. This also means that if you wish to instill self-discipline in students, you must model self-discipline. This is especially essential when you are confronted with unnerving events or inappropriate behaviors in the classroom. The way you respond to these events or behaviors is likely to be copied by students. If you respond sarcastically to a student gaff, you have set the standard for responding to gaffs and have given the students license to respond in similar ways. By the same token, if you exhibit patience and tolerance in all of your interactions, students are more likely to do so as well.

Ginott does not suggest that teachers become automatons who never show any emotion. Rather, he encourages teachers to express their feelings, but to do so in rational ways. He urges the use of "sane messages," in which teachers point out problems in a situation, rather than criticizing the individuals involved in the situation. Teachers should explain to students their anger or frustration, and they should model reasonable ways of venting these feelings. Instead of getting angry and yelling at the class when they are too talkative and unfocused, communicate your annoyance to students calmly. You might use an "I" message, such as "I'm very upset with all the noise and inconsiderate behaviors in the classroom right now. I don't think we'll be able to _____ (a desirable activity) because so many people are being uncooperative."

## Be Consistent

Inevitably, some students in your classroom will irk and provoke you. Other students will delight you and brighten your day. But as the teacher, you have to impose the same expectations and the same treatment on all students. You have to implement the rules consistently and equitably. This means that on the rare occasions when Julio violates the class rules, he meets with the same consequences as do Johnny and Kate, who break rules far more frequently.

Some teachers have a hard time with consistent implementation of the rules, arguing that the rare offender should be forgiven for the unusual infraction and that the chronic offenders deserve the punishments. But anyone familiar with children and teenagers knows only too well their heightened sense of fairness. When teachers act "unfairly" by implementing the rules inconsistently, the message students receive is that students are not all equal in the classroom, and that some students are more respected by the teacher than others. Such a message can create a difficult classroom environment where some students become less motivated to conform to the norms of appropriate behaviors and grow even more aggressive and angry toward the teacher.

Some schools have adopted school-wide discipline and classroom management programs that call for all students to be held to the same standards by all of the adults in the school. These programs can help teachers be consistent in their enforcement of the rules. They may also save teachers time and energy that the teachers would otherwise have had to spend devising and implementing their own classroom management procedures. If students are already familiar with the school's guidelines and rules, they do not have to learn new rules every year. In fact, if the program has been in place for a few years, new teachers may even have to rely on the students to help them implement the program. The biggest potential drawback of school-wide programs is that they leave little opportunity to develop one's own classroom management system, which may be a problem when there is a mismatch between the school-wide program and individual teachers' preferences for classroom management.

**Video Case**

The video case, *Elementary Classroom Management: Basic Strategies,* shows how kindergarten teacher Amy Moylan uses morning meeting time to address individual student issues to prevent them from escalating and to prevent behavior problems on an upcoming class trip. As you watch the clips and study the artifacts in the case, reflect on the following questions.

**QUESTIONS**

1. How is this teacher being proactive?
2. How is modeling desirable behavior different for students in higher grades than for students in kindergarten? How do *you* plan to model desirable behavior?

## Be Proactive

Address student misbehavior immediately, quickly, and efficiently. Let students know that you are well aware of everything that is going on in the classroom. (Even if, in fact, you are only aware of most things, you still want them to think you are aware of everything!) Educational researcher Jacob Kounin undertook studies of classroom management in the 1970s. He found that the teachers who were most effective classroom managers were those who seemed to have the proverbial "eyes in the back of their heads." He labeled this awareness of everything that was going on in the classroom **withitness.**[6] To be "with it," you should regularly do a quick scan of what's happening in all parts of the room, even if you are working with an individual student or a small group.

**Withitness** Jacob Kounin's term for the effective teacher's awareness of everything that is going on in the classroom.

Being "with it" also means that you notice and respond to inappropriate behaviors as soon as they happen. If you do not address inappropriate behaviors immediately, the implicit message is that these behaviors are acceptable or at least not worth bothering about. Students are looking to you for guidance. Many will try to test the boundaries of acceptable behavior. (And to be honest, some students are simply testing you to see how firmly and consistently you will implement the rules.) You must communicate—promptly—just where those boundaries lie and what the parameters of acceptable behaviors are. In most classrooms, this requires a fair amount of explicit instruction from the teacher, as well as timely responses.

At the beginning of the school year, you will probably find yourself spending considerable time addressing inappropriate behaviors. In fact, some days it may feel like you did nothing but correct students' behavior (and that may actually be the case). But the sooner and more efficiently you address student behaviors and clarify for students what is and what is not appropriate—what will and what will not be tolerated—the sooner you can move on to actual teaching and learning activities. The next section of this module contains practical tips for dealing with misbehavior.

# Dealing with Misbehavior

Despite your best efforts to create and maintain a harmonious classroom environment, you are sure to experience misbehavior occasionally. You may also face one or more students who have particular trouble following classroom rules.

## Guidelines for Correcting Occasional Misbehavior

Numerous specific suggestions and strategies have been proposed for dealing with misbehavior. As we mentioned at the beginning of the module, we advise you to make an effort to learn as many of these specific strategies as possible, because some of them work with some students some of the time, whereas others work with other students some of the time. In the meantime, we'd like to present the following general approaches to, and guiding principles for, managing student misbehavior. They can help you choose and formulate your own effective strategies.

- *Be clear, firm, and calm.* In his studies on classroom management, Jacob Kounin found that when teachers dealt effectively with student misbehavior, there was a positive "ripple effect" on other students' behavior.

When a student breaks a rule in class, the teacher's response can help not only to correct the behavior of the offending student but also to discourage such behavior on the part of other students in the class. Kounin found the ripple effect to be most influential when the teacher is *clear* and *firm* regarding student misbehavior. Being clear means that the teacher explicitly states the offending behavior. Rather than simply saying, "Stop that" or making another, equally vague comment, the teacher specifies the inappropriateness of the offending behavior: "In this classroom, we don't use that kind of language" or "We listen when someone else is talking; we do not talk." To be firm, the teacher needs to convey a serious commitment to following through with appropriate consequences for the offending behavior. The benefits of the ripple effect are lessened, according to Kounin's research, if the teacher shows too much anger or frustration when dealing with the offending student. Kounin's research, then, tells teachers to be not only clear and firm, but also calm, when responding to student misbehavior.[7]

- *Focus on the behavior.* Educational researcher Haim Ginott urges teachers to give "sane messages," focusing on the situation rather than the individuals involved in it, when addressing student misbehaviors. These messages avoid any attack on the character of the offending student, while emphasizing appropriate and inappropriate behaviors in a given situation. For example, instead of saying, "Johnny, stop being so mean," try "Johnny, stop hitting Carlos, and open your book to page 47."

- *Repeat and clarify the rules.* You've set up classroom rules, explained them to the students, discussed the importance of the rules and the consequences for violating the rules, and even had all students express their commitment to the rules. Now you can expect the students to follow the rules. Right?

  Well, yes and no. Yes, you should expect the students to abide by the rules. At the same time, however, we urge caution in assuming that students have understood the rules exactly as you want them to be followed—even after your thorough and detailed explanation and discussion. It may also be too optimistic to assume that all students will remember the rules.

  When a student violates a rule, you should remind, or in some cases explain to, students how the particular action or behavior violated one of the classroom rules. Some students will genuinely not realize that an action violates a rule. Others may have forgotten about the rule, and still others are intentionally violating the rules to determine how firmly and consistently you will implement them. Even if students do know, the more reminders they receive, the more the offending students (as well as the other students in class) will realize the importance of the message and your commitment to it.

## Tips for the Tough Ones

Despite your best efforts to be consistent and proactive, respectful, and noticing of students, you may occasionally have a student or two who refuse to comply with any of the classroom rules, for whom all threats of punishment fall on deaf ears, and the threat of punishment itself seems ineffective. We'd like to suggest here that a large part of managing students resembles a chess game or any other game of strategy. You have to think like your opponent, anticipate his or her next move, and respond accordingly. In a classroom setting, that might translate into trying to understand why a student is acting out in a particular way. Here are some steps you can follow as part of your strategic thinking:

1. *Begin by identifying potential stimuli that might provoke a student's undesirable behavior.* Once you've identified these stimuli, try to avoid putting this student in situations that feature them and that could, therefore, lead to the undesirable and inappropriate behavior. That might mean isolating the student within the classroom, a common practice in many elementary classrooms where some students do not yet have the self-control to sit next to another student without talking or getting into trouble. Or it might mean allowing a student to take periodic breaks and step out of the classroom for a few minutes.

2. *Try to determine what the student is trying to achieve through his or her behavior.* Rudolph Dreikurs identified four "mistaken goals" that explain chronic student misbehavior: attention, power, revenge, and learned helplessness. Dreikurs suggested that students move through these goals sequentially. If the attention-seeking misbehavior does not achieve the desired effect, the offending student will seek power, and so on. Dreikurs also examined adults' reactions to these misbehaviors, which range from annoyance to threat to despair. Further, he suggests that as students adopt increasingly mistaken goals, their behavior becomes increasingly difficult to rectify.[8] Again, this suggests that a prompt response is the best response, when mistaken goals and the misbehavior associated with them are easier to correct.

   Dreikurs urged teachers to recognize both students' mistaken goals and their own feelings provoked by the misbehavior. The teacher should formulate responses that can effectively address the behaviors without validating the mistaken goals. Suppose a student wants attention and figures that one way to get noticed is to act out. The attention is negative, but at least the student is noticed. Thinking like your student and then figuring out why he or she is seeking attention can help you formulate an effective response. You can try, for example, to think of more productive ways for this student to get attention. At the same time, you should avoid responding to misbehaviors in ways that will bestow attention on behaviors you do not want the student to continue. One strategy to try is to "catch them being good"—to comment on the presence of *desirable* behavior in the offending student, rather than responding to the undesirable behavior that got your attention in the first place.

3. *Look for carrots and sticks.* Still thinking like your student, what might be a positive motivator for him or her? What could you, the teacher, offer to this student if he or she refrains from the inappropriate behavior? It needs to be something that he or she would genuinely be interested in having. In other words, what bargaining leverage, or "carrot," do you have? Perhaps the student enjoys taking on extra responsibilities within the classroom. An elementary school student may enjoy caring for the class pets. A student of any age might want more computer time. At the same time, think about what might be a negative motivator for the student. What consequence or punishment (the "stick") would be a sufficient deterrent to keep this student from continuing the inappropriate behavior? Taking away certain privileges until the student exhibits appropriate behavior might serve as a deterrent for misbehavior.

   Put your ideas to the test by presenting them to the student. First try the carrot, because most students will respond positively to rewards (if you've found the right reward). Allow the student to earn the extra computer time or class job by following the rules. If that fails, try withdrawing

## Video Case

The video case, *Secondary Classroom Management: Basic Strategies,* shows high school American history teacher Henry Turner discussing his personal classroom management strategies, which are also demonstrated in clips showing him teaching American history. As you watch the clips and study the artifacts in the case, reflect on the following questions.

### QUESTIONS

1. How does this teacher follow the advice given earlier in this module to help his students remain focused during class?
2. How does this teacher demonstrate the advice in this module to plan ahead and communicate expectations to students?
3. How does this teacher remain calm while being clear and firm about violations of rules? What are some specific ways you can use to be clear, firm, and calm when your students violate your rules?

***Online Study Center***

rewards. If rules are broken, take away the students' computer privileges or class job. Punishment should be your last resort because it is often ineffective and sometimes produces negative side effects.

Planning ahead and communicating with students are keys to helping them behave well. Avoid making up rewards, and especially punishments, on the spot. Not only does this come as a surprise to the student, but you also run the risk of overreacting and making a punishment too harsh for the particular violation. If consequences for rule infractions are known in advance, then when a student chooses to break a rule, he or she is also choosing the consequences associated with that rule infraction. As we noted in Module 8, Establishing the Classroom Environment, psychologist William Glasser's "choice" theory suggests that students choose behavior that meets their needs. Glasser recommends that teachers help students realize that the choices they may be making are unproductive and are not helping to meet their needs.[9] Communicating ahead of time the consequences for bad choices is one way to show students that their needs will not be met through misbehavior.

Consistency is another essential element in working with students who present you with management challenges. Some students' lives have been characterized by so much inconsistency that they have developed a distrust of all adults. Being consistent, even if at times it seems like you are being harsh, can help such a student develop a sense of trust, especially if you are able to convey the consistency and fairness of your actions. Other students may suffer from physiological or psychological challenges that prevent them from being as responsive and as disciplined as desired. For these students as well, consistency and routine help them develop the behavior patterns to be successful in a school setting. In all instances, make sure that you follow through on any promise of reward or punishment. Without that follow-through, your integrity with the student is compromised, along with the likelihood of your getting the student to behave appropriately.

Let's Sum Up

Classroom management is the biggest challenge that new teachers face and is a primary reason why teachers leave the classroom. It is also the area for which new teachers feel the least prepared. Many teacher educators argue that classroom management is a "hands-on" learning experience and cannot be taught in a college classroom. We agree that classroom management is a trial-and-error process that depends not only on the teacher's individual classroom style but also on the makeup of the student population in the classroom and the ethos of the school itself. As we noted at the beginning of the chapter, the ever-changing nature of the classroom requires teachers to develop a large repertoire of classroom management skills from which they can draw to fit specific situations.

Nevertheless, we believe that the guidelines we have laid out in this chapter are applicable in all situations. As recommended in Module 8, Establishing the Classroom Environment, carefully planning and arranging the physical space and establishing and implementing the daily procedures for the things you and your students regularly do in the classroom are your first big steps toward managing classroom behavior. Following the guidelines in this module will also help you to actively implement the classroom culture you wish to have. When one of the many specific techniques that you will acquire does not work, take some time to revisit and reflect on these underlying principles as a way to determine which other technique might be more effective in your current situation.

## Further Resources

Numerous books have been written about classroom management, and various educators and researchers have developed specific approaches and programs they tout as effective management strategies. All of these approaches have merits and ardent followers, and all probably have some skeptics. Our goal here is not to add to these approaches or to promote one program over another but simply to acquaint you with several popular approaches that you are likely to encounter during your career as a teacher.

- Linda Albert, *Cooperative Discipline,* rev. ed. (Circle Pines, MN: American Guidance Service, 1996). Dr. Albert presents a realistic approach to discipline and classroom management, one in which students are held responsible for their behavior.
- Carol M. Charles, *Building Classroom Discipline,* 8th ed. (Boston: Allyn & Bacon, 2005). A look at eighteen different approaches to classroom management, based on different theories and assumptions of how humans learn.

- *Discipline Help: You Can Handle Them All.* Available at: **www.disciplinehelp.com.** This website presents explanations for misbehaviors and proposes strategies to help teachers and parents address and correct misbehaviors.
- Edmund T. Emmer, Carolyn Evertson, and Murray E. Worsham, *Classroom Management for Secondary Teachers,* 7th ed. (Boston: Allyn & Bacon, 2006). A well-researched book on effective classroom management practices.
- Carolyn Evertson, Edmund T. Emmer, and Murray E. Worsham, *Classroom Management for Elementary Teachers,* 7th ed. (Boston: Allyn & Bacon, 2006). The counterpart to the book for secondary school teachers mentioned above.
- Adele Faber and Elaine Mazlish, *How to Talk So Kids Can Learn: At Home and in School* (New York: Simon & Schuster, 1996). Faber and Mazlish present practical, easy-to-follow advice on how to frame conversations with students to create optimal learning environments.

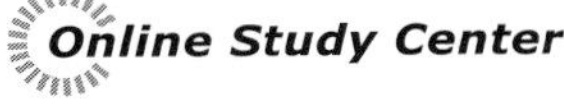


- *Learning Network.* Available at: **http://www.teachervision.fen.com/lesson-plans/lesson-5776.html.** This section of the Learning Network website presents advice from teachers about various aspects of classroom management.
- Robert J. MacKenzie, *Setting Limits in the Classroom: How to Move Beyond the Classroom Dance of Discipline* (Roseville, CA: Prima Pub., 1996). MacKenzie offers an alternative to a cycle of punishment and misbehaviors and proposes a step-by-step guide to create structure that works to stop power struggles, motivate students, and solve problems with homework.

- *Teachnet.* Available at: **http://www.teachnet.com/index.html.** The "Classroom Management" section of this website presents a range of suggestions about behavior and discipline from a variety of viewpoints.

Scenario

After he was hired last spring for his "dream position" teaching high school English, Chris could hardly wait to start introducing his students to new worlds of literature. He spent all summer thinking about which works he would have the students in his ninth- and tenth-grade English classes read. He composed and recomposed lists so often that he couldn't remember which was the most current. Finally, he decided on a list of the books that he wanted his students to read and sent it to his department chair, requesting that the books the school did not already own be purchased for the fall.

A few days later, Chris was asked to meet with Ms. Bradley, his department chair. Full of confidence and excitement about the new school year, Chris arrived early for his meeting. The tone of the meeting was not, however, what Chris was expecting.

"You put together a great list of literature, and I'd love for you to be able to teach all of these books," Ms. Bradley began. Then she delivered the bad news. "Unfortunately, there are certain considerations. First, we have to follow the state guidelines. That means you have to teach the books in the school curriculum guide first. I believe you were sent a copy of this with the faculty handbook and other materials." Ms. Bradley pointed to a two-inch binder on her desk.

Chris remembered looking through the guide when he had received it. He had been hoping, however, that it contained only a suggested, rather than a required, list. "These books are so predictable and outdated," he thought to himself. "How can I get students interested when even *I* find these books boring?"

Ms. Bradley noticed Chris's fallen expression, and she smiled sympathetically. "Sorry," she said, "but it's like when you were a kid, you have to finish your vegetables before you can have dessert. If you have any time left at the end of the year, you can teach any of the books on your list that we have in the storeroom. I'm afraid the budget for books has already been spent for this year, so we can't order anything new."

"Keep in mind, too, that you have two Level 3 tenth-grade classes," added Ms. Bradley. "These students have to take the graduation exam at the end of the school year. You will probably need to spend a lot of time preparing them for that test. They will need a lot of work with writing, grammar, and vocabulary development."

"Grammar lessons," Chris thought to himself. "How I *hated* those when I was a student!"

As Chris so abruptly discovered, teachers don't have sole discretion in determining what to teach their students. Half a century or more ago, teachers had greater leeway in choosing the topics they taught, as well as in how they taught them. Today, however, the curriculum is pretty much determined by state and local standards and guidelines, as well as by the textbooks used. In fact, some wags assert that we have a national curriculum and that it is expressed in the textbooks produced by large publishing firms. Yet, even though textbooks do provide many ideas and resources, teachers still have some choice of how and when they will teach the curriculum that addresses state standards.

You'll learn in this module that organizing what you will teach requires considerable planning on your part, beginning with the overarching purposes or goals and following up with specific learning objectives students are expected to master. Sequencing the curriculum and organizing it in such a way that both the whole and its parts are clear to your students will require considerable effort and creativity on your part. Depending on your teaching circumstances, you may even have the opportunity to work with fellow teachers to combine goals and objectives from different subjects to provide interdisciplinary instruction.

**This module emphasizes that:**

- **To plan effectively, you must take into consideration the content to be taught, the resources available, the time allotted, and the characteristics of your students.**
- **The content to be taught is determined by a number of different players: your state, your local school district, the individual school, and the community.**

- Effective planning starts with the broad purposes (goals) for learning and moves to the specific (objectives).
- Interdisciplinary teaching both provides rewards and poses challenges for teachers and students alike.

# Planning to Plan: Influences on the Planning Process

As in many other pursuits, preparation is the key to success in planning what you will teach. Before you begin making actual plans, you should spend some time learning more about the context in which your plans will be implemented. What goals do your state and school district require your students to meet? What is expected by stakeholders in your school and in the community? What resources are available to you? Once you have gathered all of these data, you will be in a position to use the information wisely as you make some specific plans for the year.

## State Standards and State Tests

One of your first and foremost considerations when planning your course for the year is to find out what students are expected to know and be able to do, according to the state guides for the discipline and grade level(s) you will be teaching. As Chris learned the hard way, one of the current realities of K–12 teaching in the United States is that teachers are expected to teach a prescribed course of study, or teach to a set of standards that have been approved by the state board of education.

**No Child Left Behind (NCLB) Act** the name of the 2001 reauthorization of the Elementary and Secondary Education Act. NCLB adds many new requirements for states and school districts.

The **No Child Left Behind (NCLB) Act** of 2001 created a federal influence that makes knowing your state's curriculum guidelines or standards even more important to you. NCLB mandates that state educational agencies develop curriculum standards that specify the content and skills students are expected to gain at each grade level or cluster of grades. Further, this federal law requires that states measure students' progress via annual testing of students in grades three to eight in math, English/reading, and science. States must report annually on students' academic progress as measured by these state exams. States also need to verify academic qualifications of their high school graduates by requiring them to pass an exit exam. (For more details on NCLB, see Module 1, Reflective Teaching for Student Learning.)

**High-stakes tests** tests that are required of students and that have serious consequences, such as eligibility for promotion to the next grade or graduation from high school, attached to the outcomes of the tests.

Because of these **high-stakes tests,** as they have come to be known, school district officials are expecting their teachers either to follow a prescribed district-developed curriculum or, at a minimum, to base their curriculum on the state standards. As Ms. Bradley noted, teachers generally have some leeway in what else to teach after all the standards have been addressed. Do not expect, however, to have much free time; most state guides are rather extensive.

When you examine the state curriculum guide or standards, do not focus only on the course or grade level you are teaching.[i]

[i] It is also helpful to find out what the students were to have learned the previous year. It would be very frustrating to plan your entire year, only to discover that students had already learned most of that material the year before!

All state standards place heavy emphasis on reading instruction in the primary grades.

Some disciplines, such as foreign languages, have an obvious hierarchy of concepts and skills, whereas for others the sequencing of topics may be less rigid. If you do not check the state guides, and instead assume, from your personal experience with sequencing topics, that students have covered particular concepts, you may find that they do not have the knowledge base you expected. For example, a typical mathematics sequence for high school is algebra 1, geometry, algebra 2; but in some states, the curriculum guide may call for an integrated approach to mathematics concepts, so that high school mathematics courses cover topics in algebra, geometry, trigonometry, data analysis, and statistics at increasing levels of complexity. That could mean that students in an integrated program may not have learned as much algebra in grade nine as students who took a full year of algebra during grade nine. If you were a tenth-grade mathematics teacher, this information would be very valuable to you in planning for the year.

Likewise, it is important to know what topics students will encounter in *subsequent* courses in your subject area so that you can help them develop an appropriate conceptual base for these topics. If you teach at the secondary level, it is also useful to try to find out what concepts and skills are tested on any state-mandated standardized test that students have to pass in order to graduate. If content that is likely to appear on an exit exam is part of your course of study, you will probably want to be sure that you cover it fully to help students prepare.

For examples of current state standards in different subject matter and grade levels, see Table 10.1. Complete listings of state standards are available at **http://www.education-world.com/standards.**

## Local Curriculum Guides

In addition to state guidelines, school districts often have curriculum guides that prescribe the course of study for a given course or a sequence of courses. These guides are generally based on the state standards, but they may also include local topics or make use of local features in the teaching of key concepts or skills. For example, a school located next to a wetlands area may make use of the setting to teach some key concepts in biology, chemistry, or environmental studies. School districts that are close to places of historical

## TABLE 10.1 Examples of Content Standards from Several States

### LANGUAGE ARTS

| Grade Level | |
|---|---|
| K–3 | Distinguish among different forms of texts (such as lists, newsletters, and signs) and the functions they serve. (Texas) |
| 2–5 | Use consonant blends, digraphs, and diphthongs to orally decode words. (Georgia) |
| 8 | Produce work in at least one literary genre that follows the conventions of the genre. (Pennsylvania) |
| 9–11 | Apply knowledge of Greek, Latin, and Anglo-Saxon roots and affixes to determine the meaning of unfamiliar vocabulary. (Kansas) |
| 9–12 | Identify strategies used by the media to present information for a variety of purposes (e.g., to inform, entertain, or persuade). (California) |

### MATHEMATICS

| Grade Level | |
|---|---|
| 2 | Use place value concepts to represent whole numbers using physical models, numerals, and words, with ones, tens, and hundreds. (Ohio) |
| 7 | The student will solve consumer application problems involving tips, discounts, sales tax, and simple interest, using whole numbers, fractions, decimals, and percents. (Virginia) |
| K–12 | All students will regularly and routinely use calculators, computers, manipulatives, and other mathematical tools to enhance mathematical thinking, understanding, and power. (New Jersey) |
| Advanced Placement Calculus | The student will use integration to solve problems. This will include areas bounded by polar curves, length of a path (including parametric curves), work (Hooke's law), and improper integrals. (Virginia) |

### SCIENCE

| Grade Level | |
|---|---|
| K–5 | All students will measure and describe the things around us, explain what the world around us is made of, identify and describe forms of energy, and explain how electricity and magnetism interact with matter. (Michigan) |
| 6–8 | Students will know how cells function as "building blocks" of organisms and describe the requirements for cells to live by stating how cells work together to keep the organism alive. (Illinois) |
| 9–12 | All students will analyze claims for their scientific merit and explain how scientists decide what constitutes scientific knowledge, how science is related to other ways of knowing, how science and technology affect our society, and how people of diverse cultures have contributed to and influenced developments in science. (Michigan) |
| 9–12 | The student will identify the independent variables, dependent variables, and controls in an experimental set-up. (Oklahoma) |

*Continued* ▶

▶ *Table 10.1 continued*

| SOCIAL STUDIES | |
|---|---|
| **Grade Level** | |
| 1–3 | Construct and interpret maps and other geographic tools, including the use of map elements to organize information about people, places, and environments. (Arizona) |
| 6–8 | Describe the social, economic, and political characteristics of Western European society that led to the exploration of the Americas. (Maryland) |
| 9–12 | Explain how the design of the U.S. Constitution is intended to balance and check the powers of the branches of government. (Connecticut) |

Source: Education World. Available at: **http://www.education-world.com/standards/**.

Visit this chapter of the Online Study Center to link to more examples of both national and state content standards.

significance may focus more of their social studies/history curriculum on personalities or episodes related to these historical events. Rural communities may have a greater emphasis on agricultural concepts than would an urban community, just as seaside communities may stress aquatic ecologies.

Local curriculum guides are often developed by a committee of teachers and administrators or by a group of community members. Regardless of who participated in their development, they have been approved by the local educational agency, such as the district school board, and must therefore be followed by teachers in the district. The district guides are as binding as the state frameworks, so it is important to become well-acquainted with them.

## School Expectations

Next, you will want to find out whether there are any school-specific practices or expectations that will affect your planning. Some schools may have implemented a common course of study for certain courses that requires the alignment of content, pacing, or even teaching activities. The high school, for example, may expect all students in ninth-grade English to read the same books in the same order. Biology classes may all take a common midterm exam

Teachers often work together to plan curricula and to coordinate teaching efforts.

or final exam, or both. The same may hold at the lower grades. All fifth-grade teachers might follow the same course of study in science, social studies, math, or reading. These expectations help schools to ensure equity in academic offerings and to avoid even the hint of preferential treatment for one group of students over another.

**Collaborative teaching** (co-teaching) two or more teachers working together to plan and deliver instruction to a group of students. Collaborative teaching often involves a regular education teacher working with a special education teacher to provide appropriate instruction to students with disabilities.

Another common practice at the school level is **collaborative teaching,** in which two or more teachers work together to help all of their students master the required content. Consult your department chair or a grade-level colleague before you begin the planning process to find out what the expectations for collaborative teaching are. Collaborative teaching is quite common when working with children with disabilities. A regular education teacher and a special education teacher may work together to ensure that students with disabilities get the attention they need. Some of these expectations may be based on past practices and may not exist in any written form. For example, the fifth-grade teachers may have established the practice of semi-departmentalizing instruction, so that one teacher teaches science to all three classes, another does social studies, and you, as the new teacher, may be expected to take over math instruction.

## Community Expectations

A fourth, but in no way lesser, consideration is community expectations about what students will be taught. This is often a complex constraint to consider, because there may not be consensus among community members on what they want the school to teach. Some community members may want controversial topics, such as intelligent design, taught, whereas other community members may be strongly opposed to the inclusion of these topics in the curriculum. A sector of the community may expect the school to offer their children a course of study that will help them gain acceptance to highly selective universities, whereas another sector may find the academic expectations that such a course places on their children too demanding.

As important as learning what the community expects you to teach is determining what the community expects you *not* to teach. These unspoken expectations are sometimes even more difficult to uncover until a teacher (and let's hope it is not you) violates one of them. A community uproar may be provoked when a teacher presents a lesson on tolerance for homosexuality or understanding of a different religion. Sometimes, seemingly innocuous topics or well-known pieces of literature, such as Mark Twain's *The Adventures of Huckleberry Finn,* can create an uncomfortable controversy within a community. Consider that among the authors most frequently challenged by libraries or schools in the past five years have been J. K. Rowling, author of the *Harry Potter* series, Toni Morrison, author of *Beloved,* and Judy Blume and Maurice Sendak, both of whom are best known as children's authors.[1] Other topics that can sometimes raise the community's ire include health lessons on sexually transmitted diseases or birth control.

Community expectations are, as we mentioned earlier, difficult to discern and adhere to. In addition, these expectations are often dynamic and shifting, sometimes rapidly. What was desirable one year may be disdained the next. Your best source of guidance will be veteran teachers, grade-level team leaders, or your department chair, who are likely to have a sense of community expectations for both what should be taught and what shouldn't.

## Available Resources

Yet another consideration in planning your course of study is available resources. As the opening scenario illustrated, your curricular decisions may be influenced by the books, computers, lab space, and other materials that are available for you to use.

***Print Resources*** A key question is what texts and supplemental materials your school has at its disposal, and in what quantity. In the opening scenario, Chris soon learned that his summer planning was premature, because many of the books that he wanted his students to read were not part of the school inventory and the book budget had been used up the previous spring. (It is not uncommon for public schools to place book orders for the fall before the end of the previous school year.) Had Chris been aware of these constraints on the school's resources, he would have been able to plan more efficiently.

Further, you will want to find out whether the existing print resources have already been "claimed" by veteran teachers. Returning teachers may have already decided what print materials they will be using and may have earmarked certain resources for a unit of study, a semester, or even the entire school year. Therefore, even though the school may have the resources that you need and would like to use, they may not be available for your use at all or may be available only at a particular time during the school year. In this case, you will need to rethink the sequence in which you will study these topics.

***Technology and Information Resources*** In addition to print resources, you will want to find out what other resources the school or district has, which are available for your use, and when they might be available. These would include resources such as computers, overhead projectors, TV/DVD players, and access to the school's and the community's library. You may have to plan a lesson or unit of study well in advance in order to secure use of certain resources, or if resources are not available, you may have to find alternative teaching activities to help students gain the requisite knowledge or skills. A teacher who wants all students to carry out extensive Internet research, for example, should be certain that all students can get access to Internet-linked computers for extended periods of time. Be sure to check details, such as whether or not filtering software is in place that would limit students' access to websites they need for research, and whether the movie you want to show is available on the same day as the TV or DVD player.

***Community Resources*** We encourage you to investigate community resources that you could use. A pharmaceutical research lab located nearby might offer students the opportunity to see practical applications of the sciences they are studying, or a foreign language center could provide students with a place to practice their developing language skills. When considering the use of community resources, be sure to familiarize yourself with the school's policy and practice on educational field trips or on any class meetings outside of the regularly scheduled class time and the school premises.

## Now You Do It

Visit the Education World website at **http://www.education-world.com/standards** and look up some of the content standards listed for the subject and grade level that you intend to teach in the state in which you will be teaching. Print out some of these standards. Then go to a different state, and compare and contrast the standards for the two states in the same subject and grade level. How similar or different are they? Is there anything there that surprises you?

# The Planning Process

You have familiarized yourself with all of the factors that you know will influence your plans. Now you can actually begin to plan for your courses. As we have pointed out, you will probably be responsible for teaching concepts and skills specified in the state curricular guides. The organization of these concepts and skills within the curriculum guides may be based on a structure that makes sense from a discipline perspective, but not from a teaching and learning perspective. One of your first tasks, therefore, may be to come up with a logical plan for teaching the requisite topics. We recommend that in developing your plan, you proceed from the general to the specific. Think first about your overall vision for your course or term. Next, plan the sequence in which you will present topics. Finally, decide on the pace at which you will move from topic to topic, keeping in mind that several factors can affect your progress, including unanticipated events such as snow days or illnesses, and the rate at which your students learn the material.

## Overall Purpose or Vision for the Course

From a holistic perspective, think about what your students are to take away from the term, semester, or year of study. No matter how expertly you teach, not all of your students are likely to master *all* of the content and skills that you will be teaching over the course. Identify the essential understandings that your students should have gained at the end of the course of study. What are the "big ideas" that are important for students to grasp and why are these big ideas important? Knowing the answers to these questions prepares you not only to teach your course, but also to provide an answer to your students' unending plaint, "Why do we have to learn this?"

Thinking about the "big ideas" of your course can also help you to situate the course you are teaching along a continuum of studies in the particular subject matter, or even among the different courses that your students are likely to be taking at the same time. For instance, a science teacher who wants her students to perform statistical analyses of data collected would need to know what data analysis concepts her students have already learned. An English teacher can help his students get a better sense of a piece of American literature if he knows what the students have learned in their history course about the time period in which the work was written.

## Topics and Their Sequence

Having a vision for the course(s) you will teach can be useful in helping you determine what topics you will include in your plan for the course, and in what order you will present these topics. As we have noted often, state or district curriculum guides may specify concepts or skills, but, depending on the subject, there still may be quite a bit of leeway in planning the actual topics that you will have students learn about as they are mastering the required material.

The first step is to make a list of topics that you consider essential and important for the course you are to teach. Base this list on the purpose of the course and your vision for it. At the same time, read the relevant state standards or objectives carefully, and make a second list of the standards and objective you need to address during the academic year. (You might also want to list the standards that were addressed in the previous course and those that will be addressed in the next course.) Now look at your two lists. Try to find points of intersection between topics and concepts. Determine how—and how well—you can integrate the state standards into the list of topics that you have developed.

Consider, for example, a Spanish teacher who believes it is important for his students to learn about *Día de los Muertos,* the Day of the Dead, celebrated in many Spanish-speaking countries. He looks through the state curriculum guide and finds a number of relevant objectives that would allow for the inclusion of this important Mexican celebration. The guidelines specify, for example, that students "explain the cultural significance of traditions and celebrations in the target culture" and that they "access and describe local and national activities of the target culture." Another objective requiring students to recognize "information from authentic materials" can be met by having students read newspaper accounts about the Day of the Dead.

Once you have a list of topics, you will need to think about the order in which students will study these topics. Some disciplines, such as history, foreign languages, and mathematics, may have a fairly natural (but not necessarily fixed) sequence of topics to study, but others, such as English and the natural sciences, may not. To help you decide on a logical sequencing of topics, you may wish to consult sources such as the following:

- *Colleagues.* Take advantage of the collective years of experience of your department or grade-level colleagues. Ask them for feedback as you think through different options for sequencing topics. They may see connections, considerations, or constraints that you do not.
- *Textbooks.* Look at the sequencing of topics in several different textbooks, if possible. Analyze any similarities and differences you find. Ask yourself why the topics are presented in this particular order. See whether you can determine what principle of organization was used when the textbook was developed.

Armed with the information you gathered from these sources, consider the topics on your list once again. Analyze each topic in terms of the prerequisite skills and knowledge that students need in order to benefit from instruction. Think about the level, familiarity, and complexity of the topics on your list. Learning theory suggests that learning is more effective when new information can be linked to existing knowledge. Learners should also progress through increasing levels of complexity as they master concepts, beginning with recognition and comprehension, then moving on to analyzing or applying the ideas they have learned.

We encourage careful deliberation when deciding on the order of topics and recommend that you share your thoughts with at least one colleague who teaches the same subject or grade level. You want to be able to justify your course of study to your department chairs, to administrators, and even to parents, if need be.

## Pacing

In August, the end of the school year may seem very far away: ten whole months! In reality, though, students in most places in the United States attend school for 180 days. That means you will have *at most* 180 class periods (middle school and high school teachers) or 180 days (elementary school teachers) to cover essential content. Making allowances for chapter and unit tests, midterm and final exams, state-mandated testing, special school programs, unexpected events, and weather-related school closings, you can count on maybe 150 to 160 days or class meetings to teach all of the topics you have identified as being important. Thus you must use your allotted time wisely.

> **Video Case**
>
> In the video case, *Reading in the Content Areas: An Interdisciplinary Unit on the 1920s*, you'll see how two high school teachers join forces to create a unit focused on the "Roaring 20s." You'll also hear students' reflections on how this interdisciplinary approach has increased their learning in both language arts and social studies. As you watch the clips and study the artifacts in the case, reflect on the following questions.
>
> **QUESTIONS**
>
> 1. How do the comments of the students (in the main video) and of the social studies teacher (in the bonus videos) reflect the benefits of interdisciplinary instruction described on the next page? Do they note any further benefits? Are there any that *you* would add?
> 2. What evidence do you see of the planning process that these two teachers must have employed to develop this cooperative lesson on *The Great Gatsby*?
>
> ***Online Study Center***

Now you are ready to look at your list of topics and decide how much time you will need to spend on each one. Think again about the levels of familiarity and complexity of the topics on your list. Mark those concepts that you expect to be more challenging for students to grasp. Maximize the time you plan to spend on those topics. Then mark those concepts that you think may be more familiar to students or easier to grasp. Estimate how much time you will need to spend on these topics. As you allocate time to each topic, think also about logical breaks for exams, especially if you need to give midterm and final exams in the course.

The next step is to break each topic into subtopics and allot time to each subtopic. Be sure to plan time not just for instructional activities but for assessment as well. Continue breaking down the topics until you get to a daily plan. Keep in mind that your pacing plan is tentative and approximate. Factors that may affect your pacing include the achievement levels of your learners, the types of instructional activities you want to conduct, and, of course, unexpected events. Unexpected though they may be, we urge you to plan for some "surprises" by allowing some room for adjustments in your schedule.

***Level of Learners*** Your selection of topics and your pacing plan will have to be reviewed and revised as you get to know the interests and abilities of your students. In some instances, your planning will have been overambitious, and you will have to expand the time allotments. You may even need to eliminate some subtopics and fold others together to focus on the most essential concepts. In other instances, you will find that your students grasp concepts more quickly than anticipated and that what you expected to take, say, two weeks takes under a week.

***Instructional Activities*** Although an interactive lesson in which students actively engage with content can be a most effective learning activity, it is often not very time-efficient. This kind of lesson may require two or even three class periods to complete, compared to the single class period that would suffice if the same material were covered via a teacher lecture or teacher-led discussion. Similarly, expect that learning will occur at a slower pace when students work in groups. To save yourself some frustration, plan more time than you initially expect for interactive instructional activities.

***The Unexpected*** Think about what might possibly go wrong with a lesson, and then plan what you will do if it happens. Imagine your ideal lessons, and develop plans to ensure the perfect execution of these lessons. But at the same

time, imagine stumbling blocks that could impede the progress of the lesson and plan for alternative activities.

A major key to good planning is flexibility. Plan extensively, but do not be *too* wedded to your plan. You need to be willing to adjust your plans as the situation warrants.

## Now You Do It

Referring to the state curriculum guide that you will use in your position, propose a sequence of topics for a year of study. Be sure you can explain the rationale for the sequence you propose. Think about the purpose of each topic you include. Explain the importance of the topic to your students' subject matter knowledge.

# Interdisciplinary Planning

**Interdisciplinary teaching** integrating the subject matter from two or more subject areas, such as English and history, often by using themes such as inventions, discoveries, or health.

In some schools, teachers at certain grade levels may work in **interdisciplinary teams** and may be expected to plan their curricula in concert with one another and to align their topics of study to complement topics in other disciplines. Some schools adopt an organizing theme or focus for a particular grade or period of time and expect teams of teachers to organize their courses of study around that theme. For example, a middle school might

## In Your Classroom

### Steps in Planning Interdisciplinary Instruction

1. *Develop an organizing theme or vision for the course of study.* In the same way that we urge you to have a vision for your individual course, we urge the similar development of a vision for the interdisciplinary study.
2. *Decide which content subject will serve as the primary content base.* For some themes, the content base is more obvious than for others. In the example of civil rights, the most logical primary content base is social studies. For other themes, such as environmental studies, the primary content base could be science.
3. *As a team, brainstorm topics, within each of the disciplines, that are related to the primary content base in a meaningful way.* The brainstorming sessions may help you discover connections that are not immediately obvious. You may want to start with the table of contents of discipline-specific textbooks and then expand on these topics. Draw also on the collective expertise, experiences, and interests of the educators on your team.
4. *Identify the points of intersection among the disciplines.* Consider the list of topics that the team formulated during your brainstorming session(s), and identify concepts and skills in each content area that are related to or complement these topics. These points of intersection should be highlighted often to help students recognize the interconnections among these topics.
5. *Coordinate Teaching Plans.* In order for students to grasp the interrelatedness of the disciplines, they need to learn these interconnected concepts at the same time. Thus the coordination of instruction is essential. The team should develop a pacing plan to which all team members agree.

adopt civil rights as an organizing theme for its eighth-grade students. Teams of teachers, consisting of an English and social studies teacher, would plan a course of study with civil rights as the organizing theme. The English teacher might have students read biographies of civil rights leaders in the United States or other countries, or study the writings of these leaders, and the social studies teacher might have students study civil rights movements in the United States or other countries.

Educators often praise the benefits of interdisciplinary learning. Students are able to see the interconnectedness of concepts and skills from the perspective of different subjects, and teachers have an opportunity to work more closely and productively with one another. At the same time, the planning of interdisciplinary instruction presents a host of challenges. As multifaceted as planning for your own course is, coordinating the planning of different subject areas with one or more of your colleagues is even more complex. The "In Your Classroom" feature offers a set of steps to help with this planning.

Veteran teachers often do not seem to do any planning at all, and less experienced teachers may be tempted to think that teaching requires little or no planning. But things are not always what they seem. Indeed, most veteran teachers are *constantly* planning their next class, their next week, month, and unit, even if they do not write down their plans. They are constantly adding to a reservoir of ideas that they have already used. We encourage less experienced teachers to follow their example and integrate planning into their daily reflections. We remind you, too, that not every teacher has the ability to remember plans without writing them down. We suggest that you develop a process for planning both short- and long-term courses of study, and that you commit your plans to writing until you determine how much you can remember without written reminders. Furthermore, many school principals require probationary teachers to submit written lesson plans on a weekly basis.

## Further Resources

- Richard I. Arends, *Learning to Teach* (New York: McGraw-Hill Higher Education, 2004). A good general guide and reference book. See especially Chapter 3 on planning.

- Education World. Available at: **www.education-world.com.** This site contains links to state content standards and lesson plans.
- Greta Morine-Dershimer, "Instructional Planning," in James M. Cooper (Ed.), *Classroom Teaching Skills,* 8th ed. (Boston: Houghton Mifflin, 2006). A good chapter on effective short- and long-range planning.

- *New York Times.* Available at: **www.nytimes.com/learning/teachers/index.html.** The *New York Times* creates daily lesson plans based on current events for a variety of grades and subject matter. The website also identifies academic content standards that each lesson addresses.

MODULE 10 Planning What to Teach

# Module 11

# Planning Lessons

**Scenario**

"What am I going to do? That lesson was awful! And I have three more classes that are supposed to do the same activity. I don't understand! In Ms. Johanssen's classroom, this lesson would have gone perfectly." On the verge of tears, Angie was trying to recover for a disastrous first class as a new teacher at Macomber Middle School.

During her student teaching last spring, Angie had worked with Ms. Johanssen, and now she was hoping to implement the same approach Ms. Johanssen had used for teaching science to middle schoolers. Ms. Johanssen would have students do an "exploration," during which they made careful observations. After the exploration, each team of students would have five minutes to talk about their observations and formulate some hypotheses about the science involved. Finally, Ms. Johanssen would lead a discussion, during which students would share their observations, conclusions, and emerging hypotheses.

Angie remembered being constantly amazed at how engaged the students were in each lesson, and how excited they had been when they found that their hypotheses were valid. The class discussions were so lively that Ms. Johanssen hardly had to say anything. That was the easiest part of the lesson, Angie remembered thinking. The discussion practically ran itself.

The most challenging part was deciding which student to call on next, because all of them wanted to share their thoughts. "I can't wait to get my students doing these kinds of activities," Angie had said to herself.

Angie had decided to do a classification that she had seen in Ms. Johanssen's class. The class, as a whole, would make of list of the different shoes the students were wearing. Each group would have the task of sorting the shoes into categories, then sub-categories, then sub-sub-categories. Once each group had decided on these categories, its next task was to describe the characteristics of the categories and sub-categories.

But nothing had gone as she had planned or imagined. The problems began with the groups. Angie had planned on just four groups of students, but she ended up having to make five groups, so she did not have enough handouts and had to take time to make another set. Then, the students in the first class did not understand what Angie wanted them to do, and she had to explain it three times. Ultimately, she wrote the task on the board so the students could remember what to do.

Once the students finally got started on the exploration, they seemed pretty interested. But Angie had to spend so much time getting them started that they didn't have much time for the exploration.

The discussion—the part Angie was most looking forward to—was the biggest disappointment of all. Students had no ideas, drew no conclusions, and came up with no hypotheses. The only comments they offered were about what groups of shoes they made. The last five minutes of the class were the most painful to relive. Angie did not know what questions to ask, so she kept asking the same ones over and over.

Angie thought back on the different comments Ms. Johanssen would make about planning out the details of the lesson. "Maybe this is what Ms. Johanssen was talking about when she kept telling me to write down the questions I wanted to ask. I just thought she was telling me that because that's what the university kept telling us." Maybe not, though. She was beginning to understand what Ms. Johanssen was talking about. Well, at least I've got the next forty minutes to get ready for my next class and avoid a second disaster today," she thought to herself, as she sat down to write out some questions.

**Preview**

As Angie found out the hard way, lesson planning is an essential part of your work as a teacher. Being prepared and organized is a new teacher's best attribute. Many of the problems that occur in classrooms arise because teachers haven't adequately planned lessons and activities. Planning well also communicates caring to students. They take disorganization as a sign that the teacher either is incompetent or doesn't care enough to prepare for class. In either case, this is a situation you can easily avoid by thoughtful planning.

Like Angie, you may think that writing lesson plans is more of an academic task rather than one that will be useful to you as a teacher. You may even have had the opportunity to work with veteran teachers who did not seem to write or use lesson plans. In fact, most veteran teachers plan their lessons in great detail, although they may or may not write them out. They usually plan the details of the lesson in their minds, including the questions they want to ask and the time they want to spend on each phase of the lesson. Some principals, however, require all teachers to hand in lesson plans each week so that the plans can be examined to ensure that state standards are being addressed.

Making a good lesson plan helps you determine and remember exactly what you want to accomplish in a given lesson and how you intend to accomplish it. It identifies what students will be learning or practicing during the lesson, and it specifies ways to know whether students have in fact learned the targeted concepts or skills. It can also chronicle what students have (or should have) learned and what they will (or should be able to) master next.

Numerous formats exist, but most lesson plans contain, at a minimum, learning goals or objectives of the lesson and the procedure to be followed to help students meet these learning objectives. In their most detailed form, lesson plans

- **Specify what students are expected to know and what they will learn from the proposed learning activities.**
- **List the state standards that the lesson addresses.**
- **Describe the materials needed for the lesson.**
- **Provide a step-by-step outline for the teaching and learning activities to be carried out.**
- **Propose enrichment, extension, or re-teaching activities for the exceptional students.**
- **Tell how students will be assessed.**

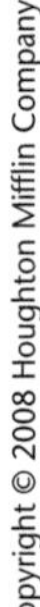

This module will explain how to create each of these elements of a detailed lesson plan. You can also view several examples of complete lesson plans at your Online Student Center.

**This module emphasizes that:**

- **There are basic parts of a lesson plan that need to be addressed, including an overview, lesson objectives, state standards addressed, materials needed, planned activities, enrichment or extension activities, closings, and assessment procedures.**
- **Lessons should include opportunities for student cognitive development at different levels of complexity.**

## Now You Do It

Analyze Angie's first class. What do you think led to the problems she encountered? What can she do *before* her next class to avoid a recurrence of the same problems? What can she do *during* the class to make the lesson more productive?

# Lesson Plan Overview

The overview portion of a lesson plan provides a brief synopsis of the lesson. It describes the principal learning activity of the lesson, as well as the phases of the learning activity. It may also present the purpose and the assessment for the lesson. Writing the overview is a useful way to check that the activity planned is clear in your mind and that it does indeed match the purpose you have identified. Table 11.1 gives examples of lesson overviews.

**TABLE 11.1 Examples of Lesson Overviews**

| Subject and Grade Level | Lesson Overview |
|---|---|
| Social studies—middle school | Students will research inventions by African American inventors. They will first complete a graphic organizer about the inventors and the inventions with a partner. Next, each student will choose one invention to research. Each student will be expected to write a minimum of one page about the effect the invention had on people's lives. |
| Science—high school | Students will see Newton's First Law of Motion in action. They will carry out prescribed activities and will make careful and detailed observations of the results of the activities. As a class, students will make inferences about their observations and will relate them to Newton's First Law. |

# Learning Goals and Objectives

**Learning goal** a broad statement of what students will know or be able to do as a result of engaging in the learning activities being proposed.

**Learning objective** a narrow, specific statement identifying discrete behaviors that students will be expected to demonstrate as evidence of their mastery of particular concepts or skills.

A **learning goal** is a broad statement of what students will know or be able to do as a result of engaging in the learning activities being proposed. A **learning objective** is a narrower, more specific statement identifying discrete behaviors that students will be expected to demonstrate as evidence of their mastery of particular concepts or skills. Learning objectives are useful because they provide direction for the teacher and, if communicated to them, for students as well. By articulating learning objectives, teachers can be clear about what they expect of the students at the beginning of the lesson. Learning objectives also provide the basis for evaluating student learning.

The problem, though, for most of us is that when we think of broad goals such as learning about African American inventors or about motion and then try to narrow those broad goals down to learning objectives, the issue gets complex and confusing. There are so many possible objectives, so much to learn even about these limited goals. What is needed is a framework to sort out the numerous possibilities, a tool to guide our building of the lesson plan. Luckily, there is help here.

## Bloom's Taxonomy

**Bloom's taxonomy** a classification of educational objectives in the cognitive domain, including knowledge, comprehension, application, analysis, synthesis, and evaluation. Other taxonomies exist in the affective and psychomotor domains.

In the 1950s, a group of educators and educational psychologists headed by Benjamin Bloom developed a way to classify objectives that are often the goals of education. His classification system, which is known as **Bloom's taxonomy,** is still popular today as a basis for developing learning objectives. (A taxonomy is an orderly classification of phenomena in terms of their presumed relationships to one another.)

Bloom and his colleagues began by identifying three areas or domains of educational activity:[1]

- *cognitive:* intellectual activities
- *affective:* socio-emotional states and activities
- *psychomotor:* manual and physical dexterity skills

Their plan was to develop a taxonomy for each of these three domains. They started with the cognitive domain and developed a taxonomy in 1956. The taxonomy for the cognitive domain consists of six levels of thinking. From the simplest to the most complex, these six levels are *knowledge, comprehension, application, analysis, synthesis,* and *evaluation.* For each of these six levels, Bloom and his colleagues described what "competence" would entail and proposed a list of behaviors that would constitute evidence of competence. The levels and behaviors are summarized in Table 11.2.

As an example, a student competent in a given area at the comprehension level in mathematics can translate or interpret material from one form to another, such as from a word problem to a graph, and can estimate future trends. For evidence of competence at this level, a teacher might ask students to predict a subsequent event, such as the next point on a graph.

The affective domain, published in 1964, has five levels: *receiving, responding, valuing, organizing,* and *characterization.* The psychomotor domain was developed by Simpson in 1972 and has seven levels: *perception, set, guided response, mechanism, complex or overt response, adaptation,* and *origination.* These

## TABLE 11.2 Bloom's Taxonomy of Cognitive Objectives

| Level | Definition | Key Words | Examples |
|---|---|---|---|
| Knowledge | The ability to remember previously learned material | Arrange, define, duplicate, label, list, memorize, name, order, recall, recognize, relate, repeat, state | Know common terms, know specific facts, know basic concepts |
| Comprehension | The ability to grasp the meaning of material | Classify, describe, discuss, explain, express, identify, indicate, locate, recognize, report, restate, review, select, translate | Understand facts and principles, interpret charts and graphs |
| Application | The ability to use learned material in new and concrete situations | Apply, choose, demonstrate, dramatize, employ, illustrate, interpret, operate, practice, schedule, sketch, solve, use, write | Apply concepts and principles to new situations, apply laws and theories to practical situations, solve mathematical problems |
| Analysis | The ability to break down material into its component parts so that its organizational structure may be understood | Analyze, appraise, calculate, categorize, compare, contrast, criticize, differentiate, discriminate, distinguish, examine, experiment, question, test | Recognize unstated assumptions, recognize logical fallacies in reasoning, distinguish between facts and inferences, analyze the organizational structure of a work |
| Synthesis | The ability to put parts together to form a new whole | Arrange, assemble, collect, compose, construct, create, design, develop, formulate, manage, organize, plan, prepare, propose, set up, write | Write a well-organized theme, integrate learning from different areas into a plan for solving a problem, formulate a new scheme for classifying objects |
| Evaluation | The ability to judge the value of material (such as a statement, novel, poem, or research report) for a given purpose | Appraise, argue, assess, attach, choose, compare, contrast, defend, estimate, evaluate, judge, predict, rate, select, support, value | Judge the adequacy with which conclusions are supported by data, judge the value of a work (art, music, or writing) by using external standards of excellence |

Source: Adapted from Benjamin S. Bloom and David R. Krathwohl, *Taxonomy of Educational Objectives: The Classification of Educational Goals, by a Committee of College and University Examiners, Book 1*. Published by Allyn and Bacon, Boston, MA. Copyright © 1984 by Pearson Education. Reprinted by permission of the publisher.

two domains are used less often than the cognitive domain in preparing learning objectives, especially in the upper grades. Primary school teachers may, however, want to take these domains into account in their lesson preparation.

Bloom's taxonomy is useful to keep in mind when writing learning objectives for lessons. Teachers should structure learning activities so that initial activities in a new concept or skill require lower-level thinking and later activities require more complex thinking. At the beginning of a new unit of study, students may be expected to meet objectives that are at the knowledge or comprehension levels. Then, as they become more competent with the concepts and skills in the unit, they can be expected to perform activities at the application or analysis level. Your task as a teacher is to ensure the learning activities and lessons you plan allow for and facilitate this cognitive growth.

In a high school biology class studying photosynthesis, for example, the following tasks require students to think at different levels of Bloom's taxonomy.

- *Knowledge level.* Ask students to define photosynthesis and to list the reactants and products of the process.
- *Comprehension level.* Have students explain, in their own words, each step of the process.
- *Application level.* Ask students to illustrate what happens to water molecules in the photosynthetic process.
- *Analysis level.* Require students to break down the process into its component parts. Students could be expected to compare and contrast photosynthesis and plant respiration.
- *Synthesis level.* Require that students design or create. A sample task might be to illustrate the interrelationship between producers and consumers to explain why photosynthesis is essential to consumers, such as humans.
- *Evaluation level.* Have students assess the impact that increased levels of carbon dioxide in the atmosphere could have on plant life.

At the elementary school level, a teacher whose class was studying the solar system might assign the following tasks to address the levels of Bloom's taxonomy.

- *Knowledge level.* Require students to name the planets in order of increasing distance from the sun.
- *Comprehension level.* Show the students pictures of the planets and ask them to name the planets.
- *Application level.* Require students to create a model of a particular planet.
- *Analysis level.* Have students decide which planets are most apt to be warmer or colder.
- *Synthesis level.* Ask students to write a short story imagining what kind of creatures might live on each of the planets.
- *Evaluation level.* Students could debate which planets might be most hospitable for human colonization.

## Writing Learning Objectives

Robert Mager was one of the pioneers of instructional or learning objectives in the early 1960s.[2] Basing his thinking firmly in behaviorist learning theory (described in Module 6, Key Principles of Learning), Mager insisted that these objectives must be *observable* and *measurable*. He identified three essential elements of the learning objective:

1. *The observable act or behavior*—that is, what students will do to show that they have acquired the requisite knowledge or skill.
2. *The conditions* under which the act is to occur—that is, the material and resources available to students to carry out the task, and any time constraints placed on completing the activity.
3. *The criteria* that define an acceptable level of performance.

Table 11.3 gives some examples of learning objectives that contain these three elements.

## TABLE 11.3 Examples of Learning Objectives

| Objective | Conditions | Behavior | Criteria |
|---|---|---|---|
| Given a map of the United States, students will label the fifty states with 90 percent accuracy. | Given a map of the United States, | students will label the fifty states | with 90 percent accuracy |
| Given five music clips, students will correctly identify the music genre of each clip. | Given five music clips, | students will correctly identify the music genre | of each clip |
| Students will identify correctly the ingredients in a mixture of chemicals prepared in advance by the teacher. | Given a mixture of chemicals prepared by the teacher, | students will identify ingredients | correctly |

The key to learning objectives, as Mager envisioned them, is the verb used to describe the behavior students are expected to perform. The verb, Mager insisted, is an *action* verb describing behaviors. Selecting the appropriate verb for learning objectives is one of the challenges of writing them. The verb needs to indicate observable and measurable behavior that shows a student has internalized the concept or skill well. The verbs presented in Table 11.2, showing Bloom's taxonomy, are good examples of appropriate action verbs to use in learning objectives.

Learning objectives are student-focused and outcomes-oriented. They describe what students will know or be able to do after engaging in the lesson. They do *not* describe what students or the teacher will do during the lesson; that information may be found in the overview of the lesson. The focus on outcomes is important because learning objectives form the basis for assessing student learning, which is described later in this module and in detail in Module 15, Assessment for Learning, and Module 16, Tools for Assessment.

### Now You Do It

Write one learning objective for the lesson that Angie, the teacher described at the beginning of the chapter, was planning. Be sure your learning objective has the three criteria specified by Mager, and decide which level of Bloom's taxonomy is reflected in the objective. Now try writing a learning objective for your own subject and grade level.

## State Standards in Your Lesson Plans

In Module 10, Planning What to Teach, we discussed the importance of using state curriculum guides or standards as a foundation for your planning. With heightened levels of accountability and increased pressure on schools to ensure that students pass state-mandated tests, teachers are being scrutinized ever more closely to ensure that the curriculum they teach includes the concepts and skills that students are expected to know when they take their yearly tests.

One way of showing school administrators and parents that your curriculum is carefully aligned with the state standards or benchmarks is to identify the standards addressed in any given lesson. This is also a useful way for you to keep track of the standards that have been covered and of those that still need to be addressed.

## Materials Planning

Think about what you will need to carry out the planned learning activities—that is, materials beyond what is commonplace in the classroom (handouts, texts, paper, pens or pencils, chalk, graphing calculators or rulers in math class, and so on). Listing these materials in your lesson plan can help you get organized for the lesson. Angie, for example, might have used her class lists to determine how many handouts she would need and thus have saved herself some time.

This is especially important for technology-related materials. Some schools have a limited number of TVs/VCRs/DVDs or tape recorders, and teachers sign up for them in advance. If the planned learning activity involves audio or video recordings, for example, having listed these materials can remind you to get the appropriate technology to play the recording. If you plan to use the computers in a computer lab, you will need to schedule this activity well in advance. You want to be sure you have the equipment you will require to carry out your lesson when planned and as planned.

## Procedure

This is the nitty-gritty of the lesson plan: what exactly you will do, and what you will have the students do, during the time that you are responsible for their learning on any given day. There are at least three distinct parts to think about: the beginning, the middle, and the end of the lesson. As we consider these different parts of the lesson, ask yourself questions such as these:

- How will you introduce the ideas and objectives of this lesson?
- How will you get students' attention and motivate them in order to hold their attention?
- How can you tie lesson objectives in with student interests and past classroom activities?
- What will be expected of students and how will you communicate this to them?

### The Beginning: Getting Students Focused and Engaged

**Anticipatory set** an activity that focuses the students' attention for the instruction that will follow.

Often overlooked in both the planning and implementation stages, the opening of the lesson is an essential first step in getting students ready to learn. These beginnings are sometimes referred to as **anticipatory sets.** The anticipatory set conveys to students the usefulness and excitement of the concepts they are being taught. Its explicit purpose has two dimensions, the cognitive and the affective.

- *Cognitive.* To get students thinking about the focus of the lesson. Students at nearly all grade levels are presented with information in four to seven subject areas on any given day. For many students, the shift from one subject to another requires some cognitive processing. After all, how many of us can make a seamless transition from trigonometric ratios to anaerobic respiration to the Treaty of Versailles in the course of a morning?

  Thus, before engaging students in the learning activity, you should help them shift their cognitive processes to the requisite discipline, be it mathematics, science, history, or foreign languages. Specifically, help students recall key concepts and skills that they will need for the planned learning activity. For some lessons, you will want to review the content of the previous lesson. For others, you will want to remind students of previously studied topics that are prerequisite for or related to the focus of the day's lesson.

- *Affective.* To get students interested in the learning they will undertake. Out of school, students exist in a media-dense world of advertising and entertainment, where some extremely creative minds vie for their attention. As a result, educators are forced to compete. Research tells us that we remember better what we are interested in learning and want to learn.[3] Sparking students' interest can thus make learning more effective and comprehensive. One way to spark students' interest is to show them the relevance of the concepts or skills they are about to learn.

Table 11.4 offers some sample lesson openings. Also visit the video case to see one teacher opening a lesson.

## TABLE 11.4 Examples of Lesson Openings

| Subject and Grade Level | Lesson Overview |
|---|---|
| Eleventh-grade American history | Show a few segments of the video *Pearl Harbor*. Encourage students to imagine what it was like when the military base at Pearl Harbor was surprised by the Japanese attack. After viewing the segments of the video, have students write in their journals for five minutes about how they would have felt if they had been at Pearl Harbor on that day. |
| Fourth-grade science | Ask students to flex their arms by bending their lower arms up from the elbow. Then have them extend their arms by raising their arms straight above their heads. Make sure students understand the terms *flex* and *extend*. As they do so, have them observe their arms closely. Ask what they notice as they flex and extend their arms. Ask students whether they know which muscles they use to perform each action. If they are unfamiliar with the terms *biceps* (flex) and *triceps* (extend), introduce the terms now. Ask students to vote on whether the following statement is true: "Most people's biceps are stronger than their triceps." |
| Eleventh-grade statistics (mathematics) | Present the following problem: Imagine that you are about to board an airplane. You find out that the plane is a Boeing 737, with 162 seats in coach. That means there are 27 rows with 6 seats in each row, 3 on either side of the aisle. Your seat is 12D, an aisle seat about halfway back. As you wait to board, you look around the gate area to see who else will be on your plane. In the crowd, you notice 5 very young and crying children traveling with one parent, 2 very large men, and 3 young people about your age. How likely is it that you will be seated next to or in the same row as any one of these groups? What is the mathematical probability? |

## Video Case

In the video case, *Classroom Motivation: Strategies for Engaging Students,* seventh-grade teacher Josh Baker shares his main strategy for motivating students, which is to engage students by drawing on important aspects of their lives and relating them to the curriculum. Teaching a lesson on Rosa Parks, he connects it to a larger unit on civil rights. As you watch the clips and study the artifacts in the case, reflect on the following questions.

**QUESTIONS**

1. What does Josh do at the beginning to capture students' attention and engage them in the lesson?
2. What evidence do you see that the students are engaged?
3. How might you have begun this lesson differently?

## The Middle: The Learning Activity

This is the main event of the lesson, where the learning objectives are addressed and, with luck and good planning, met. The activity may range from a lecture to a discussion to a small-group activity to a long-term research project. (See Module 12, How to Teach, for different types of learning activities.) Whatever activity you plan, you want to be sure that it does, in fact, help students achieve the learning objective that you set. Ask yourself, "How does this learning activity help students master the concept/skill of the lesson?" Table 11.5 is an example of a learning activity from a lesson plan.

Writing your lesson plan can help you clarify and specify exactly what will take place during the minutes that you have with the students. Knowing what will take place can help you determine what materials and resources you will need, as well as what time allotments you should make. The better you plan before the lesson, the more smoothly the lesson will go.

We strongly recommend that during your first few years of teaching, you prepare detailed plans for learning activities, including such specific organizational details as those described in the "In Your Classroom" feature. This may seem like an overly tedious task, but it is an extremely important and useful one. The act of planning in such detail brings to light other details that may need to be addressed for the lesson to be effectively implemented. For example, Angie, the teacher in the opening scenario, would probably have been less disappointed with her class discussion if she had written out, in advance, the questions she needed to ask. The more thoroughly you plan lessons, the easier it will be for you to anticipate areas of concern. Eventually, you may be able to do most of your planning mentally, as do many of your experienced colleagues.

That being said, the detailed plan that you develop should not be seen as an intractable script that must be adhered to at all costs. It is, as we have noted, a *plan*, and like all plans, it is subject to change. Circumstances may arise that require you to alter or even abandon your plans in favor of something else. Still, those events are more the exception than the rule, and a well-thought-out and detailed plan will make your lessons flow much more smoothly, allowing for optimal student learning.

### TABLE 11.5 Example of a Learning Activity Plan

Have students attach the garden hose to a tap and adjust the flow of water to a constant pressure. Starting at an angle of 0 degrees to the ground, measure and record the distance the stream travels in the horizontal direction along the ground. Repeat this process at 20, 30, 45, 60, and 75 degrees.

**Questions**

1. Which angle allowed you to achieve the maximum distance?
2. Can you think of a method to determine the maximum height the water achieved at the optimum angle? Briefly describe your method.
3. Draw the approximate path that the water followed in its flight. What is the shape of the path?
4. If you were to increase the pressure on the water in the hose, what effect would it have on the angle you would use to achieve maximum distance at the new pressure?
5. Do you think that, in order to achieve maximum distance, a shot put or a javelin would need to be thrown at some angle different from that at which the water was projected? Why or why not?

## In Your Classroom

### Don't Forget the Details

As you write lesson plans, pay particular attention to organizational details such as the following:

- If you are planning to have students work in groups, be sure you have decided how the groups will be formed, who will decide on the makeup of the groups, where the groups will be located, how the groups will function, and what task(s) the groups will carry out.
- If you anticipate a class discussion on a topic, think carefully about the key points you want students to get out of the discussion and the questions you will need to ask to ensure that these points are brought to light.
- If the day's activity consists of students working independently on a project, anticipate what materials and resources students will need, where they will work on the project, and how to respond to students who are not prepared to work on the project.
- If the lesson is a demonstration or lecture, think about materials, such as graphic organizers, that can make it easier for students to be engaged and to stay "on task."

### Closing

As important as the opening is the closing, or wrap-up, of the lesson. The closing of the lesson gives you an opportunity to reinforce for students the key concepts or skills addressed in that day's lesson. It can make explicit the new knowledge that students were expected to gain from the learning activity. One typical activity in the closing is revisiting the question or situation presented in the opening. Another is asking students to make a "3-2-1 list": a list of three things they did during the lesson, two things they learned, and one thing they want to know more about. The closing is also a good time to present homework assignments that can reinforce and extend the learning of the lesson.

Too often, teachers lose track of the time and must hastily close the lesson as the school bell rings and students are stampeding toward the door. Be aware of time as the lesson unfolds so that you will have enough time for a good closing.

## Assessment

As you plan your lesson, think carefully about how you will assess student learning. Remember that one of your first tasks when writing a lesson plan is to identify learning objectives. The purpose of the lesson is to help students achieve the learning objectives that you set. In order to know whether the students met the learning objectives, you have to provide some sort of assessment activity. The assessment may not necessarily be a formal exercise or activity; it may in some cases be based on informal observations of individual or group work. In all cases, you want to ask yourself questions such as "How will I know that the students have met the learning objectives I've set?" or "What can students do to show that they have met the learning objectives?" Module 15, Assessment for Learning, and Module 16, Tools for Assessment, offer more information and guidelines on assessing student learning.

# Extensions/Differentiations

In most cases, the learning activities you plan are designed for the "average" student in your classroom. When they plan lessons with this average student in mind, most teachers feel confident that a majority of the students in the class will be able to complete the learning activities and achieve the learning objective set. Still, in most groups of students, there will be some whose academic abilities or cognitive processes are substantially less developed or notably more developed than those of the majority of the students. Some students will be over-challenged by the lesson planned, whereas others will be under-challenged and bored by it. And often, students at either of these extremes—lost in the lesson *or* bored by it—become disruptive. Therefore, it is doubly important to consider them in planning.

To ensure that *all* students benefit from instruction, and to minimize the potential for disruption to the lesson, plan ahead for modification to the learning activities to help those students whose abilities differ from average.

- Design extension activities for those students who are able to complete the planned activity more quickly than the other students.
- Prepare modifications of the activity for students who work more slowly or whose prerequisite skills are less developed.
- Think also about adaptations to the activity for students whose command of the English language or of American school culture is tentative. For example, you might want to use a parent or a teacher's aide to translate materials or give oral directions to English language learners.

The more you can anticipate before the lesson, the more likely it is that the lesson will go smoothly and that all students will achieve the learning objectives you have set.

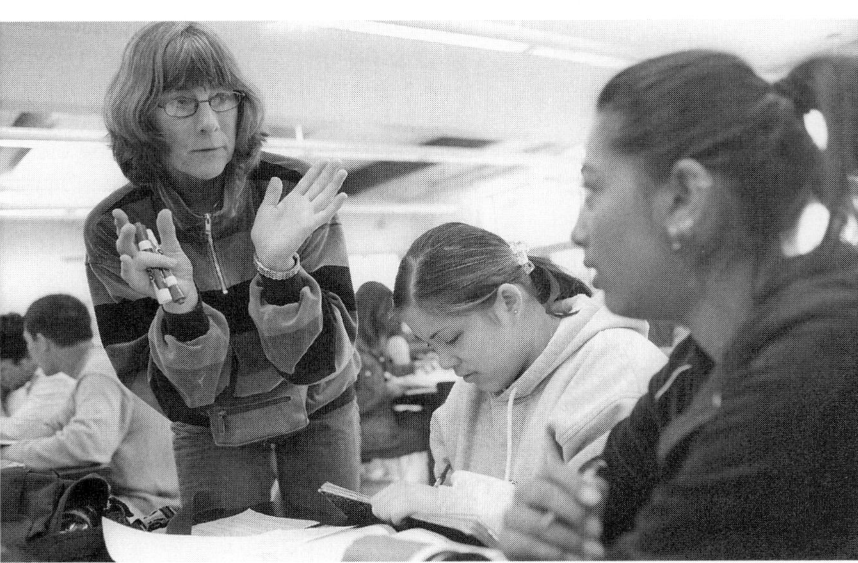

This teacher provides some extra help for two students who require special attention.

## Transitioning

Transitions pose challenges for many students. Some have difficulty making the cognitive switch from one subject to another. Others are challenged by the idea of changing from one type of activity, such as working independently, to another type, such as working in a small group. As you plan your lessons, be attuned to the transition challenges that your students face, and think of ways to minimize disruptions and maximize student learning. The smoother and easier the transitions from one topic to another or from one learning activity to another, the more time students spend on academic endeavors.

At the younger grades, transitions are made more easily when routines are established from one activity to another. For example, students come to expect that after morning seatwork comes morning meeting; after lunch is silent reading for fifteen minutes. Even for older students, the more familiar they are with a format for an activity, the easier the transition. At any age, transitions can be eased with advance warning, either by verbal cues or by a visual cue that signals to students the approaching end of one activity and the start of another.

With that in mind, think of what you can say or do, as you move students from one part of the lesson to the next, to optimize academic engagement time. You may want to make explicit to students the connection between one activity and the next one, or between one phase of the lesson and the next, so that students see one as a continuation of the other, rather than as an entirely different activity requiring a shift in thinking or content.

## Connections Among the Subjects

Just as important as the connections between parts of the lesson are the connections between and among subject-matter areas. As you plan your lesson, think of connections among the content areas that you can make evident to students. If you are teaching a math lesson, what connections with science or music can you highlight? If teaching a history lesson, think of connections with English or science; if teaching an English lesson, highlight connections to other languages. At the elementary level, these connections are easier to make, because the elementary teacher is often the sole teacher of these different content areas. At the secondary level, making the connections

### Now You Do It

Pick a topic that is taught in the grade or subject matter you want to teach. Develop a lesson plan that incorporates all or most of the elements of a good lesson plan that have been discussed in this module. Use the portions of sample lesson plans in this module and the full plans available through your Online Study Center as models for writing yours. Exchange your lesson plan with another prospective teacher and critique each other's plans, or ask your instructor to provide you with feedback.

becomes more challenging, because individual teachers are generally responsible for one content area only. At the same time, this differentiation makes the connections even more important. Helping students recognize the interconnectedness of content areas facilitates and strengthens the learning of content.

As you become more experienced and build up a repertoire of learning activities, you may find yourself writing shorter and shorter lesson plans, using a lot of shorthand to remind yourself of what you want students to do in a given lesson. For the first few years of teaching, though, we recommend that you write out detailed lesson plans—not only to remind you of what you want to accomplish in the lesson, but also as a record of what you have covered in terms of content. These may come in handy when an upset parent complains that you never covered a key concept that was on a state assessment. And they surely will be helpful when you begin planning your lessons the following fall.

## Further Resources

- Greta Morine-Dershimer, "Instructional Planning," in James M. Cooper (Ed.), *Classroom Teaching Skills,* 8th ed. (Boston, MA: Houghton Mifflin, 2006), pp. 20–54. An excellent chapter on how to plan lessons and units.

- Teacher's Net, Lesson Bank. Available at: **http://www.teachers.net/lessons/post/posts.html.** This website contains approximately 200 prepared lesson plans from teachers around the world.
- Terry D. TenBrink, "Instructional Objectives," in James M. Cooper (Ed.), *Classroom Teaching Skills,* 8th ed. (Boston, MA: Houghton Mifflin, 2006), pp. 55–78. This chapter provides lots of practice in writing good instructional objectives.

- Yahoo's Directory of K–12 Lesson Plans. Available at: **http://dir.yahoo.com/Education/K_12/Teaching/Lesson-Plans.** This website contains many lesson plans and resources for a variety of subjects.

MODULE 11 Planning Lessons

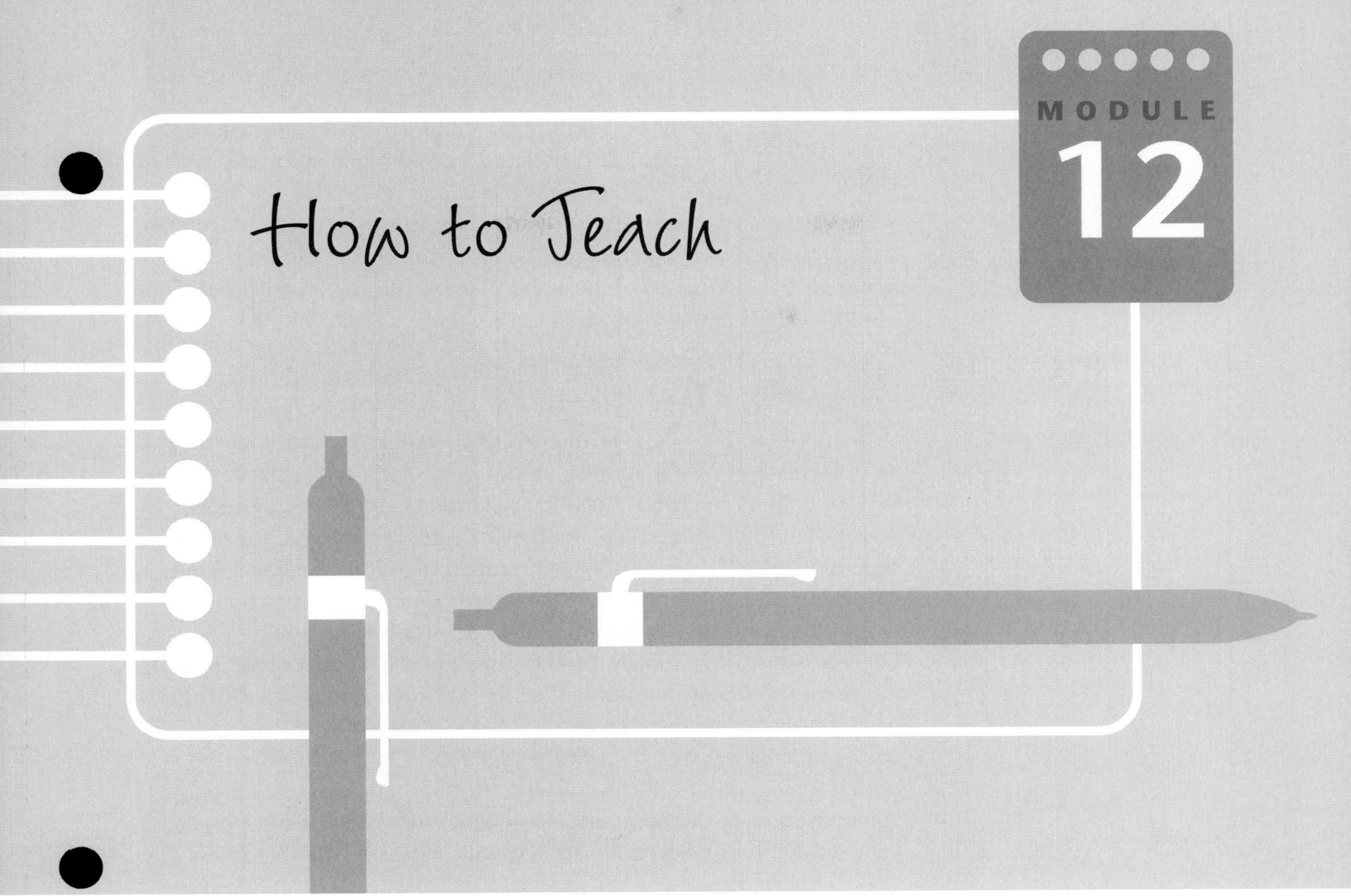


"Scenario"

It's the first day of classes after the winter break, and fifth-grade teacher Carla Thompson is beginning a new social studies unit in American history. The first three months of the school year were spent learning about the early explorers and the pre-Columbian civilizations. Carla had students research the different explorers and write reports about them. Carla has sensed her students' interest waning and is concerned that they will just shut down if she does not find some way of getting them engaged in the next unit of study, which is on the early colonies. Carla has been toying with some ideas.

"Scenario"

For the past two and a half weeks, Marc Wilhammer has been introducing trigonometric ratios in his eighth-grade math class. He explained to his students how these ratios were derived. He taught them an acronym to help them remember how to find sine, cosine, and tangent values. Although students seem to have memorized the acronym (SOH CAH TOA) and are generally able to find the missing value when they are given the other two, Marc is not convinced that they grasp the importance of these ratios in math and other fields. He is looking to find some way of helping students understand this.

Scenario

Charles Macomber, a high school English teacher, has just completed a month-long study of Shakespeare's *Hamlet* and is ready to give his students the end-of-unit exam. The day before an exam, Mr. Macomber always spend the class period reviewing for the exam. This time, he wants to be sure that all of the students are involved and *really* benefiting from the review session.

Preview

As each of these scenarios illustrates, deciding *how* to teach a particular lesson involves a number of considerations beyond the listing of concepts and skills that make up the curriculum. These considerations include content questions, such as "What do students already know about the topic?" and "What are they expected to know at the end of the school year?" They also include process questions, such as "How can students best interact with the information? What instructional activities can effectively and efficiently help students internalize key concepts and skills?" Finally, teachers need to consider students' interest in the topics. Topics that have little inherent interest for students (such as trigonometric ratios) may need to be presented in ways that can show students the usefulness of the knowledge so that they may be more motivated to learn the concepts. In this module, we will propose some instructional activities and approaches that we recommend adding to your repertoire of teaching strategies.

**This module emphasizes that:**

- **How you teach is as important as what you teach.**
- **How best to teach a concept depends on a number of considerations, among which are the purpose of the lesson and the students' level of familiarity with the concepts or skills involved.**
- **Different lesson types may be more appropriate or less appropriate for different purposes.**
- **Different lesson types require different degrees of direct teacher involvement in the instructional activity.**

## The Purpose of the Lesson

Deciding how to teach is as important as deciding what to teach. After all, *how* you teach concepts and skills often makes a difference in *how well* students learn the concepts and skills. One of the first considerations when deciding what kind of lesson to present is the purpose of the lesson. Some common purposes of lessons are listed below.

- *Introduce a new concept or start a new unit of study.* The purpose of the introductory lesson is to establish the framework for new concepts that students will be learning. For such a lesson, the teacher might decide to explain the new concept to students or have students recall and practice previously learned concepts that are related to the new concept.

For example, before teaching about graphing quadratic equations, an algebra teacher might spend some time reviewing graphs of linear equations. The teacher could also have the students carry out a simulation that highlights the concepts or skills to be learned. As an opening activity for a unit of study on force and motion, the teacher might have students investigate the movement of Slinky toys under different conditions.

- *Practice of a previously introduced skill.* The purpose of such a lesson is to help students develop facility with a previously taught skill. For these lessons, a teacher would plan to have students work with less guidance and oversight from the teacher. Our aforementioned algebra students might be expected to graph equations on their own or to determine which equations match which graphs. The physics teacher might have students carry out a more disciplined investigation of force and motion with the Slinky toys.
- *Application or synthesis of concept(s) or skill(s) learned previously.* The purpose of these lessons is to have students expand their knowledge of a concept or skill and be able to use that knowledge in various situations and contexts. These lessons generally entail less direct involvement of the teacher. For example, physics students might carry out their own projects involving force and the motion of a variety of objects.
- *Review of concepts learned in preparation for an assessment.* With the purpose of recalling recently introduced concepts and skills, review lessons can be teacher-led or student-led.
- *Assessment of students' levels of mastery of concepts learned.* The purpose of these lessons is to assess students' understanding of concepts either during or after teaching a unit. (See Module 15, Assessment for Learning.) Assessment lessons tend to have little direct involvement by the teacher.

## Now You Do It

Refer to Scenario One at the start of this module. Ms. Thompson is introducing a new unit of study on colonial America. In light of her concerns about her students' waning interest in history, she wants to find a way to get students at least interested in, or even excited about, the new unit of study.

1. What do you see as the primary purpose of this introductory lesson? What suggestions could you make to Ms. Thompson for this lesson?
2. Look again at Scenarios Two and Three. What are the primary purposes of these lesson?

## Learning Activities

After deciding on the purpose of the lesson, you need to choose a learning activity that fits the purpose and engages the students. In this section, we will present a sampling of activities and strategies that you may want to include in your repertoire: lectures, teacher-led discussions, group work and cooperative learning, and individual work. These are certainly not the

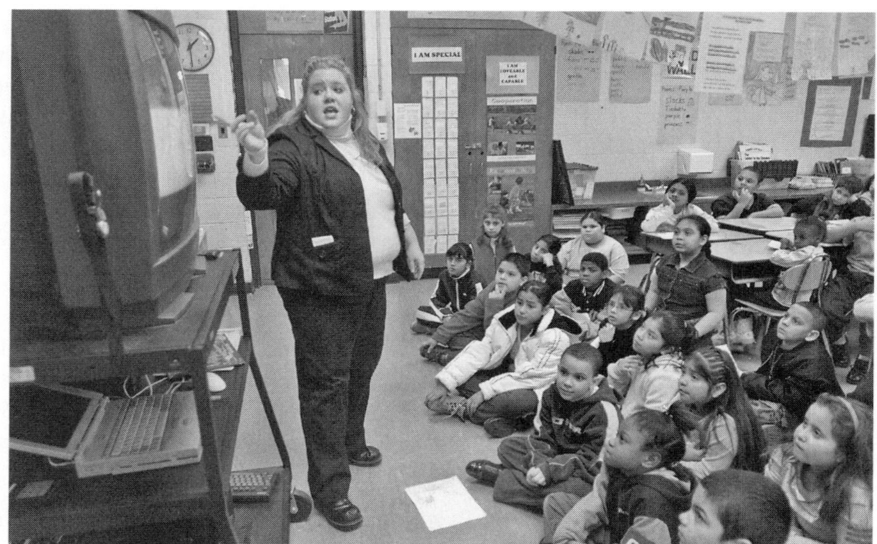

Using visual media can provide a powerful way to explain new concepts and capture student attention.

only options available, and we recommend that, throughout your career as a teacher, you continue to look for new activities that work for you and your students. However, those four "basics" should be in every teacher's toolkit.

When picking activities, remember that "variety is the spice of life." One of your responsibilities as a teacher is to keep students interested and engaged in the learning process, and one way to do so is to offer them a range of learning activities. When this approach is implemented effectively, all of the learning activities presented are viable and productive structures that help students expand their knowledge base. However, too much of a good thing is a bad thing. Having students carry out cooperative learning tasks too often can become as unproductive as lecturing every day. As you plan your lessons for the week, month, or term, plan a variety of learning activities so that students do not become bored or complacent.

At the same time that we urge you to vary the learning activities in your classroom, we want to remind you that students are more productive if they are familiar with the expectations and structure of the learning activity. The first time you have a classroom discussion, you may be dissatisfied with students' participation. The first time you have students carry out a cooperative learning activity, you may be disappointed with the level of off-task behavior you observe within the different groups. And the first time you have students work independently, you may be disappointed by the level of talking and sharing among the students.

Keep in mind that as you are teaching students content, you are also teaching them how to learn within a particular structure. The more they practice with these formats, the better they become at them (assuming, of course, that you give them productive feedback to help them become skillful at these activities). Be patient with students. Give them time and opportunity to learn both the content and the structure of the learning activities.



## Lecture

**Lecture** a lesson in which the teacher presents information, while students listen attentively and take notes; also known as a transmission lesson.

Probably the most recognizable lesson type is the teacher-led **lecture,** during which the teacher presents information while students listen attentively and take notes. Sometimes referred to as a transmission lesson, the lecture is an efficient way of conveying important information to students. It is also an often (perhaps unfairly) maligned lesson type and is described by many as ineffective. In fact, some critics insist that the uninterrupted transfer of information from teacher to students saps both interest and motivation.

Without necessarily championing the virtues of the lecture/transmission lesson, we have found definite benefits to these lessons. The key is to avoid the common pitfalls that make them onerous or off-putting to your students. Keep in mind that the large majority of us are visual rather than auditory learners; that is, we remember what we see better than what we hear. With that important principle in mind, the following pointers can help make these lessons as effective as they are efficient.

**Graphic organizer** a visual representation to help students understand the "structure" of the information presented to them and the relationship between the main points and secondary points included.

1. *Provide a visual structure to the lecture.* A visual structure makes it easier for the students to follow the lecture by giving them cues to the key topics. This is particularly helpful to students with underdeveloped listening skills. One helpful visual structure is the **graphic organizer.** The graphic organizer can take a number of forms, but all forms are designed to help students identify more readily the main points and secondary points of the lecture. One common and useful graphic organizer is an outline listing some or all of the main topics and subtopics of the lecture. As the teacher presents information, students fill in the outline with the important information gleaned from the lecture. Another common graphic organizer consists of a graphical representation of the outline with one shape representing main topics, a second shape for subtopics, and still other shapes for details. Figure 12.1 shows two possible formats—one vertical and one horizontal—for graphic organizers that can help students navigate a lecture.

2. *Provide auditory cues.* For most students, learning by listening is not their dominant learning style, so it is a useful strategy to include unmistakable auditory cues (such as "First," "Second," and so on) or transition words and phrases (such as "Because of this") that draw attention to main points or sequential ideas.

3. *Keep the lecture purposeful, focused, and cogent.* Your students are depending on you to follow the outline you presented. That means you should present only relevant information and present it in a clear, sequenced, and specific order. Use the graphic organizer you have distributed to the students as a guide to keep yourself focused and on track.

4. *Be "environmentally aware."* As adults, most of us have a sustained attention span of, at most, about thirty minutes. Students, be they of elementary school age or high school teens, probably have a sustained attention span of about ten or fifteen minutes. (Many sociologists insist that students of the TV generation have a sustained attention span of approximately seven minutes, the average length of an uninterrupted segment in a television show before a commercial break.)[1]

   Rather than fighting this trend, use it to your advantage. Plan your lecture in seven- to ten-minute segments. After each segment, include some kind of marker to signal the end of that segment and the beginning of the next. You may even want to stop lecturing for a minute or two (not unlike a commercial break, but without the commercials). You could use the break to check students' understanding of the information that you have just presented, or you could ask them to share with a neighbor what they thought were the main points of the lecture.



**Class discussion** a lesson format in which the teacher engages students in a dialogue about an assigned reading, a previously taught concept, or a completed experiment.

## Teacher-Led Discussions

As familiar to most of us as lectures are teacher-led **class discussions,** lessons in which the teacher engages students in a dialogue about an assigned reading,

**Figure 12.1**
**Examples of Graphic Organizers**

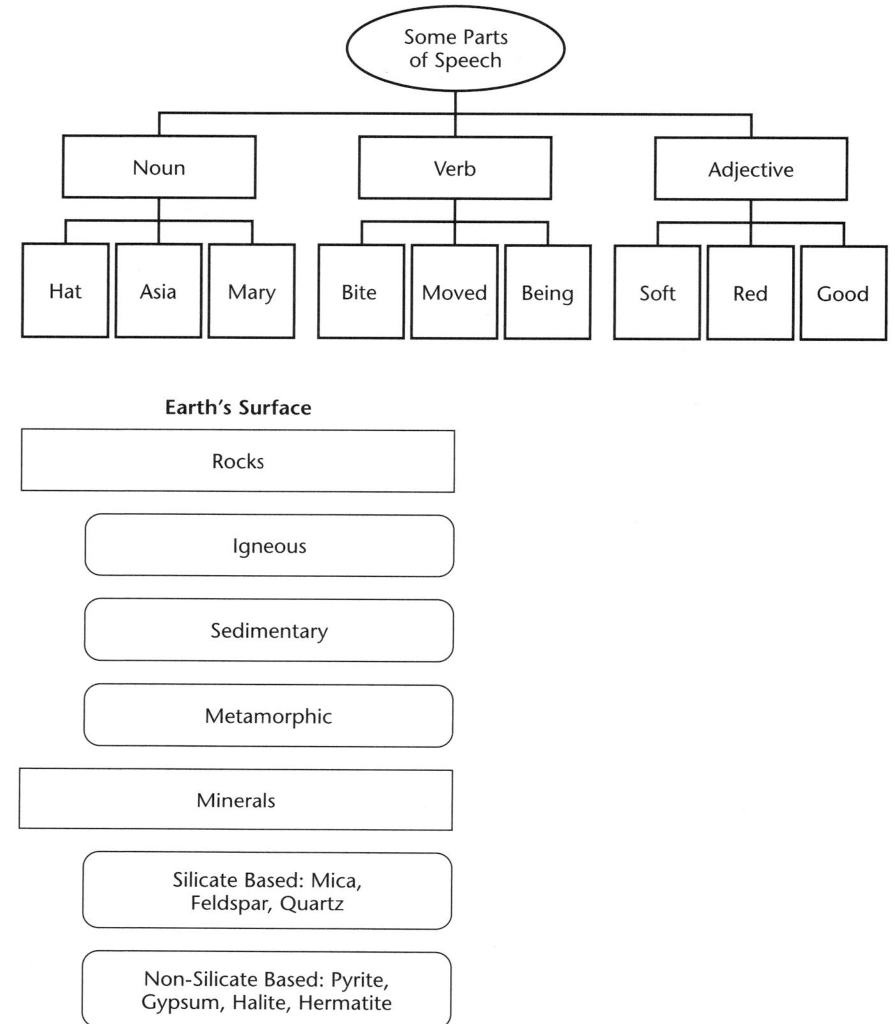


a previously taught concept, or a completed experiment. One purpose of the class discussion is to check and/or enhance students' understanding of concepts presented. Unlike the lecture, during which students generally remain passive, a class discussion requires the active participation of the students as they respond to the teacher's or one another's questions and comments.

The key to an effective discussion is the questions that the teacher asks. Although we all ask many questions in our daily interactions with others, asking questions that encourage discussion and enhance student learning is not as easy as it may seem. New teachers often become frustrated with students' lack of responsiveness in class discussion, but the problem may have less to do with lack of student interest in the topic and more to do with the kinds of questions being asked or how they are asked. Here are some pointers to help make your class discussions effective:

**Convergent questions** questions that have one clear correct answer; also known as closed-ended questions.

- *Mix convergent and divergent questions.* Simple yes/no and either/or questions are called **convergent questions** or closed-ended questions. Convergent or closed-ended questions are useful in checking students' recall of facts or their basic comprehension, the lower-level thinking skills in Bloom's taxonomy. (See Module 11, Planning Lessons.) Examples of such questions include "What were the key events that brought Europe into the Enlightenment?" and "So when we solve this equation for *x*, what is the answer?" They generally have just one correct answer, and the discussion tends to be a quick, staccato-like exchange between the teacher and students. For each question the teacher poses, one (and only one) student gives a one- or two-word response, and consequently, the teacher often dominates the discussion.

**Divergent questions** questions that do not have one clear correct answer, but instead call for interpretation or analysis; also known as open-ended questions.

Open-ended questions, or **divergent questions,** require longer and more descriptive responses. Examples of such questions include "Why do you suppose the author decided to name the main character _____?" and "What factors might have contributed to the results we got in our science experiment?" These questions move students beyond the comprehension level to make inferences, draw conclusions, speculate about causes, and/or predict effects. When used in a teacher-led discussion, divergent questions allow for greater student participation than do convergent questions. Because open-ended questions require interpretation or analysis, they often do not have a single correct answer. Because responses can vary, more than one student can be prompted to offer an answer. The answers that students offer can give teachers significant insight into their understanding of concepts.

- *Vary the content of your questions.* Many of your questions will be directly aimed at uncovering, clarifying, and even enhancing students' understanding of the topic being studied, from literary or historical analysis to the interaction of different biological, chemical, or physical variables in a life cycle. An equally important goal, however, is helping your students relate this understanding to their immediate surroundings and experiences. As they read about the actions of a literary or historical figure, you can ask them to think about the effect that similar actions would have in their world. Ask them to imagine themselves in a similar situation and to explain how they would react to the challenges confronting the characters they are studying. In the sciences, your questions can help students see the application of the concepts in their lives and daily activities.

- *Plan your questions.* As you plan for a class discussion, you want to prepare your questions with great care to make sure that you have a good assortment of question types, from convergent to divergent, from factual or literal to interpretive, analytical, or even evaluative questions. You should also vary the focus of the questions so that students recognize the connection and relevance of these concepts to their out-of-school lives.

- *Limit the number of questions you ask.* Look for quality, not quantity, in your questions. If the question–answer pattern is one teacher question to one student answer, each student will have about one minute of "talk time," while the teacher will have up to twenty-five minutes. Because one goal of a discussion-type lesson is to give as many students as possible as much talk time as possible, the fewer questions the teacher asks, the more opportunity students have to talk. By asking open-ended or probing questions, you can get responses from more than one student, increasing the student participation in the discussion.

- *Use wait time.* Silence is golden—at least for a little while. Wait time is one of the few teaching techniques that has been found to have a demonstrable effect on student learning.[2] When you ask a question, give students enough time (at least five seconds) to think about the answer. Some students will be ready to answer (right or wrong!) as soon as the last word leaves your lips, but others need some time to think about the question and formulate a response or, in some cases, to get up the courage or confidence to offer an answer. That five-second wait time may at first seem very uncomfortable for you, but you will notice more and more hands going up the longer you wait. (Up to a point, that is. We do not recommend a five-minute wait period!)

- *Monitor student participation.* Keep in mind that you want to maximize the participation of *all* students. To do so, you must carefully monitor which students are participating and how much each student is participating. We all probably remember classes in which a small group of students dominated any discussion. As students, some of us were quite content that there were such willing speakers in the class, for that freed us from having to talk or think about the questions, or even listen to the questions being asked. Others, who had many thoughts to share, may have resented the teacher calling on the same students over and over again (or so it seemed).

  In one of his trilogy of books on life in schools, Theodore Sizer describes the tacit understanding that often exists in classrooms: those students who want to talk raise their hands and are called on, while those who do not want to talk do not raise their hands and are not called upon to participate. Everyone, from teacher to students, is comfortable with the arrangement. The problem with this less-than-perfect arrangement is that it also allows some students to sit passively in the classroom and barely engage in the learning process.[3]

  Sizer's findings suggest that you may have to compromise student comfort for learning. Instead of calling only on students who raise their hands, even with the extra wait time, you may want to consider calling on some students who are *not* raising their hands. We recommend caution and care, however, when using this practice. Younger students, particularly, may not be used to such a practice and may find it threatening, at least at first. We know of some teachers who alert their students to this practice before implementing it so that students will know what to expect and what is expected of them.

- *Provide students with specific feedback.* In their study of classrooms, researcher John Goodlad and his team found that the classroom environment was typically neither full of praise nor full of criticism; in fact, they described it as flat. They found that teacher feedback to students' responses was most often nonspecific comments such as "Good," "Excellent," or "Super," which were largely ineffective in helping students learn.[4] Educational researchers Myra and David Sadker suggest that students need feedback that is specifically related to a particular answer or a response that is honest and sincere so that they can gauge how well they are understanding concepts and mastering skills.[5]

## Cooperative Learning and Group Work

**Group work** a type of lesson in which students work together in small groups to complete an assigned task.

Of growing prominence over the past twenty or thirty years is **group work,** during which students work with a small group of classmates to complete an assigned task. Rather than having the teacher in front of the room managing an activity that involves all the students, group work affords the teacher an opportunity to interact with these small groups of students in a more relaxed setting.

## Now You Do It

Look at these examples of teacher feedback. Comment on the effectiveness of each, judging on the basis of the criteria suggested on the previous page.

**Scene 1**

| | |
|---|---|
| *Teacher:* | *On page 188, Nick refers to Gatsby's mansion as "that huge incoherent failure of a house." What do you think he means?* |
| *Student 1:* | *That Gatsby's life doesn't make any sense?* |
| *Teacher:* | *Good. Anyone else?* |

**Scene 2**

| | |
|---|---|
| *Teacher:* | *On page 188, Nick refers to Gatsby's mansion as "that huge incoherent failure of a house." What do you think he means?* |
| *Student 1:* | *That Gatsby's life doesn't make any sense?* |
| *Teacher:* | *I'm not sure I follow. Can you explain a bit more?* |
| *Student 1:* | *Well, Gatsby worked so hard to have all these riches so he could win Daisy, but in the end, he wasn't successful, so maybe to Nick, Gatsby's life was a failure and that didn't make sense to him.* |



**Cooperative learning** structured learning opportunities in which students work in groups to achieve academic advancement and social growth.

It is important at this point to distinguish between group work and **cooperative learning groups**. All cooperative learning is done in groups, but not all group work is cooperative learning. Cooperative learning groups typically have a structured organization with very specific learning expectations. When teachers informally assign students in small groups to discuss an idea, to share the results of an experiment, or to generate questions about a topic, these examples of group work are not necessarily cooperative learning activities. Because cooperative learning activities require more specific structure and organization than does group work, we will devote most of this section to discussing cooperative learning.

***Characteristics of Cooperative Learning*** Various educators and educational researchers have defined cooperative learning activities in different ways, but most agree that they share at least the following essential elements.

- *Group interdependence.* Cooperative learning is grounded in the belief that collaboration will bring about greater student learning than competition. For this reason, cooperative learning activities are designed so that the students within a group depend on one another in all aspects of the task. They share resources, responsibility for one another's learning, and rewards. In order for one member of the group to succeed, all members must succeed, and in order for a group to be successful, each member of the group must succeed individually.
- *Group and individual accountability.* Each member of a group is assessed individually on his or her mastery of the academic content. In addition, the group is assessed on how well it achieved the group goals. Unlike group work, in which some students may contribute more to a task while others contribute less, cooperative learning requires that all members of the group contribute to the best of their ability. To ensure that this expectation is met, the teacher looks not just at the product of the group work but also at the learning that each individual member of the group gained.

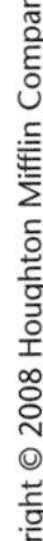

- *Focus on social and interpersonal skills.* Because cooperative learning requires students to work collaboratively, they can do so most effectively if they have well-developed interpersonal skills, such as communicating effectively through listening and speaking as well as in written form, team building, and negotiation and conflict resolution skills.

***Types of Cooperative Learning Activities*** Several specific formats for cooperative learning activities are summarized in Table 12.1. All of them share the dual goals of academic advancement and social growth, but some types of cooperative learning focus primarily on academic achievement, whereas others focus more on developing students' interpersonal skills. Strategies, such as Student Teams Academic Divisions (STAD), Jigsaw, and Team-Assisted Instruction (TAI), that focus primarily on academic achievement have a specific task structure so that every member of the group participates.[6] In these strategies, the success of the group is linked to the academic performance of the individual. Each member of the group is also assessed individually on his or her mastery of the content presented. In contrast, strategies such as Think-Pair-Share (TPS) are designed to help students develop their social skills while focusing on academic content.

A third group of strategies tries to balance these two goals. These activities, such as Number Heads Together, typically are divided into different parts, some of which require cooperation and others of which do not. In this type of activity, the success of the group often depends on the performance of an individual member, so groups have to work together to make sure that all members have mastered the content.

### TABLE 12.1 Formats for Cooperative Learning Activities

| Name | Brief Description |
|---|---|
| Student Teams Achievement Divisions (STAD) | Four-member, mixed-ability learning teams. Teacher presents lesson, students work within teams to make certain all team members have mastered the objectives. Students take individual quizzes. Points are awarded on basis of improvement over previous quizzes. |
| Team-Assisted Individualization (TAI) | Similar to STAD, students are in four-member, mixed-ability teams. However, students are assigned work at their level and work at their own pace. Team members check one another's work and provide assistance as needed. Students are tested individually, but the team receives points for the progress of individual members. |
| Jigsaw | Each student on a team becomes an "expert" on one topic by working with members from other teams assigned the same topic. Upon returning to the home team, each student-expert teaches the group, and students are all assessed on all aspects of the topic. |
| Think-Pair-Share | Students think to themselves about a topic provided by the teacher; then each one pairs with another student to discuss it; then they share their thoughts with the class. |
| Number Heads Together | The teacher groups students into four-member teams and assigns each member of the team a number (1, 2, 3, or 4). The teacher next poses a question and gives the teams time to make sure that all members of the team know the answer. The teacher then calls a number. For each team, the member assigned that number (for example, all 4s) must respond to the question for the team. |

***Managing Cooperative Learning Activities*** The success of all cooperative learning strategies depends on how well students can work together in their groups. The "In Your Classroom" feature offers some suggestions for creating groups that work well together. You may also need to help students develop group process skills, including

- *Organizational skills.* To get organized on their own, students need to be able to get started on the assigned task. They also need direction on how to assign and fulfill roles within the group, such as summarizer, checker, explainer, and the like.
- *Communication skills.* Group members must understand and follow directions independently. In addition, many groups, especially groups of younger students, may need instruction in such skills as taking turns within the group, responding appropriately to others' comments, and speaking at an appropriate volume level so as not to disturb other groups.
- *Interpersonal skills.* Group members must learn to respond appropriately and constructively to other members' contributions. For example, they should be taught to paraphrase other members' comments or to ask for or give clarification before responding.



## In Your Classroom

### Grouping Students for Cooperative Learning Activities

One of the keys to effective management of cooperative learning activities is the makeup of the groups and the directions you provide. We offer you the following suggestions and strategies to consider.

- *Assign students to groups.* We strongly discourage you from letting students group themselves. The voluntary formation of groups can create social tension and stress for students, especially in the middle-school years. Too often there is at least one social outcast with whom no one wants to work. When the teacher decides on the makeup of the groups, at least one layer of tension can be removed.
- *Consider grouping students heterogeneously by ability level.* In a four-person group, for example, include one student of high ability, a second whom you consider of low ability, and two of average ability. The hope is that this composition will allow for maximum learning and maximum participation from all members of the group.
- *Place English language learners with special care.* As a general rule, it is best not to put more than one English language learner in any one group, especially if all your ELL students are from the same linguistic background. Otherwise, the temptation to converse in their primary language could lead to off-task behavior during the group work, frustrating the other members of the group. You may want to make an exception to this rule, however, if you have an ELL student with a very rudimentary understanding of English. It may be more useful to put this student with a more fluent ELL student of the same linguistic background, allowing the more fluent student to act as an interpreter. The complexity of the task the students are to undertake may be a factor in your decision making here.
- *Balance social characteristics.* Try to have groups as gender-balanced as possible. (In some instances, of course, it is just not possible to do so.) A similar rule of thumb holds for other characteristics, including work habits and sociability.

Classroom management is another key to effective and productive cooperative learning activities. You must be well organized and well prepared when implementing such an activity. You also must manage the classroom so that students function effectively in groups. Key management concerns include noise levels, student movement, and control issues.

- *Noise.* Students have to talk to one another, and if there are four or five groups in the classroom, at least four or five students may be talking at any given time. That usually leads to a noisy classroom, certainly noisier than one would expect to find during a lecture or even a teacher-led discussion. In addition, as students become more engrossed in their task, they may get excited and speak more animatedly. As the teacher, you want to manage the noise level so that students can interact freely without, however, disturbing their classmates in other groups. This is likely to be a chronic management issue when students are engaged in cooperative learning activities.
- *Movement.* In a lecture or teacher-led discussion, the expectation is that students remain seated, allowing them to focus on the lecture or discussion. In a cooperative learning activity, students may need to procure materials or resources; they may be in search of information either in the library or from the Internet; or they may be creating a poster or jointly writing a paper. Any of these tasks may lead to a lot of movement in the classroom. You will need to figure out a way to manage the movement of students to maintain a productive classroom environment.
- *Control.* For some teachers, cooperative learning activities challenge their understanding of appropriate behavior and norms of interaction within the classroom. Teachers are often used to being in control of student learning. They give the lecture, they lead the discussion, they decide what will be taught and how it will be taught. When students are engaged in cooperative learning activities, the teacher has less control over their learning. The students are not all being presented the same information, so students are not all learning the same concepts. Students are exploring concepts on their own, they may be following different pathways to find answers to questions, and they may learn different concepts from those that the teacher expected they would learn.

  You may simply have to give up some control of student learning and trust that the activities you design are engaging enough to excite students' interest in the topics presented and that your students are motivated enough to want to learn. Given a measure of responsibility for their own learning, most students respond positively and perform well.

Another key management concern is how you give directions when introducing cooperative learning activities. We recommend that you always begin by telling students *why* they are doing the activity. Students cannot read your mind, so they may not know the purpose of a learning activity. They may also not have the foresight to understand how the cooperative learning activity you have designed will lead them to greater understanding of particular concepts.

We also suggest that you provide both verbal *and* written directions. The most effective approach (we think) is first to explain to students what they are to do and then to hand out written, bulleted, step-by-step instructions for the activity. The clearer you can make the directions at the beginning, the less time students will need to spend trying to figure out just what they are supposed to do. Remember, too, that you want to explain not only what students are to do, but also what they will be accountable for at the end of the activity.

## Video Case

The Jigsaw model is one example of a cooperative learning strategy that can be particularly effective for students in the middle elementary grades. In the video case, *Cooperative Learning in the Elementary Grades: Jigsaw Model,* you'll see how veteran fifth-grade teacher Ilene Miller dispatches students to small expert groups to study the ancient Olympics. Students then return to their "home group" to teach their classmates what they've learned. Throughout the video, Ilene reflects on how this strategy has increased student learning and made her a better teacher. As you watch the clips and study the artifacts in the case, reflect on the following questions.

**QUESTIONS**

1. Which of the characteristics of cooperative learning described in this module are demonstrated in this video case?
2. How does this teacher manage the classroom environment during cooperative learning?
3. How are group composition and group-skills training important to the success of these groups?
4. What new things about cooperative learning did you learn from this video case?

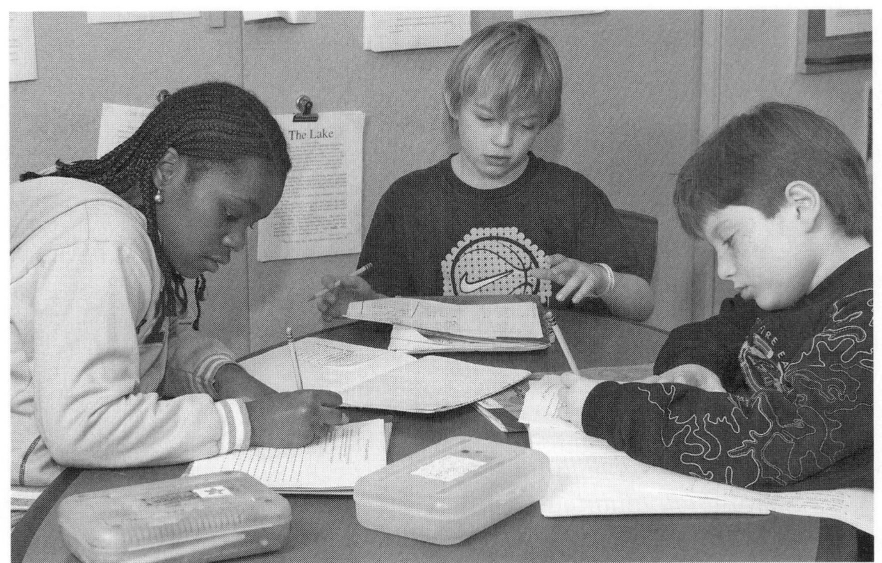

Teachers often use the work students produce individually as a way to assess how well students are learning.

Cooperative group activities can be a powerful tool for learning, or they can be management nightmares for the teacher. Students can gain important new insights on concepts, or they can waste a class period learning new ways to tease one another. The key is careful, thoughtful planning, clear and unambiguous tasks, and disciplined management. Keep in mind, as well, that the more familiar students are with group work, the better they are at doing it.

## Independent Work

**Individual work** a type of lesson in which students work alone to complete an assigned task.

A fourth learning activity, one that is familiar to many of us, is **individual or independent seat work.** As the name suggests, individual work activities have students working alone to complete an assigned task. The teacher assigns a task that students are expected to complete unassisted and on their own. This type of activity is often used to assess student progress or achievement. (See Module 15, Assessment for Learning.) Because students work on their own, the teacher can use the work they produce to determine how well they are grasping the concepts presented and, toward the end of a unit, how well they have mastered those concepts.

As with the other learning activities we have considered, individualized tasks are more effective when the task is clearly defined, the directions are specific and easy to follow, and the classroom management is structured and purposeful. Again, students' familiarity with working independently also helps to ensure greater on-task behavior.

# Timing and Pacing

As any good performer will tell you, timing is everything. Much as good performers practice their timing, good teachers study the timing and pacing of learning activities. They plan enough time to allow students to complete the activity without feeling either too rushed or too relaxed. Either situation can result in students going off-task and not achieving the learning objective you have set for the activity. The "In Your Classroom" feature offers some suggestions for planning the timing of your activities.

## In Your Classroom

### Tips for Pacing Learning Activities

- *Divide your time.* In order to allow enough time for a learning activity, plan in small chunks. Break down the total lesson time available to you into smaller segments, and assign each segment a specific task or part of a task. Determine how much you can accomplish in the time you have available, and adjust your plans if necessary.
- *Share timing information with students.* As you give instructions for the task or the activity, communicate the amount of time students have to complete it. This helps students remain focused on the task before them and pace themselves to work through it at a reasonable rate.
- *Tune in to your audience.* As students complete assigned tasks, look and listen carefully for cues indicating confusion, frustration, or accomplishment. This careful monitoring enables you to make adjustments to the time allotment of a task on the basis of collective student reactions.

# Adjusting Learning Activities to Learning Styles

As we have discussed elsewhere, teaching and learning are not one-size-fits-all enterprises. Teachers have preferences for certain learning activities, derived in part from fond memories of activities they did during their student careers. In addition, teachers take into account their own philosophy about learning when they design or plan these activities. As a result, one teacher's lecture lesson or cooperative learning activity may be noticeably different from the lecture or cooperative activity planned by another teacher.

Your students also vary in their preferences for learning. Some students are more productive when they work alone; others learn better in groups. Some students need to talk about concepts in order to understand them; others understand better when they can interact with a text. Some students are visual learners; others may be auditory or kinesthetic learners. An awareness of and appreciation for this diversity is essential when you are planning and implementing lessons. Consider creating options for individual lessons that allow you to adapt them to the learning preferences of your students. In addition, be sure to vary the learning activities so that all learning preferences are addressed over the course of a week or a unit of study.

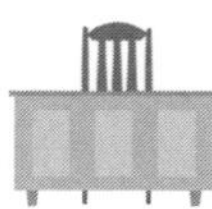

## Now You Do It

In your high school chemistry course, you are in the middle of a unit on chemical bonds. You have a lab activity in which students draw different molecules and identify the types of bonds between the atoms. You believe the activity is a good one for many of the students in the class, but you want to think of some way to address the different learning preferences of other students. What adaptation could you make to the activity? How would the adaptation(s) you propose address students' varying needs?

Let's Sum Up

Student learning of concepts taught is not automatic. The mere fact that you planned and taught a brilliant lesson (at least you thought it was) does not mean that your students internalized or even understood the concepts you presented. Providing a good variety in terms of lesson types, adapting learning activities to draw on different learning preferences, and maintaining a quick pace and rhythm in the classroom are all strategies that can enhance the likelihood that most of your students will master most of the concepts you teach.

And it is becoming increasingly important to ensure that they *do* master the material. In an era of high-stakes testing based on state standards, student performance on these tests becomes an essential component of effective instruction. Students' academic performance can be enhanced when they learn effectively and thoroughly the concepts being taught, making the *how* of teaching *what* students are expected to learn even more crucial.

## Further Resources

- The Cooperative Learning Center. Available at: **http://www.co-operation.org/**. On the website of the Cooperative Learning Center, directed by Roger Johnson and David Johnson, are research findings of studies on cooperative learning, practical guides for implementing cooperative learning groups, and examples of effective practices in cooperative learning.

- The Cooperative Learning Network. Available at: **http://home.att.net/~clnetwork/**. This website offers links to a host of references and resources on cooperative learning strategies.
- George Jacobs, Michael Power, and Wan Inn Loh, *Teacher's Sourcebook for Cooperative Learning: Practical Techniques, Basic Principles, and Frequently Asked Questions* (Thousand Oaks, CA: Corwin Press, 2002). The authors present numerous practical and easily implemented strategies to help make cooperative learning activities useful and productive for students and easy to manage for the teacher.
- Donna E. Tileston, *What Every Teacher Should Know About Effective Teaching Strategies* (Thousand Oaks, CA: Corwin Press, 2004). Tileston offers teaching tips for each phase of the teaching process, from planning to implementation.

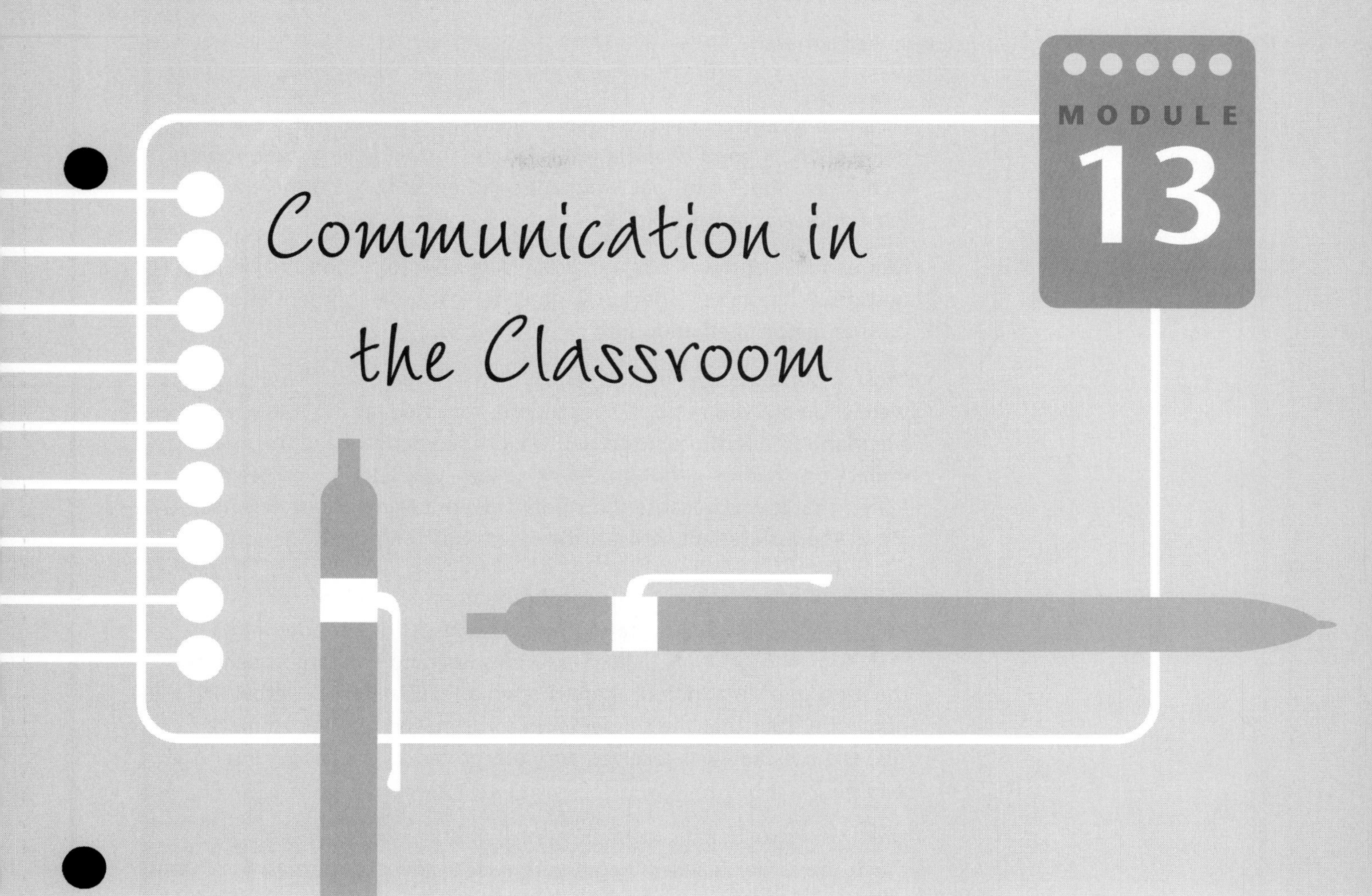


Scenario

"Okay, guys, enough talking. It's time to get to work." Meghan's voice was lost in the chatter of students laughing and joking with one another. "Hey, you guys," Meghan said, more loudly. A few students looked her way, but no one stopped talking. "Guys!" she shouted. Slowly students stopped their conversations and turned toward her.

"Hey, Ms. Sullivan, we were just talking about the weekend. But you didn't tell us about your weekend yet." Snickers filled the classroom as other students joined in with, "Yeah, Ms. Sullivan, tell us about your weekend."

"Not now, guys. It's time to get to work. I want to get the first part of the assignment done today,"

"Aw, come on. You always tell us. We tell you what *we* do over the weekend."

"Yeah, well, we're gonna have to cut down on that. We gotta cover three more chapters before the midterms. It's a department midterm, remember? And, you know, we have to get through Chapter 14. We're only on 10."

"Yeah, but you'll be grading ours, right? So it's not like we really have to study. You always tell us not to worry about grades—it's the learning that's important, right? Well, we're learning a lot." Eric was the ringleader of the class and always seemed to have an answer for everything. Meghan enjoyed Eric a good deal. He was a bright and engaging student with a cocky air about him that Meghan found endearing, but he always looked for ways to get out of work.

Meghan just glared at Eric, not really sure how to respond to his suggestion. "C'mon. Let's get to work. Please? Your assignment and your partner are on the handout."

"You're getting to be like the rest of them—a real drag. We thought you were cool, but you're not." The students resumed talking to one another. Meghan's frequent urging to get to work seemed to have minimal impact on anyone, although the noise level was a lot lower. Meghan feared that it was because the students were talking about her, not about the assignment. At least they were quiet, Meghan thought.

Preview

At its most fundamental level, the communication process consists of a sender and a receiver, a message and a means of sending the message.[1] In addition, there is often a feedback loop: verbal or nonverbal cues that the sender looks for from the receiver to make sure the message was received and interpreted as the sender intended it to be.

Effective instructional communication—in other words, teaching—is much the same. Teachers begin with a clear and cogent message that is delivered through appropriate media to a class full of receptive listeners. The students demonstrate, perhaps immediately, by responding to the teacher's questions, or later, through their performance on homework

**Figure 13.1**
**Factors Involved in the Communication Process**

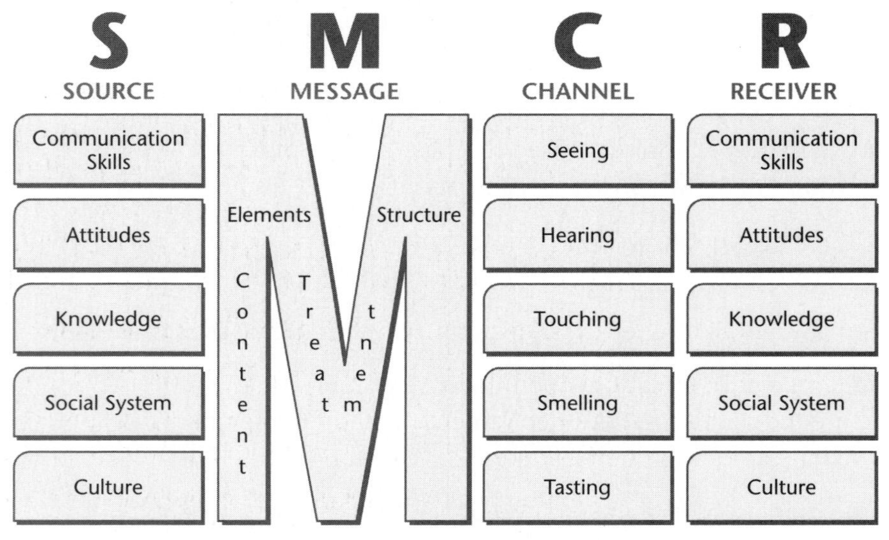


Source: From *Process of Communication,* 1st edition, by Berlo, David, 1960. Reprinted with permission of Wadsworth, a division of Thomson Learning: **www.thomsonright.com.** Fax: (800) 730-2215.

and tests, that they have successfully received the message. As simple as that may seem, there are nevertheless a number of variables that can compromise the effectiveness of the communication.

In this module, we will consider variables related to each of the major components in the communication process: the source (the teacher), the message itself, the channel or the means of sending the message, and of course the receivers (the students). We'll discuss variables that can compromise the effectiveness of the process and propose strategies to address these variables. We'll also describe ways for teachers to determine whether and how well their messages are being received. We'll also briefly examine the advanced communication skills you'll need to negotiate and resolve conflicts in your classroom.

**This module emphasizes that:**

- **Effective communication is at the heart of effective instruction.**
- **Instructional communication, like interpersonal communication, consists of a sender, a message, a means of sending the message, and a receiver.**
- **In instructional communication, unlike in interpersonal communication, the sender or teacher has to seek out feedback from the receiver to verify the effectiveness of the communication.**
- **Planning how to communicate information and instruction is as important as planning what to teach students.**
- **In addition to their instructional communication skills, teachers need to be skilled in negotiation and conflict resolution.**



## Teachers as Communication Senders

The first element in the communication process is the sender of the message. In instructional communication, the sender is most often the teacher, who is a primary source of information in the classroom and the initiator of most of the communication that takes place there. It is important that the teacher, as sender of messages, be perceived by his or her students as a knowledgeable and authoritative source. For some teachers who are just a few years older than their students, viewing themselves as the authority figure is sometimes a challenge. Like Meghan, the teacher in the scenario at the beginning of this module, some teachers try to adopt a more egalitarian relationship with their students. But also like Meghan, these teachers often have difficulty getting students to focus on learning tasks when their students do not see their teacher as having authority over them. The effectiveness of the communication depends in part on how willing the receivers are to accept the message of the sender.

We are not suggesting that you have to be heavy-handed and dictatorial toward students or that you cannot allow them to make some decisions about rules and regulations governing the classroom. You must, however, continuously make clear the status differences between you and your students. Your communications to them should reflect your confidence in yourself as an authority figure. All aspects of communication can contribute to students'

Teachers are the primary source of information in the classroom.

perceptions of you, but two that are very important for getting and keeping students' attention and respect are your voice and your movements about in the classroom.

## Voice Manipulation

One of your most important teaching tools, if not *the* most important, is your speaking voice. By manipulating your voice efficiently and effectively, you can not only engage students and keep their attention but also safeguard your vocal cords. Let's look at some of the voice characteristics that you should keep in mind.

- *Volume.* In most instances while teaching, you are addressing a group of at least twenty individuals, all of whom need to be able to hear clearly the message being conveyed. That means your voice must be loud enough for all of the students in the classroom to hear without effort. Speaking loudly, however, does not mean that you shout. Shouting may make students think you are angry, are upset, or have "lost your cool." Shouting also puts excessive strain on your voice and can damage your vocal cords.

  Instead, you want to learn to *project* your voice, as do singers or actors in the theater. Projecting amplifies your voice without increasing the strain on your vocal cords. To project your voice, breathe deeply from your diaphragm, so that your lungs are filled. Use the air pressure from your deep breath to project your voice. The increased volume comes not from your vocal cords, as it does when you shout, but from your lungs. To maximize the amount of air in your lungs, stand up straight (yes, your mother was right). With more air coming out of your lungs, your voice will have more power and will project farther.

- *Pitch.* Your voice will be easier to hear and will last longer if it is neither too high-pitched (most common among females) nor too low-pitched (more likely among males). Our human ears are most attuned to sounds in the middle range, and producing speech in this range inflicts less strain on your vocal box. You may want to seek feedback from a friend or colleague about the pitch of your voice. Then, practice lowering the pitch of your voice if it tends to be very high or raising it if it tends to be very low.

- *Inflection.* Voice inflection deals with the changes in pitch and intonation that people use in social conversation. Voice inflection helps to clarify meaning or intent and to convey emotions. Consider how the meaning of a declarative sentence can change depending on which word the speaker emphasizes:

  - "*I* didn't say she was angry." The speaker is suggesting that someone else made the statement.
  - "I didn't *say* she was angry." The speaker may have implied the statement but did not state it overtly.
  - "I didn't say *she* was angry." The speaker may have made a similar statement about a different person.

  Inflection can also convey whether the sentence is a statement or a question. When spoken with a falling intonation, the sentence "She said that" is a statement; it conveys information. If the speaker uses a rising intonation, however, the sentence conveys surprise or disbelief: "She said that?" Your rising intonation at the end of a question also provides students with a cue that their participation or response is expected.

  Voice inflection can provide listeners with clues about the most important parts of the message. Words that are spoken more emphatically or with a different pitch are key words, and information that is delivered after a pause is usually key information.

  Finally, varying your voice inflection creates a more melodic and engaging experience for the listeners, increasing the likelihood that they will continue to pay attention.

## Movement Within the Classroom

Effective teachers keep moving. They use their movement around the classroom to create a variety of benefits for themselves and their students:

- *Substitute for student movement.* A typical classroom setting requires students to be physically inactive, sitting in their seats for much of the day, listening to the teacher, participating in a discussion, or working with a partner. Physical and mental activity seem to be connected. Just think of how easy it is to find yourself drifting off when you sit down to watch television. This relationship suggests the need for movement within the classroom if students are to be active listeners. However, as we described in Module 8, Establishing the Classroom Environment, allowing students to move about freely can present some classroom management challenges. Thus, many teachers choose to do most of the moving about the classroom themselves as a way of providing vicarious physical motion within the classroom.

- *Keeping students' attention.* From a visual standpoint, teacher movement gives students some variation in what they see. When the teacher remains at the front of the classroom, students have only the blackboard and the backs of their classmates' heads for visual stimulation. When the teacher moves around the classroom, students look at other parts of the classroom and other classmates. Some students may even have to turn physically to see the teacher. Even though the students' movement within their seats may be minimal, it does provide some new stimulation and keeps them alert.

  From an auditory perspective, teacher movement contributes to the effect of voice inflection. As the teacher moves, the source of the auditory stimulus moves. For some students, the stimulus is now louder because the source is closer to them; for others, the stimulus assumes a different tone or pitch with the relocation of the source. For all students, the shifts in auditory stimulus can help them remained engaged.

- *Engaging the whole class.* A normal classroom discourse pattern has the teacher ask a question to which one or a few students respond. The student respondents generally direct their comments to the teacher, often creating more of a dialogue between the teacher and individual students. If the teacher remains at the front of the room most of the time, nonresponding students may have difficulty hearing the comments of their classmates, especially if they are seated behind the speaker. As a result, the nonresponding students may not feel involved in the discussion and may not feel compelled to listen to the response given. When the teacher moves around to different parts of the classroom, the student respondents will turn toward the teacher as they speak, making it easier for the nonrespondents to hear and even listen to the comments being made and hence creating a more inclusive conversation.
- *Encouraging good behavior.* In addition to contributing to more effective communication, teacher movement also has benefits in terms of classroom management. The proximity of the teacher to students tends to reduce students' tendency to be off-task.

# Instructional Messages

The second element in the communication process is the message. In instructional communication, the message is the heart of the process, and ensuring its reception in a form similar to its transmission is essential to effective teaching. Instructional communication is not so much about how well the teacher teaches as about how well learners learn—in other words, how well students receive the messages the teacher sends. The message must be received as intended in order for the communication to be effective. To go from teacher to student in essentially the same form, a message must be both clear and phrased appropriately for the audience.

## Clarity of Message

Keeping in mind the importance of the message in instructional communication, you want to be sure that you are clear about what you want to say. You may be thinking, "Of course, I know what I want to say. I'm teaching about light-dependent photosynthesis." Or perhaps you are teaching about the Battle of Stalingrad during World War II. Those, we would argue, are the topics that will be the focus of your communication, but they do not constitute the *message*.

When we talk about clarity of the message, we are suggesting that you articulate for yourself the specific "take-home" message—a summary statement—that you want your students to receive and internalize about the topic you are teaching. What, exactly, do you want your students to internalize about the light-dependent reactions in photosynthesis? Precisely what should they take away from their study of the Battle of Stalingrad? Choose the one most important message you want to convey.

## Appropriate Language

Once you have clarified your message, think about the language you will use to communicate that message. In the classroom, the message—what you want students to learn—can be made more accessible by your use of appropriate language. When choosing your words, consider the level of formality that you will use, the age of the students, and the ethnic, cultural, and gender composition of the class.

- *Formality.* As we noted earlier in this module, it is important that your students perceive that you are in a position of authority in the classroom. The language you use can help you create and reinforce this perception. In the classroom, your language and style of speaking will need to be more formal than the language you use with your friends and family. At the same time, you do not want to convey an egotistical attitude by speaking in a condescending manner.

  A good rule of thumb is to use proper English and to avoid slang and incorrect grammar, even though both may be generally acceptable. Besides being responsible for conveying academic content, teachers are also modeling for their students how to converse in their own future public lives. Using slang or sloppy speech may give students a false impression that this informal language will be appropriate for them in their workplaces. The "In Your Classroom" feature offers specific tips.

- *Age-Appropriateness.* You should use words that are neither insultingly simple nor overwhelmingly complex. This happy medium will vary not just from one grade to the next but also, in some instances, from one group of students to another at the same grade level! Finding the right level will take some time and patience, as you assess the vocabulary comprehension levels of your students. A good rule of thumb is to err on the side of simplicity, at least at first. As you and your students get to know one another better, you can make the necessary adjustments to your language use.

- *Neutral Vocabulary.* You need to be sure that your language does not offend anyone because of his or her religious affiliation, ethnic identity, cultural background, political convictions, or sexual orientation. Be gender-neutral in your language, never suggesting, say, that boys are

### In Your Classroom

**Dos and Don'ts of Classroom Language**

Here's a short list of considerations to keep in mind when communicating with your students. These apply not just to the classroom, but also to any situation, such as sporting events, extracurricular activities, or field trips, in which you are in contact with your students.

- DO speak clearly, concisely, and fluidly.
- DON'T address your students as "you guys" or "guys." Rather, use terms such as "everyone/everybody," "boys and girls," "children," or "class," depending on their ages.
- DO use words that are gender-neutral and inoffensive.
- DON'T use filler words such as "like," "you know," and "um."
- DO use proper grammar. Avoid using idiomatic expressions or slang.
- DON'T ever use even mild or commonly used expletives or profanity.

more likely than girls to participate in sports, to do well in math, or to have trouble appreciating poetry. Avoid any hint of ethnic or cultural mocking, and allow none from the students in your class, even if the comments are made in jest. Do not belittle the interests of any of your students. Save your commentary about political events for the teachers' room or, better yet, for weekend outings with your friends.

## Means of Communication

The importance of the means cannot be overstated in instructional communication. As we noted earlier, teaching is not just lecturing or conveying information. Students must internalize the messages conveyed with the same meaning given the messages by the teacher. In light of the importance of receiving the message, the means of sending a message become key. There are four principal means of communication, each with its own strengths and weaknesses.

- *Oral communication* is the principal medium of instructional communication. Teachers communicate their messages by lecturing, asking and answering questions, leading discussions, and giving directions. They also use voice inflection to indicate emotions and to cue learners/listeners on their responsibilities for participation. Oral communication requires of the receiver good listening skills and a reasonable auditory memory: students must hear and internalize the message and retain it.
- *Written communication* records the verbal message in print, whether on a chalkboard, projector screen, in a handout, or in a book. Written communication allows for greater permanence, and to some extent clarity, of the message, because it can be revisited and reviewed by the receiver. Written communication requires of the receiver age-appropriate reading skills to "decode" the written message. Because the message can be revisited as often as needed, however, the receiver does not necessarily need to remember the message, as one does with oral communication.
- *Visual communication* presents the message graphically—through pictures, drawings, or graphs and charts. Visual communication offers a permanence similar to that of written communication. When visual communication is the only means used to convey a message, however, there is a high potential for misunderstanding, because visual messages can be ambiguous, resulting in competing, or even conflicting, messages being understood by receivers. Think how different people react to works of art. Because the message being conveyed in visual communication is not explicit, the receiver makes use of his or her background knowledge and cultural understanding to decipher the message.
- *Nonverbal communication* includes the sender's style of dress, spatial distance from the receiver, eye contact, and facial expression. Such "body language" is by far the most ambiguous form of communication. The messages communicated through body language all have multiple interpretations and meanings. As we noted in Module 3, Teaching Culturally Diverse Learners, many of these interpretations are linked to a student's cultural background. Thus nonverbal communication suffers from even greater ambiguity than visual communication. Try to be aware of your nonverbal messages and the varying messages that your students may be receiving. For example, a teacher who decides to stand

near a student and offer helpful strategies while he works through math problems may be surprised to learn that, rather than finding the teacher's presence reassuring, the student finds such proximity intimidating or threatening.

Because different students have different preferences for receiving information, you can help guarantee that the messages sent are accurately received by using multiple means to communicate your messages. For example, when giving students instructions about how to construct a geometric model, consider using at least two or three of the means of communication: describing the process as you do it yourself, and then handing out written instructions accompanied by diagrams.

## Your Students: Receivers of Instructional Communication

The fourth element in the communication process is the receiver. In instructional communication, the receivers, your students, are not always willing participants in the communication process. In order for your message to be received as it is delivered, your students must be *ready, able,* and *willing* to receive the message. Problems with any of these three can create barriers to effective communication.

- *Ready.* Students are ready to receive messages when competing messages or other distractions have been eliminated—or at least minimized—and when their attention has been focused on the relevant topics.
- *Able.* Students are able to receive messages that are understandable. Understandable messages use language that is accessible to the students, are delivered with consideration to the developmental cognitive abilities of the students, and respect the attention span of the students.
- *Willing.* Students are willing to receive messages when the messages are of interest to them or the delivery is engaging and enjoyable.

Your students are inundated daily with a staggering number of visual, verbal, and (to a lesser extent) written messages. From television, video games, and Internet surfing, to text and instant messaging, to the ubiquitous iPods and other MP3 players, today's students experience constant sensory stimulation, if not sensory overload. To survive this chronic onslaught, many young people have learned to filter messages, selectively internalizing only those of interest. Your "messages" may not be ones that they readily opt to allow in. A potential consequence of the message overload that young people experience may be strategies for filtering aural messages. In addition, many young people are prone to "sensory surfing," jumping from one auditory stimulus to another as their interest wanes. As a result, some of your students may not have much experience focusing for very long on a single event. Do not be surprised to see them start to tune you out after about five or seven minutes.

You can help your students develop their listening skills by planning relatively short learning activities with frequent comprehension checks at the beginning of the school year and then gradually extending the length of the learning activities and decreasing the frequency of comprehension checks. Further, if your school system does not have guidelines for student use of electronics in the classroom, you may want to impose policies for their

use within your classroom. Make it clear to students when, if ever, certain electronic devices can be used in the classroom. While certain of these devices can be very powerful learning tools, they can also be a source of distraction for many students.

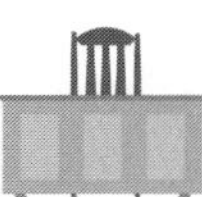

## Now You Do It

Refer to the opening scenario, and apply what you have learned in this module to answer the following questions.

**QUESTIONS**

1. What do you think has led to Meghan's current situation in the classroom? What did Meghan do, or fail to do, with her students to contribute to the current difficulty?
2. What can Meghan do to change the classroom environment? What immediate action should Meghan undertake? What long-term action would you suggest?

# Feedback: Confirming Delivery of Your Message

Because the received message is as important as the sent message in instructional communication, it is essential that teachers take steps to determine the success of their communication efforts. In order to make sure your messages get across to students as you intend them to, you need to check that students are listening by asking questions to assess their comprehension. You will also want to decode conscientiously the messages your students send you. Often messages have meanings that can be hidden in the content or delivery of the message.

## Check for Listening

Your students, if they are to learn the information you are presenting, need to be very good listeners. Good listeners are active listeners who are able to restate accurately the message sent. You may assume naively that your students have, over the course of their school career, developed good listening skills, but that may not be the case. Initially, at least, we suggest that you assume the contrary: that at times your students' listening skills are not as finely honed as they ought to be.

Observe your students during the lesson to see whether they look as though they are actively listening. Then verify your impressions by asking students to restate the message you just presented. As you come to know your students better, you will develop a more intuitive sense of how well students are listening. In the meantime, stop frequently throughout a lesson and have students restate your message. Although this may slow down your lessons at first, the benefits to student learning can be significant.

## Ask Questions . . . and Expect Answers

In social communication, a person asks a question to get information. In most instances, the answer to the question is unknown to the person asking

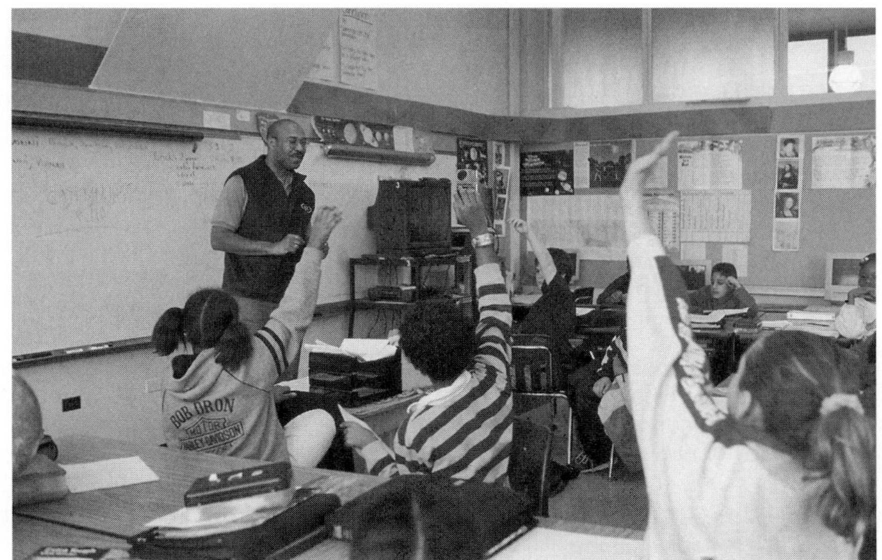

Asking questions is a great way to check for students' listening, but be sure to wait for students to answer them.

it, which is why he or she asks it. In instructional communication, the situation is different; the questioner, the teacher, asks questions to which he or she already knows the answer. In fact, the teacher is often the source of the information about which he or she is asking the question. The teacher's purpose in asking questions is not to get information but to verify that those being questioned, the students, possess the information needed to answer the question.

Consider the following scenario:

> "So, now who can tell me the answer?" Stone silence. Not a hand raised. Peter thought to himself, "I know they understand this. Why doesn't anyone ever answer my questions?"
>
> He forged on, "First, we subtracted 27 from both sides of the equation. And then we divided both sides by 4. What's left?" Still no response. Peter waited another thirty seconds to see if anyone would volunteer. Finally, he gave in and told them, "As you can see, we're left with $x = 3$. That's the answer. Let's try another one. How about number 21?"
>
> Peter continued explaining the solutions to the equations, knowing full well that his students could also do it but, for some reason, would not even attempt to answer his questions.

Perhaps because students know that the questions being asked of them are not "real" questions, it is not uncommon for students to be sluggish in responding to questions, even though they may well possess the knowledge needed to answer the questions. Other factors may also contribute to the ringing silence that teachers sometimes hear when they pose a question. Some students may have an aversion to speaking in class. Others may simply be overwhelmed by the number of questions they have already been asked that day. The situation is aggravated when the teacher gives in, loses the "waiting game," and answers his or her own questions.

We firmly believe it is important that you maintain the social communication protocol, so when you ask a question, make sure that at least one student answers it. You may have to wait literally a minute or two, or you may have to call on a student to answer the question, but you want to be sure to establish the practice of having students—not you, the teacher—answer the questions you ask.

**Video Case**

In the video case, *Classroom Management: Best Practices,* a student emphasizes the importance of listening to students. As you watch the clips and study the artifacts in the case, reflect on the following questions.

**QUESTIONS**

1. Does this student's perception agree with the information in this module? Why or why not?
2. How can you, as a teacher, make students feel comfortable coming to you with personal concerns, while maintaining your status as an authority figure?

***Online Study Center***

### Learn to Decode Student Messages to You

Students often express their frustration over understanding concepts or skills in indirect ways. Consider some typical student comments:

"Math is such a waste of time. I'll never use it once I'm out of school."

"How can anyone like poetry? It's so stupid!"

"Can I go to the nurse? I don't feel well." (Student asks just before physical education class.)

When you hear a student voice these feelings, think about what the student is really trying to express to you. Rather than trying to convince a student of the usefulness or value of learning these concepts, it might be more beneficial to ferret out the difficulties the student is having learning the concepts or skills. It may well be that the student who sees math as "such a waste of time" feels overwhelmed and unable to understand the concepts being presented. Rather than admit his or her difficulty understanding, the student targets the subject as the problem. Similarly, a student who cannot see the worth of a poem may never have developed the strategies or skills needed to analyze and appreciate poetry. Finally, the student who makes frequent requests to visit the nurse, especially if these requests often come at the same time of day or just before the same class period, may be communicating fear or frustration with whatever course or classroom situation is on her or his schedule at that time.

When your students make comments like these, it may be worthwhile to pursue the conversation, time permitting of course, to try to identify the source of concern or frustration for the student. Then you will be better able to direct the student to resources that may be useful in helping him or her be more successful academically, socially, or even emotionally. For example, students who are struggling to understand particular concepts may be afforded additional instructional support.

In addition, "listen" to what your students are communicating to you nonverbally, especially when their nonverbal communication seems to send a different message from their words. A normally engaged student who becomes silent and stops participating, or a reliable student who starts forgetting homework, should be encouraged to speak with a counselor. Recognize that a student's outburst of anger is more than likely not directed at you but may, rather, indicate that the student needs help in finding the resources to address a problem. In these instances, we do not encourage you to try to solve the problem yourself. Instead, direct students to the necessary professional resources. Few teachers are trained therapists, and attempts to help students with personal problems can backfire, often placing the teacher in a compromising situation.

## Negotiating and Conflict Resolution Skills

Any time there are twenty or more people in a confined area for an extended period of time, such as an entire school year, there will inevitably be conflicts. Small conflicts can easily escalate into larger ones that compromise the learning environment and stifle your attempts to communicate important instructional messages. Although it is far from a comprehensive approach to conflict resolution, the "In Your Classroom" feature offers

## In Your Classroom

### Steps to Take in a Conflict

Use the acronym CLERS to help you remember the following steps. You can use them to be the teacher who "clears" up conflict.

1. *Check your own attitude.* Maintain a calm and even-tempered demeanor. The situation is already volatile, and your goal is to diffuse the tension. You must set the tone by being calm, objective, analytical.
2. *Lower the stress levels.* Encourage those involved in the dispute to curb their emotions. Remind participants frequently to lower their voices, to breathe deeply, and to take breaks between statements. Having participants sit down can also help to reduce the tension. Your goal is to have the participants discuss dispassionately the issues that led to the conflict.
3. *Establish the ground rules.* Develop a process for discussing the issues that is fair and, even more important, *appears* fair to all participants. Your effectiveness depends on your ability to appear unbiased. Make sure all participants have a clear understanding of the rules and of your expectations for the conversation.
4. *Restate and rephrase.* As each participant presents his or her position, rephrase what you understand to be the core issues of the conflict. A major stumbling block in resolving conflicts is misunderstanding. When you rephrase others' positions, you clarify for all involved what the core issues are. After all participants have presented their issues, restate once more what you understand to be the core of the conflict. ("Belinda, you think that Angie should have told you she was going to the dance with Carla and her friends. Angie, you were afraid to tell Belinda because you knew she would be upset with you, but you were excited that Carla and her friends included you.")
5. *Suggest solutions.* After everyone agrees on the core issues, you can propose possible solutions to the group, asking each individual whether he or she would be willing to accept the resolution. If a compromise solution is reached, restate the resolution for all. You may also want to have all the participants restate what they believe they have agreed to or what they understand they are expected to do.



a few guidelines for negotiating and resolving conflict among students and with colleagues or parents. We also urge you to learn to recognize early signs of conflict and to be proactive in dealing with these situations before they become full-blown disputes that require much energy and detract from instructional time.

Your communication skills lie at the heart of your effectiveness as a teacher. As a teacher, you must hone your oral and written skills so that you convey effectively important messages that include not just discipline-specific information, but also attitudes and beliefs about learning. You want to sharpen your listening skills so that you can check for students' understanding of concepts taught. You'll also want to "hear" what your students are telling you, either verbally or nonverbally, and can address their needs and concerns adequately.

Keep in mind that some of the norms and expectations of instructional communication differ from those of interpersonal or social communication. Because the flow of communication in the classroom is more often one-way than two-way, you must be sensitive to the messages that students are conveying and respond to them effectively.

## Further Resources

- Pamela Cooper, Carolyn Calloway-Thomas, and Cheri J. Simonds, *Intercultural Communication: A Text with Readings* (Boston: Allyn & Bacon, 2006). Using a narrative approach, Cooper, Calloway-Thomas, and Simonds explore the multifaceted and complex world of intercultural communication.
- Pamela Cooper and Cheri J. Simonds, *Communication for the Classroom Teacher,* 7th ed. (Boston: Allyn & Bacon, 2002). Cooper and Simonds help teachers, both current and prospective, develop the knowledge and skills necessary for effective communication within the classroom.
- Ro Neff (Ed.), *Classroom Communication: Collected Readings for Effective Discussion and Questioning* (Madison, WI: Atwood Publishing, 1989). These essays offer suggestions for enhancing discussion in the classroom.
- Robert Powell and Dana Caseau, *Classroom Communication and Diversity: Enhancing Instructional Practice* (Mahwah, NJ: Lawrence Erlbaum Associates, 2004). Powell and Caseau offer a framework for helping teachers find ways to communicate effectively in a diverse, multicultural classroom.

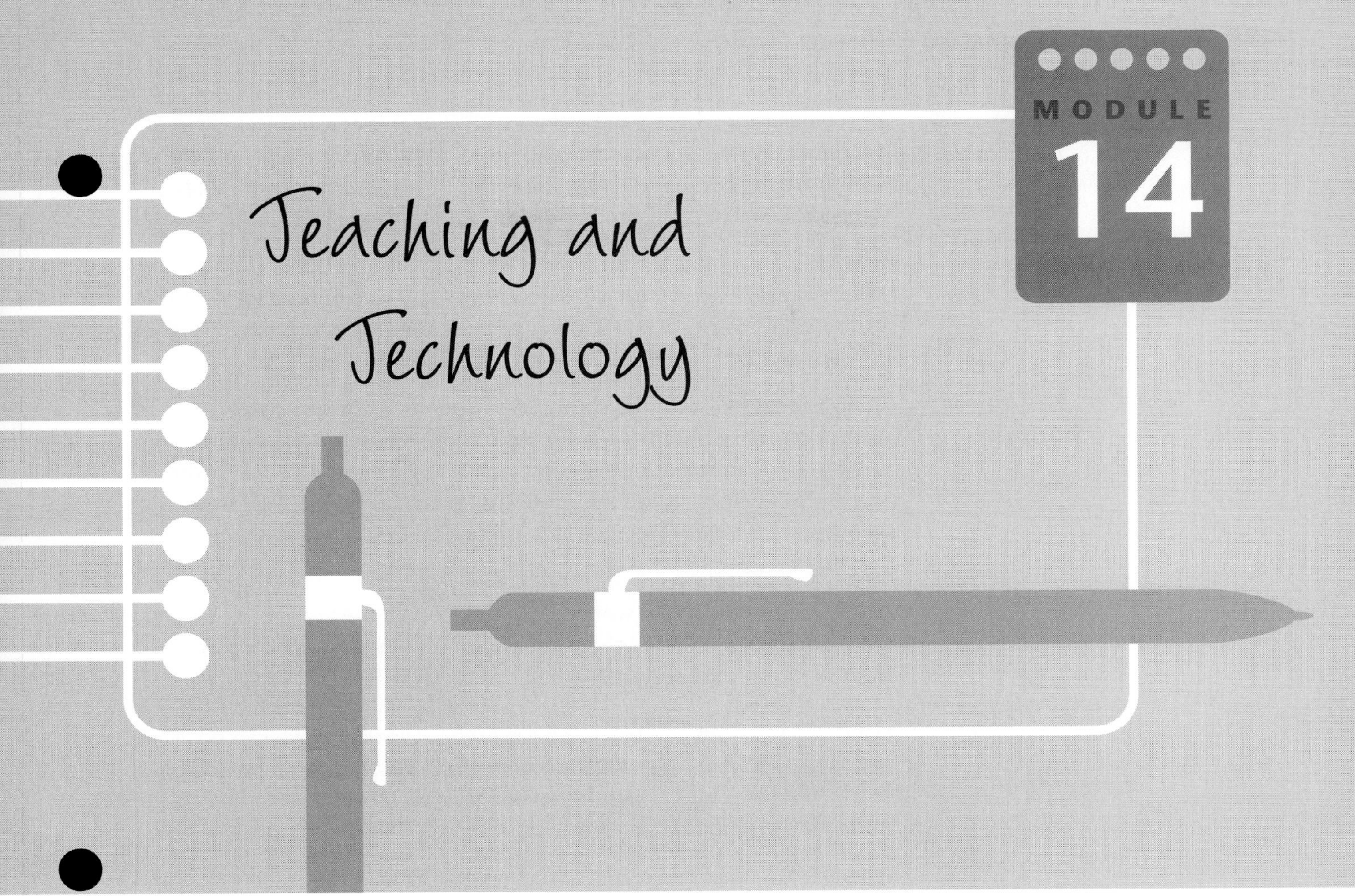


Scenario

"Okay, everyone, it's time to save what you were working on and put your keyboards away. We'll begin our math lesson in three minutes." Mr. Burke's fourth-graders have just spent the last forty minutes working on their social studies projects. Most of them were researching their topics on the Internet. Some had started writing their reports, while others were looking for images and pictures to include in their multimedia presentations.

In Mr. Burke's classroom, each student has a cordless keyboard at his or her desk. The students' computer monitors are encased in their desks, under transparent plastic desktops, giving every student easy access to his or her computer.

"Are we ready to begin?" asks Mr. Burke as he turns on the LCD projector. Students focus on the images that appear on the screen in the front of the room as Mr. Burke reviews the previous day's math lesson. "Let's review solid shapes. Yesterday, we talked about the shapes that make up a rectangular prism." Behind him, on the interactive white board, an image of a rectangular prism appears. "Who wants to remind us what we talked about yesterday?" Mr. Burke chooses a student from the many hands that go up. "Ally, come on up and tell us about a rectangular prism."

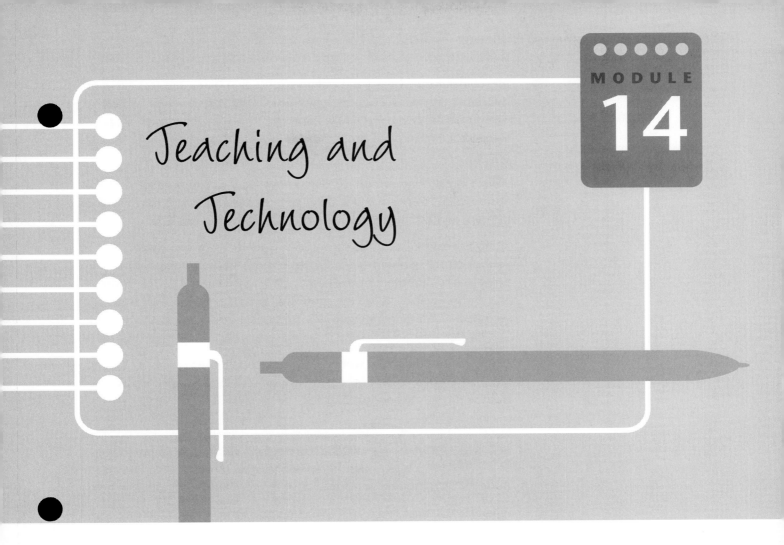

Ally comes to the board and points out the two bases and four faces of the prism. As she touches the white board, the parts are highlighted. "These are the two bases," Ally points out. "They are congruent shapes." Her verbal explanations are translated into words that appear on the board.

"That's great, Ally. You can sit down now. Now let's look at some of the attributes of the prism. How many vertices does the prism have?" Hands pop up, and Mr. Burke calls on Jung Lee, who answers, "Six."

"Jung Lee says a prism has six vertices. How many of you agree? Use your electronic pointer to answer yes or no." Students take out their pointers and aim them at the board, clicking on either the YES or the NO on the screen. Individual responses, as well as class totals, are recorded on Mr. Burke's computer. He takes a quick look at the monitor.

"Dakota, you said you disagree with Jung Lee. Can you tell us why?" Dakota comes up to the white board and counts the vertices by touching them. As she touches the vertices, each is highlighted. "I count eight vertices," responded Dakota.

Preview

The classroom in the scenario above can be called a "connected" classroom. Technology is used as an educational tool to facilitate both students' learning and performance of the teacher's administrative tasks.

When people hear "educational technology," they most often think of computers, such as those in the scenario, but if we define technology in a more general sense, as the application of new scientific knowledge to practical purposes, then technology has been a part of the classroom for a long time. One of the first technological advances introduced into schools was the chalkboard, which first appeared in the early nineteenth century. The wall-mounted chalkboard replaced individual student slates and changed the way teachers and students interacted. Now, teachers could write lessons or problems a single time for all students to copy, rather than having to write on each student's slate. With the advent of electricity and the widespread adoption of electrical appliances, many new technologies became available for use in schools by the mid-twentieth century. And ever since, from overhead projectors to educational television, from electric typewriters to laptop computers and graphing calculators, these new tools have significantly influenced what happens in the classroom.

Nearly every new technology has been enthusiastically heralded as something that will transform education, and nearly every new technology has been met with various levels of excitement and anxiety by the teachers who are expected to implement this transformation. The same is true of today's technology. In this module, we will summarize the different technologies available today and examine how these technologies are currently used in the classroom. Our hope is that this overview will familiarize you with a wide variety of technological enhancements to instruction and will spotlight any skills you need to develop to put such tools to their best uses in your classroom.

**This module emphasizes that:**

- **Teachers today must be familiar with the workings of a variety of hardware tools and must understand the uses of several types of software.**
- **Increasing use of computers and the Internet in the classroom is likely to lead to changes in the teacher's role and responsibilities.**
- **Technology tools can help you, as a teacher, streamline some of your instructional and administrative tasks.**
- **Technology is useful in nearly every subject area across the curriculum, with specialized applications available for many subjects.**
- **Distance learning is an increasingly popular way for schools to pool resources and for students to find opportunities that are not available to them locally.**
- **Assistive technology of many kinds can help students with disabilities perform the same tasks as their peers without disabilities.**

### Now You Do It

Read through the opening scenario again, and identify ways in which the technology used in this classroom seems to facilitate students' learning. Also list ways in which the technology contributes positively to the teacher's administrative duties. Make a second list of any drawbacks you notice about the use of technology in this classroom.

# Technology Terminology, or What Might You Find in Your Classroom?

Classrooms such as the one in the opening scenario are still the exception, rather than the rule. In most American schools, you are more likely to find a mix of old and new technologies. You will still find overhead projectors, slide projectors, televisions, and VCRs or DVD players, and you will need to know how to work them and use them effectively in your lessons. You are increasingly likely to encounter some of the newer technologies described in this section, however. And you will need to know not only how to work the hardware gizmos but also how to choose and use software effectively to enhance the learning of your students.

## Technology Hardware

You will almost certainly be working with computers as a teacher. As the opening scenario of this module demonstrates, however, "educational technology" encompasses more than just computers; other tools are becoming more and

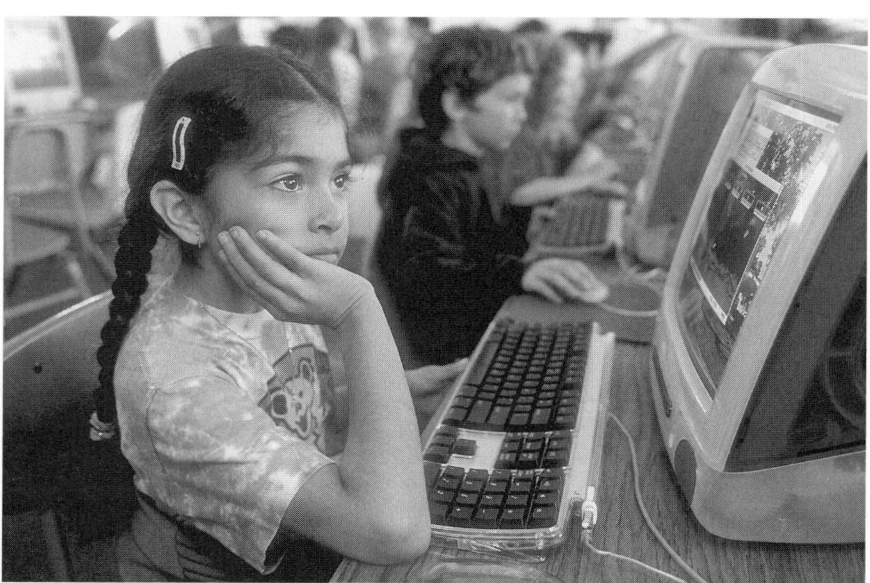

Students use computers for a variety of learning tasks.

more common in the elementary and secondary school environment. Here's a rundown of hardware you might see soon:

- *Computers.* Some might argue that computers, which have been a familiar sight in schools since the early 1980s, are hardly "new technologies." Nevertheless, their role within the classroom continues to evolve as their capabilities increase and their potential for enhancing the learning experiences of students is studied and assessed. At this point, schools vary in their computer-to-student ratios and choices of machines. At some schools, every student has a computer. Some of these may be desktop models, like those in Mr. Burke's classroom in the scenario. Others may be laptops. The portability of laptops allows secondary students to carry them from class to class and enables teachers to plan the use of activities involving computers during trips or other out-of-classroom lessons. Most schools, however, cannot afford a computer for each student. In these schools, each classroom may be equipped with a few computers, usually desktop models, or all the computers may be grouped in one or two computer labs or the library/media center. Some schools have opted to combine these approaches, installing a few computers in each classroom and adding a computer lab with up to thirty computers. With a fixed number of computers in each classroom, students can access the computers at any time during the school day, but only a limited number of students can use the computers at any given time. You will need to devise methods to ensure fair access for all students. The computer lab option allows all of the students in a class to work individually on a computer; however, they may have access only once or twice a week. You will need to plan carefully what you want students to accomplish during their lab time.

**AlphaSmart** a computer companion that consists of a keyboard with an LCD display that displays text; AlphaSmarts are most often used as word processors.

- *AlphaSmarts.* An **AlphaSmart** is a computer companion that consists of a keyboard with an LCD display that displays text. AlphaSmarts are most often used as portable word processors because they can be used as stand-alone processors. Files can be saved to the memory of the AlphaSmart and later uploaded to a computer. One model, *Dana,* allows students to browse the Web or check email. A number of advantages have made AlphaSmarts increasingly popular in schools. They are small, light, readily portable, and easy to store. They are also fairly rugged and able to withstand the rough use to which students may subject them.

Finally, AlphaSmarts represent a low-cost option for giving all students access to word processing capabilities.

- *Handheld Devices*. Handheld devices, such as the following, are gaining in popularity in schools for their portability, limited versatility, and low cost.

  - *Personal Digital Assistants (PDAs)* can help both teachers and students organize tasks and assignments and keep track of important information. PDAs can usually run versions of productivity applications, such as Microsoft® Word and Excel, allowing users to use them as miniature computers. Most of the models also have wireless communication capabilities, from sending and receiving email to browsing the Internet. In addition, most have infrared beaming capabilities, enabling users to "beam" information to other users who are within range of one another. As an alternative to beaming, PDAs can be connected to a network, and with the appropriate software, they can be used to take quizzes, answer teachers' questions as in the opening scenario, or provide feedback to teachers.

    Some peripherals, or attachments, are available that make PDAs an even more attractive technology option. An extended keyboard makes the PDA easier to use as a word processor or communication device to send emails. Scientific probes can be attached to the PDA to help students collect data. Applications that can be purchased for PDAs include graphic organizers, ebook readers, and reference resources (encyclopedia, dictionary, thesaurus). Teacher tools include grade books, lesson planners, and quiz and worksheet generators.

    Current PDAs have limited wireless capabilities, so users are unable to engage in such activities as downloading songs or using instant messaging (IM). Some may view this limitation as a drawback, but many teachers appreciate the reduced options for nonacademic distraction! Perhaps the most significant disadvantage of PDAs is that they have small screens, and without the use of extended keyboards, it can be difficult for students to input information.

  - *Pocket personal computers (PCs)* have many of the same uses as PDAs, and they frequently offer greater functionality and greater wireless capabilities for cellular communications, file sharing, and downloading. Their cost is proportional to the level of functionality and the number of features available.

  - *Handheld graphing calculators* are still prominent in the mathematics classroom, but they have become more versatile via the development of mini-applications, or "apps," related to other content areas, such as science, history, and geography. Handheld graphing calculators can also be turned into portable calculator-based laboratories (CBLs) with the purchase of scientific probes and a CBL cradle in which the calculator sits. The data can later be uploaded to a computer for manipulation and analysis.

**Interactive white boards** dry-erase writing surfaces connected to a computer. The white board has a driver that can be connected to a computer to make the board interactive.

- ***Interactive white boards*** offer a dry-erase writing surface connected to a computer. Many white boards can be connected to a computer to make the board interactive so that touching an area of the white board, as the student did in Mr. Burke's class, will activate the corresponding software application or open the corresponding web page. Other boards can digitize, and convert into text on a computer, words that are written on their surface.

- Projectors are especially useful for teachers who have only one or two computers in their classroom. When data or information from the computer is projected onto a large screen, all the students in class can see and have access to the information. Teachers can then ask questions of students and anticipate lively discussions.

With the constant advances under way in miniaturization, we expect great innovations in technology over the next generation. It seems safe to say that educational technology will continue to play an important role in helping students access information more readily and streamline the learning process.

## Technology Software

The world of educational software is filled with applications of variable content and quality. The challenge for educators is to find applications that match the needs and wants of both teachers and students. Here is a brief overview of the types of educational software available.

- *Skills development* applications help users develop and improve basic or core skills, generally in the areas of literacy and numeracy. The *Clifford the Dog* reading series and the *Reader Rabbit* math series are examples of skills development software.
- *Knowledge presentation* applications present information in an engaging and often interactive format to help students understand important concepts. Knowledge presentation applications tend to focus on the social sciences (history, geography, economics) or the natural sciences (biology, chemistry) and hard sciences (physics, engineering). The *Carmen Sandiego* series and the *Magic School Bus* series engage students in visually rich educational adventures as they teach key concepts in their different content areas. At the secondary school level, knowledge presentation applications can be particularly useful to illustrate concepts in science or mathematics.
- *Multisubject by grade* programs offer both skills development and knowledge acquisition in different content areas and at different grade levels. The *Reader Rabbit*, *JumpStart*, and *Cluefinders* series are examples of this type of application. Users practice basic skills and test their understanding of discipline-specific concepts that are appropriate for students at that grade level.
- *Early learning* programs target children from age 3 to 6 years. These programs generally focus on helping young learners develop preliteracy and prenumeracy skills, such as letter and number recognition and production. Some programs help learners develop habits of mind and thinking skills that can help them be successful students.
- *Thinking and problem-solving* programs are designed to develop logical thinking processes or creative thinking skills. They present users with a construction to create or a problem to solve. Some applications that fit in this category are *I Spy*, *Reader Rabbit Thinking Adventures,* and the *Zoombinis Logical Journey*.
- *Creative arts and multimedia* programs allow users to engage in the creative arts. These applications might teach users the basics of music notation and help them write a music score that they can play back on the computer. Other applications offer users an artist's palette and a blank screen on which they can create unique designs and drawings. Multimedia applications allow users to manipulate and enhance still photography or create video clips of varying length and complexity.

- *Simulation* programs are among the most popular applications. These applications also make best use of the power and capabilities of computers. From building a city from the infrastructure up to creating one's own animals, communities, schools, or amusement parks, simulation programs help users to see the inevitable consequences of decisions and actions and to appreciate the delicate interaction among elements of any community or system.
- *Textbooks.* Some state legislatures are investigating the possibility of having computer software take the place of textbooks. Because textbook publishers often provide interactive versions of textbooks, these states are considering investing more of their resources in computers and less in textbooks. The outcome of these initiatives could have important implications for textbook publishers, schools and their budgets, and computer makers.

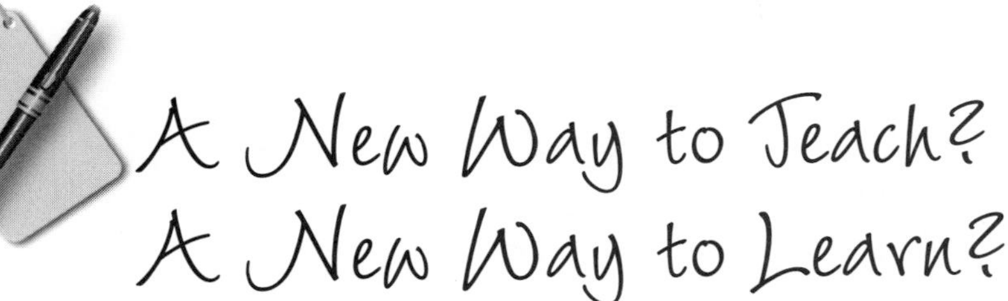

# A New Way to Teach? A New Way to Learn?

There is much speculation about how new technologies, especially computers and the Internet, will affect not just the physical structure of schools, but also the very nature of teaching and learning. Schools tend to be conservative and conserving institutions, reluctant to change rapidly or dramatically. Still, current trends suggest that the computer technology wave may be difficult for schools to withstand. Let's look at what some educators are predicting for the schools of the future.

- *Teacher's role.* As the Internet makes more and more inroads into the learning environment, the role of the teacher may well shift from that of the source and deliverer of information to that of an educational manager. When students have ready access to the Internet, they have access to much more information than the teacher could ever possess. Instead of trying to compete with these many sources of information, the teacher may focus more on managing students as they access essential information.

  This shift in the teacher's role by no means suggests that the teacher's responsibilities will be any less important than before. You may have a less visible, less prominent role during the interactive part

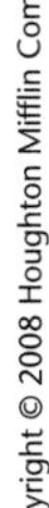

of the lesson, but as the teacher, you will still design learning activities and determine what topics students will study and what important concepts all students should know. You may also find that you have more preteaching responsibilities, such as finding relevant websites or checking links to make sure they are still live.

**Electronic grade book** a cross between a database and a spreadsheet that enables the teacher to store information on students and to compute grade averages.

It is likely that your role will also expand, and you will become an information arbiter, helping your students to reconcile conflicting pieces of information. The Internet, as we all know, contains millions of bytes of information, much of which may be inaccurate or inexact. As

## In Your Classroom

### Using Technology to Enhance Your Productivity

Beyond the primary responsibility of educating their students, teachers have to respond to administrative directives, parent queries or requests, and community concerns. Educational technology can help teachers be more efficient and more productive during the school day as well as after school hours. Many teachers use technology tools to streamline such tasks as the following:

- *Curriculum and lesson planning.* Nearly every state department of education has its state curriculum standards posted to the Web, allowing teachers easy access to curricular expectations. Most state departments of education also post released test items from state-mandated tests. In addition, databases of lesson plans on specific topics and grade levels have become available through numerous websites. Just as readily available are suggestions and ideas for differentiating activities to meet the needs of diverse learners at all grade levels.
- *Assessment.* Test generator software enables you to customize publisher-supplied tests to create exams that match the particular topics you cover in class. Most software of this type allows teachers to specify the type of assessment items to include, from multiple-choice to open-response to essay questions, the number of items of each type, and the specific topics to be tested. Teachers can generate different versions of a test that cover the same topics at the same level of difficulty. These different versions can be used for make-up tests, for example.
- *Recordkeeping.* One of the most popular productivity tools is the **electronic grade book,** often a cross between a database and a spreadsheet. The database function allows the teacher to store key contact information for his or her students, such as mailing addresses, parent contact information, emergency contact information, and school-related information such as locker numbers and combinations and textbook numbers. The spreadsheet function serves as the grade book.

  With an electronic grade book, you can quickly access statistical information about students' performance on individual tasks or their performance over time, and you can calculate students' term average each time you enter a graded assignment. As a reflective teacher, you can analyze these statistics to gain insight into individual students' academic and assessment strengths and weaknesses.

  Your grade book may also simplify your reporting tasks. More and more school systems are moving toward electronic report cards, generated from grades or narratives that teachers submit electronically.
- *Communications.* Teachers can post daily or weekly homework assignments, test and project dates, and class events at the course website, a practice that helps students and their families stay well informed about the activities in the classroom. You can send bulk emails to parents reminding them of certain events, and you can communicate more efficiently with parents about particular students, as needed. Email is also useful for efficient communication with colleagues, administrators, and your school district.

students encounter conflicting pieces of information, the teacher will have to help them discern which information is more credible and which sources more reliable. The teacher will need to acquaint students with criteria for determining the credibility or reliability of websites. The teacher will also need to help students understand the importance of discerning nuanced or biased presentations of information.

- *Teacher's responsibilities.* In the classroom of the future, the teacher will need to possess even greater knowledge of his or her subject matter and related disciplines. Although teachers may not explicitly transmit information to students as much as in the past, they will still be responsible for what students are learning and for ensuring that what students learn is accurate information. This task may present even greater challenges to teachers because they will have less control over the information that students are encountering.

  In addition, students are likely to delve into topics in greater depth or explore topics only distantly related to the main focus of their learning. Teachers will be expected to appreciate the interrelatedness of disciplines and to understand the impact that an outbreak of animal virus, for example, can have on the economy and political stability of a country. The demands on teachers will be greater, not less.

- *Teacher's resources.* Just as more resources are available for student learning, more resources are available for teachers. Lesson plan databases offer teachers ideas for learning activities. Online communities can provide teachers with discipline-specific information or teaching hints and ideas. The ubiquitous blogs can also provide a source of help, support, and information for teachers—or they can be a complete waste of your time. You will need to know how to evaluate and make the best use of these resources. The "In Your Classroom" feature summarizes current teacher productivity tools and how you can use them.

# Technology Across the Curriculum

In addition to helping teachers perform numerous tasks more efficiently, technology has contributed to making students more efficient and productive in their work, and it offers a wide variety of enriching resources and engaging educational activities and experiences. We present an overview of the contributions that technology can make to the various disciplines.

## English and Reading/Language Arts Education

Probably the most important contribution that computers have made to English education is their facilitating of writing tasks. Word processing software has made writing more efficient for all writers, from student writers to professionals. Most educators agree that word processing software also frees student writers to think more about substantive issues rather than focusing on mechanical tasks. Gone are the days of having to write an assignment out by hand and then hand-write it again (and maybe again and again) in response to feedback. Revisions are much easier on an electronically saved document. Student writers can easily test various alternatives for organizing ideas within a paragraph, or paragraphs within an essay, to find the most expressive and cogent organization of ideas.

Most word processing applications have built-in spelling and grammar checks that can help students verify the accuracy of the spelling and grammar they have used in their written work. These add-ons are not without controversy, however. Some teachers are concerned that the spelling and grammar checks cause students to become complacent in their writing and to pay little attention to the correct spelling of words, thinking that the spelling check will catch all errors. Unfortunately, the spelling and grammar check do *not* catch all errors—and they may even "correct" a word incorrectly. Teachers must help students learn to use their own judgment when considering the suggestions made by a spelling checker or grammar checker. These technological tools may call the writer's attention to typographical errors, but in the long run, the student who has internalized the rules of accurate and effective English expression will save time and write better.

Other technology tools that contribute to student learning in the English/language arts classroom are presentation applications, such as Microsoft's PowerPoint, and multimedia software, such as HyperStudio. With these tools, students can express themselves using graphics and video and audio clips, in addition to text.

A host of multimedia options are available to help students develop critical reading skills in both decoding and comprehension. Tools such as the following can be used with young students learning to read or for older students who are experiencing difficulty with reading.

- *LeapPad Learning Systems,* developed by the LeapFrog Company, are interactive learning tools that help young readers learn to read. Students place a specially made book on the LeapPad, insert a cartridge, and then use the stylus that is provided to hear the book read to them.
- *The Living Books series,* published by Broderbund, consists of CD-ROMs with interactive presentations of various books. Students can click on words to have the story read to them. Most of the images on the screen page are also linked, so students can click on any object on the page to hear its name or a description of it.
- *Games.* Many educational software products target key concepts and skills in reading and English, such as decoding, vocabulary development, or word usage. In nearly all instances, the skills development is embedded in engaging, animated adventure, or arcade-like games.

## Mathematics Education

Math educators have been at the forefront of technology use since the advent, in the mid-1960s, of handheld electronic calculators, which replaced the slide rule, itself a new technology in the seventeenth century. As these simple calculators became ubiquitous, their use in the math classroom became more and more controversial. Still a point of contention for some math educators and community members, calculators remain a staple of many middle school and high school math classrooms. Even more prominent now are graphing calculators, on which students can carry out simple and complex calculations, see graphs of equations and functions, or run applets (small programs that deal with other math concepts).

Mathematics teachers are also making use of a variety of software products.

**Integrated software suites** groups of programs that combine word processing, spreadsheet, database, and presentation applications.

- ***Integrated software suites,*** groups of programs that combine word processing, spreadsheet, database, and presentation applications, find frequent use in the math classroom. The spreadsheet application is used to record data sets and to create different graphical displays of the data. The word processing and presentation applications may be used to create text analysis of the data sets and to present the findings in an

In addition to mathematics classrooms, graphing calculators are increasingly being used in other subjects.

integrated format. An example of a graphics suite is CorelDRAW Suite, which includes programs for vector illustration, layout, image editing, animation software, and painting.

- *Math-specific software* helps students develop computational fluency or master key mathematics concepts. Like educational software developed for reading/language arts, math software is often embedded in a game environment to engage and motivate students. These drill-and-practice software applications help students develop understanding of math concepts and skills fluency, while maintaining interest and motivation. Other math-specific software programs target particular concepts in mathematics. Geometer's Sketchpad is a mathematics visualization application that allows students to construct geometric elements and explore their attributes. A host of software applications, such as 3D Grapher and FindGraph, allow students to create graphs of data sets.
- *Online tutorials and test preparation portals* are more recent additions to the educational technology toolbox. In response to the federal mandate that students in grades three through eight be tested yearly in math, reading/English, and science, educational publishers have developed online tutorials and assessment programs that address all of the standards or benchmarks for a given state. Students sign in to the website and take a diagnostic test. On the basis of their results, they are assigned to complete certain skills tutorials available at the site. Teachers can track students' progress and assessment results electronically and prescribe further skills practice, if needed.

## Science Education

The miniaturization of technologies has perhaps benefited science education more than any other field. Data probes are available for various handheld tools, such as Palm handhelds and Calculator-Based Laboratory System (CBL) that Texas Instruments produces. Students can use these probes to collect, first-hand, rich data related to actual environmental conditions, rather than working with hypothetical data manipulations generated by their teachers or textbooks. The data can then be uploaded to a spreadsheet for manipulation and analysis.

**Video Case**

In the video case, *Using Technology to Promote Discovery Learning: High School Geometry Lesson,* you'll see how high school teacher Gary Simons promotes geometry learning through a discovery learning approach. (See Module 6, Key Principles of Learning, for a description of discovery learning.) As you watch the clips and study the artifacts in the case, reflect on the following questions.

**QUESTIONS**

- Mr. Simons maintains that technology is an essential tool for promoting discovery learning. Is his statement consistent with your experiences? Why or why not?
- What aspect of using technology tools to support discovery learning do you think will be most challenging to you as a new teacher? How will you approach this challenge?

***Online Study Center***

Other technologies, such as digital microscopes and digital cameras, have enhanced students' opportunities to visualize such science phenomena as the reproduction of microscopic organisms and the composition of molecules or atoms. Schools need not purchase these more expensive tools to benefit from them. Digital images are readily found on the Internet and can be downloaded for use in the classroom.

In addition to making information and images available, the Internet offers students and teachers access to professional scientists. For example, Scientific American **(http://www.sciam.com/askexpert_directory.cfm)** offers anyone the opportunity to log on and ask a question in most science disciplines. The Center for Innovation in Engineering and Science Education **(http://www.ciese.org)** offers a similar opportunity. You and your students may be able to participate in exchanges of queries and comments or in scheduled live chats with scholars working on a project or subject of interest to you. When students have the opportunity to ask scientists and scholars about their research and their findings, they are more likely to recognize the relevance and applicability of concepts they are learning in the classroom.

## Social Studies Education

Historians and the study of history may be the greatest beneficiary of the rapid expansion of the Internet. Many groups make digitized archives of primary documents available, so that almost any student with Internet access can readily retrieve primary source documents on almost any historical event. With these documents, the study of historical events is enriched and expanded. For example, students studying immigration into the United States during the late nineteenth and early twentieth centuries can find, on various websites, newspaper articles from this time period, as well as political cartoons, personal diaries of immigrants, and historical analyses about the period. These sources can help students understand these historical events from a richer human-interest perspective than that provided by the sparse historical facts often found in textbooks.

As we noted earlier in this module, however, the sheer amount of information about historical events and other key social studies topics creates an important new role for teachers: that of information arbiter. You must find ways to help your students locate accurate information and evaluate other materials they find online. One way teachers can guide students through Internet research is with a **WebQuest,** an inquiry-based learning activity that has students navigate through different websites to gather and analyze information on a theme or topic. The advantage of a WebQuest is that students are directed to specific websites where relevant information can be found, rather than spending important class time looking for sites that *might* contain useful information.

**WebQuest** an inquiry-based learning activity in which students navigate through a set of websites to collect and analyze information on a theme or topic.

For computers that are not connected to the Internet, several different kinds of software packages often involve topics that are germane to social studies.

- *Simulation software* can be a very engaging tool. In *Decisions, Decisions: Local Government* by Tom Snyder Productions, users must make decisions about the economic, political, and social well-being of a community confronted with a dilemma. *Real Lives* by Educational Simulations introduces students to living conditions in different locations throughout the globe and helps them appreciate the interaction among geographical and climatic features, economic conditions, and quality of life in these locations.

- *Geography and map-making software* familiarizes students with important geographical features of different regions of the United States or other countries.
- *Virtual field trips* enable students to "visit" key locations when distance or funding limits their ability to go on actual field trips. Students from distant parts of the country can visit virtually places such as Plimoth Plantation, a recreated village from 1620, and Colonial Williamsburg, a recreated village from the mid-eighteenth century.

## Distance Learning

**Distance education** using technology to link students and teachers in separate locations.

**Distance education** involves using computers and the Internet to link students and teachers in separate locations. In some cases, distance education may consist of a video and audio hook-up between two sites, enabling students to participate in a lecture or discussion with a scholar in another part of the country. In other instances, students take a full-semester or full-year course online. Students log in to the course site, where they receive assignments, download readings, submit essays, take online exams, and engage in virtual discussions.

Distance learning is a rapidly growing alternative to the traditional face-to-face class. Although more commonly found at the college level, distance, or online, learning has been gaining ground at the secondary school level as well. Creating online learning communities allows schools to share resources and to provide a more flexible learning environment and a wider range of course offerings.

One of the largest online high schools is the Virtual High School (VHS), established in 1997. Since its inception, it has expanded its curricular offerings to more than 160 different courses in all content areas, including AP and honors courses, as well as gifted and talented courses for middle school students. VHS currently enrolls approximately 190,000 students both in the United States and worldwide. VHS can address the needs of small groups of students within a school district who may have advanced academic abilities or unique talents that the school district cannot afford to address.

Other school districts and consortia of schools are developing their own online learning communities, suggesting that this flexible option for delivery of instruction may become more common in the future.

## Assistive or Adaptive Technologies

**Assistive or adaptive technology** devices and services that help people with disabilities to perform better in their daily lives. Such devices include motorized chairs, remote control units that turn appliances on and off, computers, and speech synthesizers.

New technologies play an important part in the education of many individuals with disabilities. Tools and services have been created and refined to help these individuals perform many of the same tasks that their peers without disabilities are able to do. Particularly useful are tools that help students with disabilities communicate more effectively, through reading, writing, or even speaking.

- *Screen readers* use text-to-speech software to vocalize text that is shown on the computer screen. Most are designed for blind users, but they can also be useful for students with visual processing disabilities who experience difficulty reading.
- *Screen magnifiers,* designed for users who are not blind but have visual impairments, are software applications that enlarge the images and texts on the screen.
- *Refreshable braille displays* are tactile devices that produce a line of braille that changes regularly to allow the individual who is deaf-blind to "read" the text displayed on a computer screen.

- *Voice recognition software* translates the spoken word into text, enabling users with motor disabilities to compose text without having to make use of a keyboard or other input device. Voice recognition software also benefits users with language production disabilities, such as dyslexia or spelling difficulties. (See Module 4, Teaching Students with Disabilities.) These users can dictate the text they want to write without getting overwhelmed by preoccupation with knowing which letters, in what order, make up the words.
- *Adaptive keyboards* of various kinds have been developed for use by students with motor disabilities. Some adaptive keyboards display a keyboard on the screen that the user can access with a mouse or by tapping the screen either with a stick or by hand.
- *Single switches* are devices for users with severe physical disabilities. Single switches are generally used in conjunction with scanning software and allow the users to control the computer with one or two specific strokes. The user triggers the switch when the desired option is highlighted.

As described in Module 4, Teaching Students with Disabilities, schools are required by federal law to provide adaptations, such as these technological devices, to students who require them because of disabilities. Because federal law also requires students with disabilities to be included in regular classrooms to the greatest extent possible, you are likely at some point to have to learn how to help students work with their adaptive technology. We advise you to seek help from special-education personnel at your school.

Electronic technologies have changed the way businesses operate, and it appears that they are influencing—if not revolutionizing—the way schools educate children. The key to the effective use of these technologies is the teacher who knows how to use them to enhance student learning. Simply having technological tools in the classroom doesn't mean they will be used effectively. Teachers are the key element in how, and whether, these technologies will help students learn. As a new teacher, it is incumbent on you to familiarize yourself with the hardware and software that exist in your subject field and to learn how to use them effectively.

## Further Resources

- Richard. C. Forcier and Don. E. Descy, *The Computer as an Educational Tool: Productivity and Problem Solving,* 4th ed. (Upper Saddle River, NJ: Prentice-Hall, 2005). This is an introductory book in the use of computers as a tool in education.

- International Society for Technology in Education (ISTE), *ISTE's Electronic Resources.* Available at: **http://www.iste.org/resources/**. A superb list of links that covers a wide range of issues, including standards, the "digital divide," professional development, and technology integration.

Online Study Center

- Kathy Schrock, *Guide for Educators.* Available at: **http://school.discovery.com/schrockguide/**. A very well-organized list of useful links, with an especially helpful section broken down by subject area.
- Sharon Smaldino, James Russell, Robert Heinich, and Michael Molenda, *Instructional Technology and Media for Learning,* 8th ed. (Upper Saddle River, NJ: Prentice-Hall, 2006). Now in its eighth edition, this is one of the seminal books on the "how to" of using media in the classroom.

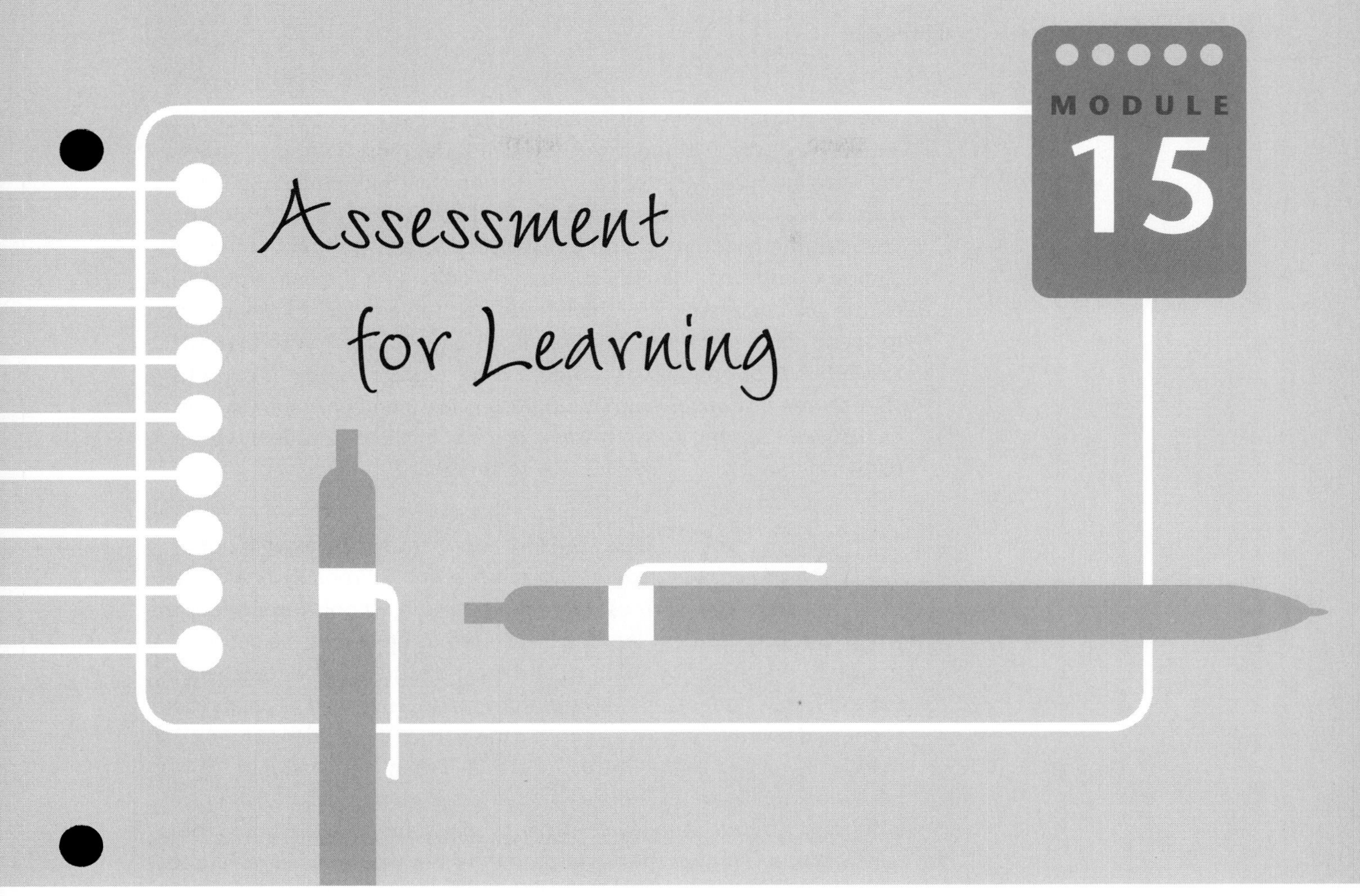

# MODULE 15
# Assessment for Learning

**Scenario**

It's almost the end of third-period English class, and the teacher is returning the most recent essay assignment. This was one of your finer essays, you thought when you handed in the paper, so you await your paper with confident anticipation. As Mr. Motlin places the paper face down in front of you, his expression gives you no clue to your grade. You turn the paper over eagerly, only to encounter an all-too-familiar C+ at the top of your essay. You flip through the essay and note the usual few, if any, comments and a smattering of surface error corrections. "I can never get a good grade in this class, no matter how much time I spend on the paper! I don't get it! Mr. Motlin just doesn't like me!" you sigh as you walk out of class.

**Scenario**

"Think we'll get our tests back today?" your friend asks as you shuffle into your fifth-period algebra II class. "I'm sure of it," you respond. "I asked Mr. K. yesterday." "How do you think you did?" your friend inquires. "Did you get those problems on the last two pages?" "I think I did okay on one of them. The second one, the lighthouse one, I was clueless. Good thing Mr. K. always goes over the tests or I'd never understand anything!"

The bell rings and, after his usual greeting to the class, Mr. Kelvin announces, "We're going over the exam today. First, let me talk about the overall results. Most of you did well on the trigonometric ratios and reciprocal ratios—the laws of sines and cosines—and most of you got the straightforward problems, but we need to revisit some of the more complex problems. Many of you had difficulty with the two problems on the last page, especially the lighthouse problem, so I think we need to spend some more time on these kinds of problems." With that, Mr. Kelvin hands out the tests amid groans and sighs of relief. "Okay, let's start on the first page. Who's going to explain number one to us?" As hands shoot up, Mr. Kelvin tosses a piece of chalk to a student, who deftly catches it and makes his way to the board.

Preview

These scenarios represent typical assessment episodes in many schools. Probably one of the most common events in schools throughout the world, assessing student learning tends also to be one of the activities most misunderstood by students and most disagreeable for teachers. For too many students, the awarding of grades is viewed as a capricious event, unrelated to any real effort on the part of the student and only marginally related to the instructional activities in the classroom. As Scenario One illustrates, tests and other assessment measures can create a defeatist attitude in many students, who assume that the grade they earn is based more on the whim of the teacher than on their ability to recognize, recall, or analyze information. For some teachers, assessment measures, especially standardized tests, are a necessary evil that interrupts the instructional flow and can create tension in an otherwise supportive and productive teacher–student relationship.

But, as the teacher in Scenario Two shows us, assessment practices can be effective and beneficial. They can help teachers determine how effective their instructional activities have been and gauge how well students are understanding and internalizing the information presented. In addition, effective assessment practices help students identify key concepts in a unit of study, realize what they do and do not understand, and appreciate the progress they are making in achieving the instructional goals of the course.

To make optimal use of assessment activities, teachers need to plan them carefully and thoughtfully, design tasks that focus clearly on the goals and objectives, and, most important, explain to students (and administrators and parents) the purpose of the assessment activities. We'll see in this module that assessment can provide teachers with useful information before, during, and after instructional activities and units. We'll also discover that, in addition to the obvious assessment events, such as tests, effective teachers engage in ongoing, informal assessments and use a variety of ways to gather information about how well their students are learning.

**This module emphasizes that:**

- **Assessment and instruction are partners in promoting student learning.**
- **Instructional activities are sometimes confused with assessment activities. Both are important, but they serve different purposes.**
- **Assessments serve three major purposes: diagnostic, formative, and summative.**
- **Teachers use both formal and informal means to assess student learning.**
- **Four primary information-gathering techniques used by teachers are inquiry, observation, analysis, and testing.**
- **Most tests represent one of two types: standardized or teacher-made.**

# What Is Assessment?

**Assessment** the process of gathering information about behavior, skills, ideas, and attitudes, using such tools as rubrics, checklists, rating scales, and portfolios.

**Measurement** the systematic collection of data or information.

**Evaluation** making judgments about, or assigning value to, the data or information collected in the measurement phase of assessment.

Although people often equate assessment and evaluation, **assessment** in fact consists of two separate yet related components:

- **measurement,** the systematic collection of data or information
- **evaluation,** judging or assigning value to the data or information collected

A familiar assessment experience can help to frame this discussion. Perhaps you were surprised when you first received your scores from one of the popular standardized college admissions tests. Accustomed to a 100-point grading system, you may have been confused to see a score of 550 or 650. What exactly did those scores mean? It was hard to be sure until someone explained to you that the scale for these tests runs from 200 to 800 and that the institution you wanted to attend preferred to accept students with scores above a certain level. Your 550 or 650 was a *measurement.* Your preferred school then *evaluated* that measurement as either above or below its cut-off score.

As a teacher, you will use a variety of methods to measure the learning of your students. You will also assign value to the information you collect, most often in terms of grades on homework, tests, or report cards.

Educational assessment takes place on a variety of levels: within the classroom and at the district, state, and even national level. Although the tools used to assess may be similar, the purpose of assessment, and consequently the uses to which the data collected are put, differ significantly between the classroom and larger-scale levels. A middle school social studies teacher may give students a multiple-choice quiz to see how well they have mastered key topics from a unit on the Civil War, whereas a multiple-choice test taken by the same students later in the year may also be given to thousands of others all over the country and then used by a government agency to compare the progress of U.S. students from year to year.

## Standardized Tests

**Standardized tests** tests or inventories that have invariant characteristics, such as specific procedures for administering the test and a fixed set of questions.

**Standardized tests** are so called because their most important characteristic is their "standardization," which includes the procedures under which the test is administered, the set of questions, the time limitations, and a set of norms against which the performance of your group is compared. There are three types of standardized instruments: *aptitude* tests; *achievement* tests; and *interest*, *personality*, and *attitude* inventories. Aptitude tests try to predict how well someone might do in a particular area, such as creativity or writing. Achievement tests measure how well an individual has achieved in some specific area, such as reading, mathematics, or science. Interest, personality, and attitude inventories are not tests, because there is no right answer to any given question. Instead, they seek to measure typical rather than maximum performance, such as learning style or study habits.

For standardized test scores to be interpreted effectively, the classroom teacher must follow directions exactly in administering the test. The test must be started and finished precisely in keeping with the test's directions so that all students have the same amount of time. The conditions must also be the same. If calculators are to be used on a portion of a math test, students must be given calculators, whether or not they choose to use them. Most standardized tests are scored by the commercial test company, and you may receive charts and graphs showing the distribution of scores of your students, as well as the norm scores.

Large-scale assessment via standardized achievement tests, particularly at the state level, has become a dominant element in the lives of public school teachers and administrators. As described in Module 1, Reflective Teaching for Student Learning, the federal No Child Left Behind (NCLB) Act requires states to annually test and report the academic progress of their students and to take steps to ensure that students make "adequate yearly progress." It is important for you as a teacher to be familiar with the large-scale achievement assessment systems in your particular state and with the uses to which the results are put. We strongly encourage you to seek out information on these tools from school administrators. The focus of this module (and of Module 16, Tools for Assessment), however, will be on classroom, rather than large-scale, assessment.

GRAND AVENUE BY STEVE BREEN

Grand Avenue: © United Feature Syndicate, Inc.

# Assessment as Part of Teaching

As we noted in Module 11, Planning Lessons, assessment is one of the principal tasks in the teaching process, and it warrants as much planning and design as curriculum development or instructional planning. As shown in Figure 15.1, the starting point in most teachers' planning process is to identify goals or outcomes—the concepts and skills that students are to master by the end of a unit, marking term, or year. Once these outcomes have been determined and the curriculum has been written, two equally important and essential considerations must be addressed:

- *Learning activities.* What activities will students engage in to lead to their achievement of the goals?
- *Assessment.* How it will be determined that students have indeed mastered the concepts and skills?

In other words, the curriculum, instruction, and assessment need to be planned and aligned thoughtfully and carefully *before* the actual teaching gets under way.

## Instructional Activities versus Assessment Activities

Some teachers confuse instructional activities with assessment activities. Although they are certainly related, these are two separate activities with two distinct purposes. Instructional activities help students master skills and knowledge, whereas assessment activities collect information on how well students have mastered these concepts and skills. Good instructional activities do not necessarily make good assessment activities, nor do appropriate assessment tasks make for good instruction.

Consider the example of an upper elementary class that studies the American Revolutionary War as part of the social studies curriculum. The state curriculum standards specify that students are to learn about six key battles of the war. The teacher divides the students into groups and assigns each group the task of researching a particular battle of the war and presenting that information to the rest of the class. Each group will decide on the format of its presentation. Students will present their research to their classmates, and each presentation will be evaluated on the basis of a rubric developed by the teacher in collaboration with the students.

**Figure 15.1**
**Assessment and Instruction in Learning**

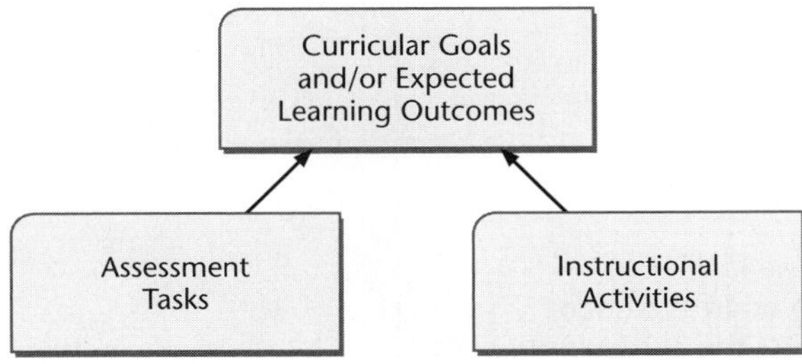

This activity can be an excellent instructional activity, helping to facilitate students' learning about the selected battles. However, it would not make a good assessment activity. Because students are making presentations about only one battle, the teacher has evidence only about their knowledge of the specific battle chosen for their presentation. He or she needs to find a way to gather evidence about each student's knowledge of *all six* key battles.

### Using Assessment to Guide Instruction

Beyond grade attribution, student assessments provide valuable information to guide teachers' instructional practices and help students become better learners. Assessments can provide the information you need for purposes such as

- (re)structuring the curriculum or unit of study to better address what students do and do not know, what they can and cannot do
- modifying instructional activities to optimize students' learning
- rethinking your own assumptions about student learning
- refining and enhancing your instructional practices
- helping students recognize principal and secondary concepts and skills
- helping students become more astute and responsible learners

## Purposes for Assessment

Depending on the point at which they are used, and on how the information gathered is put to use, assessments can serve three main purposes: diagnostic, formative, and summative.

**Diagnostic assessment** assessment used to determine a student's strengths and weaknesses.

### Diagnostic Assessment

As its name suggests, a **diagnostic assessment** is used to *diagnose* or uncover a student's areas of strength and weakness. Diagnostic assessment is

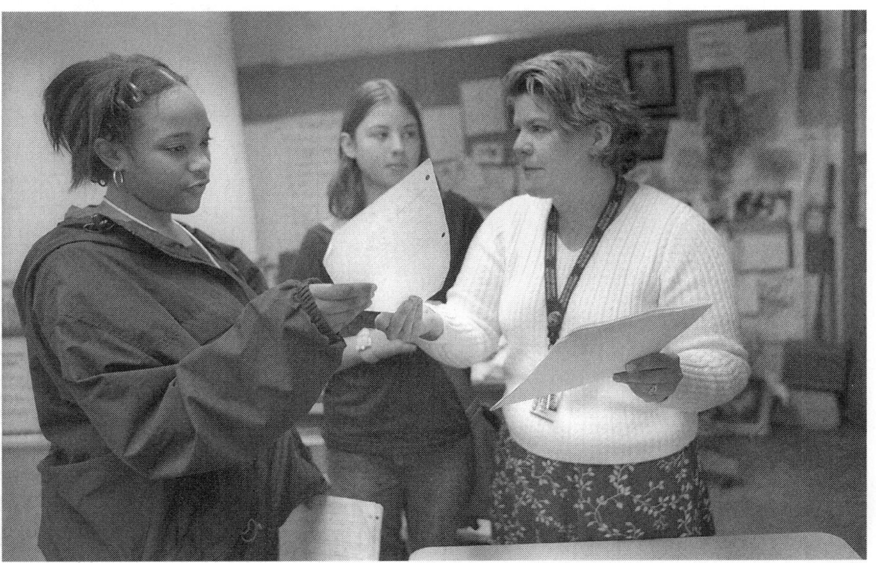

Teachers can use formative assessments to address student needs and adjust the curriculum.

an essential data-gathering process that helps teachers to determine a starting point for a unit of study. Just as a medical professional collects information about a patient's physical or mental well-being, teachers need to collect information about a student's intellectual and, sometimes, social state. We would not ask a doctor to prescribe a medical treatment until he or she had collected enough data to make an informed conjecture about the patient's condition. The same is true in teaching.

The purpose of diagnostic assessment is to ascertain the depth and breadth of students' preparedness, in terms of knowledge and skills, for a particular unit of study or a particular grade level. As much as we'd all like to think that students learn everything they are taught, we know that such is rarely the case. A diagnostic assessment lets you know *exactly* what your students have and have not internalized from previous units of study in the same or prior years of school. Elementary teachers might give diagnostic assessments to find out how well their students can carry out math operations, decode text, or work in groups. Middle school and high school teachers may administer a diagnostic assessment to measure how well students can organize their ideas, solve multistep math problems, or analyze causes of historical events.

Teachers collect and make judgments about data through diagnostic assessments, but they do not necessarily communicate to others the results of the assessment. Rather, teachers may simply use the data to determine the preparedness of their students to undertake a unit of study. They use the information they have gathered to structure their curriculum or unit of study to help students learn better.

You may want to carry out a diagnostic assessment at the beginning of the school year to find out what your students know and can do in specific areas. The information collected from this assessment can help you set your instructional plan for the month, semester, or even the year. It can also help you avoid frustrating yourself and your students by asking them to do tasks that are beyond their cognitive abilities or require a greater knowledge base.

It is also useful to do a diagnostic assessment at the start of a new unit of instruction to help you situate your instructional plan. If you are starting a new unit on atomic structure in seventh grade, a diagnostic assessment can tell you what your students already know about atoms, and this information will enable you to make optimal use of instructional time. If the majority of the students already know the parts of the atoms, it may be that you can move quickly through a review of the parts and spend more time on other, less familiar concepts. If, on the other hand, students show tenuous or inaccurate understanding of atomic structure, you will want to spend more time teaching these fundamental concepts.

## Formative Assessment

**Formative assessment** assessment used to monitor learning progress during instruction.

**Formative assessment** is carried out while instruction is taking place. It is meant to help the teacher gauge how well students are understanding concepts presented and how well they are achieving the instructional objectives of the unit. With this information, teachers can confidently maintain the curricular structure and pace they have set, or they can modify instructional activities if they find that a majority of students are not on track or if most students are more advanced in their skills development than anticipated.

Formative assessment is somewhat analogous to the behavior of a hiker on a several-day hiking excursion. Just as the hiker has fully planned his trip, including the trails he will hike, the number of miles he will hike in all and on each day, and the amount of food and water he will need, a teacher fully plans an instructional unit, including the learning objectives, a time line for the unit, and engaging learning activities that focus on each of the objectives. Along the way, the hiker stops to gauge his actual progress against his plan: Has he stayed on the right trail? Has he traveled as far as he had planned? Has he rationed his food and water supply adequately? Depending on the answers to these questions, the hiker may continue as planned or make adjustments to his plans. Similarly, you want to gauge your students' learning throughout your instructional unit to monitor their progress toward the instructional objectives you have set. You'll want to make sure, all along the way, that your students understand the content accurately and are internalizing the skills being taught.

Formative assessment can help you, the teacher, carry out three important activities:

1. *Evaluate learning activities.* Your data can give you important insights into the effectiveness of your teaching approaches and strategies. If a large number of students have failed to grasp a particular concept, you may want to rethink your teaching of the concept. Perhaps you presented it too quickly or too abstractly for some learners. Perhaps you assumed prerequisite knowledge that many of your students did not possess. Perhaps you did not provide enough practice or application of the concept to allow for student mastery. Discovering this gap between what you are teaching and what the students are learning *before* you reach the end of a unit enables you to back-track easily and re-teach the concept in a timely manner and thus saves you from jeopardizing subsequent learning objectives of the unit of study.
2. *Check your pacing.* On the basis of the data collected, you can set the pace of instruction. If your data show that most of the students have grasped the essential concepts being presented, you can move on to new concepts. If your data show that students have at best a tenuous grasp of the concepts being taught, you'll want to slow down and re-teach them.
3. *Help students prioritize learning.* A third, equally important reason for formative assessment is to make clear to students which are the key concepts and the relative importance of the concepts being presented. Students are often bombarded with so much information, both in and out of school, that they have difficulty prioritizing the concepts and knowing which information they need to focus on. Through formative assessment, students can see which concepts you, the teacher, consider important. After all, if it's on the test, it must be important, right?

**Video Case**

What is formative evaluation and how can it shed light on student progress on a more immediate basis than formalized tests? In the video case, *Formative Assessment: High School History Class,* you'll meet high school history teacher Henry Turner, who believes in the value of frequent testing. You'll see how Henry uses informal measures such as an open-note quiz to evaluate students' understanding of a particular historical period. You'll also hear from two students who have just taken a quiz. As you watch the clips and study the artifacts in the case, reflect on the following questions.

**QUESTIONS**

1. What elements of formative assessment can you identify in Henry's program?
2. What do the students see as the advantages of this approach? What are the disadvantages?
3. What types of formative assessment can you see yourself using with your students?

## Summative Assessment

**Summative assessment** assessment that usually occurs at the end of a unit of instruction and is designed to determine whether students have learned what they were supposed to learn. This assessment is generally used to assign grades.

**Summative assessment** generally occurs at the end of an instructional unit. Summative assessments are designed to measure how many students met the learning objectives for the unit and to indicate how well students met these objectives. Unlike formative assessment, which provides *feedback* that can be used to make adjustments to learning activities as the unit is being taught, summative assessment provides *evidence* of student learning once the unit of study has ended. Recalling our analogy to a hiker, a summative assessment enables the hiker to determine whether he attained his goal and to decide how well his performance stacked up to what he had hoped to achieve.

# Formal and Informal Assessment

**Formal assessment** assessment that occurs at set times during a term and seeks to determine what students have learned.

**Informal assessment** assessment that is not scheduled but is based on teacher observation of how students are doing and what difficulties they may be having.

Most often when we think of assessment, we think of a written exercise or a planned oral presentation—a **formal assessment** event. Formal assessment, be it diagnostic, formative, or summative, occurs at set dates over the course of the term and is, in most instances, carefully designed to measure specific content or skills that students are expected to learn.

Between these formal assessment events, teachers are engaged in constant and ongoing assessment of both student learning and teacher instructional practices. These data-gathering events, which are called **informal assessments,** can be as informative as formal assessments, while often being more intuitive.

Informal assessment consists principally of anecdotal evidence of student performance, as opposed to the systematic and traceable evidence provided by formal assessments. The primary tool used to collect the data is observation. Teachers look at students' ability to complete classroom activities or assignments, answer teachers' questions, work with classmates, understand directions, manage work time, internalize information presented, and many other skills. Then, on the basis of these observations, teachers make tentative judgments about how well students have internalized the concepts and skills being taught.

Teachers of elementary students, especially lower elementary students, tend to make frequent use of informal assessment. Traditional pencil-and-paper tests require that student test-takers be able to *read* the test items and *write* with some fluency in order to show their understanding of concepts. For students in the early grades, whose literacy skills are still emerging, formal assessments may not be able to measure student performance in many content areas accurately. Consider, for example, a fourth-grade student who participates frequently during math lessons and shows evidence of being able to solve computation problems accurately but scores poorly on written pencil-and-paper tests. Does the student score poorly because of a lack of understanding of the math concepts or because, as a consequence of poor reading skills, she or he misunderstands the task presented? The teacher's anecdotal evidence of the student's performance can help to pinpoint the dominant area of weakness and to develop strategies for addressing it.

Other sources of information for informal assessment include (but are certainly not limited to) homework, class discussion, and cooperative group work. In large part, though, informal assessment relies on observation of students: their behavior, interactions or reactions, and performances. We discuss observation, and other information-gathering techniques, in more detail next.

# Information-Gathering Techniques

As we stated earlier in this module, assessment consists of *measurement*, collecting the information you need regarding student learning, and *evaluation*, making judgments about the information collected and using those judgments to make decisions and prepare reports. Just how do teachers collect the information they need? Four techniques are commonly used in the classroom: *inquiry*, *observation*, *analysis*, and *testing*. Each requires a different level of engagement from the teacher, and each provides different kinds of information that can be used to make inferences about various areas of learning.

## Inquiry

**Inquiry** asking questions of individual students or small groups of students to collect information.

**Inquiry** consists of asking questions of individual students or small groups of students. Of course, most teachers ask questions routinely all day long. Inquiry as an information-gathering technique, however, focuses on collecting data about students' self-perceptions and attitudes, their opinions of events or social trends, and even their self-evaluations of their strengths and weaknesses, rather than their understanding of taught concepts or their ability to perform set tasks. Inquiry requires a one-on-one engagement between the teacher and student to ensure that the information gathered is as accurate as possible.

From an assessment perspective, information collected through inquiry can offer insights into students' social and emotional states and into motivational variables that can affect their performance. Because teaching is an interpersonal event, motivational variables are an important component of helping students learn. Teachers can use information gathered via inquiry to design instructional activities that are more likely to interest students, thereby potentially enhancing their learning of skills and concepts.

Inquiry as an information-gathering technique does have some weaknesses:

- *Subjectivity.* Because inquiry is so strongly dependent on interpersonal interaction and exchange, personal views can easily color the information gathered. A student who is even slightly uncomfortable talking one-on-one with the teacher may not be forthright and open in such exchanges, perhaps leading the teacher to mistaken conclusions about the student's emotions or motivations.
- *Unreliability.* Students' attitudes may vary markedly from one week to the next.
- *Time.* This information-gathering technique is time-consuming, given that the teacher must interview each student individually or in a small group for a significant period of time.

**Video Case**

In the video case, *Assessment in the Elementary Grades: Formal and Informal Literary Assessment,* you will see how Chris Quinn, a second-grade teacher, administers both a formal assessment (a standardized test on phonics) and an informal literacy assessment (a running record) to her students. Throughout, Chris explains why different types of assessments are important for gauging students' learning and for planning instruction. As you watch the clips and study the artifacts in the case, reflect on the following questions.

QUESTIONS

1. How do you anticipate combining formal and informal assessments in your classroom?
2. How does this teacher show that she is using assessment as a key part of instruction?
3. Do you agree that students should help determine the assessment process? Why or why not?

*Online Study Center*

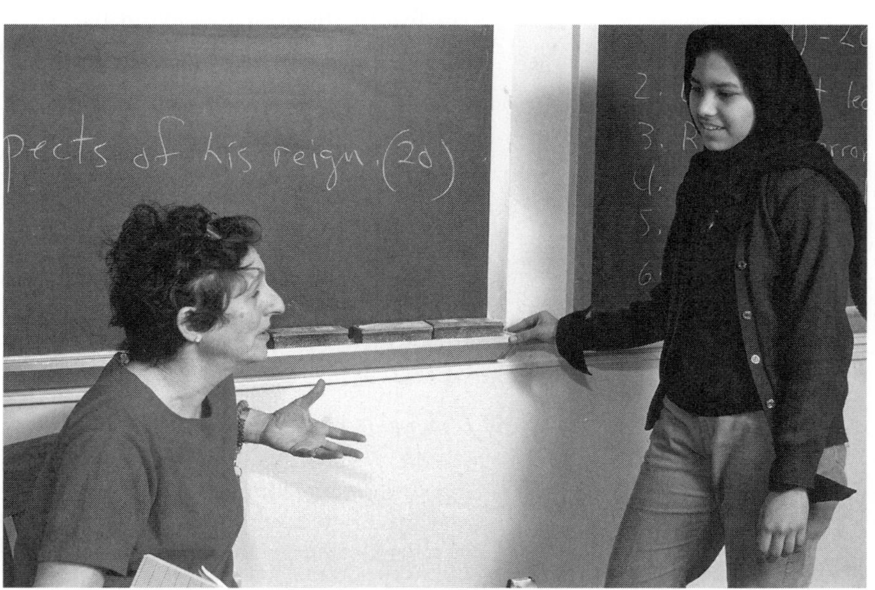


Inquiry and observation are informal ways of assessing students' emotions and understanding.

## Observation

**Observation** the process of looking and listening, noticing the important elements of a performance or product.

A second information-collecting technique, observation, may also seem like a pervasive classroom activity of teachers. After all, don't teachers constantly monitor students throughout all phases of the school day? Monitoring students, however, does not mean that teachers are *observing* them. **Observation** consists of a careful study of interactions and behaviors. If students are working independently, the teacher monitors them when she verifies that they are on task and completing their work. She is observing when she looks at how students engage in the given task, how well they follow directions on their own, or how much they participate in class discussions and interact with one another and with adults.

From an assessment perspective, observations can help teachers understand how students structure given tasks, how they organize their time and resources, or how they process information presented to them. They can also yield insights into students' emotional and social development, as teachers observe students interacting with their classmates, negotiating work flow in small groups, or resolving conflicts in the classroom or on the playground. Unlike inquiry, observation is not dependent on interpersonal interaction. In fact, the more unobtrusive the teacher can be while observing students, the more authentic the students' actions and behaviors and the more reliable the information. Observations do require a time commitment on the part of the teacher, but they can be integrated into the teacher's daily routine more easily than inquiry. Although observations may suffer from subjectivity because it is up to the teacher to ascribe meaning to observed actions and behaviors, teachers can use tools, such as checklists of desirable behaviors or listings of expectations, to help make their observations more objective.

## Analysis

**Analysis** the process of breaking something down into its component parts.

The two remaining techniques, analysis and testing, make use of written artifacts and evidence in the information-gathering process. **Analysis** consists of breaking down a task performed by students into various sub-tasks to determine students' areas of strength and weakness or their preferred process for undertaking a particular task. One teacher may analyze mathematics exercises to see how well a student is able to differentiate among operations, carry out computations, or apply processes. By analyzing an English essay, another teacher can gain insight into a student's ability to organize and prioritize ideas, defend positions, or write cogent sentences.

From an assessment perspective, analysis of tasks gives the teacher important information on students' understanding of learning processes. Used for formative assessment, analysis can help the teacher track students' progress in mastering targeted skills. It allows for a more uniform, and therefore objective, collection of information about all students. Such information collection does not impinge on teachers' instructional time; rather, teachers can analyze tasks during times not devoted to instruction.

## Testing

**Testing** determining aptitude or achievement by presenting a common situation to which all students respond.

**Testing,** probably the most familiar of information-gathering techniques, supposes that all students in the class carry out the same task, following the same set of instructions. Their performance is described using a common set of rules. Testing provides teachers with the same information on all students: how well they mastered skills or concepts taught. Testing is used primarily for determining achievement and aptitude. As we noted earlier in this module,

**Teacher-made tests** tests developed to measure student learning related to particular objectives the teacher selected and specific material the teacher taught.

standardized tests have been developed by test publishers and are often used to assess student achievement of state standards or benchmarks. In contrast to standardized tests are **teacher-made tests,** developed to measure student learning for particular objectives and material that the teacher has taught. Teacher-made tests have several different formats, which are described in detail in Module 16, Tools for Assessment.

## Now You Do It

Which of the information-gathering strategies described in this module (inquiry, observation, analysis, or testing) would you choose to determine each of the following?

1. How well a swimmer executes the backstroke
2. A student's aptitude for mathematics
3. A student's memory for historical events
4. What misunderstandings a group of second-graders have regarding addition problems
5. Who the most popular child in the class is
6. To which chairs, in order of their skills, the violin players in the school orchestra should be assigned
7. A student's ability to implement proper safety precautions when operating a radial-arm saw in shop class
8. How students in a government class feel about the outcome of the latest national election
9. How well students can compute the volume of a cube
10. A student's ability to write a well-constructed paragraph

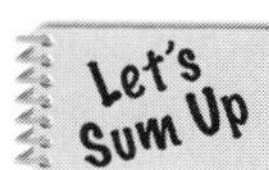


Assessment has always played a key role in effective teaching and learning, for teachers must gauge students' starting points and progress if they are to determine how successful instruction is—that is, how well students are learning. Today, the growing importance of formal assessments (particularly those used for high-stakes decisions about the futures of students, teachers, and schools) means that teachers must prepare for those events by aligning their lessons carefully with the standards students must meet, and by developing their own effective assessments, to ensure that students are indeed being adequately prepared to perform their best on the critical standardized achievement tests. We believe that effective assessment possesses the following characteristics and provides the following benefits.

- *Effective assessment is grounded in clear, explicit learning goals.* Before assessment can be designed, teachers need to know what exactly students are to learn. Important questions that can help guide instructional practices include "What do I want the students to know?" and "How will I know the students know it?"
- *Effective assessment communicates educational values.* Effective assessment conveys to students information about the value of knowledge in general and about which specific knowledge is of most value to them. Assessment tasks are one way to remind students what topics are important to learn and what skills are important to possess.
- *Effective assessment communicates to students expectations for performance.* Students should know exactly what they are expected to know and be able to do, and they should understand just what constitutes the various levels of performance from poor to excellent.

- *Effective assessment helps to improve student learning.* As we saw throughout this module, effective assessment helps teachers know what concepts students are internalizing and what skills they have mastered. Armed with this information, teachers can design learning activities to help students address areas of misunderstanding or can re-teach concepts or skills that have been only superficially learned. Effective assessment also helps students to realize the depth and breadth of their own learning, and it can often help them identify effective learning strategies.
- *Effective assessment stresses processes as well as outcomes.* Effective assessment enables teachers to discover not only what students know and can do, but also how they connect concepts and ideas, how they recall information, and how they apply skills.
- *Effective assessment gives students feedback on their progress.* Students should be able to determine how well they are progressing toward meeting the instructional objectives of the unit or the curriculum. Beyond providing students with numeric or letter grades, effective assessment helps students to recognize their growth and progress, their areas of strength, and the areas in need of strengthening.
- *Effective assessment gives teachers feedback on their performance.* In addition to providing feedback for students, effective assessment gives teachers valuable information about their instructional practices. From the results of an assessment, teachers can make inferences about how clearly they have presented concepts and skills.
- *Effective assessment is fair, reliable, and valid.* In Module 16, Tools for Assessment, we explain what makes an assessment tool fair, reliable, and valid.
- *Effective assessment tools are regularly reviewed and refined.* In most classrooms, the curriculum undergoes some revision from one term or one year to the next. The change may be subtle and minor, or it may be significant. In either case, any change in the teaching of the curriculum is likely to require a change in the assessment tools or tasks.
- *Effective assessment is ongoing and continuous, not episodic.* Even when no formal assessment is scheduled to take place, some kind of assessment is occurring in most classrooms. Effective teachers are always eager to determine what students have internalized, how well they can apply new skills, and how fully they have understood the concepts taught.



## Further Resources

- Norman E. Gronlund, *Assessment of Student Achievement,* 8th ed. (Boston: Allyn & Bacon, 2006). A balanced, concise, and practical guide for testing and performance assessment linked to effective classroom instruction and learning.
- James H. McMillan, *Classroom Assessment: Principles and Practice for Effective Standards-Based Instruction,* 4th ed. (Boston: Allyn & Bacon, 2007). Provides prospective and current teachers with a concise, nontechnical, and practical guide to conducting a full range of high-quality classroom assessments.

- The National Center for Research on Evaluation, Standards, and Student Testing. Available at: **http://cresst96.cse.ucla.edu.** This website contains numerous articles and reports that discuss current assessment and evaluation issues.
- Terry TenBrink, *An Educator's Guide to Classroom Assessment* (Boston: Houghton Mifflin, 2003). A concise booklet on the essential elements of classroom assessment.

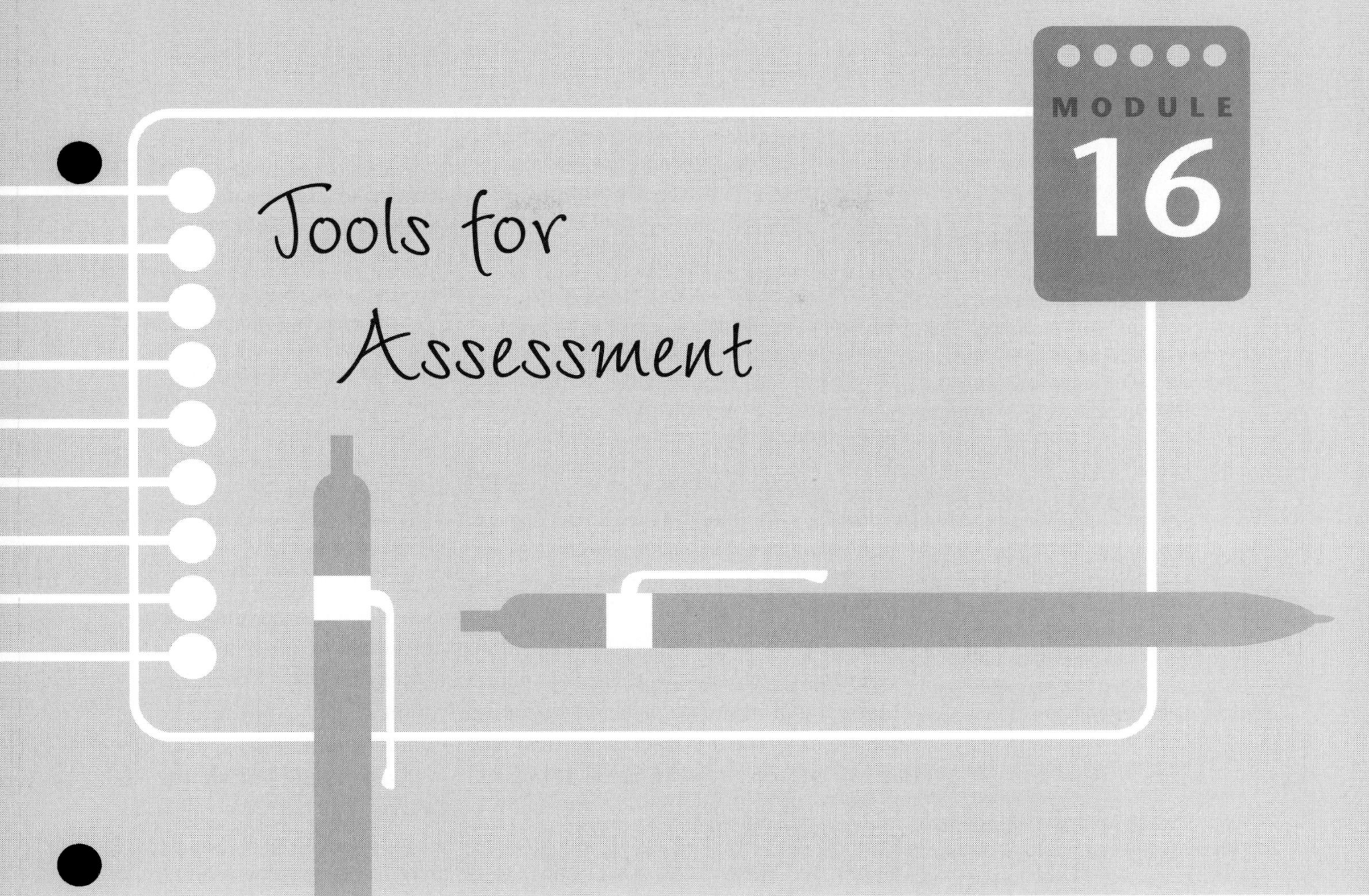


# Tools for Assessment

Scenario

Mr. Sanchez was worried about the conference he was about to have with Debra's parents. He had given Debra Cox a C+ for the last grading period, and she had challenged him on the grade. Debra was accustomed to earning nothing less than a B. Her parents had called and asked to see him, and he was sure that was what it was about. "That's OK," he thought, "I've got all of her grades and can show her parents how she averaged a C+."

"Hello, Mr. and Mrs. Cox," Mr. Sanchez said as he ushered them into his room. "You sounded on the telephone as if this was a matter of some urgency. How can I help you?"

"Mr. Sanchez," said Mr. Cox, "my wife and I are quite concerned about the C+ you gave Debra for the last grading period. That was the lowest grade she has earned in middle school, and we'd like an explanation of how she got that grade, if you don't mind."

"I thought that might be the issue that concerned you, so I made copies of Debra's grades for each of her tests and assignments for you to examine," said Mr. Sanchez. "As you can see, Debra got a B and a B– on her two major tests but only a D+ on her homework assignments."

"I don't understand," said Mrs. Cox. "How could she do so poorly on the homework?"

"Actually, she did OK on the homework she handed in, but she didn't hand in two assignments, so she took zeros for those two homework pieces. When you average in the two zeros, it dropped her homework grade to a D+. Because the homework counted the same as the tests, she had a B, a B–, and a D+, which averaged out to a C+ for her final grade."

"But the rest of the homework assignments look like they average Bs. Doesn't adding in two zeros give undue weight to those assignments?" inquired Mr. Cox.

"Yes, I suppose it seems that way," said Mr. Sanchez, "but the numbers don't lie."

Preview

In Module 15, Assessment for Learning, we defined assessment as consisting of two elements: *measurement*, the systematic collection of information, and *evaluation*, the assigning of value to the information collected. That module discussed the importance of planning for assessment as a part of learning and the different purposes of general types of assessment. In this module, we will look in more detail at the nuts and bolts of assessment: the variety of techniques that can be used to collect information. We will consider what kinds of information each of these tasks can give you, the teacher. We will also discuss how to evaluate the data generated by each measurement tool and how to make sense of and give meaning to the information you gather.

Keep in mind that the information collected during the assessment process is being used to make important decisions about students' academic performance and to draw inferences about future steps and strategies. In all cases, the tools you use to collect information need to be fair, valid, and reliable—characteristics that we describe in this module. Finally, we shall see that the fair assignment of grades is not as clear-cut as Mr. Sanchez seems to think.

**This module emphasizes that:**

- **The tools used to assess student learning are varied, but all those you use should fit the learning objectives you have chosen.**
- **Tests typically exhibit one of two formats: selected-response tests or constructed-response tests.**
- **Many educators urge using "authentic" assessment, which asks students to provide evidence of learning in the form of demonstrations, exhibitions, portfolios of work, and other "real-life" illustrations.**
- **Assigning value to student performance requires a rubric, which states both the criteria and the standards for assessment.**
- **Determining grades is a difficult task that requires an understanding of certain basic principles of fairness.**

# Measurement: Choosing Assessment Tools

When planning the measurement component of the assessment process, you must make some decisions about the nature of the data you will collect. First, you'll have to decide what information you want or need to collect. This decision should be guided by your learning goals for the students and by the stage of the instructional process you are about to implement.

Next, you'll have to figure out what tools will give you the information that you want to collect. The key criterion to consider when choosing assessment tools is the "fit" between the information you want to collect and the assessment tool you are considering. You want to be sure that the assessment tool you decide to use can in fact provide the kind of information you need to determine how well students have met the instructional goals. Numerous assessment tools are available, but they can be divided into two general categories: traditional assessments and alternative, or authentic, assessments.

## Traditional Assessment Tools

Traditional assessment tools are pencil-and-paper tests. You are probably very familiar with several types from your own educational history. The format of these assessment tools may vary, but most are either selected-response tests or constructed-response tests.

**Selected-response tests** tests in which the person being tested can choose from among a set of answers, one of which is correct. Multiple-choice and true/false tests are examples.

***Selected-Response Tests*** With **selected-response tests,** students are given the task of selecting the correct or most appropriate response from a series of possible responses. One familiar format is *multiple choice* (or, as many students dryly call these tests, multiple guess), for which the test-taker chooses the "most appropriate" answer from a group of four or five possible answer choices. A second format is *true/false,* for which the test-taker decides whether a statement is true or false.

One familiar assessment tool is the pencil-and-paper test.

The essential skill required for a selected-response task is discrimination between accurate and inaccurate statements in order to select the correct response. Students may recognize the appropriate response, or they may "find" the most appropriate response through a process of elimination. Regardless of the process used, the assessment task consists entirely of selection and does not require that students produce any answers on their own.

Selected-response tests have several strengths:

- Because all students complete the same task, selected-response tests are a fair assessment tool.
- They are a fast and efficient means of collecting information.
- Selected-response tests are easy to score.
- Multiple-choice tests can be reliable.

The drawbacks or weaknesses of selected-response tests include the following:

- Test-taking savvy can sometimes substitute for knowledge of content. In the absence of content knowledge, selected-response items are also subject to guessing.
- Too often, the focus is on recall of information, rather than higher-level thinking processes such as analysis, application, synthesis, and evaluation of knowledge.
- It is difficult to write good questions, especially multiple-choice questions.

**Constructed-response tests** tests that require the person being tested to respond to the questions by coming up with his or her own answers. Short-answer and essay tests are examples.

***Constructed-Response Tests*** Another pencil-and-paper assessment activity, the **constructed-response test,** consists of two types of test items: *short-answer* questions, requiring students to write responses of about fifty to one hundred words, and *essays*, requiring longer, more developed written responses. Constructed-response tests require a more active engagement on the part of the test-taker than selected-response tests. On a constructed-response test, the test-taker composes, or constructs, a response, instead of recognizing the correct response from a list of possible answers. The test-taker has to draw on his or her knowledge base to identify essential concepts that address the topic and must use a number of thinking and writing skills to formulate a response.

The strengths of constructed-response tests include the following:

- They can be used to assess learning at all levels of complexity, including abstract thinking and creativity.
- Constructed-response items can assess students' abilities to organize, and present in an effective sequence, logically essential and relevant ideas.
- They are often easier to create and write than selected-response tests.

Constructed-response tests also have several drawbacks or weaknesses:

- They require considerable time to grade.
- Scoring can be unreliable. Essay questions are often scored differently by different teachers, and even the same teachers may score the same answer differently at different times.
- Because so few questions can be included in a given test, constructed-response tests have limited sampling ability; some important objectives may not be assessed.
- Quality of handwriting may influence how the teacher scores the essay.

The general consensus is that selected-response tests are good for measuring factual information, but, because of their limited sampling ability, constructed-response tests are not. Instead, constructed-response tests (essay tests and short-answer tests) should be reserved for measuring complex achievement.

## Authentic Assessment Tasks

In the recent past, a movement to rethink the tasks used to assess student learning has been fueled by dissatisfaction with the breadth and quality of the information that can be collected from pencil-and-paper tests. Many educators and assessment specialists argue that because pencil-and-paper tests too often focus on recognition or recall of disconnected skills or concepts, the information collected from these tasks is of limited value. Thus any inferences they suggest about students' abilities or knowledge base are tenuous at best. A particularly apt example is the English language learner who earns nearly perfect scores on selected-response grammar tests, but does not or cannot apply these same rules to written work, let alone order dinner in a restaurant. From the student's scores on the grammar tests, a teacher might be tempted to infer that the student had a good command of the English language, but this inference would not be supported by the student's oral or written performance.

**Authentic assessment** assessment that seeks to evaluate tasks that most directly measure learning outcomes.

To provide teachers with information that is more comprehensive, many educators propose that students be asked to carry out **authentic assessment** tasks that require using or applying knowledge and skills in more realistic situations. Often called "performance tasks," these newer assessment tasks, which can include such products as demonstrations, exhibitions, and portfolios, allow for the collection of different kinds of information about student learning.

***Demonstrations and Exhibitions*** *Demonstrations* require students to display, or demonstrate, their understanding of concepts and skills in some visible form, be it a project, an oral presentation, or a performance task of some kind (such as a science experiment, a dramatic presentation, or even an interpretive dance). *Exhibitions* are most often visual or oral displays of student learning and may take the form of paintings, drawings, sculptures, music, videotapes, or models.

For both demonstrations and exhibitions, students are encouraged to present evidence of learning in any format, from written to oral to kinesthetic. These types of assessments are especially popular among educators because they incorporate the ideas of Howard Gardner's theory of multiple intelligences. That is, they aim to convey knowledge in ways that appeal to a variety of intelligences—not just linguistic, but also musical, interpersonal, and more (see Module 5, Teaching Academically Diverse Learners, for further information on Gardner's theory).

Students must take a much more active role in authentic assessments than they would in traditional assessments. They are often expected to decide what form their presentation of their learning will take and to plan, design, and organize the content of the presentation. Proponents argue that these assessment tasks require students to think more fully about what they have learned as they decide on the substance and format of their presentation.

These tasks can offer teachers more information about student learning beyond their understanding of the concepts presented. From a student demonstration or presentation, teachers can find out not only what students know about particular concepts related to the unit of study, but also how they prioritize and connect the information embedded in their presentations. This

Demonstrations, performances, and exhibitions can all be used as forms of authentic assessment.

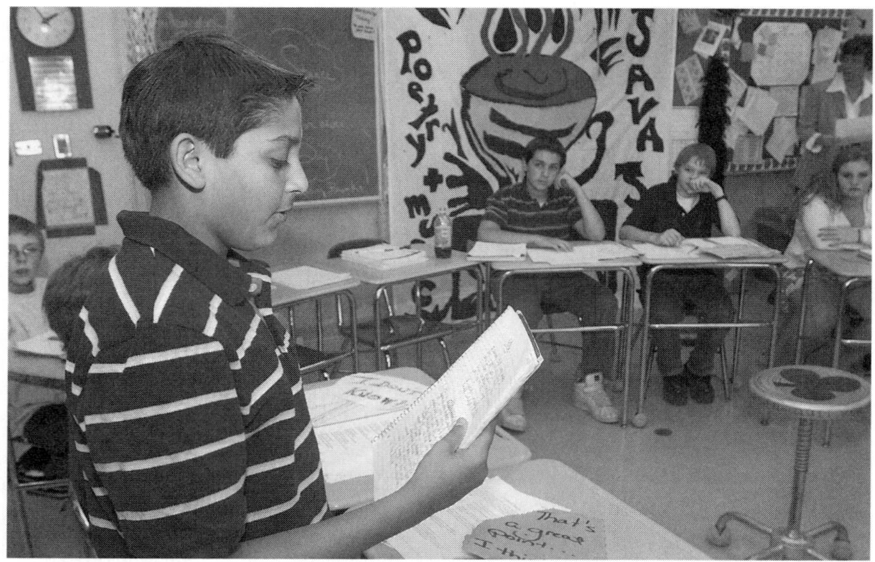

**Portfolio** a collection of work assembled over time to demonstrate the meeting of a learning standard or the acquisition of a skill. Portfolios can be developed by both students and teachers.

**Video Case**

What does portfolio assessment look like in the elementary classroom? In the video case, *Portfolio Assessment: Elementary Classroom,* you'll see how teacher Fred Park helps students develop their writing for a piece that will become part of their portfolios. Through an interview with Fred, you'll gain insight into the strengths of portfolio assessment, as well as the classroom management challenges inherent in this approach. As you watch the clips and study the artifacts in the case, reflect on the following questions.

**QUESTIONS**

1. From this teacher's description, which of the types of portfolios described in this chapter are the students assembling?
2. Do you agree with Fred Park that portfolios are the most meaningful way for students and teachers to assess students' work? Why or why not?
3. What benefits and drawbacks do you see in a portfolio system like the one this teacher is using?

*Online Study Center*

richer body of information allows teachers to make more tenable inferences about student learning.

***Portfolios*** Another authentic assessment task has students put together **portfolios** of their work. Students may present a discipline-specific portfolio (at the secondary level) or a multidisciplinary one (at the elementary or middle school level). Portfolios tend to be in one of two formats:

- *Exemplary Work Portfolio.* The pieces of work in an exemplary work portfolio represent the best efforts or best work of the student. Students, either on their own or in consultation with an adult (a teacher, an aide, or even a parent), select from the work done over a set period of time (a grading period, a semester, or the entire school year) those pieces that they believe constitute their best work. This portfolio is similar to those in the fine arts or advertising—a showcase of exemplary work of the artist.
- *Progress Portfolio.* Rather than showcasing the best pieces, a progress portfolio seeks to trace the development of the student's skills and content knowledge over a grading period, semester, or school year. Pieces are usually arranged chronologically to show the evolution of the student's skills.

Advocates insist that because portfolios contain numerous pieces that are often constructed by students, they are more revealing of the students' actual capabilities than a selected-response test. In addition, because the pieces are usually produced and assembled under relaxed conditions, rather than test-taking conditions, they represent a more studied sampling of students' actual capabilities. In many instances, the tasks completed are more authentic than those in a selected-response or constructed-response test. For example, a portfolio may contain a persuasive letter to town leaders, in which a student argues in favor of or against a particular position on a key issue facing the town. This is often viewed as a more authentic task than having the student identify parts of a formal letter on a worksheet or test or write a persuasive letter with a fictitious scenario (even if it is realistic).

These alternative assessment tasks are not, however, without their challenges. Logistically, the most obvious challenge is time. Unlike pencil-and-paper tests that can be administered to an entire class at once, performance tasks require time for each student to display his or her work from which the teacher collects information about student learning. Portfolios present a similar challenge. If a portfolio has five to ten pieces of work, the assessor has to read through all the pieces. If each portfolio requires, on average, forty-five to sixty minutes to read and assess, it will take one teacher over twenty hours to read through one class set of portfolios. Imagine the elementary teacher who has students put together a portfolio for reading/language arts, social studies, *and* science, or the secondary English teacher who has five classes and receives portfolios from all the students in all of them. We recommend using authentic assessment tools in moderation!

As we will see, authentic assessments also present challenges in terms of fairness, reliability, and validity.

# Fairness, Reliability, and Validity of Assessment Tools

When designing or selecting an assessment tool, be it a traditional pencil-and-paper test or an authentic task, teachers want to be sure that the tools being used to assess student learning are fair, reliable, and valid. Let's look at what each of these qualities means in the context of the assessment process.

## Fairness

On a fair assessment, no student has an advantage because of his or her ethnic or cultural background, race, gender, or religious affiliation. Thus a fair assessment shows no bias toward or against any particular individual or group of individuals.

Reading tests that include passages containing geographically or culturally specific details are often accused of unfairness or bias. These passages confer an unfair advantage on students who are familiar with the context of the passage and disadvantage students who are not. A student who shows poor comprehension of such a passage may simply lack the cultural background that would help him or her understand its meaning.

The fairness of authentic assessment tasks can also be a bit problematic. On the one hand, students get to select either the format (performance tasks) or the actual pieces (portfolio) to show their knowledge gain. Thus these tasks can be considered fair; all can undertake the task from a position of strength. On the other hand, these tasks may be considered unfair for the less creative students, who may not be able to think of ways to exhibit their knowledge in authentic tasks.

## Reliability

**Reliability** consistency of measurement—that is, how consistent test scores or other evaluation results are from one measurement to another.

**Reliability** reflects the consistency of data. An assessment measure is reliable if it gives scores that are consistent, either across students or over time.

Reliability across students does not mean that every student gets the same score. It means that the assessment materials or circumstances give every student the same opportunities. Reliability is of significant concern with standardized tests that offer different versions of the same test. If half of the third-grade students in a school district take version A of the annual state reading test, and the other half take version B, the teachers and administrators in the district want some assurance that the two versions of the test will give similar results, so that the scores of all students will be comparable, no matter which version they took.

Teachers who create their own assessments should also try to ensure reliability by applying the same criteria and expectations for all students. Let's say a lower elementary school teacher wants to assess his students' skills at decoding written words. He decides to have students choose a book from which they will read some pages aloud to the teacher. Students will be assessed on their fluency of decoding. Although students may be more interested in the book and motivated to read well if they choose their own book, such a procedure does not allow for consistent, or reliable, results because the readability levels of the books that students choose are likely to vary considerably. The teacher will not have a consistent standard against which to measure students' decoding skills.

Reliability should also be reflected in the consistency of a student's scores over time. Suppose Phil took a college admission test and scored 600 the first time, but 780 on his second try two months later, even without any interventions such as test-prep classes in between. We might question the reliability of the test.

Authentic assessment tasks present special reliability concerns. As we've noted, for traditional assessments, reliability suggests uniformity of tasks. With alternative assessments, students are presenting individualized tasks, with little or no uniformity. Imagine you are teaching a unit on ancient civilizations and have given your students the option of choosing a demonstration or exhibition to illustrate their understanding of the concepts. One student decides to build a model of a Mesopotamian town, a second studies Sanskrit and replicates an ancient writing tablet, while a third creates a market scene from ancient Babylon. The information collected for each presentation will be as varied as the projects.

**Inter-rater reliability** the degree to which different raters, looking at the same information or evidence, would come to similar judgments about its quality.

Another reliability issue for authentic assessments is **inter-rater reliability.** That is, would one teacher looking at the same task gather the same information and draw the same inferences as another? If not, then the value assigned to a particular task depends largely on the judgment of the teacher, which makes the task unreliable.

## Validity

**Validity** the extent to which the results of an evaluation procedure serve the particular uses for which they are intended.

**Validity** is concerned with whether the information gathered actually measures what it was intended to measure. Validity also focuses on the inferences about student knowledge or ability that can be made on the basis of the assessment tool. A valid assessment tool measures what has been taught; teachers are able to infer that students who score well on the assessment tool have internalized the content presented. If a student scores well on the test that covers photosynthesis, and the test is valid, we can infer that the student has an understanding of the photosynthetic process.

A particular tool may be a valid measure for one aspect of student learning and an invalid measure of another aspect. This is a concern for both traditional and authentic assessment tools. Asking students to write an essay analyzing a character from a novel could be a valid measure of their analytic and reasoning skills, and it might also be a valid measure of their grammar and mechanical skills, but it would not be a valid measure of their creative writing skills. Similarly, if a student builds a three-dimensional structure as a geometry project, this model probably will not shed insight into how well the student can solve proofs or visualize geometric transformations.

**Content validity** the extent to which the knowledge taught matches the knowledge tested by an assessment tool.

Specifying what knowledge and skills are to be assessed can help you to ensure that the assessment tool is valid.

**Content validity** reflects a match between the knowledge taught and the knowledge tested. If the unit of study just completed was on the United States Constitution, the assessment tool should ask only about the Constitution. Including items about the Declaration of Independence would undermine content validity.

Content validity is often easier to establish for traditional assessment tools than for authentic assessments. Each test item, whether a selected-response or constructed-response item, can be linked to a particular lesson, which shows that the knowledge tested does indeed correspond to the knowledge taught. With authentic assessment tasks, validity becomes more problematic, especially when students have the freedom to select the format for providing evidence of knowledge gained. Does crafting a model of an Egyptian pyramid provide sufficient evidence that the student creator has met the instructional objectives for the unit on ancient Egypt? Could any student have successfully completed the pyramid project? If the answer to the second question is yes, then the assessment tool is not valid.

## Now You Do It

For each learning objective in the table below, use what you have learned in this module to determine if the assessment task is a fair, valid, and reliable means for determining whether the learning objective has been met.

| Learning Objective | Proposed Assessment Task |
|---|---|
| Students will discern the differences between a protective tariff and a revenue tariff. | Ask students to write the definitions of the terms *protective tariff* and *revenue tariff.* |
| Students will make a minimum of ten baskets in a one-minute basketball drill. | Time each student as he or she tries to sink ten baskets. |
| Students will identify the vanishing points in a three-point perspective drawing. | Present students with three pictures that contain vanishing points, and ask them to identify these points by pointing to them. |
| Students will name the planets of our solar system, in order, starting with the closest to the sun. | Give students a list of planets, and ask them to order them from the sun outward. |
| Students will diagram a simple sentence. | Write a sentence on the chalkboard and ask students to identify the parts of the sentence. |
| Students will translate the first two pages of *Don Quixote* from Spanish to English. | Ask one student to read aloud the first two pages of *Don Quixote.* |
| Students will sing the words to *The Star-Spangled Banner.* | Ask students to listen to an instrumental version of the national anthem and write down the words. |
| Students will analyze the allegorical meaning of Joseph Conrad's *The Heart of Darkness.* | Have students read *The Heart of Darkness* and discuss it in small groups. |

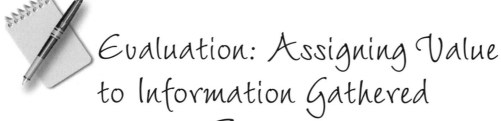

# Evaluation: Assigning Value to Information Gathered

The second part of assessment consists of *evaluation*, assigning values to the information or evidence gathered. How you go about assigning value depends on what kinds of information you have gathered from the various information-gathering techniques. Assigning value to student performances on a multiple-choice test is different from how you would assign value to an oral report. This section will offer some guidelines to help you in this process.

## Assigning Value to Test Performance

Good pencil-and-paper tests are written in such a way that test items are specifically related to targeted instructional goals, so the number of items a student has answered correctly represents the extent to which that student has met the goals of the instructional unit or subunit. In other words, a student who answered eighteen out of twenty questions correctly receives a higher value and is thought to have learned more than one who answered fourteen out of twenty questions correctly.

***Assigning Value to Selected-Response Tests*** One advantage of selected-response tests, according to some educators, is the objectivity associated with grading them. Because each test item has a clearly identified correct answer, grading of these tests is completely independent of the test assessor, and concerns about potential teacher bias are eliminated. Teachers prepare answer keys to multiple-choice and true/false tests so that scoring the tests can be done quickly (and even, in some cases, by machine). Teachers can then total the number of correct responses that each student makes and convert the number of correct responses into a percentage. Thus, for example, a student who answers eighteen of the twenty questions correctly has scored 90 percent on the test.

But what does "90 percent" mean and how should it count? Many school districts establish a grading scale that translates the percentage correct into a letter grade. Having a grading scale makes it easy for teachers to assign a value to a score on a multiple-choice or true/false test. Ninety percent would be in the B range if the specified B range was 85–92 percent, for example. Districts establish such scales so that there is an appearance of consistency throughout the school district. Such uniformity is difficult to achieve in practice, however. Some teachers construct very difficult tests; others write easier ones. A 90 percent score may represent different levels of achievement in different classes, but because of the uniform grading scale, students in different classes would receive the same grade.

***Assigning Value to Constructed-Response Tests*** Constructed-response tests tend to be more prone than selected-response tests to reader bias and subjectivity of interpretation, which often leads to variability in assigning grades to essay questions and hence compromises to some extent the reliability of this assessment tool. As mentioned earlier, critics fear that the information collected and evaluated with constructed-response tests is too often related more to a student's writing ability or linguistic skills than to his or her knowledge of specific content. In such a situation, those students who write well have a clear advantage over those whose linguistic skills are less refined. Wittingly or not, teachers frequently take into consideration the quality of the student's writing when they attribute value to the written response. Therefore, the student's grade may reflect the quality of his or her writing as much as, or more than, his or her understanding of ideas or concepts being tested.

To overcome this potential bias, teachers should develop a "model answer" to be used as a guide when students' answers are graded. The model answer should contain all the content that students are expected to include, and it should specify any important organizational features that would be expected. Some teachers find it helpful to create a checklist of major points that would appear in an ideal response and then to put check marks next to these points as students mention them in their answers. This process reduces the influence of a student's writing style on the teacher's perception of the quality of the answer. The teacher can predetermine how many points a student would need to mention to receive an A, B, and so on.

## Assigning Value to Authentic Assessment Information

Authentic assessment presents an even greater challenge in deciding the value of the information collected. Two key considerations need to be addressed.

1. *Criteria for assessment.* Assessing student learning via authentic tasks requires that you specify what constitutes measurable evidence that students have met the instructional objectives you set. For example, if you have students put together a portfolio, what will you look for in the pieces that will allow you to know with some confidence that students achieved the objectives? Going back to the example on ancient civilizations, you have to decide what you will look for in the scale model, the Sanskrit document, and the marketplace re-enactment to determine that the creators of these projects have met the objectives you set for them.

2. *Standards of assessment.* You also have to think about how you will differentiate qualitatively between one portfolio and another or between one presentation or demonstration and the next. Why would Georgia's portfolio be given a value of "superior," whereas Angelina's is "adequate"? Why would you label the document in Sanskrit "excellent" but the town model "very good"? You want to be sure that you are assigning value to these variable projects in a fair and consistent manner and that, when evaluations differ, one student's work shows evidence of more student learning than the other.

These two elements are often presented in a tool referred to as a rubric.

**Rubric** a set of rules for scoring student products or student performance. A rubric typically takes the form of a rating scale or checklist.

***Rubrics*** **Rubrics** provide a scoring system to assess performance (or products of performance). They generally take the form of a rating scale or checklist. Rubrics provide assessment guidelines specifying what constitutes visible evidence of the criteria listed and indicating how to distinguish among levels of quality in student performance. The criteria of a rubric are most often content-specific, but some may also be generic, designed to be used in any content area. These descriptors for each level of performance are intended to provide an unbiased and reliable foundation for assessing student performance. In some cases, indicators may be used to provide examples of each level.

As an example, let's look at the rubric shown in Table 16.1, which was developed by the Northwest Regional Educational Laboratory to assess the

**TABLE 16.1 Rubric for Assessment of Oral Reading**

**FLUENCY**

| 1 | 3 | 5 |
|---|---|---|
| The emerging reader reads aloud with awkward pauses, stops, and starts. There are usually few signals for transitions.<br>• The reader reads each word as a single entity, limiting the flow of the passage. Meaning is usually obscured by this flow.<br>• Line breaks and/or hyphenated words are confusing and usually halt the progress of the oral reading.<br>• Substitutions are typically "guesses" at words with little attempt to maintain meaning or context. | The developing reader reads aloud with some appropriate pauses, stops, starts, and signals for transitions.<br>• The reader reads in "chunks," applying meaning to phrases of single sentences instead of whole passages.<br>• Line breaks or hyphenated phrases are often broken and noticeable.<br>• Substitutions are sometimes inappropriate in maintaining the context, and meaning is sometimes blurred. | The reader advanced in fluency reads aloud with appropriate pauses, stops, starts, and signals for transitions.<br>• The reader reads whole passages for meaning, as opposed to single words or phrases.<br>• Line breaks or hyphenated phrases are smooth and unnoticeable.<br>• Substitutions or corrections are silently made, and meaning is always maintained. |

**RATE**

| 1 | 3 | 5 |
|---|---|---|
| The emerging reader is not yet able to select an appropriate rate and speed for an oral reading.<br>• The rate does not correspond to the meaning of the passage, and sometimes a monotone or excessively hurried speed is the result.<br>• Meaning and context are actually obscured by the difficult rate and speed employed by the reader. | The developing reader sometimes selects an appropriate rate and speed for an oral reading.<br>• The rate does not always correspond to the meaning of the passage, and attempts to add emphasis through rate sometimes produce a "bumpy" oral reading.<br>• The rate and speed do not always correspond to the meaning of the text, and it can sound "forced." | The advanced reader selects and maintains an appropriate rate and speed for an oral reading.<br>• The rate corresponds to the meaning of the passage, and the reader uses the ability to speed up or slow down different sections of text to create an appropriate emphasis on the meaning of the text.<br>• The rate and speed are well coordinated and enable the oral reading to sound "natural." |

Source: Northwest Regional Educational Laboratory. Available at: **http://www.nwrel.org/assessment/pdfRubrics/k3devcontoral.PDF.** Used by permission of Northwest Regional Educational Laboratory.

oral-reading skills of younger children. Two criteria are listed: (1) *fluency*, the flow of a reader's delivery in an oral reading, and (2) *rate*, the speed and pattern a reader follows in an oral reading. For each criterion, three standards are given. A rating of 1 is given to emerging readers; a rating of 3 indicates a developing reader; and a rating of 5 indicates an advanced reader. Descriptors are also provided for each criterion and rating to provide more complete information for both the teacher and the student or the student's parents.

A second common format for a rubric is shown in Table 16.2. This rubric was developed to assess student presentation posters. The criteria are listed in one column on the left, and the ratings or standards are found in subsequent columns. Some important criteria include evidence of student understanding

**TABLE 16.2 Rubric for a Student Poster**

| | Advanced (4) | Proficient (3) | Basic (2) | Unsatisfactory (1) |
|---|---|---|---|---|
| **Understanding of key concepts** | Student demonstrates a thorough knowledge of all important concepts. | Student demonstrates satisfactory knowledge of most concepts. | Student demonstrates adequate knowledge of key concepts. | Student demonstrates little knowledge of key concepts. |
| **Variety of details** | Student uses a wide variety of relevant and compelling details. | Student uses a variety of relevant details. | Student uses an adequate number of details. | Student provides an inadequate number of details. |
| **Annotations** | Student provides complete documentation of a variety of appropriate sources. | Student provides documentation of a variety of sources. | Student provides adequate documentation of a limited number of sources. | Student fails to provide documentation of sources. |
| **Grammar** | Student always uses correct grammar in written work. | Student usually uses correct grammar in written work. | Student makes some grammar errors in written work. | Student makes numerous grammar errors in written work. |
| **Charts, graphs, and pictures** | Student provides an appropriate number of pertinent and illustrative graphics. | Student provides a sufficient number of pertinent graphics. | Student provides graphics, some of which are pertinent. | Student fails to provide pertinent graphics. |
| **Computer-generated text** | All student text is word processed, using correct format. | Most student text is word processed, using correct format. | Student text is not consistently word processed. | Student failed to use word processing. |

Source: Science Learning Network. Available at: **http://www.sln.org/guide/dukerich/rubrics/student_display.pdf.** Used by permission of Science Learning Network.

of concepts, variety of details, and quality of text and graphics. (It is interesting to note that one of the criteria listed is "computer-generated text," indicating that the preparer considers it important for students to develop word processing skills.) The standards range from advanced to unsatisfactory, and the rubric provides descriptors for each standard level of each criterion.

A third kind of scoring rubric is the *holistic rubric.* A holistic rubric may have descriptors similar to those shown in Table 16.3 but often does not specify criteria for assessment. A holistic rubric may be used to evaluate student open-response items or writing samples on standardized tests. Many holistic rubrics use a 3-, 4-, or (as in this case) 5-point scale.

### *Challenges in Assigning Value to Authentic Assessment Information*

The challenge with any authentic assessment task is determining how to assign value to students' performances in a consistent, standard, and doable way. The descriptors in the rubrics are designed to be objective and specific, but they are subject to variability depending on the evaluator. Deciding what constitutes "thorough" understanding as opposed to "satisfactory" or "adequate" understanding requires interpretative judgments on the part of the evaluator that lack the "objectivity" that traditional pencil-and-paper tests may offer. The presence of the evaluator and her or his consequent interpretation of the information collected leads some critics to discount rubric

## TABLE 16.3 Holistic Scoring Rubric

| Points | Criteria for Scoring |
|---|---|
| 5 | • The student demonstrates in-depth understanding of the relevant and important ideas.<br>• The answer is fully developed and includes specific facts or examples.<br>• The answer is organized around big ideas, major concepts, or key principles in the field.<br>• The response is exemplary, detailed, and clear. |
| 4 | • The student shows a good understanding of the topic.<br>• The answer demonstrates good development of ideas and includes supporting facts or examples.<br>• The answer may demonstrate some organization around big ideas, major concepts, or key principles in the field.<br>• The response is good, has some detail, and is clear. |
| 3 | • The student demonstrates some knowledge and understanding of the topic, but may show gaps in his or her understanding and knowledge.<br>• The answer demonstrates satisfactory development of ideas and includes some supporting facts or examples.<br>• The response is satisfactory, containing some detail, but may be vague or underdeveloped and may include misconceptions or some inaccurate information. |
| 2 | • The student demonstrates little knowledge or understanding of the topic.<br>• The student may include an important idea, part of an idea, or a few facts but does not develop the ideas or deal with the relationships among the ideas.<br>• The response contains misconceptions or inaccurate or irrelevant information.<br>• The response is poor and lacks clarity. |
| 1 | • The student shows no knowledge or understanding of the topic.<br>• The student writes about the topic using irrelevant or inaccurate information.<br>• The response has numerous grammatical and usage errors. |
| 0 | • The student failed to provide an appropriate response. |

Source: National Center for Research on Evaluation, Standards, and Student Testing. Available at: **http://www.cse.ucla.edu/CRESST/pages/Rubrics.htm.** Used by permission of CSE/CRESST.

assessment as overly subjective and biased. One way to address the potential variability is to have multiple evaluators assess a given task; this is the procedure used with most state-mandated authentic assessment systems.

As we have noted, the variability of data presents several other significant challenges in assigning value to authentic assessments. How, for example, could the model of a Mesopotamian town, the document in Sanskrit, and the market scene in ancient Babylon all provide evidence that students have achieved the same learning goals? The first student may have learned about the social structure or architectural and civil engineering advances of ancient civilizations, while the second became familiar with writing systems, and the third found out about the economic monetary system used. All three students are probably meeting learning objectives of the unit of study on ancient civilizations, but each may be meeting *different* objectives.

It is also important to consider a second and perhaps even more basic question: Can these projects, in fact, provide you, the teacher, with reliable information about whether students are learning the concepts that you want them to learn? In constructing a model of a Mesopotamian town, has a student actually understood the prominent position of religion in this civilization or the major advances in civil engineering that it achieved? Or has the

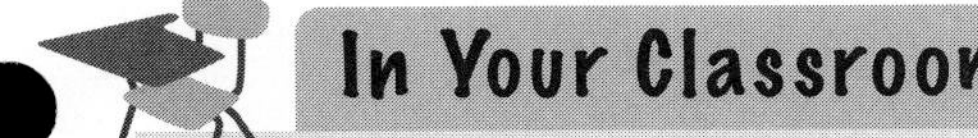

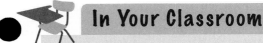

## In Your Classroom

### Overcoming the Challenges of Evaluating Authentic Assessments

To address some of these challenges in the information-gathering and evaluation processes for authentic assessments, consider the following ideas:

- Decide *before* you assign the task exactly what you'll be looking at and looking for during the assessment process (what information you will be systematically collecting) and how you will assign value to the information collected.
- On the basis of your decisions, develop a rubric consisting of a list of criteria and a set of standards.
- Share the rubric, or at least the criteria, with your students as they begin the task, so that they will also know what skills and knowledge are important and valued.
- Consider including, as part of all projects, demonstrations, and presentations, some kind of an oral presentation or question-and-answer period from which you can find out what students learned from their projects. These might be one-on-one question-and-answer sessions, or other students in the class might be invited to ask questions. As you hear from the students about their projects, you can listen for specific information that can tell you what learning objectives students have met.
- Plan to evaluate portfolios, demonstrations, or presentations in small batches, if possible, to preserve your alertness and stamina.



student merely done an art project, building three-dimensional structures from a picture or drawing found in a book? In making a document in Sanskrit, has the second student learned about a word-based writing system? Or has the student merely copied a series of symbols onto a piece of paper?

In addition to the problematic information about student learning that authentic assessment tasks may offer, many teachers find it difficult to assign value to such qualities as a student's creative talents, attention to detail, and overall neatness.

Finally, sustainability of the evaluator's focus and stamina is yet another challenge. In the case of portfolio assessment, even with a detailed list of elements, the astuteness with which value is assigned can vary over time as the teacher's determination to read attentively through the many pages of numerous portfolios wanes.

## Grading

Assigning grades is a task that few teachers enjoy. No matter how objective you try to make them (for instance, by averaging grades as Mr. Sanchez did in our opening scenario), grades are always subject to many kinds of interpretation problems.

As we noted earlier, for example, the ease or difficulty of tests and other evaluation devices varies from teacher to teacher, so that a grade of B probably means something different in Mr. Sanchez's class from what it means in another teacher's class. Even if a school district has a standard grading scale, earning an A in Ms. Hardgrader's class might be more difficult than earning an A in Mr. Easy's class.

The practice of averaging grades can produce inaccurate results because the results don't take into account the difficulty level of the tests or other assignments. Another problem occurs when an extreme score is averaged along with other scores, as happened to Debra in Mr. Sanchez's class. Assigning a zero score to a work assignment and then including the zero along with the other scores when calculating a **mean,** the arithmetic average, is a very unfair educational practice. A measure of central tendency that is fairer to use is the **median,** the middle score in a distribution of scores.[1]

**Mean** the arithmetic average of a set of scores, determined by dividing the sum of the scores by the number of scores.

**Median** the 50 percent point in a distribution of scores—that is, the point that divides a set of scores exactly in half.

Teachers also have to decide whether they will grade "on the curve" or, alternatively, establish certain cut-off points for each grade. This issue concerns the source of comparison used to assign a grade. Three different options are possible: norm-referenced grading, criterion-referenced grading, and self-referenced grading.

## Norm-Referenced Grading

**Norm-referenced grading** determining grades by comparing information about an individual with information you have about a group of similar individuals, usually the other members of the class.

Grading on the curve is referred to as **norm-referenced grading.** With a *norm-referenced perspective,* students' performances are assigned values by comparing each student's performance to the "normal," or average, performance of students in a comparison group. For your grading purposes, the norm will probably be the average of the other students in the class. As we note in Module 15, Assessment for Learning, standardized tests are also norm-referenced. In those cases, comparison groups are larger and may include all the students in a school district, the state, or even the whole country. Some commercially prepared standardized tests use, to find the norm, the scores of all the students who have taken the test over the years.

Norm-referenced grading is called grading on the curve because the scores are based on a statistically normal distribution (also known as a bell curve because of the shape the scores make when shown on a graph). Most of the students are clustered around the mean, or average, with a gradually decreasing number of students scoring progressively higher or lower than the norm or the mean.

Let's say, for example, that the teacher of an honors English class uses a norm-referenced perspective to assign grades for the term. The teacher would first determine the average of the class and then compare each student's performance to the class average. Most of the students in the class (68 percent, according to a statistically normal distribution) would cluster around the average, earning Cs. Some students would have Bs, some would have Ds, a few would have As, and a few would have Fs.

The major drawback of norm-referenced grading is that some students will always get higher or lower grades, even if the class as a whole all performs similarly. In the honors class, for example, all of the students might do very well. The actual score difference between an A and a B or between a C and a D may be very small, but because all students were compared to the average, some would still end up with low grades, even though they had learned quite effectively. A similar problem could arise with a class where all the grades were low. A student who had not fully mastered the learning objectives could end up with an A.

A second criticism of the norm-referenced perspective is that it discourages the less academically able students because, no matter how hard they try or how much they improve, they are likely to score lower than the best students; they are thus doomed to low grades. Proponents might disagree, insisting that such a perspective provides a reasonable challenge and healthy competition among students without favoring any group of students.

Students who receive a B or C, they maintain, will be motivated to try to match or exceed the performance of students who receive a higher grade.

## Criterion-Referenced Grading

**Criterion-referenced grading** determining grades by comparing information about an individual with some performance criterion; that is, some description of expected behavior.

A second type of grading is referred to as **criterion-referenced grading,** whereby the teacher establishes criteria for achievement that will represent a particular grade. Thus, if all the students in the class meet the criteria for an A grade, they will all get As.

One way of assigning grades using a criterion-referenced system is to establish certain cut-off points for each grade. For example, you can assign points for every assignment and every test. Important assignments or tests would be worth more points. Next, you determine how many total points a student must get to receive an A, how many for a B , and so on. At the end of the marking period, you add up each student's points and compare this number to the cut-off levels to assign report card grades.

Many large-scale, statewide assessments use a criterion-referenced perspective to measure students' yearly progress. Standards are set for each grade level in different disciplines, and the statewide assessment is designed to measure whether students meet the specified standard, indicating that they possess a body of knowledge appropriate for their grade level.

The advantage of this type of grading is that each student's achievement is measured against a standard, and students are not measured against one another. This type of grading is compatible with the notion of standards of learning that nearly all states have established.

Critics of this perspective raise concerns about the quality of the standards set. If the standards are set too low or too high, then the grades attributed are not very reliable indicators of the students' knowledge. In addition, disagreement over what standards to set at each grade level can lead to inconsistency in what exactly the attributed grade signifies from one class or school to another.

### Video Case

In the video case, *Assessment: Grading Strategies and Approaches,* high school social studies teacher Henry Turner shares his thoughts on assessing students' learning and on grading their efforts. As you watch the clips and study the artifacts in the case, reflect on the following questions.

QUESTIONS

1. What is Henry's belief about the importance of the role of tests in determining student grades? Do you agree or disagree with him? Why?
2. What do you most like and most dislike about his grading system?
3. What questions would you like to ask Mr. Turner about his assessment philosophy?

***Online Study Center***

## Self-Referenced Grading

**Self-referenced grading** grading based on progress or improvement. The student's previous work is set as a benchmark against which to compare current work.

Some teachers incorporate an element of improvement, or **self-referenced grading,** into their evaluations. Self-referenced grading takes the student's previous work as a benchmark against which to compare current work. With this perspective, each student's performance is measured in terms of the progress made since the previous assessment. Such a perspective acknowledges that students acquire knowledge and skills at different rates, and it suggests that one important consideration in the learning equation is that students make steady and regular progress in their knowledge acquisition.

As you think about evaluating student work or performance, you will want to decide which perspective best reflects your beliefs about learning, while being adequately aligned with the expectations and beliefs of the school system in which you are teaching. All three perspectives have their proponents and their critics. All three are grounded in a set of beliefs about teaching and learning. All three are used in various classrooms, schools, and school districts throughout the country. Your task is to find the approach that works best for your situation.

Assigning grades is a complex process and deserves your thorough study to ensure that you have done everything you can to make the process fair and the results as meaningful as possible. Consult some of the references listed at the end of this module to explore further the many issues connected with grading.

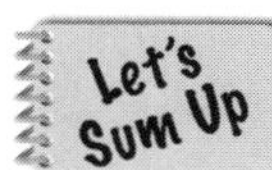


Assessment is an integral part of the teaching/learning experience. Assessing student learning frequently, through both formal and informal means, provides you with information about how well your students are doing. This information enables you to make judgments and decisions about how to proceed in your instructional activities. Should you review the concepts because half the students didn't understand them? Or should you move on to the next unit in the curriculum? If one instructional approach didn't seem to work, what should you try next? In other words, gathering information about student learning puts you in a better position to determine how to proceed instructionally, and your students will benefit from your good assessment techniques and procedures.

## Further Resources

- Peter W. Airasian, *Classroom Assessment: Concepts and Applications* (New York: McGraw-Hill Higher Education, 2005). An excellent, teacher-friendly book on testing, grading, and interpreting tests.

- Central New York Regional Information Center. Available at: **http://www.nysed.gov.** Go to this website and search on "authentic assessment" for interesting articles about the value of authentic assessment procedures.
- Terry D. TenBrink, "Assessment," in James M. Cooper (Ed.), *Classroom Teaching Skills,* 8th ed. (Boston: Houghton Mifflin, 2006), pp. 330–374. A fine overview of assessment issues and tools.
- Russell G. Wright, "Success for All: The Median Is the Key." *Phi Delta Kappan,* May 1994, 723–725. Makes a strong case for using the median, rather than the mean, as a measure of central tendency when averaging student grades.

- Yahoo!'s Directory of K–12 Lesson Plans. Available at: **http://dir.yahoo.com/Education/Standards_and_Testing.** This website contains a wide variety of resources for testing, assessment, measurement, and benchmarking.

MODULE 17

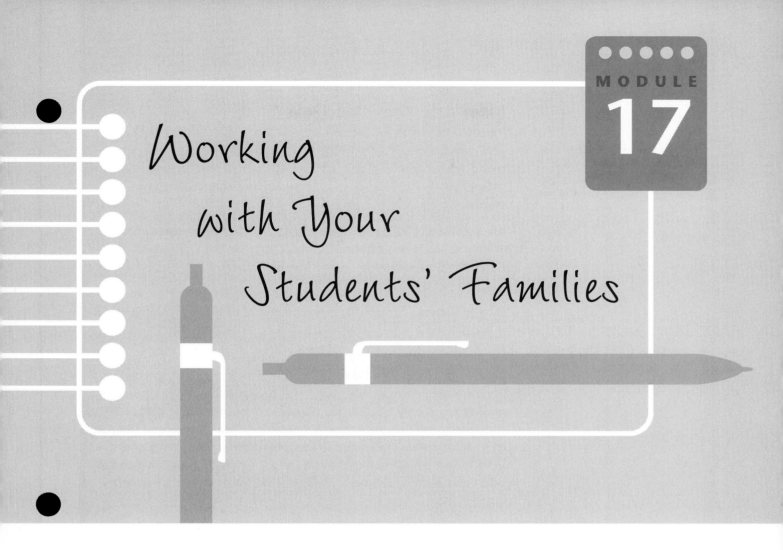

# Working with Your Students' Families

"Mr. MacGwyre, my mother wants to talk to you. She's going to call you today."

"Thanks for letting me know, Carrie."

Tim MacGwyre had met Carrie's mother only briefly at the Open House earlier in the school year. However, Mrs. Matherson was well known in the school community. She had been president of the PTA for many years and was always very successful at rallying the community and spearheading fund-raising efforts. When they had learned that her daughter Carrie was in Tim's third-period history class, his colleagues had warned Tim that Mrs. Matherson was "a force to be reckoned with."

The meeting time having been set, Tim tried to imagine what Mrs. Matherson might want to talk about. It was almost the end of the first marking period, and Tim feared that the purpose of the meeting was not to talk about planning a field trip to the local museum to supplement the next unit of study in Tim's history class.

He reviewed the curriculum he had planned and satisfied himself that he was covering all of the state-mandated topics. He went through all the assignments he had planned and felt prepared to defend each as a viable learning activity. Last, he carefully reviewed the grades he had given Carrie so far in the term and found that he felt all were justified.

Tim could hear Mrs. Matherson approaching. She stopped at nearly every classroom to chat with the teacher there. Tim was just in his second year of teaching at Branford High School, and he was not nearly as friendly with his colleagues as she was. He began to feel even more nervous.

"Mr. MacGwyre! So good to see you again. Thanks for agreeing to meet with me on such short notice." Tim could sense the energy and power of Mrs. Matherson, and he realized he did not want, nor could he afford, to get on her bad side.

"Nice to see you, as well. Please come in and sit down. What can I do for you?"

"I wanted to talk to you about Carrie's grade on her last history project. You see, she and Jessica Adams worked on their projects together, and they proofread each other's papers; yet Jessica got an A– on her project and Carrie got only a B. Carrie and Jessica have been best friends for years, and Carrie has always done better than Jessica in school. So you can imagine Carrie's disappointment when she got a lower grade. I've talked to some of the other parents, and their children all seem to have gotten about the same grade as Carrie. But Carrie always does better than they do."

Tim was prepared to talk with Mrs. Matherson about Carrie's work, but not about everyone else's work. And yet, he did not really know how he was going to avoid that conversation.

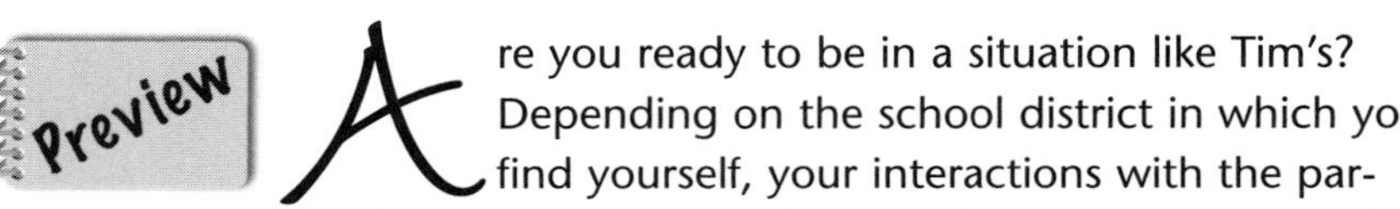


Are you ready to be in a situation like Tim's? Depending on the school district in which you find yourself, your interactions with the parents or guardians of your students may be anywhere from rare to daily, from antagonistic to welcoming, from hostile to responsive. You may long for any sign that the adults in your students' lives are interested in what their children are learning. Or, like Tim, you may find yourself wishing that your students' parents showed a bit *less* enthusiasm for their children's academic performance. Even if you are among those fortunate educators whose students' parents are supportive of your work to educate their children, you may wonder how to make the best use of all that support.

Whatever the nature of the dynamics between the school and the parents, interacting with the parents or guardians of your students is an integral part of your job as a teacher. Developing the skills and strategies to communicate well with the caregivers of your students can help make your work more effective in helping their children learn. Educators agree, and research supports, that parental/guardian involvement increases student learning, so finding ways to involve parents and guardians effectively in their children's learning is extremely important. Involving parents and guardians who avoid the extremes of parental apathy and "helicopter parents" (those who always seem to be hovering around) will make your teaching life more enjoyable and effective.

Knowing that you want to make parents your allies and co-educators, you need to think carefully about how to win them over. In some school districts, this may require little or no effort. You may have parents beating down your door to offer assistance, support, and guidance. Or you may find what is all too often the case: that it is very difficult to gain parent and guardian involvement.

Some communication challenges can result from differences in experience or culture between teachers and families. Some parents may not have had positive school experiences, either as students or as parents. Their lingering antagonism may be apparent in their initial interactions with you. You may also have a significant population of English language learners whose parents are only marginally fluent in English, if that. These parents may have cultural as well as linguistic reasons for rarely communicating with you or the school. You may find that establishing productive relationships with your parents will take some skill and effort on your part.

**This module emphasizes that:**

- **Communication with parents and guardians of your students requires considerable planning and effort on your part. One method won't work with all parents. Communication with families can be face-to-face, written, or electronic.**
- **If run effectively, parent–teacher conferences offer a great opportunity to establish good relationships, but if handled poorly, they can have negative consequences.**
- **You need to spend considerable time thinking about how you want families to be involved in the work of your classroom and giving them opportunities to become involved.**
- **There are general guidelines to help you succeed in involving families in the work of the school.**

# Benefits of Maintaining Good Communication

***In loco parentis*** a Latin phrase referring to the responsibilities of the teacher to function "in the place of parents" when a student is in school.

From their inception, schools have been given the responsibility of educating students ***in loco parentis.*** That Latin phrase means that educators are acting *in the place of parents* when they interact with students. For many years, this phrase was taken literally. Teachers were viewed as substitute parents during the time that students were at school, and they were expected to educate students as though the students were their own children. Teachers were expected to be concerned not only about students' academic

Easy and open communication with parents is a major asset in teaching.

understanding of concepts and skills but also about the moral upbringing of the students in their charge. In more recent times, the extent of the educator's responsibilities has been redefined and, in some instances, limited. The process continues, as educators' responsibilities regarding students' physical, intellectual, and moral well-being are being hammered out in different venues, from state legislatures to federal courts.

Of course, teachers will always be very influential in the education of the young people they find before them. They therefore have an obligation to maintain frequent and open communication with the parents or guardians of these young people. This communication is important for several reasons:

- *Sending consistent messages.* Teachers, as well as other community members such as clergy, coaches, and club leaders, are expected to contribute to the education and socialization of the young so that they can become productive and contributing adult members of society. This enormous task requires consonance among the many participants so that young people receive a consistent message about the core beliefs, values, and behaviors that are important in their culture.

- *Enlisting cooperation and help.* You want the family members of your students to be your allies in the educational process, not adversaries. Making sure the parents understand exactly what you are looking to accomplish can help you enlist their aid in helping students achieve the goals you have set for them.

- *Encouraging good conduct.* Good teacher–home communication also helps to bring together two worlds that many students, typically older ones, would prefer to keep separate. When students know that parents have ready access to their teachers, and vice versa, they often respond by being more cautious in their behavior and more appropriate in their interactions, both at school and at home.

- *Sending messages directly.* Young people are not always the most reliable of communicators, so what is reported at home about the goings-on in the classroom, and what is reported to the teacher about events at home, may not be completely accurate. Some students have a flair for the dramatic and tend to exaggerate reality, and others opt for selective memory loss and "forget" key events, happenings, or assignments. Communicating directly with parents and guardians helps avoid these

© Baby Blues Partnership

kinds of strategic retellings and memory lapses. Also, by letting families know what you will be doing from week to week, you help them minimize the classic conversation of a parent asking, "What did you do in school today?" and the child answering, "Nothing."

# Communication Methods: It's Not Just What I Say, It's How I Say It

As we emphasized in Module 13, Communication in the Classroom, the bottom line in all communication is delivery of the message. You have a message that you want to send: information, an idea, a point of view, a suggestion or recommendation. You want to make sure the intended audience—the parents and guardians of your students—get the message you intend them to receive. Therefore, you must find the most effective method for delivering that message.

Several factors will affect how you choose to deliver messages to the family members of your students. Some occasions, such as parent–teacher conferences and the situation described in the opening scenario, require face-to-face meetings. Other information may be delivered in writing, whether on paper or through email. You may even wish to enlist the other multimedia capabilities of the Internet.

## Verbal Communications

Depending on the age of your students, you may have more or less opportunity to communicate verbally with their parents. The trend seems to be "the older the student, the less contact between teacher and parent." This trend can be a double-edged sword. On the one hand, you may have fewer interruptions from parents and fewer demands placed on you by parents. On the other hand, you may have less support from home for the educational process. As we discuss later in this module, written communication, especially electronic communication, can help bridge the gap and get more parents actively involved in their adolescent children's schooling. Although you will certainly talk informally with parents, many schools have formalized opportunities to meet the families of your students at such events as Back-to-School nights and parent–teacher conferences.

***Back-to-School Night*** Many schools host open houses or Back-to-School nights shortly after the beginning of each academic year. At these events, parents typically hear short presentations about course goals and expectations from each of their child's teachers. At the elementary level, parents may hear one long presentation from the classroom teacher and shorter presentations from specialists. At the secondary level, parents hear shorter presentations from each of their child's content teachers and specialists.

Many teachers find these evenings intimidating and nerve-wracking, but they are important opportunities for you to get family members "on your side," as partners in helping their children achieve the goals you set for them. Thorough preparation is the best way to relieve some of the nervousness you may experience before your "performance." Here are a few guidelines:

- Plan carefully what you want to say.
- Make a list of the main points you want to share with the parents. Class policies are particularly important to share with parents.
- Let them know the penalties you impose for tardiness, late work, and missing assignments.

## Now You Do It

Read this scenario and reflect on your answers to the questions that follow.

*With just a few minutes to go, Marissa gave the classroom one final look. Good: it looked neat and organized. She had moved the usual piles of papers off her desk and decorated the bulletin boards with new displays. Open House always filled Marissa with dread. In her third year of teaching middle school math, however, she was starting to feel a bit less nervous about the evening. After all, she knew what topics she wanted to cover with parents and had her script pretty much memorized.*

*As parents of her first-period class filed in, Marissa quickly scanned their name tags and greeted them by name, mentally matching each adult with the student he or she represented. It was amazing how similar some of the students and their parents looked. She invited the parents to visit the classroom and then take a seat anywhere. As Marissa waited at the front of the room for the parents to get settled, she gave herself a mental pep talk. "See, there's nothing to be nervous about. I know what I'm doing here."*

*Marissa started with her presentation by talking about the curriculum. New this year, the curriculum was designed to address all the concepts covered on the state test scheduled for May. She had paused to shift to class policies when a voice rang out from the back: "What are you going to do to help my son pass this test in May? He scored low last year and this is an important year. If he doesn't score higher this year, he won't be able to take geometry next year."*

*Startled by the interruption, Marissa strained to see who the man was. She could not see his name tag, so she had no idea which student was his son. That was okay, she thought. She wanted to avoid talking about individual students in front of the whole group, anyway. She began to respond in general terms. "Well, as I mentioned, we spent last year redesigning the middle school math program to address that very issue, and we are confident that this new curriculum is more comprehensive and will help students be more successful on the test."*

*"I don't really care about the 'new curriculum,'" the man persisted. "I'm concerned about my son and whether I'll have to pay for summer school so that he can take geometry next year."*

**QUESTIONS**

1. How would you deal with the insistent parent if you were in this teacher's situation?
2. Propose strategies to help the teacher defuse the situation and resolve the conflict.

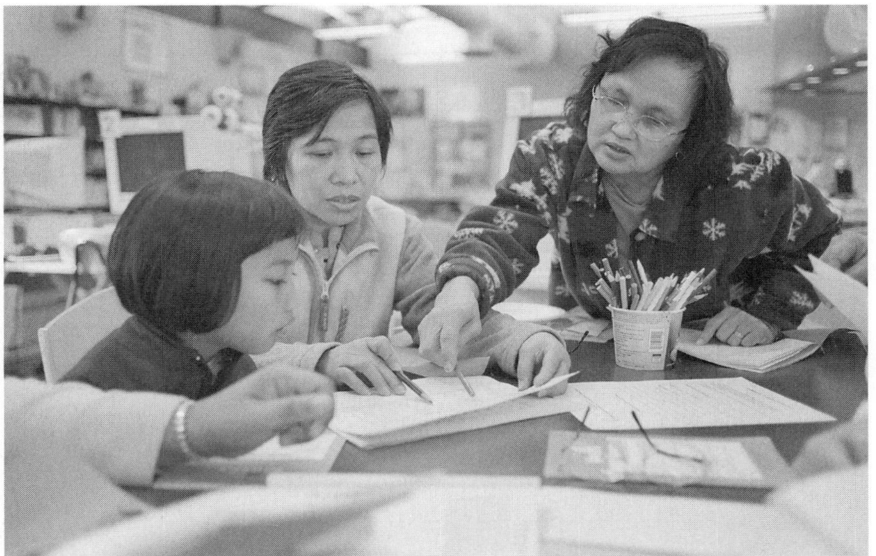

With preparation and care, you can comfortably discuss the performance of individual students with their family members during parent conferences.



- Present a cogent overview of the course or courses you teach to their children.
- Explain the rationale behind the tasks and assignments you have set.

You should also be aware of some of the pitfalls of these events. Some parents see Back-to-School night as an opportunity for a parent conference. Some like to get feedback on how their child compares academically to the other students in the class. Others may want to air their own disagreements with school policies or personalities. These are conversations you want to avoid! Draw on your best negotiating skills to turn the conversation deftly to more general topics.

***Parent Conferences*** Another opportunity for face-to-face verbal communication occurs at parent conferences. At these conferences, discussion of individual student performance is not just acceptable; it is expected. Parents come to find out how their child is doing. As you prepare for these conferences, keep in mind that most parents want to hear positive things about their child. Many also want to hear that their child is superior to others in the class. With these desires in mind, here are some tips to help you hold successful parent conferences.

- *Keep the discussion focused on the child of the parent(s) with whom you are meeting.* Expect parents or guardians to try to compare their student with other students in the class. Be prepared to respond tactfully, yet firmly, to divert attention from other students and back to their child.
- *Maintain a positive or constructive tone.* Avoid talking about what a student does not do and frame your comments to indicate what the student needs to do. For example, avoid telling Jillian's parents that she always hands in her work late. Instead, tell them Jillian's work would benefit if she were more punctual. Do not complain that George never studies for his math test; instead, suggest that George would do well if he regularly spent thirty minutes a night on math homework and review.
- *Remain objective.* Never personalize a student's behavior or work. There is every likelihood that the student's behavior in your class has nothing

to do with you as an individual and may have more to do with you as a teacher or an adult. For example, don't say, "I think Damon is just trying to aggravate me when he yells out answers to my questions." Instead, try something like this: "When Damon yells out answers without raising his hand, he deprives other students of the opportunity to respond."

- *Consider inviting the student to attend the conference.* In some school systems, students participate in the discussion about their academic

## Now You Do It

Read this scenario and reflect on your answers to the questions that follow.

*"Let's see, who's next? Oh, the Hollingsworths," Angela Gordon muttered to herself. It was the second day of parent conferences. Only a few parents in any of Angela's four classes had signed up for conferences, despite numerous reminders and urgings. Family apathy was a serious concern at the school, and the teachers and administrators hoped that having parent conferences would get more parents involved. So far, however, most of the parents Angela had seen were the ones who were already highly involved in their children's educational experiences. The Hollingsworths were a surprise, because they did not seem to fit this mold.*

*Angela had yet to meet Mr. and Mrs. Hollingsworth or to have any communication with them. Their daughter Tara was an average student, both in academics and in class participation. Tara generally handed in assignments on time, was usually present in class, and sometimes participated on her own initiative. Her tests and quizzes were in the B–/C+ range, with an occasional high or low score.*

*As Angela leafed through Tara's folder in preparation for the meeting, she had to admit that she did not know Tara very well. Tara was one of those students who placed few demands on Angela's time, and for that Angela was, to some extent, grateful. Angela rarely interacted with Tara on a one-on-one basis, although Tara did come to her writing conference as required. Angela remembered the conference as being fairly one-sided, with Angela doing most of the talking.*

*Angela was still pondering what to say about Tara when the Hollingsworths appeared at the open door of the classroom. "Mr. and Mrs. Hollingsworth? I'm so glad to meet you. I'm Ms. Gordon, Tara's English teacher. Please come in and sit down." After the couple were seated, Angela launched into her usual conference opener. "I have Tara's folder of work here for you to review. We can also talk about her grades to date and talk about her strengths and . . . ."*

*She was surprised to be interrupted by Mrs. Hollingsworth, whose face was stony. "Tara tells us you don't like her and that you pick on her all the time in class when you're not ignoring her. She hates the class and comes home crying every day," Mrs. Hollingsworth informed Angela. "We try to not interfere in our children's schooling, but English has always been Tara's favorite subject, and now she can't stand it. We want to know why you dislike our daughter so much," the mother continued, before ending with what sounded to Angela like a threat. "We thought it was only right to talk to you first before we go to the principal and demand that Tara be put in a different English class."*

*Angela was stunned by the Hollingsworths' comments. Why would Tara think she hated her? Angela mentally reviewed the daily classes to try to understand what she was hearing. She called on Tara, but she tried to call on everyone in the class, whether they raised their hands or not. Did Tara see that as picking on her? And of more immediate concern, what in the world should Angela say to Tara's angry parents?*

### QUESTIONS

1. How would you deal with the parents if you were in this teacher's situation?
2. Propose strategies to help the teacher defuse the situation and resolve the conflict.

performance. In student-led conferences, the student may be the first to talk, responding to the grades he or she earned in a given term and then answering questions by parents and teacher. It is important to keep the emotional climate positive and to avoid the student's being embarrassed in front of his or her parents. Before implementing any new practice, however, check with your school administrator to be certain it is acceptable.

**Video Case**

How can you be an effective communicator during parent conferences? In the video case, *Home–School Communication: The Parent–Teacher Conference,* you'll see teacher Jim St. Clair's approach firsthand. You'll see how he weaves actual examples of the child's work and his own observations into his discussion of the child's strengths and weaknesses. You'll also see him listen and respond to the mother's concerns. As you watch the clips and study the artifacts in the case, reflect on the following questions.

**QUESTIONS**

1. How does this teacher employ the advice given above? Could he apply any of the advice better, in your opinion?
2. What is the value for the teacher of asking family members what the student says about school when they are at home?
3. What, if anything, would you do differently in parent conferences, to reflect the age of students you teach and your own personal teaching style?

***Online Study Center***

## Written Communications

One way to establish open communication with the families of your students is through regular written communication. This may take the form of a weekly or monthly newsletter, an open letter to parents at the start of each term, or personalized notes sent to each parent or guardian at regular intervals. Through this written communication, you can keep parents informed about the topics of study and about assessment dates, two areas of most concern to parents.

When communicating in writing, it can sometimes be difficult to choose the appropriate style and tone. Without seeming arrogant, you want to convey confidence in your ability to teach effectively. Or you may want to let parents know that you are solicitous of the needs of students and their families, but without seeming patronizing or overly accommodating. You also need to use language that makes you sound professional, and yet avoid using so much jargon or "educationese" that some parents feel inadequate or your message becomes inaccessible. Finding the appropriate discourse level for your communications with parents is a dynamic process. You may wish to ask colleagues who have more experience with the families of your school for advice. The "In Your Classroom" feature includes some other tips.

## Electronic Communications

Some school districts encourage electronic communication between teachers and parents. Teachers may be required to have a course or class website and may be expected to communicate with parents electronically as well. Even if your school does not require it, you can use these communication tools to your advantage. Do not, however, assume that all parents and guardians have access to the Web or to email communication. Be sure to plan other methods to communicate with those who do not.

***Email*** Email communication can be fast, efficient, and often more reliable than depending on students to deliver a note home to parents. Problems, potential or actual, can be addressed more quickly in the hope of a faster and more productive resolution. Email communications also offer the possibility of closer monitoring of student work, especially when students face challenges to their academic performance. Be sure to secure parents' permission to use their email addresses if you plan to communicate this way.

At the same time, if it is not managed carefully, email communication with parents can become the bane of your existence. Some parents may come to expect easy, direct, and constant access to their child's teacher, and supplying these parents with immediate responses could consume all of your nonteaching hours. To avoid this potential predicament, we suggest first that you correspond with parents using only your school email account, and refrain from giving parents your personal email address. Second, establish an email policy with your students' parents. Your policy might be to respond to emails once a day or twice a week, for example. We also suggest that you make this policy known to the school administration as well as to students

## In Your Classroom

### Guidelines for Writing to Students' Families

As useful as written communication with parents is, it can also be a public relations nightmare if the communication is not carefully reviewed before being sent out. Here are a few guidelines to consider.

- *Use formal language in writing.* Although you may be friendly with the parents of your students, and some may even be your friends, the tone in your written communication should always be formal.
- *Talk about the class as a whole.* Celebrate the achievements of the whole group rather than those of individual students. Speaking about specific students may give the impression that you are showing favoritism toward some students and not others. This could be an especially thorny issue for students in the college application/acceptance cycle.
- *Proofread, proofread, and then proofread again.* Make sure that your written communication is grammatically correct in all aspects—spelling, punctuation, and usage. If you are uncertain about anything, ask a colleague to look over what you have written. Few things are more damaging to a teacher's reputation than a written communication with grammatical errors, no matter what discipline you teach. Remember that spell-checkers are not foolproof; they often overlook words used inappropriately, such as "lead" incorrectly used for "led."
- *Presentation is crucial.* Not only should the tone be formal and the language grammatically correct, but the presentation of written communication also needs to look professional. Do *not* handwrite any written communication, even if it is a very short note. Do *not* make hand corrections on a typed note, even though you have already made copies.
- *Follow school policy.* In some school districts, all written communications with parents must be cleared with the school administration. Make sure you know what the policy is and adhere to it.

and their families, so that any potential complaints about your "lack of responsiveness to parents" can be addressed appropriately. Your policy does not prevent you from answering urgent emails immediately, but it can give you some breathing room for less critical communications from parents.

We also urge you to keep in mind that all email correspondence leaves a "paper trail," or lasting record of your words. Even deleted email messages can be retrieved from a computer's hard drive. Be cautious when writing emails to parents, especially if you are dealing with a conflict or dispute. Put in an email message *only* information that you are willing to acknowledge and own. In heated or complicated situations, it is prudent to have a colleague read through your email before you send it, to make sure the message is unambiguously clear and is free of any tone of accusation or blame. In a similar vein, we suggest you keep hard copies of any emails from parents that present the potential for conflict or are the result of a conflict.

***Class Website*** A course or class website is also a fast and efficient way to maintain close communication with parents. The course website can list the course outline for the term and provide students and their families with information about course expectations, class policies, assignments, and due dates. At least in theory, the class website can also help to alleviate email overload from parents seeking information about your classes.

To be effective, however, the course or class website needs to be updated on a regular basis. As you plan the website for your course(s) or class, plan also for its maintenance. If you are well versed in web design, you may decide that you can maintain the site. If not, then (except in primary grades) there is likely to be at least one student, if not many, in your class or course who is skilled in web design and interested in maintaining the site. Some teachers offer extra credit to the student(s) who maintain(s) the site.

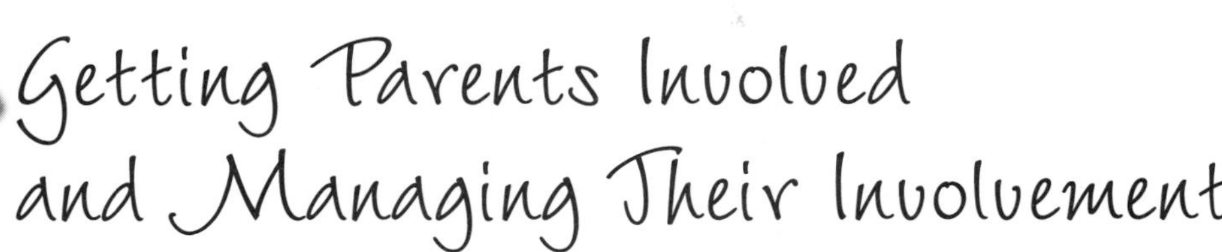

## Getting Parents Involved and Managing Their Involvement

Research tells us that getting parents involved in their children's schooling reaps benefits for the school. These benefits include more regular student attendance, a higher graduation rate from high school, fewer retentions in the same grade, better diagnosis of student needs and better placement of students, and improvement in student performance on math and reading tests.[1] If your school does not have a program to encourage parental participation, you might want to invite parents to spend a few hours a week helping in the school or classroom. The "In Your Classroom" feature lists a number of ways in which family members can help at school.[2]

### In Your Classroom

#### Ways Parents Can Help at School

- Share information with a student or class about a hobby.
- Share information with a student or class about a career.
- Share information with students about a country the parent visited or lived in.
- Tutor a student or a small group of students in reading, math, or another area.
- Help coach an athletic team.
- Help check a student's written work.
- Help put out a school or classroom newsletter (can also be done at home).
- Help sew or paint a display.
- Help build something (such as a loft in a classroom).
- Help students work on a final exhibition or project. (This can also be done at home or in a workplace.)
- Help answer the school's phones.
- Help plan a new playground for the school.
- Help plan a theme-based presentation for students.
- Help present a theme-based program for students.
- Demonstrate cooking from a particular country or culture.
- Share a particular expertise with faculty (such as use of computers or dealing with disruptive students).
- Help students plan and build an outdoor garden or other project to beautify the area outside the school.
- Help coach students who are taking part in an academic competition (such as Odyssey of the Mind, Future Problem Solving, or Math Masters).
- Help bring senior citizens to school to watch a student production.

Having parents involved in the classroom, however, does require some management on your part. You will need to decide what exactly you want these parents to do. Many of your parents may not be trained educators and will need specific direction if they are to help productively. Depending on how many parents you have volunteering, you may want to set up a mini-training session for them either during a free period or after school. Before you do so, think strategically about the best way to make use of these parents. In particular, if you are having volunteers work with students, make it clear just how much help is appropriate. If you have any concerns about parents being able to maintain confidentiality about students' academic work, you may want to limit parental involvement to more managerial or housekeeping tasks. Do not discourage any parents from volunteering, but be strategic in how you channel their enthusiasm and participation.

Let's Sum Up

We want to leave you with a general set of suggestions to help you frame your interactions with parents.

- *Be respectful and never condescending.* The temptation may at times be strong to respond to some parents or guardians in ways that convey to them your disapproval of their parenting skills. As a teacher, you may come to believe that you possess good insights into young people's behaviors and a wealth of knowledge about viable strategies. You very well may have greater insights into the minds of children or adolescents than some of their parents do. After all, the numbers are on your side, because you deal regularly with so many more of these minds at one time. Remember, however, that few parents welcome parenting tips from teachers. If you are a young or childless teacher, you may find this is particularly true.

  Being respectful in your interactions is not limited to the way that you talk, the words and intonation that you use, or the facial expressions and gestures that you display. It also consists of realizing the limitations of your own knowledge and accepting the breadth and depth of the knowledge that parents possess. Remember, for example, that although you may be an expert on children in general, the parents are experts on their own child. When you convey respect for the ideas and viewpoints of your students' parents, you will very often find that parents reciprocate and show respect for your views and ideas.

- *Develop a thick skin.* At times, you may encounter parents or other community members who fail to show what you consider appropriate respect for you or the school. You may notice, too, that teacher-bashing has become something of a popular sport. Expect to hear comments such as "It must be nice to work only a half-day" and "I wish I had as much vacation as you teachers do" and "I can't believe our teachers want higher salaries! For the work they do, I'd be happy to get that salary" and other comments or viewpoints on the state of teaching and schooling in the United States.

  You will have to decide on what approach you will take if and when you receive similar comments. Some teachers respond to comments of this nature by sharing with their interlocutor the number of hours spent beyond the school day grading papers, planning lessons, calling parents, and arranging field trips. Others will share a typical school day: the back-to-back classes of instruction, the twenty-three minute lunch period, the hectic pace dealing with administrative demands, student and parent needs, and state mandates.

  Keep in mind, though, that these sorts of comments are probably not a personal attack on your work ethic or your effectiveness as a teacher. As much as it might frustrate you to do so, it may be in your best interest simply to ignore many of these criticisms and biting remarks. Your task is not to change these people's minds about teachers' compensation or qualifications, but to communicate clearly and effectively with them about their child.

- *Be guarded in what you say to, and share with, parents.* To put it in terms of time-honored clichés, honesty may be the best policy, but discretion is the better part of valor. No matter how friendly you may be with the parents or guardians of your students, keep in mind that when you communicate with parents about school happenings or school-related events, you are communicating as a representative of the school system. Remind yourself—as often as you need to—that as long as you are at school or a school-sponsored function, and whenever you are asked to speak as a public school teacher, anything you say carries the weight of the school district with it. Avoid criticizing school policy or the practices of any of your colleagues or administrators. Also refrain from commenting on state mandates regarding topics such as testing, curriculum frameworks, or teacher licensure.

  Other land mines to avoid are discussions about other students in the class. Some parents, such as Mrs. Matherson at the beginning of this module, are inclined to seek comparisons of their child to other students in the class, in terms of academic ability or performance, teacher assistance or support, or even social standing among peers. Engaging in these kinds of discussions can backfire and cause damage in more ways than one:

  - From a legal perspective, revealing information about a student's academic performance to someone other than that student's legal guardians violates the Family Educational Privacy Act, so you would be opening yourself up to a potential lawsuit.
  - Engaging in such a conversation compromises your reputation as an impartial and discrete evaluator of student performance and as a fair assessor of student needs.
  - You could cause a serious rift among the parents, who can sometimes be highly competitive about their children.
  - Although you may believe you are communicating these views to a parent in confidence, you cannot be sure that the parent will keep that confidence. As a result, the parents of your students may become reluctant to entrust you with confidential information about their children—information that you may need to teach effectively.

- *Show no favoritism.* Be aware of the potential for perceptions of favoritism not just among your students, but among parents as well. If you are teaching in a public school, some of the parents of your students are at least acquaintances, and more likely friends, who talk and compare notes about their children's experiences in school, sports, or extracurricular activities such as music, dance lessons, and community events. Others may be involved in fierce rivalries. The last thing you want to do is contribute to breaking up a friendship or exacerbating a rivalry by inadvertently conversing significantly longer with one parent than with another or revealing seemingly innocent information to one parent and not to another.

  You will probably have parents for whom you feel more or less affinity, and we certainly do not expect you to like *all* of the parents and guardians of your students. What we do expect is that you interact with all of them in the same way, with the same enthusiasm and attention, just as you do with all of your students.

## Video Case

The video case, *Parent Involvement in the School Culture: A Literacy Project,* shows literacy specialist Linda Schwertz working with a group of parents on a book publishing project. You'll also hear from parents who explain why they are so eager to become involved in this and other school events. As you watch the clips and study the artifacts in the case, reflect on the following questions.

### QUESTIONS

1. How do the benefits of parent–teacher communication and cooperation described by the parents in this video case compare to those listed earlier in this module?
2. What steps do you think this teacher needed to take to manage the involvement of these parents?
3. Compare the teacher's assertion that the culture of a school is created by the families of the students with the remarks of the parent who suggested that teachers need to help families feel welcome and get involved. What are the respective roles of teachers and families in creating the culture of the school?
4. Do you feel comfortable with having family members of students involved in your class? In what ways? What potential drawbacks do you see to parent involvement, and how might you overcome these drawbacks?

**Online Study Center**

## Further Resources

- Joyce L. Epstein, *School, Family, and Community Partnerships: Preparing Educators and Improving Schools* (Boulder, CO: Westview, 2001). A good information source from one of the top scholars in the field of school–parent partnerships.

- The Family Involvement Network of Educators (FINE). Available at: **http://www.gse.harvard.edu/hfrp/projects/fine.html.** FINE is a national network of over 5,000 people who are interested in promoting strong partnerships among children's educators, their families, and their communities.

- Janie E. Funkhouser and Miriam R. Gonzales, *Family Involvement in Children's Education: Successful Local Approaches* (Washington, DC: OERI, U.S. Department of Education, 1997). Available at: **http://www.ed.gov/pubs/FamInvolve/index.html.** This "idea book" catalogues successful approaches that schools can use to help overcome barriers to family involvement in their children's education—regardless of family circumstances or student performance.

- National Network of Partnership Schools. Available at: **http://www.csos.jhu.edu/p2000/.** Established by researchers at Johns Hopkins University, the National Network of Partnership Schools brings together schools, districts, and states that are committed to developing and maintaining comprehensive partnerships among school, families, and community.

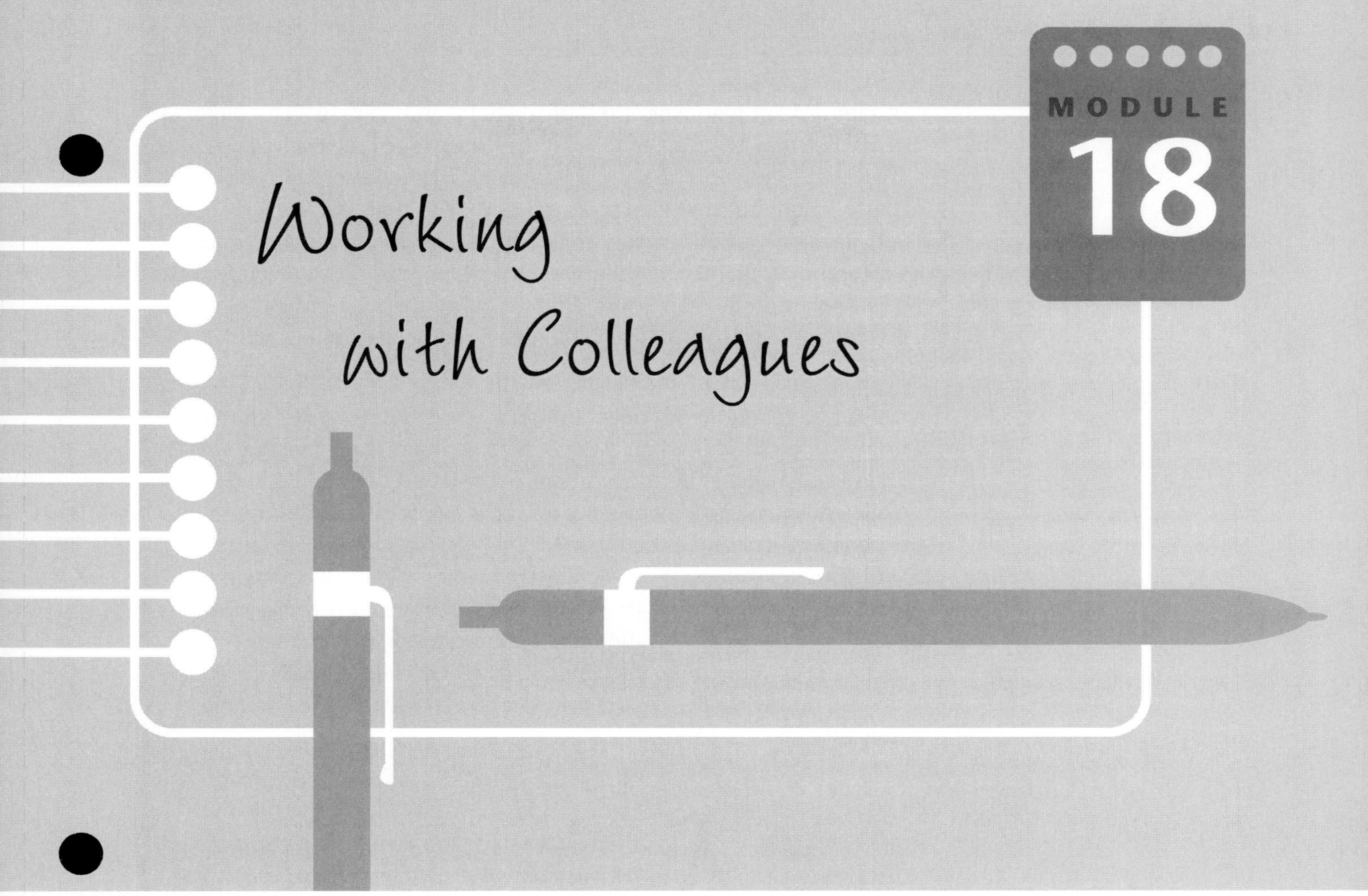


Scenario

"Martha, want to join us for lunch in the teachers' room?" Janice peered into Martha's classroom and found her new colleague hidden behind a stack of papers. When she got no acknowledgment of her invitation, Janice moved into the classroom and repeated the invitation.

"What? Oh!" Martha jumped when she saw Janice. "I didn't hear you come in. I'm trying to get these papers graded before my next class. It seems to take me forever to get a stack of papers graded."

"I stopped by to see if you wanted to join us for lunch in the teachers' room."

"Oh no, I can't. I have to get these papers done." Martha said no more and returned to her piles of papers. A bit disappointed, Janice left Martha's classroom in silence.

Once in the teachers' room, Janice joined her usual lunch partners. "I stopped by Martha's room, but she was too busy grading papers."

"You can tell this is her first year, can't you? She'll figure it out soon enough," commented Clare, a twenty-seven year veteran of the school system. "I've seen dozens like her who work through every lunch break the first couple of years. But they all come around, if they don't burn themselves out! But, anyway . . . you won't believe what my class comedian said today. I try not to laugh, but that kid cracks me up!" With that, the usual lunchtime conversation was under way. Topics occasionally included weekend or vacation plans, family members' accomplishments, a film recently seen or a book recently read. More often, though, the subject tended to gravitate to particular difficult students or complaints about school administrators or board decisions.

Janice had taught at Springfield Middle School for five years and had been one of those teachers who worked through lunch her first year. Then a colleague in her department encouraged her to, as she put it, "take advantage of the collective words of wisdom" that her more experienced colleagues could offer her. "It's important to socialize with your colleagues," she explained to Janice. "They understand what you're going through and can give you good advice if you're having problems with a student, an administrator, or a parent. You want to know them well enough to feel comfortable asking them for help or advice. Besides advice, they can give you hands-on help sometimes."

Preview

As a new teacher, you have many resources to fall back on: your own long experience as a student, the example of former teachers, and your professional coursework and reading, to name just a few. Once you are in your own classroom, however, those memories and experiences may sometimes seem quite far away. But you will have another powerful source of knowledge, wisdom, and help all around you: your fellow teachers. This rich reservoir of support could elude you if, like Martha, you hesitate to interact with your colleagues.

This module discusses the steps you can take to recognize your colleagues as a rich resource and to make them useful to your development as a professional teacher.

**The module emphasizes that:**

- **There is a distinctive culture of teaching, and beginners need to understand the dynamics of this culture.**
- **Isolation from colleagues and other adults is one of the unique characteristics of their profession with which teachers must cope.**
- **Because of the "flat" career structure and the lack of hierarchy among teachers, the profession exhibits considerable egalitarianism.**
- **Advice-giving among teachers is a primary means of communicating the culture of a school and the craft of teaching.**

## Now You Do It

Read the following continuation of the opening scenario, and then reflect on your answers to the questions that follow.

*Martha finally took Janice's advice and made a conscious effort to eat in the teachers' room at least once or twice a week. So far, she hadn't needed to call on her colleagues for support or assistance, but she appreciated the camaraderie that the teachers' room afforded, even though she was not always "in sync" with the topics discussed or the tone of the conversation. It was a relief to take part in adult conversations after listening to and trying to decipher the disjointed utterances of pre-adolescents and adolescents.*

*Eating with her colleagues also helped Martha feel a part of the community at her school, and she liked that sense of belonging. She even found that it helped her solidify her professional identity. By listening to her colleagues talk about their interactions with their students, Martha became better able to find the words and phrases to respond to her own students' challenges and infractions.*

**QUESTIONS**

1. What, specifically, do you anticipate learning from your fellow teachers?
2. How important do you think it will be to feel a part of the school community in which you find yourself? What benefits do you believe you will gain from feeling a part of a school's teacher community? What drawbacks might exist?
3. Is it important for teachers to participate in social events organized for or by teachers in the school district? Explain your view.

## The Culture of Teaching

As a work environment, schools are quite different from most other work settings. Staff in an office, in a hospital, and even at a construction site generally enjoy and benefit from collegial interactions with coworkers. These social interactions and exchanges among workers are particularly useful for less experienced employees, who can gain essential knowledge and insights about the work from their veteran colleagues. In most of these workplaces, the expectations for newer members of the work community are quite different from those placed on the more experienced members. Finally, the easy access to colleagues and the greater visibility of one's work tend to make it easier for supervisors to notice and address difficulties that might arise for these new workers.

In schools, as we all know, teachers spend their workday teaching students, and many, like Martha in the opening scenario, remain alone in their classrooms even when the students are out. Many teachers spend at least 75 percent, and up to 90 percent, of their workdays in isolation from their colleagues. This and other elements of schools as workplaces have led sociologists to define and describe a **"teaching culture,"** a workplace environment with its own customs, routines, and ways of behaving. Let's take a close look at these patterns. Later, we will review efforts to bring about change in schools as a work environment.

**Teaching culture** as in other workplaces, the world of teachers has its own culture, a special pattern of routines, behaviors, customs, and mores that sets it apart from other types of employment.

Schools as work settings have been frequently studied and described. As early as 1932, Willard Waller[1] wrote about the teachers in schools, describing common images of teachers. Then, over thirty years ago, Dan Lortie carried

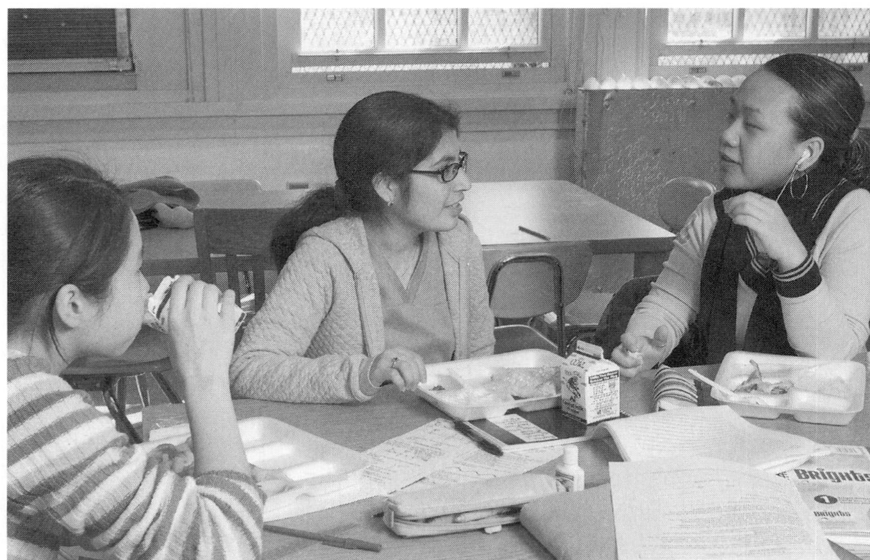

Your fellow teachers can be an immensely rich source of information and knowledge.

out an enduring, classic sociological study of teachers, which he published as the book *Schoolteacher* (1975). Among other findings, Lortie identified three characteristics that defined the teachers in his study: individualism, presentism, and conservatism.

- *Individualism.* At the time Lortie conducted his research, he found that teachers generally worked alone, deciding on their own what to teach and when and how to teach it. In recent years, however, state- and district-wide curricula have become more prominent, such that what (and sometimes how) to teach is typically laid out in the school district's curriculum guidelines. Although this particular generalization is somewhat dated, most of Lortie's other insights still apply. For instance, teachers rarely intrude on the work of a colleague and infrequently offer unsolicited support or advice to other teachers.

**Presentism** a tendency to focus principally on present events and tasks without much consideration for the future.

- *Presentism.* **Presentism** is a tendency to focus principally on present events and tasks without much consideration for the future. Lortie found that teachers exhibited this tendency to work and think primarily in the here and now. Many focused principally on what they needed to teach in the short term without necessarily thinking about the connection between what they were teaching students and what students would be learning in two years or five years. Moreover, in the absence of any career path in teaching, teachers rarely thought in terms of future goals or advancing within their profession. As a result, many teachers developed efficient, energy-conserving routines and practices and stuck with them year in and year out.

- *Conservatism.* By conservativism, Lortie did not mean that teachers tended to be politically conservative. Rather, his research suggested that teachers tended to maintain the status quo—to conserve the same learning environment that they had known as students. As he put it, "Teachers teach the way they were taught."[2]

Since Lortie's research was published, other educators and researchers have continued to study the work of teachers. Key findings emphasize the isolation that many teachers experience and the egalitarian nature of teachers as colleagues.

## Teacher Isolation

**Isolating nature of teaching** a characteristic of the teaching profession; teachers tend to be cut off from contact with professional peers and therefore do their work "in isolation."

Few studies have contradicted the findings of Lortie and others about the **isolating nature of teaching.** Some sociologists attribute this to the "egg crate" architecture of schools that were built in the late nineteenth century and much of the twentieth century: square, box-like classrooms all opening off a central hallway. Others insist that teacher isolation can be traced all the way back to the colonial origins of schools, where a lone teacher taught all the students in a single schoolhouse. Further isolating early teachers was the expectation that they would be models of virtue within the community. Teaching, it would appear, has been an isolating profession for many, many years.

Whatever its source, the isolating nature of teaching is an oft-heard criticism of the work, and it is echoed in frequent complaints about the lack of social interaction with adult colleagues. At the same time, it is not uncommon for teachers, like Martha, to seek that isolation. This is one of several contradictions in the world of teachers: they seek to be alone yet long for adult interaction. In order to understand this contradiction, let us take a closer look at the work demands that may explain this confusing finding.

Unlike office workers, who can often manage their work pace, teachers have limited control over the pace of work. Also, during the interactive part of the school day, when teachers have students before them, the energy demands on them are substantial. Teachers constantly and continually have to be teaching, monitoring, assessing, responding, and making decisions. They must be concerned not only with students' academic progress but also with their physical and social well-being. In many situations, teachers cannot leave the classroom to take a break, get a cup of coffee, make or answer a phone call, or even, as is the perennial joke in teaching, go to the bathroom.

It is not surprising, then, that when they do *not* have students before them, teachers often feel a need to be alone—just to "decompress" as well as to get the necessary work done for the next phase of the workday. Teachers have to plan for upcoming lessons, grade papers, and take care of administrative tasks such as record keeping, sorting and organizing student work, and spelling out lesson plans. Although they may be spent alone, the parts of the school day when student are not present are nearly as fast-paced as the parts spent in front of students.

The challenge for all teachers is to balance these two competing needs. New teachers are especially vulnerable, because many have not yet developed personal routines and practices to streamline their handling of administrative tasks. They also often do not have the repertoire of learning activities that veteran teachers have, so they need to spend more time planning learning activities, as well. We do not suggest that teachers wiggle out of their responsibilities, but we strongly urge them to keep their own needs in mind and to make conscious efforts to interact with colleagues.

## Egalitarianism Among Teachers

**Egalitarianism** a value that is widely subscribed to in the teaching profession and is fostered by the lack of hierarchy in teaching.

Another attribute associated with the teaching culture is **egalitarianism**—that is, a working environment characterized by a spirit of equality. Lortie noted the flat career path of teaching and cited it as one reason for what he labeled presentism. Lortie suggested that teachers do not often think in terms of future career goals or advancement because there are no formal, hierarchical differentiations among levels of teachers. Thus there is "nowhere to go" professionally unless one moves out of teaching into school administration. More recently, sociologists and other researchers have also linked the flat career path of teaching to the egalitarian nature of the culture. All teachers are equal, at least in terms of their status within a school district. Beginner or veteran, all have the same rights and responsibilities, work expectations, and decision-making authority. The exceptions, department chairs and curriculum coordinators, are fulfilling administrative functions in addition to their teaching functions. As teachers, they do not necessarily have a higher status than their colleagues.

For new teachers, the notion of equality can be intimidating. Although few new teachers possess the breadth and depth of content knowledge, pedagogical skills, or simple, old-fashioned savvy about teaching that their more experienced colleagues possess, they are given the same responsibilities as their veteran colleagues and are expected to achieve the same results. Some new teachers find themselves overwhelmed by the challenges of the first year of teaching and intimidated by the notion of equality with their more experienced colleagues. (The full array of issues and potential problems faced by new teachers is discussed in Module 24, The First Year.)

This notion of equality sometimes discourages new teachers from asking for guidance or advice from their colleagues, because they believe that doing so would be an admission of incompetence and a sign of failure. They are, after all, full-fledged, licensed teachers, on par with their veteran colleagues. They should, so their thinking goes, be able to cope just as well.

## In Your Classroom

### Tips on How to Join the Team

Every new social situation holds new promises and new hazards. This is particularly true of a beginning teacher's initial teaching assignment. The experienced teachers you encounter have the potential to be either a tremendous asset or a disappointing liability. The following tips are offered to help ensure that your new colleagues contribute to the successful launching of your teaching career.

- *Actively join the faculty.* Once hired, you will officially be "on the faculty," but that is different from being accepted as "one of the team." Often, acceptance hinges on active steps taken by the new teacher, such as introducing yourself to teachers you haven't yet met or sitting with other teachers at lunch and joining in the conversations.
- *Ask questions.* Few beginners have all the answers. On the other hand, teachers are teachers because they like to help others. Be open to their answers and their advice.
- *Be aware of your responsibilities for confidentiality.* A teacher hears things from students, from parents, and (unfortunately) from gossip among teachers that simply should not be shared unless there is a compelling reason.
- *Don't isolate yourself.* New teachers can make two "isolation" mistakes. One is to stay in their classrooms, like Martha in the opening scenario, using every minute on planning and paperwork, and remaining separated from fellow teachers. A second mistake is to isolate oneself with one other teacher or a small group of teachers, cut off from most of the faculty. All too often, the small group is made up of other new teachers, and their separateness is misinterpreted as a sense of superiority or rejection of the more established teachers.
- *Don't be too opinionated.* Many experienced teachers are put off by or suspicious of "Ivory Tower" ideas about education, particularly when they are announced by those with no "battlefield experience." We suggest that during the first year of teaching, you be a listener and a questioner.
- *Find a mentor.* We describe mentoring and how to find a mentor later in this module.

For similar reasons, the egalitarian principle can also inhibit veteran teachers from offering advice or support to a struggling new teacher. Veteran teachers may feel that they will insult or offend a new teacher if they offer unsolicited advice. Offering assistance might signal to others that the new teacher is having difficulties, suggesting that the teacher is ineffectual or inept.

This egalitarian quality of the teacher culture can make experienced teachers feel frustrated and even resentful that their practical and content knowledge—developed over many years—is not recognized or appreciated. Many have been able to develop very effective teaching strategies and techniques that they want to share with their newer counterparts, but the culture of teaching does not always encourage such sharing. The "In Your Classroom" feature on the previous page offers some tips for bridging this gap between experienced teachers and yourself, the new kid on the block.

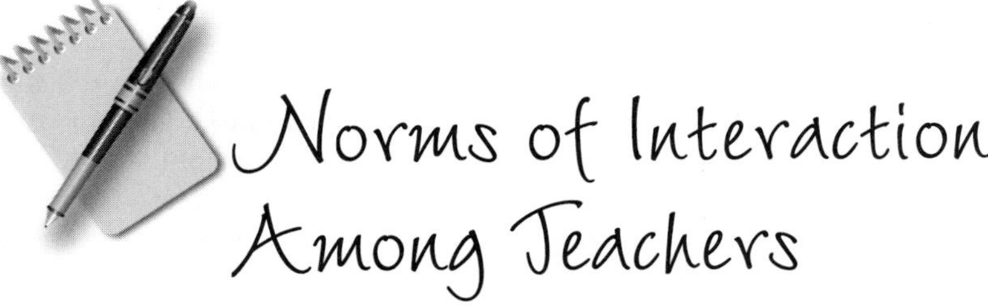

# Norms of Interaction Among Teachers

In light of our brief description of the culture of teaching, how do teachers interact with one another? As we saw in the scenario at the beginning of the module, teachers understand and appreciate the need for solitude in order to get work done, but they do not necessarily look kindly on teachers who repeatedly and continually opt to be alone. Teachers generally believe that social interaction among colleagues is not just a good idea but is essential to survival.

The expectation among teachers, whether it is explicitly stated or implied, is that everyone will spend some time in areas where teachers congregate away from students, such as the teachers' room, department office, or teachers' lunchroom. For new teachers, the prodding of a colleague or weekly reminders may be necessary to get them away from their desks or out of their classrooms to mingle with their peers. Eventually, Wednesday lunch or Friday breakfast will become a regular, eagerly anticipated event.

## Congeniality

Teacher discourse—the way teachers speak among themselves—has been described as *congenial* rather than *collegial*. It serves a social need without addressing the professional need. Teachers are encouraged and expected to talk to one another, and indeed they do, but their exchanges tend to be social, expressed in everyday language. Unlike the discourse of other professionals, such as lawyers or doctors, whose interactions are characterized by the use of technical or theoretical terms, teachers' interactions typically reflect congeniality, rather than fostering a more professional style of exchange among colleagues.

Anything related to one's family, free time, or even personal relationships is generally acceptable. Stories about student infractions or misbehaviors and complaints about administrators or district policies, although the telling of such tales can be unethical and unprofessional, are common. On the other hand, conversations about teaching strategies and theories, successful learning activities, ideas for curriculum planning, or assessment are frequently considered off limits. "No shoptalk" is the unstated rule in many teachers' lounges. To talk about a successful learning activity or an idea for curriculum integration could be viewed as showing off or inappropriate boasting. Still, as described in the next section, teachers have developed indirect ways to share their ideas, theories, and solutions to professional problems.

## Advice-Giving

In the opening scenario, Janet recollects that she has learned much from her social conversations with colleagues during lunch. Numerous teachers will share similar reflections on how much they have learned from colleagues, even in schools that abide strictly by the "no shoptalk" rule. How, then, do teachers share their collective words of wisdom and provide guidance and support for their less experienced colleagues? Consider the following case study.

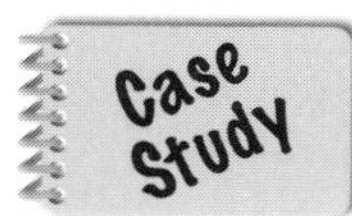


### *Someone Help Me with Brian ... Please!*

"That Brian is going to be the death of me!" Sheila ranted as she entered the teachers' room. "He must spend all of his waking hours trying to figure out how to drive me nuts! I swear I was ready to lose it in class today. Arrgghh!"

"Now what did he do?" asked Joyce, who was deep in a stack of math tests but knew that Sheila would continue ranting unless she asked her about Brian. The other teachers in the room stopped what they were doing to listen.

"He's such an instigator. During the entire class, he was cracking jokes under his breath, making comments about the so-called 'brainiacs,' distracting everyone near him. Then he started flicking pieces of paper around the classroom. Of course, every time I looked over at him, he was sitting there with an arrogant smirk on his face, daring me to accuse him of something or send him to the office. He is so disruptive! I didn't get through half of what I wanted to cover today because of him."

"I had a 'Brian' last semester," commented Arlene, a science colleague. "I know exactly what you're going through. It was getting so I could hardly stand the class. You should have seen this kid in chem lab! I never knew what he was going to try to do. I was seriously going to ask Mr. DiMarco if I could ban him from lab, but I knew DiMarco would never go for that. And the last thing I wanted him to think was that I couldn't control my own classroom. So what's Brian's story?"

"You mean besides his life mission of driving me crazy?" answered Sheila. "Don't really know. He's new to the school. Moved here in the fall from somewhere out of state. He seems bright enough and usually does well on tests, but for some reason, he's always disrupting the class. If I say anything to him to get him to stop, he just seems to get worse. And if I ignore him, he seems to think I've given him license to continue."

"I tried those with Aubrey, too," said Arlene. "They didn't work with him, either. I even tried calling his parents, but they were only concerned about his grades, and his grades were okay. They were no help at all." Arlene paused for a minute as if recalling the experience. "Then I found the hook. Aubrey was on the basketball team, so I started asking him about his workouts and training program and talking about some of the college and pro players. He was like a completely different kid. He would come to class a few minutes early to tell me about this player or that player, about how many baskets he made in practice, and his 'game stats.' He even started yelling at other students who were disrupting the class! Amazing, really. He still comes by to talk basketball with me, even though I don't have him at all this year."

"I had a 'Brian' this year, too," Joyce reported. "Luckily for me, I know his mother, and ever since he found that out, he's been pretty quiet in class. His mother isn't afraid to punish him if she hears he acts up in class. All I have to do is suggest that his mother might like to hear about what he's doing in math class and he straightens right up. Thank goodness there are still some of those kinds of parents around."

"Well, I've got to figure out some way of dealing with Brian or the entire year will be wasted."

This case illustrates a very common advice-giving exchange among teachers. Although teachers might rarely give advice directly, they often share "war stories," as some like to call them. On one level, these stories help to foster a sense of community, of shared experiences and feelings among teachers. They can help teachers realize that their experiences are not unique or insurmountable, because others have had similar experiences and have been able to cope with them with a modicum of success.

On a less obvious level, though, these war stories provide other teachers, such as Sheila, with strategies and techniques for addressing particular situations. They constitute the primary advice-giving approach in teaching. In this case, Sheila was given two options for dealing with the problem student in her class. Arlene suggested that Sheila find a "hook," a topic of interest for Brian. From the story she told, Arlene is implying that appealing to a student's interest can ease a teacher–student power struggle, leading to a more positive relationship between the teacher and student and to a more productive learning environment in the classroom. Joyce offered a completely different approach: playing the "parent card." Joyce reminded Sheila that home and school can be allies in the cause of education. Finally, Arlene advised Sheila not to send her problem student to the office, because the principal seemed to expect teachers to be able to handle discipline problems on their own.

Sheila is likely to share her frustrations with Brian with other teachers, who will probably offer her suggestions and advice in a similar manner—by recounting their own experiences in a comparable situation. Sheila will weigh these different options and select one or more to try in her dealings with Brian. Eventually, with the "Brian problem" behind her, Sheila will be able to share her own experiences with other teachers who encounter their own "Brians."

As the case illustrates, advice-giving is frequently couched in sharing of similar experiences. It is self-referential, as teachers tell how they responded to a situation. It is rarely direct or heavy-handed. It is rarely theoretical or given an abstract name, such as "the disruptor neutralization technique." For these reasons, although advice-giving among teachers occurs frequently, it may not be recognizable to the untrained eye.

## Now You Do It

The slice-of-life conversation from a teachers' lounge above is not atypical of the way teachers interact. As you reflect on it, answer the following questions.

**QUESTIONS**

1. Is Brian's teacher, Sheila, being professional here? Is it ethical to discuss individual students in this way, even though it is not in a public forum, but in the teachers' lounge?
2. How would you describe the language or terms of the exchange? If we were overhearing a conversation in a "psychologists' lounge," rather than a teachers' lounge, how do you suppose the language would be different?
3. How would you compare the remarks of Sheila, Joyce, and Arlene?
4. What, if anything, do you think Sheila learned from this exchange?

# A New Teaching Culture?

The description of teacher and school cultures that we have presented applies to a majority of schools, but not to all. Many schools have been successful in instilling a culture of professional *collegiality* rather than simple *congeniality*. In these schools, teachers regularly work together, share teaching successes and challenges, and support one another to optimize student learning.

## Collaborative Initiatives

In some schools, initiatives by individuals or small groups of teachers have led to pockets of collaboration among the faculty. Among these initiatives to enhance the level of collegiality and collaboration among teachers are school-based management programs, co-teaching situations, teacher induction, mentoring, and peer coaching programs. Here is a brief summary of each.

**School-based management (SBM)** a school reform effort that allows for greater decision making about programs and budgets at the local school level rather than the district level.

**Co-teaching** an instructional arrangement wherein two teachers share educational responsibilities for a student or a group of students.

**Peer coaching** an arrangement whereby teachers help one another with instructional issues through observation and consultation. This coaching between equals tends to be collegial and nonthreatening.

- **School-based management (SBM)** is a school reform effort, borrowed from the business world, to move some decision-making authority about programs and budgets to the individual school level, from the district level. As a result, teachers tend to have greater involvement in the actual decisions about what happens at their schools.
- **Co-teaching** occurs when two teachers work in close concert with each other to plan and implement lessons for students in the same classroom. Teachers in such situations are working collaboratively throughout the school day, and they are likely to engage in frequent conversation about teaching strategies and approaches. One situation in which co-teaching often occurs is special education, where a student or students are mainstreamed; the regular classroom teacher and the special education teacher jointly plan and take responsibility for instruction.
- **Peer coaching** in schools involves teachers who observe one another teach and then share thoughts, suggestions, and strategies. Through

Formal programs, such as peer coaching and teacher induction, can serve to infuse collegiality into teacher interactions at a school.

peer observations and discussion and reflection, teachers can gain new insights into their own teaching beliefs, evaluating and rethinking their current practices. Peer coaches can also help teachers implement new strategies or approaches. Peer coaching initiatives, however, tend to be limited to small groups of teachers within a school, so, as in co-teaching, the effect on the school culture as a whole is limited.

**Teacher induction** a program designed to initiate new faculty members into the profession and the routines of a particular school or district through informational meetings and other activities.

- **Teacher induction** programs are designed to ease the transition of beginning teachers into the profession and to foster a more supportive, collaborative school culture. They typically consist of periodic meetings for teachers new to the school or district, at which teachers engage in professional conversations about relevant topics, such as teaching approaches, strategies, and concerns.

**Mentor** usually an experienced colleague who gives personal and professional guidance to a beginner. Often such an individual is part of a district-wide mentor program.

## Mentoring

Another initiative designed specifically to help new teachers is **mentor** programs. A mentor teacher is usually an experienced colleague who gives personal and professional guidance to a beginner. In a typical mentor program, a teacher new to the school system is paired with a veteran teacher who helps the new teacher adjust and adapt to the school environment. The mentor teacher may offer insights into the school district, make procedural and administrative suggestions, give advice on teaching, or simply provide emotional support as the new teacher adjusts to the expectations of the work environment.

Through the mentor relationship, teachers learn to converse about teaching, instilling a habit of collegiality among participants in the program. As more and more teachers participate in such programs, either as mentor teachers or as new teachers, these habits can be institutionalized throughout a school so that collegiality becomes the norm.

If you find yourself in a school without a mentor program, we strongly urge you to seek out your own mentor. This is *the most important advice* we have to offer. The following suggestions should guide your choice.

- Take your time and choose carefully. The first teacher who offers advice or befriends you may not make the best mentor.
- Select someone who has the *time* and *energy* to work with you.
- Ideally, select someone from your grade level or from within your department who is familiar with the content you are teaching. As far as possible, try to match your mentor's strengths (such as extensive acquaintance with subject matter or very effective lesson planning) with your needs.
- Look for someone with solid experience who is respected for her or his professionalism.
- Try to find someone you can be comfortable confiding in—someone who will be candid with you, while always being "on your side."

New teachers are often reluctant to seek out a mentor because they realize that acting in that capacity makes demands on the individual. This is true, but you should also realize that many teachers enjoy being a mentor and sharing their expertise. Having acquired skill and understanding, they find the opportunity to work with newcomers stimulating and enriching. It is also tangible evidence of their excellence! Finally, remember that "down the line," you may have the opportunity and professional obligation to mentor a new teacher yourself.

### Video Case

In the video case, *Teaching as a Profession: Collaboration with Colleagues,* you'll hear teachers talk about the importance and the "how-tos" of collaborating with colleagues. You'll also see a formal collaborative work group in action. As you watch the clips and study the artifacts in the case, reflect on the following questions.

**QUESTIONS**

1. How do these teachers' definitions of collaboration compare to the initiatives described in this module? How do they compare to your own ideas about collaboration?
2. Watch the bonus videos on challenges of collaboration and on advice about collaboration. How do you anticipate overcoming the challenges mentioned?
3. Are there any other challenges you foresee? What additional advice would you like to have?

***Online Study Center***

As a teacher, you are part of a community that extends beyond your classroom and involves more people than the students you greet every day. This school community, although it may seem boringly familiar to you, who have spent so many years in schools as a student, may become jarringly unfamiliar as you experience it from the perspective of a teacher and an adult member of the school community. You will uncover intricacies of this culture to which you were never privy as a student.

First-time American travelers to foreign countries often experience feelings of discomfort and even frustration upon finding themselves in a culture that seems so much like American culture and yet does not function in the same way. It is not uncommon for new teachers to experience similar feelings of **culture shock.** The environment is familiar, yet it functions according to different rules and has different norms from those they are used to. (This issue of culture shock is also addressed in Module 24, The First Year.)

**Culture shock** the feeling of disorientation that people may experience when initially immersed in a society that is somewhat familiar but exhibits subtle differences in values, customs, and norms.

Spend some time getting to know this new culture. Spend time with your colleagues. Listen to them so you can find out what the norms of communication and interaction are. Getting to know this new culture will also make it easier for you to envision and implement the kind of learning environment you want to set up in your own classroom.

## Further Resources

- Esme Raji Codell, *Educating Esme: Diary of a Teacher's First Year* (Chapel Hill, NC: Algonquin Books, 1999). One of a rich literature of books by beginning teachers, which chronicles what a great resource—and occasionally, what a source of frustration—one's new colleagues can be.
- Dan Lortie, *Schoolteacher* (Chicago: University of Chicago Press, 1975). Although over thirty years old, this classic sociological study of the teacher culture and the dynamics of the teaching profession is still a valued resource for understanding the work and life of the American teacher.

- **TeachersFirst.com.** This site is an excellent source of tips, advice, and materials for teachers. It is one of many sites on the Internet that enables beginning teachers to get help from more experienced teachers.

MODULE 19

# School Governance and Funding

Scenario

Tara Givens had spent her first two years of teaching in a well-funded, upper-middle-class school system with a state-of-the-art school building, computers in every classroom, and a host of curricular offerings for students. Parental support was very strong, with parents organizing and overseeing many of the extracurricular activities. The students competed fiercely for grades, top honors, and acceptance to prestigious colleges and universities. Tara had found the pressure from students and parents overwhelming, and she longed to be in a school system where she could make a difference and really help students learn. Now, in her third year, she was looking forward to teaching English/language at a middle school in a new school district. This one was not as well funded, so the resources available in the schools were somewhat limited. Still, the district was more racially and ethnically diverse, something that Tara was specifically looking for. Tara felt confident that she would be able to help students learn and inspire them to go to college, just as she had been inspired by her own teachers.

The first month or so of the year went just as she had hoped. The students in her seventh-grade language arts class seemed to appreciate the attention she showed them and the excitement for learning that she conveyed. Homework was nearly always done; the few chronic offenders growled when they had to come to her after school, but they made their work up. She was able to get through units of study in the time she had planned. Even better, she got in most of the activities she had planned as well.

By the end of the second month, however, Tara noticed a significant slowdown in what she was able to accomplish in a given week. The number of missing homework assignments had increased, too.

"I need to do something to get these students interested again," she decided. Many of the books she had had her students read in her last school district were not available at her current school. A careful search of the titles in the department storeroom turned up enough copies of *Somehow Tenderness Survives* by Hazel Rockman, a collection of short stories about living in South Africa under apartheid. Although the book was published in 1988, Tara thought that the stories could still be relevant to her students because the authors of the stories were both white and black. Tara thought these stories would give students different perspectives and insights into apartheid.

"I'll have students keep a journal in which they respond to each of the stories we read. Then at the end, they can choose their favorite story and write a review of it," thought Tara. "The students should be able to keep up with the work, so I won't have to nag them or make them stay after school."

Tara's intuition proved right. Most of the students seemed to be enjoying the stories, although Tara sometimes felt a bit uncomfortable with the direction the discussions occasionally took, especially regarding racism. But the students were keeping up with their reading and their journals.

"Ms. Given, my mother wants to meet with you after school today," said Henry, one of Tara's brighter students, as he came into class.

"That's fine. I have no meetings planned," Tara responded, privately excited that one of her parents showed interest in what the children were doing in school. Tara mentally ran through her plans for the rest of the term, just in case Henry's mother wanted to know. But when Henry's mother arrived, the conversation was nothing like what Tara was expecting. In fact, Tara was quite surprised by what Henry's mother had to say.

"Ms. Given, I've been talking to some of the other parents in the class, and we all feel that the book you are having our children read is inappropriate," Henry's mother began. "Our children do not need to be reading any more about institutional racism. They live that every day. I asked Dr. Roemer about the book and he knew nothing about it. He said it was not on the list of books for seventh grade."

"Besides," she continued, "It seems Henry never has any homework. I ask him what he's supposed to do, and he tells me he's got no homework except to write in his journal about the stories. I looked at his journal and was appalled at all the grammar and spelling errors. How is he ever going to learn to write well if you don't have him correct his work? How is he, or any of the students in the class, ever going to pass the end-of-year test?"

"We've sent a letter to the principal and the superintendent complaining about the choice of book and the lack of work being done," she concluded. "We demand that you stop reading this book and start teaching students so they can pass the end-of-year test."

Henry's mother handed Tara a copy of the complaint the parents had sent. Tara looked at the letter, but she was too stunned to focus on the words. She couldn't believe what she was hearing.

"Why didn't Dr. Roemer say anything to me about the parents' concerns?" Tara wondered. "Why didn't the parents get in touch with me earlier? Why did they send this letter to the superintendent?" Tara was ready to burst into tears, but she had to say something to Henry's mother.

"Thank you for letting me know. I will certainly take your concerns seriously. Now if you'll excuse me, I have another meeting in a few minutes," Tara lied, leading Henry's mother to the door of her classroom. As she turned back to her empty classroom, she thought, "What a great way to start at a new school: complaints to my department chair, principal, and superintendent all within the first term!"

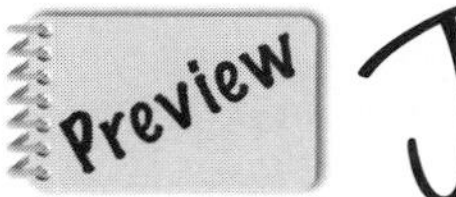


Teachers do have a certain amount of autonomy within the classroom and can (and must) make decisions about what to teach and how to teach. At the same time, teachers work in an organization that is highly visible and accessible to many stakeholders, from students and parents to community members. These many stakeholders may have conflicting expectations of the schools and may place contradictory demands on them.

As a member of an educational organization, you should be aware of how the organization works: how it is structured, governed, and financed. In this module, we will present an overview of the typical structure and governance of schools. We will also discuss financing sources and options for America's public schools.

**This module emphasizes that:**

- **Schooling in the United States is a state responsibility.**
- **Schools are organizations with many different layers of governance, from the state to the district to individual schools.**
- **Schools have hierarchies that teachers need to understand and respect.**
- **Financing of schools is primarily a state or local responsibility. In some states, it is also a political and controversial topic.**

# Governance of Schools

In many countries, public education is governed by a central agency, typically called the Ministry of Education, that ensures that the curriculum taught throughout all public schools (and sometimes all private schools) in the country is consistent. In the United States, however, the legal governance of public schooling is the responsibility of the individual states, rather than the federal government. States have the legal responsibility and authority to make decisions in most key areas of schooling, including

- what students learn
- how many years students must be in school and how many days each year
- what prospective graduates need to know in order to receive a high school diploma
- what qualifications teachers must have in order to teach in the state

## State Education Authorities

A number of different entities and individuals at the state level play a role in the delivery of educational services in the state.

- *State legislatures.* The legislature of each state is generally regarded as its chief educational policy-making body because the legislature funds education and makes the laws that govern and affect it. When state economies are strong, more money is usually invested in public education. Conversely, when state economies experience recessions, public education typically takes a financial hit.
- *Governors.* Governors also play a policy role by choosing to focus on particular educational issues and including these issues as part of the budgets they submit to legislatures. They also determine the makeup of the state board of education in states with appointed boards.

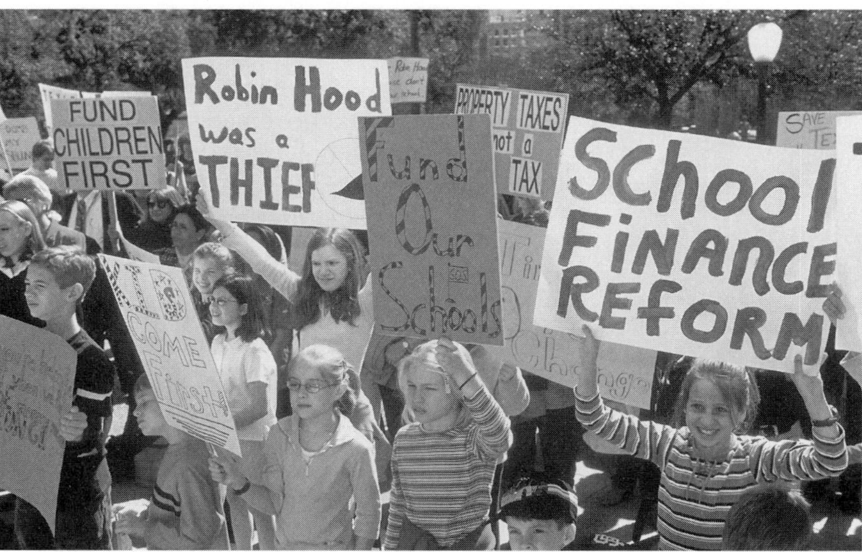


The local community participates in the governance of the local school districts.

**State board of education** The state board of education sets and reviews policy that governs the schools within the state. Members of the state board of education may be elected or appointed.

**Chief state school officer** the principal education official in the state. The chief state school officer, who may hold the title of commissioner or state superintendent of education, oversees the state education agency.

**State educational agency (SEA)** or state department of education the agency responsible for implementing the policies set by the state board of education, the legislature, or the governor's office.

**Local education agency (LEA)** the local school administrative group. The local education agency may be a town, a city, or a group of towns.

**School board** a group of community members charged with the oversight of the schools in that community. Alternately called the school committee, the school board is responsible for setting educational policy for the schools, approving curriculum, and hiring and evaluating the district superintendent. Its members may be elected or appointed.

**Superintendent of schools** the chief academic and administrative officer of a school district. The superintendent is responsible for the quality of education in the school district and for the effective implementation of all the school district's policies and practices. The superintendent directly supervises all building administrators and indirectly supervises all teachers in the district.

- *State boards of education.* Because governors and legislatures have many responsibilities in addition to public education, most states have a **state board of education** to exercise general control and supervision of public elementary and secondary schools. The state board of education usually sets goals and priorities for education in the state, establishes academic standards, determines qualifications for teachers and administrators, and makes recommendations to the governor and legislature for the improvement of education. Members of the state board of education are elected in some states but appointed by the governor in others.

- *Chief state school officer.* This position has various names in different states. The individual may be called the **chief state school officer,** commissioner of education, superintendent of public instruction, secretary of the state board of education, or superintendent of education. Whatever his or her title, this person is responsible to the state board of education for the administration of public education. The chief school officer identifies educational problems and recommends solutions to those problems to the state board of education. The chief state school officer also reports to the governor and legislature on the status of education in the state. This officer exercises little direct control over local educational officials but does exert considerable influence.

- *State departments of education.* The chief state school officer also heads the **state education agency (SEA),** most commonly called the state department of education or department of public instruction. The SEA is responsible for carrying out the policies of the state board of education and the laws passed by the state legislature. It consists of a bureaucracy of officials, often numbering in the hundreds. The SEA has a great many responsibilities, including administering and distributing state and federal funds to local school districts, licensing teachers and administrators, administering special programs and state assessments, accrediting college and university educational licensure programs, issuing reports, and generally monitoring the implementation of state educational policies.

## Local Education Authorities

Most state education authorities leave much of the day-to-day management of schools to the local school districts or **local educational agencies (LEAs).** There are approximately 15,000 LEAs in the United States. They vary in size from huge urban school districts, such as New York City and Los Angeles, to small rural districts with only a few schools. Whatever the size of your own school district, you are likely to encounter a variety of different players involved in governing education at the local level.

- *School boards.* Each local school district establishes a policy-making group—called a board of education, school board, or school committee—that is responsible for running the public schools in the district and for ensuring that state laws are followed. The local **school board,** which may be elected or appointed, has the authority to set curricula and programs of study within the schools; to hire, evaluate, and (when necessary) terminate school personnel; and to set the starting and ending times of the school day and the school year. Their decisions must adhere to the state education laws.

- *School superintendents.* One of the most important decisions that local school boards make is the hiring of the **superintendent of schools.**

The superintendent is both the chief academic and the chief administrative officer of the district. This is probably the most important and powerful individual in your school district. School superintendents are generally highly trained education professionals, knowledgeable about national schooling trends and practices. Because school board members often do not have a background or expertise in education, they often depend heavily on the superintendent to provide current and relevant information on educational trends and happenings so that the board can make informed decisions about policy and practices.

In addition to providing information and advice to the local school board, the superintendent is the chief academic officer and oversees the course of study at each grade level and each school of the district. The superintendent ensures that the course of study conforms to state curriculum requirements and is appropriately taught by the teachers in the district. Depending on the size of the school district, the superintendent may delegate the actual design of the curriculum to other school personnel, but he or she will generally review the proposed curriculum and give it final approval. Superintendents may also delegate the hiring and supervision of teachers to building administrators, but once again, they are ultimately responsible for the quality of education within the schools and for the academic achievement of all students within the school district. In these days of state-mandated testing and the reporting of students' academic performance to state and federal agencies, this responsibility is an enormous one.

The superintendent is also the chief public relations officer of the school district, responsible for maintaining a positive image of the school district and productive relations with community members. This role becomes especially important when districts are looking for additional funding from the community for building renovations or construction of a new school and when results from state testing need to be communicated to the public.

## School-Level Authorities

Your interaction with your district's superintendent is likely to be minimal once you have been hired. (In fact, you may not even be interviewed by the superintendent when you are hired.) Rather, the administrators with whom you will have the most frequent interaction are likely to be your **department chair** or cluster coordinator and the **principal** and assistant principal of your school.[i] As described in the "In Your Classroom" feature, these individuals will be the most directly involved in your daily work and will be able to assist you with problems or concerns that you may encounter. They will also be responsible for supervising your teaching and (as described in Module 20, Professional Performance Assessment) for evaluating your performance.

**Department chair** within a school, an administrator charged with oversight of a content area department. The department chair is delegated some of the principal's authority. The department chair may or may not have teaching responsibilities in addition to having an administrative role.

**Principal** the highest-ranking administrator in a school building. May also be referred to as the head (master/mistress) or the school director. The principal supervises the work of all the teachers and is responsible for ensuring the quality of education within the school. The principal reports directly to the superintendent.

- *Principals.* At the top level of the school hierarchy are your building administrators. Large schools often have both a principal and one or more assistant principals or vice principals. In this situation, one individual (most often the principal) may be responsible for supervising and evaluating teachers, while another person (such as the assistant principal) deals with student issues, especially disciplinary problems. At smaller schools, the principal does it all.

[i]The building administrators may have different titles, such as director, headmistress/master or head, vice principal, assistant head, and so on. Their functions and responsibilities are likely to be very similar in spite of the variations in titles.

## In Your Classroom

### Working Within Your School Hierarchy

Respecting the hierarchy of the school is crucial to maintaining good working relationships with students, colleagues, administrators, parents, and community members. It is especially important in the following situations:

- *Problems with students.* If you have a conflict with a student that you are unable to resolve, talk to your department chair before going to the assistant principal or principal. These administrators may be able to resolve the issue, and if they cannot, they can advise you about how to take your concerns to the next level in the hierarchy. In elementary schools where you may not have a department chair or cluster coordinator, consider the informal hierarchy of schools and consult a veteran teacher before going to one of the building administrators.
- *Problems with adults.* Likewise, if you have a grievance with a parent, a colleague, or even your department chair, speak to the department chair before moving up the chain of command. Once again, in schools with flat hierarchies, rely on your veteran colleagues for guidance and support.

Ignore the hierarchy at your peril. Although skipping over levels may seem more expedient and efficient, it can also cause strained relationships that can make your work environment less productive, or even antagonistic.

Principals hold decision-making authority over various aspects of school policy and practices, and they supervise how state and district laws are put into action in the classroom. Principals are also expected to be the instructional leaders in their schools. In this era of high-stakes testing, this role can place considerable pressure on principals to ensure that their students achieve at expected levels of competence.

Your principal and assistant or vice principals, if you have them, will be important resources for you as you negotiate some of the challenges of the first years of teaching. They can provide you with instructional and practical assistance. Keep in mind, however, that they are also responsible for evaluating your performance in the classroom.

- *Department chairs.* If you are teaching at the high school level, you will probably be in an academic department and will have a department chair. Your department chair will be your first point of contact for any questions or concerns. He or she can tell you about policies and practices in the school, as well as offer valuable insights into dealing with problematic students. He or she is likely to be the one most closely responsible for your supervision and will carry out the classroom observations that may be required during your first year. (See Module 20, Professional Performance Assessment, to learn more about classroom observations.)

Middle schools and elementary schools do not typically have department chairs, because they are not organized into departments as high schools tend to be. Middle schools may be organized into clusters; a cluster is a group of four or five teachers, each from a different discipline, who teach the same group of students. Depending on the size of the middle school, there may be cluster coordinators or curriculum coordinators whose responsibilities include supervision and evaluation of the teachers in a cluster. These individuals may also perform functions similar to those of department chairs in a high school.

Elementary schools generally have flatter hierarchies and rarely have any kind of formal administrative position between the teachers and the building administrators. In these schools, there may be an informal hierarchy with which you will want to familiarize yourself. Find out who the veteran teachers are—those on whom the principal often calls. Consult them for information and advice. A few elementary schools have been experimenting with adding a more formal hierarchical layer of **lead teachers.** These teachers most often play an instructional role, rather than an administrative or supervisory one.

**Lead teachers** teachers who provide instructional leadership, rather than serving in an administrative or supervisory capacity.

All of these key individuals and entities at the state, local, and school-building levels are shown in Figure 19.1.

Because each school district can decide on its supervision structure, there is no one model applicable in all schools. We have presented common supervision structures that your school may or may not have. You will need to find out what the hierarchy is for your particular school.

**Figure 19.1**
**Organizational Structure of a Typical State School System**

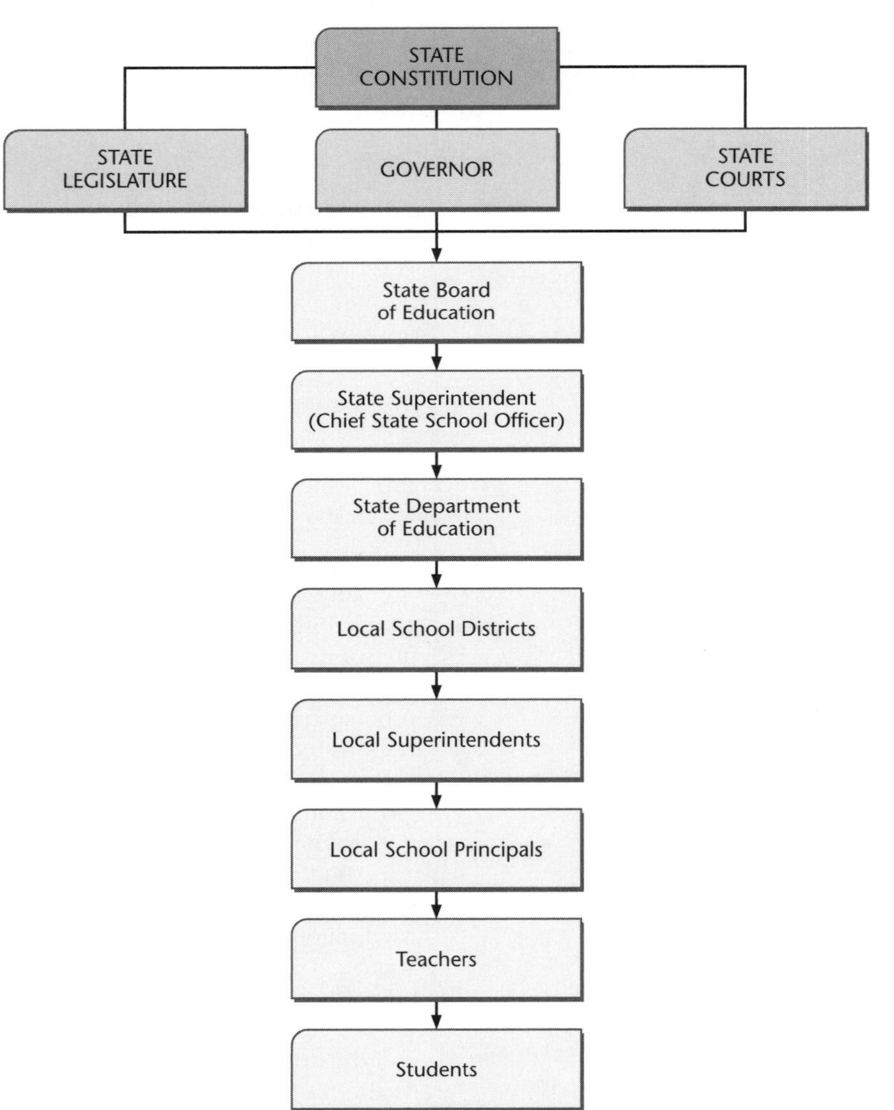

## Now You Do It

Refer to Tara's situation in the opening scenario and apply what you have just learned about school governance to answer the following questions.

**QUESTIONS**

1. In what way(s) did Tara forget to respect the school hierarchy? What did she neglect to do that led to her current situation?
2. How should Tara deal with this situation? To whom should she talk first?
3. What should she say to Dr. Roemer, her department chair? To the principal?
4. Should she speak with the superintendent? If so, what should she say? If not, why not?

# School Funding

In countries with a centralized administration for public schooling, funding for the schools comes from the nation's central government. The Ministry or Department of Education hires, assigns, and pays the salaries of school personnel. It also procures most material resources, such as texts and technology, for the public schools.

In the United States, as we noted earlier, the federal government plays a much smaller role. Public schooling is primarily the responsibility of the states. The federal government contributes a small portion of the total funding for public education. Although the No Child Left Behind Act substantially increased the federal obligation to education, funding from the federal government still accounts for no more than 8 percent of the budgets of public schools at the K–12 level. This means that more than 90 percent of the money for public schools comes from state and local sources.

**Figure 19.2 Contributions to School Funding**

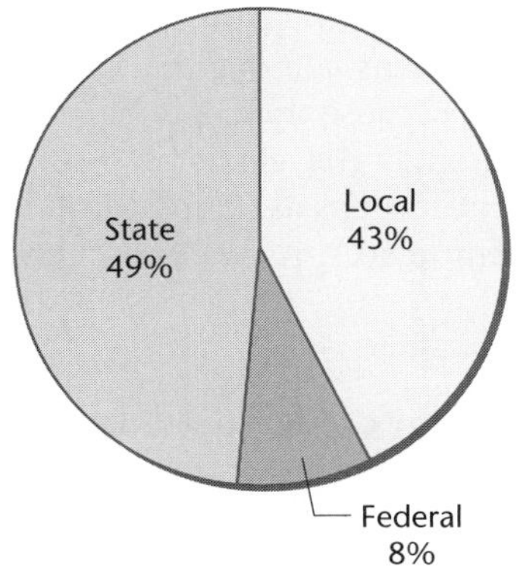


**Property tax** a tax imposed on property owners within a community. The tax is collected annually. In many states, individual communities set and collect property taxes and use the money collected to run the services within the community, among which are the schools. The tax rate can vary from one community to another.

## State and Local Sources of School Funding

State governments pay for about 49 percent of public schooling costs, and local monies pay for approximately 43 percent. From one state to another, however, the funding structure can vary significantly. In some states, the majority of money for public schooling comes from state funds. The state government of Hawaii, for example, provides almost 90 percent of funds for schools in that state. In other states, more of the revenue comes from local funds (see Figure 19.2). In about half the states, state and local contributions to public schooling are close to equal.[1]

The amounts of money spent on schools also vary widely from state to state. The national average expenditure per pupil is around $7,800, but this figure ranges from a high of $13,000 in the District of Columbia to a low of $5,000 in Arizona and Utah.[2]

*State* monies for education generally come from tax revenues collected, most commonly via a state income tax or state sales tax. In some states, revenues from state lotteries are reserved for school funding. *Local* contributions generally come from local **property taxes,** annual taxes that homeowners pay on the value of their homes and that corporations pay on their businesses. Cities and towns where property values are high collect more money from property taxes than those towns with lower property values. These

Inequities in school funding can lead to disparities in resources available to a school district.

towns are able to allocate more monies to their public schools. As described in the opening scenario, such well-funded districts often can provide better buildings and other facilities, pay higher salaries, and furnish newer resources for students and teachers.

Differences in local funding ability have led, in recent years, to numerous charges throughout the country that the educational opportunities afforded to students in poorer districts are not equal to those enjoyed by pupils in wealthier districts. In a number of states, lawsuits have been filed in both state and federal courts on behalf of students in poorer districts. Many courts have ruled in favor of the poorer school districts and ordered states to make changes in their funding structures. Some states try to address local funding imbalances by giving more state monies to towns that raise less in property taxes. A common funding formula is to determine the expenditure per pupil for each school district and then compensate towns whose expenditures per pupil are below a set standard. Other states have attempted to redistribute local property taxes from affluent to less affluent towns, a move that is often opposed by residents of the more affluent towns. Because the changes generally require legislative or popular approval through the electoral process, opponents are often successful in defeating the proposals. Thus, funding inequities among school districts persist in many places. As we'll see, these variations can affect your work as a teacher.

## Impact of School Funding on Teachers

Variations in local and state funding of schools affect the salaries that districts are able to pay their teachers, as well as the districts' decisions about resource allocation and the level of influence teachers can exert on those decisions.

- *Teacher salaries.* The local financing of public schooling leads to a wide range of teacher salaries. From state to state, the annual salaries of teachers with similar years of experience may vary by as much as $20,000. Nationally, the average teacher salary is approximately $48,000.[3] The highest average salaries tend to be found in states with the highest cost of living, such as California, Connecticut, and the District of Columbia. Conversely, states where the cost of living is low, including South and North Dakota and Oklahoma, have some of the lowest average salaries. Within a state, teacher salaries also vary, although these differences may

Online Study Center

not be as marked as the differences from one state to another. You can link to the latest available salary reports from your Online Study Center.

- *Resource allocation.* Differences in funding structure also lead to differences in resources, in terms of both spending priorities and monies available. Some school districts spend more of their resources to update textbooks and print materials, whereas others opt to upgrade their technology resources. Some districts allocate funds to paraprofessional staffing to lower the teacher–student ratio, whereas others place greater emphasis on expanding curricular offerings. Many districts also must allocate a substantial percentage of their money to meeting the educational needs of all their students. (See Module 4, Teaching Students with Disabilities.)
- *Teacher input.* In some districts, teachers are able to request that certain materials, such as library resources, software applications, or supplemental books, be purchased. In other districts, teachers are allotted a yearly sum that they can use to order classroom supplies or supplemental materials. In still other districts, teachers have no input into the selection of the materials that are purchased for use in their classrooms. Be sure to learn the policies in your district.

## Now You Do It

In the opening scenario, Tara decided to leave a well-funded school district, in which resources were abundant, for one where resources were older and more limited. Consider these questions as you think about the kind of school district you want to teach in.

**QUESTIONS**

1. How essential are a variety of resources to your intended or actual approach to teaching?
2. How easy would it be to find alternatives to the resources that you would need to teach in the way you envision?
3. What kind of school district would you prefer to teach in?

In teaching, as in any other career, understanding the structure and hierarchy of your workplace—in this case, your school district—is essential to helping you work successfully in that environment. It is especially important that you know who is responsible for supervising and evaluating teachers in your school. You must also be aware of and respect the decision-making hierarchy if you are confronted with any problem or grievance.

School financing tends to be an emotional issue at both the local and state levels. On the one hand, complaints of inadequate funding of schools are frequently heard, especially from those most intimately involved in schools. On the other hand, many critics insist that too much money is being "wasted" in public schools and that teachers are overpaid while students remain undereducated. The reality probably lies somewhere between these two extremes, but it is important for you, as a new teacher, to understand the parameters of the debate and its impact on your work. The level of funding can affect not just how much money you earn but also the resources, from textbooks to paper, that you have available to do your job well.

## Further Resources

- Michael Berkman and Eric Plutzer, *Ten Thousand Democracies: Politics and Public Opinion in America's School Districts* (Washington, DC: Georgetown University Press, 2005). Berkman and Plutzer offer a comprehensive look at local school governance based on empirical data collected in thousands of school districts.
- Susan Moore Johnson, *Leading to Change: The Challenge of the New Superintendency* (San Francisco, CA: Jossey-Bass Education Series, 1996). In this book, Johnson presents a thoughtful analysis of the leadership styles of twelve superintendents.
- Jonathan Kozol, *Savage Inequalities: Children in America's Schools* (New York: HarperPerennial, 1992). Kozol presents his findings about funding inequities and their effect on the quality of the education that students in underfunded schools receive.
- Jonathan Kozol, *The Shame of a Nation: The Restoration of Apartheid Schooling in America* (Phoenix, AZ: Crown Press, 2005). Kozol again looks at the condition of education in some urban districts. Funding inequities, Kozol argues, have led to greater and greater disparity in the quality of education that students in America receive.
- Deborah Meier and George Wood (Eds.), *Many Children Left Behind: How the No Child Left Behind Act Is Damaging Our Children and Our Schools* (Boston, MA: Beacon Press, 2004). Meier and her colleagues weigh in on the impact of the No Child Left Behind Act on America's schools.

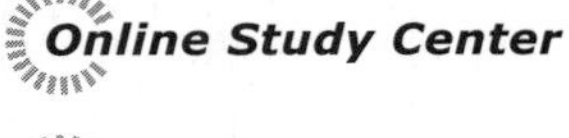


- National Center of Educational Statistics. Available at: **http://www.nces.ed.gov.** This website offers statistics on the condition of education in the United States.

Online Study Center

- National Education Association. Available at: **http://www.nea.org.** The NEA website contains annual reports on the state of education in the United States with statistics on the condition of education in each of the fifty states.
- Joel Spring, *Conflict of Interests: The Politics of American Education* (New York: McGraw-Hill, 2004). Spring looks at the various stakeholders who influence and shape educational policy in American schools.

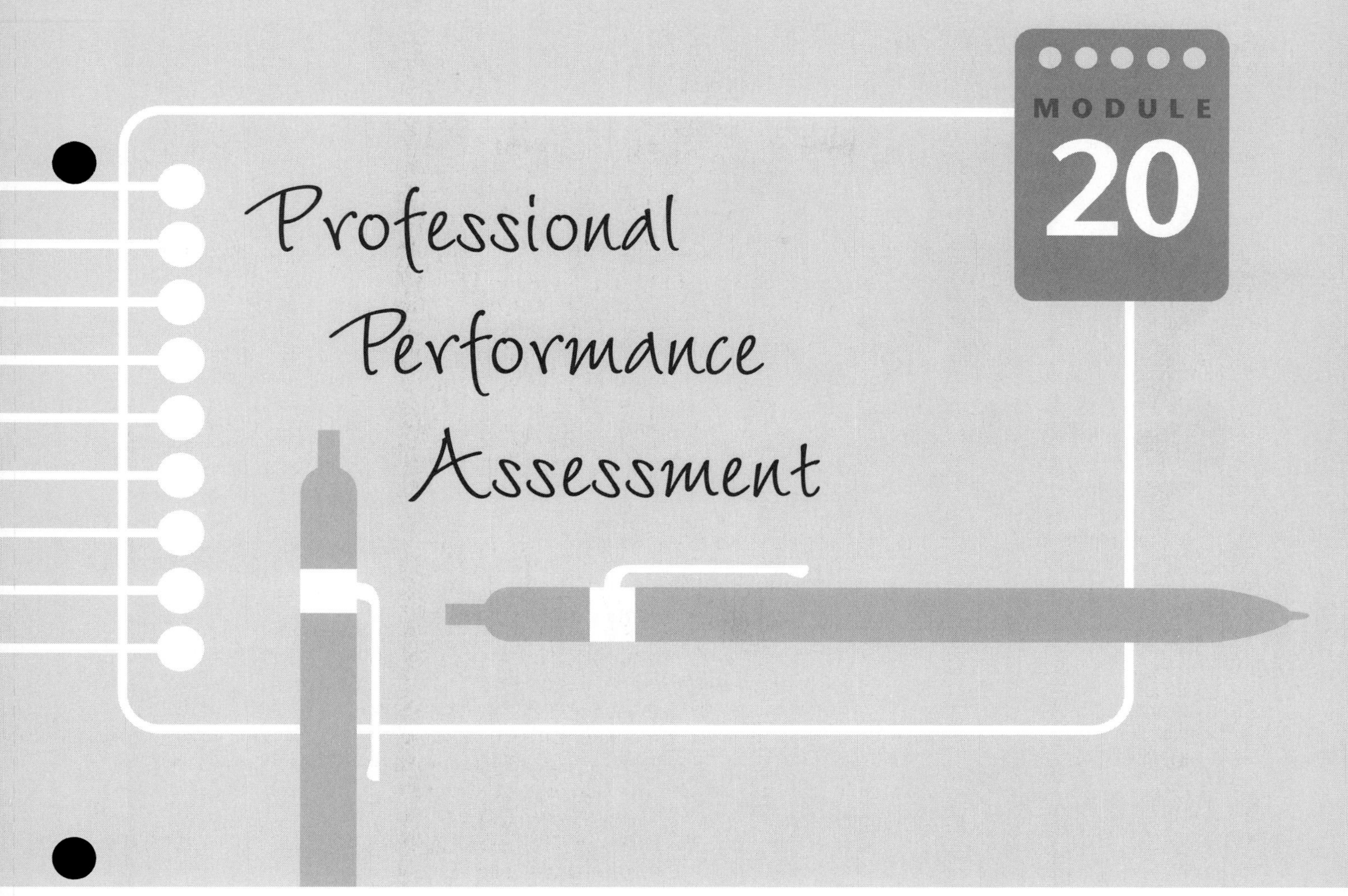


# Module 20: Professional Performance Assessment

Scenario

Margaret Spellman, the principal of Middletown High School, settled in to read through this year's teacher evaluations written by the department chairs. The first one on the pile was for Joe Campione, a veteran English teacher and a legend in the school system. With his fiery, somewhat impulsive personality, Joe was known for his passion in teaching, in conversation, in life.

Joe had been at the school for nearly twenty years. He was an awe-inspiring, yet intimidating, teacher for most students. His passion for literature and learning inspired many students to become English majors in college. His strong beliefs about teaching, learning, and life had also led to numerous confrontations with colleagues, parents, and administrators, not to mention students. But his students learned, and the number of students earning advanced-placement credit in English was quite high, a result that was frequently attributed to Joe's demanding expectations. It was rumored that no student ever went to Joe Campione's class unprepared.

Margaret was caught off-guard as she started to read Joe's evaluation, which was written by the new department chair, Tom James. Since his hiring two years ago, Tom had shown himself to be a conscientious worker, a dedicated teacher, and an effective administrator. The evaluations he had done last year were thorough and suggested a keen observer's eye. His evaluation of Joe's teaching, much to her surprise, was very critical of Joe's teaching style and even called into question Joe's understanding of English and literature pedagogy. Joe's forceful, interactive style, the hallmark of his teaching, was summarily dismissed as being abusive and threatening to the students, thereby creating a "negative learning environment." Tom also faulted Joe for "failing to take attendance in accordance with district policies" and "neglecting the state-mandated curriculum" in his selection of reading assignments for his American literature class.

In terms of teaching, Tom noted that Joe "cut off students in mid-sentence," "dominated the discussion," and "imposed certain views on students, while discounting or ignoring students' views or opinions." Joe's classroom management was, according to the evaluation, "in need of attention." According to Tom's report, students came in late and got up at any time and walked out of the class. Even worse, Tom reported that "many of the students were engaged in activities other than the discussion and were consequently not participating in or benefiting from the instruction."

Margaret sat, wondering. She had observed Joe teach a number of times, and Tom's observations were all consistent with what Margaret had seen. But Margaret had always considered Joe an edgy, yet inspiring, teacher who was able to extract the best from his students. Tom's evaluation, however, rated him a mediocre—even ineffective—teacher. Which was he?

**Performance assessment** an evaluation that is based on actual measurement of what is done and its outcomes.

Like nearly all professionals, teachers undergo a periodic **performance assessment** to evaluate the quality of their work. High-quality teaching is important. Teachers are entrusted with the intellectual, social, and (in some cases) physical development of young people, and the effect they have on students can be far-reaching. Research on value-added benefits of schooling has found that the most important factor affecting student learning is the teacher.[1] In fact, the effect of having either a good or a bad teacher two years in a row is significant in terms of student learning.

As described in the opening scenario, however, evaluating the performance of teachers is not as cut and dried as evaluating the performance of some other workers. One factor complicating the evaluation of teachers' performance is the absence of any quantitative standard for quality teaching. Teachers do not have sales goals to achieve, clients to woo, cases to win, or operations to perform. Instead, as the scenario above suggests, there are many definitions of "effective teaching." Another complication is that teachers are rarely the only ones responsible for the achievements of their students. In any given year, their students may be taught by many other adults within the school, not to mention the effect of their past teachers and those outside of the school. All of these teachers, as well as the students themselves, contribute to varying degrees to the academic performance of students.

We will see, however, that schools and school districts have developed ways to assess teachers that deal, in varying degrees, with these complications.

**This module emphasizes that:**

- **There are currently several efforts under way to define effective teaching.**
- **Teachers have long gone through a particular process of evaluation and assessment that has recently been enhanced by the requirements of No Child Left Behind (NCLB).**
- **Teacher assessment may draw on several different processes and information sources.**
- **There are ways to prepare for and respond to an evaluation.**
- **The habit of reflection-on-action, or becoming a reflective practitioner, is the key to improved professional performance.**

## Now You Do It

Reflect on the following questions:

**QUESTIONS**

1. Think about exemplary teachers you have had. What qualities do these teachers have? What criteria would you list for an exemplary or effective teacher?
2. Judging on the basis of the limited information in the scenario above, would you agree or disagree with Tom James's evaluation of Joe Campione? Can Joe be an effective teacher if he intimidates students? Can he be effective if he does not implement school policies?
3. In your opinion, do the knowledge and skill necessary to become a competent teacher differ from what is required to be an outstanding teacher? If so, *how* do the two differ?

# Defining Effective Teaching

Some teachers are quiet and others are boisterous; some are strict disciplinarians, while some are lax about enforcing rules. Some are patient and nurturing, while others are fiery and demanding. Yet all of these teachers can be exemplary teachers, and they can all be ineffective teachers. How can we tell which is which? What are reasonable criteria and standards to use when determining the quality of a teacher's work?

The first step in teacher evaluation is to choose a set of indicators of quality, the criteria by which teachers should be judged. One set of criteria comes from the federal government. According to the No Child Left Behind Act, schools are required to have "highly qualified" teachers in all classrooms. These are teachers who have met state licensure requirements, which often include a subject-matter test in the subject they seek to teach. Individual states, however, decide on licensure requirements and on the acceptable level of subject-matter knowledge for their teachers, so there is variability from state to state. As we'll see next, educational researchers and professional organizations have also attempted to define effective teaching.

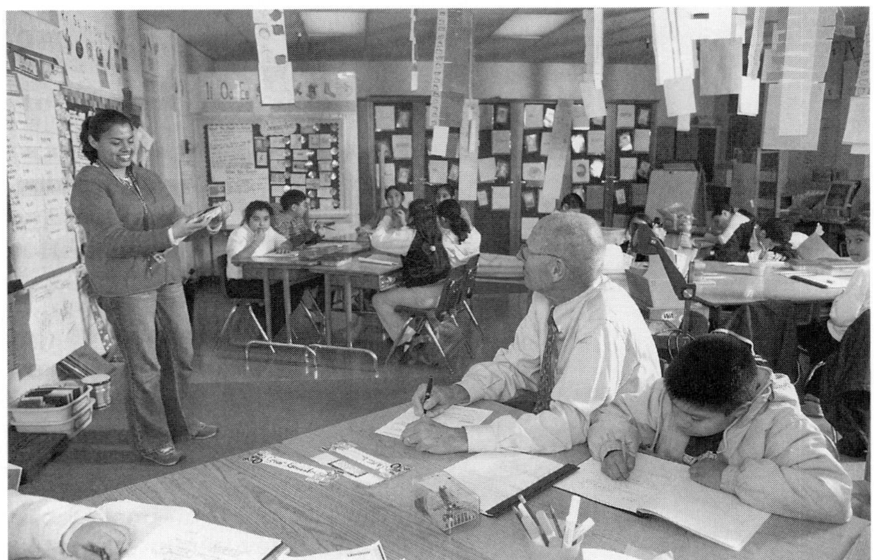

While initially stressful, being observed by colleagues and supervisors can be a major source of improvement.

## Research on Effective Teaching

Educational research has yielded lengthy lists of criteria for both the knowledge teachers should possess and the things teachers should be able to do. One researcher and theorist, Charlotte Danielson, has attempted not only to define, but also to categorize, what an accomplished teacher does.[2] Danielson's "framework for teaching" lays out the various areas of competence in which professional teachers need to develop expertise. Danielson organizes the complex activity of teaching into twenty-two components, which are then clustered into four domains of teaching responsibility.

1. *Domain 1: Planning and Preparation.* How does a teacher design instruction and organize the content of what students are expected to learn? To be effective in this domain, teachers need to demonstrate that they know their content, pedagogy for teaching that content, their students, how to select instructional goals, what resources they have available to them, how to design coherent instruction, and how to assess student learning.
2. *Domain 2: The Classroom Environment.* Domain 2 consists of the interactions occurring in a classroom that are not specifically instructional. Effective teachers create an environment of respect and rapport among the students, establish a culture for learning, manage classroom procedures and student behavior, and efficiently organize the physical space.
3. *Domain 3: Instruction.* This domain constitutes the core of teaching—the engagement of students in learning content. To be effective here, a teacher needs to communicate clearly and accurately, use appropriate questioning and discussion techniques, engage students in learning, provide feedback to students, and demonstrate flexibility and responsiveness.
4. *Domain 4: Professional Responsibilities.* This domain addresses the wide range of teacher responsibilities outside the classroom. They include reflecting on teaching, maintaining accurate records, communicating with families, contributing to the school and district, growing and developing professionally, and showing professionalism. Teachers who demonstrate these competencies are seen as true professionals and are highly valued by their colleagues and administrators.

This framework for professional practice provides several benefits. First, it offers the teaching profession a shared vocabulary for talking about excellent teaching. This is particularly helpful for performance evaluators. Second, it assists novice teachers by providing a roadmap to excellence in professional practice. Third, the framework establishes a structure for discussions among teachers and sharpens the focus for professional development. Finally, it communicates to the larger community the array of competencies needed to be an effective teacher.

Researchers and evaluators do not, however, always agree on the specifics of each item in these lists. Consider, for example, the criterion that teachers demonstrate that they know the appropriate methods for teaching their subject-matter content. Some history teachers believe the most appropriate teaching method is one in which the teacher lectures for most of the class. Other history teachers are convinced that the appropriate methodology is discussion-based. Still others would insist that the most appropriate approach to teaching history is to have students "become" historians, engaging in their own research and study of primary documents. Similar ranges of understanding hold for nearly all, if not all, of the criteria listed in Danielson's framework.

Once criteria are defined, evaluators must establish a standard for each of the criteria selected. All who are involved in the educational process would agree that teachers must have knowledge of their content area to teach effectively, for example. But how much content knowledge must the teacher have? Does a middle school math teacher need to have mastery of differentiation and integration? Should a high-school biology teacher be expected to explain the intricacies of kinetic molecular theory? How fluent in Spanish or French does a foreign-language teacher who is teaching introductory-level courses need to be? These questions provoke even greater debate when content knowledge standards must be set for elementary school teachers, who rarely delve into concepts beyond a basic level.

Schools, districts, and states must all come to their own conclusions. Although sometimes it may seem that decisions about criteria and standards are arbitrary and confusing, they are usually the result of extensive negotiations and compromises among educators of differing theoretical and philosophical camps. In some instances, these criteria and standards are dynamic, as educators who are involved in the process seek to adjust and refine them.

## National Efforts to Define Effective Teaching

Even though teacher performance reviews remain a local responsibility, attempts have been made in the recent past to consolidate and standardize the criteria and standards that define a highly effective or highly competent teacher. Two groups in particular have made significant contributions to developing a uniform language to describe the qualities and skills that highly qualified teachers possess. These are the Interstate New Teacher Assessment and Support Consortium (INTASC) and the National Board for Professional Teaching Standards (NBPTS).

**Interstate New Teacher Assessment and Support Consortium (INTASC)** an organization that aims to provide a nationally uniform set of criteria for new teachers, to be used by both teacher preparation programs and state licensing authorities.

***INTASC*** The **Interstate New Teacher Assessment and Support Consortium (INTASC),** created in 1987, focuses on the skills and competencies that a well-prepared new teacher should possess. The aim of the organization is to provide a nationally uniform set of criteria for new teachers—guidelines to be used by both teacher preparation programs and state licensing authorities. INTASC has developed a set of core standards for what all beginning teachers should know and be able to do, as well as standards that are specific to particular subject-matter areas. The INTASC core standards are listed in

## TABLE 20.1 INTASC Core Standards

1. **Content Pedagogy** The teacher understands the central concepts, tools of inquiry, and structures of the discipline he or she teaches and can create learning experiences that make these aspects of subject matter meaningful for students.
2. **Student Development** The teacher understands how children learn and develop, and can provide learning opportunities that support a child's intellectual, social, and personal development.
3. **Diverse Learners** The teacher understands how students differ in their approaches to learning and creates instructional opportunities that are adapted to diverse learners.
4. **Multiple Instructional Strategies** The teacher understands and uses a variety of instructional strategies to encourage student development of critical thinking, problem solving, and performance skills.
5. **Motivation and Management** The teacher uses an understanding of individual and group motivation and behavior to create a learning environment that encourages positive social interaction, active engagement in learning, and self-motivation.
6. **Communication and Technology** The teacher uses knowledge of effective verbal, nonverbal, and media communication techniques to foster active inquiry, collaboration, and supportive interaction in the classroom.
7. **Planning** The teacher plans instruction based upon knowledge of subject matter, students, the community, and curriculum goals.
8. **Assessment** The teacher understands and uses formal and informal assessment strategies to evaluate and ensure the continuous intellectual, social, and physical development of the learner.
9. **Reflective Practice: Professional Growth** The teacher is a reflective practitioner who continually evaluates the effects of his or her choices and actions on others (students, parents, and other professionals in the learning community) and who actively seeks out opportunities to grow professionally.
10. **School and Community Involvement** The teacher fosters relationships with school colleagues, parents, and agencies in the larger community to support students' learning and well-being.

Source: The Interstate New Teacher Assessment and Support Consortium (INTASC) standards were developed by the Council of Chief State School Officers and member states. Copies may be downloaded from the Council's website at **http://www.ccsso.org.** Council of Chief State School Officers. (1992). Model standards for beginning teacher licensing, assessment, and development: A resource for state dialogue. Washington, DC: Author. **http://www.ccsso.org/content/pdfs/corestrd.pdf.**

### Video Case

What does it mean to be an effective teacher? In the video case, *Teaching as a Profession: What Defines Effective Teaching?*, you'll see vivid examples of the various dimensions of teaching excellence—from developing command of one's subject matter, to drawing on one's own emotional intelligence, to setting up an effective learning environment. As you watch the clips and study the artifacts in the case, reflect on the following questions.

**QUESTIONS**

- How do the characteristics of effective teachers mentioned in this video fit into Charlotte Danielson's framework for teaching?
- Evaluate yourself on the criteria listed in Table 20.1. What are your strongest and weakest areas? How will you emphasize your strengths as a teacher, and how will you strengthen your weaker areas?

***Online Study Center***

Table 20.1. For each principle, key indicators for knowledge, disposition, and performances are given. For a complete listing of the standards, go the INTASC website at **http://www.ccsso.org/projects/Interstate_New_Teacher_Assessment_and_Support_Consortium/.**

From its standards, INTASC has worked to develop a performance assessment that can be used to measure the competencies and skills of beginning teachers, which is currently being field-tested in a limited number of disciplines with plans to expand to other licensing areas. The primary tool for the assessment is a portfolio of materials that the candidate uses in teaching. Candidates include in their portfolios examples of student work, videotapes of the candidate teaching in his or her classroom, assessment tools that the candidate uses, and written reflections of the candidate's thinking about teaching and learning.[i]

[i]INTASC website.

**National Board for Professional Teaching Standards (NBPTS)** a professional agency that is setting voluntary standards for what experienced teachers should know and be able to do in the major disciplines.

***NBPTS*** Unlike INTASC, which looks principally at beginning teachers, the **National Board for Professional Teaching Standards** has focused on developing standards for national certification of more experienced teachers. (See Module 25, Professionalism in Teaching.) In fact, a candidate for national certification must have taught for a minimum of three years.

The NBPTS awards national certification to experienced teachers in twenty-seven different subject-matter/grade-level areas, and it plans to add more. It has a set of standards and competencies for each area. For more information on the standards for a specific discipline and level, consult the NBPTS website at **www.nbpts.org.**

Like INTASC, the NBPTS relies on a portfolio as the principal tool for assessing a candidate's teaching effectiveness. The content of the portfolio is similar to that used in the INTASC program: examples of student work, learning activities, assessments used; videotaped lessons; and a written reflection or self-evaluation. Both groups use trained veteran teachers to rate the content of the portfolios.

## The Evaluation Process

Teacher evaluation is often part of the teacher contract and is therefore negotiated with the school board or its representative (generally, the superintendent). As a result, just as there is no definitive set of criteria or standards, there is no standardized procedure for assessing teachers' performance. The process sometimes even varies among different groups of teachers within a single school district! We will describe a fairly typical process to give you an idea of what to expect, and you can link to more examples of evaluation processes from your Online Study Center. But because of this variability, it is essential that you become well versed in the process used in *your school system*. Be sure that you fully understand the process before the time comes for your first performance review.

Teacher performance assessment can be divided into three phases:

1. *Before the evaluation.* This is your chance to prepare yourself and your evaluator.
2. *The evaluation itself.* All evaluation processes includes some method of gathering information about the teacher's performance. Most commonly, an evaluator observes a teacher in his or her classroom for a short period. We'll describe classroom observations in detail and review a variety of other information sources that are often used with or as alternatives to observations.
3. *After the evaluation.* This is when you learn how the evaluator has rated you and have your opportunity to respond to the assessment.

Like your own assessments of students (see Module 15, Assessment for Learning, and Module 16, Tools for Assessment), assessment of your performance as a teacher can be formative or summative.

**Formative evaluation** an evaluation conducted to identify particular points of difficulty and suggest areas in need of further work or development.

- A **formative evaluation** is designed to help the individual being evaluated develop as a professional. Its purpose is supervisory: to help the individual grow and improve. Although judgments about the quality of the teacher's performance are made, these judgments are used as a basis for providing constructive feedback to improve performance or, in some cases, remediate weaknesses.

**Summative evaluation** a process used to make a judgment about the outcomes or quality of an individual's work.

- A **summative evaluation,** on the other hand, is not necessarily a learning tool. Its purpose is evaluative: to make a value judgment about the quality of an individual's teaching. The performance of the individual is measured against a set of criteria and standards that indicate exemplary work.

Our discussion of teacher evaluation assumes that the evaluation is *summative* rather than *formative*. In fact, though, it is not always clear whether the evaluation a teacher is undergoing is formative or summative—whether it is to help you improve or to make a judgment about your competence.

Note also that in most school districts, newer teachers are evaluated more often and more regularly than veteran teachers. A typical schedule might have a new teacher being observed up to four times in the course of one year, with one formal evaluation yearly. More veteran teachers might be on a two-year evaluation cycle, as was Joe Campione in the opening scenario, or even on a three-year cycle, with formal evaluations occurring every two or three years. In the "off" years, the teacher may be expected to write a self-evaluation based on improvement goals set by the teacher himself or herself.

## Before the Evaluation: How to Prepare

**Classroom observation** an information-gathering process during which the evaluator observes the teacher teaching in his or her classroom.

As we have pointed out, there is no one evaluation process, but a nearly universal component of the process is the **classroom observation,** in which the evaluator observes you teaching in your classroom. It is commonly assumed that the lesson observed is indicative of the teacher's better efforts. Choose the lesson you will teach during the observation carefully. It should be representative of the teaching style that works best for you in bringing about optimal student learning. This is not the time to experiment with new teaching approaches or techniques. Stay with what you know and feel comfortable with and, most important, what you know works for you with this particular group of students.

A good way to prepare for the classroom observation is to prepare your evaluator. In some school districts, teachers are required to submit a lesson plan for the class being observed. It's a good idea to do so, even if it is not required in your district. We recommend that you also provide the evaluator with the additional written materials described in the "In Your Classroom" feature. Providing this information to the evaluator well before the observation can serve a number of useful purposes:

- *Preparing yourself.* At the most basic level, preparing documentation helps you get prepared for the observation. The summary of the previous, current, and subsequent lessons, for example, can help you review the sequencing of concepts and skills, ensuring that there is a logical progression through a study of topics.

- *Explaining your situation.* Preparing summary documents also gives you an opportunity to present any extenuating circumstances or conditions that may affect the lesson, or to explain any digression from the approved or expected curriculum for the grade level. For example, you may want to point out that LeDawn and Shantelle, lifelong friends, are in the middle of a falling out that is affecting the classroom environment. Or that Clark may be experiencing a difficult home situation that

## Preparing Your Evaluator Before a Classroom Observation

Provide written documentation that can help the evaluator follow the lesson easily. Communicate the focus of the lesson, your goals for the lesson, and what students will be expected to do. Preparing the evaluator in this way enables him or her to follow the lesson in a productive way. Here's what to include:

- A short summary of the lesson to be observed, describing how it fits in the unit. Give a short recap of what concepts and skills were taught in the previous lesson, and give an overview of what concepts and skills the subsequent lesson will target.
- Copies of any documents that you will use during the lesson. If your lesson involves a group discussion of a reading, for example, make a photocopy of the reading and any discussion questions that students were asked to consider.
- If the lesson will grow out of a homework assignment, be sure to give the evaluator a copy of the assignment.
- You may also want to include a class list or a seating chart if students have assigned seats.

is affecting his work in class, so you are allowing him to be less participatory than usual for the time being.[ii]

- *Getting organized.* Pulling together the requisite materials for the class helps you get organized before the observation, ensures that all the necessary materials are readily available, and conveys to the evaluator the sense that you are organized and prepared.

## Sources of Information

Judgments about the quality of a teacher's work are based on a variety of information sources. Some (such as classroom observations) provide direct, if limited, evidence of the quality of work. Others (such as student ratings, a teacher's portfolio, student achievement, or even self-evaluation) provide additional information that needs to be carefully pieced together to ensure a reliable and accurate judgment. Let us look at some of these sources of information. We will focus first on classroom observations because they are still the primary source of information that evaluators consider.

***Classroom Observations*** A classroom observation is the bread and butter of teacher evaluations. Throughout your teaching career, expect to be observed numerous times. You may already be used to being observed from your student teaching or internship days or from other work experiences. That experience can help you be more comfortable in on-the-job teaching evaluations.

In nearly all instances, these observations are planned; the evaluator will give you sufficient notice of the day and period of the planned observation. In fact, teacher contracts in some school districts require that the evaluator give adequate notice of a classroom observation. The evaluator may schedule a pre-observation conference to find out about your goals for the lesson, but such a conference is more likely to take place when there is to be a supervisory, or formative, rather than a summative evaluation. There may also be a post-observation conference, but once again, that would be more common in a formative evaluation.

[ii]If such a situation does arise, be sure to inform the school guidance staff as well.

The observation generally lasts for a single class period at the secondary level and for the duration of a content-specific lesson at the elementary level. Generally, evaluators try to be unobtrusive, allowing the class to flow as close to normally as possible. Some evaluators take copious notes as they observe, scripting the lesson fully. Others may make use of a standardized form, commenting on the different criteria as they observe them.

***Other Sources of Information*** Just as some teachers rely solely on test scores to determine students' grades, some school systems rely solely on classroom observations to determine the quality of a teacher's performance. Other districts consider several sources of information. Any combination of the sources listed below may be used. Again, we urge you to become familiar with the policies of *your school district.*

The following sources of information are among the most commonly used today.

- *Self-evaluation.* As we noted, self-evaluations are common for experienced teachers. They may also be part of the process for evaluating new teachers. You may be asked to evaluate your progress toward meeting short- or long-term goals set for you in a previous evaluation, or you may be expected to evaluate your performance on the basis of the district criteria.

  In either case, it is important to be balanced in your self-evaluation. You want to highlight your strengths and accomplishments with pride and, at the same time, judiciously identify areas in which you want or need to grow. Be sure to provide ample examples of specific activities to illustrate both accomplishments and areas of growth. Be careful to be neither overly critical of your performance nor overly self-satisfied.

- *Teacher interview.* Your evaluator may believe that an interview is a better way of gathering information about you than your writing a self-evaluation. Or your evaluator may decide that a more comprehensive way of gathering information is to interview you *about* your self-evaluation or about the classroom observation he or she did.

  The disadvantage of an interview is that you may not accurately anticipate the questions that will be asked and may be caught off-guard by one or more of them. Your responses may not be as thoughtful or as focused as you would have liked them to be, or as smooth as they could have been if you had had more time to reflect on the questions and prepare responses.

  If an interview is part of the evaluation process in your school district, we recommend that you ask your more experienced colleagues what kinds of questions to expect. You could even ask one of them to role-play the evaluator in a mock interview.

- *Teacher portfolio.* You may be asked to put together a portfolio of work that evaluators can review. In some districts, you will be given a list of components or items to include in your portfolio. (Some districts may even require or expect you to include a videotaped lesson.) If the contents of the portfolio are not specified, you will want to include items that show the quality of your teaching based on the criteria that your school district has established for teacher evaluation. These may include lesson plans you have written, student work flowing from learning activities you have implemented, tests and quizzes or any other assessments you have designed, or modifications you have made for students with special needs.

For each item that you consider for inclusion in your portfolio, ask yourself, "What does this item say about the quality of my teaching? How does this item show that I have reached a high level for the criteria used?" If the item does not show you have reached a high level, or that you have grown or improved in some way, you may not want to include it. If your district also requires a self-evaluation, this culling-of-materials exercise may be a useful first step in writing it. For more on developing portfolios, see the Online Study Center.

- *Written artifacts.* In the absence of a teaching portfolio, you may want to submit to your evaluator samples of lessons plans, student activities, and assessments that are representative of the quality of your work.

The following sources of information are being increasingly used by school districts, especially to evaluate new teachers.

**Peer review** a system of evaluation in which the perceptions and judgments of fellow teachers contribute to salary decisions.

- *Peer review.* To date, it is rare for a **peer review** be a part of the summative evaluation process at the K–12 levels. Peer reviews tend to be more common in supervisory, formative evaluations. In teacher mentor or peer-coaching programs, for example, a teacher will observe a colleague and then provide feedback on a particular skill area or range of skills.

  If peer review is part of your district's summative evaluation, it is a good idea to ask a veteran colleague in the school district to be a mock evaluator and to observe you teach once or twice before your formal evaluative observation. This "practice evaluation" may make you less nervous about there being observers in the classroom. In addition, your colleague can provide insights into the evaluative process in the school district, can warn of potential pitfalls to avoid, and can stress important skill areas. Your mentor teacher can be an especially useful source of feedback and advice.

- *Student achievement.* Using the learning outcomes of their students as a way to measure a teacher's quality is still in the proposal stage in most states. However, in view of the greater accountability being placed on students for the achievement of certain outcomes, and with more responsibility being placed on schools to ensure that students achieve these outcomes, many people suggest making teachers more—and more directly—accountable for the academic achievements of their students. Such a plan would define teacher quality on the basis of the number of students who achieve passing scores on state-mandated assessments. In extreme situations, a teacher's license would not be renewed if the percentage of students in his or her class who received a passing score on the state assessment were consistently low.

  Whether student achievement can, or should be, a valid indicator of the quality of a teacher's performance is a debate we will leave for others. We do want to point out, however, that the issue is being raised more and more frequently and that, in the not-too-distant future, student outcomes may become a criterion for teacher evaluation.

- *Student ratings.* To date, ratings of teachers by their students have been used mainly as a way to evaluate college instructors. The maturity level of most K–12 students, even at the high school level, calls into doubt their ability to evaluate the performance of their teachers objectively.

**Competency testing** an assessment strategy aimed at gauging the acquisition of particular skills or knowledge.

- *Competency testing.* **Competency testing** is more commonly used at the initial licensure phase to ensure that teachers entering the profession have the knowledge base to be effective educators. However, in light of recent trends toward greater accountability of teachers, and the requirement of the NCLB for highly qualified teachers in every classroom, it is not inconceivable that competency testing will become a requirement for re-licensure as well.

## After the Evaluation

As we mentioned earlier, you may have a conference with your evaluator in which you discuss elements of your classroom observation or other data gathered by the evaluator, as well as other issues related to your yearly performance review. In some cases, you may simply be given the written review and will have the option of meeting to discuss its contents.

In either case, you will review the ratings given to you by the evaluator at this time. You will probably be rated on a scale of 1 to 5 or 1 to 10 on each of the criteria for teacher effectiveness, and you will also receive an overall rating. Teachers whose overall rating on their first evaluation indicates that they are less than competent are generally required to develop an improvement plan, with the help of their supervisors. Such plans typically include specific short- and long-term goals designed to help the teacher reach the competent level. If a second evaluation finds a teacher still less than competent, with unachieved goals in the teacher's professional growth plan, the teacher in question may be in jeopardy of being dismissed, especially if the teacher has not yet been granted tenure. (See Module 23, Hiring, Firing, and the Educational Law, for more information on tenure and dismissal.) In such a situation, the individual in question may want to consider alternatives to teaching.

In some districts all teachers, as part of their continuous professional growth and development, and regardless of their level of experience teaching, are expected to set short- and/or long-term goals. If you are asked to set goals, whether for improvement or for professional growth (or if such goals are set for you), be aware that the goals may be considered binding, which means that progress toward meeting them will be an integral part of your next performance review. As is always the case, be careful what you agree to, and be especially careful what you sign.

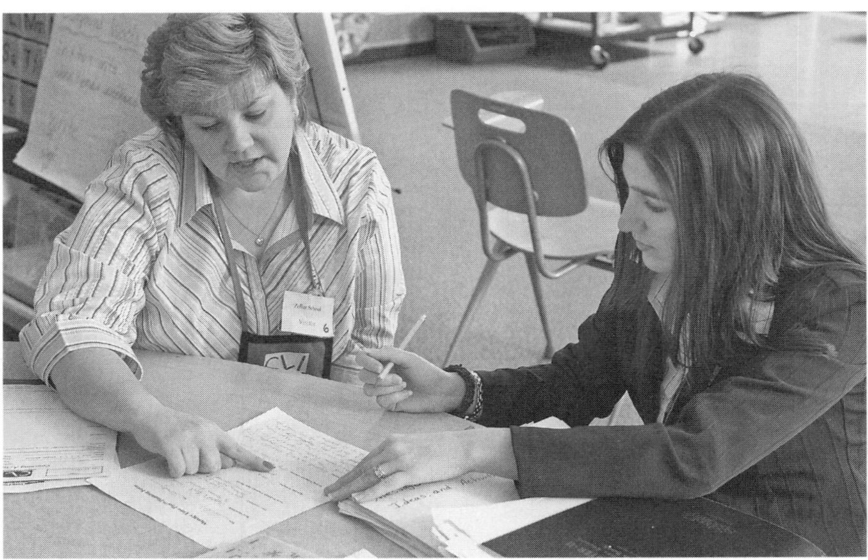

If you have a chance to discuss your evaluation with the evaluator, be certain to use the opportunity to ask any questions and make sure you fully understand the evaluation and its implications for your teaching future.

## Can You Disagree with Your Evaluator?

Whatever the criteria and standards your district uses to asses teachers, they are always open to the interpretation of the evaluator. What may look like skilled classroom management to one evaluator may seem to another like an overly strict learning environment. A "meaningful learning activity" for one evaluator may strike another as a waste of time. A viable and valid assessment activity for some may seem to others like a useless game. What can you do if you believe your evaluator gave you low ratings simply because he or she has a different philosophy of teaching from yours? It depends on the policies of your school district.

In nearly every district, you will be asked to sign a copy of your evaluation, and the copy will be kept in your personnel file. The form will have a statement similar to the following: *I have read this evaluation and agree/disagree with its content. My comments are/are not attached/included.* If you are unhappy with the evaluation and are convinced that it is unfair or incorrect, what should you do when the evaluator asks you to sign it?

1. *Stall for time.* Let the evaluator know you are surprised by the report, and ask for time to study and think about it.
2. *As calmly and rationally as you can, review what has been said and "evaluate the evaluation."* At this stage, you may want to share the evaluation with a wise and experienced colleague.
3. *Respond taking the "long view."* Don't give in to the emotions of the moment. Realize that your evaluator probably had as hard a time writing the evaluation as you have had reading it.
4. *If you disagree, do it respectfully.* Focus on the content of the evaluation, and make no statements about the evaluator. Try to be clear and concise.
5. *If you are convinced that you have been misjudged or misevaluated, respectfully take your case to a supervisor or to the representative of the teachers' union.* In all cases, we strongly urge you to avoid a reaction like Joe's in the continuation of the opening scenario that appears in the accompanying "Now You Do It" feature. Not only would it not improve your situation, but it could also create an antagonistic relationship between you and the principal.

Some of the options that may be available to you for further action are listed below.

- In many districts where collective bargaining is allowed, teacher evaluations may be part of the agreement between the district and the teacher's union. Such agreements generally specify a procedure and a mechanism for teachers to disagree with their performance reviews. These agreements are designed to protect teachers from subjective performance reviews that can compromise their reputation and future employment.
- In some districts, teachers have the opportunity to appeal an evaluation. In such districts, teachers may be able to request that a different evaluator carry out a second evaluation, using the same sources of information.
- Some districts may have a process for "grieving" an evaluation (filing a grievance about the evaluation).

In some districts, none of these options is available. Our familiar advice applies once again: become very familiar with the entire evaluation process in your own school district.

## Now You Do It

Read this continuation of the opening scenario, and reflect on the questions that follow.

*High school principal Margaret Spellman knew it was going to be bad day. She was starting to get a cold, and she felt sluggish. Furthermore, she was still troubled by the annual evaluation that Joe Campione had received from his department chair. She wondered how Joe had reacted to it.*

*As she pulled up to the high school, her question was answered. There, just outside the administrative building, was Joe, pacing back and forth. She just knew he was waiting for her.*

*"Have you seen this garbage?" Joe shouted at her before she was even close enough for him to speak in a normal tone.*

*"Good morning, Joe. I assume you're talking about your evaluation. Yes, I saw it yesterday. Why don't we go inside my office and talk about it?" she replied, walking up to him.*

*"I can't. I have a first-period class. But this is garbage. I will never sign this. This guy knows nothing about teaching." Joe threw the papers at Margaret's feet and stormed off to class. Margaret sighed as she watched Joe's retreating back. Then she stooped to pick up the evaluation report.*

**QUESTIONS**

1. If you were advising Joe before he indulged in this outburst, what would you say to him? What are his better options?
2. If you, as an untenured teacher, received a performance evaluation that you believed was unfair and might hurt your career, what would you do?

# Self-Assessment: Being a Reflective Practitioner

It is more than likely that you will be expected to write a self-evaluation as part of the performance review process. It may be that you have had to write self-evaluations in your teacher education program or for your application for licensure. In any event, we strongly encourage you to do self-assessments on a regular basis. Doing so can help you become the reflective practitioner we have described and urged you to be in many other modules, particularly Module 1, Reflective Teaching for Student Learning. Research has shown that teachers who are reflective about their work think critically about their teaching and are able to effect productive changes to their teaching.[3]

Researcher Donald Schön refers to two reflective processes: reflection-in-action and reflection-on-action.[4]

- *Reflection-in-action* occurs while the teacher is in the act of teaching a lesson and generally leads to immediate decisions about action.
- ***Reflection-on-action*** is a more deliberate process that takes place after the actual teaching act is over. Teachers engage in reflection-on-action when they plan for instruction or think through a previously taught lesson.

**Reflection-on-action** an inner process in which the individual thinks back on events, attempting to see them in a more objective manner with a view toward improvement.

As we have stressed throughout this book, the habit of reflection, or what Schön calls reflection-on-action, is a crucial ingredient of successful teaching.

Schön maintains that through reflection-on-action, teachers gain greater self-understanding and evolve new approaches to teaching as they examine the assumptions on which they base their teaching.

Despite its formal name, reflection-on-action can take as simple a form as thinking through your day with a quiet, after-school cup of coffee, or reviewing your class performance while driving home from school. Many teachers also employ tools such as teaching journals, video recordings of their lessons, and discussions with other teachers as part of their reflection process. (See Module 1, Reflective Teaching for Student Learning, for descriptions of tools for reflection.)

Performance assessment is an integral part of any profession. Your performance reviews may be more critical to your job security than any other single thing. In teaching, formative and summative evaluations of teachers (as well as assessments of students) are key processes for monitoring the quality of education that students are receiving. Annual evaluations help teachers recognize what they are doing well and identify how they can (or must) improve.

At the same time, evaluations can be problematic, because there is no agreed-upon set of specific criteria to define quality teaching and there are no definitive landmarks that can be used to measure the quality of a teacher's instruction. The opening scenario highlights the ambiguity that can plague teacher evaluations. That is why we strongly encourage you to become as familiar as you can with the evaluation process in your school or district—both the written, formal description of the process and the more informal clues your colleagues can give you about it. Be proactive in preparing for your evaluations by providing your evaluator with as much information as you can offer before the evaluation, so that your purposes and goals will be clear and easy to follow. As a precaution, also become familiar with the appeals process—just in case.

## Further Resources

- Association for Supervision and Curriculum Development (ASCD). Available at: **http://www.ascd.org/portal/site/ascd/index.jsp.** This leading educational association is an excellent resource on a wide range of issues related to teaching and learning and has been a leader in teacher performance assessment.
- Charlotte Danielson and Thomas L. McGreal, *Teacher Evaluation to Enhance Professional Practice* (Princeton, NJ: Educational Testing Service, 2000). A comprehensive and clear presentation of the authors' system of teacher assessment, which focuses on student learning. In addition, there is a special section on beginning teachers.

- Elizabeth McCay, *Teacher Evaluation,* Commonwealth Educational Policy Institute. Linking teacher performance assessment to the educational reform movement, the author lays out the alternatives and complexities in a fine, short article available at: **http://www.cepionline.org/policy_issues/staffing/p_teacher_eval.html#.**
- Pamela D. Tucker and James H. Stronge, *Linking Teacher Evaluation and Student Learning* (Alexandria, VA: ASCD, 2005). This book not only describes a system of linking teacher evaluation to student learning, but also explains how it has been adapted by four different school systems.

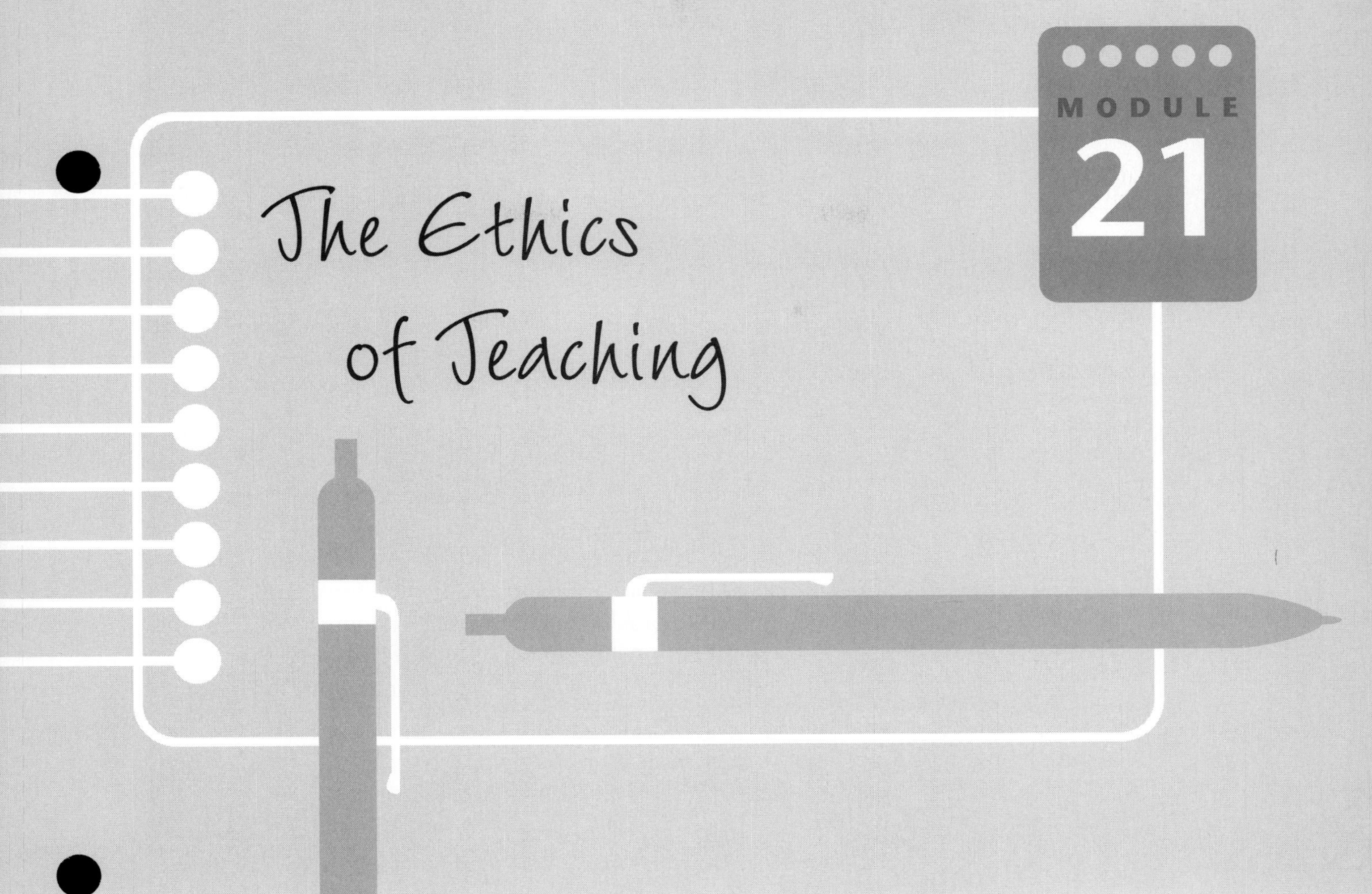


Scenario

As Helen Finn walked into the girls' bathroom, she heard, "Quick, a teacher's coming. Flush it down the toilet! Now!" A loud swish of a toilet flushing followed, and a group of tenth-grade girls strutted defiantly out of the bathroom. One of the last in the line was Siobhan, who had been in Helen's chemistry class last year. Because she was the only one Helen knew very well, she decided to ask her about the situation. "Wait. Siobhan, I'd like to talk to you."

"But I've got French right now and I don't want to be late."

"OK, then come see me after school."

Although Helen had the rest of the day to figure out what to say to Siobhan, she was still uncertain how she would approach the topic when her former student showed up. The school had been plagued by a growing drug problem, and all teachers had been asked to be especially vigilant in the bathrooms and around the school grounds for any evidence of drugs. Helen strongly suspected that the girls in the bathroom were flushing some kind of drugs down the toilet, but she had no way to prove it. From what Helen remembered of Siobhan from last year, she was a hard-working, diligent student. She never missed class, always seemed to be well prepared, and had all her work done on time. "Maybe I can appeal to her sense of honesty and honor to tell me what they were doing in the bathroom," Helen hoped.

"Siobhan, what were you girls doing in the bathroom?"

"I was going to the bathroom and fixing my hair," Siobhan replied innocently.

"And the other girls?"

"The same, I guess. I didn't ask."

"Why did I hear someone say, 'Flush it down the toilet, quick'?"

"I don't know. I didn't hear that."

Helen had thought that Siobhan would tell her the truth. Instead she seemed determined to protect her friends. "Siobhan, I'm really disappointed. I thought you would tell me the truth. I know what I heard, and I distinctly heard someone say, 'Flush it down the toilet.' I'm sure you think you are doing a service to your friends by not telling on them, but you aren't." Siobhan stared at Helen blankly, waiting for a pause in her "lecture."

"Can I go now?" Siobhan asked. Helen realized that she probably wasn't going to get any information from Siobhan and let her go.

Helen sat for a few minutes debating with herself. "What should I do? Should I convey my suspicions to Ms. Foster (the principal)? Is it fair to accuse these students without proof?" She knew that Ms. Foster had acted before on suspicion and had handed out long suspensions to offenders. Helen was convinced that Ms. Foster tended to overreact in these situations, a practice that Helen strongly opposed. But there was a real and growing drug problem in the school, and Helen was concerned that these students were jeopardizing their education and even their health.

Preview

This scenario illustrates one of the innumerable ethical dilemmas you may face on a regular basis in the classroom and school. Teaching is a social endeavor, and you are constantly interacting with students, other teachers, administrators, parents, and other community members. That means that you will frequently confront situations in which you will have to make decisions based on your beliefs about good and bad, right and wrong. Studying ethics now can help you clarify those beliefs.

**Ethics** a branch of philosophy that examines questions of right and wrong.

**Ethics** is a branch of philosophy that examines questions of right and wrong. The term is also used to mean a code of behavior based on a set of beliefs about good and bad, right and wrong. Although some philosophers insist that there is a natural code of ethics to which all societies should adhere, ethics tends to have a culture-specific flavor based on what a particular group of people value in terms of behaviors and actions. On the whole, however, the ethics of one cultural group is generally similar to that of another cultural group, at least in its core beliefs, such as the need for honesty, integrity, loyalty, and kindness.

**Ethical dilemma** a situation in which two or more different moral principles compete, making it difficult to define one clearly "right" path.

In some instances, the right course of action is easy to determine (although it may not be quite so easy to follow). An **ethical dilemma** arises when the right action or behavior is not obvious. Two or more different moral principles compete, making it difficult to define just one clearly right path. We suggest in this module that practice in identifying and weighing the competing moral principles that create an ethical dilemma can help you to be better prepared to face the ethical dilemmas that inevitably arise in any teacher's career. Practice, too, is important in developing everyday habits of good character in you and your students, as you will also see in this module.

**This module emphasizes that:**

- **There are six characteristics of ethical thinking in teaching.**
- **Ethical dilemmas present the teacher with particular problems.**
- **Opportunities exist in the everyday work of teaching to ethically influence the lives and character of students.**

# The Characteristics of Ethical Teaching

In a sense, individuals lose their "freedom" when they get married, and in a similar sense, people lose their freedom to do as they please when they become teachers. In both situations people make commitments, and ethical constraints come with these commitments. Constrained by ethics, the teacher is not always able to act in a manner that he or she finds most satisfying. For instance, the teacher should not respond with sarcasm to a student's foolish or rude remark. Even though a child—sometimes even a very small child—can provoke a rush of anger, the teacher should not act on that anger.

In another, more positive sense, ethics consists of principles that call the teacher to higher modes of professional behavior. It is the ethical principles that teachers follow that mark the teacher's character and the social significance of the profession. Researcher Kenneth Howe suggests that in dealing with issues involving ethical judgment, we as teachers need to exhibit six characteristics: appreciation for moral deliberation, empathy, knowledge, reasoning, courage, and interpersonal skills.[1]

## Appreciation for Moral Deliberation

We need, first, to discern that a situation has an element of right and wrong. We need to see the complex moral dimensions of the problem and appreciate that care must be taken to protect the rights of all parties. Helen

Ethical teaching requires courage, empathy, and interpersonal skills, as well as an appreciation for moral deliberation, knowledge, and reasoning.

was making a routine check on the girl's bathroom, and she sensed that some rule-violating behavior, or possibly something immoral, was going on.

## Empathy

*Empathy* is the ability to mentally "get inside the skin" of another. We need to feel what the others in an ethically troublesome situation are thinking and feeling. Siobhan's silence may be attributed to a sense of loyalty to her friends, an important moral quality. The teacher acknowledges Siobhan's loyalty toward her friends when she comments, "I'm sure you think you are doing a service to your friends by not telling on them," but she also suggests that such loyalty is misplaced.

## Knowledge

One of the tools of a teacher who is able to deal effectively with ethical issues is raw knowledge. Collect as much information about the situation as you can, and try to avoid making unwarranted assumptions. Remember that facts will enable you to put an issue in context. In the above scenario, it would be easy for the teacher to assume that the girls were engaging in illegal activities in the bathroom, given the comment she believes she overheard. Consider, however, what other information could be collected that could help clarify the situation. For example, were there other people in the bathroom besides that group of girls? Was there any smoke odor in the bathroom? Any ashes on the floor? The teacher might also want to talk to other girls who were in the bathroom at that time.

## Reasoning

To reason is to reflect systematically on an issue. When we reason about an issue, we move through it step by step and draw conclusions, or we may compare a particular event or action with some moral principle and come to some conclusion. As a teacher, you need to be thoughtful and deliberate when making a decision. Weigh carefully and thoughtfully the merits and possible negative consequences of each course of action you consider. Ask yourself whether the merits outweigh the potential fallout. In this scenario, Helen doesn't appear to have thought out the consequences of Siobhan's flat denial that anything wrong was going on. She should have considered each possible alternative open to Siobhan and should have been ready with a way of responding to each.

Each situation will present you with new and unique circumstances and challenges, so hard and fast rules for reasoning through ethical dilemmas are hard to come by. Three types of reasoning—ends-based, rule-based, and care-based thinking—are often employed by teachers and others confronted by ethical dilemmas.

- *Ends-based thinking* is best captured by the phrase "Do whatever provides the greatest good for the greatest number."
- *Rule-based thinking* asks, "If everyone in the world were to do what I am about to do—to follow the rule that I am about to follow—is that the kind of world I would want to live in?" Rule-based thinking is opposed to ends-based thinking. It challenges the idea that we can ever really know what the consequences of our actions will be. Instead, the rule-based thinker says, we must always stick to our principles and let the chips fall where they may.
- *Care-based thinking* demands that we do to others what we would want others to do to us, a principle most commonly known as the Golden Rule.

Although there are arguments for and against each of these methods of moral reasoning, there are no iron-clad criteria for applying them to particular cases. Nevertheless, it is important, first, to respond to ethical situations with reason rather than emotion and, second, to be aware which method of reasoning we are using.

## Courage

To feel, to know, and to reason are not enough. To be ethical, we must act, and action sometimes takes courage. To be ethically correct often requires the willpower to act in what we perceive to be the right way, rather than in the

The ethical person has learned how to service others.

comfortable way. Frequently, when confronted with a seemingly no-win dilemma such as the one involving Siobhan, we tend to ignore it in the hope that it will simply go away. However, as the theologian Harvey Cox sees it, "Not to decide is to decide."[2]

### Interpersonal Skills

Once you have decided on a course of action, you will have to implement your decision. Acting on ethical principles demands sensitivity, as well as courage. You need the communications skills to state your decision and the reasoning behind it carefully and clearly. You also need to be able to call up the right words, with the right feeling and tone, and to address the issue at hand openly and honestly. Not having thought through the situation, Helen had no response to Siobhan's request, "Can I go now?" In fact, she has probably lost face with the student.

### Now You Do It

Imagine you are the teacher in the above scenario. How would you respond to this situation? What other information would you want to have? What else would you say to Siobhan? What action, if any, would you take? Would you, for example, report your suspicions to the principal? If so, on the basis of what moral principle? How would you defend your actions? What words would you say? How would you face potential negative reactions?

## Ethical Dilemmas

In some instances, the ethical, or right, course of action is easy to determine, although it may not be easy to follow. If you found a wallet full of money in a parking lot, you would know that the right course is to try to return the wallet, intact, to its owner. It would probably also be clear to you that neither keeping the wallet nor giving yourself a "small reward" for finding the wallet is included in the right course of action, tempting though these responses might be. Thus, finding a wallet does not present an ethical dilemma for someone with the habit of honesty.

Often, it is not so easy to determine the right action or behavior. In the everyday world of teaching, most ethical situations are rather straightforward (someone bullies someone else, a mean rumor is spread, an iPod is stolen, a locker is vandalized), but sometimes they are more complex. Sometimes, they present you with a troubling dilemma.

As we noted earlier in the chapter, an ethical dilemma arises when two or more different moral principles compete, making it difficult to define just one clearly "right" path. Convincing—even compelling—arguments can be made to support two, or sometimes several, different options. The dilemma, then, is deciding which of the two competing moral principles to select and which action to take.

Ethical dilemmas force you to make difficult decisions. They will challenge your belief system and set of moral principles and will at times require you to prioritize these ethical guidelines by which you live, which can be a very difficult task. At the same time, these dilemmas can help you clarify what you believe in and what behaviors and actions you consider most important.

Like any difficult task, however, ethical decisions can become somewhat less daunting with practice and preparation. Although the situations you encounter will undoubtedly be unique, the following case studies can help you prepare for the task of confronting moral dilemmas. Pondering the issues involved will give you an opportunity to identify, ahead of time, your dominant moral principles and styles of thinking.

The competing principles faced by Siobhan's teacher are, on the one hand, fairness in the treatment of student behavior and, on the other hand, adherence to laws and school rules and responsibility for the well-being of the community. If fairness is the more compelling moral principle, then the teacher would not report the incident, because she already has evidence that the principal has a history of acting unfairly toward students. If adherence to rules and social responsibility are the more compelling principles, then the teacher would report the incident. Even without hard evidence of wrongdoing, she would be driven by the probability of illicit activity and a concern for the well-being of these students, as well as that of the larger student body.

At the same time, either course of action is fraught with potential fallout—that is, residual responses that evoke other moral principles. If the teacher reports the students to the principal in the name of social responsibility, she risks losing the respect of and alienating the students, who may very well feel unjustly accused or even betrayed by the teacher's actions. If she does *not* report the incident, she may compromise her reputation within the school community. She still risks a loss of respect from many students, who may see her as someone who lets some students get away with illegal activities. Her commitment to the well-being of the community may be called into question.

Such a conflict, between the needs of an individual or a small group and those of the larger community, is a common source of ethical dilemmas. Other clashes of moral principles that can leave you in a dilemma include

- *Truth versus loyalty.* Personal honesty or integrity is at odds with responsibility and keeping promises to others.
- *Short-term versus long-term considerations.* Real and important requirements of the present come up against foresight, stewardship, and deferred gratification.
- *Justice versus mercy.* Fairness, consistent expectations, and an equal application of the rules are opposed to empathy, compassion, and a desire to make exceptions.

In deliberating ethical dilemmas, it may be useful to try to focus on which course of action can lead to the *greater good.* This question often pits short-term considerations against long-term concerns. Siobhan's teacher, for example, might decide that the greater good will be served by *not* reporting the girls to the principal and keeping a closer eye on the bathroom during the school day. With that course of action, the teacher might reason, "I can show students that I am fair but am also committed to enforcing the rules. My integrity with the students is not compromised, so I can be influential in helping them see the importance of respecting school rules." Or the teacher might decide that the greater good will be served by reporting the incident to the principal, arguing, "Students need to see that the administration is strongly committed to addressing the drug problem at school. We need to let students know how serious we are about not tolerating any infractions, or even suspicions of infractions, of the rules."

The following case studies offer familiar ethical dilemmas that you may face (or may already have faced). Consider thoroughly the different courses of action, weighing the benefits and potential repercussions of each option. Discuss your chosen course of action with others.

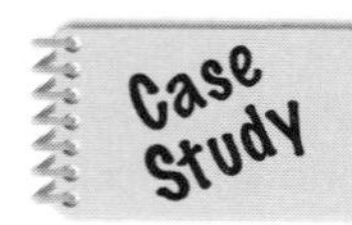


## *Bad Reputation or Bad Behavior?*

While grading papers during your free period, you hear shouting outside your door. You open it to find a group of eighth-graders arguing passionately, with one student about to take a swing at another. You catch his arm.

"Roger, what are you doing? You know the school rules about fighting!"

"Mark started it!" Roger insists. "I caught him in my locker. He was trying to steal something from my locker!"

"I was not!" Mark insisted.

"You were too! I saw you!" Roger retorted.

You quickly realize that your papers will not get graded any time soon. You could send both of the boys to the office, but you know that both the principal and the assistant principal are out for the morning, so the two will just sit in the office or, worse, be sent back to their classes. "You two, in here," you command, still hoping to wrap this up quickly. "The rest of you—get back to where you're supposed to be."

You have Mark and Roger take seats in your classroom, being careful to keep them safely apart. As they take their seats, you review what you know about the situation and the two students. You saw Roger ready to hit Mark, a clear violation of school rules. You have an accusation that Mark was trying to steal something, another violation of school rules. Both students seem to be in the wrong. Or are they?

As for the students involved, you taught Roger last year and know him to be an honest, principled student. You know his parents, too, and feel confident that Roger would not have tried to punch Mark without strong provocation. You have never had Mark in class, so you have not had any direct interactions with him. He is fairly well known among teachers and administrators as someone who is often in trouble. You have heard conversations in the teachers' lounge about him. You suspect that he was, in fact, trying to steal something out of Roger's locker, although you do not have any proof. You decide you need more information.

"All right, let's hear it, one at a time. No interruptions allowed when one person is talking. Understand? Mark, you first."

Mark gives what you find to be a tenuously plausible explanation: he noticed a piece of paper sticking out of Roger's locker and was trying to push the paper back into the locker. He didn't open the locker. How could he? He doesn't know Roger's combination. As he was pushing the paper back in, Roger and his friends came up and started shouting and pushing him.

"Roger, your turn." Roger insists that he saw Mark turning the combination lock on his locker and that Mark was trying to get into his locker to steal something. "He's always stealing things! Everyone knows it!" You are dismayed but not surprised by the personal, *ad hominem* attack. You remember hearing that Mark does not have many friends in school and is struggling to fit in.

## *Be a Whistle-Blower or Disloyal Colleague?*

Johanna is not one of the strongest students in your Level 3 English class, but she is probably one of your hardest working. She is striving to be the first in her family to be accepted into college. Her grades are average or slightly above in all subjects except U.S. history, where she has Mr. Cronin. Mr. Cronin is known as one of the more crotchety teachers at the high school. Throughout your five years at Milkwood High School, you have heard chronic complaints from students about his teaching and grading practices. A few weeks ago, Johanna delivered one of the most heartfelt of these complaints.

"Ms. Woodworth, I'll never get into college! Look at this paper! I worked so hard on it and I got a D+! I just don't get it. I can never get a good grade with him, no matter how hard I try. He just has it in for me!" Johanna had burst into tears as she entered your classroom, slumped into a desk, and threw her paper on the floor.

You read through the paper, noticing some grammatical errors as well as some well-argued points. "Well, it's not an A paper," you thought to yourself, "but it's not a D paper, either." Looking at the dejected and broken student sitting in your room, you wondered what, if anything, you could do to help her.

"Do you have any more papers to write for Mr. Cronin?" you had asked Johanna.

"Yes, one more that counts for 25 percent of our grade."

"Well," you offered. "Maybe I can give you some suggestions to help you write this last paper. You'll have to do all the work, but I can help you get organized and then give you some feedback on your first draft."

"Oh, would you? Really? Thank you sooooo much!"

Over the next three weeks, Johanna came in once or twice a week, with her paper at various stages of completion. Her first draft was a bit disorganized, but after the two of you talked about the paper, she was able to revise it so that it flowed more smoothly. When she showed you her second draft, you circled some grammatical errors that she needed to correct, but you found that she had done a good job making and supporting her points. "She has to get a decent grade on this paper," you thought to yourself.

A few days later, however, Johanna has returned, again in tears. "I told you, Ms. Woodworth. He just doesn't like me. I don't even know why I try. I could hand in *anything* and get the same grade."

You take the paper from Johanna and look through it. There are no marks or comments on the paper except a "D" on the last page. You are dumbfounded. How could he give this paper a D? Based on what criteria? As an English teacher, you know the paper had few, if any, grammatical errors. Maybe history is not your field, but you know what a well-supported argument looks like, and Johanna had well-supported arguments in her paper.

"Maybe Johanna is right about Mr. Cronin," you think to yourself. "But what can I do about it? I can't go to the principal to complain about a colleague, even one who seems to be totally unprofessional! And I could confront Mr. Cronin, but what would I say? Accuse him of bias or laziness? Me! A new teacher! He'd eat me for breakfast! But it's so unfair to Johanna—and I wonder to how many other students."

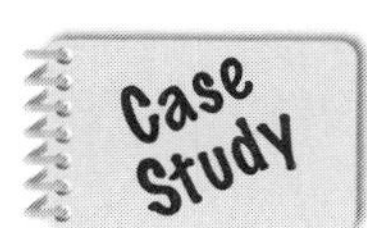


## *Make a Small Accommodation or Defy Your Principal?*

"Mr. Mathers, can we have a word with you?" You turn and see a very well-dressed couple standing at the door of your classroom.

You think to yourself, "Just when I was hoping to get out at a reasonable time," but you respond, "Certainly. What can I do for you?"

"We're Devin's parents and we'd like to talk to you about his math grades for the first semester." Devin McPratt is one of the more challenging students in your eleventh-grade pre-calculus course, not because he has difficulty understanding the math, but because he seems to devote so very little time to his studies. He comes to class late, pays attention only sporadically, and rarely, if ever, hands in his homework. His test and exam scores are mediocre at best. Often he completes only about half of the test, seemingly losing interest before he finishes.

You have never met Devin's parents before, but you have had numerous conversations with Devin about his poor work habits. You tried to convey to him your confidence in his ability, while bemoaning his wasted talent, but to no avail. He earned a C− in the first quarter, but you gave him the benefit of the doubt—and a grade of C. For the second quarter, with an F for a homework grade and a D for attendance, Devin's math grade was a D+. His midterm grade was a 70 percent.

## Video Case

The video case, *Legal and Ethical Dimensions of Teaching: Reflections from Today's Educators,* shows a roundtable discussion among a diverse group of educators who describe some of the ethical and legal dilemmas they have encountered in their own schools. As you watch the clips and study the artifacts in the case, reflect on the following questions.

**QUESTIONS**

1. How could you apply the principles described in this module to the dilemmas these teachers describe?
2. What is your dominant principle in personal ethical decisions? Is it the same one you apply in professional ethical choices? Why or why not?
3. The assistant principal in the video recommends that teachers be proactive in asking for help and advice about ethical and legal issues. Do you know where you could get such help? How would you ask for advice in a way that would not compromise an already delicate ethical situation?

***Online Study Center***

"Devin's math grade is unacceptable to us," Mr. McPratt begins.

"So far, so good," you think. "It *is* unacceptable, especially from someone as bright as he is."

"I agree," you jump in quickly. "Devin is a very bright young man, capable of doing far better. But as I explained in the mid-quarter progress report, Devin rarely hands in his homework or completes class work. His test are most often graded in the C range because he does not finish them."

"Yes, we'd like to talk about that. We'd like you to give Devin an opportunity to complete those tests and to hand in missing homework assignments. Devin needs more time to complete tests and should be allowed extra time when taking tests."

"Oh, I'm sorry. I didn't realize that Devin required extra time on tests. I never received any notice about that from the special education department or the guidance counselor."

"Devin doesn't have any learning problems. He just works better when he has more time."

"Don't we all?" you think to yourself. Aloud, however, you reply, "Mr. and Mrs. McPratt, I can appreciate your concern for Devin, but I don't think that I can make special arrangements for one student and not allow the other students in the class the same opportunity. It wouldn't be fair to the other students."

"We're not interested in fairness. You are compromising Devin's chance of getting into Harvard, where three generations of McPratts have gone. This is one of those cases of 'reverse discrimination.' We will not tolerate anything that jeopardizes his application. If you do not allow Devin to retake the tests, we will take the matter to the principal and, if necessary, the superintendent."

"Let me look at Devin's work, and I'll get back to you in a day or two." You realize that a protracted conversation at this point will not lead to a resolution, and you need time to think about this unexpected turn of events.

The next day, you find a note in your box from the principal, asking you to stop by and talk to her. When you walk in, she gets right to the point, "What's going on with the McPratts?" You recount the meeting that you had with them the previous afternoon.

"They've already called me and the superintendent and are quite adamant about their request. Devin has all As and Bs, except in your class. They're saying the low grade is personal and that Devin doesn't deserve it. I would strongly advise you to consider granting their request."

"What are you telling me? That I have to change his grade?"

"Not at all. But you might want to honor the requests that the McPratts have made."

"But that wouldn't be fair to the other students in the class."

"They wouldn't know about it."

"How could they not?" you wonder. You also wonder what you should do.

## The Everyday Ethics of Teaching

As we hope the preceding case studies make clear, serious ethical issues strongly influence the lives of teachers. Few teachers get very far into their careers without having to deal with situations like these. But these cases do not exhaust the ethical responsibilities of the teacher. There are everyday events that occur in the classroom and in school life that have an even greater ethical impact on students.

Although it is clear that parents and guardians have the primary responsibility for the ethical training of their children, schools do have a clear impact on the character and moral lives of students. Classrooms and schoolyards teem with issues of right and wrong: a student submits a report that is downloaded from an Internet site; a group of girls start a rumor that another girl is pregnant; a bus driver allows a few older students incessantly to pick on the other students; a teacher continually and harshly picks on a particular same student. Events like these send strong ethical messages to students. How the teacher and the rest of the school respond to these ethical dimensions of schooling is what we refer to as the *everyday ethics of teaching*. In particular, teachers ethically influence students in three ways: by example, by the classroom climate they create, and by the dialogue they establish.

1. *Personal example.* The personal example provided by teachers includes the care and manner with which they do their work, the way they treat students and others, and their use of examples from history and literature to enrich the ethical understandings of students. Remember the old adage that "actions speak louder than words." One of the most powerful ways that you influence your students is through your actions. If you want your students to be fair with one another, you have to be fair with them. If you want your students to be honest and trustworthy, you have to be an exemplar of honesty and trustworthiness. If you want your students to be respectful, you have to act in respectful ways with them.

2. *Classroom climate.* Teachers can establish a good classroom climate by creating an environment of safety and trust where students are free from fear and ridicule, where a spirit of cooperation and friendly competition prevails, and where students are working hard and feeling the satisfaction of learning. For many students, a personal sense of safety is often lacking in their lives. Creating a "safe zone," a climate of trust and safety, is a first step to their becoming serious learners.

3. *Ethical dialogue.* Teachers can establish an ethical dialogue in their classrooms by discussing with students the core ethical values, such as honesty, respect for others, and responsibility, that come into play not only in the study of literature and history, but especially in the real-life events of the school and beyond.

The *everyday ethics of teaching,* then, means *doing the job as it ought to be done.* It means realizing that the minutes and hours you spend with students are precious and making sure that they do not waste their time with you.

On a daily basis, you and your students will experience events that can have immeasurable impact on them. You want to be sure that the impact is positive and that students gain helpful guidance as they form their own sets of moral principles. Because the effect of an action or behavior may not be immediate, it is often hard to know how much of an impact you have had on particular students. But "better safe than sorry" might be a useful maxim: we encourage you to assume that *all* of your actions and behaviors will influence some students. That means that everything you do or say can contribute to the shaping of your students' ethical outlook and character.



## Further Resources

- Character Education Partnership (CEP). Available at: **www.character.org.** This Washington-based organization is an advocacy group and clearinghouse for educators interested in character formation and the ethical domain of teaching.

- Thomas Lickona, *Character Matters: How to Help Our Children Develop Good Judgment, Integrity, and Other Essential Virtues* (New York: Touchstone, 2004). This book contains fourteen strategies for helping students succeed academically while building character and much more. A valuable classroom resource.
- Kenneth Strike and Jonas Soltis, *The Ethics of Teaching,* 4th ed. (New York: Teachers College Press, 2004). This short book is an excellent source for ways to approach the topic of ethics in teaching—and it contains a number of practice cases.
- Hal Urban, *Positive Words, Powerful Results: Simple Ways to Honor, Affirm, and Celebrate Life* (New York: Fireside, 2004). This paperback book by a former classroom teacher is inspiring and offers long lists of tested ideas and strategies.

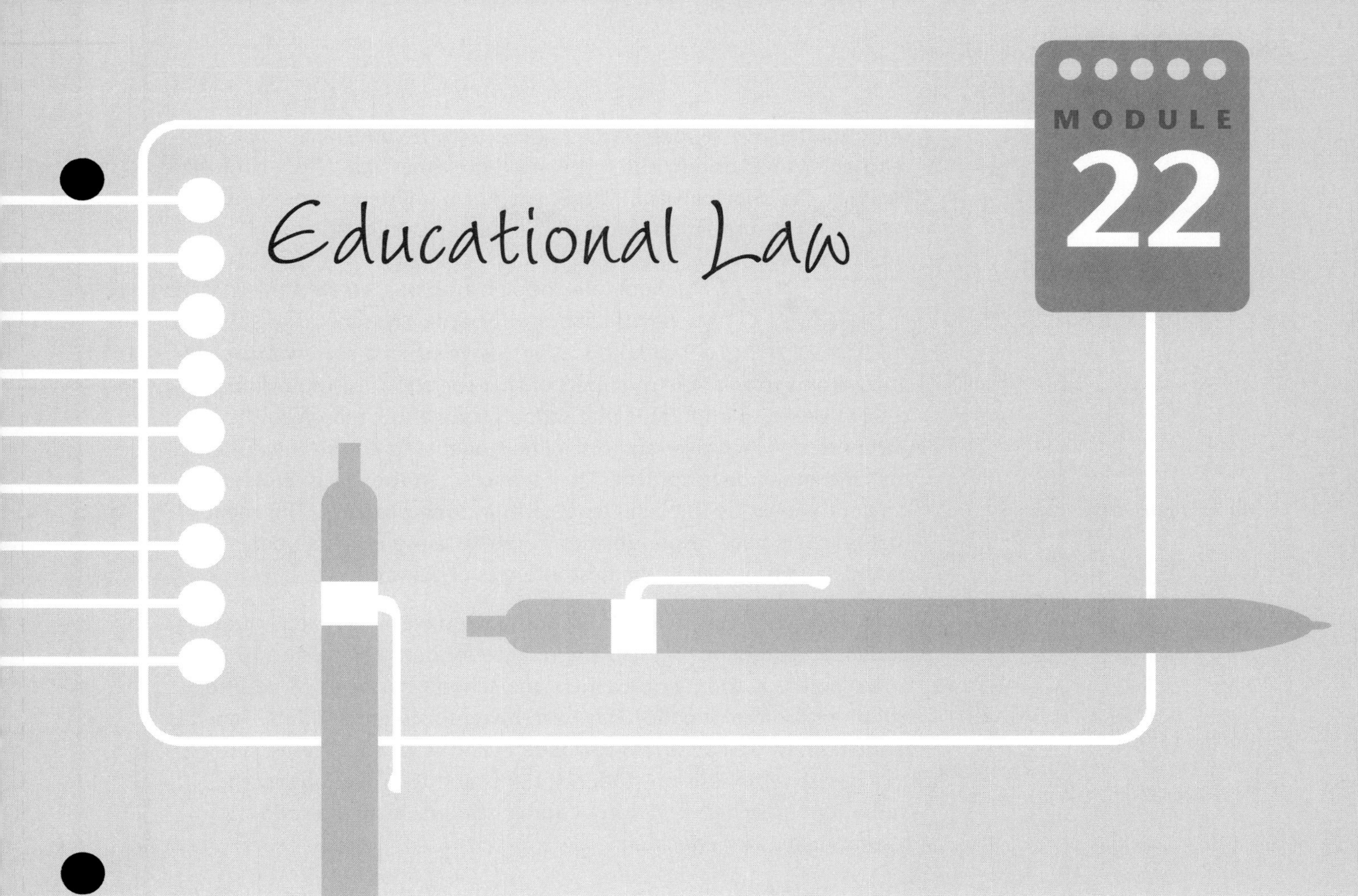

# MODULE 22
# Educational Law

Scenario

If truth be told, Heather was a little afraid of the middle school students. She loved the little ones and felt perfectly in control dealing with a class full of 5- or 6-year-olds. But the bigger students, the sixth-, seventh-, and eighth-graders, frankly made her nervous. She had worried about this when she accepted the position teaching at a K–8 school, but she had convinced herself that because the K–2 wing was in a different part of the school building, it was unlikely that she would see the older students much, if at all. She found that if she arrived early enough and went straight to the K–2 wing, she was usually able to avoid any encounters with these older, more intimidating students.

This seemed to work fine until one November morning. She was running a little late and had just entered the building from the parking lot. She turned the corner and saw two sixth-grade boys squaring off to have a fight. Heather hesitated a moment and then quickly reminded herself that these were not her students. She turned around, went back out the door, and entered the building from the front.

About mid-morning, Heather received a message to see the principal before going to lunch. The principal was furious with her. Apparently, the boys had fought; one had suffered a bloody nose, and both had got their clothing ripped. The mother of one of the boys was threatening to sue the school. To make matters worse, one of the fighters told the principal, "That new teacher saw us fighting and just walked the other way." To a confused Heather, the principal said, "Don't you know anything about your legal obligations in a situation like that!?" In fact, Heather didn't.

Preview

Schools are social institutions, created to serve the needs of society. Specifically, schools are charged with educating the youth of a society to be productive and responsible members of that society. This responsibility is seen as being so important that schools have also been given the authority to watch over and discipline students to ensure their intellectual and moral development. They are to act in the place of parents, a concept known by the Latin legal term ***in loco parentis.*** This means that teachers have responsibilities similar to those of the students' parents and must act in the best interests of the students.

***In loco parentis*** the responsibility of the teacher to function "in the place of the parents" when a student is in school.

Until the recent past, teachers' actions or motives were rarely questioned, and students' rights were rarely considered. Since the 1960s, however, the authority of teachers and schools has been called into question as more attention has been given to students' rights. Federal legislation, as well as several key federal and state court cases, has led to a greater emphasis on students' rights and to limitations on the authority of teachers and school administrators, as well as additional responsibilities for educators.

This module explores those responsibilities. We will examine key federal and state laws and court rulings that affect your rights and responsibilities as a teacher.

**Specifically, the module focuses on:**

- **The legal responsibilities of teachers and, in particular, their liability to legal action.**
- **Their responsibilities for the intellectual, emotional, and social development of students, both inside and outside the school.**

## Now You Do It

As you prepare to study this module, reflect on what you know about educational law. Also, take time to consider your answers to the following questions about the opening scenario.

**QUESTIONS**

1. In your school experience, have you had teachers who unknowingly "gave off signals" that they were afraid of students? How did this affect their effectiveness?
2. How would you act if you were in a situation similar to Heather's? Reflecting on your answer, how would you evaluate this possible behavior?
3. Legally, what do you believe Heather should have done? Ethically, what do you believe she should have done? What is the difference?

- The legal rights both of students and of teachers.
- The meaning and limits of teachers' academic freedom and lifestyle freedom.
- The laws related to copyrighted material and the fair use doctrine.

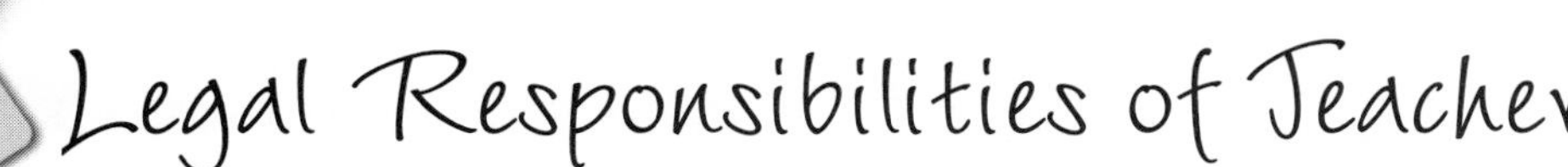

# Legal Responsibilities of Teachers

Although the rights of teachers to act *in loco parentis* may not be as sweeping as they were decades ago, you, as a teacher, are still responsible for your students in many of the same ways their parents are at home. We'll examine teachers' responsibilities for the physical, emotional, and social well-being of students, both in and out of school; their responsibilities regarding their students' academic performance and the privacy of student records; and their responsibilities to protect students' legal rights. We'll also see that teachers have a responsibility to protect themselves, and we'll discover just how that might have affected Heather, the teacher in the opening scenario.

## Responsibility for the Physical Well-Being of Students

Because schools are social institutions with the purpose of forming the youth of the society into productive, responsible citizens, they are also charged with ensuring the well-being of the youth while they are at school or at any school-sponsored event, from a sporting event to a field trip. Teachers and the schools have a duty to protect students from harm, to use due care when interacting with and monitoring students, and to eliminate any foreseeable dangers. Teachers must create classroom and school environments that are

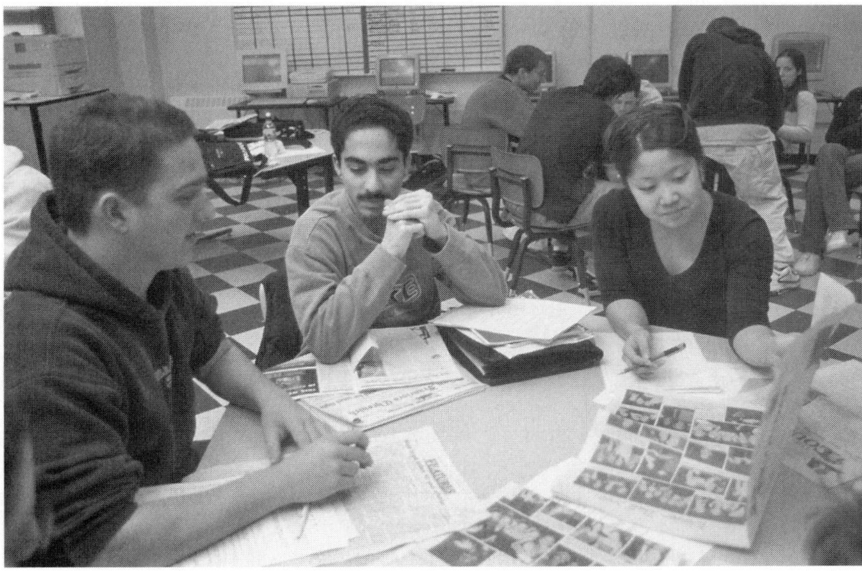

It is important for new teachers to get clarification about their legal responsibilities.

## In Your Classroom

### Your Duty to Keep Students Safe

As a teacher, you not only are charged with teaching students about specified topics in a given discipline but also are legally responsible for the physical and emotional well-being of students while they are in your care. That means that you are expected to do all of the following:

- Provide proper supervision.
- Establish and implement rules for acceptable behavior and consequences for breaking those rules.
- Give appropriate warning when students violate rules.
- Take reasonable precautions to prevent injury.

physically, intellectually, and emotionally safe for all students. They are expected to act quickly to put a stop to behaviors, actions, or comments that might reasonably be expected to lead to harm or injury, whether physical or emotional. In the words of the court, they are to "exercise reasonable caution and foresight in supervising students."[1] The "In Your Classroom" feature lists some ways in which you can show such reasonable caution.

Even so, accidents are an unavoidable part of life, and schools and classrooms have their share of accidents. The question for you as a teacher is to what extent you are responsible—or **liable,** in legal terminology—for an injury a student might sustain while in your classroom or under your supervision at recess or lunch, for example.

**Liability** a legal obligation incurred by an individual.

In general, the courts have ruled that teachers are liable for student injuries if all of the following conditions are met:

1. The teacher had a duty to protect the student(s).
2. The teacher failed to use reasonable care.
3. The teacher's carelessness led to the student's (students') injury.
4. The student(s) sustained a provable injury.[2]

**Reasonable care** a legal term for the level of supervision and care that a teacher must exercise over pupils.

The courts have acknowledged that the level of **reasonable care** that the teacher is to use depends on the circumstances of the situation; the age, maturity, and experience of the students; and the level of potential danger involved in the activity. Some school activities have a greater potential for injury or danger (examples include physical education class, industrial arts or domestic science class, and lunch or recess), so teachers supervising these activities are expected to be especially vigilant to prevent injury. Other situations do not present as great an expectation of danger, so less vigilance is appropriate. Various court cases and findings have helped to define some of these variables.

In the case of *Sheehan* v. *St. Peter's Catholic School* (1971), Margaret Sheehan's teacher at St. Peter's Catholic School brought her class outside during recess to watch a group of students playing baseball. Once outside, the teacher directed her class to sit and watch the game. The teacher then returned to the school. In her absence, some of the students started throwing pebbles, one of which hit Margaret, an eighth-grader, in the eye. Her parents sued, claiming that the teacher and the school failed to provide adequate supervision for the students and were therefore liable for their daughter's injury.

The jury agreed, ruling that the teacher had not used reasonable care when she left the students alone outside. The teacher should have foreseen that leaving students unsupervised on an athletic field might lead to a potentially harmful situation.

The extent of school or teacher liability has, in most cases, been limited to activities that take place during school hours and activities that are sponsored by the school or related to the school. When a 12-year-old boy was fatally injured at a school playground after school hours, the family sued the school for negligence in leaving the school grounds accessible after hours. The California court ruled in favor of the school, stating the schools do not have to supervise the school grounds at all times, but only during school-related activities that take place during school hours. As we'll see next, rulings are less clear about activities that take place away from school.

The case of *Mancha* v. *Field Museum of National History* (1971) arose from an incident that occurred when a group of students from a Chicago middle school were on a field trip to a local museum. Once at the museum, the teachers allowed the students to visit the museum's rooms on their own. While viewing the exhibits, Roberto Mancha was attacked by a group of boys from a different school. His parents sued, claiming that the teachers and the school were negligent when they let the students visit the museum without direct supervision and were therefore liable for their son's injuries.

The Illinois court disagreed, finding that the level of danger and likelihood of injury while visiting a museum were "minimal" and that the teachers therefore could not have reasonably foreseen any danger to the student.

Athough Roberto Mancha's teachers and school were not held liable for his injuries, you should not assume that this ruling applies to all cases. Some field trips may require more direct or even constant supervision, depending on the circumstances. A field trip to a factory where heavy or dangerous machinery is used would warrant closer supervision than one to a museum.

Teachers may also be held liable if they assign or encourage potentially dangerous activities for homework. A Louisiana court found a science teacher liable for injuries sustained by a 13-year-old who was building a model volcano at home. The teacher had done a volcano demonstration in class and then allowed the student to take his volcano model home to experiment on his own. The teacher should have foreseen the potential danger, especially in that the teacher did not know what chemicals the student would be using.

***Responsibility to Protect Oneself*** Even though you are responsible for maintaining a safe environment and protecting the well-being of the students in your care, you also have an abiding interest in keeping yourself free from harm. At one time or another, you may find yourself exposed to a potentially dangerous situation, and you will want to protect or defend yourself. Imagine that two students are fighting or that an angry student moves toward you in a threatening way. What is an appropriate response?

The guiding principle set down by the courts for potentially dangerous situations is that of "reasonable force." Teachers can use reasonable force to protect themselves or others in a dangerous or threatening situation. Reasonable force, like due care, is not a set standard. Rather, it is defined by the circumstances and especially by the individuals involved in the situation. A 220-pound high school teacher would not use the same force on a 120-pound freshman as he might with a 190-pound senior. Likewise, a petite female teacher, such as Heather in our opening example, should exercise prudence when trying to stop an altercation between two burly high school football players. Common sense and a very loud voice can help you deal with many situations that appear to be getting out of control, without the need to physically intervene (for, as we have seen, legally you must intervene). Prompt action can be useful in avoiding serious injury to all parties. Sometimes, that prompt action may involve sending for help if you feel you are at personal risk.

## Now You Do It

Read the following scenario and apply what you now know about teachers' liability as you reflect on your answers to the questions that follow.

*Sandra Blanchett's sixth-period English class was particularly animated today after lunch. "Something must have happened at lunch," Sandra thought to herself. "Best to get them thinking about something else."*

*Sandra sternly admonished the class to get working on their small-group projects, and they reluctantly took their seats to begin working. Sandra moved from group to group, checking on their work, giving suggestions and guidance as needed.*

*"Hey, what the hell—"*

*Sandra turned around quickly, recognizing the voice as that of Roger. "Excuse me!" she chided him. "What are the rules about language in the classroom?"*

*"But Alexandra just bit me! Look! I'm even bleeding!" Sandra's mind raced. After a short pause, during which the class watched in stunned silence, she sent Roger to the school nurse.*

*"Alexandra, you need to go directly to the principal's office," she directed. "Tell the principal that I'll be there at the end of the period. The rest of you need to get back to work. The show is over."*

*As things settled down and Sandra's heart stopped racing, she began to reflect on the incident. "What kind of punishment do they have for biting? I can't believe she just bit him in class . . . and I didn't even see it. Gee, I wonder if I'll be held liable?"*

**QUESTIONS**

1. Did Sandra take the appropriate action? Why or why not?
2. Given what you have learned in this module, do you believe Sandra is liable?

## Responsibility for the Emotional and Social Well-Being of Students

How would you, as a teacher, respond to the student in the following situation?

### *Sexual Harassment in the Classroom*

"Mr. Johannsen, the boys keep making fun of me and calling me names! And George keeps trying to touch me!"

Mr. Johannsen immediately recognized the voice as that of Heidi, a seventh-grader who had developed physically much more rapidly than most of her classmates.

"You have to tell them to stop!" she pleaded.

"Heidi, just ignore them and they'll stop. They only do it because they know you'll get upset. Don't let their teasing bother you. Besides, it's harmless."

"No, it's not! It really bothers me!" she shouted back, nearly in tears. "You don't know what it's like!"

The days of "boys will be boys" and advice like "just ignore them" are long gone, as well they should be. Teachers today must create a classroom environment that keeps students safe from any physical danger or harm and from any kind of harassment, sexual or otherwise. According to U.S. Department of Education guidelines issued in 1997, a school or school district can be found liable if it is made aware of the existence of harassment and fails to take action.[3] In the above scenario, Mr. Johannsen was made aware of the offending behaviors of groups of boys but failed to take action. Heidi and her parents would have legitimate grounds for a lawsuit under Title IX of the Elementary and Secondary Education Act.

In some unfortunate cases, teachers themselves have been the source of harassment or, even worse, have acted inappropriately with students of the same or the opposite gender. As a consequence of this outrageous behavior, all teachers now face increased scrutiny of their interactions with students. We strongly urge caution when you interact with students, especially middle school and high school students, who are more apt to want to be friendly with their teachers, to avoid *any* behavior that might be questionable.

It also goes without saying that teachers cannot make any disparaging comments to students, or use any kind of foul language with them—even if the teacher meant the comments in jest. Students or other adults present may not recognize the lightheartedness with which the teacher made these comments, and even if they do, they may be offended. School is a place where no one should be embarrassed or offended.

We also strongly urge you appreciate the limitations of your role as teacher and refer students in distress to appropriate counselors or mental health professionals. By nature, teachers want to help students, especially those students who may have challenging emotional issues. Some teachers try to serve as confidential counselors to these students, with the sympathetic intention of helping them through a difficult time. Unfortunately, some people (such as the student himself or herself, the parents of the student in question, and/or school administrators) may not view the teacher's actions in the same light. Such misperceptions may cause serious problems for the teacher.

***Protecting Students' Physical and Emotional Well-Being Outside of the School*** Laws and the courts call on teachers to be, in some ways, the eyes and ears of society. Teachers who detect that their students are in potentially dangerous situations outside their school lives must work to eliminate the danger themselves or inform appropriate authorities of the danger. Two situations are especially important.

- *Child neglect or abuse.* Every state in the United States and all U.S. territories legally require teachers to report any and all known or suspected cases of child neglect or child abuse. It is important to note that the reporting individuals' names remain confidential (assuming that the reports are made in "good faith") to protect school personnel from frivolous lawsuits. On the other hand, a teacher who fails to report evidence, or even suspicions, of neglect or abuse can be prosecuted under the law.
- *Threats from a student.* A teacher or any employee of the school district who has any information that a student intends to do harm to himself or herself or to others is obligated to report that information to the appropriate authorities. A teacher who does not report this information can be found liable if, in fact, injury or death does occur. Teachers and guidance counselors *cannot* keep such information confidential, even to honor promises made to students who confide in them.

## Responsibility for Students' Academic Progress

**Educational malpractice** failure to adequately educate a student.

An area of teacher liability that has arisen recently is **educational malpractice,** or failure to adequately educate a student. Educational malpractice cases tend to fall into two categories: (1) failure to teach and (2) misclassification and improper placement of students. Cases in the second category often stem from accusations that a school failed to provide requisite services for a student with undiagnosed special needs or it placed a student, either with or without special needs, in the inappropriate classroom setting. Because the case law for cases related to special education is so extensive and complex, we will focus primarily on a teacher's responsibility for an individual's student academic performance. In other words, if a student has "failed to learn," can a teacher be liable for a "failure to teach"?

Two court cases have to date defined the legal response to claims of educational malpractice. In both cases, the courts ruled against the students and their families, who were suing the respective school districts for failure to teach.

The case of *Peter W.* v. *San Francisco School District* (1976) concerned a student, Peter W., who graduated from high school with a fifth-grade reading level even though the state of California had a statute requiring graduates to read at an eighth-grade level. Peter and his family sued, claiming negligence on the part of the school and the teachers who taught him. They also claimed that the school system violated the state statute by allowing him to graduate with only a fifth-grade reading level.

The court, however, ruled in favor of the school district, finding that "classroom methodology affords no readily acceptable standards of care, or cause, or injury."[4] Without a workable and generally accepted standard of care, the courts cannot determine whether a teacher or school system used reasonable care in the education of a student. In this case, the court further noted that learning to read and write are influenced by many factors, only one of which is the instruction received. Finding the schools liable for academic achievement of each and every one of their students, the court found, would allow any student to file a lawsuit and that "would burden them [the schools]—and society—beyond calculation."[5]

In the case of *Donohue* v. *Copiague Union School District* (1977), Edward Donohue graduated from a public high school, earning a graduation certificate, even though he could not read or write well enough to fill out employment applications. The student and his parents sued the school district for negligence and educational malpractice. The court dismissed the complaint for reasons similar to those put forth in the *Peter W.* decision: the absence of a workable standard of care. The court found that Donohue's classmates who were exposed to the same teaching did not fail to learn. From that finding, the court inferred that the plaintiff's failure to learn must have been due to causes other than failure to teach. Noting (as did the judges in the *Peter W.* ruling) that learning is influenced by a range of variables, including social, emotional, and economic factors, in addition to innate intelligence and ability, the court found it nearly impossible to attribute responsibility to the school district alone.

At present, educational malpractice should not pose a threat to teachers, but it may in the not-too-distant future. Some legal scholars expect that a workable standard of care may be soon formulated. Largely because of the No Child Left Behind Act, more and more states are specifying what a qualified teacher needs to know in order to teach and are requiring that teachers pass a standardized test to be granted a teaching license. At the same time, many states are defining what high school students need to know in order to earn a diploma and are requiring students to pass a standardized test to be granted their diplomas. As they take such steps, states come closer to defining a workable standard of care.

## Responsibility for Maintaining Confidentiality of Students' Academic Performance

Consider the following scenario.

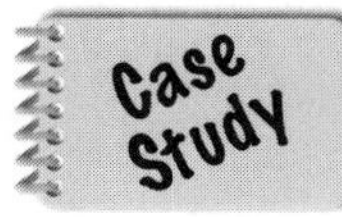


### *Confidentiality in the Classroom*

"Has everyone finished? Does anyone need more time?" You do a check around the room to see whether any student is still working on the weekly quiz. You recently decided to give weekly quizzes in your eighth-grade Level 3 math class, in hopes of keeping better track of how well students are internalizing the important concepts.

You wait a few more minutes for those who may still be writing. "If everyone's done, exchange papers with your neighbor, get a different-colored pen, and write your initials at the bottom of the paper. When everyone's ready, we'll go over each problem on the quiz. Remember to mark any incorrect answers on the paper you're grading." You go through the quiz, item by item, having a student read the item and then give the correct answer.

"Now count up the number of correct answers, and that becomes the numerator. Write the total number of questions as the denominator. You should all have a fraction with 25 as the denominator on the paper you are checking."

Suddenly a student yells out, "Look at this. The dweeb got five right this time. Hey, Huey! You got five right this time. What a loser! My dog could do better than you!"

"What did I say about those kinds of comments, Rudolpho? You are not to talk about the paper you graded." Despite your admonitions, you hear students giggling and talking about how some of the students in the class did on the quiz.

"Okay, that's enough. Let me have the quiz papers." You quickly collect the papers and resume the day's lesson.

This common practice of peer grading may seem like an efficient way of giving students prompt feedback and relieving the teacher of the piles of papers in need of grading. Yet it was the focus of a federal court case that was eventually heard by the U.S. Supreme Court. The question raised in *Owasso Independent School District No. I-001* v. *Falvo* (2002) was whether the practice of peer grading violates the Family Education Rights and Privacy Act (FERPA) passed in 1974.

FERPA, also referred to as the Buckley Amendment, is federal legislation that protects the rights of students to the privacy of records related to their educational performance. It also gives students and their parents unlimited access to all official educational records kept by the school. You yourself may recall having signed waivers at various times in your academic career—for example, if you asked teachers for their recommendations to support a college application. Depending on which box you checked, you may or may not have waived your right to view the recommendations that people sent in on your behalf.

FERPA also restricts access of people outside the school system to these records without the written permission of the parents of the student in question. (Once students reach 18 years of age, the privacy rights become theirs.) Records can be viewed by school personnel for educational use but cannot be shared with people outside the school or with other students.

In *Owasso Independent School District No. I-001* v. *Falvo* (2002), the U.S. Supreme Court ruled in favor of the school district, finding that the peer grading did not violate FERPA because the grades on the quizzes were not part of

## In Your Classroom

### Protecting Your Students' Confidentiality

FERPA affects you in the classroom in important ways. Here are some things to remember:

- You are required by law to keep students' grades confidential.
- Neither students nor their parents should have access to your grade book. If you have a pencil-and-paper one, keep it in a secure place. If yours is an electronic one, make sure it is password-protected or on a secure computer to which students do not have access.
- During parent conferences, when a parent asks you how another student performed in comparison to his or her child, resist the temptation to respond! Tactfully point out that you legally cannot discuss the performance of other students but speak only about the academic work of his or her child.
- Do not announce students' grades or post them in any public place.
- Finally, resist the temptation to talk about particular students in the teachers' rooms or other open areas. You never know who is listening and what will be repeated or, even worse, misrepresented.

a student's official educational record. In the decision, the justices helped to clarify the extent of educational records, defining them as information kept in permanent files. All grades recorded on report cards would be part of a student's official educational record, but grades on tests and quizzes would not. Comments that a teacher makes on a student's report card are part of a student's educational record, but notes that teachers may make to help them determine a student's grade for a marking period would not be.

## Responsibility to Protect Students' Legal Rights

Prior to the 1960s, the courts were rarely involved in the day-to-day operation of the schools, and issues of students' rights were rarely if ever considered. Over the past fifty years, however, the courts have been asked to rule more and more frequently on issues related to student rights within the schools. From free expression to due process to search and seizure, the breadth and depth of students' constitutionally protected rights in schools have been debated, and decisions have been handed down at various levels in the state and federal judicial systems. Although we cannot present an exhaustive explanation of students' rights in schools, we will address key considerations that teachers need to keep in mind.

***Due Process*** The Fourteenth Amendment to the U.S. Constitution states in part that citizens shall not be deprived of "life, liberty, or property, without due process of law." Because we do not have a constitutional right to education, the courts have ruled that students have a property right to attend school and receive an education, much the same as a person's right to ownership of other property. Accordingly, students cannot be deprived of their right to education without **due process.**

**Due process** the deliberative process that protects a person's constitutional right to fair and equal protection under the law.

Due process means that, before any action can be taken that would remove a student from school (such as a suspension or expulsion), the school system must ensure that the student's rights have been respected and that all processes required by the law have been followed. Specifically, the student—and the student's parents, for minor students—must be informed of the charges against him or her and afforded a hearing in which the evidence against the offending student is presented and the student is given the opportunity to respond to the charges.

Even though you may not be in an administrative position, you may be called on to participate in some way in disciplinary action against students. In all cases, be mindful of students' due process rights, to spare yourself the unnecessary headache that a lawsuit can bring.

***Freedom of Expression*** The defining case of student free speech was decided by the U.S. Supreme Court in 1969. In *Tinker* v. *Des Moines Independent School District,* the Court held that neither teachers nor students "shed their constitutional rights to freedom of speech or expression at the schoolhouse gate."[6] The Court also noted that because schools are responsible for "educating the youth for citizenship,"[7] they should instill in students an appreciation of and respect for their constitutional rights.

Still, students' freedom of expression is not absolute. The test for limiting student free speech or expression is whether the expression "materially disrupts class work or involves substantial disorder or invasion of the rights of others." In subsequent cases, the courts have ruled that schools do not have to wait until a disruption occurs; rather, if there is sufficient evidence to suggest that a disruption will occur, the schools can ban the expression.

Individual student expression may be protected speech, but school-sponsored publications and plays are a different issue. In the landmark case *Hazelwood School District* v. *Kuhlmeier* (1988), the U.S. Supreme Court ruled that educators can exercise substantial control over school-sponsored activities, such as publications and plays, as long as their censorship has "valid educational purpose"[8] or is reasonable. It is important to point out that the *Hazelwood* decision does not *require* educators to censor school-sponsored publications, but it does *allow* them to do so. Navigating the waters of free expression is rarely clear-cut or explicit. If you are the faculty advisor for any school publication, it is probably wise to err on the side of caution and to censor questionable material.

## Legal Rights of Teachers

Although teachers are agents of the school system and are charged with the appropriate education of the youth of a community, they are also members of that same community and may have abiding interests in certain decisions affecting the community. As private citizens, teachers benefit from all of the rights afforded them and all people living in the United States by the U.S. Constitution. This means, for example, that teachers, like everyone else, should be able to openly support, and even campaign for, their political candidate or to comment publicly on community or national issues.

Still, it is important to understand that our constitutionally guaranteed rights are not absolute. For example, the Supreme Court has ruled that a person cannot yell, "Fire!" in a crowded theater, because doing so poses a serious threat to the other people in the theater. When deciding challenges to our constitutional rights, the courts weigh the interests and rights of the individual against the interests, rights, and well-being of the larger society. The same holds when they consider the extent of teachers' constitutionally protected rights while they are in schools or are acting as agents of the school.

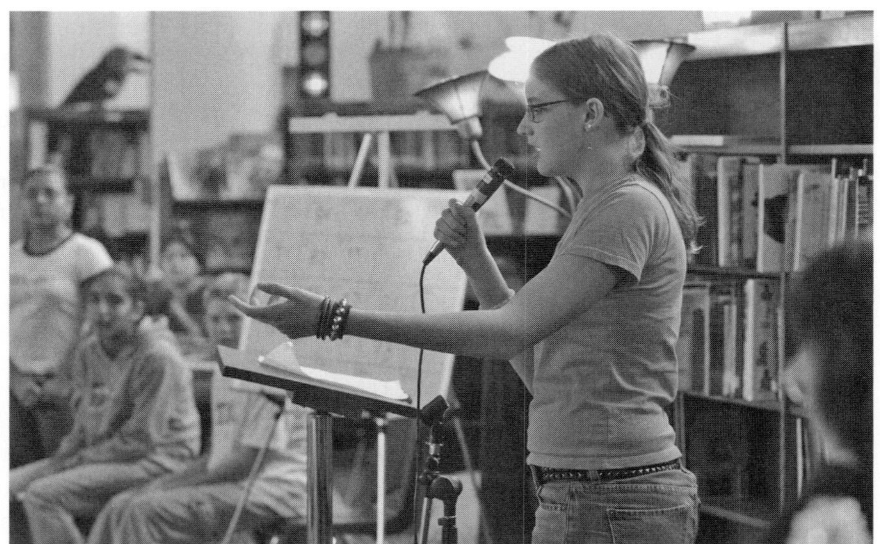

Teachers and students, as members of a community, have the right to speak out on issues that concern them, as long as they do it outside school activities and school hours.

## Freedom of Expression

The First Amendment to the U.S. Constitution states that "Congress shall make no law . . . abridging the freedom of speech. . . . " Freedom of speech includes symbolic, verbal, and written expression. Symbolic freedom of speech means one can wear a symbol that conveys an idea or point of view. A black armband, a yellow ribbon, and (in some instances) facial hair can all be symbols that may constitute protected speech. The courts have ruled, however, that freedom of expression is not limitless.

***Right to Speak Out on Issues of Public Concern*** Members of a community have the right to express their views on matters of public concern. We can place posters for political candidates on our lawns, speak in favor of or against a proposed law, or wear pins or buttons that advance an idea. Teachers, as members of a community, also have the right to express their points of view. They cannot, however, express these views in the classroom or when they are acting as agents of the school.

The defining case regarding teachers' rights in this area, *Pickering* v. *Board of Education,* was heard by the U.S. Supreme Court in 1968. Marvin Pickering was an English teacher at a public high school. He wrote a letter to the local newspaper in which he severely criticized the way the superintendent of schools and the school board spent school funds. The school board took offense at Pickering's letter and claimed that the letter "was detrimental to the efficient operation . . . of the schools."[9] The board opted not to rehire Pickering at the end of the school year. Pickering insisted that his letter was protected speech and sued the school system.

The Court ruled that the issue about which Pickering had written the letter was indeed a matter of public concern so that *as a citizen,* Pickering had a right to comment on the issue. The question the Court had to address was whether these comments made by an employee of the school system negatively affected the efficient operation of the school. The Supreme Court looked for a balance between the interests of the teacher to comment on issues of public concern and the interests of the school board to run the schools efficiently. The Court found that Pickering's comments did not jeopardize his working relationship or his effectiveness as a teacher. As a result, the Court ruled that the letter was in fact protected by the First Amendment, and Pickering was reinstated.

## In Your Classroom

### Free Speech "Dos and Don'ts" for Teachers

The following guidelines are based on the *Pickering* case and subsequent cases.

Teachers can:

- comment on issues of "public concern" related to the school or school district.
- campaign for political candidates in public *outside* of the school and school hours.

Teachers cannot:

- make public confidential information about the school or school district.
- malign or denigrate their superiors in public.
- campaign openly for political candidates or causes during school hours or at school.

**Academic freedom** the freedom of teachers to teach an issue or to use a source in teaching without fear of penalty, reprisal, or harassment.

***Right to Teach Freely, or Academic Freedom*** **Academic freedom** has been described by the courts as being fundamental to a democratic society. The courts acknowledge that teachers need to be free to experiment with new teaching methodologies and select appropriate teaching materials in order to teach their discipline in the most effective and efficient manner. At the same time, the courts have ruled that, like the other rights, academic freedom is not absolute, but limited. A teacher's right to academic freedom has to be balanced with other and potentially competing educational priorities, one of which is the ability of the school district to efficiently educate those in their charge. A look at some landmark court cases can help to clarify these limitations.

In the case of *Keefe* v. *Geanakas* (1969), a Massachusetts English teacher, Robert Keefe, assigned a provocative article from the *Atlantic Monthly* to one of his classes. Some of the students' parents complained about the language in the article, which they found offensive. Mr. Keefe's principal instructed him not to assign the article again. He refused, arguing academic freedom. The school district disagreed and removed him at the end of the school year.

The court ruled in favor of Mr. Keefe, who was reinstated. The court found that the offensive language to which the school board objected was already present in the school, because it could be found in books in the library. In addition, the school board had not informed the faculty that such language was prohibited. Finally, the court found that the language in question was not particularly offensive.

In the case of *Parducci* v. *Rutland* (1970), Marilyn Parducci, a high school English teacher in Alabama, assigned *Welcome to the Monkey House,* by Kurt Vonnegut, to her eleventh-grade class. The high school principal and the associate superintendent both thought the book was "literary garbage" and told Ms. Parducci not to use the book again. Ms. Parducci disagreed with their opinion of the book and continued to assign it. Ms. Parducci was fired, so she sued, claiming a violation of her right to academic freedom.

The court ruled in her favor. It found that the school did not show that assigning the book was inappropriate for juniors in high school or that it significantly disrupted the educational process in the school. Ms. Parducci was ordered reinstated.

In the case of *Boring* v. *Burncombe County Board of Education* (1998), Margaret Boring, a high school drama teacher, sued her school system for an end-of-year transfer. She claimed that the district was retaliating against her for selecting a play with questionable language for students to perform in a state-wide drama competition, which created some controversy in the school community. In this case, the court ruled against Ms. Boring, finding little evidence to link the play and the transfer. Moreover, the court did not find the transfer to be punitive.

When deciding challenges to teachers' academic freedom, the courts consider all of the following factors:

1. The teacher's purpose in assigning the task
2. The educational relevance of the assignment
3. The age of the students
4. The quality of the material and its effect on the students

The courts have been consistent in recognizing that school boards (or school committees) have the authority to decide the curriculum and to expect that teachers will teach that curriculum. Likewise, school boards have the authority to dictate which instructional materials will be used and which cannot be used. They can also specify inappropriate language and topics in the classrooms. The caveat is that if the school board has not made it clear what is and what is not allowable, it will not be able to remove a teacher for using questionable material.

Teachers, on the other hand, have the right to decide teaching *methods* and to present topics and materials relevant to the decided curriculum. They also have the right to supplement the curriculum with relevant materials or topics. They do *not* have the right to teach topics or distribute materials that are contrary to the decided curriculum and/or forbidden by the school board. Also, materials that might be appropriate for high school students may be judged inappropriate for elementary school.

## Use of Copyrighted Materials

Teachers often look for materials to supplement and enhance the texts that the school district purchases. They may draw from a host of sources, including other textbooks, chapters from books, essays or articles from newspapers and magazines, television and radio shows, and articles posted on websites. With the proliferation of photocopiers, computers with printers, recordable DVD players, and the ubiquitous Internet, finding and redistributing these materials has become quite easy.

The problem is that many of the materials that are so freely distributed and used in the classroom belong to individuals who spent much time, thought, and money producing them. To protect the investments of authors, artists, and software designers, the U.S. Congress has enacted copyright laws. These laws are not meant to prevent the use of such materials; rather, they are meant to ensure that the use of such intellectual property is authorized by its owners.

Use of copyrighted materials is more lenient for educators than for the general public. Teachers can generally legally redistribute printed or videotaped material if they get permission from the owner(s) of the material (which usually entails paying a fee). In addition, the doctrine of **fair use** allows for the limited educational use of copyrighted material without permission.

**Fair use** a legal principle defining specific, limited ways in which copyrighted material can be used without permission from the author.

Teachers can always make one copy of any printed material, be it a chapter from a book, a poem, or a newspaper or magazine article, to use in preparation for teaching the material. Teachers can also make multiple copies of copyrighted material if the material meets the tests of *brevity, spontaneity*, and *cumulative effect* and includes a notice of copyright. Table 22.1 provides some examples of printed materials that meet these tests. Some practices, such as creating a class anthology by copying material from several sources, making

**TABLE 22.1 Tests to Determine Eligibility of Copyrighted Material for Fair Use**

| Test | Examples of Items that Pass This Test |
|---|---|
| Brevity: The materials must be brief. | • An entire poem of 250 words or fewer, printed on no more than two pages<br>• An excerpt of a longer poem if it is fewer than 250 words<br>• An entire article, essay, or short story of 2,500 words or fewer<br>• An excerpt of an article, essay, or short story if it is fewer than 1,000 words or less than 10 percent of the whole work<br>• One chart, diagram, cartoon, or picture per book or periodical |
| Spontaneity: The time between deciding to use a particular work and using it is too short to allow for a response to a request for permission. | • Recently published news articles related to a class topic |
| Cumulative Effect: The materials are not used so much that they deprive the copyright holders of benefits to which they are entitled. | • The copied material is for only one course taught by one teacher in the school.<br>• No more than one copyrighted piece by the same author is used.<br>• No more than three excerpts or pieces from the same anthology, text, or periodical issue can be copied in a semester.<br>• No more than nine instances of multiple copying are allowed for one course during a term. |

multiple copies of weekly newspapers or magazines expressly for classroom use, and copying consumable materials (workbook pages, for instance), are definite violations of copyright laws.

Similar fair use guidelines also regulate the use of television and radio shows, nearly all of which are copyrighted. Videotaped television shows can be used for no more than forty-five days without obtaining permission. After forty-five days, the show(s) must be erased or taped over. During the first ten days after the taping, the teacher may show the video no more than twice. Copying a commercially produced videotape, DVD, video game, or software application is allowable only as a backup of the original. Such copies cannot be distributed, even in an educational setting.

Guidelines are still being developed to address copyright issues for material on the Internet, including websites and components of websites. Keep in mind, though, that online versions of newspapers, magazines, and other print material are still protected by copyright laws and require the same procedures for use as their traditional counterparts.

## Teachers' Appearance at School

Imagine yourself in the following situation. What advice would you give your colleague?

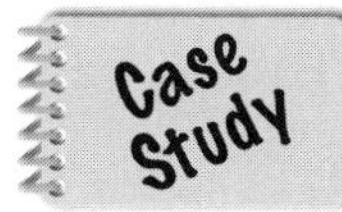


### *When Is a Rule a Rule?*

It is the first day of school, and your colleague has finally returned after spending two and a half months hiking a section of the Appalachian Trail. As he walks into the department office, you catch sight of his full beard and mustache. "Hey, Paul. What's with the new look?" you ask.

"Oh, you mean the beard? You know, while I was hiking, there wasn't any way to shave, so I guess I just got used to not shaving."

"So how was the hiking?" you ask politely, still somewhat fixated on the beard.

"Amazing!" Paul explains. "I can't wait to go back next summer and finish the Trail." The first-period bell interrupts your conversation. "I'll tell you more at lunch," Paul shouts as he heads to his first-period class.

At lunchtime, you start eating, anticipating that Paul will join you. Halfway through the lunch period, Paul arrives, looking deflated. "What a way to start the school year!" he exclaims as he slumps down in a chair.

"A class-from-hell already?" you ask sympathetically.

"No, problems with the principal already. He's not very fond of my new beard. Told me it had to be gone by tomorrow or *I* would be."

"Can he do that?" you ask. "That doesn't seem right."

"That's what I thought, too. He says otherwise. It's not that I love this beard so much, but I just don't like being told what I can and cannot wear or how I can look."

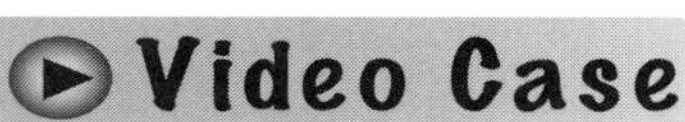


What aspects of the law will be relevant to you as a teacher? In the video case, *Legal and Ethical Dimensions of Teaching: Reflections from Today's Educators,* you'll have an opportunity to listen in on a conversation with a diverse group of teachers, an attorney who became a teacher (the moderator), and an elementary school administrator. The participants will discuss everyday issues they've encountered, including ethical dilemmas, concerns about child abuse, and how the law affects their course of action. As you watch the clips and study the artifacts in the case, reflect on the following questions.

**QUESTIONS**

1. How do these teachers' concerns reflect the laws and court rulings described in this chapter?
2. Did you find the advice offered to these teachers practical? What, if anything, would you add?
3. What kinds of questions would you pose to a school district attorney? Who else at your school do you think will be able to help you with legal questions?

Should the principal be able to require Paul to shave his beard? If Paul refuses and is fired, is his dismissal legal? The answer to *both* of these questions is "yes and no." As in most cases challenging the schools' authority in different arenas, the courts have looked to balance the interests and rights of the individual teacher with the educational mission of the schools.

Courts have generally ruled that schools and school systems may impose grooming and dress codes, as long as these codes are reasonable. They must also be explicit, in writing, and equitably imposed on all employees. The courts have not, in most instances, found that teachers have any constitutionally protected right to dress as they please. In fact, various courts have ruled that teachers have an obligation to dress in ways that are not detrimental to the educational process and that encourage appropriate respect from students.

At the same time, the courts have also ruled that a teacher's grooming preferences can be constitutionally protected if they reflect racial or ethnic values. In *Braxton* v. *Board of Public Instruction of Duval County, Florida* (1969), a Florida court ruled in favor of Booker Peek, an African American teacher who wore a goatee. Mr. Peek was not rehired after failing to comply with repeated requests from school officials that he shave his goatee. Peek insisted that his goatee was a symbol of racial pride and therefore constituted free speech, which is protected under the First Amendment. The Court agreed, ruling that Peek's goatee was protected under the First Amendment and that the school district's decision not to rehire Peek appeared to be racially motivated.

## Teachers' Lifestyles

In the first half of the twentieth century, teachers were expected to be moral exemplars for the young students they taught. They were not permitted to do anything of questionable morality, even when they were outside of the school. Female teachers were commonly forbidden to be seen in public with a man who was not a relative unless an older woman was accompanying them. In more recent times (as recently as the 1950s and 1960s), female teachers in some places were expected to resign if they got married or, as married women, became pregnant.

Fortunately, such restrictions on teachers' lifestyles have almost totally disappeared—at least with regard to their private lives. While they are in school or are attending school-sponsored or school-related activities, teachers are still held to a moral standard in their position as educators and as role models for the students. The courts, however, have been less likely to rule in favor of the schools' attempts to restrict teachers' private behavior. The goal of the courts, once again, is to weigh the interests and rights of the individual against the needs of the school system to carry out its educational responsibility efficiently and effectively. Trying to find this balance is not always an easy task. Both sides can and do present convincing arguments to support their positions.

Consider the case of *Morrison* v. *State Board of Education* (1969). Marc Morrison, a high school teacher, had a brief homosexual relationship with another teacher employed at his school. A year later, the other teacher reported the relationship to the superintendent, who then revoked Morrison's license to teach, on grounds of "immoral, unprofessional" conduct.

The court ruled in favor of Morrison, finding that the terms of the school district's policy on immoral and unprofessional conduct were too vague. It also found that the school district did not show that Mr. Morrison's lifestyle was in any way detrimental to the educational process at school.

In sum, the ruling of that court and the rulings of other courts in subsequent cases have generally been understood to mean that a teacher's private life and lifestyle cannot be grounds for dismissal unless the school administration can show that the lifestyle has a detrimental effect on the educational process at school.

Law and regulations are general, broad guidelines; they cannot cover every detail of every situation that may occur. There may even be competing laws or regulations that apply to a given situation. When this occurs, courts are asked to examine the situation and decide how a law or regulation applies. In court cases involving teachers, students, and school systems, the courts try to balance the interests of the individual with those of the institution, while remaining faithful to the relevant law. The findings of different courts illustrate the complexity and challenge of trying to strike this balance. However, because the law is dynamic, it is important for teachers to keep up with legal rulings and changes. We suggest that you regularly read an educational journal with a legal column or the newsletter of your professional association for notices and features related to school law. Major cases, of course, are reported on the network and cable news stations, so keep abreast of the news, too.

## Further Resources

- *Acceptable Use Policies: A Handbook.* Available at: **http://www.pen.k12.va.us/VDOE/technology/AUP/home.shtml.** This handbook is produced by the Virginia Department of Education and is a rich source of information on using the Internet in schools and developing acceptable use policies.
- *Deskbook Encyclopedia of American School Law* (Rosemont, MN: Data Research, annually). This excellent annual reference book is an easily accessible source on the current law and legal issues surrounding all aspects of public and private education.
- Louis Fischer, David Schimmel, and Cynthia Kelly, *Teachers and the Law,* 6th ed. (New York: Longman, 2002). This book, written by scholars who are lawyers and professors of education, bridges the worlds of the courts and the classroom with great detail and clarity.

- Michael W. LaMorte, *School Law: Cases and Concepts,* 8th ed. (Boston: Allyn and Bacon, 2004). This text covers both key legal opinions and dissenting opinions and also adds valuable commentary and explanations.

**Online Study Center**

- *The Legal Information Institute's Supreme Court Collection.* Available at: **http://www.law.cornell.edu.supct.** This website gives you access to the most important Supreme Court school-related decisions.
- Perry Zirkel, "De Jure" column in *Phi Delta Kappan* (Bloomington, IN: Phi Beta Kappa International). This regularly published column reports on important issues of school law and offers an excellent way to follow recent developments.

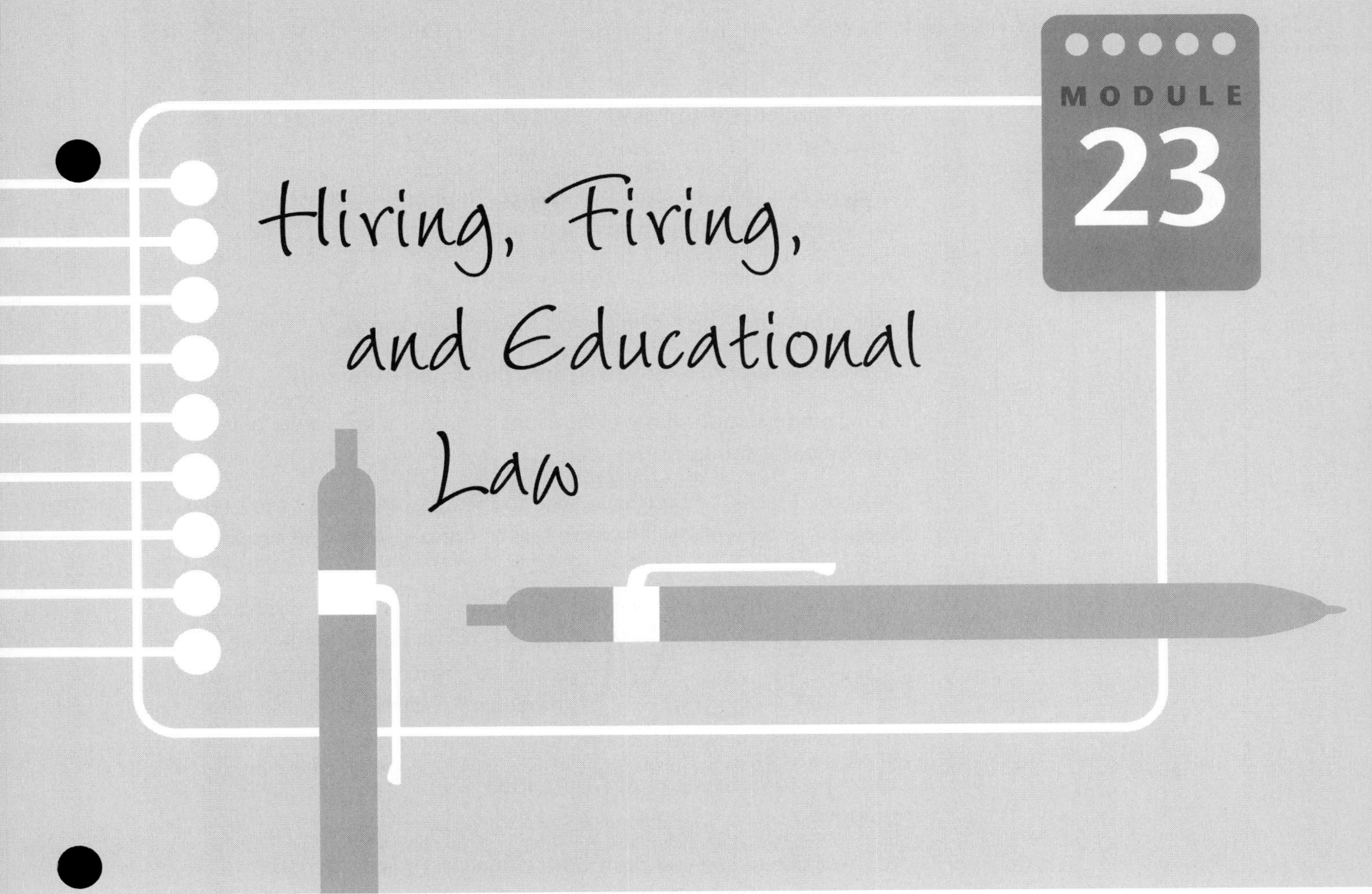


Scenario

Friday could not come soon enough for Marisa Borden this week. Spring vacation began today, but the students, it seemed, had already been on vacation since Monday. Trying to get them to focus on Spanish verb conjugations had taken every bit of energy she possessed. She had never thought that her first year of teaching would be so exhausting or that she would have to spend so much time getting—and keeping—students on task. She had always thought that by high school students would be able to stay focused for longer than fifteen minutes.

Marisa straightened up her desk, packing up a big pile of papers to grade over the break. She stopped in the office to check her mailbox for any late papers before leaving. In her box, she found a sealed envelope with her name typed on it.

"What's this?" she wondered. School communications were rarely in sealed envelopes; in fact, they were rarely in envelopes at all. She opened the letter and began to scan the contents: "letter . . . contract . . . not be renewed . . ."

"What? That can't be," she thought to herself, in shock. She reread the letter, carefully scrutinizing every word this time, but the message was still the same: "This letter is to inform you that your contract will not be renewed at the end of this school year."

Marisa rushed into the principal's office, hoping to find her still there. "Ms. Wrainwright, do you have a minute?"

"Oh, hello, Ms. Borden. Looking forward to the break?"

"I was, until I got this." She waved the letter in the air.

"Yes, not the best day to deliver that. But it had to go out."

"I don't understand. All my evaluations have been favorable, haven't they? At least I thought they were."

"I'm sorry, Marisa. I don't have time to talk about it. And I *can't* really talk about it, either. You'll have to talk to the people at the superintendent's office."

Scenario

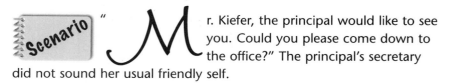

"Mr. Kiefer, the principal would like to see you. Could you please come down to the office?" The principal's secretary did not sound her usual friendly self.

"I'm trying to get a set of papers graded. Can it wait?" DeLayne Kiefer responded.

"No, he'd like to see you right now, during your prep period." Mr. Halliday, the principal, was new to the school, and he had quickly earned a reputation as not very approachable. In fact, DeLayne's few encounters with the principal had been less than pleasant experiences. He was a strictly-by-the-book administrator and seemed to allow for little, if any, leeway for students or teachers in any of the school policies. DeLayne was glad now that he had earned tenure last year rather than being up this year.

"I'm on my way down," DeLayne replied. Heading down to the office, he wondered why he had been summoned so urgently. "Has a student complained about something? Or maybe a parent?" he wondered.

"Come in, Mr. Kiefer. Sit down. Let me get right to the point. You were absent last Thursday at the mandatory professional development session."

"Yes, I told you I had a family emergency that I had to attend to. Do I need to give you a note?" DeLayne asked, half jokingly.

"Yes, so you said. But I heard from a reliable source that you did *not* in fact have a family emergency and had simply decided that you had better things to do than attend the professional development session. Not only did you violate your contractual obligation by failing to attend a mandatory session, but you also lied about your absence. I've already spoken to the superintendent, and your contract will not be renewed at the end of the school year."

"What? I don't know who your supposed 'reliable source' is, but I did have a family emergency."

"So you say. But I'm afraid you're not very credible. You should start looking for another teacher position for next year. That'll be all." DeLayne left the principal's office, his head swimming in utter disbelief. On his way back to his office, he met Alice Hurley, a veteran teacher at the school. In response to her casual greeting, DeLayne spewed out an account of the events of the last half hour.

"What did you say to him?" Alice asked.

"Nothing. I was in shock. I couldn't believe what I was hearing."

"You've got to see Alan, our union rep, right away. Interrupt him if he's in class. Halliday can't do this."

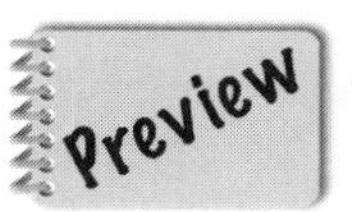


The events in these two scenarios are somewhat atypical, but such things do happen in today's schools. Like most organizations, schools are faced with hiring and firing personnel, laying people off, and dismissing employees whose job performance is less than satisfactory. And like most organizations, schools have to comply with legal regulations and respect their workers' constitutionally protected rights.

In this module, then, we want to acquaint you with the realities and the law related to the hiring and dismissal practices of public schools.

**Specifically, we focus on:**

- **A description of the hiring process, from interviews to the signing of a contract.**
- **The provisions of teaching contracts and what is meant by breach of a teaching contract.**
- **The nature of teacher tenure and its legal grounding.**
- **The conditions under which a teacher can be dismissed.**

## Now You Do It

Before you begin this module, reflect on what you already know about hiring and firing, and consider your opinions about the opening scenarios.

**QUESTIONS**

1. Can you recall being a student and hearing about a teacher being dismissed? What were the circumstances? Do you believe you got the "full story"?
2. If you were Marisa Borden, in Scenario One, what would you do?
3. If you were DeLayne Kiefer, in Scenario Two, what would you do?

# Hiring Practices

To be hired as a teacher, you will need to work with not only the authorities of the school where you will teach, but also those of the local school district, and your state. (See Module 19, School Governance and Funding, for more information on the role of authorities at all these levels.)

## State Licensure

If you plan to teach or are currently teaching in a public school setting, you will at some point have to be licensed to teach by your state educational agency. Some states do allow for short-term waivers for high-demand disciplines, such as math, science, foreign languages, and special education, but possessing a valid teaching license is generally a prerequisite for teaching in public schools throughout the country.

Requirements for licensure vary from state to state. The state educational agency, typically called the Department of Education, decides what skills and knowledge a person needs to teach and proposes regulations for licensure, which are then passed by the state legislature.

Every state, however, has an abiding interest in ensuring that its students receive a quality education. The federal No Child Left Behind (NCLB) legislation also requires that all teachers be "highly qualified," which means that a teacher has been licensed and has demonstrated a high level of competence in the subject(s) he or she teaches. For this reason, many states require prospective teachers to pass tests designed to assess the competencies and skills of beginning teachers. One popular set of tests is the Praxis series developed by Educational Testing Services (ETS). The Praxis I and II are written tests that measure the candidate's overall literacy (Praxis I) and content knowledge (Praxis II) of the discipline in which the candidate seeks licensure. Praxis III is a performance assessment that uses live classroom observations, portfolios, and teacher interviews as sources of information. Veteran teachers evaluate candidates on a set of nineteen criteria in four domains: planning to teach

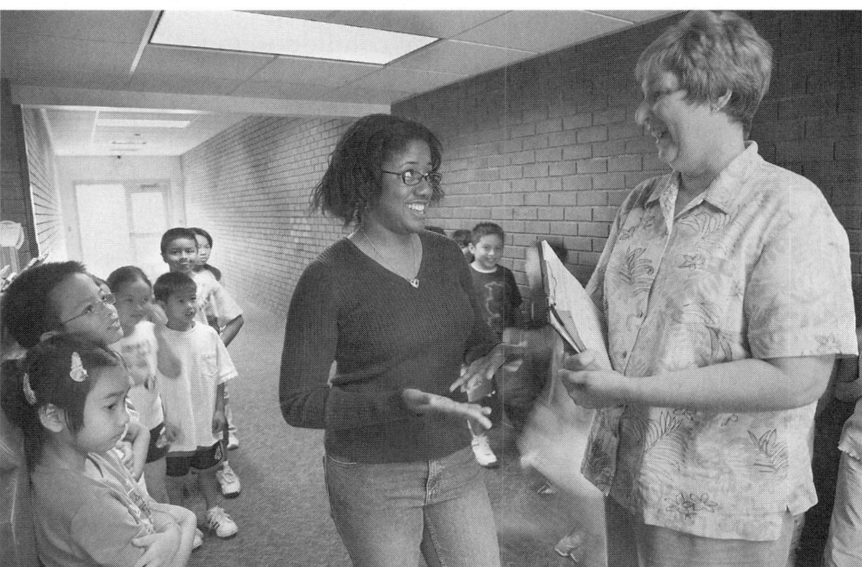

Before accepting a teaching contract, it is important to talk with the school's teachers.

(i.e., the quality of lesson planning), the classroom environment, instruction, and professional responsibilities.

## School District Hiring Processes

School systems are like most employers. When they are hiring a new teacher, they look for the person who, in their estimation, is the most qualified and whose philosophy of and approach to teaching best match those of the school system. In most school systems, the number of applicants far exceeds the available positions, so school administrators are usually able to be selective in their hiring practices. And, of course, certain disciplines, such as English, history, and the social sciences, tend to be far more competitive from the teacher's perspective than other disciplines, such as math, science, and foreign languages.

Typically, the hiring process begins when the school district determines its teaching needs for the following school year by analyzing information on enrollment, budget, and teaching vacancies. In periods of tight school budgets, districts will look for personnel who can serve the schools in a variety of positions. Therefore, candidates with multiple licenses tend to be very attractive.

After assessing its needs, the school district notifies the public of the anticipated vacancies and urges interested applicants to apply. Applicants are typically required to send in cover letters and résumés. Some districts ask for college transcripts and letters of recommendation at this point; others do not ask for them with the initial application. Even if the school district does not request letters of reference, it is always a good idea to include the names and contact information for several references.

The district personnel then select applicants to invite for interviews. For a particular job, you can expect to participate in one to three interviews. You may be interviewed by one person at a time or by a group of people; you may be asked to teach a class or to explain how you would teach a class. The interviews are as varied as the school districts, so when you are invited for an interview, try to get as much information as you can about the process the district uses. The "In Your Classroom" feature provides a few tips for interviewing.

The hiring process can take from a few weeks to a few months to complete, depending on the time of year. Many school districts like to begin the hiring process in April or May, before the end of the school year, so

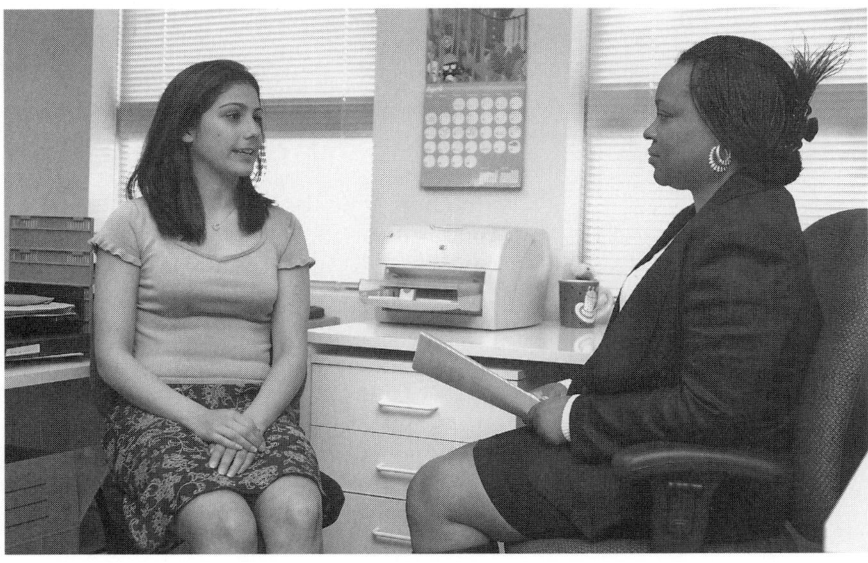

Interviews are an important part of the hiring process, so be sure you are prepared to get the most out of yours.

## In Your Classroom

### Preparing for Job Interviews

It is a grave mistake to underestimate the importance of a job interview. Even if you are convinced you are the ideal candidate for a particular teaching position, it is the opinion of the hiring agent that counts! Here are some interviewing pointers to consider:

- *Don't limit yourself to interviewing for "the perfect job."* Better to cast a wide net and get experienced and comfortable in the interview setting.
- *Role-play interviewing with a classmate or friend.* Prepare answers to likely questions, such as the following: What are your strengths as a teacher? What is your philosophy of teaching? What are your ideas about discipline and about classroom control? What can I tell you about our district (or our school)?
- *Find out as much as you can about the actual position, the school, and the district before the interview.* Use the Web. Don't be shy about asking knowledgeable acquaintances what they know about the job.
- *Dress appropriately.* If you are not sure what "appropriately" is, by all means, get advice!
- *Ask questions.* Be prepared not only to answer the interviewer's questions but also to pose questions of your own. Remember, you are not trying just to get any job; you want one that is a good "fit" with your skills and talents. Your good questions will impress the interviewer.

that returning teachers can participate in the process. Some districts find that returning teachers are more often available to participate if the district does most of its hiring in mid- to late June, once the school year has ended. It is also quite common to have a late hiring period in July or August to fill unexpected vacancies.

## Contracts

**Contract** a binding agreement between parties.

Once both you and the school district have determined that there is a good fit between you, a representative of the school district offers you a **contract.** At this point, legal rights and responsibilities come into play.

### Provisions of Teaching Contracts

Teaching contracts vary from district to district and from state to state. At a minimum, your contract will specify your teaching assignment, including maximum class size, and any other duties that you will be required to perform. It should also state your yearly salary and pay periods; your benefits, such as health insurance and sick leave; and the grievance procedures you should follow in case of conflicts related to the contract. If the contract is the result of collective bargaining, there is usually mention of the union as the recognizing and sole bargaining agent. In some "right to work" states, primarily in the South and West, collective bargaining by public employees is illegal. Teacher unions exist in these states, but they do not represent the teachers at a bargaining table.

Other conditions of employment may also be a part of your contract. In some states, certain conditions, such as regular updating of your teaching license, are dictated by state law. In some school districts, the faculty policy handbook may be considered contractually binding. For this to be the case, teachers must be made aware of the provisions within the handbook, and the provisions must be clear and specific. In other school districts, the faculty handbook carries a disclaimer that the policies within are not contractually binding. As with all contracts, be sure to read this one thoroughly and make sure you understand all its provisions before signing to indicate your acceptance.

## Breach of Contract

From a strict legal perspective, a contract is created once an offer with definite terms, such as salary and teaching assignment, is made and accepted. The contract may not be binding, however, until it is approved by the school board. Until the contract is binding, either the teacher or the school district can withdraw from the contract. For this reason, it is worthwhile to ask, *before* you sign, whether a contract has already been approved by the school board. Some school boards may give their agents (that is, principals or superintendents) blanket approval to offer contracts. Other school boards may devote part of a board meeting to approving contracts.

If you have a valid, binding contract, both parties are obliged to honor its terms. If either the school district or you renege on the contract, it is considered a **breach of contract,** and the offending party can be held liable for damages. The employer breaches the contract if it violates a provision of the contract or tries to change the terms of the contract after it is in effect. For example, if your contract specifies social studies as your teaching assignment, and a week before school starts, you are given two science classes, that could constitute a breach of contract. If you do not want to teach a subject that is outside your specific area of expertise, make sure your teaching assignment is explicitly stated on your contract.

**Breach of contract** a failure to fulfill the requirements of a legal agreement.

A teacher breaches a contract if he or she signs the contract and then refuses the position. If you have already signed a contract with one school district, you are legally bound to fulfill that contract. You cannot suddenly decide to return to school, accept a different job, or simply take a year off. If you do, you will be in breach of contract and can be sued by the school district.

## Duration of Contract

Your contract may have a fixed duration of one year. If you have such a fixed-term contract, then you need to receive a new contract every year. In some districts, all contracts are renewed yearly. In others, some teachers may be offered a "continuing contract" or **tenure.** With a continuing contract, you are automatically rehired for the following year unless the school district informs you by a specified date that your employment will not be renewed.

**Tenure** a legal right to permanent employment as a teacher, protecting that teacher from dismissal without adequate cause.

Tenure, the right to permanent employment, was instituted to protect teachers from arbitrary action by a principal, superintendent, or school board. Most public school systems in the United States still subscribe to the practice of granting tenure to their teachers after a fixed period of probationary service—usually, but not always, three years. In fact, tenure is part of the state regulations in a number of states, where school districts are required to grant teachers tenure after they successfully complete their probationary period.

During the probationary period, a teacher is hired on a year-to-year basis, and the school system has the option of not renewing a teacher's contract. Nothing obliges a school system to renew a teacher's contract, although in most cases the contract is renewed. The school district is also not required to give a reason when it declines to renew a contract of a teacher on probation.

In fact, as a result of various court rulings, school districts generally *avoid* giving any reasons for nonrenewal of contracts. This is what happened to Marisa Borden, the first-year teacher in Scenario One at the beginning of this module. When she queried her principal about the reason for her contract not being renewed, she received no explanation from Ms. Wainwright.

Once the probationary period is ended, the school system has to decide whether it wants to grant the teacher tenure. The decision is an important one for both teachers and the district, because once a teacher has been granted tenure, she or he is very likely to teach in the district until retirement or until he or she decides to leave. Tenure is also an important psychological milestone for teachers. Many feel that they can focus more fully on designing lessons that truly stimulate and enlighten students, rather than fearing political repercussions or striving excessively to please their supervisors. The job protection offered by tenure is not unlimited, however. Keep in mind these two important limitations:

1. *Tenure is granted only for service in a specific school district.* If a tenured teacher leaves that district to teach in another district, he or she loses tenure.
2. *Tenure does not guarantee exactly which job you will have.* Tenure guarantees employment within the district *only*. It does not guarantee that a teacher

## Now You Do It

Read the following scenarios and apply what you have learned in this module as you reflect on the questions that follow.

### Scenario One

*Imagine that you are offered a position teaching two classes of biology and three of chemistry at a high school in a lower-socioeconomic school district. You accept the position, mostly because you are anxious about having a job in the fall, not because you think the school is a particularly good fit for you.*

*Months later, in August, you get a call out of the blue from a different school system, about a position for which you had applied and were interviewed back in May. They did not make you an offer, but the person they did hire for the position had an unexpected change of plans and is moving out of state. You were the principal's second choice, you are told, and because his first choice backed out, he is offering the position to you.*

*You would love to teach in that school district! The high school is exactly the kind of school where you see yourself teaching most happily. The position would be all biology, which is what you really want to teach. And you would earn about $3,000 more there.*

#### QUESTIONS

1. What would you do and why?
2. Is your chosen action legal? Why or why not?
3. Is your choice ethical? Why or why not?

### Scenario Two

*"Thank you for coming to see me on such short notice, Mr. Grey. As you are surely aware, we have been looking at some ideas for restructuring and reorganizing the middle school and high school. After much debate and discussion, the school board and the school administration have decided to move you to the middle school and—"*

*"What? To the middle school? I don't think so. I didn't request a transfer to the middle school. I've been teaching at the high school for six years, and I'm tenured. You have no right to transfer me against my wishes."*

*"Actually, we can," replies the principal. "And if you refuse the transfer, I'm afraid you will not have a teaching position in this district next year."*

#### QUESTIONS

1. Does tenure allow Mr. Grey to refuse the transfer to the middle school?
2. What would you do in this situation? Would your decision be legal?

will always have the same teaching assignment at the same school in the same classroom under the same conditions. Teachers can be transferred to another school within the district or can be asked to teach other classes, as long as they are qualified to do so and no additional training is required.

## Termination of Service

As we have noted, nontenured teachers usually do not have the right to continued employment. The situation is different for tenured teachers. They are protected by the due process clauses of the Fifth and Fourteenth Amendments to the U.S. Constitution, which protect citizens' rights to life, liberty, and property. With tenure, there is an expectation of continued employment, which the courts have defined as a property right. Tenured teachers also have an expectation of good standing within a community, which the courts have defined as a liberty right. Any action that threatens an individual's liberty or property rights must follow the procedures of **due process.**

**Due process** the deliberative process that protects a person's constitutional right to fair and equal protection under the law.

There are two kinds of due process:

- *Procedural due process* is related to how the laws are applied. Broadly defined, procedural due process guarantees to all individuals the right to a fair and public trial with an impartial jury, the right to be present at the trial, and the right to be heard in their own defense.
- *Substantive due process* looks at the substance of a law to see whether, for example, the law in any way limits an individual's constitutional rights. Substantive due process ensures that laws are clear and explicit in terms of what is and what is not permissible and the consequences of violating the law.

In labor law, due process is usually evoked when doubts are raised about the fairness or the fair implementation of an organization's hiring and dismissal policies and procedures. Schools are required to protect tenured teachers' due process rights in any action that could potentially lead to loss of employment or dismissal. Thus, tenured teachers can be dismissed only under certain circumstances: violations of their contracts, incompetence, or pressing financial needs of the school district.

### Dismissal for Cause

For tenured teachers to be **dismissed for cause,** they have to have violated contractual obligations related to their teaching responsibilities.

**Dismissal for cause** the removal of an individual from a paid position on the grounds of her or his having broken a contractual obligation or failed to meet commitments.

The actual grounds for dismissal vary from district to district and from state to state, but generally they must be job related and must be explicitly stated in state laws, district policies, and/or faculty policy documents. Common grounds for dismissal include (but are not limited to) insubordination, incompetence, immorality, incapacity, inefficiency, and conduct unbecoming a teacher. The courts have usually held that the cause for dismissal cannot be based on a teacher's private life. In recent years, dismissals for cause based on a teacher's private life have been overturned by the courts unless the teachers have engaged in actions and behaviors in public that constitute conduct unbecoming to a teacher by compromising the integrity of the individual or school district.

The procedure for dismissing a tenured teacher for cause is often spelled out in state laws and, as we have seen, must respect due process. This means that, among other requirements, the employer must present a clear statement of the charges, as well as evidence to support the charges. In turn, employees must have the opportunity to present evidence before an impartial authority to defend themselves against the charges. The second scenario at the beginning of this module presents a situation in which an employee's procedural due process rights were violated. DeLayne Kiefer was accused of violating his contractual obligations but was not given the opportunity to defend himself against these charges. The principal, as an agent of the school system, had an obligation to present to DeLayne the charges against him, to set up a hearing with an impartial arbiter, and to allow DeLayne to defend himself. Ms. Hurley's advice—that DeLayne should talk to his union representative—is more than appropriate in this situation.

## Dismissal Due to Deficiencies

The primary responsibility of teachers is to educate their students to the best of their ability. School administrators generally try, during a teacher's probationary period, to determine that teacher's competence. Despite this process, however, tenured teachers are sometimes found to be incompetent in fulfilling their responsibilities.

An incompetent teacher is one who lacks the knowledge or skills needed to perform professional duties adequately. Evidence of incompetence must be convincing. A bad day or two in the classroom is not sufficient to show incompetence. Failure to maintain classroom discipline is often accepted as evidence of teacher incompetence, with the courts maintaining that a teacher cannot teach effectively in a chaotic classroom. Still, an out-of-control classroom alone is not enough evidence to show teacher incompetence. Administrators must provide ample evidence to show that a teacher is not fulfilling his or her professional obligations and that students are not learning.

Courts have tended to view incompetence as a *remediable* problem, one that can be fixed. They require school administrators to design and implement an action plan to help the teacher develop the requisite teaching knowledge. If, after every effort has been made to help the tenured teacher (a process that may take one or two years), there is still evidence of incompetence, the school district can then attempt to dismiss the teacher. In all likelihood, however, the teacher will challenge the dismissal.

## Reduction in Force

**Reduction in force (RIF)** the elimination of teaching positions in a school system because of declining student population or funding.

**Reduction in force** (or RIF-ing, as it has come to be known) happens during periods of economic slowdown when the budgets of school districts do not fully cover all the expenses. In such instances, school districts have to find creative ways with limited resources of providing an appropriate education to all students. Schools may decide to eliminate entire programs—such

### Now You Do It

Consider carefully the following scenarios. For each, decide whether you think the dismissal would be upheld in state or federal courts, and why or why not.

**Scenario One**

*"Ms. Murphy, we need to talk about your students. This is the third year in a row that a majority of your students have failed to pass the*

*state standards assessment. Their performance is affecting the school's rating. Last year, we talked about changes you were going to make in the classroom to help more students pass the test."*

*"Yes, we did, and I carried out the plan to the letter. We did sixty minutes a day of test preparation. The students wrote essays nearly every day. But, as I told you when you came to observe me, this is one of the weakest classes I've ever taught. They've made good progress, but they are still far behind where they need to be."*

*"Well, we all have that challenge. Unfortunately, your students performed the worst of all the classes. The superintendent is quite upset, and the district is being threatened with state receivership unless the scores rise. He is looking for some real changes in the teaching staff, starting with bringing in some new blood. I'm afraid you will be let go at the end of the school year."*

*"But I'm tenured! You can't let me go!"*

*"Apparently the superintendent seems to think otherwise."*

QUESTION

1. Can Ms. Murphy be dismissed because her students perform poorly on the state-mandated test?

### Scenario Two

*"Ms. Smythe, it has come to my attention that you have a second job," Ms. Finkelstein, the principal, states.*

*"Yes. I do. But I don't see how that is anyone's business but mine."*

*"Normally, I'd agree. But unfortunately, a parent of one of our students saw you at your other job and reported it to the superintendent. She does not think that working in a strip club is appropriate for—"*

*"It's not a strip club; it's a cabaret."*

*"It doesn't really matter. The superintendent has told me to tell you that if you want to keep your job in the district, you'll have to quit the other job."*

*"You can't do that. I have tenure. All of my evaluations have been excellent. You yourself have praised my teaching many times. You can't fire me for waitressing a few nights a week."*

*"Do you serve drinks and wear a very short shirt at your cabaret job?"*

*"Yes, but what does that have to do with my teaching?"*

QUESTION

1. Can Ms. Smythe be dismissed if she refuses to quit her second job as a cabaret waitress?

### Scenario Three

*A large school district with four middle schools and two high schools is facing severe budgetary difficulties. After many long and difficult sessions, the superintendent and school committee have finally decided that they will increase class size and consolidate some classes. Two English positions will be eliminated at the high school level. Because of growing enrollments at the middle school, no positions will be eliminated there.*

*You are in your fourth year of teaching English at the middle school and recently have been given tenure. Although you feel bad about the high school teachers, most of whom are at least ten-year veterans of the school district, you were relieved to hear that no positions would be cut at the middle school.*

*A few days later, you find a letter in your mailbox. Much to your surprise and chagrin, you are informed that you have been "riffed" as the "last hired" English teacher. At lunch, you go to see the union rep to find out why you got this letter.*

*"Oh, you got it. I meant to give you a heads up, but I've been so busy with all the riffing. Besides, I figured you'd be expecting it since you were the last English teacher hired in the district."*

*"But I teach at the middle school. The layoffs are at the high school! Why am I being let go?"*

*"Three of the English teachers at the high school are also licensed to teach middle school. And they have been in the district longer than you have. You and one teacher at South High, who was the second-to-last hired, will be laid off. Sorry about that, but we didn't have any choice."*

QUESTION

1. Is the school district right to choose you as the English teacher who must be laid off?

as certain sports programs, courses in the arts, physical education, or foreign languages—in order to reallocate necessary resources to core content areas. (If you have ever seen the movie *Mr. Holland's Opus*, you may remember that "riffing" of the arts programs was a central theme.) Some schools may decide to increase class size to consolidate classes and eliminate teaching positions.

When positions are eliminated, the teacher in that position does not necessarily lose his or her job. On the contrary, a reduction in the teaching force is most often subject to seniority rights, guaranteeing that teachers with the most seniority will preserve their jobs within the district. Those who are let go first are those with the least seniority, the fewest years of service. The teachers who are kept may be shifted from one school to another or reassigned to a different grade level or subject area, if appropriate.

We strongly recommend that when you begin your job search, you research the school districts you are considering. Once you have been offered a contract, you want to be certain that the position is one that you want. Don't immediately jump at a job. Try to talk with other teachers in the district—ideally, teachers from the school where you are slated to teach. Work hard to find out all you can about the work environment, the fit between your teaching philosophy and the school's, the benefits available, and teacher longevity within the district. Teacher longevity may suggest that teachers find the district a good employer and hence have not looked for other teaching positions.

In addition, work to understand fully the contractual obligations and professional duties of the position. Once you accept a position, talk to your new colleagues, your immediate supervisor, and your mentor to inform yourself of all job expectations, particularly in terms of nonclassroom obligations. During your first few years of teaching, be especially careful to ensure that you understand and meet all of the district expectations.

## Further Resources

- *Deskbook Encyclopedia of American School Law* (Rosemont, MN: Data Research, annually). This excellent annual reference book is an easily accessible source on the current law and legal issues surrounding all aspects of public and private education.

- Louis Fischer, David Schimmel, and Cynthia Kelly, *Teachers and the Law,* 6th ed. (New York: Longman, 2002). This book, written by scholars who are both lawyers and professors of education, bridges the world of the courts and the work of the teacher with realism and clarity.

- *Job Search Handbook for Educators.* Available at: **www.ipfw.edu/adlc/JobSearchHandbook.PDF.** Published online by the Advising and Licensing Center of Indiana University-Purdue University of Fort Wayne, this handbook is an outstanding resource, offering practical information on writing résumés, searching for jobs, and getting useful interview tips.

- Teachers-Teachers.com. Available at: **www.teachers-teachers.com.** This is a free service designed to help educators find new and varied teaching jobs. Through Teachers-Teachers.com you can view job postings from 2,100 school systems and private schools nationwide.

- Perry Zirkel, "De Jure" column in *Phi Delta Kappan* (Bloomington, IN: Phi Beta Kappa International). This regularly published column reports on important issues of school law and provides an excellent way to follow recent developments.

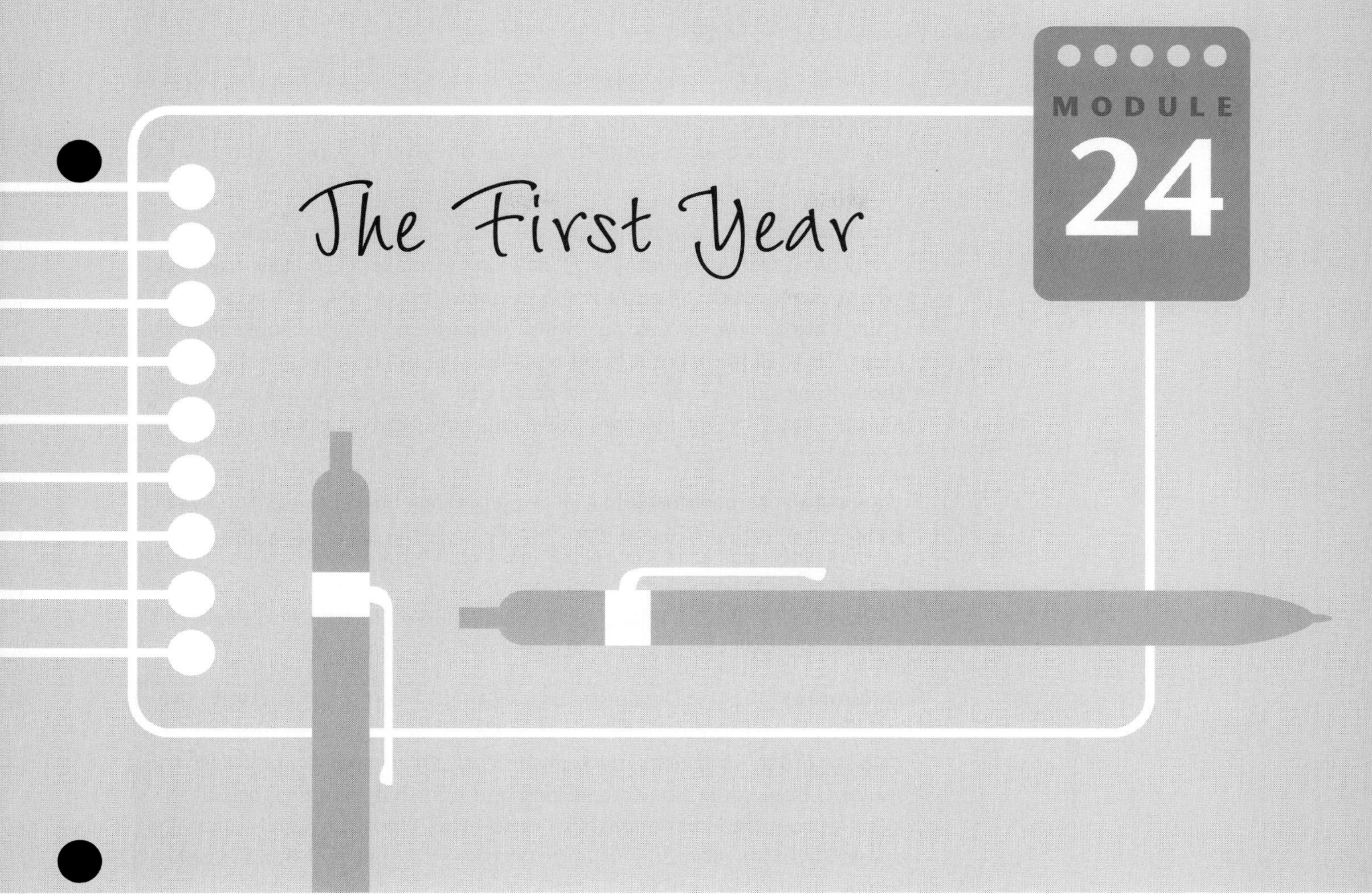


Scenario

**September 1.** Whew, spent most of last week setting up the classroom. Now I'm ready to meet the kids and their parents tomorrow. I'm so excited! I'm so nervous!!

**September 22.** Wow, all that time I spent over the summer planning lessons seems to be paying off. I think I might be a pretty good teacher!

**October 11.** What a drag today was! Well, everybody's got to have one lesson that doesn't work out. I'll spend this weekend planning some new things for next week.

**October 27.** Will I ever have a good night's sleep again? I'm so worried about the first-term grading. Darrel, the custodian, made me leave AGAIN today because he had to lock up the building. And it's going to take me until midnight to get through just today's stack. Then, I've got to plan next week's lessons. Sure wish there was a magic "extra time" fairy I could call!

**November 19.** Well, I guess the "honeymoon" is over with the students. Classroom rules seem to have been totally forgotten, and discipline has all but disappeared! Maybe it's not too late to become a stockbroker, like cousin Dale. Or—wait—a travel agent, like my friend Tammy. Yeah, that's it . . . "scouting" trips to sunny islands, civilized conversations with other adults. . . .

**November 20.** I just DREAD going to school tomorrow morning. Thank heavens there are only two more days until Thanksgiving break!!

**November 27.** Wow, the break really helped. I hope the smile I plastered on at the family reunion didn't look too fake. I felt like such a liar whenever anybody asked how it was going, and I said, "It's good. Things are . . . moving along." But it was sure nice to see some friendly faces. They all think I'm a good teacher, at least. The sleep really helped, too! I think now I know what to do to get the students back on the learning track—I'm sure I was just too tired to come up with a strategy before.

**December 4.** Surprising how glad I was to see the kids again—even though half of them are sniffling from colds. The new management strategy seems to be working.

**December 9.** Rotten little germ spewers! Now I'm sick! And worse yet, they won't even listen to me. Again!

**December 17.** The December break canNOT come fast enough!!! My students have mutated into fearless beasts that respond to nothing—no calls for order, no threats, no punishments. Or maybe it's me who's the mutant. How could I be threatening and punishing these poor kids! Who lets people like me teach?? I'm so tired, I'm not even emotionally stable anymore—forget alert and competent! I'm lucky I don't dissolve in tears before lunch!!

**December 20.** We must all really need this break. The kids somehow became human again today—probably the prospect of being away from me and being safe with their families again. But they were so sweet, bringing me cards and saying "Happy Holidays!" Eileen and Harry even brought surprise gifts. Eileen and Harry, out of all of them! The two who are my biggest challenges—wow! Well, Happy Holidays, indeed, if it means two weeks of rest!! Well, relative rest—only six more months of lessons to plan.

**January 4.** Sleep is SO wonderful!!! I think I've rested up enough to make it through the next six months. After that, I am definitely looking for a new job. Maybe I'll ask Tammy about what it takes to be a travel agent.

**January 8.** My students (yes, *my* students—I'm still surprised to hear myself say that) were so excited to share stories about their vacations that I was surprised how easy it was to get them settled back to work. Are these the same kids I had before the break?

**January 24.** The students still haven't reverted to the "December doldrums." They're still tons easier to manage and more attentive. Lessons go so much more smoothly when they behave! Now, I just wish I knew: am I learning how to work with them, or are they just growing up or something?

**February 20.** FINALLY, I've figured out a system for keeping track of homework.

**March 9.** Today went SO well!! I think I've finally found some activities that genuinely interest these students. And almost nobody interrupted me today!

**April 12.** I've started getting home before dark!! Of course, it stays lighter longer now, too, but still. And I had an hour left before bedtime tonight after I finished grading. Oh, the excitement of being able to watch the evening news.

**April 29.** Spring break was a blast! Great reunion with Neil, Maria, and Lili from college. And my horror stories about teaching were nothing next to some of theirs! But strange how similar the first year has gone for all of us. Maybe I should stop taking this all so *personally*.

**May 17.** Today, the principal oh-so-casually asked if I would be the faculty sponsor for the students' Thanksgiving Charity Drive, a big deal in this community. I was a little stunned, although not so much about the Charity Drive. Finally, I managed to mumble, "This means I'm coming back next year then?"

"Oh, sure!" she chirped, like I should never have doubted. "The contracts will be coming from the district office any day now."

But do I WANT to come back?

**May 20.** Still pondering whether to keep doing this. The more I think about it, the more I realize how much I've learned. And I've definitely already put in a TON of work!! All the other teachers say it gets easier after the first year. And the way Tammy complains about those infantile clients at the travel agency—they sound like they're even worse than actual children!

**May 27.** The contract came in the mail today. I signed it quickly, before I could think too much, and sent it right off. Guess I'll be back.

**June 7.** Boy, the end of the year sure seemed to come fast! After we emptied all the desks and lockers and bulletin boards this week, the room looked positively naked. I don't remember it looking so bare last summer. Ah, summer . . . I can hardly wait to get away to the lake house with those two other teachers—what great friends they've turned out to be! I just have to get everything packed away for September. . . .

One of the authors of this text wrote a book, entitled *The Roller Coaster Year*, about the experiences of first-year teachers.[1] The title is an especially apt one. For most new teachers, like the author of the fictional journal above, the first year of teaching is like a roller-coaster ride with very high highs and very low lows. Sometimes the transition from a high to a low is as frightening and fast as the roller-coaster car plummeting down a hill and whipping around a curve.

A new teacher's highs and lows may come at different times during the course of the year and will last for varying periods of time, but we can almost guarantee that every beginner will experience them. Some decide that the highs are not enough to make up for the lows and eventually opt for a different profession. Others become resolutely convinced, perhaps even more than before, of the goodness of fit between themselves and a career in teaching. Still others remain uncertain about their future in the classroom but decide to continue teaching for another year or two.

Whatever your decision at the end of your first year of teaching, we urge you to keep in mind the fact that the first year of teaching is, indeed, special. Most teachers report that it was by far their most trying and most difficult year of teaching. Thus, as you weigh the highs and the lows in an effort to decide what to do, remember that your first year of experience is a poor standard on which to base a career choice.

**This module emphasizes that:**

- **First-year teachers tend to experience some unexpected feelings and reactions.**
- **There are some common "stages" to a teacher's initial year, and a body of practical advice and specific suggestions exists to guide new teachers through their initial year.**
- **There are specific sources of support and help that new teachers should seek out.**

## Now You Do It

As you reflect on the opening journal entries, consider your answers to the following questions.

1. Can you recall having had a brand-new teacher? How could you tell? What made his or her status as a new teacher unmistakable? Did you and your fellow students behave differently toward the new teacher?
2. As you contemplate your first year of teaching, what highs and lows do you anticipate? What can you do now to keep your potential "lows" from causing you real trouble?

# Overcoming Initial Disorientation

Nearly all of us spend on average thirteen years in elementary and secondary schools, but we spend them as *students*. Shifting your perspective to that of a teacher can be complicated, and one of the major stumbling blocks to that shift can be your student perspective itself. You may have known schools so well as a student that you do not realize how different they will be when you take on the role of teacher. Many teachers assume their experiences will be an extension or continuation of their student experiences, which, for the large majority of teachers, were overwhelmingly positive. As a

The beginning months of teaching can often be tiring and demanding.

result, it is not uncommon for new teachers, excited and energized at the start of their first school year, to experience many unexpected and even unpleasant feelings as they begin their teaching careers. Three of the most jarring are culture shock, physical exhaustion, and social isolation.

## Culture Shock

**Culture shock** the feeling of disorientation initially experienced when one is immersed in a society with different values, customs, and mores.

One of the most unexpected and unpleasant feelings new teachers encounter is **culture shock.** Just as travelers experience culture shock when visiting a foreign country, new teachers often feel that same disquieting sense of being in a familiar, yet "foreign," culture. You have been here before; in fact, at one time you were a "native," fully fluent in the culture. But now you find yourself on the outside, unable to crack that invisible barrier blocking you from full participation in this seemingly familiar culture. You think you "speak the language" but soon discover that when you speak, the "natives" do not seem to understand you in the way you expect them to. And although you understand the principal activities of this culture, you are unable to join in them fully, at least not in the way the natives do. Your frustration and confusion may be tremendous. And all of this is particularly true if the school you are teaching in differs in size, composition of the student body, and other characteristics from the ones you attended as a student.

However, all is not lost! Following the tips of experienced travelers, the first step in overcoming culture shock is to realize that you are in a foreign culture with different norms, values, and beliefs. You now officially belong to the teacher culture, whereas your previous "cultural" knowledge of schools was of the student culture. Think of it as going to Italy after having lived in Spain for many years. You hear the language and it sounds eerily close to Spanish, and yet when you try to speak in what you think is a recognizable language, you are met with unresponsive stares. You are no longer part of the student culture but are not yet part of the teacher culture.

Once you make that distinction, you can begin to identify the differences between the two cultures and use that information to your advantage. To carry on our example, in Italy you would study Italian, trying to learn some key words and phrases quickly, even though you might still think "in Spanish." In the school setting, that means you want to think like a student but act like a teacher. Make use of your extensive knowledge of your old culture to help you be more effective in your new culture, in these and other areas:

- *Lessons.* When designing or planning a given lesson, think about what lessons interested or bored you as a student. What activities did you and your classmates enjoy? Then revert to your teacher role and think of how you can design the lesson to make it interesting for your students. Think also about those lessons or activities that created the most mayhem in the classroom, and carefully avoid them.
- *Management.* When dealing with a disruptive student, refer to your student cultural knowledge to recall what consequences had the most and the least impact on you or your friends. Did assigning detention or sending a student to the principal or dean of students help to eliminate negative behaviors? If not, what did? Use this information in your teacher role to help you decide on appropriate consequences.
- *Reputation.* Although you find it useful to think like a student in many cases, you should definitely avoid trying to speak like a student! One of the most important challenges facing a new teacher is to find the appropriate **social distance** between him or her and students. Your language is key to establishing you as an authority figure, and this is one area where you cannot switch back and forth between the student culture and the teacher culture.

**Social distance** the psychological relationship between individuals, ranging from the familiar to the formal.

## Physical Exhaustion

Teaching is a high-energy endeavor, and we stress *high*. When the students are in the classroom, the teacher is busy maintaining the flow of the lesson. When students are not in the classroom, the teacher is busy getting ready for the next time they are there, as well as taking care of administrative details and trying to maintain contacts with parents, administrators, and colleagues. The demands on your energy reserves, both physical and intellectual, are enormous.

Expect to be *very* tired in your first weeks and months of teaching. Physical exhaustion is especially acute for teachers in the elementary grades, although teachers at the middle school and secondary school levels also experience intense fatigue. We have heard many stories of student teachers or first-year teachers getting home from school in the late afternoon and deciding to lie down for "just a minute," only to wake up the next morning!

Like professional athletes, teachers may need an initial training period to get "in shape" for their work. To help you cope with the fatigue, be good to yourself. Go to bed early, take vitamins, and exercise when you can. All of these habits will give you greater energy and more stamina, which we guarantee you will need. And expect your favorite Friday night activity to be "vegging out" on your couch.

## Social Isolation

A third feeling that is common among new teachers is social isolation. Normal social interaction is a luxury that few teachers are able to enjoy during the school day. They spend most of their day apart from peers, working with people who are not yet adults. In addition, as we noted in Module 13, Communication in the Classroom, verbal interactions in the classroom do not adhere to typical conversational patterns. They tend to be characterized by a one-way flow of information from the teacher to students, or a teacher-question/student-answer pattern in which the teacher already knows the answers to the questions.

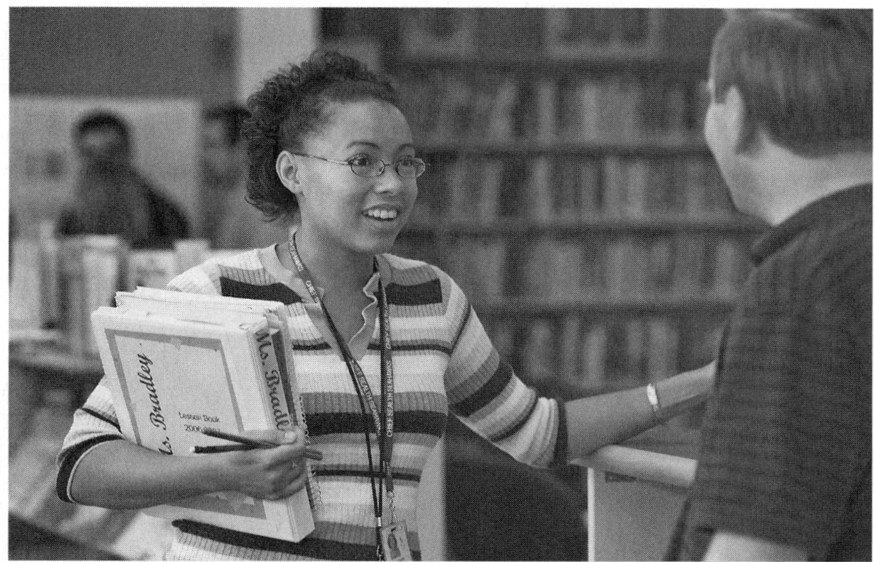

Your first years of teaching will be more satisfying if you take advantage of every available opportunity to enjoy the company of your colleagues.

As we noted in Module 18, Working with Colleagues, most teachers also have few opportunities to engage in conversation with their coworkers. Leisurely discussions about weekend events, popular movies, or the latest reality show on TV are often supplanted by harried exchanges about incidents in the classroom, problematic students, or challenging parent conferences. On those limited occasions when teachers do actually find time to converse with other adults, such as during lunch in the teachers' room, the topics too frequently revolve around incidents in the classroom or problems with administrators or parents. The "In Your Classroom" feature offers some tips for reducing, if not entirely overcoming, the isolation that can plague you as a new teacher.

## In Your Classroom

### Reducing Social Isolation

Knowing the limitations of the classroom, we make two suggestions to help reduce in small ways the social isolation you may feel.

1. *Take the time to engage your students in chitchat.* Even young children can engage in social conversation, and these short interludes may help you feel less isolated in the classroom. Ask your students about community events, about their extracurricular activities or interests, and about what they did or are going to do on the weekend. Share with them selected (and we stress *selected*) interests and events in your life to allow for some normal conversation.
2. *Relish adult company whenever possible.* Have conversations with your colleagues about non-school-related topics. Find out about their families and weekend activities. Discuss current events, be they sports events, political happenings, or the latest movie or novel. Of course, you will also want to take advantage of your senior colleagues' wealth of experience, which can be a priceless source of advice and support during the first year or two, and you may even need to bend an ear once in a while to vent periodic frustrations. But we strongly encourage you to make a conscious effort to engage your colleagues in conversations *unrelated to work* to help reduce social isolation.

# How to Prepare for Your First Year

Careful planning and organization are critical to a productive first year. To get you started, we offer the following series of checklists. Each checklist suggests key questions you should ask yourself.

## Before School Begins

Table 24.1 lists a number of decisions you should make and tasks you should accomplish before the school year begins. Be sure to add any further items that apply to your own situation.

**TABLE 24.1 What to Do Before the School Year Begins**

**Classroom Set-up**

Make sure you have enough desks for all the students.
- At the secondary level, what will be your largest group?
- At the elementary level, will you have additional students coming into your classroom at any time?

Arrange the desks in the classroom.
- Will you place them in rows? In clusters? In semicircles?

Decide how you will use the available classroom space.
- Will you have a classroom library area?
- At the elementary level, will you have a meeting area? Centers?
- At the secondary level, will you have areas for different activities?
- Where will you place your classroom computers? What rules will you have for their use?

Decorate the classroom.
- How will you use the bulletin board(s)? What will you put on the board(s) for the first days of school?
- Will you make use of the inside/outside wall areas? If so, how?

Post key information in your classroom.
- Where in the classroom will your name be posted?
- Where will your students' names be posted?
- How will students know where their desks are?
- Will classroom rules be posted? If so, where?
- Where will you post fire emergency information?
- Will you post a daily schedule? If so, where?
- What other information will you post in conspicuous places in the classroom? Where will this information be placed?

### Classroom Supplies

Place consumable supplies (e.g., writing paper, construction paper, pencils, facial tissue).

- What consumable supplies will you have in your classroom?
- Where will you place consumable classroom supplies?
- Will you label the location/placement of consumable supplies?
- Will students have unlimited access to the supplies or will they need your permission to use them?
- How will students dispose of consumables, especially excess paper? (Will there be a recycling bin? For what kind of paper?)

---

Place nonconsumable supplies (e.g., scissors, staplers, three-hole punch, paper cutter, calculators, markers).

- What nonconsumable supplies will you have in your classroom?
- Where will you place nonconsumable classroom supplies?
- Will students have unlimited or permission-only access to the supplies?
- Will you label the location/placement of nonconsumables?

---

Decide on use and placement of instructional materials (textbooks and supplemental curriculum materials, class library books).

- What are the school or department policies regarding distribution of instructional materials?
- Will students be given textbooks and be expected to be responsible for them, or will texts remain in the classroom, to be distributed to students when needed and collected afterward?
- If classroom sets of reading books are used, will students be held responsible for the books, or will the books remain in the classroom?
- Will students have access to supplemental materials?
- If you have a classroom library, will students be able to take books home? If so, how will you keep track of these books?

---

### Classroom Procedures

(See Module 8, Establishing the Classroom Environment, and Module 9, Maintaining the Classroom Environment.)

---

Decide on homework flow.

- How will homework be communicated to students? Daily notices on the blackboard or homework board for students to copy? Daily, weekly, or monthly homework assignment sheets? Class website?
- Will homework assignments be communicated to parents?
- How will homework be collected? Who will be responsible, you or your students?
- Where will homework be collected? Will you have a central location, or will you personally collect each day?
- How often will homework be collected? Every day? Once a week? Whenever specified when assigned?
- How will homework be returned to students? Who will be responsible for returning homework, you or your students?
- How often will homework be returned? Every day? Once a week? As soon as graded?
- How will students who are absent find out about homework assignments?
- How much time will absent students be given to do missed homework assignments?
- How will homework be graded? How much weight will it have in determining students' grades for the marking period?

---

Decide on class work flow.

- How will completed classwork be collected? Who will be responsible, you or your students?
- Where will classwork be collected? Will you have a central location for students to place their completed class work, or will you collect each day? If you teach more than one group of students (upper elementary or secondary), will there be a separate location for each group of students?

---

*Continued* ▶

▶ *Table 24.1 continued*

- How will work-in-progress be handled? Will students be responsible for work-in-progress, or will students have individual folders, or will you establish a central location for all students' work-in-progress?
- How will classwork be returned to students? Who will be responsible for returning classwork, you or your students?
- How often will classwork be returned? Every day? Once a week? At the end of the grading period? As soon as graded?
- Will classwork be graded? How much weight will it have in determining students' grades for the marking period?
- If you do not have your own classroom, how will you manage classwork?

Think about class rules.

- Who will decide on class rules: you alone, the students, or both you and the students?
- When will the rules be decided?
- Where will you place the class rules within the classroom?
- Will students have individual copies of the class rules?

Establish classroom jobs.

- Will you assign classroom jobs or let students volunteer?
- How will you assign these jobs or pick from those who volunteer?
- How often will you change job assignments?
- Will these jobs be seen as privileges or responsibilities?
- Will there be any consequences for students who do not carry out their jobs?

Decide on class schedule (elementary).[i]

- What will your daily schedule look like? When will you schedule learning in the core curriculum areas?
- How much time per week will you devote to the core curriculum areas? To other curriculum areas?
- What other instructional activities will you include in the weekly schedule?

Establish a process for communication between home and school. (See Module 17, Working with Your Students' Families.)

**Instructional Planning**

(See Module 11, Planning Lessons, and Module 12, How to Teach.)

Become familiar with the school or district curriculum and the state standards for your discipline area.

Determine school and department policies for sharing available resources (class sets of books, videos) or scheduling of tests, exams, and papers.

Get copies of the instructional materials you will be using, especially the teachers' editions.

Plan thoroughly (in explicit detail, including approximate times) for at least the first month, and for the first two months if possible.

- What instructional activities will you implement?
- What instructional support (handouts, websites, etc.) will you use in the instructional activities?

[i]You may have little flexibility in deciding the daily or weekly schedule. Some schools or school districts impose common times for core curriculum subjects, in particular, math and reading.

Make sufficient copies of the handouts you will use during the first month.

Decide on a grading policy for each class (secondary) or discipline (elementary) you teach. (See Module 16, Tools for Assessment.)

- How much will tests and quizzes count?
- How many papers or projects will you have students do over the course of a grading period? How much weight will these have?
- How much weight will homework and classwork have?

**Get to Know Your School**

Introduce yourself to the school staff, the administrative assistants, and the custodial staff.

Find out about school supplies.

- What supplies are available to you? In what quantities?
- How do you order school supplies? Of whom do you make requests?
- Do teachers have a budget for ordering supplies? If so, how much does each teacher have? By when must the supplies be ordered?

Find out about classroom maintenance and accessibility.

- Who is responsible for cleaning your classroom?
- How often will it be cleaned? Exactly what will and what will not be cleaned in the classroom?
- What is the procedure (if there is one) for accessing your classroom during nonschool hours?

Read thoroughly the school handbook to become familiar with the school rules and policies.

Read thoroughly the faculty handbook to be aware of your rights and responsibilities.

Read the local paper, the school paper (if there is one), and/or the school yearbook to find out about local traditions, events, and sports teams.

Introduce yourself to colleagues in your discipline or grade level. Set up times to meet with your colleagues to find out about curricular and behavioral expectations.

Find out about common practices in the teacher's room.

- Is there a coffee maker? If so, how does coffee making "work?"
- Is there a common refrigerator for teacher lunches? How "safe" is the refrigerator? (Do lunches often mysteriously disappear?)
- Is there a common fund for snacks, coffee, birthday cards, and so on?

**Get to Know Your Students**

(Review Modules 2 through 5.)

Memorize your students' names, first and last. Doing so makes it much easier to match names with faces after you finally meet the students.

Find out salient information about your students.

- Which students, if any, are on IEPs? Ask for copies of the IEPs to read through. Get in touch with the special education department to find out what services will be given to your students.
- Which students, if any, have family histories of which you need to be aware?
- Which students, if any, have other situations of which you should be aware?

Continued 

▶ *Table 24.1 continued*

Decide on a seating arrangement for your students. If possible, show your arrangement to a colleague who has taught your students in the past.

Send a greeting or letter of introduction to your students (and their parents).

**Personal Preparation**

Look at yourself in the mirror and call yourself Ms. or Mr.—to start getting used to your new role.

Map out your driving route to work. Time how long it takes you to get to work, and double that time. (Once school starts, the traffic will be heavier than it is in the summer months.)

Invest in clothing that looks professional but is also practical and not overly expensive. Between chalk, pens, and students' hands (particularly if you teach in the lower grades), your clothes may take quite a beating.

Develop your teacher voice. Practice giving commands in a serious yet gentle manner. Make sure your voice drops at the end of sentences. (Review Module 13, Communication in the Classroom.)

Learn to project your voice without shouting. You need to be heard by twenty or more students, but you do not want to lose your voice or sound angry doing it. (Review Module 13, Communication in the Classroom.)

## The First Day(s) of School

We cannot overstate the importance of the first few days of school. First impressions may not last forever, but they do linger for a long time and can often set the tone for the rest of the school year. Our best advice is to be overly organized. Better to have too much planned than not enough. It's important that you convey to students that even though they may know you are new, at least to the school, you know what you are doing and you are in charge. We have witnessed a few unfortunate new teachers who were not fully prepared for that first day, and it has not been a pretty sight. Again, we have drawn up another checklist to help you. Be sure to customize it by adding items that are important to your particular situation.

## The First Months of School

Just as there is much for your students to learn about you and your classroom routines and procedures, there is much for you to learn about school practices and procedures. Expect that it will take some time for both you and your students to feel comfortable in your new environment. Encourage your students to ask questions if they are uncertain about something, just as you should ask questions of colleagues or other school personnel when you are uncertain about a practice.

Table 24.3 lists some topics that you will want to find out about as the weeks and months pass. As with the other checklists in this module, we urge you to add topics that apply specifically to you.

## TABLE 24.2 What to Do on the First Day(s) of School

***ARRIVE EARLY!***

***Make sure your classroom is all set up***

At a minimum, you want to have the following information clearly displayed to students as they enter:

- Your name
- Students' names, their desks, and their lockers or cubbies (elementary)
- Students' seating chart (secondary)

Greet students at the door of the classroom as they arrive. Introduce yourself to your students, and have them introduce themselves to you.

Begin an instructional activity as soon as the bell rings (secondary).

Have students begin an academic task as soon as they arrive (upper elementary and secondary) or have settled (lower elementary).

Plan a time in the day to get to know your students. (You might want to do this during the first week, rather than the first day.) Begin by telling students about yourself, and then have them tell about themselves: their interests and hobbies, and their families (if appropriate). You may want to let students ask you questions about you. If you do so, be careful to deflect any questions related to your personal life. (Walk especially gingerly around questions about personal relationships or your social life.)

Keep students busy for the period or the day. Remember that the first day sets the tone for the rest of the year.

Introduce your students to the classroom. Show them where different items can be found. Let them know about any areas or items in the classroom that are *not* accessible to them.

Explain to students the classroom routines and procedures. (The ones you decided before the first days of school, remember?) Prioritize these, and introduce procedures and routines progressively, one or two each day, so that students do not become overwhelmed.

Progressively introduce the nonverbal cues you will use in the classroom. Be sure that students know what each cue is and what their response is to be.





## TABLE 24.3 Key Topics to Learn About Early in Your First Year

Field trips

- What do you need to do if you want to take your students on a field trip? Who needs to approve the field trip? How do you inform colleagues? Do you need to get colleagues' okay if students will be missing their classes? How do you arrange for transportation? How many chaperones do you need? How do you arrange for chaperones?

Sports events (secondary)

- What is the school policy for students being dismissed early for sporting events? How do students make up work? What do you do if you have a test scheduled for that day?

*Continued* ▶

▶ *Table 24.3 continued*

Tests and grading practices (Review Module 16, Tools for Assessment.)

- What is the school policy for number of tests that a student may have on a given day?
- What is the school policy for make-up tests?
- What is the grading scale used in the school?
- What is the school policy with regard to cheating on a test?

Report cards, reporting to parents on students' academic progress (Review Module 16, Tools for Assessment.)

- What is the grading scale used in the school?
- How are grades reported at the end of the marking period?
- If comments are usually written, what kinds and of what extent are they?

Parent conferences (Review Module 17, Working with Your Students' Families.)

- Are there regularly scheduled parent conferences?
- How many parents normally come to parent conferences?
- How does the scheduling of parent conferences usually take place (parents set a time, teacher assigns a time, etc.)?
- What can you expect from parent conferences?
- How should parent conferences be structured?
- Do students usually, sometimes, or never attend parent conferences?
- Which topics are appropriate and which are inappropriate?

Back-to-School night (Review Module 17, Working with Your Students' Families.)

- How is Back-to-School night organized? Do students and parents attend or just parents?
- How long does it last?
- What kind of information is normally shared with parents?
- What kind of information is *not* normally shared with parents?
- What is the usual attendance rate among parents?

Disciplinary issues

- Is there a school-wide disciplinary system in place? If so, of what does it consist?
- How can you deal with academic dishonesty (cheating on a test, plagiarizing papers)?
- How do you deal with violations of class or school rules, especially repeat offenders? (What support do you have from the administration?)

## What Help Can You Expect?

Teaching is one of the few professions that gives full responsibility to its new members. There is no gradual assuming of responsibilities, as is often the case in many other professions. (Imagine a brand-new sales representative being expected to sell as much as a veteran sales rep.) There are also no lighter loads, less demanding expectations, or limited accountability.

**Induction program** a structured series of events and activities aimed at easing the transition of beginners into their new work.

**Mentor** a person who gives both personal and professional guidance to a beginner.

(Imagine a newly graduated surgical resident performing a quadruple bypass.) New teachers typically are expected to perform the same duties and meet the same obligations as veteran teachers. They are given the same responsibilities and held to the same standards as their colleagues with twenty or even thirty years of experience!

Not too long ago, most new teachers were left on their own to "sink or swim." They were issued district curriculum guides, given the requisite textbooks, handed the keys to their classroom, and sent on their way until the time the school administrator came by to officially observe and evaluate their performance. Some of the luckier beginners had sympathetic colleagues who, vividly recalling the misery of their first year of teaching, took pity on their inexperienced counterparts and provided them with support and advice.

Fortunately, the needs of new teachers have been largely recognized, and most (but not all!) school systems have created **induction programs** to eliminate the "baptism of fire" quality of the first year and to help make the transition into teaching easier. These induction programs vary in scope and breadth, but they often include a new teachers group, a **mentor program,** or both.

- *New teachers groups.* Common activities for a new teachers group include regular meetings, which all new teachers are expected or required to attend. During these meetings, you will be introduced to various aspects of the school system (the school administration, the district curriculum, special services available, school and district procedures and practices), receive training in specific district- or school-wide programs (reading, science programs, or assertive discipline, for example), or be coached in effective teaching techniques.
- *Mentor programs.* In a teacher–mentor program, a new teacher is matched with a more experienced colleague who serves as a mentor, generally for the duration of one school year. In some systems, all new teachers are systematically assigned a mentor; in others, the new teacher has to request a mentor. Teacher–mentor matches are generally based on grade level or discipline taught, but other matches have been beneficial as well. In any case, the mentor is expected to provide whatever support and guidance the new teacher needs or requests. In general, it is understood that the conversations between the mentor and the new teacher are confidential, which enables the new teacher to share openly any concerns or difficulties he or she may be experiencing without the fear that others will be made aware of any temporary challenges.
- *Combined programs.* Some school systems offer both a mentor program and a new teachers program as part of the induction of new teachers. A combined program offers the benefits of each method; mentors help new teachers transition more easily and quickly, and groups allow new teachers to share with one another common challenges and triumphs. In some situations, mentors join such meetings, in effect providing all the new teachers with multiple mentors.

When you are investigating job opportunities or have been offered a position, be sure to ask about the district or school's induction program. Find out whether there is a teacher–mentor or a new teachers program. Ask about the district's commitment to these programs and the expectations for new teachers. Making this inquiry will *not* make it seem that you lack confidence. It will be interpreted as evidence that your expectations are realistic and that you are committed to being the best teacher you can.

## Video Case

What are some of the challenges and rewards that first-year teachers might experience? How can new teachers capitalize on their enthusiasm and energy for teaching, while at the same time drawing on the wisdom of more seasoned teachers? In the video case, *The First Year of Teaching: One Colleague's Story,* you'll meet fourth-grade teacher Will Starner, who speaks candidly about his first year—what he has learned about himself, what he finds is the best way to approach difficult situations, and the value he places on camaraderie with his fellow teachers. As you watch the clips and study the artifacts in the case, reflect on the following questions.

**QUESTIONS**

1. View the bonus video, *Mr. Starner Reflects on His First Year of Teaching.* How do his observations compare with the descriptions you have read so far in this module?

- Does this teacher offer any new information about the first year of teaching?
- What is the most important advice or information you feel this teacher conveyed to you?

***Online Study Center***

## In Your Classroom

### Surviving Your First Year

Here are some suggestions for surviving the first year:

- *Know what to expect and be forewarned.* Expect that your first year will be similar to those experienced by other first-year teachers. In other words, expect the worst and hope for the best. Anticipating difficulties and challenges will make it easier to face them if and when they do present themselves.

- *Find a mentor.* As we have already noted, teaching can be an isolating experience. To combat this isolation, we strongly encourage you to take advantage of any offer for a mentor to help you through your first year or two. If your school does not have a mentor program, you may have to take the initiative and seek out a more experienced teacher. We describe how to find your own mentor in Module 18, Working with Colleagues. In the early days and weeks of the school year, your mentor can familiarize you with routines, structures, personnel, administrative and logistical expectations, and available resources. Once the rush of the new school year has passed, your mentor will be a valuable resource for pedagogical advice, suggestions about managing your classroom and your administrative duties, and curricular ideas. And at *all* times, call on your mentor to help you avoid the political land mines that lurk in every job.

- *Look for strength in numbers.* We encourage you not only to find a mentor but also to join with other new teachers in your district to share successes and struggles. No matter how overwhelmed you may feel, make time to talk to other new teachers. These conversations will help you realize that your struggles are not unique and will reduce the social isolation that plagues many new teachers. If your school district does not have a new teachers group, ask an administrator to help organize one. And if all else fails, invite some of your new colleagues for a get-together at a local watering hole or cafe on a Friday afternoon.

- *Invest some time and effort in establishing your reputation.* Much of your first year will be spent establishing yourself within the school district. In some districts, parents view new teachers with a fair amount of skepticism and suspicion. Some new teachers feel they're being tested. Others describe the first year as an initiation or a hazing. There is a sports strategy that claims the best defense is a good offense. This is particularly good advice for new teachers in dealing with parents. Be accessible to parents. Keep them informed about what is being taught. Invite them to come meet you at set times. Try a breakfast meeting as a way of introducing yourself to your students' parents. Accept offers to help out (even though you may find the idea incredibly intimidating). The sooner you are given the tacit "stamp of approval" from the parent community, the easier your life will be.

- *Make yourself known within the school.* Even though you may feel swamped and overwhelmed with work, you should make an effort to get out of your classroom and get to know those with whom you work. And this doesn't mean just your teaching colleagues, but also your administrators and the support staff at the school. Never forget that the secretaries and custodians are among the most important people in a school! Getting to know them will be time well spent.

Grand Avenue: © United Feature Syndicate, Inc.

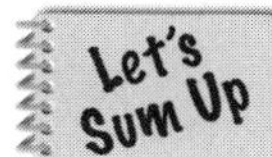


We have presented what some may see as a negative portrayal of the first year of teaching. We do so not to discourage you from becoming a teacher but in the hope of helping you achieve your goal of becoming a teacher. As we mentioned, our description may or may not resemble your experiences, but we prefer to present you a starker image of what *can happen* during one's first year of teaching. Knowing what challenges you are likely to face will, we hope, provide you with a sense of comfort, or at least a feeling of camaraderie, if you encounter similar difficulties. This knowledge may also make it easier to handle these times of stress and help you put the year in proper perspective.

We firmly believe that teaching is a richly rewarding profession. The spark in the students' eyes as they marvel at the results of their science experiment and the glow of pride on their faces for a well-deserved grade can hardly be replicated in any other profession. We offer the information in this chapter to help you be able to experience these moments.

## Further Resources

- *EZ School.* Available at: **http://www.EZSchool.com.** This website, which is associated with Amazon.com, is a treasure trove of resources for the new teacher. It is filled with good ideas, teaching plans for a range of subject matter, and worksheets.
- Erma S. Hershman and Dyan M. McDonald, *The Survival Kit for New Teachers: A User-Friendly Handbook,* 2d ed. (Garland, TX: ITPA, 2001). The title says it all. Although this book focuses largely on elementary school classrooms, the authors have another 2001 book with a similar title except that it is for "new secondary teachers."
- "Supporting New Teachers," *Educational Leadership* [special issue] 56/8 (May 1999). This special issue includes several articles that focus on the plight of first-year teachers and how schools can help them get over their initial difficulties.

- *What to Expect Your First Year of Teaching.* Available at: **http://www.ed.gov/pubs/FirstYear/index.html.** This website is an excellent resource for beginning teachers. It combines many of the practical tips and much of the advice in this module with several resources helpful to beginning teachers.
- Harry K. Wong and Rosemary T. Wong, *The First Days of School: How to Be an Effective Teacher* (Sunview, CA: Harry Wong Publishing, 1998). This highly acclaimed handbook abounds with tips and strategies to help the new teacher get a strong start. It is especially effective in discussing motivation and ways to minimize discipline problems and other issues that plague new teachers.

Scenario

Hank Taylor had not been sure he would like teaching sixth-graders, but he had been pleasantly surprised. Although he'd hoped for eighth-graders, his principal, Mrs. Weaver, had changed his assignment at the last minute. A summer's planning went out the window. His fellow teachers had rolled their eyes and sympathized, but they had told Hank to expect more of the same, because "That's the way Mrs. Weaver treats new teachers." Still, he had adjusted quickly and found good material to teach, and now he really liked his students.

He liked Mrs. Weaver, too, but lately she was getting under his skin. Mrs. Weaver treated Hank and the other two "wet-behind-the-ears rookies," which she smilingly called them in the presence of anyone who'd listen, as her personal assistants. But that's not all. She regularly asked them to "volunteer" their free time, coming in on Saturdays to sort and repackage the canned goods and other foods for the "Fight Hunger" drive or to tutor lagging students who weren't even in their classes.

Today she came into the lunch room and said that, with the secretary sick, she was having a crisis and needed her "rookies to give me a couple of hours this afternoon." It turned out that she needed help photocopying and getting the conference room ready for a meeting that night with the Parents'

Council. Hank sensed that, besides it being quite annoying, there was something deeply wrong with the way he and the other new teachers were being treated, but he couldn't put his finger on it.

Preview

We live in a world of specialists. Doctors usher us into the world. Dentists take care of our teeth. Farmers and grocers address our need for food. Ministers and priests attend to our spiritual needs. Gravediggers are handy at the end of life. And, of course, teachers specialize in meeting the educational needs of our society.

**Profession** an occupation or occupational group that meets certain criteria. Among other things, a profession requires training and knowledge, performs a social service, has a code of ethics, and embodies a sense of autonomy and personal responsibility.

Some of these specialists are more highly trained than others and are recognized as *professionals,* meaning they have qualified to be part of a **profession,** a group that has special characteristics. Even though the title *professional* has undergone some "stretching" in recent years (as in the case of the "professional bartender" and "professional rug cleaner"), it remains an important designation that reflects how society should acknowledge and value particular groups of specialists. In the scenario above, what is troubling Hank is that he is not being treated as a professional. As the scenario makes clear, being a *professional teacher* is not just an abstract idea, but one with very real everyday consequences. In this module, we explore in some depth exactly what it means to be a professional teacher.

We begin by considering to what extent teaching has the characteristics commonly attributed to professional occupations. We also consider the opinions of "Joe and Jane Public" about teachers as professionals. A chronic impediment to professional status for teachers is public perception of the field, which too often sees teachers as part-time workers who have months of vacation and do a job that "anyone can do." The old adage "Those who can, do, and those who can't, teach" stubbornly persists in the minds of many. Media coverage of failing schools and U.S. students' underperformance on international tests contribute to the negative perception.

On the other hand, most people appreciate the fact that the quality of children's education is intimately linked to the quality of America's teaching force and are therefore sympathetic to the greater professionalization of teachers. We review some efforts to professionalize teaching. Finally, we consider how you, as a teacher, can contribute to your own **professional development.**

**Professional development** efforts by a school or school district to improve the professional skills and competencies of its professional staff. Also called staff development or in-service training.

**This module emphasizes:**

- **The qualities that distinguish a profession from any other occupational group.**
- **Public perceptions of the status and societal contributions of teachers.**
- **The current drive to raise the level of professional skill of teachers.**

- **The major associations dedicated to the interests and improvement of teachers.**
- **The wide array of vehicles for professional development currently available to teachers.**
- **How reflection on your philosophy of teaching and on your teaching performance can contribute to your professional development as a teacher.**

# Qualities, Attributes, and Activities of the Complete Professional

Before we can engage in the debate over the professional status of teachers, we need to determine what attributes define a professional and what activities are characteristic of a professional. Then we can look at how the teachers measure up.

Here are some agreed-upon attributes of professionals:[1]

1. A professional renders a unique and essential service to society. This service is so important that it must be accessible to all members of society.
2. A professional possesses mastery of a complex body of knowledge and specialized skills, gained through formal education and practical experience.
3. The period of education and training required to become a professional is generally long. In many instances, mastery of the body of knowledge requires formal education and training beyond the undergraduate experience.
4. A professional relies on intellectual rather than physical skills to carry out services.
5. Members of a profession enjoy a degree of autonomy and decision-making authority.
6. Professionals are self-regulating. Members of the profession often decide on criteria for entry into the profession and establish requirements for remaining in good standing within the profession. Members are responsible for removing those who fail to live up to the standards set.
7. Professionals follow a code of ethics established by the members of the profession. The members are responsible for disciplining those who fail to adhere to this code of ethics.
8. Professionals accept personal responsibility for their behaviors and actions. Because the service they render is generally related to human welfare, their behaviors and actions can have far-reaching consequences.
9. Professionals usually work without supervision. They may work alone, but even when they work in groups, they are usually autonomous and report to other professionals principally as colleagues.
10. Professionals are more concerned with the services they render than with the remuneration they receive.

Enjoying young people is an important quality in a teacher.

Let's look at how teachers measure up in terms of these qualities and attributes of professionals.

1. *Do teachers render a unique and essential service to society?* Few would disagree that the education of a society's young people is an important service to that society. The perpetuation of any culture depends on the socialization and education of the young. However, teachers are not the only group of people in society who educate the young; their service is not unique. Many others in society help prepare the youth for their adult roles in society. Parents are the primary educators (and, in the case of homeschooled children, the sole educators) of their children. Other community members, such as clergy and sports coaches, also participate in the education of young people. Other "educators" include the media, both print and visual.

2. *Do teachers possess a complex body of knowledge and specialized skills, gained through an extended period of formal education and practical experience?* One view of teaching that still persists is that it is a technical occupation. This view is based on the premise that specific behaviors on the teacher's part will predictably lead to desired student behaviors and learning. Research findings over the past thirty years, however, have suggested that teaching is a far more complex and unpredictable undertaking, requiring teachers to make a multitude of decisions, often very quickly. To make these decisions, teachers draw on their knowledge about the nature of the content they are teaching, pedagogy, child psychology, and learning theories, as well as their previous experiences.[2] Research findings have confirmed that through experience, training, and reflection, veteran teachers develop a complex body of knowledge and specialized skills.[3]

   What is the complex body of knowledge that a teaching professional possesses and uses to make these decisions? Drawing on the work of educational researcher Lee Shulman and others, we consider five areas essential:

   - Knowledge of subject matter being taught
   - Theoretical knowledge about teaching and learning
   - Personal practical knowledge

- Practical knowledge of effective teaching techniques and approaches
- Attitudes and frames of mind that foster learning[4]

As we stressed in Module 1, Reflective Teaching for Student Learning, effective teachers not only draw on these skills to make moment-by-moment decisions, but they also *reflect* on their decisions. As they consider the appropriateness and possible alternatives to their choices, these teaching professionals use their knowledge, skills, and experience to continue to learn and improve their teaching.[5]

**3.** *Do teachers undergo an extended period of formal education and practical training?* In the majority of states, a bachelor's degree is the minimum requirement for licensure. Four years of undergraduate education do not, however, constitute an extended period of formal education. Some states (California and New York, for example) have set a master's degree as the minimum requirement for licensure, but this trend has not yet gained much momentum.

Teachers also do not undergo an extended period of practical training like that experienced by many other professionals, such as medical practitioners. Some teacher education programs require a year-long internship in conjunction with their formal education courses, but the dominant model for practical training in teacher education programs throughout the country is one semester of experience as a student teacher.

One impediment to a more universal requirement for an extended period of education and training is the financial burden this could impose on future teachers. Some teacher-educators observe that, compared with other professions, the average starting salaries of teachers are not high enough to support the financial strain incurred with an extended training requirement.

**4.** *Do teachers rely on intellectual rather than physical skills to perform their services?* This is clearly an attribute of teaching. Teaching is by its very nature an intellectual endeavor. Teachers are responsible for helping to expand students' intellectual development.

**5.** *Do teachers enjoy autonomy and decision-making authority?* Within the classroom, teachers enjoy a great deal of autonomy and decision-making authority. They often decide the sequence of topics to teach, if not the topics themselves. They decide the learning activities in which students will engage. They decide on most of their classroom practices and policies and on the appropriate disciplinary actions for violation of the rules. And, as every student knows, they decide what grades students will receive!

Beyond the classroom, the decision-making power of teachers grows progressively smaller. They may have some decision-making authority in setting school-wide policies and practices, although the teacher's voice is generally only one voice of many. At the district level, teachers have little, if any, decision-making authority. These decisions are made by the local school board and superintendent of schools.

**6.** *Do teachers self-regulate and self-govern?* Teachers have little to no input or influence in their own governance. As we note in Module 19, School Governance and Funding, schooling in the United States is under the control of state governments and local school boards. These governmental bodies regulate entry into and removal from teaching, through their policies on licensure requirements, professional development expectations, and reasons for dismissal.

As we describe later in this module, teachers are often represented at the bargaining table by local chapters of one of two national professional groups for teachers, the National Education Association (NEA) and the American Federation of Teachers (AFT). Neither of these groups, however, serves as a regulatory or governing body for teachers.

7. *Do teachers follow a code of ethics established by members of the profession? Is there a group that disciplines those who violate the code of ethics?* The NEA has developed and refined a code of ethics that teachers are encouraged to follow. It addresses two key principles—commitment to students and commitment to the profession—and presents a series of statements of what an ethical teacher will not do. You can link to the NEA Code of Ethics from your Online Study Center. The AFT does not have a code of ethics. Many states have developed their own codes of ethics for teachers. Some schools of education also have codes of ethics for their graduates, and teachers are encouraged to follow the principles laid out therein.

   Unlike the members of other professions, however, all teachers are not obliged to live by a code of ethics. In addition, there are no consequences imposed by any organization when a teacher violates any of the principles of the code. On the contrary, the local chapters of the NEA or AFT are expected to defend teachers against any charges that they failed to live up to their professional obligations.

***Online Study Center***

8. *Do teachers accept personal responsibility for their behaviors and actions?* To date, teachers have had to assume little accountability for the academic performance of their students. Individually, some teachers may feel a heavy responsibility to help all of their students be successful in high-stakes testing, as well as in their daily studies. Legally, however, teachers have not yet been held responsible for individual students who fail to meet minimum requirements set for their particular grade or age group. (See Module 22, Educational Law.) Nor are the majority of teachers' professional evaluations currently based on the success of their students.

   With the recent implementation of state-mandated annual tests in nearly every state, however, talk of **teacher accountability** for student performance has become more commonplace. Teachers' performance reviews may soon include information on the number of students who scored at each level on the annual state assessment, and, as we will see later in this module, some districts are proposing basing teacher salary decisions on student performance as well.

**Teacher accountability** the relatively new idea that teachers are responsible for their students' learning and should be held liable if their students fail to learn.

9. *Do teachers work without supervision?* Rarely do teachers work without supervision, at least in theory. In most school districts, teacher supervision and evaluation is part of the negotiated contract with the school district. In elementary schools, teachers are usually supervised by a principal or by an assistant principal. At the secondary level, teachers may be supervised by their department chair or by one of the school administrators.

   In the last few decades, supervision among peers has become more common on the educational landscape. Many school districts across the nation have instituted **mentoring** or peer coaching. (See Module 18, Working with Colleagues.) These programs are designed to make support and guidance from their peers available to teachers and to give them a greater sense of responsibility for the quality of instruction in all classrooms. Still, teacher supervision by a nonteaching administrator is a more familiar model.

**Mentoring** the process and practice of an older, more experienced person giving advice and guidance to a beginner.

10. *Are teachers more concerned with the service they render than with the pay they receive?* Given that the average starting salary is a little over $30,000, teaching does not draw too many with the promise of huge financial gains. It would be fairer to say that most teachers have opted to become teachers in order to serve the students they teach and to make positive contributions to their community and to society as a whole.

Thus our assessment of whether teaching exhibits the ten characteristics of a profession yields mixed results. Teachers do render an important, though perhaps not a unique, service to society; they are more concerned with service than with personal gain; their work relies principally on intellectual skills; and a growing body of research suggests that they do possess a body of complex knowledge.

On the other hand, this body of knowledge is not developed through an extended period of education and training; it is more often developed "on the job," while the individual is actually teaching. Teachers do not enjoy much autonomy or decision-making authority; they do not self-regulate or self-discipline; and they are not legally bound to live by a code of ethics set forth by a governing body.

From this analysis, we conclude that teaching falls somewhere between a profession and an occupation or a trade. Some have suggested that teaching is a "semi-profession," whereas others see it as a profession-in-progress or an evolving profession. As we will see next, this in-between view of teaching also seems to reflect the views of teaching held by many members of the public.

**Now You Do It**

1. Judging on the basis of your experience and observations, which of these ten criteria of a profession "fit" teaching and which do not?
2. Now, based on your careful judgments of each of these criteria, does teaching, in fact, qualify as a profession? Why or why not?

# Societal Views of Teaching and Teachers

As you join the teaching force, do not be surprised (or discouraged) to hear comments from friends or acquaintances disparaging your choice of profession. You may even have already heard comments along the lines of "You can do better than that." In the minds of these people, the rewards of teaching, particularly the financial rewards, are not enough to compensate for the drawbacks. There is, though, another significant sector of American public opinion that is highly respectful and appreciative of the work that teachers do, realizing the terrific challenges of managing and teaching a group of twenty or more students. From them, you may hear quite different comments: "Teaching is such a crucial profession. I've always thought about teaching, but . . ." or "When I retire, I'm going to look to teach." For these people, the rewards are not necessarily linked to any monetary scale but, rather, are related to other, less tangible things.

## Historical Views

The history of the teaching profession in the United States can shed some light on these contradictory views of the social status of teachers. In the early days of schooling, from the late 1600s through the struggle for America's independence, the teaching force consisted of young men studying for the ministry. At that time, teaching was considered a respectable, yet temporary, profession—a step in the pathway to a successful career as a minister.

In the period following the Revolutionary War, universal schooling was promoted as the means by which young citizens would learn about their new government and develop feelings of belonging and patriotism. Achieving these goals required an increase in the numbers of public schools and people to teach in them. This large need for teachers led the leaders of the new nation to turn to young women as a source of educators. Because the role of women in society at this time was a subservient one (remember that women did not win the right to vote in the United States until 1920), female teachers could be paid less than male teachers, which also made them a more affordable option. As more and more women came to populate the classrooms as teachers, fewer and fewer men joined the teaching force, even temporarily. The status of teachers in U.S. society became synonymous with the low status of women, who eventually constituted 90 percent of the teaching population.

The demographics of the teaching population in the United States did not change until the 1960s and 1970s. Two key events of these times contributed to this change: the women's movement and the Vietnam War. The women's movement spurred many women to join the nation's work force and opened up to women many occupations that previously had been the unique domain of men. Teaching became a less attractive option for them, and the percentage of educated women pursuing a career in teaching declined. At the same time, the Vietnam War opened up the classroom to men, who were given a draft deferment if they were teaching. The gradual exodus of women from and influx of men into the teaching profession led to small changes in the social status of teachers.

Today, 79 percent of all teachers and 91 percent of elementary teachers in U.S. public schools are still female.[6] Perhaps the continued predominance of females in the classroom contributes to the fact that teachers are paid less than members of many other professions where a similar level of education is required. Despite efforts of some states to boost teachers' salaries, most teachers still choose teaching for reasons other than the money. Low pay, in turn, contributes to the perception of many that teaching is not a high-status occupation.

## Modern Views

At the same time that many people accord teachers little social status, surveys show that the majority of the public—the people whose taxes pay our public school teachers—overwhelmingly acknowledge and support the nation's teachers. When asked, on one major national survey, to select which group provided "the most benefit to society," 62 percent of respondents selected teachers, whereas only 17 percent selected physicians, the second choice. Only 5 percent chose people in business, 3 percent chose lawyers, and journalists and politicians were selected by only 1 percent each.[7]

Members of the public are also aware of the direct importance of teachers to their students' learning. When asked to rate the factors that have the greatest impact on student learning, 44 percent selected the qualifications of the teacher over other factors, such as class size, socioeconomic status of the family, and the family's involvement and support.[8]

Finally, the public has a great deal of trust in teachers. According to the *National Credibility Index*, when asked which of several categories of people are "the most believable when speaking out on public issues," respondents rated teachers the highest, above members of the armed forces, national experts, and community activists.[9]

The conflicting views held by many citizens seem to reflect our initial evaluation of teaching as an evolving profession. We'll examine next some of the efforts to drive that evolution in the direction of greater professionalism.

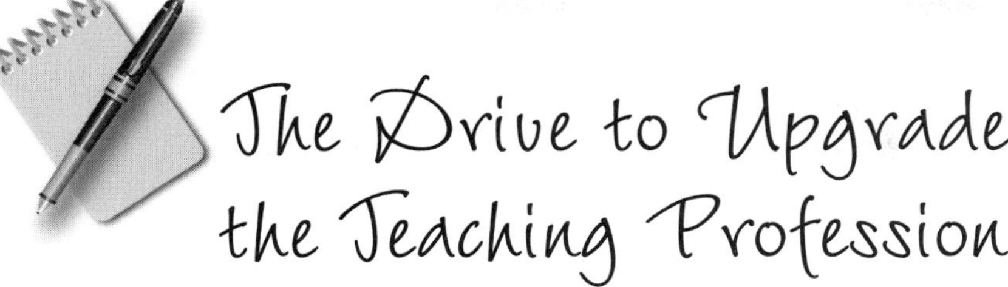

# The Drive to Upgrade the Teaching Profession

Today, many groups both inside and outside education are devoted to upgrading the skills and knowledge base of American teachers. Two key initiatives in this upgrading effort include certifying exemplary teachers and paying teachers for outstanding performance.

## Teacher Certification

**National Board for Professional Teaching Standards (NBPTS)** a professional agency that is setting voluntary standards for what experienced teachers should know and be able to do in the major disciplines.

In Module 20, Professional Performance Assessment, we discussed the efforts of the Interstate New Teacher Assessment and Support Consortium (INTASC) and the **National Board for Professional Teaching Standards (NBPTS).** While INTASC concentrates on establishing standards for those entering the teaching profession, the NBPTS has been active in establishing standards by which to measure and certify excellence in experienced teachers. Made up largely of classroom teachers, the NBPTS has compiled a list of five core propositions that define excellence in teaching. These are listed in Table 25.1, along with descriptors of each one. These five core propositions are used as the basis for standards to evaluate experienced teachers for NBPTS certification. NBPTS certification is recognized by many school districts as evidence of excellence among experienced teachers and is often financially rewarded.

To be eligible to apply for NBPTS certification, a teacher must have taught for a minimum of three years. Candidates complete an extensive series of performance-based assessments, submitting samples of their students' work, videotapes of themselves teaching, and portfolios. In addition, the teacher candidates submit lengthy analyses of their teaching practices and complete written tests of their subject-matter knowledge.

As of 2006, nearly 50,000 teachers nationwide had received board certification, with approximately 8,000 teachers becoming certified each year.[10] Currently, board certification is offered in twenty-seven different teaching fields, and there are plans for adding more. The work of the NBPTS is important in helping teachers become and be seen as professionals, but it is not without its critics. Some argue that the standards are too vague and superficial. Others question the objectivity of the assessment process. Still other critics suggest that certification serves to reinforce the status quo rather than to reform teaching in any meaningful way. Nevertheless, even though the NBPTS may not have found the perfect definition for excellence in teaching, the core propositions serve as a viable starting point in identifying what teachers need to know and be able to do in order to be effective.



## Pay-for-Performance Plans

**Pay-for-performance plans (merit pay)** teacher salary plans in which teachers whose performance meets district-set criteria at a high standard receive a higher percent salary increase than those who are evaluated as simply competent or do not meet the standards.

**Pay-for-performance,** or merit pay, plans have been part of the educational debate since the 1950s. Drawing from practices used with success in the private sector, pay-for-performance plans are designed to reward teachers who excel in their work. Rather than having a single salary schedule in which all teachers

## TABLE 25.1 Core Propositions of the National Board for Professional Teaching Standards

| | |
|---|---|
| 1. Teachers are committed to students and their learning. | • Teachers recognize individual differences in their students and adjust their practice accordingly.<br>• Teachers have an understanding of how students develop and learn.<br>• Teachers treat students equitably.<br>• Teachers' mission extends beyond developing the cognitive capacity of their students. |
| 2. Teachers know the subjects they teach and how to teach those subjects to students. | • Teachers appreciate how knowledge in their subjects is created, organized, and linked to other disciplines.<br>• Teachers command specialized knowledge of how to convey a subject to students.<br>• Teachers generate multiple paths to knowledge. |
| 3. Teachers are responsible for managing and monitoring student learning. | • Teachers call on multiple methods to meet their goals.<br>• Teachers orchestrate learning in group settings.<br>• Teachers place a premium on student engagement.<br>• Teachers regularly assess student progress. |
| 4. Teachers are mindful of their principal objectives. | • Teachers think systematically about their practice and learn from experience.<br>• Teachers are continually making difficult choices that test their judgment.<br>• Teachers seek the advice of others and draw on education research and scholarship to improve their practice. |
| 5. Teachers are members of learning communities. | • Teachers contribute to school effectiveness by collaborating with other professionals.<br>• Teachers work collaboratively with parents.<br>• Teachers take advantage of community resources. |

Source: National Board of Professional Teaching Standards. Reprinted with permission from the National Board for Professional Teaching Standards, **www.nbpts.org.** 

receive a same percentage salary increase each year, a school district that adopts a pay-for-performance plan bases teachers' salary increases on predetermined criteria. Those who meet the criteria at a high standard receive a higher percent salary increase than those who are evaluated as simply competent. Those who do not meet a minimum standard receive no increase in salary at all.

Some merit pay proposals are based on the same criteria already in use for evaluating teachers in the district, so that merit is based solely on the qualities that teachers exhibit. (See Module 20, Professional Performance Assessment, for a description of common criteria.) Proponents of these pay-for-performance programs insist that such an alternative to a set salary schedule for teacher compensation is essential to bringing about much-needed improvement in teacher quality. Opponents of these programs argue that the potential for favoritism and arbitrary awarding of merit pay is too great, largely because of the subjectivity involved in assessing teacher quality.

In an attempt to address some of the concerns and potential shortfalls of pay-for-performance plans, some school districts have been experimenting with multifaceted plans that provide more objective criteria for salary increases. *Career ladder* plans offer stipends or salary increases for teachers who take on additional responsibilities within the school, such as serving as lead teacher for a curriculum area or grade level, or as a mentor for their less experienced colleagues.

Other pay-for-performance proposals stress teacher accountability, as discussed earlier in this chapter, by basing teacher compensation partly on the performance of their students on measures such as state achievement tests. Using student outcomes on such standardized tests is often presented as a more objective basis for awarding merit pay. Opponents counter that teachers are not the only factor influencing student performance. They also express concern that such an arrangement might prompt highly competent teachers to shy away from teaching low-performing students, because these students would be less likely to achieve the requisite passing scores. They argue that such merit pay schemes harm low-achieving students or their teachers or both.

Currently, only a few local districts and the states of Minnesota and Texas have launched pilot merit pay programs with some success.[11] These plans reward not just teacher quality, as assessed via evaluation, but also added responsibilities that teachers may take on. It may be difficult to scale these successful programs up to a state or even national level, but you should expect to see more attempts to implement merit pay, as part of a continuing effort to motivate and reward excellence in teaching.

## Now You Do It

Visit the website of the NBPTS **(http://www.nbpts.org)** and learn the requirements for certification in your subject area and/or grade level of teaching.

# Professional Associations

Like other professional groups, teachers have a number of associations whose purposes range from protecting the interests of their members to promoting their professional growth and development to communicating new research findings in areas of interest to teachers. Two large professional organizations, the National Education Association and the American Federation of Teachers, both purport to represent all teachers, while several other associations aim to appeal to smaller groups of teachers.

## National Education Association

**National Education Association (NEA)** the older and larger of the two major teachers' associations. Founded in 1857, it has a membership of approximately 2.7 million.

The largest group representing the interests of educators is the **National Education Association (NEA).** Founded in 1857 "to elevate the character and advance the interests of the profession of teaching and to promote the cause of popular education in the United States," the NEA currently has a membership of approximately 2.7 million educators, from classroom teachers to teacher aides, administrators, and college professors. It has 51 state affiliates and more than 14,000 local affiliates.[12] The NEA describes itself as "committed to building broad-based support for quality public education, to generating business and community partnerships that promote excellence in public schools, and to supporting initiatives that focus on quality teaching and learning for all students." It provides a wide range of services to its membership, from publications to comparative analyses on working conditions and benefits of teachers throughout the country to research on new trends in education. It also provides many special services for its members, such as travel programs, insurance policies, and book club programs.

Attending meetings and conventions of professional organizations can contribute to your professional development.

Perhaps one of the most important and controversial services that the NEA provides is protecting and defending the interests and rights of its members. The NEA offers legal advice and support to local affiliates that are negotiating contracts with their districts. It also comes to the defense of teachers who have filed grievances against their school districts or who have been charged with any kind of violation. Although the NEA sees these actions as an integral part of advancing the interests of the profession, others see them as union activities, which are incongruous with a profession.

Another controversial activity of the NEA is its political lobbying on issues on the national education agenda. It has taken stands on such issues as vouchers (it opposes them), competency testing for teachers (it opposes it), and national certification (it is in favor of it). In 1976, the NEA for the first time formally backed a presidential candidate, Jimmy Carter. It has formally supported the Democratic candidate in every presidential election since then. Arguing that these stands serve to "advance the interests of the profession," the NEA insists that raising its voice on these issues of national importance to education helps promote an educational environment that is consistent with the purpose of public schooling in the United States.

Critics, however, have a different interpretation and accuse the NEA of being overly political and more interested in the welfare of its members than in the education of the young people in its members' care. They insist that the political stances and candidate backing of the NEA represent the views of a small group of national decision makers, and not those of its 2.7 million members, whose political views span a wide range.

## American Federation of Teachers

**American Federation of Teachers (AFT)** the second-largest teachers' association or union in the United States, having been founded in 1916 and currently affiliated with the AFL-CIO, the nation's largest union.

The second-largest educator association is the **American Federation of Teachers (AFT),** which boasts a membership of approximately 1.3 million educators. The AFT was founded in 1916 as a teacher union. Since its formation, it has been associated with the labor movement, and today it is an affiliated international union of the AFL-CIO. Although the AFT has 43 state affiliates and 3,000 local affiliates, its members tend to be concentrated in large urban areas, such as New York, Chicago, Boston, Philadelphia, and Washington, DC.[13]

The AFT makes no claim that it is anything other than a union representing the interests of its member teachers. It regularly bargains for teachers in contract negotiations in many urban centers. At the same time, the AFT, under the leadership of its long-time president, Albert Shanker, advocated for a number of educational reforms, including national certification through the NBPTS, merit pay for teachers, higher standards for licensure, and reform to teacher education programs. Up until his death, Shanker worked tirelessly for educational reform.

## Additional Professional Associations

There are a host of other professional organizations or associations for teachers and educators. We have listed several that may be of interest to you in Table 25.2. Some, such as the National Council of Teachers of Mathematics, the International Reading Association, and the National Science Teachers Association, focus on helping teachers stay abreast of trends in their subject-matter areas. They have local and state chapters and hold regular meetings. Other associations, such as the National Association of School Administrators

### TABLE 25.2 National Organizations or Associations

| Organization | Website |
|---|---|
| National Science Teachers Association | **http://www.nsta.org** |
| National Council of Teachers of English | **http://www.ncte.org** |
| National Council for the Social Studies | **http://www.ncss.org** |
| National Council of Teachers of Mathematics | **http://www.nctm.org** |
| National Association for Music Education | **http://www.menc.org** |
| National Association for the Education of Young Children | **http://www.naeyc.org** |
| International Reading Association | **http://www.reading.org** |
| American Council on the Teaching of Foreign Language | **http://actfl.org** |
| National Art Education Association | **http://www.naeareston.org** |
| American Alliance for Health, Physical Education, Recreation and Dance | **http://aahperd.org** |
| Association for Education Communications and Technology | **http://aect.org** |
| Council for Exceptional Children | **http://www.cec.sped.org** |
| National Association of Gifted Children | **http://www.nagc.org** |
| National Association of Elementary School Principals | **http://www.naesp.org** |
| National Association of Secondary School Principals | **http://www.nassp.org** |
| American Association of School Administrators | **http://www.aasa.org** |
| American Educational Research Association | **http://www.aera.net** |
| Association for Supervision and Curriculum Development | **http://www.ascd.org** |
| Council of Chief State School Officers | **http://www.ccsso.org** |
| Association of Teacher Educators | **http://www.ate1.org** |
| American Association of Colleges for Teacher Education | **http://www.aacte.org** |
| Association of American Educators | **http://www.aaeteachers.org** |
| Association for Childhood Education International | **http://www.acei.org** |
| National Association of State Boards of Education | **http://www.nasbe.org** |
| National School Board Association | **http://www.nsba.org** |
| National Congress of Parents and Teachers | **http://pta.org** |
| National School Public Relations Association | **http://nspra.org** |
| National Middle School Association | **http://nmsa.org** |

and the Council of Chief State School Officers, are more broad-based organizations that look to keep educators informed about research and trends in the field of education.

Some professional associations are honorary and are open to prospective, as well as current, teachers. These include Phi Delta Kappa, Pi Lambda Theta, and Kappa Delta Pi. These groups often present a more scholarly perspective on educational issues. Still other associations, such as the Association of Supervision and Curriculum Development, have a practitioner orientation and attempt to address directly what goes on in classrooms.

## Now You Do It

Visit the website of the NEA (**http://www.nea.org**) or AFT (**http://www.aft.org**), as well as those of any other professional associations that interest you. Find out what it takes to join the organization and what benefits you would gain from membership.

# Your Own Professional Development

One quality of a professional is an appreciation of the dynamic nature of the knowledge necessary to work effectively. Professionals tend to be committed to the constant renewal and improvement of their skills and intellectual competence. Like other professionals, many teachers are committed to their professional development and seek out every opportunity to enrich their knowledge base. Many states also recognize the importance of professional development by requiring teachers to show evidence of continuing learning when they renew their state teaching licenses. Teachers may participate in classes or workshops offered by their school or district or in those offered by professional groups or organizations. Colleges and universities often provide professional development workshops or graduate-level courses for teachers. As a teacher, you will also find many informal opportunities to continue your learning.

## District- or School-Based Programs

The first place to explore for professional development opportunities is your school district. Many school districts have long recognized the importance of promoting teachers' professional development. Find out what seminars, workshops, or other activities are available to you. Here is a sampling of what you may find:

- *Induction programs.* These regular seminars, which are often held after school, provide technical advice and emotional support for new teachers.
- *Mentor programs.* Some schools have structured mentor programs, in which veteran teachers are partnered with novice teachers to provide one-on-one, confidential advice, professional assistance, and emotional support. If your school does not, we strongly urge you to consider

carefully seeking out a mature and experienced teacher to guide you during your initial teaching.

- *School-wide seminars.* School districts may offer seminars or workshops that focus on any of a number of topics. Some, such as training in the use of a new math or reading series, are designed for all teachers in a given discipline or grade range. Others may be required of all teacher, and some offerings are for targeted, smaller groups. Check your district's website or printed calendar to get details about what is available, or required, for you.

## Professional Associations

Professional groups or organizations hold conferences and offer workshops and seminars that can be a major source of professional development. These offerings may be discipline-specific or more generically related to schools, teaching, and learning. Associations such as the NEA, the AFT, and the Association of Supervision and Curriculum Development address issues and topics of interest to teachers across disciplines and grade levels. We encourage you to join at least one of these professional organizations, especially the local branch, and to take advantage of professional development opportunities that they may offer. Attending these workshops is also a good way to network and to share experiences and ideas with other teachers. These informal conversations are often sources of great learning as well.

## Colleges and Universities

Local institutions of higher learning frequently offer summer workshops for teachers. Some workshops are grant-funded and thus may be offered at little or no cost to participants. In addition, participants often have the option of enrolling in the workshop for graduate course credit, which can contribute to salary increases. In nearly all school districts, earning a graduate degree advances the teacher to a higher pay scale.

Working on an advanced degree during the school year is a professional development option that a large number of teachers choose. Graduate courses in education generally meet once a week and are often scheduled in the late afternoon or evening in order to be accessible to working teachers. Some school districts offer partial or full tuition reimbursement to teachers who satisfy certain criteria in completing a graduate course.

## Informal Professional Development Opportunities

Other professional development opportunities may be more informally organized and yet offer many benefits for teachers. Teachers may organize book clubs or study groups to learn more about a new practice or trend. Some teachers engage in **action research,** carrying out research projects based in their own classrooms or schools.

**Action research** carrying out informal experiments in one's own classroom in order to improve one's teaching.

You may have to be proactive in seeking out professional development opportunities. We encourage you to ask questions, join organizations, and seek out opportunities for professional growth. Networking, talking to colleagues, and joining professional listservs or online bulletin boards are all good ways to find out what opportunities are available at what cost. If you find out about an interesting seminar that has a high registration fee, check with your administrator to see whether school funds might be available to cover the costs.

# Professionalism and Your Philosophy of Teaching

The essence of your work as a professional educator is to help foster the intellectual, physical, social, and emotional development of the students in your classroom. Because of the idiosyncratic and individualistic nature of learning, defining a single effective way of achieving this end is nearly impossible. As a professional, you will draw on your knowledge and experiences to formulate ideas about the most effective and efficient ways to bring about student learning. These ideas will become the basis for your beliefs about teaching and learning—in other words, for your educational philosophy.

Although we do not want to impose a particular set of beliefs on you, we strongly encourage you to think carefully and reflectively about your successes and failures in the classroom as you begin to formulate a philosophy of teaching. When a lesson goes well, ask yourself why. What was it about the organization, content, and/or structure of the lesson that made it successful? Likewise, when a lesson does not go well, ask yourself the same questions. From these interior conversations, you will expand your personal practical knowledge, while developing rationales and explanations for your beliefs. You will also be articulating a personal philosophy, which can guide you, as well as serving as a topic, in future reflections.

Whether or not teaching is a profession is one of those profoundly important issues, such as global warming and international political relationships, that, though worthy of much attention, may not be at the top of your agenda as you get ready to be a teacher. Undoubtedly, too, many wonderful teachers have never given it much attention. And although these teachers may not spend any time wondering whether or not they are members of a profession, they nevertheless do their work as professional teachers, incorporating the essence of professionalism into the manner with which they interact with students, colleagues, and the community.

The crucial question, then, is not the abstract issue of professionalism but whether you are going to measure up to the profession's high standards of service, of ethics, and of high-quality teaching for all children. As you begin your career, the essential question is "Can I make myself a professional teacher?" It is a question only you can answer.

## Further Resources

- American Federation of Teachers. Available at: **http://www.aft.org.** The AFT's website provides information on the organization and its programs, commentary on current issues, and links to other interesting websites. Contact the American Federation of Teachers, 555 New Jersey Avenue, NW, Washington, DC 20001.

- National Education Association. Available at: **http://www.nea.org.** This website offers a great deal of information about the NEA and its programs. Contact the National Education Association, 1201 16th Street, NW, Washington, DC 20036, (202) 822–7200, FAX: (202) 822–7292.
- National Education Association, *Status of the American Public School Teacher: 2000–2001* (Washington, DC: National Education Association, 2000). This report is one in a series of studies conducted every four years. It contains a massive amount of information on who teachers are, what is on their minds, and the conditions of their work.
- Eugene F. Provenzo and Gary McCloskey, *Schoolteachers and Schooling: Ethoses in Conflict* (Norwood, NJ: Ablex, 1996). This short book gives a thoughtful and detailed picture of the ways in which teaching changed in the last third of the twentieth century and the forces that affect a teacher's life.
- Public Agenda, *A Sense of Calling: Who Teaches and Why, 2000* (New York, Public Agenda, 2000). An encouraging and current report on new teachers' attitudes about their chosen profession, their satisfactions, and their concerns. The report also deals with the perceptions that administrators have of new teachers and their performance.

# Endnotes

## MODULE 1

1. The Public Agenda, *A Sense of Calling: Who Teaches and Why* (New York: Public Agenda, 2000), 12.
2. Richard Ingersoll, *Teacher Turnover, Teacher Shortages, and the Organization of Schools* (Seattle, WA: Center for the Study of Teaching and Policy, University of Washington, 2001). **http://www.ctpweb.org.**

## MODULE 2

1. Raymond L. Cohen, "Immigration to the United States," *EH.Net Encylopedia*, Table 1: Immigration Volume and Rates. Available at: **http://www.eh.net/encyclopedia/article/cohn.immigration.us.**
2. Jacqueline Jordan Irvine, "Still Standing in the Schoolhouse Door," *Education Week* (May 19, 2004): 38.
3. U.S. Bureau of the Census, *Selected Age Groups for the Population and Hispanic Origin for the United States, July 1, 2003*. Available at: **http://www.census.gov/Press-Release/www/releases/img/cb04-98-table2.pdf.**
4. Thomas D. Snyder and Charlene M. Hoffman, *The Digest of Education Statistics 2002* (Washington, DC: National Center for Education Statistics, 2003), 8.
5. **http://www.ncela.gwu.edu/policy/states/reports/statedata/2003LEP/GrowingLEP_0304.pdf.**
6. Jim Cummins, "Cognitive/Academic Language Proficiency, Linguistic Interdependence, the Optimum Age Question and Some Other Matters," *Working Papers on Bilingualism* 19 (1979): 121–129.
7. Shirley B. Heath, *Ways with Words: Language, Life, and Work in Communities and Classrooms* (Cambridge: Cambridge University Press, 1983).
8. Ruby Payne, "Understanding and Working with Students and Adults from Poverty," *Instructional Leader* IX, no. 2 (March 1996). Available at: **http://www.infoplease.com/ipa/A0193727.html.**
9. Myra Sadker and David Sadker, "The Issue of Gender in Elementary and Secondary Education," in *Review of Research in Education* 17, ed. Gerald Grant (Washington, DC: American Educational Research Association, 1991): 269–334.

## MODULE 3

1. Christine I. Bennett, *Comprehensive Multicultural Education: Theory and Practice* (Boston: Allyn & Bacon, 1999).
2. James A. Banks, *Cultural Diversity and Education: Foundations, Curriculum, and Teaching,* 5th ed. (Boston: Pearson Education, 2006), 59–62.
3. James A. Banks and John Ambrosio, "Multicultural Education," in James W. Guthrie (Ed.), *Encyclopedia of Education,* 2d ed. (New York: Macmillan Reference USA, 2003), 1703–1709.
4. Geneva Gay, "The State of Multicultural Education in the United States," in K. A. Moodley (Ed.), *Beyond the Multicultural Education: International Perspectives* (Calgary, Alberta: Detseting Enterprises, 1992), 41–65.
5. Geneva Gay, *Culturally Responsive Teaching: Theory, Research, and Practice* (New York: Teachers College Press, 2000); Gloria Ladson-Billings, *The Dreamkeepers: Successful Teachers for African-American Children* (San Francisco: Jossey-Bass, 1994).

## MODULE 4

1. *Twenty-Fifth Annual Report to Congress on the Implementation of the Individuals with Disabilities Education Act* (Washington, DC: U.S. Department of Education, 2005), I-13. Available at: **http://www.ed.gov./about/reports/annual/osep/2003/25th-vol-1-sec-1.pdf.**

## MODULE 5

1. Robert J. Sternberg, *Intelligence, Information Processing and Analogical Reasoning: The Componential Analysis of Human Abilities* (Mahwah, NJ: Lawrence Erlbaum Associates, 1977).
2. Howard Gardner, *Frames of Intelligence* (New York: Basic Books, 1985) and Howard Gardner, *Multiple Intelligences: The Theory in Practice* (New York, Basic Books,1993).
3. Kathy Checkley, "The First Seven . . . and the Eighth," *Educational Leadership* 55 (September 1997): 12.
4. *Digest of Educational Statistics, 2004* (Washington, DC: National Center for Educational Statistics, U.S. Department of Education), Table 55.
5. J. S. Renzulli, "What Is This Thing Called Giftedness, and How Do We Develop It? A Twenty-Five Year Perspective," *Journal for the Education of the Gifted* (1999).
6. Ellen Winner, "Catching Up with Gifted Kids," *Cerebrum*, The Dana Foundation, Winter 2001.
7. Spyros Konstantopoulos, Manisha Modi, and Larry V. Hedges, "Who Are America's Gifted?" *American Journal of Education* 109, no. 3 (May 2001): 344–382.
8. Carolyn Callahan, "Identifying Gifted Students from Underrepresented Populations," *Theory Into Practice* 44, no. 2 (Spring 2005): 98–104.
9. N. D. Fleming and C. Mills, "Not Another Inventory, Rather a Catalyst for Reflection," *To Improve the Academy* 11 (1992): 137–149.
10. **http://www.vark-learn.com/english/page.asp?p=multimodal.**
11. David A. Kolb, *Experiential Learning: Experience as the Source of Learning and Development* (Englewood Cliffs, NJ: Prentice-Hall, 1984).
12. Adapted from Carol Ann Tomlinson, *The Differentiated Classroom: Responding to the Needs of All Learners* (Alexandria, VA: Association for Supervision and Curriculum Development, 1999).

## MODULE 6

1. B. F. Skinner, "The Science of Learning and the Art of Teaching," *Harvard Educational Review* 24 (1954): 88–97.
2. Benjamin Bloom, *All Our Children Learning* (New York: McGraw-Hill, 1980).
3. Jean Piaget, *The Psychology of Intelligence* (London: Routledge & Kegan Paul, 1950).
4. Jean Piaget and Barbel Inhelder, *The Psychology of the Child* (New York: Basic Books, 1969).
5. Lev Vygotsky, *Mind in Society: The Development of Higher Psychological Processes* (London: Harvard University Press, 1978).
6. Jerome Bruner, *The Process of Education,* rev. ed. (Cambridge, MA: The Belknap Press of Harvard University Press, 2004).

7. William H. Kilpatrick, "The Project Method: Child-Centeredness in Progressive Education," *Teachers College Record* 19 (1918): 319–334.
8. Albert Bandura, *Social Learning Theory* (Englewood Cliffs, NJ: Prentice-Hall, 1977).

**MODULE 7**

1. NCLB Act of 2001. Available at: **http://www.ed.gov/nclb/accountability.**
3. Daniel G. Bates and Fred Plog, *Cultural Anthropology,* 3d ed. (New York: McGraw-Hill, 1990), 7.

**MODULE 8**

1. William Glasser, *Choice Theory in the Classroom,* rev. ed. (New York: HarperPerennial, 1998).

**MODULE 9**

1. Abraham Maslow, *Motivation and Personality,* 3d ed. (New York: HarperCollins, 1987).
2. Carl Rogers, *Freedom to Learn,* 3d ed. (Needham, MA: Prentice-Hall, 1994).
3. Nel Noddings, *Caring: A Feminine Approach to Ethics and Moral Education* (Berkeley: University of California Press, 1984), 180.
4. Haim G. Ginott, *Teacher and Child: A Book for Parents and Teachers,* 1st Collier Books ed. (New York: Colliers, 1993).
5. Rudolf Dreikurs, *Maintaining Sanity in the Classroom: Classroom Management Techniques,* 2d ed. (Washington, DC: Accelerated Development, 1998).
6. Jacob S. Kounin, *Discipline and Group Management in Classrooms* (Huntington, NY: R. E. Krieger, 1977).
7. Op. cit.
8. Rudolf Dreikurs, *Maintaining Sanity in the Classroom: Classroom Management Techniques,* 2d ed. (Washington, DC: Accelerated Development, 1998).
9. William Glasser, *Choice Theory in the Classroom,* rev. ed. (New York: HarperPerennial, 1998).

**MODULE 10**

1. American Library Association, *Challenged and Banned Books.* Available at: **http://www.ala.org/ala/oif/bannedbooksweek/challengedbanned/challengedbanned.htm#mfcb.**

**MODULE 11**

1. Benjamin S. Bloom and David R. Krathwohl, *Taxonomy of Educational Objectives: The Classification of Educational Goals, by a Committee of College and University Examiners. Handbook I: Cognitive Domain* (New York: Longmans, Green, 1956); David R. Krathwohl, Benjamin S. Bloom, and Bertram B. Masia, *Taxonomy of Educational Objectives: The Classification of Educational Goals. Handbook II: Affective Domain* (New York: David McKay, 1964); and Elizabeth J. Simpson, *The Classification of Educational Objectives in the Psychomotor Domain* (Washington, DC: Gryphon House, 1972).
2. Robert F. Mager, *Preparing Instructional Objectives: A Critical Tool in the Development of Effective Instruction,* 3d ed. (Atlanta, GA: Center for Effective Performance, 1997).
3. For example, see Jack Snowman and Robert Biehler, *Psychology Applied to Teaching,* 10th ed. (Boston: Houghton Mifflin, 2003), 412–416.

**MODULE 12**

1. Dorothy Singer and Jerome Singer, *Handbook of Children and the Media* (Thousand Oaks, CA: Sage Publications, 2000).
2. Mary Budd Rowe, "Wait-Time and Rewards as Instructional Variables, Their Influence on Language, Logic, and Fate Control: Part One—Wait-Time," *Journal of Research in Science Teaching* 11, no. 2 (1974): 81–94. This study was conducted with elementary school teachers and students. Studies with high school populations yielded similar results.
3. Theodore Sizer, *Horace's Compromise: The Dilemma of the American High School* (Boston, MA: Houghton Mifflin, 1984).
4. John Goodlad, *A Place Called School* (New York: McGraw-Hill, 1984).
5. Myra Sadker and David Sadker, "Questioning Skills," in James M. Cooper (Ed.), *Classroom Teaching Skills,* 8th ed. (Boston: Houghton Mifflin, 2006), 101–148.
6. Robert Slavin, *Cooperative Learning: Theory, Research, and Practice* (Englewood Cliffs, NJ: Prentice-Hall, 1990).

**MODULE 13**

1. David Berlo, *The Process of Communication: An Introduction to Theory and Practice* (New York: Holt, Rinehart, and Winston, CBS College Publishing, 1960).

**MODULE 17**

1. Joyce L. Epstein, *School, Family, and Community Partnerships: Preparing Educators and Improving Schools* (Boulder, CO: Westview, 2001) and Diana Hiatt-Michael (Ed.), *Promising Practices for Family Involvement in School* (Greenwich, CT: Information Age Publishing, 2001).
2. North Central Regional Educational Laboratory, *50 Ways Parents Can Help Schools.* Available at: **http://www.ncrel.org/sdrs/areas/issues/envrnmnt/famncomm/pa1lk20.htm.**

**MODULE 18**

1. Willard Waller, *The Sociology of Teaching* (New York: John Wiley, 1932).
2. Dan Lortie, *Schoolteacher* (Chicago: University of Chicago Press, 1975).

**MODULE 19**

1. National Education Association, Ranking & Estimates, 2003. Available at: **http://www.nea.org/edstats/images/04rankings.pdf.**
2. The Condition of Education, 2006, National Center for Educational Statistics. Available at: **http://nces.ed.gov/programs/coe/.**
3. Op. cit.

**MODULE 20**

1. S. Paul Wright, Sandra Horn, and William L. Sanders, "Teacher and Classroom Context Effects on Student Achievement: Implications for Teacher Evaluation," *Journal of Personnel Evaluation* 11, no. 1 (1997): 57–67.
2. Charlotte Danielson, *Enhancing Professional Practice: A Framework for Teaching* (Alexandria, VA: Association for Supervision and Curriculum Development, 1996).
3. Kenneth Zeichner and Daniel Liston, *Reflective Teaching: An Introduction* (Mahwah, NJ: Lawrence Erlbaum Associates, 1996).
4. Donald Schön, *The Reflective Practitioner: How Professionals Think in Action* (New York: Basic Books, 1983).

**MODULE 21**

1. From Kenneth R. Howe, "A Conceptual Basis for Ethics in Teacher Education," *Journal of Teacher Education* 37 (May/June 1996): 6.

2. Harvey G. Cox, *On Not Leaving It to the Snake* (New York: Macmillan, 1967), viii.

## MODULE 22

1. Louis Fischer, David Schimmel, and Cynthia Kelly, *Teachers and the Law,* 6th ed. (New York: Addison-Wesley Longman, 2002).
2. Op. cit.
3. U.S. Department of Education, Office of Civil Rights, *Revised Sexual Harassment Guidance,* Title IX, January 19, 2001. Available at: **http://www.ed.gov/about/offices/list/ocr/docs/shguide.html.**
4. Peter W. Airasian and George F. Madaus, "Linking Testing and Instruction: Policy Issues," *Journal of Educational Measurement* 20/2 [Linking Achievement Testing] (Summer 1983): 103–118.
5. Op. cit.
6. *Tinker* v. *Des Moines Independent Community School District,* 393 U.S. 503 (1969).
7. Op. cit.
8. *Hazelwood School District* v. *Kuhlmeier* 56 U.S.L.W. 4079, 4082 (12 January 1988).
9. *Pickering* v. *Board of Education,* N.E. 2d 1 (1967); 391 U.S. 563 (1968).

## MODULE 24

1. Kevin Ryan (Ed.), *The Roller Coaster Year: Tales by and for Beginning Teachers* (New York: HarperCollins, 1991).

## MODULE 25

1. Myron Lieberman, *Education as a Profession* (Englewoood, NJ: Prentice-Hall, 1956).
2. Christopher Clark and Penelope Peterson, "Teacher-Stimulated Recall of Interactive Decisions" (paper presented at the annual meeting of the American Educational Research Association, San Francisco, 1986); Richard Kindsvatter, William Wilen, and Margaret Ishler, *Dynamics of Effective Teaching* (White Plains, NY: Longman, 1996), 2–3.
3. Richard J. Shavelson, "What Is the Basic Teaching Skill?" *Journal of Teacher Education* 24 (Summer 1973): 144–149; Richard J. Shavelson, "Review of Research on Teachers' Pedagogical Judgments, Plans, and Decisions," *Elementary School Journal* 83/4 (1983): 392–413.
4. Lee Shulman, *The Wisdom of Practice: Essays on Teaching, Learning, and Learning to Teach* (San Francisco: Jossey-Bass, 2004).
5. Walter Doyle, "Themes in Teacher Education Research," in W. R. Houston (Ed.), *Handbook of Research on Teacher Education* (New York: Macmillan, 1990), 6.
6. *The Status of the American Public School Teacher: 2000–2001* (Alexandria, VA: National Education Association, 2002), 103.
7. David Haselkorn and Louis Harris, *The Essential Profession: A National Survey of Public Attitudes Toward Teaching, Educational Opportunity and School Reform* (Belmont, MA: Recruiting New Teachers, 1998), 2.
8. Ron Ferguson, "Paying for Public Education: New Evidence of How and Why Money Matters," and "Professional Development IQ Test-Answers," *National Staff Development Council,* at **http://www.nsdc.org/library/basics/pdiqan. cfm.**
9. Belden Russonelio and Stewart, "Teacher Quality: A Review of Existing Data," *Research and Communications* (August 1999).
10. National Board of Professional Teaching Standards. Available at: **http://www.nbpts.org.**
11. Holly K. Hacker and Terrence Stutz, "Incentive Pay Enters Classroom: Other States Watching as Texas Ties Teacher Bonuses to Test Scores," *Dallas Morning News,* June 12, 2006.
12. National Education Association. Available at: **http://www.nea.org.**
13. American Federation of Teachers. Available at: **http://www.aft.org.**

# Index

**Now You Do It** are interactive features designed to allow opportunities for you to consolidate the knowledge you learned in the text module, and engage in more thinking on key topics.

### Now You Do It

What have been your experiences with multicultural education? What non-Western curricular offerings were available in your high school? Did your undergraduate education require that you take a non-Western history, literature, art, or music course? What arguments would you advance to support the inclusion of non-Western cultures and civilizations in the K–12 curriculum? What arguments would you advance to oppose the inclusion of these courses?

### Now You Do It

Pick a topic that is taught in the grade or subject matter you want to teach. Develop a lesson plan that incorporates all or most of the elements of a good lesson plan that have been discussed in this module. Use the portions of sample lesson plans in this module and the full plans available through your Online Study Center as models for writing yours. Exchange your lesson plan with another prospective teacher and critique one another's plans, or ask your instructor to provide you with feedback.

**In Your Classroom** boxes provide practical ideas and application tips for use in classrooms.

### In Your Classroom

#### Adapting to Students with Disabilities

There are very likely to be students with disabilities in your classroom. How will you deal with their different needs?

- *Do not stereotype these students.* For example, consider two students identified as having learning disabilities. One may have below-average intelligence and have difficulty in mathematics; the other may have high intelligence and have trouble reading. Although each has learning disabilities, you would need to provide different instruction for each.
- *Get to know them.* Learn all you can about each student's limitations and potential and about what instructional approaches and technologies might be particularly effective.
- *Consult the special education teachers in your school.* The more you and the special education teacher can coordinate instruction and services for your students with disabilities, the better the students' educational experiences will be.
- *Try to co-teach with a special education teacher* whenever feasible.
- *Insist that any needed services be provided.* After all, it is the law.
- *Pair students who have disabilities with students without disabilities who can help them.*
- *Use a variety of teaching strategies,* including hands-on activities, peer tutoring, and cooperative learning strategies.

### In Your Classroom

#### Tips for Pacing Learning Activities

- *Divide your time.* In order to allow enough time for a learning activity, plan in small chunks. Break down the total lesson time available to you into smaller segments, and assign each segment a specific task or part of a task. Determine how much you can accomplish in the time you have available, and adjust your plans if necessary.
- *Share timing information with students.* As you give instructions for the task or the activity, communicate the amount of time students have to complete it. This helps students remain focused on the task before them and pace themselves to work through it at a reasonable rate.
- *Tune in to your audience.* As students complete assigned tasks, look and listen carefully for cues indicating confusion, frustration, or accomplishment. This careful monitoring enables you to make adjustments to the time allotment of a task on the basis of collective student reactions.